Public School Law

Public School Law

Teachers' and Students' Rights

FIFTH EDITION

Nelda H. Cambron-McCabe

Miami University (Ohio)

Martha M. McCarthy

Indiana University

Stephen B. Thomas

Kent State University

PEARSON

Boston • New York • San Francisco • Mexico City
Montreal • Toronto • London • Madrid • Munich • Paris
Hong Kong • Singapore • Tokyo • Cape Town • Sydney

Series Editor: *Arnis E. Burvikovs*
Editorial Assistant: *Christine Lyons*
Marketing Manager: *Tara Whorf*
Production Editor: *Michelle Limoges*
Compositor: *TKM Productions*
Composition and Prepress Buyer: *Linda Cox*
Manufacturing Buyer: *Andrew Turso*
Cover Designer: *Linda Knowles*

For related titles and support materials, visit our online catalog at www.ablongman.com.

Library of Congress Cataloging-in-Publication Data

Cambron-McCabe, Nelda H.
    Public school law : teachers' and students' rights / Nelda H. Cambron-McCabe, Martha
M. McCarthy, Stephen B. Thomas.—5th ed.
    p. cm.
    Mc Carthy's name appears first on the 4th edition.
    Includes bibliographical references and index.
    ISBN 0-205-35216-2
    1. Students-Legal status, laws, etc.—United States. 2. Teachers—Legal status, laws,
etc.—United States. I. McCarthy, Martha M. II. Thomas, Stephen B. II. Title.

KF4119.M38 2004
344.73'0793—dc21   2002043726

ISBN 0-205-35216-2

Printed in the United States of America

10 9 8 7 6 5 4 3 2 1   07 06 05 04 03

Contents

Preface   xiii

1 *Legal Framework of Public Education*   **1**

State Control of Education   **1**
Legislative Power   2
State Agencies   3
Local School Boards   5
School-Based Councils   8

Federal Role in Education   **9**
United States Constitution   9
Federal Legislation   14
Federal Administrative Agencies   17

Function and Structure of the Judicial System   **17**
State Courts   20
Federal Courts   20
Judicial Trends   22

Conclusion   **23**

2 *Church/State Relations*   **25**

Constitutional Framework   **25**

Religious Influences in Public Schools   **29**
Silent Prayer Statutes   30
School-Sponsored versus Private Devotionals   31
Religious Displays and Holiday Observances   37
Proselytization in the Classroom   39
Equal Access for Religious Expression and Groups   42

Accommodations for Religious Beliefs   **48**
Release-Time Programs   48
Excusal for Religious Observances   49

Religious Exemptions from Secular Activities   50

Religious Challenges to the Secular Curriculum   **53**
Defining What Is "Religious"   53
Challenged Curriculum Components   54

State Aid to Private Schools   **57**
Aid for Student Services   58
Aid to Encourage Educational Choice   62

Conclusion   **65**

3   *School Attendance and Instructional Issues*   **67**

Compulsory School Attendance   **67**
Alternatives to Public Schooling   68
Exceptions to Compulsory Attendance   71
Health Requirements   72

Residency Requirements   **74**

School Fees   **77**
Transportation   78
Textbooks, Courses, and Materials   78

The School Curriculum   **80**
Requirements and Restrictions   81
Censorship of Instructional Materials   82

Student Proficiency Testing   **89**

Educational Malpractice and Instructional Negligence   **93**

Instructional Privacy Rights   **96**
Student Records   97
Pupil Protection and Parental Rights Laws   103

Conclusion   **104**

4   *Students' Rights in Noninstructional Matters*   **107**

Freedom of Speech and Press   **107**
Unprotected Conduct and Expression   109
Commercial Expression   113
School-Sponsored (Governmental) Expression   114
Protected Private Expression   117
Student-Initiated Clubs   125

Student Appearance   **128**
    Hairstyle   128
    Attire   130

Extracurricular Activities   **134**
    Attendance, Training, and Recruitment Regulations   135
    Restrictions on Eligibility   136
    Fees for Participation   139
    Other Conditions   140

Conclusion   **140**

5   ***Student Classifications***   **143**

Legal Context   **143**

Classifications Based on Race   **146**
    Pre-*Brown* Litigation   146
    De Jure Segregation in the South   149
    Distinguishing between De Jure and De Facto Segregation   151
    Fashioning Appropriate Remedies   152
    Achieving Unitary Status   159
    Postunitary Transfer and School Assignment   161

Classifications Based on Native Language   **163**

Classifications Based on Ability or Achievement   **166**
    Tracking Schemes   166
    Gifted and Talented Students   168

Classifications Based on Age   **170**

Classifications Based on Gender   **171**
    Interscholastic Sports   172
    Academic Programs   177
    Sexual Harassment of Students   180
    Marriage and Pregnancy   183

Conclusion   **184**

6   ***Rights of Students with Disabilities***   **187**

Legal Context   **187**
    Rehabilitation Act   188
    Americans with Disabilities Act   191
    Individuals with Disabilities Education Act   192

Free Appropriate Public Education   **193**

Individualized Education Programs   **196**
Initial Identification   196
Evaluation   197
IEP Preparation   199
Public and Private Placement   200

Related Services   **205**
Transportation   206
Psychological Services   206
Health Services   207

Extended School Year   **208**

Participation in Sports   **209**

Discipline   **212**
Suspension   213
Expulsion   214

Procedural Safeguards   **216**
Stay-Put   216
Mediation   218
Impartial Due Process Hearing   219
State Review   220
Civil Action   220
Remedies and Attorneys' Fees   221

Conclusion   **222**

7   **Student Discipline   225**

Conduct Regulations   226

Expulsions and Suspensions   230
Expulsions   230
Suspensions   235

Corporal Punishment   240
Constitutional Issues   240
State Law   242

Academic Sanctions   243
Absences   244
Misconduct   245

Search and Seizure   248
Lockers   251
Search of Personal Possessions: Purses, Book Bags,
and Other Property   253

Personal Search of a Student   255
Use of Metal Detectors   257
Drug-Detecting Canines   258
Drug Testing   261
Police Involvement   263

Remedies for Unlawful Disciplinary Actions   **266**

Conclusion   **268**

8   *Terms and Conditions of Employment*   **271**

Licensure or Certification   **272**

Employment by Local School Boards   **276**
Employment Requirements   277
Assignment of Personnel and Duties   279

Contracts   **282**
Term and Tenure Contracts   284
Supplemental Contracts   287
Leaves of Absence   289

Personnel Evaluation   **289**

Personnel Records   **292**

Other Employment Issues   **294**
Using Copyrighted Materials   294
Reporting Suspected Child Abuse   299

Conclusion   **303**

9   *Teachers' Substantive Constitutional Rights*   **305**

Freedom of Expression   **305**
Legal Principles   306
Application of the Legal Principles   309
Prior Restraint and Channel Rules   315

Academic Freedom   **318**
Course Content   318
Expressing Personal Views in the Classroom   321
Teaching Strategies   322

Freedom of Association   **326**
Political Affiliations   327
Political Activity   329

Personal Appearance   **333**

Privacy Rights   **335**
    Search and Seizure   337
    Lifestyle Choices   340

Conclusion   **344**

10   *Discrimination in Employment*   **346**
___

Legal Context   **346**
    Fourteenth Amendment   346
    Title VII   347

Race and National-Origin Discrimination   **352**
    Hiring and Promotion Practices   359
    Adverse Decisions   355
    Affirmative Action   357

Gender Discrimination   **359**
    Hiring and Promotion Practices   359
    Compensation Practices   361
    Termination, Nonrenewal, and Denial of Tenure   363
    Pregnancy Discrimination   365
    Sexual Harassment   367
    Retirement Benefits   369

Sexual Preference Discrimination   **370**
    Access to Benefits   370
    Harassment   371
    Adverse Employment Decisions   371

Religious Discrimination   **372**
    Hiring and Promotion Practices   372
    Accommodation   373
    Adverse Employment Decisions   376

Age Discrimination   **376**
    Hiring and Promotion Practices   378
    Compensation and Benefits   378
    Adverse Employment Actions   379
    Retirement   381

Disability Discrimination   **382**
    Qualifying as Disabled   384
    Otherwise Qualified   386
    Reasonable Accommodation   387
    Termination and Nonrenewal   389

Conclusion   **390**

11 *Termination of Employment*   **392**

Procedural Due Process in General   **392**
    Dismissal   394
    Nonrenewal   394
    Establishing Protected Property and Liberty Interests   396

Procedural Requirements in Discharge Proceedings   **402**
    Notice   404
    Hearing   406

Dismissal for Cause   **412**
    Incompetency   412
    Immorality   413
    Insubordination   416
    Neglect of Duty   418
    Unprofessional Conduct   420
    Unfitness to Teach   421
    Other Good and Just Cause   422
    Reduction-in-Force   423

Remedies for Violations of Protected Rights   **425**
    Liability of School Officials   426
    Liability of School Districts   428
    Remedies   430

Conclusion   **434**

12 *Labor Relations*   **436**

Employees' Bargaining Rights in the Private and Public Sectors   **437**

Teachers' Statutory Bargaining Rights   **442**

Scope of Negotiations   **444**
    Governmental Policy   445
    Selected Bargaining Subjects   447

Union Security Provisions   **452**
    Dues and Service Fees   452
    Exclusive Privileges   456

Grievances   **459**

Negotiation Impasse   **461**

Strikes   **463**

Conclusion   **466**

13 *Tort Liability*   468

Negligence   468
    Duty   469
    Breach of Duty and Standard of Care   476
    Proximate Cause   479
    Injury   480
    Defenses against Negligence   480

Intentional Torts   486
    Assault and Battery   487
    False Imprisonment   488
    Intentional Infliction of Mental Distress   489

Defamation   490
    Private and Public Persons   491
    Veracity of Statements   491
    Fact versus Opinion   492
    Privilege   493

Damages   494

Conclusion   495

14 *Summary of Legal Generalizations*   497

Generalizations   497

Conclusion   503

Glossary   505

Selected Supreme Court Decisions   509

Index   513

Preface

The fifth edition of *Public School Law: Teachers' and Students' Rights* provides a comprehensive treatment of the evolution and current status of the law governing public schools. The content of all chapters has been updated, and some new sections have been added to capture emerging issues of legal concern. Additionally, **a new chapter on the rights of children with disabilities** has been added to reflect the continuing expansion of litigation in this arena. The newly reorganized student classification chapter now includes desegregation.

Since World War II, lawmakers have significantly reshaped educational policy. Most school personnel are aware of the burgeoning litigation and legislation, and some are familiar with the names of a few landmark Supreme Court decisions. Nonetheless, many teachers and administrators harbor misunderstandings regarding basic legal concepts that are being applied to educational questions. As a result, they are uncertain about the legality of daily decisions they must make in the operation of schools. Information provided in this book should help alleviate concerns voiced by educators who feel that the scales of justice have been tipped against them.

Public School Law differs from other legal materials currently available to educators because it addresses legal principles applicable to practitioners in a succinct but comprehensive manner. Topics with a direct impact on educators and students are explored, and the tension between governmental controls and the exercise of individual rights is examined within the school context. The analysis of specific school situations relies on applicable constitutional and statutory law and judicial interpretations of these provisions. Implications of legal mandates are discussed, and guidelines are provided for school personnel.

We have attempted to present the material in a nontechnical manner, avoiding the extensive use of legal terms. However, the topics are thoroughly documented through extensive notes that appear at the bottom of pages should the reader choose to explore specific cases or points of law in greater detail. These notes provide additional information on selected cases and should assist the reader in understanding specific concepts. Also, a glossary of basic terms and a table of Supreme Court cases are provided at the end of the book.

A few comments about the nature of the law might assist the reader in using this book. Laws are not created in a vacuum; they reflect the social and philosophical attitudes of society. Moreover, individuals who have personal opinions and biases make laws. Although we may prefer to think that the law is always objective, personal considerations and national political trends do have an impact on the development and interpretation of legal principles.

Also, the law is not static but rather is continually evolving as courts reinterpret constitutional and statutory provisions and legislatures enact new laws. In the 1960s and early 1970s, courts and legislative bodies tended to focus on the expansion of personal rights through civil rights laws and constitutional interpretations favoring the individual's right to be free from unwarranted governmental intrusions. However, since 1975, judicial rulings have supported governmental authority to impose restraints on individual freedoms in the school context in the interest of the collective welfare. Although the themes of educational equity and individual rights, which dominated litigation earlier, remain important, efforts to attain educational excellence have generated a new genre of legal activity pertaining to teachers' qualifications and performance standards for students. Moreover, the educational agendas promoted by the religious and political right, such as prayer in public schools and curriculum censorship, have provoked substantial legal activity.

Throughout this book, much of the discussion of the law focuses on court cases because the judiciary plays a vital role in interpreting constitutional and legislative provisions. Decisions are highlighted that illustrate points of law or legal trends, with particular emphasis on recent litigation. A few cases are pursued in depth to provide the reader with an understanding of the rationale behind the decisions. Reviewing the factual situations that have generated these controversies should make it easier for educators to identify potential legal problems in their own school situations.

As we complete this book, judicial decisions are being rendered and statutes are being proposed that may alter the status of the law vis-à-vis teachers and students. Additionally, some questions confronting school personnel have not yet been addressed by the Supreme Court and have generated conflicting decisions among lower courts. It may be frustrating to a reader searching for concrete answers to learn that in some areas the law is far from clear.

In spite of unresolved issues, certain legal principles have been established and can provide direction in many school situations. It is important for educators to become familiar with these principles and to use them to guide their decisions. Although the issues generating legal concern will change over time, knowledge of the logic underlying the law can make school personnel more confident in dealing with questions that have not been clarified by courts or legislatures.

We have attempted to arrange the chapters in logical sequence for those reading the book in its entirety or using it as a text for school law courses. An introductory chapter establishes the legal context for the subsequent examination of students' and teachers' rights, and a concluding chapter provides a summary of the major legal principles. Subheadings appear within chapters to facilitate the use of this book for reference if a specific topic is of immediate interest. The reader is encouraged, however, to read the entire text because some topics are addressed in several chapters from different perspectives, and many of the principles of law transcend chapter divisions. For example, litigation involving various aspects of teachers' rights has relied on precedents established in students' rights cases; the converse also has been true. Throughout the text, various sections are cross-referenced to alert the reader that a particular concept or case is discussed elsewhere in the book. Taken together, the chapters provide an overall picture of the relationship among issues and the applicable legal principles.

Although the content is oriented toward practicing educators, the material should be of equal interest to educational policymakers because many of the legal generalizations pertain to all educational personnel. In addition, *Public School Law* will serve as a useful guide for parents who are interested in the law governing their children in public schools. Given its comprehensive coverage of students' and teachers' rights, this book also is appropriate for use as a basic text for university courses or in-service sessions.

The material will assist school personnel in understanding the current application of the law, but it is not intended to serve as a substitute for legal counsel. Educators confronting legal problems should always seek the advice of an attorney. Also, there is no attempt here to predict the future course of courts and legislatures. Given the dynamic nature of the law, no single text can serve to keep school personnel abreast of current legal developments. If we can provide an awareness of rights and responsibilities, motivate educators to translate the basic concepts into actual practice, and generate an interest in further study of the law, our purposes in writing this book will have been achieved.

Acknowledgments

A number of individuals contributed to the completion of this book. We are extremely grateful to our students who reacted to various drafts of the chapters and assisted in checking citations. Our sincere thanks go to several education graduate students and law students who provided valuable assistance in reviewing drafts of chapters, locating legal materials, and verifying citations: Griffin Dunham, Rozlind Gallaspie, Tonya Gendin, Lisa Lee, Jennifer Nobles, Jacob Rigny, Kathy Sears, Darin Sider, and Ran Zhang. In addition, we appreciate the cheerful and conscientious assistance provided by staff members Jan Clegg and Peggy Bower at Miami University and Susan Hanns at Indiana University. We also thank the following reviewers of the text: Tony Armenta, Southeastern Louisiana University; Benjamin Baez, Georgia State University; and David A. Williams, Northern Arizona University.

This book would not have been completed without the support of our families. Our parents offered constant encouragement, as they do in all our professional endeavors. The contributions of our spouses, Harry McCabe, George Kuh, and Yvonne Thomas, simply cannot be measured. They assumed far more than their share of family responsibilities during the writing of this book, as they did for the earlier editions of the book. Also, throughout this project, our children, Patrick McCabe, Kari and Kristian Kuh, and Kyle Thomas, provided support as well as much needed diversions from long hours of legal research.

Public School Law

1

Legal Framework
of Public Education

The authority for the establishment and control of American public education, which serves about 46,900,000 students,[1] is grounded in law. State and federal constitutional and statutory provisions provide the framework within which school operational decisions are made. Policies and practices at any level of the educational enterprise must be consistent with legal mandates from higher authorities. The overlapping jurisdictions of federal and state constitutions, Congress and state legislatures, federal and state courts, and various governmental agencies (including local school boards and school-based councils) present a complex environment for educators attempting to comply with legal requirements. In an effort to untangle the various legal relationships, this chapter describes the major sources of law and how they interact to form the legal basis for public education. This overview establishes a context for subsequent chapters in which legal principles are discussed more fully as they apply to specific school situations.

State Control of Education

The Tenth Amendment to the United States Constitution stipulates that "the powers not delegated to the United States by the Constitution, nor prohibited by it to the states, are reserved to the states respectively, or to the people." The Supreme Court has recognized that this Amendment was intended "to allay fears that the new national government might seek to exercise powers not granted, and that the states might not be

---

1. National Center for Education Statistics, *Overview of Public Elementary and Secondary Schools and Districts: School Year 1999–2001* (Washington, DC: U.S. Department of Education, 2001) (http://nces.ed.gov/pubs2001/overview/#2).

able to exercise fully their reserved powers."[2] Since the United States Constitution does not authorize Congress to provide for education, the legal control of public education resides with the state as one of its sovereign powers. The Supreme Court repeatedly has affirmed the comprehensive authority of the states and school officials "to prescribe and control conduct in the schools" as long as actions are consistent with fundamental federal constitutional safeguards.[3] The state's authority over education is considered comparable to its powers to tax and to provide for the general welfare of its citizens. Although each state's educational system has unique features, many similarities are found across states.

Legislative Power

All state constitutions specifically address the legislative responsibility for establishing public schools. Usually the legislature is charged with providing for a uniform, thorough and efficient, or adequate system of public education. In contrast to the federal government, which has only those powers specified in the United States Constitution, state legislatures retain all powers not expressly forbidden by state or federal constitutional provisions. Thus, the state legislature has plenary, or absolute, power to make laws governing education.

Courts have recognized the state legislature's authority to raise revenue and distribute educational funds, control teacher certification, prescribe curricular offerings, establish pupil performance standards, and regulate other specific aspects of public school operations. Moreover, states can mandate school attendance to ensure an educated citizenry. Presently, all 50 states require that students between specified ages (usually 6 to 16) attend a public or private school or receive equivalent instruction. In addition, legislatures are empowered to create, reorganize, consolidate, and abolish school districts, even over the objections of affected residents.[4]

Legislatures also can authorize other school governance arrangements, such as state-funded charter schools that operate outside many regulations on the basis of a charter granted by the state or local board of education or other entities. The charter school movement has been characterized as one of the fastest-growing education reform efforts nationally. Since 1991, 39 states and the District of Columbia have enacted laws authorizing charter schools, usually specifying a cap on the number of charters granted to existing public or private schools or groups starting new schools. The number of charter schools ranges from one in a few states to more than 200 in Arizona and California. In the District of Columbia, over 8 percent of the students

---

2. United States v. Darby, 312 U.S. 100, 124 (1941).

3. Tinker v. Des Moines Indep. Sch. Dist., 393 U.S. 503, 507 (1969).

4. State laws, however, can place restrictions on making changes in school district boundaries. *See, e.g.,* State v. Bd. of Educ., 741 S.W.2d 747 (Mo. Ct. App. 1987) (holding that Missouri law requires voters in affected districts to approve boundary changes).

were enrolled in charter schools in 2000.[5] Enrollment nationally reached over 575,000 students during fall 2001.[6] Although this represents less than 1 percent of the students enrolled in public schools, the number continues to increase as states approve new legislation and expand the provisions of existing laws.

In some instances, when state laws are subject to several interpretations, courts are called on to clarify legislative intent. If the judiciary misinterprets the law's purpose, the legislature can amend the law in question to clarify its meaning. However, if a law is invalidated as abridging state or federal constitutional provisions or federal civil rights laws, the legislature must abide by the judicial directives. A state's attorney general also may be asked to interpret a law or to advise school boards on the legality of their actions. Unless overruled by the judiciary, the official opinion of an attorney general is binding.

Although the state legislature cannot relinquish its law-making powers, it can delegate to subordinate agencies the authority to make rules and regulations necessary to implement laws. These administrative functions must be carried out within the guidelines established by the legislature. Some states are quite liberal in delegating administrative authority, whereas other states prescribe detailed standards that must be followed by subordinate agencies. It is a widely held perception that local school boards control public education, but local boards have only those powers conferred by the state. Courts consistently have reiterated that the authority for public education is not a local one, but rather is a central power residing in the state legislature. School buildings are considered state property, local school board members are state officials, and teachers are state employees. Public school funds, regardless of where collected, are state funds.

State Agencies

Since it has been neither feasible nor desirable to include in statutes every minor detail governing public schools, all states except Wisconsin have established a state board of education that typically supplies the structural details to implement broad legislative mandates. In most states, members of the state board of education are elected by the citizenry or appointed by the governor, and the board usually functions immediately below the legislature in the hierarchy of educational governance.

Accreditation is an important tool used by state boards to compel local school districts to abide by their directives. School districts often must satisfy state licensure or accreditation requirements as a condition of receiving state funds. Though accreditation models vary among states, the most common approach involves the establish-

---

5. *See* National Center for Education Statistics, *Overview of Public Elementary and Secondary Schools and Districts: School Year 1999–2000* (Washington, DC: U.S. Department of Education, 2001) (http://nces.ed.gov/pubs2001/overview/#2). John Ericson and Debra Silverman, *Challenge and Opportunity: The Impact of Charter Schools on School Districts* (Washington, DC: Office of Educational Research and Improvement, June 2001).

6. *Charter School Highlights and Statistics* (Center for Education Reform, 2002) (http://edreform.com/pubs/chglance.htm).

ment of minimum standards in areas such as curriculum, teacher qualifications, instructional materials, and facilities. In some states, different grades of school accreditation exist, with financial incentives to encourage local schools to attain the highest level. Since the mid-1980s, there has been a movement toward performance-based accreditation under which a school's performance is assessed against predicted outcomes calculated for the school in areas such as pupil achievement, absenteeism, and student retention.

Within legislative parameters, the state board of education can issue directives governing school operations. In some states, rules pertaining to such matters as proficiency testing for students and programs for children with disabilities are embodied in state board rules rather than state law. Courts generally have upheld decisions made by state boards of education, unless the boards have violated legislative or constitutional mandates. For example, the Kansas Supreme Court recognized that the state constitutional grant of general supervisory power to the state board of education meant that enabling legislation was unnecessary for the board to require local school districts to develop student and employee conduct regulations.[7] The Supreme Court of Pennsylvania acknowledged the state board of education's authority to issue and enforce uniform student disciplinary regulations governing all schools in the state.[8] Also, the Sixth Circuit upheld the Ohio State Board of Education's authority to compel a school district to be annexed to a neighboring district because it failed to meet minimum state standards.[9] The appeals court reasoned that the annexed district had no federal constitutional right to remain in existence.

State boards of education, however, cannot abrogate powers delegated by law to other agencies. In 1991, the North Carolina Supreme Court held that the state board's prohibition on local board contracts with Whittle Communications interfered with school districts' statutory authority to enter into contracts for supplementary materials.[10] The school board in question contracted to air daily classroom broadcasts of Channel One (a news program including advertisements) in return for television equipment. The court reasoned that the contract was within the local board's statutory authority and could not be circumscribed by action of the state board of education.

In addition to the state board, generally considered a policy-making body, all states have designated a chief state school officer (often known as the superintendent of public instruction or commissioner of education) to function in an executive capacity. Traditionally, the duties of the chief state school officer (CSSO) have been regulatory in nature. However, other activities, such as research and long-range planning, may be part of this role. In some states, the CSSO is charged with adjudicating educational controversies, and citizens cannot invoke judicial remedies for a grievance pertaining to internal school operations until such administrative appeals have been

---

7. State *ex rel.* Miller v. Bd. of Educ., 511 P.2d 705 (Kan. 1973).

8. Girard Sch. Dist. v. Pittenger, 392 A.2d 261 (Pa. 1978).

9. Wilt v. Ohio State Bd. of Educ., 608 F.2d 1126 (6th Cir. 1979).

10. State v. Whittle Communications & Thomasville City Bd. of Educ., 402 S.E.2d 556 (N.C. 1991), *reh'g denied,* 404 S.E.2d 878 (N.C. 1991). *See* text accompanying note 36, Chapter 4.

exhausted. When considering an appeal of a CSSO's decision, courts will not judge the wisdom of the decision or overrule such a decision unless it is clearly arbitrary or against the preponderance of evidence.[11]

Each state also has established a state department of education, consisting of educational specialists who provide consultation to the state board, CSSO, and local school boards. State department personnel often collect data from school districts to ensure that legislative enactments and state board policies are properly implemented. Most state departments also engage in research and development activities to improve educational practices within the state.

Local School Boards

Although public education in the United States is state controlled, it is for the most part locally administered. All states except Hawaii have created local school boards in addition to state education agencies and have delegated certain administrative authority over schools to these local boards. Nationwide, there are approximately 14,900 local districts, ranging from a few students to several hundred thousand.[12] Some states, particularly those with a large number of small school districts, have established intermediate or regional administrative units that perform regulatory or service functions for several local districts.

As with the delegation of authority to state agencies, delegation of powers to local school boards is handled very differently across states. Some states with a deeply rooted tradition of local control over education (e.g., Colorado) give local boards a great deal of latitude in making operational decisions about schools. In states that tend toward centralized control of education (e.g., Florida), local boards must function within the framework of detailed legislative directives. State legislatures retain the legal responsibility for education and can restrict the discretion of local boards by enacting legislation to that effect.

The citizenry within the school district usually elects local school board members.[13] The United States Supreme Court has recognized that the Equal Protection Clause requires each qualified voter to be given an opportunity to participate in the

---

11. *See, e.g.,* Botti v. S.W. Butler County Sch. Dist., 529 A.2d 1206 (Pa. Commw. Ct. 1987); Eisbruck v. N.Y. State Educ. Dep't, 520 N.Y.S.2d 138 (Sup. Ct. 1987).

12. There also are approximately 600 special school districts operated by state or federal agencies. National Center for Education Statistics, *Overview of Public Elementary and Secondary Schools and Districts: School Year 1999–2000* (Washington, DC: U.S. Department of Education, 2001), Table 2 (http://nces.ed.gov/pubs2001/overview/#2).

13. In some cities, school board members are appointed by the mayor. Also, in a few states, such as Virginia, local board members are appointed by other agencies, such as the city council, county board of supervisors, or a selection committee chosen by a local circuit court judge. *See, e.g.,* Irby v. Va. State Bd. of Elections, 889 F.2d 1352 (4th Cir. 1989) (upholding state's method of appointing members of local school boards as not intentionally discriminatory). *See also* Vereen v. Ben Hill County, Ga., 743 F. Supp. 864 (M.D. Ga. 1990) (rejecting claim that the Georgia statute authorizing grand juries to select members of county boards of education was enacted for racially discriminatory reasons).

election of board members, with each vote given the same weight as far as practicable.[14] When board members are elected from geographical districts, such districts must be established to protect voting rights under the "one person, one vote" principle. If "at-large" elections result in a dilution of the minority vote, an abridgment of the federal Voting Rights Act may be found.[15] However, the Supreme Court in 1996 struck down congressional redistricting plans drawn on the basis of race,[16] so the creation of race-based voting districts to ensure that a majority of the voters for designated school board seats are people of color would likely abridge the Fourteenth Amendment.[17]

The state legislature can specify the qualifications, method of selection, and terms and conditions of local school board membership. Board members are considered public school officers with sovereign power, in contrast to school employees, who are hired to implement directives. Public officers cannot hold two offices if one is subordinate to the other, cannot have an interest in contracts made by their agencies, and in some states cannot occupy more than one paid office. Generally, statutes stipulate procedures that must be followed in removing public officers from their positions. Typical causes for removal include neglect of duty, illegal performance of duty, breach of good faith, negligence, and incapacity.

A local board must act as a body; individual board members are not empowered to make policies or perform official acts on behalf of the board. School boards have some discretion in adopting operational procedures, but they are legally bound to adhere to such procedures once established. Although courts are reluctant to interfere with decisions made by boards of education and will not rule on the wisdom of such decisions, they will invalidate any board action that is arbitrary, capricious, or outside the board's legal authority (i.e., an *ultra vires* act).

School board meetings and records must be open to the public. Most states have enacted "sunshine" or "open meeting" laws, acknowledging that the public has a right to be fully informed regarding the actions of public agencies. Certain exceptions to open meeting requirements are usually specified in the laws. For example, in many states, school boards can meet in executive session to discuss matters that threaten public safety or pertain to pending or current litigation, personnel matters, collective bargaining, or the disposition of real property. Although discussion of these matters

---

14. Hadley v. Junior Coll. Dist., 397 U.S. 50 (1970).

15. 42 U.S.C. § 1971, *et seq.* (2002). Section 1973 states that "no practice or procedure shall be imposed or applied . . . in a manner which results in a denial or abridgment of the right . . . to vote on account of race. . . . " *See, e.g.,* Johnson v. Desoto County Bd. of Comm'rs, 204 F.3d 1335 (11th Cir. 2000); Clark v. Calhoun County, Miss., 88 F.3d 1393 (5th Cir. 1996); Blytheville Sch. Dist. No. 5 v. Harvell, 71 F.3d 1382 (8th Cir. 1995). *See also* Reno v. Bossier Parish Sch. Bd., 528 U.S. 320 (2000) (ruling that, in the vote-dilution context, § 5 of the Voting Rights Act does not prohibit the Justice Department's preclearance of a redistricting plan as long as it is no more dilutive than the plan it replaces; plan, however, can be challenged after implementation under 42 U.S.C. § 1973).

16. Bush v. Vera, 517 U.S. 952 (1996); Shaw v. Hunt, 517 U.S. 899 (1996).

17. *See, e.g.,* Cannon v. N. C. State Bd. of Educ., 917 F. Supp. 387 (E.D.N.C. 1996) (holding that creation of race-based single board member voting districts threatened equal protection rights).

may take place in closed meetings, statutes usually stipulate that formal action must occur in open meetings.[18]

Local school boards hold powers specified or implied in state law and other powers considered necessary to achieve the purposes of the express powers. These delegated powers generally encompass the authority to determine the specifics of the curriculum offered within the school district, raise revenue to build and maintain schools, select personnel, and enact other policies necessary to implement the educational program pursuant to law. Courts have recognized that even without specific enabling legislation, local boards have discretionary authority to establish and support secondary schools, kindergartens, and nongraded schools; to alter school attendance zones; and to close schools. Local boards also can contract with private companies to provide various services and even to manage total school operations.[19]

Some decisions have been challenged as beyond a local board's lawful scope of authority. For example, school board decisions to alter the length of the instructional week have been contested, and several courts have ruled that in the absence of any state regulations specifying a minimum length of instructional time, school boards have the power to lengthen or shorten the instructional week.[20] Courts also have upheld local school boards' authority to impose a community service requirement as a prerequisite to receipt of a high school diploma.[21]

Nonetheless, local school boards cannot delegate their decision-making authority to other agencies or associations. In an illustrative case, a New Jersey court ruled that a school board could not relinquish to the teachers' association responsibility for determining courses of study or settling classroom controversies.[22] Also, the Iowa

---

18. *See, e.g., In re* Kansas City Star Co., 73 F.3d 191 (8th Cir. 1996) (holding that a closed session between the desegregation monitoring committee and school board did not violate the Missouri Sunshine Act); Connelly v. Sch. Comm. 565 N.E.2d 449 (Mass. 1991) (holding that the Massachusetts open meeting law requires school committees to select principals in open meetings, but selection committees can hold private sessions to screen applicants).

19. In recent years, corporations such as Education Alternatives, Inc. (EAI) and the Edison Project have attracted substantial attention because of their contracts to manage public schools and school districts. Also, a number of companies, such as Sylvan Learning Systems, Britannica Learning Centers, and Berlitz Language Schools, have more limited contracts with public school districts to provide intensive tutoring or specialized instruction. *See* Catherine Gewertz, "Takeover Team Picked in Philadelphia," *Education Week,* vol. 29 (April 2, 2002), pp. 1, 20, 21; Martha McCarthy, "Privatization of Education: Marketplace Models," B. Jones (Ed.), *Educational Administration: Policy Dimensions in the Twenty-First Century* (Greenwich, CT: Ablex, 2000), pp. 21–40.

20. *See, e.g.,* New York City Sch. Bds. Ass'n v. Bd. of Educ., 347 N.E.2d 568 (N.Y. 1976) (shortening the instructional week by two 45-minute periods); Morgan v. Polk County Bd. of Educ., 328 S.E.2d 320 (N.C. Ct. App. 1985) (lengthening the school day and term). Where specifications are provided in state law, however, local boards must adhere to such mandates. *See, e.g.,* Johnston v. Bd. of Trustees, 661 P.2d 1045 (Wyo. 1983) (holding that a school district's practice of compressing the school week into four days violated the state law requiring the school year to be 175 days).

21. *See, e.g.,* Herndon v. Chapel Hill-Carrboro City Bd. of Educ., 89 F.3d 174 (4th Cir. 1996); Steirer v. Bethlehem Area Sch. Dist., 987 F.2d 989 (3d Cir. 1993); text accompanying note 82, Chapter 3.

22. Bd. of Educ. v. Rockaway Township Educ. Ass'n, 295 A.2d 380 (N.J. Super. Ct. Ch. Div. 1972).

Supreme Court held that a school board could not delegate its rule-making authority to a state high school athletic association.[23]

School-Based Councils

Since the mid-1980s, the notion of decentralizing many operational decisions to the school level (site-based management) has received considerable attention. Several legal controversies have focused on the composition and authority of these councils. In 1996, the United States Supreme Court declined to review a decision in which the Seventh Circuit upheld a 1988 Illinois law creating elected school councils, empowered to hire personnel and approve budgets and programs, in the Chicago public schools.[24] The appeals court found that the law's reservation of six places on each council for parents of children in the schools and only two places for other residents did not significantly dilute the voting rights of nonparent residents. The court also rejected school principals' allegations that the law's repeal of their tenure violated protected rights.

The 1990 Kentucky Education Reform Act entails major changes in school funding, curriculum, and governance, including the creation of school-based councils with authority for policy decisions affecting school sites. Whereas local school boards retain many of their traditional powers—such as establishing schools, setting tax rates and budgets, and maintaining facilities—the school-based councils are authorized to hire the building principal, select textbooks, and make policy decisions in other areas such as curricular offerings, staff assignments, and student discipline. Determining the respective spheres of authority of local boards and school-based councils has created some tension. In 1994, teachers challenged a local board's action in requiring school-based councils to obtain board approval before implementing school improvement plans. Noting some overlap in duties between local boards and school councils, the Kentucky Supreme Court reasoned that the state did not delegate to local boards approval authority over council decisions pertaining to school improvement plans.[25] The court reasoned that the state law granting school-based councils independent policy-making powers constituted a clear delegation of legislative authority to the school level.

The relationship between community school boards and their parent school district also has been controversial in New York City. Interpreting the New York decentralization law, the state high court in 1993 found that the community boards are

23. Bunger v. Iowa High Sch. Athletic Ass'n, 197 N.W.2d 555 (Iowa 1972).

24. Pittman v. Chi. Bd. of Educ., 64 F.3d 1098 (7th Cir. 1995); text accompanying note 92, Chapter 8. *See also* Fumarolo v. Chi. Bd. of Educ., 566 N.E.2d 1283 (Ill. 1990) (striking down restrictions on eligible voters for different classes of council members). Under 1991 amendments to the law, teacher members of the council are appointed by the board of education and principal, and all adult residents of the district and nonresident parents are eligible to vote for the elected council members.

25. Bd. of Educ. v. Bushee, 889 S.W.2d 809 (Ky. 1994). *See* Charles Russo, "School-Based Decision Making Councils and School Boards in Kentucky: Trusted Allies or Irreconcilable Foes?" *Education Law Reporter,* vol. 97 (1995), pp. 603–617.

empowered to employ their respective community superintendents, but that the Chancellor of the New York City Public Schools is authorized to establish the selection process. The contested process stipulates that school-based councils will submit to the chancellor a comprehensive evaluation of each finalist for community superintendencies.[26]

Where school-based councils have been created and delegated authority in certain domains (e.g., curriculum, personnel), their decisions have the force of law. Only if councils act beyond their scope of authority or impair protected rights will their decisions be invalidated by the judiciary.

Although school district boards of education and, in some jurisdictions, school-based councils are authorized to perform discretionary duties (i.e., those involving judgment), school employees (e.g., superintendents, principals, teachers) can perform only ministerial duties necessary to carry out policies. Hence, a superintendent can recommend personnel to be hired and propose a budget, but the school board, or in some instances the school council, must make the actual decisions.[27] Although it might appear that educators at the building level retain little decision-making authority, administrators as well as classroom teachers can enact rules and regulations, consistent with policies and laws from higher authorities, to ensure the efficient operation of the school or class under their supervision.

Federal Role in Education

Unlike state constitutions, the Federal Constitution is silent regarding education; hence, individuals do not have an inherent federally protected right to an education.[28] The United States Constitution, however, does confer basic rights on individuals, and these rights must be respected by school personnel. Furthermore, Congress exerts control over the use of federal education aid and regulates other aspects of schools through legislation enacted pursuant to its constitutionally granted powers.

United States Constitution

A *constitution* is a body of precepts providing the system of fundamental laws of a nation, state, or society. The United States Constitution establishes a separation of powers among the executive, judicial, and legislative branches of government. These three branches form a system of checks and balances to ensure that the intent of the

---

26. Bd. of Educ. v. Fernandez, 601 N.Y.S.2d 56 (1993). *See also* Lavelle v. Quinones, 679 F. Supp. 253 (E.D.N.Y. 1988) (upholding the chancellor's order prohibiting the community school district from considering a principal's application for position of deputy superintendent due to the principal's alleged misconduct).

27. *See* text accompanying note 27, Chapter 8.

28. San Antonio Indep. Sch. Dist. v. Rodriguez, 411 U.S. 1 (1973) (holding that there is no explicit or implied fundamental right to an education under the Federal Constitution).

Constitution is respected. The Constitution also provides a systematic process for altering the document, if deemed necessary. Article V stipulates that amendments may be proposed by a two-thirds vote of each house of Congress or by a special convention called by Congress on the request of two-thirds of the state legislatures. Proposed amendments then must be ratified by three-fourths of the states to become part of the Constitution.

Since the United States Constitution is the supreme law in this nation, state authority over education must be exercised in a manner consistent with its provisions. In 1958, the Supreme Court declared: "It is, of course, quite true that the responsibility for public education is primarily the concern of the states, but it is equally true that such responsibilities, like all other state activity, must be exercised consistently with federal constitutional requirements as they apply to state action."[29] The Supreme Court has interpreted various constitutional guarantees as they apply to educational matters. Although all federal constitutional mandates affect public education to some degree, the following provisions have had the greatest impact on public school policies and practices.

General Welfare Clause.   Under Article I, Section 8, of the Constitution, Congress has the power "to lay and collect taxes, duties, imposts and excises, to pay the debts and provide for the common defense and general welfare of the United States." In 1937, the Supreme Court declared that the concept of general welfare is not static: "Needs that were narrow or parochial a century ago may be interwoven in our day with the well-being of the nation. What is critical or urgent changes with the times."[30] Although historically this clause has been the subject of much debate, the Supreme Court has interpreted the provision as allowing Congress to tax and spend public monies for a variety of purposes related to the general welfare.[31] The Court has stated that it will not interfere with the discretion of Congress in its domain, unless Congress exhibits a clear display of arbitrary power.[32]

Using the general welfare rationale, Congress has enacted legislation providing substantial federal support for research and instructional programs in areas such as science, mathematics, reading, special education, vocational education, career education, and bilingual education. Congress also has provided financial assistance for the school lunch program and for services to meet the special needs of various groups of students, such as the educationally and culturally disadvantaged. In addition, Congress has responded to national health and safety concerns with legislation such as the 1980 Asbestos School Hazard Detection and Control Act and the 1988 Indoor Radon Abatement Act, which require the inspection of school buildings and, if necessary, remedial action to assure the safety of students and employees. Given the increasing

29. Cooper v. Aaron, 358 U.S. 1, 19 (1958).

30. Helvering v. Davis, 301 U.S. 619, 641 (1937).

31. *See, e.g., Helvering, id.;* United States v. Butler, 297 U.S. 1 (1936); United States v. Gettysburg Elec. Ry. Co., 160 U.S. 668 (1896).

32. *Helvering,* 301 U.S. at 644–645.

number of schools that are connected electronically through the Internet, the federal government has attempted to protect the welfare of minors by policing the suitability of materials made available to them electronically.[33]

Commerce Clause. Congress is empowered to "regulate commerce with foreign nations, among the several states, and with Indian tribes" under Article I, Section 8, Clause 3, of the Constitution. Safety, transportation, and labor regulations enacted pursuant to this clause have affected the operation of public schools. Traditionally, courts have favored a broad interpretation of "commerce" and an expanded federal role in regulating commercial activity to ensure national prosperity. Interpreting congressional powers to regulate commerce, in 1985 the Supreme Court held that a municipal mass transit system was subject to the minimum wage and overtime requirements of the federal Fair Labor Standards Act (FLSA).[34] This decision, *Garcia v. San Antonio Metropolitan Transit Authority,* overturned a precedent established in 1976 when the Court limited congressional authority to enforce federal minimum wage requirements in areas of "traditional" state governmental functions.[35] Concluding that attempts to identify such state functions that would be immune from federal requirements had been unworkable and inconsistent with established principles of federalism, the Court in *Garcia* found nothing in the FLSA destructive of state sovereignty. This decision eliminated the constitutional barrier to federal regulatory efforts governing other aspects of public employment, such as collective bargaining for public employees.

Obligation of Contracts Clause. Article I, Section 10, of the Constitution stipulates that states cannot enact any law impairing the obligation of contracts. Administrators, teachers, and noncertified personnel are protected from arbitrary dismissals by contractual agreements. School boards also enter into numerous contracts with individuals and companies in conducting school business. The judiciary often is called on to evaluate the validity of a given contract or to assess whether a party has breached its contractual obligations.

First Amendment. The Bill of Rights, comprising the first 10 amendments to the United States Constitution, safeguards individual liberties against governmental

---

33. *See* Children's Internet Protection Act, H.R. 5666 § 1721; 20 U.S.C. § 9134(f) (2002); 47 U.S.C. § 254(h)(5) (2002), which requires public libraries and schools receiving federal funds to install Internet filtering software to block children's access to indecent material. In 2002, a Pennsylvania federal district court stuck down the library portion as a violation of library patrons' First Amendment rights. Am. Library Ass'n v. United States, 201 F. Supp. 2d 401 (E.D. Pa. 2002) *probable jurisdiction noted,* 123 S. Ct. 551 (2002).

34. 469 U.S. 528 (1985).

35. Nat'l League of Cities v. Usery, 426 U.S. 833 (1976). The *Usery* decision halted proposals that were pending before Congress to establish a national collective bargaining law for public school teachers. *See* text accompanying note 19, Chapter 12.

encroachment.[36] The most preciously guarded of these liberties are contained in the First Amendment, which states:

> Congress shall make no law respecting an establishment of religion, or prohibiting the free exercise thereof; or abridging the freedom of speech, or of the press; or the right of the people peaceably to assemble, and to petition the government for a redress of grievances.

The religious freedoms guaranteed by this amendment have evoked a number of lawsuits challenging governmental aid to and regulation of nonpublic schools and contesting public school policies and practices as advancing religion or impairing free exercise rights. Cases involving students' rights to express themselves and to distribute literature have been initiated under First Amendment guarantees of freedom of speech and press. Moreover, teachers' rights to academic freedom and to speak out on matters of public concern have precipitated numerous lawsuits. The right of assembly has been the focus of litigation involving student clubs and employees' rights to organize and engage in collective bargaining.

Fourth Amendment. This amendment guarantees the right of citizens "to be secure in their persons, houses, papers, and effects against unreasonable searches and seizures." The Supreme Court has recognized that the basic purpose of the Fourth Amendment is "to safeguard the privacy and security of individuals against arbitrary invasions by governmental officials."[37] This amendment has frequently appeared in educational cases involving drug-testing programs and searches of students' lockers, cars, and persons. A few cases also have involved alleged violations of school employees' Fourth Amendment rights by school officials.

Fifth Amendment. In part, this amendment provides that no person shall be "compelled in any criminal case to be a witness against himself, nor be deprived of life, liberty, or property without due process of law; nor shall private property be taken for public use, without just compensation." Several cases have addressed the application of the self-incrimination clause in instances where teachers have been questioned by superiors about their activities outside the classroom. The Fifth Amendment also has been used in educational litigation to protect citizens' rights to appropriate compensation for property acquired for school purposes. Due process litigation concerning schools usually has been initiated under the Fourteenth Amendment, which pertains directly to state action. However, many cases in the District of Columbia (involving topics such as desegregation and the rights of children with disabilities) have relied on

---

36. Several of the original states were reluctant to ratify the Constitution without the promise of a statement of individual liberties. *See* Robert Rutland, *The Birth of the Bill of Rights, 1776–1791* (Chapel Hill, NC: University of North Carolina Press, 1955), chapters 7, 8. For a discussion of the application of the Bill of Rights to state governmental action, *see infra* text accompanying note 39.

37. Camara v. Mun. Court of City and County of S. F., 387 U.S. 523, 528 (1967).

due process guarantees of the Fifth Amendment, because the Fourteenth Amendment does not apply in this jurisdiction.[38]

Ninth Amendment. The Ninth Amendment stipulates that "the enumeration in the Constitution, of certain rights, shall not be construed to deny or disparage others retained by the people." This amendment has appeared in educational litigation in which teachers have asserted that their right to personal privacy outside the classroom is protected as an unenumerated right. Grooming regulations applied to teachers and students also have been challenged as infringing on personal rights retained by the people under this amendment.

Fourteenth Amendment. The Fourteenth Amendment is the most widely invoked constitutional provision in school litigation since it specifically addresses state action. In part, the Fourteenth Amendment provides that no state shall "deny to any person within its jurisdiction, the equal protection of the laws." This clause has been significant in school cases involving alleged discrimination based on race, gender, ethnic background, and disabilities. In addition, school finance litigation often has been based on the Equal Protection Clause.

The Due Process Clause of the Fourteenth Amendment, which prohibits states from depriving citizens of life, liberty, or property without due process of law, also has played an important role in school litigation. Property rights are legitimate expectations of entitlement created through state laws, regulations, or contracts. Compulsory school attendance laws confer on students a legitimate property right to attend school, and the granting of tenure gives teachers a property entitlement to continued employment. Liberty rights include interests in one's reputation and fundamental rights related to marriage, family matters, and personal privacy. In addition, the Supreme Court has interpreted Fourteenth Amendment liberties as incorporating the personal freedoms contained in the Bill of Rights.[39] Thus, the first 10 amendments, originally directed toward the federal government, have been applied to state action as well. Although the principle of "incorporation" has been criticized, Supreme Court precedent supports the notion that the Fourteenth Amendment restricts state interference with fundamental constitutional liberties. This principle is particularly important in school litigation since education is a state function; claims that public school policies or practices impair personal freedoms (e.g., First Amendment free speech guarantees) are usually initiated through the Fourteenth Amendment.

The federal judiciary has identified both procedural and substantive components of due process guarantees. Procedural due process ensures fundamental fairness if the government threatens an individual's life, liberty, or property interests; minimum procedures required by the United States Constitution are notice of the charges, an opportunity to refute the charges, and a hearing that is conducted fairly. Substantive

---

38. *See infra* note 52.
39. *See* Cantwell v. Connecticut, 310 U.S. 296, 303 (1940); Gitlow v. New York, 268 U.S. 652, 666 (1925).

due process requires that state action be based on a valid objective with means reasonably related to attaining the objective. In essence, substantive due process shields the individual against arbitrary governmental action that impairs life, liberty, or property interests.

Since the Fourteenth Amendment protects personal liberties against unwarranted state interference, private institutions, including private schools, usually are not subject to these restrictions. For private school policies and practices to be challenged successfully under the Fourteenth Amendment, there must be sufficient governmental involvement in the private school to constitute "state action."[40]

Federal Legislation

Congress is empowered to enact laws to translate the intent of the United States Constitution into actual practices. Laws reflect the will of the legislative branch of government, which, theoretically, in a democracy represents the citizenry. Because the states have sovereign power regarding education, the federal government's involvement in public schools has been one of indirect support, not direct control.

Funding Laws.   Federal legislation affecting public education was enacted prior to ratification of the Constitution. The Ordinances of 1785 and 1787, providing land grants to states for the maintenance of public schools, encouraged the establishment of public education in many states. However, it was not until the mid-twentieth century that Congress began to play a significant role in stimulating targeted educational reform through its spending powers under the General Welfare Clause.

The most comprehensive law offering financial assistance to schools, the Elementary and Secondary Education Act of 1965 (ESEA), in part supplied funds for compensatory education programs for economically disadvantaged students. With passage of ESEA, federal aid to education doubled, and the federal government's contribution increased steadily until reaching its high point of over 9 percent of total public education revenue in 1981. In 2000, the federal share was only 7.3 percent.[41]

Congress and federal administrative agencies have exerted considerable influence in shaping public school policies and practices through categorical funding laws and their accompanying administrative regulations. Individual states or school districts have the option of accepting or rejecting such federal assistance, but if categorical aid is accepted, the federal government has the authority to prescribe guidelines

---

40. *See, e.g.,* Rendell-Baker v. Kohn, 457 U.S. 830 (1982); Burton v. Wilmington Parking Auth., 365 U.S. 715 (1961). *See also* Brentwood Acad. v. Tenn. Secondary Sch. Athletic Ass'n, 531 U.S. 288 (2001) (ruling that state athletic associations regulating interscholastic sports and other competitive activities among public and private schools are extensively entwined with state school officials and thus are considered state actors).

41. National Center for Education Statistics, *Revenues and Expenditures for Public Elementary and Secondary Education* (Washington, DC: U.S. Department of Education, 2002) (http://nces.ed.gov/pubs2002/20002367).

for its use and to monitor state and local education agencies to ensure fiscal accountability.

Much of the federal categorical legislation enacted during the 1960s and 1970s provided funds to assist school districts in attaining equity goals and addressing other national priorities. For example, the Bilingual Education Act of 1968 and the Education for All Handicapped Children Act of 1975 (which became the Individuals with Disabilities Education Act of 1990) have provided federal funds to assist education agencies in offering services for students with special needs. Although in the 1980s Congress shifted away from its heavy reliance on categorical federal aid by consolidating some categorical programs into block grants with reduced funding and regulations, aid for economically disadvantaged and English-deficient students and children with disabilities has remained categorical in nature.

In 2002, President Bush signed into law the No Child Left Behind Act, the most comprehensive reform of the ESEA since it was enacted in 1965.[42] The law, directed at improving the performance of public schools, pledges that no child will be left in a failing school. Specifically, the law requires states to implement accountability systems with higher performance standards in reading and mathematics along with annual testing of all students in grades 3 through 8. Furthermore, assessment data must be categorized by poverty, ethnicity, race, disability, and limited English proficiency to ensure that no group of children is left behind. The law greatly expands choices for parents of children attending Title I schools that do not meet state standards. If students are in a school that has been identified as low performing, they must be given the option of attending a better school within the district, including charter schools. For students attending persistently failing schools (failure to meet the state standards in three of the four preceding years), the school district must permit the students to use Title I funds to obtain supplemental educational services (e.g., tutoring, after-school or summer programs) from either public or private providers. Persistently failing schools not only lose funding as students select other schools but also face mandated reconstitution if they do not make adequate yearly progress.

Civil Rights Laws.   In addition to laws providing financial assistance to public schools, Congress has enacted legislation designed to clarify the scope of individuals' civil rights. Unlike the discretion enjoyed by state and local education agencies in deciding whether to participate in federal funding programs, educational institutions must comply with these civil rights laws. Federal antidiscrimination laws are grounded in two distinct sources of federal authority. Some are enacted to enforce constitutional rights and have general application. Others are based on the federal government's authority to place restrictions on the expenditure of federal funds and apply only to recipients of federal financial assistance. Various federal agencies are charged with monitoring compliance with these laws and can bring suit against noncomplying institutions. Under many civil rights laws, individuals also can initiate private suits to compel compliance and, in some instances, to obtain personal remedies.

---

42. 20 U.S.C. § 6301 *et seq.* (2002).

Several laws enacted in the latter part of the nineteenth century to protect the rights of African American citizens were seldom the focus of litigation until the mid-twentieth century. Since the 1960s, these laws, particularly 42 U.S.C. Section 1983, have been used by students and teachers to gain relief in instances where their federal rights have been violated by school policies and practices. Section 1983 provides a private right to bring suit for damages against any person who, acting under the authority of state law, impairs rights secured by the United States Constitution and federal laws.[43] Although Section 1983 does not confer specific substantive rights, it has been significant in school cases because it allows individuals to obtain damages from school officials and school districts for abridgments of federally protected rights. However, Section 1983 cannot be used to enforce federal laws where congressional intent to create private rights is not clearly stated.[44] In addition, Section 1981 of the Civil Rights Act of 1866, as amended in 1991, prohibits race or ethnicity discrimination in making and enforcing contracts and in the terms and conditions of contractual relationships and allows for both compensatory and punitive damages.[45]

Subsequent civil rights laws enacted since the 1960s do confer substantive rights to protect citizens from discrimination. The vindication of employees' rights in school settings has generated substantial litigation under Title VII of the Civil Rights Act of 1964, which prohibits employment discrimination on the basis of race, color, sex, religion, or national origin. Modeled in part after Title VII, the Americans with Disabilities Act of 1990 provides specific protections in employment and public accommodations for individuals with disabilities. Also, the Age Discrimination in Employment Act of 1967 protects employees over age 40 against age-based employment discrimination. Other civil rights laws pertain only to institutions with programs that receive federal funds, such as Title VI of the Civil Rights Act of 1964 (prohibiting discrimination on the basis of race, color, or national origin), Title IX of the Education Amendments of 1972 (barring gender discrimination against participants in education programs), the Rehabilitation Act of 1973 (prohibiting discrimination against otherwise qualified persons with disabilities), and the Age Discrimination Act of 1975 (barring age discrimination in federally assisted programs or activities).[46] Courts often have been called on to interpret these acts and their regulations as they apply to educational practices.

---

43. School boards as well as school officials are considered "persons" under 42 U.S.C. § 1983 (2002). *See* text accompanying note 209, Chapter 11.

44. *See* Gonzaga Univ. v. Doe, 536 U.S. 273 (2002) (finding that Congress did not intend to create privately enforceable rights under the Family Education Rights and Privacy Act, text accompanying note 166, Chapter 3.

45. 42 U.S.C. § 1981 (2002). The Civil Rights Act of 1991, Pub. L. 102–166, expanded § 1981's protections and strengthened several other civil rights mandates.

46. The Civil Rights Restoration Act of 1987, 20 U.S.C. § 1681 (2002), clarified that these four laws apply to entire institutions if any of their programs receive federal funds. This law was enacted in response to a contrary Supreme Court ruling. Grove City Coll. v. Bell, 465 U.S. 555 (1984).

Still other federal laws offer protections to individuals in educational settings and place responsibilities on school officials. For example, the Family Educational Rights and Privacy Act guarantees parents access to their children's school records and safeguards the confidentiality of such records. Federal laws also protect human subjects in research projects and require parental consent before students participate in federally supported psychiatric or psychological examination, testing, or treatment designed to reveal information in specified sensitive areas. Courts have played an important role in interpreting the protections included in these laws and ensuring compliance with the federal mandates.

Federal Administrative Agencies

Similar to state governments, much of the regulatory activity at the federal level is conducted by administrative agencies. The Office of Education was originally established in 1867, and it became part of the Department of Health, Education, and Welfare in 1953. In 1980, the Department of Education was created; its secretary, who serves as a member of the president's cabinet, is appointed by the president with the advice and approval of the Senate.

The primary functions of the Department of Education are to coordinate federal involvement in education activities, to identify educational needs of national significance, to propose strategies to address these needs, and to provide technical and financial assistance to state and local education agencies. Regulations promulgated by the Department of Education to implement funding laws have had a significant impact on many schools. The department solicits public comments on proposed regulations, and Congress reviews the regulations to ensure their consistency with legislative intent. The Department of Education administers regulations for over 100 different programs ranging from services for Native American students to projects for school dropouts. The Departments of Agriculture, Labor, Defense, Justice, or Health and Human Services administer the remaining educational programs.

Through their regulatory activities, numerous federal agencies influence state and local education policies. For example, the Office for Civil Rights and the Equal Employment Opportunity Commission have reviewed claims of discrimination in public schools and initiated suits against school districts that are not in compliance with civil rights laws. The Environmental Protection Agency also has placed obligations on schools in connection with asbestos removal and maintenance of safe school environments. School districts can face the termination of federal assistance if they do not comply with such federal regulations.

Function and Structure of the Judicial System

Judicial decisions are usually cited in conjunction with statutory and constitutional provisions as a major source of educational law. As early as 1835, Alexis de Tocqueville noted that "scarcely any political question arises in the United States that is not resolved, sooner or later, into a judicial question."[47] Courts, however, do not initiate laws as legislative bodies do; courts apply appropriate principles of law to settle disputes. The terms *common law* and *case law* refer to judicially created legal principles that are relied on as precedent when similar factual situations arise.

Although most constitutional provisions and statutory enactments never become the subject of litigation, some provisions require judicial clarification. Since federal and state constitutions set forth broad policy statements rather than specific guides to action, courts serve an important function in interpreting such mandates and in determining the legality of various school policies and practices.

The Supreme Court has articulated specific guidelines for exercising the power of judicial review. The Court will not decide hypothetical cases and will not render an opinion on issues in nonadversarial proceedings. A genuine controversy must be initiated by a party with standing to sue. To achieve such standing, the party must have a "real interest" in the outcome of the case, such as having been adversely affected by the challenged practice.

The Supreme Court also will not anticipate a constitutional question or decide a case on constitutional grounds if there is some other basis for resolving the dispute. When an act of Congress is questioned, the Court attempts to "ascertain whether a construction of the statute is fairly possible by which the question may be avoided."[48] In applying appropriate principles of law to specific cases, the Court generally follows the doctrine of *stare decisis* (abide by decided cases), and thus relies on precedents established in previous decisions. On occasion, however, the Court does overrule a prior opinion.

When a suit is initiated, the trial court holds a hearing to make findings of fact based on the evidence presented, and then applies legal principles to those facts in rendering a judgment. If the ruling is appealed, the appellate court must accept the trial court's findings of fact unless they are clearly erroneous. The appeals court reviews the written record of the evidence but does not hold a hearing for witnesses to be questioned. The appellate court may accept the trial court's findings of fact but disagree with the conclusions of law. In such instances, the case is usually remanded to the trial court for reconsideration in light of the appropriate legal principles enunciated by the appeals court.

In addition to individual suits,[49] education cases often involve class-action suits brought on behalf of all similarly situated individuals. To be certified as a class action, the suit must satisfy rules of civil procedure that specify prerequisites to establish

47. Alexis de Tocqueville, *Democracy in America,* rev. ed. (New York: Alfred A. Knopf, 1960), vol. 1, p. 280.

48. Crowell v. Benson, 285 U.S. 22, 62 (1932). *See also* Ashwander v. Tenn. Valley Auth., 297 U.S. 288, 348 (1936) (Brandeis, J., concurring).

49. Most educational litigation involves civil suits, initiated by individuals alleging injury by another private party. Civil suits often involve claims for damages or requests for specific conduct to cease because it impairs the individual's protected rights. In contrast, criminal suits are brought on behalf of society to punish an individual for committing a crime, such as violating compulsory school attendance laws.

commonality of injury and circumstances among class members. If a suit is not properly certified as a class action, and the circumstances of the original plaintiff change (e.g., a student graduates from school before a judgment is rendered), the court may dismiss the suit as moot because the plaintiff is no longer being injured by the contested practice.

Various remedies are available through court action. In some suits, a court-ordered injunction is sought to compel school officials to cease a particular action or to remove restraints they have imposed on protected freedoms. For a court to issue a preliminary injunction, evidence must indicate that the complainant would likely prevail in a trial on the merits of the case. Judicial relief also can take the form of a declaration that specific rights must be respected. In addition, courts can order personal remedies, such as reinstatement and removal of material from school records. Courts also can award damages to compensate individuals for the deprivation of their rights, and punitive damages can be assessed against state officials if such deprivations constitute a willful or reckless disregard of protected rights. Under certain circumstances, attorneys' fees can be awarded.

In interpreting constitutional and statutory provisions, courts have developed various criteria to evaluate whether the law has been violated. These judicially created standards or "tests" are extremely important and in some instances appear to go beyond the original intent of the constitutional or statutory provision in question. Judicial standards for assessing claims under various constitutional and statutory provisions are continually evolving and being refined by courts. The judiciary thus occupies a powerful position in shaping the law through its interpretive powers.

Courts, however, will not intervene in a school-related controversy if the dispute can be settled in a legislative or administrative forum. The Supreme Court has emphasized that in situations involving "persistent and difficult questions of educational policies," the judiciary's "lack of specialized knowledge and experience counsels against premature interference with the informed judgments made at the state and local levels."[50] All state educational systems provide some type of administrative appeals procedure for aggrieved individuals to use in disputes involving internal school operations. Many school controversies never reach the courts because they are settled in these administrative forums. Under most circumstances, courts require such administrative appeals to be exhausted before court action is brought.

In evaluating the impact of case law, it is important to keep in mind that a judicial ruling applies as precedent within the geographical jurisdiction of the court delivering the opinion. It is possible for two state supreme courts or two federal courts to render conflicting decisions on an issue, and such decisions are binding in their respective jurisdictions. Only decisions of the United States Supreme Court have national application.

---

50. San Antonio Indep. Sch. Dist. v. Rodriguez, 411 U.S. 1, 42 (1973).

State Courts

State courts are established pursuant to state constitutional provisions, and the structure of judicial systems varies among states. In contrast to federal courts, which have only those powers granted by the United States Constitution, state courts can review most types of controversies unless restricted by state law. State judicial systems usually include trial courts of general jurisdiction, courts of special jurisdiction, and appellate courts. All states have a court of last resort, and decisions rendered by state high courts can be appealed to the United States Supreme Court.

In most states, the court of last resort is called the supreme court or supreme judicial court. However, in New York and Maryland the highest court is the Court of Appeals, and in West Virginia it is the Supreme Court of Appeals. Courts occupying the next level in the state judicial system usually are referred to as appeals courts or superior courts. State trial courts of general jurisdiction often are called district or circuit courts, but in New York, trial courts are referred to as supreme courts of their respective counties. The most common special jurisdiction courts are juvenile, probate, domestic relations, and small claims courts. State judges are usually either elected or appointed by the governor.

Federal Courts

Article III, Section I, of the United States Constitution establishes the Supreme Court and authorizes Congress to create other federal courts as necessary. The federal court system contains courts of special jurisdiction such as the claims court, tax court, and court of international trade. There are three levels of federal courts of general jurisdiction: district courts, circuit courts of appeal, and the Supreme Court. The number of federal district courts in a state is based on population. Each state has at least one federal district court; many states have two or three; and California, New York, and Texas have four each. Judgments at the district court level are usually presided over by one judge.

On the federal appeals level, the nation is divided into 12 geographic circuits, each with its own federal circuit court of appeals.[51] A thirteenth federal circuit court has national jurisdiction to hear appeals regarding specific claims (e.g., customs; copyrights, patents, and trademarks; international trade). Federal circuit courts have from 3 to 15 judges, depending on the workload of the circuit. Most circuit decisions are rendered by a panel of the court, but in some instances the entire court (*en banc*) will rehear a case. Although a federal circuit court decision is binding only in the states within that circuit, such decisions often influence other appellate courts when dealing with similar questions. The jurisdiction of the federal circuits is as follows.

- First Circuit: Maine, Massachusetts, New Hampshire, Rhode Island, and Puerto Rico

---

51. In 1981, the Fifth Circuit was divided into the Fifth and Eleventh Circuits.

- Second Circuit: Connecticut, New York, and Vermont
- Third Circuit: Delaware, New Jersey, Pennsylvania, and the Virgin Islands
- Fourth Circuit: Maryland, North Carolina, South Carolina, Virginia, and West Virginia
- Fifth Circuit: Louisiana, Mississippi, Texas, and the Canal Zone
- Sixth Circuit: Kentucky, Michigan, Ohio, and Tennessee
- Seventh Circuit: Illinois, Indiana, and Wisconsin
- Eighth Circuit: Arkansas, Iowa, Minnesota, Missouri, Nebraska, North Dakota, and South Dakota
- Ninth Circuit: Alaska, Arizona, California, Idaho, Hawaii, Montana, Nevada, Oregon, Washington, and Guam
- Tenth Circuit: Colorado, Kansas, New Mexico, Oklahoma, Utah, and Wyoming;
- Eleventh Circuit: Alabama, Florida, and Georgia
- D.C. Circuit: Washington, D.C.[52]
- Federal Circuit: National jurisdiction on specific claims

The United States Supreme Court is, of course, the highest court in the nation, beyond which there is no appeal. It has been firmly established that the Supreme Court has the ultimate authority in interpreting federal constitutional guarantees.[53] If the Supreme Court finds a specific practice unconstitutional (e.g., intentional school segregation), this judicial mandate applies nationwide. If the Court, however, concludes that a given activity does not impair federal constitutional guarantees (e.g., corporal punishment in public schools), states and local school boards retain discretion in placing restrictions on the activity. In the latter instances, legal requirements will vary across jurisdictions.

As noted previously, if the judiciary interprets a statutory enactment contrary to legislative intent, the law can be amended to clarify its purpose. Congress has done so with a number of civil rights laws in response to Supreme Court rulings.[54] However, the legislative branch does not have this discretion in connection with constitutional interpretations. If the Supreme Court rules that a federal law conflicts with a provision of the United States Constitution, the law is invalidated, and the only recourse is to amend the Constitution.

The Supreme Court has original jurisdiction in cases in which a state is a party or that involve federal ambassadors and other public ministers. The Court has appellate jurisdiction in other cases arising under the Constitution or federal laws or entail-

---

52. Washington, D.C., has its own federal district court and circuit court of appeals; only federal laws apply in this jurisdiction.

53. *See* Marbury v. Madison, 5 U.S. (1 Cranch) 137 (1803).

54. *See supra* note 46.

ing disputes between states or parties residing in different states.[55] The Supreme Court disposes of approximately 5,000 cases a year, but renders a written opinion on the merits in less than 5 percent of these cases. The Court often concludes that the topic of a case is not appropriate or of sufficient significance to warrant Supreme Court review. It requires concurrence of at least four justices for a case to be accepted, and denial of review (*certiorari*) does not infer agreement with the lower court's decision. Since the Supreme Court has authority to determine which cases it will hear, many issues are left for resolution by lower courts. Accordingly, precedents regarding some school controversies must be gleaned from federal circuit courts or state supreme courts and may differ from one jurisdiction to another.

An individual need not exhaust state administrative appeals before initiating a federal suit if the abridgment of a federally protected right is involved, but some federal laws specify administrative procedures that must be pursued before commencing court action. Suits involving federal issues also may be heard by state courts, and the United States Supreme Court may review the interpretation of federal rights by the state judiciary. Individuals have a choice whether to initiate a federal or state suit in these circumstances, but they cannot relitigate an issue in federal court if they have been denied relief by the state judiciary. In essence, a federal suit cannot be initiated if the state judiciary has already adjudicated an issue or it could have been raised in the prior state litigation.

Judicial Trends

Traditionally, the federal judiciary did not address educational concerns; fewer than 300 cases involving education had been initiated in federal courts prior to 1954.[56] However, starting with the landmark desegregation decision, *Brown v. Board of Education of Topeka* (1954),[57] federal courts assumed a significant role in resolving educational controversies. By 1970, litigation was clearly viewed as an important tool to influence social policies, and more legal challenges to school practices were initiated in the 1970s than in the preceding seven decades combined.[58] Since the 1960s, courts have addressed nearly every facet of the educational enterprise. Much of this judicial intervention has involved the protection of individual rights and the attainment of equity for minority groups.

The volume of federal cases pertaining to school issues reached its zenith in the 1970s. Since then, it has stabilized or declined slightly in most areas (e.g., employment concerns, student discipline), except for litigation dealing with church/state

---

55. *See* text accompanying note 214, Chapter 11, for a discussion of Eleventh Amendment restrictions on federal lawsuits brought by citizens against the state.

56. John Hogan, *The Schools, the Courts, and the Public Interest* (Lexington, MA: D. C. Heath, 1985), p. 11.

57. 347 U.S. 483 (1954).

58. William Bennett, "Excessive Legalization in Education," *Chicago Daily Law Bulletin* (February 22, 1988), p. 2.

issues and the rights of children with disabilities. Indeed, cases involving children with disabilities have increased at a phenomenal rate since 1980.

There has been a notable shift in the posture of the federal judiciary during the past two decades. In the 1960s and early 1970s, federal courts expanded constitutional protections afforded to individuals in school settings, but since the 1980s the federal judiciary has exhibited more deference to the decisions of the legislative and executive branches and greater reluctance to extend the scope of civil rights. Judicial deference to policymakers nurtures diverse standards across states and local school districts. When the Supreme Court strikes down a practice under the Constitution, standards become more uniform nationally, but when the Court defers to local boards, standards vary, reflecting local perspectives. If the federal judiciary continues to exhibit restraint, volatile political controversies will be assured, because policymakers will have to grapple with issues that formerly were settled through judicial pronouncements.

The Rehnquist Court's strong federalism stance is redefining the balance of power between the federal government and states. In sharply divided decisions, the Supreme Court has strengthened states' sovereign immunity by precluding federal lawsuits against states unless Congress has abrogated state immunity through legislation enacted to enforce the Fourteenth Amendment. Such congressional intent, however, must be explicit in the federal legislation and enacted to protect a suspect class from state action. For example, in recent cases, the Court held that Congress exceeded its authority in imposing liability on states under the Age Discrimination in Employment Act[59] and the American with Disabilities Act.[60] These acts did not involve a suspect class nor were they enacted to address irrational employment discrimination by states. The new federalism limits suits against states, but school districts will not benefit from the immunity unless they are considered an arm of the state for Eleventh Amendment purposes.[61]

Although the debate will likely continue over whether courts have the competence to play a key role in shaping educational policies and whether it is legitimate for courts to play such a role, without question courts do influence school policies. Despite some deceleration in federal litigation, the volume of school cases is still substantial, far outstripping school litigation in any other nation.

Conclusion

Public schools in the United States are governed by a complex body of regulations that are grounded in constitutional provisions, statutory enactments, agency regulations, and court decisions. Since the mid-twentieth century, legislation relating to schools has increased significantly in both volume and complexity, and courts have played an

59. Kimel v. Florida Bd. of Regents, 528 U.S. 62 (2000).

60. Bd. of Trustees v. Garrett, 531 U.S. 356 (2001)

61. *See* text accompanying note 217, Chapter 11.

important role in interpreting statutory and constitutional provisions. Although rules made at any level must be consistent with higher authority, administrators and teachers retain considerable latitude in establishing rules and procedures within their specific jurisdictions. As long as educators act reasonably and do not impair the protected rights of others, their actions will be upheld if challenged in court.

School personnel, however, cannot plead "ignorance of the law" as a valid defense for illegal actions.[62] Thus, educators should be aware of the constraints placed on their rule-making prerogatives by school board policies and federal and state constitutional and statutory provisions. Subsequent chapters of this book attempt to clarify the major legal principles affecting teachers and students in their daily school activities.

---

62. *See* Wood v. Strickland, 420 U.S. 308 (1975).

2

Church/State Relations

Efforts to identify the appropriate relationship between government and religion have generated substantial controversy in our nation, and since the mid-twentieth century, schools have provided the battleground for some of the most volatile disputes. This chapter provides an overview of the constitutional framework, the evolution of legal activity, and the current status of church/state relations involving education.

Constitutional Framework

The First Amendment to the United States Constitution stipulates in part that "Congress shall make no law respecting an establishment of religion or prohibiting the free exercise thereof." Although this amendment was directed toward the *federal* government, the Fourteenth Amendment, adopted in 1868, specifically placed restrictions on *state* action impairing personal rights. In the twentieth century, the Supreme Court recognized that the fundamental concept of "liberty" embodied in the Fourteenth Amendment incorporates First Amendment guarantees and safeguards them against state interference.[1] Since education is primarily a state function, most church/state controversies involving schools have been initiated through the Fourteenth Amendment.

Constitutional scholars have extensively debated whether the framers of the Establishment and Free Exercise Clauses intended to sever civil and sectarian affairs or merely to prohibit religious discrimination and governmental promotion of a particular sect. Although this debate will likely continue, the ultimate responsibility for interpreting the restrictions imposed by the First Amendment on governmental action resides with the United States Supreme Court. Most constitutional law governing

---

1. *See* Cantwell v. Connecticut, 310 U.S. 296, 303 (1940); Gitlow v. New York, 268 U.S. 652, 666 (1925).

church/state relations has been produced since World War II, and judicial standards to assess claims under the Establishment and Free Exercise Clauses and their interaction with free speech guarantees are still evolving.

In the first major Establishment Clause decision, *Everson v. Board of Education,* the Supreme Court in 1947 reviewed the history of the First Amendment and concluded that the Establishment Clause (and its Fourteenth Amendment application to states) means:

> Neither a state nor the Federal Government can set up a church. Neither can pass laws which aid one religion, aid all religions, or prefer one religion over another. . . . Neither a state nor the Federal Government can, openly or secretly, participate in the affairs of any religious organizations or groups and *vice versa.* In the words of Jefferson, the clause against establishment of religion by law was intended to erect "a wall of separation between church and state."[2]

Whether this "wall of separation" should be the guiding church/state standard has evoked substantial debate. Jefferson's metaphor[3] was used widely by the federal judiciary for more than 30 years following *Everson,* even though this phrase does not appear in the First Amendment. During this period, the Establishment Clause seemed to be accorded greater weight than the Free Exercise Clause. Most courts supported the sentiment of Justice Douglas: "There cannot be the slightest doubt that the First Amendment reflects the philosophy that Church and State should be separated. . . . The separation must be complete and unequivocal."[4]

In a 1971 case, *Lemon v. Kurtzman,* the Supreme Court first applied a tripartite test to assess Establishment Clause claims.[5] To withstand scrutiny under this test, often referred to as the *Lemon* test, governmental action must (1) have a secular purpose, (2) have a primary effect that neither advances nor impedes religion, and (3) avoid excessive governmental entanglement with religion. This three-part test was used consistently in Establishment Clause cases involving school issues until 1992.[6]

---

2. 330 U.S. 1, 15–16 (1947).

3. This metaphor is traced to a statement made by Thomas Jefferson in 1802 in a letter refusing a Baptist association's request for a day to be established for fasting and prayer in thanksgiving for the nation's welfare. *See* Robert Healey, *Jefferson on Religion in Public Education* (New Haven, CT: Yale University Press, 1962), pp. 128–140. Chief Justice Rehnquist in 1985 asserted that the wall is "a metaphor based on bad history, a metaphor which has proved useless as a guide to judging. It should be frankly and explicitly abandoned." Wallace v. Jaffree, 472 U.S. 38, 107 (1985) (Rehnquist, C. J., dissenting).

4. Zorach v. Clauson, 343 U.S. 306, 312 (1952). *See also* Sch. Dist. of Abington Township v. Schempp, 374 U.S. 203, 219 (1963).

5. 403 U.S. 602 (1971). *See also* Walz v. Tax Comm'n, 397 U.S. 664 (1970) (applying the entanglement prong for the first time in rejecting an Establishment Clause challenge to the tax exempt status of church property).

6. *But see* Marsh v. Chambers, 463 U.S. 783 (1983); *infra* note 22.

However, a majority of the current justices has voiced dissatisfaction with the test,[7] and reliance on *Lemon* has been noticeably absent in the Supreme Court's recent Establishment Clause rulings. Support for church/state separation seems to be waning, even in school cases where separationist doctrine has received the greatest support.

Some of the current Supreme Court justices, especially Justice O'Connor,[8] favor an *endorsement standard* under which governmental action would be struck down if an objective observer would view it as having the purpose or effect of endorsing or disapproving religion.[9] The endorsement principle is not as strict as separationism. But it is easier to substantiate an Establishment Clause violation using this standard than the *coercion test,* which requires direct or indirect governmental coercion on individuals to profess a faith.[10] Both the endorsement and coercion standards focus on individual entitlements, rather than societal harms that might accrue from church/state mergers.[11] Instead of replacing the *Lemon* test with another standard or a combination, the current Supreme Court seems likely to continue to draw on various tests depending on the specific circumstances of each case. And some lower courts are attempting to cover all bases by reviewing challenged government action under multiple standards, including the three-part *Lemon* test, the endorsement standard, and the coercion test.[12]

Whereas the Establishment Clause is used primarily to challenge governmental advancement of religion, lawsuits under the Free Exercise Clause usually focus on secular (nonreligious) governmental regulations alleged to have a coercive effect on religious practices. In establishment cases, the legality of the governmental action itself is at issue, but in free exercise claims, individuals often accept the secular nature of the government regulation but assert that it burdens their religious exercise.

To evaluate free exercise claims, the judiciary traditionally applied a balancing test that includes an assessment of whether practices dictated by a sincere and legitimate religious belief have been impeded by the governmental action, and if so, to what extent. If such an impairment is substantiated, the court then evaluates whether the government action serves a compelling interest that justifies the burden imposed on

---

7. *See* Lee v. Weisman, 505 U.S. 577, 644–645 (1992) (Scalia, J., joined by Thomas, J., dissenting); County of Allegheny v. ACLU, 492 U.S. 573, 655 (1989) (Kennedy, J., concurring in part, dissenting in part); Edwards v. Aguillard, 482 U.S. 578, 636–640 (1987) (Scalia, J., joined by Rehnquist, C. J., dissenting); Aguilar v. Felton, 473 U.S. 402, 426–430 (1985) (O'Connor, J., dissenting); Wallace v. Jaffree, 472 U.S. 38, 108–113 (1985) (Rehnquist, J., dissenting). In Lamb's Chapel v. Ctr. Moriches Union Free Sch. Dist., 508 U.S. 384, 398 (1993), Justice Scalia, concurring, compared the *Lemon* standard to a "ghoul" that rises from the dead "after being repeatedly killed and buried."

8. *See* Lynch v. Donnelly, 465 U.S. 668, 687 (1984) (O'Connor, J., concurring).

9. *See, e.g., County of Allegheny,* 492 U.S. at 592.

10. *See Weisman,* 505 U.S. 577.

11. Ira C. Lupu, "The Lingering Death of Separationism," *George Washington Law Review,* vol. 62 (1994), p. 232.

12. *See, e.g.,* Doe v. Beaumont Indep. Sch. Dist., 240 F.3d 462 (5th Cir. 2001); Koenick v. Felton, 190 F.3d 259 (4th Cir. 1999); Stark v. Indep. Sch. Dist. No. 640, 123 F.3d 1068 (8th Cir. 1997); Hsu v. Roslyn Union Free Sch. Dist. No. 3, 85 F.3d 839 (2d Cir. 1996).

the exercise of religious beliefs. Even if such a compelling interest is shown, the government is expected to attain its objectives through means that are the least burdensome on free exercise rights.

In the most significant school case involving a free exercise claim, *Wisconsin v. Yoder,* the Supreme Court exempted Amish children from compulsory school attendance upon successful completion of eighth grade.[13] Although noting that the assurance of an educated citizenry ranks at the "apex" of state functions, the Court nonetheless concluded that parents' rights to practice their legitimate religious beliefs outweighed the state's interest in mandating two additional years of formal schooling for Amish youth. The Court declared that "a state's interest in universal education, however highly we rank it, is not totally free from a balancing process when it impinges on fundamental rights and interests."[14] The Court cautioned, however, that its ruling was limited to the Amish who offer a structured vocational program to prepare their youth for a cloistered agrarian community rather than mainstream American society.

In a 1990 decision, the Supreme Court modified this balancing test, ruling that the government does not have to demonstrate a compelling interest to defend a criminal law that burdens the free exercise of religious beliefs.[15] The case was initiated by two employees who had been fired for misconduct and subsequently denied unemployment benefits because they ingested peyote at a religious ceremony of the Native American Church. Distinguishing this case from *Yoder,* which involved a combination of free exercise rights and parental rights, the Court majority concluded that without such a "hybrid" situation, individuals cannot rely on the Free Exercise Clause to be excused from complying with a valid criminal law prohibiting specific conduct.[16]

Courts not only apply different criteria to assess claims under the Free Exercise and Establishment Clauses, they also impose different remedies for violations of the two clauses. For an Establishment Clause violation, the unconstitutional government activity must cease. If government action is found to impair the Free Exercise Clause, accommodations to enable individuals to practice their beliefs may be required, but the secular policy or program would not have to be eliminated.

Troublesome church/state controversies involve competing claims under the Free Exercise and Establishment Clauses because both "are cast in absolute terms, and either of which, if expanded to a logical extreme, would tend to clash with the other."[17]

13. 406 U.S. 205 (1972).

14. *Id.* at 214.

15. Employment Div. v. Smith, 494 U.S. 872 (1990).

16. Responding to this ruling, in 1993 Congress enacted the Religious Freedom Restoration Act, 42 U.S.C. § 2000bb (1996), to reinstate the compelling interest requirement, even if the government burden results from a rule of general applicability. But the Supreme Court subsequently invalidated this law because it did not simply prevent unconstitutional behavior; it overstepped congressional authority by proscribing state conduct beyond the reach of the Fourteenth Amendment. City of Boerne v. Flores, 521 U.S. 507 (1997).

17. Walz v. Tax Comm'n, 397 U.S. 664, 668–669 (1970).

The controversies become even more complex when Free Speech Clause protections are involved, as has been prevalent in recent cases.[18] Accommodations to free exercise and free speech rights can be interpreted as advancing religion in violation of the Establishment Clause, but overzealous efforts to guard against state sponsorship of religion can impinge on protections under the Free Exercise and Free Speech Clauses. This tension among First Amendment guarantees has complicated the judiciary's task in assessing claims regarding the role of religion in public schools and government relations with sectarian schools.

Religious Influences in Public Schools

From colonial days until the mid-twentieth century, religious (primarily Protestant) materials and observances were prevalent in many public schools. In two precedent-setting decisions in the early 1960s, the Supreme Court prohibited public schools from sponsoring daily prayer and Bible reading, concluding that such activities advance religion in violation of the Establishment Clause.[19] The Court reasoned that the students' voluntary participation in the religious activities was irrelevant to the constitutional impairment. The fact that daily devotional activities were conducted under the auspices of the public school was sufficient to abridge the First Amendment. These rulings "injected separationism powerfully into the political culture," stimulating public protests and congressional reactions.[20]

A number of subsequent decisions have struck down various legislative attempts to return religious activities to public schools. The Supreme Court affirmed without an opinion or declined to review decisions in which federal appellate courts struck down state laws calling for voluntary spoken prayer in public schools, a school board's attempt to permit student-led prayers in school assemblies, and state-condoned devotional activities initiated by teachers.[21] Also, the Sixth Circuit equated prayers in school board meetings with prohibited prayers during the school day rather

18. *See, e.g.,* Good News Club v. Milford Cent. Sch., 533 U.S. 98 (2001); Santa Fe Indep. Sch. Dist. v. Doe, 530 U.S. 290 (2000); *infra* text accompanying notes 41, 107.

19. Sch. Dist. of Abington Township v. Schempp, 374 U.S. 203 (1963); Engel v. Vitale, 370 U.S. 421 (1962).

20. Lupu, "The Lingering Death of Separationism," p. 232. *See also* the No Child Left Behind Act, 20 U.S.C. § 6061 (2002) (specifying that no federal funds can be appropriated under the act to be used for policies that prevent voluntary prayer and meditation in public schools).

21. *See* Ingebretsen v. Jackson Pub. Sch. Dist., 88 F.3d 274 (5th Cir. 1996) (Mississippi law authorizing student-initiated prayer); Jaffree v. Bd. of Sch. Comm'rs, 705 F.2d 1526 (11th Cir. 1983) (teacher-initiated devotional activities); Jaffree v. Wallace, 705 F.2d 1526 (11th Cir. 1983), *aff'd mem. in part,* 466 U.S. 924 (1984) (Alabama voluntary prayer law); Karen B. v. Treen, 653 F.2d 897 (5th Cir. 1981), *aff'd mem.,* 455 U.S. 913 (1982) (Louisiana voluntary prayer law); Collins v. Chandler Unified Sch. Dist., 644 F.2d 759 (9th Cir. 1981) (student-led prayers in school assemblies).

than with permissible legislative prayers,[22] due to the potential coercive effect of the prayers on students who might attend the board meetings.[23] And the Fifth Circuit found Establishment Clause violations in a school district allowing employees to lead or encourage prayers in curricular or extracurricular activities[24] and in legislation deleting the word *silent* from Louisiana's silent prayer law.[25] In the latter case, the appeals court ruled that the plain language and legislative history demonstrated that the sole purpose of the law's amendment was to return verbal prayer to public schools. These appellate courts found little constitutional distinction between the contested practices and the state-imposed devotional activities that the Supreme Court barred under the Establishment Clause in the early 1960s.

However, these rulings have not resolved many issues pertaining to religious influences in public education. Is the constitutional violation lessened if students rather than teachers initiate the devotional activities? If religious observances are occasional rather than daily, is the threat of an Establishment Clause impairment reduced? Can religious speech be distinguished from other types of speech in applying restrictions? To date, only partial answers have been provided to these and related questions in the public school context.

Silent Prayer Statutes

Students have a free exercise right to engage in *private* devotional activities in public schools as long as they do not interfere with regular school activities. Indeed, it would be difficult to monitor whether students were engaging in silent prayer. Controversies have focused on state laws or school board policies that condone silent devotionals, thus placing the stamp of public school approval on such activities.

In 1985, the Supreme Court rendered its first and only opinion to date on this issue in *Wallace v. Jaffree,* invalidating a 1981 Alabama silent prayer law under the Establishment Clause.[26] Since a 1978 Alabama law already authorized a period of silent meditation in public schools, the Court majority concluded that the only logical reason for adding the phrase *or voluntary prayer* in the 1981 amendment was to encourage students to pray. But the Court indicated that laws calling for silent meditation or prayer in public schools without a legislative intent to impose prayer might withstand scrutiny under the Establishment Clause.

---

22. Marsh v. Chambers, 463 U.S. 783 (1983) (relying primarily on "tradition" rather than the *Lemon* test, the Court rejected an Establishment Clause challenge to the use of state funds to support a chaplain to open legislative sessions with a prayer).

23. Coles v. Cleveland Bd. of Educ., 171 F.3d 369 (6th Cir. 1999).

24. Doe v. Duncanville Indep. Sch. Dist., 70 F.3d 402 (5th Cir. 1995).

25. Doe v. Sch. Bd., 274 F.3d 289 (5th Cir. 2001).

26. 705 F.2d 1526 (11th Cir. 1983), *aff'd,* 472 U.S. 38 (1985). Although several state practices were contested in this case, the Supreme Court agreed to address only the silent prayer statute. *See supra* note 21, for the disposition of the other issues.

Therefore, the constitutionality of laws calling for a moment of silence for prayer or meditation in public schools, which currently are on the books in almost half of the states, remains to be resolved on a case-by-case basis, and courts have rejected most recent challenges to such laws. For example, a high school teacher who was fired for refusing to comply with Georgia's law challenged the constitutionality of the law that requires each public school teacher to conduct a minute of quiet reflection at the opening of the school day. In upholding the statute, the appeals court concluded that the provision had the secular purpose of providing an opportunity for pupils to reflect on the upcoming day.[27]

The Fourth Circuit also upheld a Virginia silent prayer statute as being neutral toward religion since students were not encouraged to pray during the moment of silence. The contested law stipulates that each school board shall establish the daily observance of one minute of silence in all classrooms so that pupils may "meditate, pray, or engage in other silent activity which does not interfere with, distract, or impede other pupils in the exercise of individual choice."[28] The appeals court reasoned that the law provides a neutral medium—silence—during which students can be involved in sectarian or secular activities. Unlike the Alabama law struck down in *Jaffree,* which was clearly intended to return prayer to public schools, the appeals court reasoned that Virginia's law was enacted to provide time for quiet reflection—a good management strategy to settle students.[29]

School-Sponsored versus Private Devotionals

The most controversial issues currently revolve around whether the Establishment Clause concerns are eliminated if students initiate and lead devotionals in public schools. In short, what constitutes private religious expression in the public school context that does not trigger Establishment Clause restrictions? There are some mixed signals from the federal courts regarding student-led graduation devotionals and prayers in other school events.

Weisman *and Its Progeny.* The impetus for the recent wave of legislative activity pressing the limits of the Establishment Clause was the seminal 1992 decision, *Lee v. Weisman,* in which the Supreme Court struck down a Rhode Island school district's policy that permitted principals to invite clergy members to deliver invocations and benedictions at middle and high school graduation ceremonies.[30] In a five-to-four decision, the Court affirmed the appellate court's conclusion that such clergy-led devotionals at public school graduations violate the Establishment Clause. The Court majority reasoned that the policy had a coercive effect; students felt peer pressure to

27. Bown v. Gwinnett County Sch. Dist., 112 F.3d 1464 (11th Cir. 1997).

28. Va. Code Ann § 22.1-203 (2002).

29. Brown v. Gilmore, 258 F.3d 265 (4th Cir. 2001), *cert. denied,* 533 U.S. 1301 (2001).

30. 505 U.S. 577 (1992).

participate in the devotionals that were conducted at the school-sponsored graduation ceremony.[31] The Court was not persuaded that the voluntary nature of graduation exercises eliminated the constitutional infraction. According to the majority, students should not have to make a choice between attending their graduation ceremony, a milestone event in their lives, and respecting their religious convictions.

Rather than reducing devotional activities in public school graduations, the Supreme Court's decision had the opposite impact. Negative reactions to this ruling resulted in school authorities and students finding creative strategies to include prayers in graduation ceremonies. In some districts, baccalaureate services were reinstated that had not been held for many years. To pass constitutional scrutiny, such baccalaureates cannot be sponsored by the public school, but students, churches, or other groups can rent space from the school district to conduct the religious services.[32] In a Wyoming case, the federal district court ruled that students could rent the high school gym for a baccalaureate program because the event was not school sponsored, even though the school band performed and the district's graduation announcements mentioned the baccalaureate program.[33]

Because of the prohibition on school-sponsored religious activities, most post-*Weisman* controversies have involved student-led devotionals. Some school districts have given students discretion to include religious messages in their graduation speeches. In these districts the graduation ceremony has been designated a forum for student expression, so students' messages (including any religious references) are not subject to review and do not bear the stamp of school approval.[34] The Ninth Circuit upheld an Idaho school district's policy that prohibited school authorities from censoring students' graduation speeches and allowed student speakers (chosen by academic standing) to select "an address, poem, reading, song, musical presentation, prayer, or any other pronouncement of their choosing."[35] Finding the ceremony a forum for student expression, the court reasoned that the student speakers were selected based on secular criteria and were not advised to include devotionals in their

31. Although the majority opinion applied a coercion test, four of the justices who joined the majority also signed concurring opinions in which they asserted that coercion would be sufficient to abridge the Establishment Clause, but it is not a necessary prerequisite. *Weisman,* 505 U.S. at 599 (Blackmun, J., joined by Stevens and O'Connor, J. J., concurring); 505 U.S. at 609 (Souter, J., joined by Stevens and O'Connor, J. J., concurring).

32. *See, e.g.,* Verbena United Methodist Church v. Chilton County Bd. of Educ., 765 F. Supp. 704 (M.D. Ala. 1991) (holding that a school board must take all measures reasonably necessary to disassociate itself from a baccalaureate service sponsored by religious organizations and held in space rented from the school district).

33. *See* Shumway v. Albany County Sch. Dist. No. One, 826 F. Supp. 1320 (D. Wyo. 1993).

34. For a discussion of students' free expression rights, *see* Chapter 4.

35. Doe v. Madison Sch. Dist. No 321, 147 F.3d 832 (9th Cir. 1998), *vacated and remanded en banc,* 177 F.3d 789, 792 (9th Cir. 1999). *See also* Goluba v. Sch. Dist., 45 F.3d 1035 (7th Cir. 1995) (holding that student-initiated recitation of the Lord's Prayer five minutes before the high school graduation ceremony did not represent the school and thus did not violate an injunction prohibiting school personnel from authorizing, conducting, sponsoring, or intentionally permitting prayers during the graduation ceremony).

remarks. The full appellate court reheard the case and vacated the panel decision because the plaintiff had graduated, but the contested policy remained in force.

However, in another Ninth Circuit case, the appeals court upheld a school district's refusal to allow students to deliver their proselytizing graduation speeches that had been submitted to the school principal for review in accordance with school policy. Unlike the first case, this school district had a clear policy retaining school control of the graduation ceremony. Thus, the court found censorship of the proposed religious speeches appropriate to avoid an Establishment Clause violation.[36] The key distinction is whether the school has explicitly created a forum for student expression in the graduation ceremony or has retained control over students' graduation speeches.

Student Elections to Authorize Prayers. Especially volatile controversies have focused on having students decide by election to include student-led devotionals in graduation ceremonies and other school activities. The Fifth Circuit upheld the practice of allowing students to vote on whether to have nonsectarian graduation prayers selected and delivered by students, reasoning that the student election removed school sponsorship.[37] But the Third and Ninth Circuit appellate courts reached an opposite conclusion.[38] They were not convinced that the Establishment Clause could be satisfied simply by giving students control of devotional activities at school-sponsored events. These courts reasoned that school authorities could not delegate decisions to students that the Establishment Clause forbids school districts from making.[39] Also, a Mississippi law that allowed student-initiated prayers in all school assemblies, sporting events, commencement ceremonies, and other school-related events was struck down as sweeping too broadly by permitting student-led prayers at virtually all school activities.[40]

36. Cole v. Oroville Union High Sch. Dist., 228 F.3d 1092 (9th Cir. 2000).

37. Jones v. Clear Creek Indep. Sch. Dist., 930 F.2d 416 (5th Cir. 1991), *vacated and remanded,* 505 U.S. 1215 (1992), *on remand,* 977 F.2d 963 (5th Cir. 1992). *See also* Tanford v. Brand, 104 F.3d 982 (7th Cir. 1997) (rejecting challenge to invocation and benediction at university commencement, finding no coercion on adult students who have the maturity to choose among competing beliefs).

38. ACLU of N.J. v. Black Horse Pike Reg'l Bd. of Educ., 84 F.3d 1471 (3d Cir. 1996); Harris v. Joint Sch. Dist. No. 241, 41 F.3d 447 (9th Cir.1994), *vacated and remanded with directions to dismiss as moot,* 515 U.S. 1154 (1995).

39. *See also* Comm. for Voluntary Prayer v. Wimberly, 704 A.2d 1199 (D.C. Ct. App. 1997) (striking down a voter initiative that had the clear purpose of encouraging prayer in public schools because it would have authorized student-initiated voluntary prayer in most school related activities).

40. Ingebretsen v. Jackson Pub. Sch. Dist., 88 F.3d 274 (5th Cir. 1996). The impetus for this law was the public outrage over dismissal of a high school principal for allowing students to say prayers over the school's public address system. Ultimately, the school board did not ratify the termination, and the Mississippi Senate even passed a resolution commending the principal's effort to return prayer to the public schools. *See* Bd. of Trs. v. Knox, 638 So. 2d 1278 (Miss. 1994). *See also infra* text accompanying note 51, for a discussion of the fate of a similar Alabama law.

In a 2000 case of first impression, *Santa Fe Independent School District v. Doe,* the Supreme Court, in a six-to-three decision, found an Establishment Clause violation in a Texas school district's policy authorizing student-led devotionals before public school football games.[41] The controversial policy and an identical graduation prayer policy authorized two elections—one to determine whether to have invocations and the second to select the student to deliver them. Both policies subsequently removed the "nonsectarian, nonproselytizing" restriction on the prayers, but included the notation that if judicially enjoined, the prior policies with this restriction would automatically be in effect.[42] The Fifth Circuit reaffirmed its position that student-initiated graduation prayers can satisfy the Establishment Clause, but held that the football game policy abridged the Establishment Clause even if the restriction on the type of prayers was reinstated.[43] The appeals court distinguished student-led graduation prayers from such devotionals at athletic events that occur more often, involve a more diverse age span of students, and cannot be justified to solemnize sporting events.

On appeal, the Supreme Court limited its ruling to the policy authorizing student-led prayers before football games, rejecting the district's assertion that having students decide to include invocations at the athletic events and to identify a classmate to lead the devotionals removed school sponsorship. The Court majority declared that student-led expression at a school event on school property and representing the student body under the supervision of school personnel could not be considered private speech.[44] Even though the ultimate choice of speakers and content was made by the students, the school authorized the student election in the first place. The degree of school involvement gave the impression that the devotionals at issue represented the school, leading the Court majority to conclude that the practice entailed both perceived and actual endorsement of religion.[45] The majority reasoned that the current policy had a sham secular purpose and, like the school district's previous initiatives,[46]

41. 168 F.3d 806 (5th Cir. 1999), *aff'd,* 530 U.S. 290 (2000).

42. *Id.,* 168 F.3d at 812–813. The policy was modified to eliminate "prayer" from its title and to add references to student-led "messages" and "statements" in addition to "invocations."

43. *Id.* at 816–818. The appeals court emphasized that the "nonsectarian, nonproselytizing" limitation had been important when it upheld student-initiated graduation prayers in *Clear Creek, supra* note 37, but concluded that this restriction could not save the student-led prayers before football games from being invalidated under the Establishment Clause. Earlier, the Fifth Circuit had described a high school graduation as a "once in a lifetime event" contrasted with athletic events that are held in settings far less solemn and extraordinary. Doe v. Duncanville Indep. Sch. Dist., 70 F.3d 402, 406–407 (5th Cir. 1995).

44. 530 U.S. at 310.

45. *Id.* at 308.

46. The school district had a history of Christian observances in its schools. Parents initially filed suit in this case in 1995, complaining of numerous proselytizing activities (e.g., teachers promoting Christian revival meetings and chastising children of minority faiths) in addition to the school district's practice of allowing students to read overtly Christian prayers at graduation ceremonies and home football games. In 2002, the school district was again embroiled in controversy over allegations of indifference by school personnel to religious harassment of a Jewish student by classmates. The suit was settled for an undisclosed damages award. *See* Erica Goldman, "Santa Fe School District Closes Second Case Involving Religion," *Texas Lawyer,* vol. 17, no. 52 (March 4, 2002), p. 5.

was intended to promote Christian religious observances in school-related events.[47] Noting that the purpose of the Bill of Rights is to shield certain subjects from the political process, the Court held that the use of student elections intensifies the lack of representation of minority views, ensuring that they will never be heard.[48] While rejecting the argument that Establishment Clause concerns can be eliminated by delegating decisions to students, the majority emphasized that only state sponsorship of devotionals violates the Establishment Clause; nothing in the Constitution prohibits public school students from voluntarily praying at school.[49]

Post*–Santa *Fe Rulings. The *Santa Fe* decision has not settled what distinguishes protected private religious expression from unconstitutional school-sponsored devotionals. Indeed, some post–*Santa Fe* federal appellate rulings represent an expansive stance regarding the reach of the Free Speech Clause in protecting students' private religious expression in public schools. For example, in *Adler v. Duval County School Board,* after a lengthy series of court orders, the Eleventh Circuit upheld a Florida school district's policy that authorizes public school seniors to select classmates to give graduation messages and allows the speakers to choose the content, which could be religious.[50] Even though the school district's memo outlining the policy was entitled "Graduation Prayer," the court emphasized that the student elections are not to identify classmates to deliver prayers—the graduation messages are of unspecified content, which may or may not include sectarian material.

In a second Eleventh Circuit ruling, the court in *Chandler v. James* lifted the part of an injunction that had prohibited students from publicly expressing religious views in most public school settings in Dekalb County, Alabama.[51] The controversy started over a 1993 Alabama law, enacted in response to the *Weisman* ruling, that permitted nonsectarian, nonproselytizing, student-initiated, voluntary prayers, invocations, and benedictions during school-related events and extracurricular activities. The district court upheld graduation prayers but concluded that the remainder of the law swept too broadly, failing the *Lemon,* endorsement, and coercion standards.[52] The court also enjoined school officials in DeKalb County from assisting students in

47. 530 U.S. at 307–309. The Court emphasized that it is necessary to carefully review the history and context of the challenged action in determining its facial validity. *Id.* at 317.

48. *Id.* at 316–317, citing Bd. of Regents v. Southworth, 529 U.S. 217, 236 (2000) (upholding a university's mandatory student activity fees, but ruling that student elections to determine what speech is subsidized by the university run afoul of the Free Speech Clause by disenfranchising minority viewpoints). *See* text with note 53, Chapter 4.

49. 530 U.S. at 313. In his biting dissent in *Santa Fe,* Chief Justice Rehnquist not only faulted the majority for its holding but also for its tone, which he claimed "bristles with hostility to all things religious in public life." *Id.* at 318 (Rehnquist, C. J., dissenting).

50. 174 F.3d 1236 (11th Cir. 1999), *vacated with different results on rehearing en banc,* 206 F.3d 1070 (11th Cir. 2000), *vacated and remanded (for reconsideration in light of Santa Fe v. Doe),* 531 U.S. 801 (2000), *reinstated on remand,* 250 F.3d 1330 (11th Cir. 2001), *cert. denied,* 534 U. S. 1065 (2001).

51. 180 F.3d 1254 (11th Cir. 1999), *vacated and remanded (for reconsideration in light of Santa Fe v. Doe),* 530 U.S. 1256 (2000), *reinstated on remand sub nom.* Chandler v. Siegelman, 230 F.3d 1313 (11th Cir. 2000), *cert. denied,* 533 U.S. 916 (2001).

religious activities. But the Eleventh Circuit lifted the part of the injunction prohibiting all student religious expression during school, declaring that the Establishment Clause does not require and the Free Speech Clause does not permit suppression of student-initiated religious expression in public schools or relegating it to whispers or closets. The court emphasized that "the discriminatory suppression of student-initiated religious speech demonstrates not neutrality but hostility toward religion."[53]

Although the Supreme Court vacated the appellate decisions in both *Chandler* and *Adler* and remanded the cases for further consideration in light of *Santa Fe,* the appeals court subsequently reaffirmed both rulings. Distinguishing the Supreme Court's condemnation of school-sponsored student prayer in *Santa Fe,* the appeals court held that *Chandler* dealt with school censorship of private student religious expression, which is also unconstitutional.[54] The Eleventh Circuit reiterated that the district court's injunction was overly broad because it equated all student religious speech in a public context at school with expression *representing* the public school.

Even more recently, the Ninth Circuit found a school district guilty of viewpoint discrimination against a student religious club that was not treated like other student clubs in access to school supplies, audio-visual equipment, and school vehicles, and was not allowed to meet during a noninstructional period when other student clubs were allowed to hold meetings.[55] The court reasoned that equal treatment is required by the Free Speech Clause and does not abridge the Establishment Clause.

In light of *Santa Fe* and its progeny, courts will review the legislative history of school district policies to ascertain whether there has been a pattern of efforts to infuse devotionals in the public schools. Student religious expression may be considered private if truly student initiated, but the *Santa Fe* decision casts doubt on the legality of holding student elections to determine that student-led devotionals will be included in school-sponsored activities. Even though the Eleventh Circuit found the *Adler* policy permissible after the Supreme Court's *Santa Fe* decision, the appellate court emphasized that the content of students' graduation messages was not specified, so the election of speakers was not to decide whether the graduation ceremony would include religious content. Given the Ninth Circuit's expansive interpretation of Free Speech Clause protection of students' religious expression in public schools, the Supreme Court undoubtedly will be asked to provide additional guidance regarding the scope of permissible student-initiated religious activities in public schools and how to distinguish protected private religious expression from prohibited school-sponsored devotionals.

---

52. *Chandler,* 958 F. Supp. 1550 (M.D. Ala. 1997).

53. *Chandler,* 180 F.3d at 1261.

54. *Chandler,* 230 F.3d at 1315.

55. Prince v. Jacoby, 303 F.3d 1074 (9th Cir. 2002). For treatment of the Equal Access Act issues in this case, *see infra* text accompanying note 102.

Religious Displays and Holiday Observances

The display of religious documents and the observance of religious holidays in public schools also remain controversial. In 1980, the Supreme Court declined to hear an appeal of a decision allowing religious holiday observances and the temporary display of religious symbols in public education,[56] but a week later, the divided Court struck down a Kentucky law calling for the posting of the Ten Commandments in public school classrooms.[57] In the first case, the historical and cultural significance of Christmas convinced the Eighth Circuit that the prudent and objective observance of this holiday in public schools does not serve to advance religion, even though songs such as *Silent Night* are sung and the nativity scene is displayed.[58] The appeals court held that the school board's policy, allowing the observance of holidays with both a religious and secular basis, had the nonreligious purpose of improving the overall instructional program.

In contrast, the five-member Supreme Court majority in the second case was not persuaded that the Ten Commandments' cultural significance justified posting this religious document in public schools. Distinguishing the display of religious texts from the permissible use of religious literature in academic courses, the majority held that the purpose behind the Kentucky legislation was to advance a particular religious faith, which violates the Establishment Clause. The majority rejected the state judiciary's conclusion that the constitutional impairment was neutralized because the copies were purchased with private donations and carried the disclaimer that "the secular application of the Ten Commandments is clearly seen in its adoption as the fundamental legal code of Western Civilization and the common law of the United States."[59]

In spite of the Supreme Court's ruling, the controversies over such displays have not ended. In several states, policies or school board rules have recently been enacted to allow the posting of the Ten Commandments with other historic documents in public buildings, including schools.[60] The Seventh Circuit in 2001 concluded that placing a monument with the Ten Commandments on government property violated the Establishment Clause.[61] The following year, the Sixth Circuit ordered removal of

---

56. Florey v. Sioux Falls Sch. Dist. 49-5, 619 F.2d 1311 (8th Cir.1980).

57. Stone v. Graham, 449 U.S. 39 (1980).

58. *Florey,* 619 F.2d at 1314. *See also* Sechler v. State Coll. Area Sch. Dist., 121 F. Supp. 2d 439 (M.D. Pa. 2000) (rejecting an Establishment Clause challenge to holiday observance that allegedly was not "Christian enough"; the program included the Menorah and Kwanzaa candelabra as well as Christmas carols and a Christmas tree and was designed to celebrate diversity).

59. *Stone,* 449 U.S. at 41. *See* Nartowicz v. Clayton County Sch. Dist., 736 F.2d 646 (11th Cir. 1984) (barring the use of public school bulletin boards and public address systems to announce church-sponsored activities).

60. Congress has also considered legislation that would allow the Ten Commandments to be posted along with other historical documents. *See* Mark Walsh, "Commandments Debate Moves to Statehouse," *Education Week* (February 16, 2000), pp. 18, 21.

61. ICLU v. O'Bannon, 259 F.3d 766 (7th Cir. 2001), *cert. denied,* 122 S. Ct. 1173 (2002). *See also* Books v. City of Elkhart, 235 F.3d 292 (7th Cir. 2000), *cert. denied,* 532 U.S. 1058 (2001).

the Ten Commandments from displays in four county high schools.[62] Additional legislative activity and litigation on this topic seems assured.

Other religious displays also have been controversial. The Sixth Circuit held that the display of a portrait of Jesus in a public secondary school failed all three prongs of the *Lemon* test.[63] Also, a New York federal district court enjoined the display of a religious painting in the high school auditorium because it conveyed governmental endorsement of religion.[64] However, a federal district court in New Jersey found that inclusion of religious holidays, such as Christmas and Hanukkah, on school district calendars was designed to broaden students' sensitivity toward religious diversity and their knowledge of the role of religion in the development of civilization and satisfied all prongs of the *Lemon* test.[65]

Some parents have alleged that public schools promote the religion of Wicca by observing Halloween with pictures of witches and goblins. The Supreme Court declined to review a Florida court's ruling in which the state appeals court held that the display of witches does not promote a nontheistic religion or give any perception of public school endorsement of Wicca.[66] Similarly, an Establishment Clause challenge to using a devil as a public school's mascot has been rejected.[67]

A couple of recent cases have focused on requests to include religious messages in bricks purchased for school walkways or on tiles to be hung at school. In a New York case, individuals failed to secure a preliminary injunction against the exclusion of walkway bricks with Christian messages because they did not produce evidence of likely success on the Establishment Clause issue; evidence of viewpoint discrimination was insufficient to warrant an injunction.[68] Similarly, the Tenth Circuit found no Establishment or Free Speech Clause violation in not allowing persons connected with the Columbine shootings to paint religious messages on tiles to be hung in school.[69] Concluding that such expression represents the school, the court found a legitimate pedagogical reason for limiting expression that could create religious divisiveness.

In several decisions outside the school domain, the Supreme Court has condoned the use of public funds or property for certain religious displays, such as erecting a Christmas display with the nativity scene in a private park,[70] displaying an

62. Baker v. Adams County/Ohio Valley Sch. Bd., 310 F.3d 927 (6th Cir. 2002). *See also* ACLU v. McCreary County, 145 F. Supp. 2d 845 (E.D. Ky. 2001); Doe v. Harlan County Sch. Dist., 96 F. Supp. 2d 667 (E.D. Ky. 2000).

63. Washegesic v. Bloomingdale Pub. Schs., 33 F.3d 679 (6th Cir. 1994).

64. Joki v. Bd. of Educ., 745 F. Supp. 823 (N.D.N.Y. 1990). *See also* Gernetzke v. Kenosha Unified Sch. Dist. No. 1, 274 F.3d 464 (7th Cir. 2001), *cert. denied,* 122 S. Ct. 1606 (2002); *infra* text accompanying note 104.

65. Clever v. Cherry Hill Township Bd. of Educ., 838 F. Supp. 929 (D.N.J. 1993).

66. Guyer v. Sch. Bd., 634 So.2d 806 (Fla. Dist. Ct. App. 1994).

67. *See* Kunselman v. W. Reserve Local Sch. Dist., 70 F.3d 931 (6th Cir. 1995).

68. Anderson v. Mex. Acad. & Cent. Sch., 186 F. Supp. 2d 193 (N.D.N.Y. 2002).

69. Fleming v. Jefferson County Sch. Dist., 298 F.3d 918 (10th Cir. 2002).

70. Lynch v. Donnelly, 465 U.S. 668 (1984). *See also* McCreary v. Stone, 739 F.2d 716 (2d Cir. 1984), *aff'd by equally divided court,* 471 U.S. 83 (1985).

unattended cross in the capitol square,[71] and displaying a menorah with a Christmas tree and a sign saluting liberty in front of a government building.[72] Despite these decisions, courts seem likely to continue to strike down the display of sectarian documents in public schools. But the objective recognition of religious holidays will presumably withstand judicial scrutiny as long as particular faiths are not compromised.[73]

Proselytization in the Classroom

Public schools must adhere to Establishment Clause restrictions on governmental promotion of religious creeds. Because teachers and other school personnel are working with a vulnerable captive audience in public schools, their actions have been scrutinized to ensure that classrooms are not used as a forum to indoctrinate sectarian beliefs.

In 1984, the Eleventh Circuit enjoined teacher-initiated devotional activities in an Alabama school district.[74] Subsequently, the Tenth Circuit also held that school officials could order the removal of religiously oriented books from a teacher's classroom library and require the teacher to keep his Bible out of sight and to refrain from silently reading it during school hours.[75] More recently, the Second Circuit found no free exercise impairment in a New York school board's directive for a teacher to stop using religious references in delivering his instructional program,[76] and a federal district court held that school authorities properly instructed a Connecticut teacher to

71. Capitol Square Review & Advisory Bd. v. Pinette, 515 U.S. 753 (1995) (upholding the Ku Klux Klan's right to display the unattended cross on a state-owned plaza during the Christmas season as private religious expression in a traditional public forum that may be regulated only if necessary to serve a compelling state interest).

72. County of Allegheny v. ACLU, 492 U.S. 573 (1989) (upholding the display of the Menorah with the Christmas tree as celebrating religious liberty, but striking down a county courthouse display of the nativity scene with a banner proclaiming "Gloria in Excelsis Deo" as advancing the Christian faith in violation of the Establishment Clause).

73. Federal appellate courts have rendered conflicting opinions regarding laws or board policies that recognize Good Friday as a legal holiday. *Compare* Metzl v. Leininger, 57 F.3d 618 (7th Cir. 1995) (recognizing Good Friday as a school holiday conveys an impermissible message that Christianity is favored in absence of any educational or fiscal justification for the holiday) *with* Koenick v. Felton, 190 F.3d 259 (4th Cir. 1999) (upholding district policy authorizing four-day Easter holiday that coincides with Passover as satisfying the Establishment Clause and allocating school resources appropriately, because many teachers would be absent these days); Cammack v. Waihee, 932 F.2d 765 (9th Cir. 1991) (authorizing Good Friday as a legal holiday does not endorse religion any more than do Sunday closing laws).

74. Jaffree v. Bd. of Sch. Comm'rs, 705 F.2d 1526 (11th Cir. 1983). *See also* May v. Evansville-Vanderburgh Sch. Corp., 787 F.2d 1105 (7th Cir. 1986) (upholding school authorities in barring teachers from using the public school building to hold staff prayer meetings before school).

75. However, the court enjoined the school board from removing the Bible from the school library, noting that the Bible has significant literary and historical significance. Roberts v. Madigan, 921 F.2d 1047 (10th Cir. 1990).

76. Marchi v. Bd. of Coop. Educ. Servs., 173 F.3d 469 (2d. Cir. 1999).

cover a proselytizing shirt at school.[77] The judiciary has recognized that the Establishment Clause bars public school teachers' use of the "power, prestige, and influence" of their position to lead devotional activities.[78]

In several cases, teachers have been discharged for proselytizing students or disregarding selected aspects of the curriculum that conflict with their religious values. For example, the Seventh Circuit upheld a school board's dismissal of a kindergarten teacher who literally interpreted the Biblical prohibition against worshiping graven images, and thus refused to teach about the American flag, the observance of patriotic holidays, and the importance of historical figures such as Abraham Lincoln.[79] The appellate court noted that the teacher enjoys the freedom to hold such beliefs but has "no constitutional right to require others to submit to her views and to forego a portion of their education they would otherwise be entitled to enjoy."[80] A New York appeals court also upheld the dismissal of a tenured teacher based on evidence that she had tried to recruit students to join her religious organization, conducted prayer sessions in her office, and used her classroom to promote her religious faith.[81] In addition, courts have supported nonrenewal of teachers who have continued to teach the Biblical account of creation in their classes after repeated warnings to conform to school board guidelines regarding the biology course content.[82]

Although proselytization of students by public school teachers violates the Establishment Clause, the Supreme Court has emphasized that it is permissible, even desirable, to teach the Bible and other religious documents from a literary, cultural, or historical perspective.[83] Studies have indicated that the role of religion in the development of Western civilization has been given insufficient and inaccurate treatment in textbooks and courses partly due to fear of violating First Amendment restrictions.[84] Responding to these studies, several coalitions of national education, civic,

---

77. The shirt read "Jesus 2000, J2K." Downing v. W. Haven Bd. of Educ., 162 F. Supp. 2d 19 (D. Conn. 2001). *See also* Hennessy v. City of Melrose, 194 F.3d 237 (1st Cir. 1999) (upholding termination of a Fundamentalist Christian student teacher for criticizing the district's curriculum and school activities and vilifying the principal; religious beliefs cannot override compliance with reasonable school directives).

78. *See* Fink v. Bd. of Educ., 442 A.2d 837, 842 (Pa. Commw. Ct. 1982) (upholding a teacher's dismissal for refusing to comply with superintendent's directives to cease opening classes with devotional activities).

79. Palmer v. Bd. of Educ., 603 F.2d 1271 (7th Cir. 1979).

80. *Id.* at 1274. For a discussion of teachers wearing religious attire in public schools, *see* text with note 120, Chapter 10.

81. La Rocca v. Bd. of Educ., 406 N.Y.S.2d 348 (App. Div. 1978).

82. *See* Dale v. Bd. of Educ., 316 N.W.2d 108 (S.D. 1982). *See also* LeVake v. Indep. Sch. Dist. No. 656, 625 N.W.2d 502 (Minn. Ct. App. 2001), *cert. denied,* 534 U.S. 1081 (2002); *infra* text accompanying note 165.

83. *See* Sch. Dist. of Abington Township v. Schempp, 374 U.S. 203, 225 (1963).

84. *See* Timothy Smith, "High School History Texts Adopted for Use in the State of Alabama," *Religion & Public Education,* vol. 15 (1988), pp. 170–190; Paul Vitz, *Censorship: Evidence of Bias in Our Children's Textbooks* (Ann Arbor, MI: Servant Books, 1986).

and religious groups as well as the Department of Education have distributed materials addressing permissible methods to teach about the role of religion in society and attempting to clarify the legal status of various church/state issues in public schools.[85]

Comparative religion courses in high schools have seldom been controversial, but the line is not always clear between teaching about religion and instilling religious tenets in other courses.[86] Numerous Bible study courses, particularly at the elementary school level, have been challenged as a ploy to advance sectarian beliefs. Courts have carefully evaluated curricular materials and even reviewed videotapes of lessons in determining whether such instruction fosters a particular creed.[87] Courts have struck down programs where private groups have controlled the hiring and supervision of personnel or the selection of curricular materials.[88]

Performances of school choirs often have evoked controversies over alleged proselytization. A Utah choir director agreed to exempt a student from singing religious songs, but the student sought an injunction against the choir performing the songs and against holding two performances at religious sites. The Tenth Circuit accepted the school district's justification for the music, noting that a substantial amount of choral music is religious in nature and also accepted that the religious sites had superior facilities.[89] The Fifth Circuit similarly ruled that forbidding the school choir to sing religious songs would disqualify appropriate choral music, so the use of religious songs does not constitute an endorsement of religion.[90]

Some controversies over proselytization in the classroom have not challenged teachers' activities but have entailed requests for students to include sectarian materials in their presentations, artwork, or other school assignments. In most of these cases,

85. *See* Secretary Richard Riley, *Religious Expression in Public Schools* (Washington, DC: United States Department of Education 1998); *Religion in the Public Schools: A Joint Statement of Current Law,* American Jewish Congress, Chair Drafting Committee (New York: American Jewish Congress, 1995); "Religion Curriculum Addresses Liberty, Pluralism," *Education Monitor* (November 27, 1990), p. 4.

86. *See also* Doe v. Beaumont Indep. Sch. Dist., 240 F.3d 462 (5th Cir. 2001) *(en banc)* (remanding for a trial to determine if use of volunteer clergy counselors in public schools violates the Establishment Clause).

87. *See, e.g.,* Doe v. Human, 725 F. Supp. 1499 (W.D. Ark. 1989), *aff'd mem.,* 923 F.2d 2d 857 (8th Cir. 1990); Hall v. Bd. of Sch. Comm'rs, 707 F.2d 464 (11th Cir. 1983); Herdahl v. Pontotoc County Sch. Dist., 933 F. Supp. 582 (N.D. Miss. 1996).

88. Ironically, in the same district that generated the Scopes "monkey trial" in the 1920s *(see infra* text accompanying note 161), a federal district court in 2002 found an Establishment Clause violation in the school district's practice of allowing Bible teaching in its elementary schools, because the instruction entailed religious inculcation rather than the academic study of religion, Doe v. Porter, 188 F. Supp. 2d 904 (E.D. Tenn. 2002).

89. Bauchman v. W. High Sch., 132 F.3d 542 (10th Cir. 1997). *But see* Skarin v. Woodbine Cmty. Sch. Dist., 204 F. Supp. 2d 1195 (S.D. Iowa 2002) (holding that high school choir's singing of *The Lord's Prayer* at graduation ceremony and rehearsals violated the Establishment Clause).

90. Doe v. Duncanville Indep. Sch. Dist., 70 F.3d 402 (5th Cir. 1995). However, the court struck down the basketball team's policy of praying before games, practices, and pep rallies with the encouragement of school employees.

the schools have prevailed in denying the students' requests. For example, the Sixth Circuit upheld a school district's prohibition on an elementary school student showing in class a videotape of herself singing a proselytizing religious song.[91] Recognizing that the public school curriculum is supervised by faculty and designed to impart knowledge, the appeals court held that student projects can be censored to ensure that the school is not viewed as endorsing religious content. The same court backed a junior high school teacher who gave a student a zero on a report, because the student had cleared a different topic with the teacher but then wrote her report on the life of Jesus Christ. The court emphasized, however, that religious issues may be part of the instructional program. One justice observed that the student might have raised a legitimate free speech issue if the assignment had been to write an opinion piece on any topic of personal interest and religious content had been rejected.[92]

More recently, a New Jersey student alleged several grievances against the school while in kindergarten and first grade.[93] His kindergarten teacher instructed students to make posters of things for which they were thankful, and his poster was temporarily removed from the class display in the hall and then placed in a less prominent location because it depicted Jesus. Subsequently, in first grade he selected a Bible story to read to the class, and was not allowed to do so but instead was instructed to read it privately to the teacher. The Third Circuit divided evenly on the propriety of having the child read in private, thus affirming the district court's judgment in favor of school personnel. The district court had reasoned that teachers can exercise viewpoint-neutral regulations reasonably related to legitimate educational purposes to govern classroom activities. The full appellate court also found no policy or directive that would violate constitutional rights in connection with the removal of religious posters, but remanded the case for the plaintiffs to have an opportunity to substantiate a viable complaint in this regard.

Equal Access for Religious Expression and Groups

In the 1960s and 1970s, it was often assumed that the Establishment Clause demanded that religious speech be barred from government forums. More recently, however, the Supreme Court has reasoned that singling out religious views for differential treatment compared with other private expression would be unconstitutional viewpoint discrimination, which abridges the Free Speech Clause.[94] Ira Lupu has observed that "even the standard-bearers of the separationist tradition have been prepared to cede

91. DeNooyer v. Merinelli, 12 F.3d 211 (6th Cir. 1993).

92. Settle v. Dickson County Sch. Bd., 53 F.3d 152 (6th Cir. 1995). *See id.* at 159 (Batchelder, J., cconcurring).

93. C.H. v. Oliva, 226 F.3d 198 (3d Cir. 2000), *cert. denied,* 533 U.S. 915 (2001). *See also* Walz v. Egg Harbor Township Bd. of Educ., 187 F. Supp. 2d 232 (D.N.J. 2002) (rejecting contention that a student had a First Amendment right to distribute religious gifts in the classroom; reasonable accommodations were made in that religious materials could be distributed before and after school and during recess).

94. For a discussion of this notion, *see* Rosenberger v. Rector & Visitors, 515 U.S. 819, 890–899 (Souter, J., dissenting); Lamb's Chapel v. Ctr. Moriches Union Free Sch. Dist., 959 F.2d 381, 386 (2d Cir. 1992), *rev'd,* 508 U.S. 384 (1993).

territory in the name of competing rights . . . [that] include the rights to be free of official discrimination with respect to religious exercise, freedom of speech, and freedom of association."[95]

The Supreme Court started this trend in education cases in its 1981 decision, *Widmar v. Vincent,* finding no Establishment Clause violation in allowing student religious groups to have access to a forum created for student expression on state-supported college campuses.[96] The Court concluded that by providing access to a range of student groups, public institutions of higher education advance a secular purpose and do not excessively entangle the state with religion. The Court focused on the expressive aspect of the student devotional activities in *Widmar,* concluding that the university's ban on religious meetings would abridge students' free speech rights.

Equal Access Act. Below the college level, the Free Speech Clause was augmented by the Equal Access Act (EAA) in 1984, under which federally assisted secondary schools that have established a limited forum for student groups to meet during non-instructional time cannot deny school access to noncurriculum student groups based on the religious, philosophical, or political content of their meetings.[97] In 1990, the Supreme Court in *Board of Education of Westside Community Schools v. Mergens* rejected the contention that the EAA abridges the Establishment Clause, because student religious groups are allowed to meet, recognizing the law's clear secular purpose of preventing discrimination against religious and other types of private expression.[98] The Court distinguished government speech promoting religion that is prohibited by the Establishment Clause from private religious expression protected by the Free Speech and Free Exercise Clauses.[99] In subsequent cases, federal appellate courts have ruled that the EAA prevails over state constitutional provisions requiring greater separation of church and state than demanded by the Establishment Clause,[100] and have allowed student religious groups to require certain officers to be Christians to safeguard the spiritual content of their meetings.[101] The Ninth Circuit in 2002 expansively interpreted the EAA when it ruled that a school district violated the law by denying a religious club access to funds and fund-raising activities, school bulletin boards, and the public address system on an equal basis with other student groups.[102]

95. Lupu, "The Lingering Death of Separationism," p. 249.

96. 454 U.S. 263 (1981).

97. 20 U.S.C. §§ 4071–4074 (2002).

98. 496 U.S. 226, 249 (1990).

99. *Id.* at 250.

100. *See* Ceniceros v. Bd. of Trs., 106 F.3d 878 (9th Cir. 1997) (relying on the EAA to allow student religious group to meet during lunch period since it was noninstructional time and other student groups were allowed to meet); Garnett v. Renton Sch. Dist. No. 403, 987 F.2d 641 (9th Cir. 1993) (finding that the EAA prevailed over antiestablishment provisions in state law; a student religious group could not be barred from the public school's limited forum for student meetings).

101. *See* Hsu v. Roslyn Union Free Sch. Dist., 85 F.3d 839 (2d Cir. 1996).

102. Prince v. Jacoby, 303 F.3d 1074 (9th Cir. 2002). For a discussion of the Free Speech Clause issues in the case, *see supra* text accompanying note 55.

Because school districts can comply with the EAA by restricting school access to student clubs that are curriculum related, some controversies have focused on what constitutes curriculum-related clubs. Most of these cases have not dealt with religious groups, so they are discussed in Chapter 4. The religious challenges are typified by a case in which a California appeals court addressed a claim that the Fellowship of Christian Athletes should be allowed to meet in the public school during noninstructional time under the EAA because other groups not related to the curriculum were allowed school access. The court noted that the club itself would not have to be student initiated to be protected under the EAA—only its on-campus meetings would have to be initiated by students.[103]

Efforts to extend EAA coverage beyond student meetings have not been successful. For example, the Seventh Circuit in 2001 did not find an EAA violation when a principal barred a student religious group from including a large cross in the group's school hallway mural.[104] The school had invited all student groups to paint hallway murals, and sketches were reviewed by the principal, who disapproved the cross as well as other groups' use of a swastika and a brand of beer. The appeals court noted that the EAA specifies that it does not restrict the school's authority to maintain order and discipline, which justified the principal acting against three proposals he feared would lead to lawsuits or disorder.[105]

Although there are limits on the reach of the EAA, this federal law has provided substantial protection to student religious meetings in secondary schools during noninstructional time. The EAA has codified the concept of equal access and equal treatment of religious expression that is currently guiding First Amendment litigation as well.

School Access for Community Groups.   The EAA applies *only* to secondary students, so community religious groups desiring public school access during noninstructional time must rely on First Amendment protections. Since the early 1990s, the Supreme Court has made some definitive pronouncements about protecting private religious expression from viewpoint discrimination. In *Lamb's Chapel v. Center Moriches Union Free School District,* the Court held that if secular community groups are allowed to use the public school after school hours to address particular topics (i.e., family life, child rearing), a sectarian group desiring to show a film series addressing these topics from religious perspectives cannot be denied public school access.[106] In essence, school districts cannot enforce policies governing facility use during nonschool time that entail viewpoint discrimination against a religious group's message.

103. Schoick v. Saddleback Valley Unified Sch. Dist., 104 Cal. Rptr. 2d 562 (Ct. App. 2001). *See* text accompanying note 107, Chapter 4.

104. Gernetzke v. Kenosha Unified Sch. Dist. No. 1, 274 F.3d 464 (7th Cir. 2001), *cert. denied,* 122 S. Ct. 1606 (2002).

105. *Id.* at 466. But the court did not reach the merits of the allegation that suppressing the sectarian symbols violated the religion clauses.

106. 508 U.S. 384 (1993). *See also* Rosenberger v. Rector & Visitors, 515 U.S. 819 (1995).

In 2001, the Supreme Court delivered a seminal decision, *Good News Club v. Milford Central School,* allowing a private Christian organization to hold its meetings in a New York public school after school hours.[107] The Good News Club is affiliated with a national organization, Child Evangelism Fellowship, that teaches Christian values to children ages 6 to 12 and has more than 4,500 clubs nationwide.[108] The Milford School District had denied the Good News Club's request under its community-use policy that allows civic and recreational groups to use the school but not for religious purposes. The district contended that the club was engaging in religious worship and instruction that must be barred from public school facilities.

Disagreeing with the school district and the lower courts, the Supreme Court in *Milford* held that the school district's policy discriminated against religious viewpoints in violation of the Free Speech Clause. The Court majority relied heavily on *Lamb's Chapel,*[109] even though Milford school authorities attempted to distinguish the Good News Club that targets children under age 12 and involves religious instruction and prayer from the showing of films primarily to adults that was upheld in *Lamb's Chapel.* The Supreme Court did not find the distinction significant, noting that whether moral lessons are taught through live storytelling and prayers or through films is inconsequential from a constitutional standpoint.[110] The majority reasoned that the Good News Club was merely seeking access to school facilities like other community groups and that it could not be disadvantaged based on the religious content of its meetings.

The Supreme Court rejected the contention that elementary children would feel coerced to participate in the club's activities, declaring that the Court has never barred private religious conduct during nonschool hours simply because elementary children might be present. The Court did not refute Justice Souter's contention in his dissent that the clergy-led meetings were "evangelical" worship services,[111] but rather concluded that the Free Speech Clause protected the religious viewpoints expressed during the club's devotional meetings.

The Court's *Milford* decision seems to have erased the distinction between religious viewpoints and worship that some lower courts had drawn in condoning the use of public school facilities for community groups to discuss topics from sectarian per-

107. 533 U.S. 98 (2001). *See also* Culbertson v. Oakridge Sch. Dist. No. 76, 258 F.3d 1061 (9th Cir. 2001) (upholding the Good News Club's right to meet in the public school after school hours, but enjoining teachers from distributing permission slips for the meetings as encouraging the club in violation of the Establishment Clause).

108. *See* Mark Walsh, "Religious Club Seeks 'Good News' from Court," *Education Week* (February 21, 2001), pp. 1, 20.

109. 508 U.S. 384 (1993).

110. Good News Club v. Milford Cent. Sch., 533 U.S. 98, 108-110 (2001). *See also* Good News/Good Sports Club v. Sch. Dist. of Ladue, 28 F.3d 1501 (8th Cir. 1994).

111. 533 U.S. at 138 (Souter, J., dissenting).

spectives, while not allowing use of public schools for religious worship.[112] Under the *Milford* ruling, if a public school establishes a limited forum for community meetings, it cannot bar religious groups, even though students attending the school are the central participants in the devotional activities. The Court did not find a danger that the community would perceive the Good News Club's access as school district endorsement of religion.[113]

Distribution of Religious Literature.   The Supreme Court has not directly addressed the distribution of religious literature in public schools, and lower courts have rendered a range of opinions. Courts consistently have ruled that school personnel cannot give students Bibles or other religious materials,[114] and most courts have prohibited religious sects from coming to the school to distribute materials to captive public school audiences. For example, several courts have struck down school board policies allowing the Gideon Society to visit schools and present Bibles to students who wish to accept them.[115]

Departing from this trend, the Fourth Circuit upheld a West Virginia school district's policy allowing sectarian organizations along with political groups to distribute materials, such as Bibles, in public secondary schools on a designated day because the organizations were considered private entities that do not represent the school.[116] The

112. *See* Campbell v. St. Tammany Parish Sch. Bd., 206 F.3d 482 (5th Cir. 2000) (upholding the exclusion of religious services from a school district's limited forum created for community use during non-school time), *vacated and remanded for reconsideration in light of Good News Club v. Milford Cent. Sch.*, 533 U.S. 913 (2001), *remanded,* 300 F. 3d 526 (5th Cir. 2002); Full Gospel Tabernacle v. Cmty. Sch. Dist. 27, 164 F.3d 829 (2d Cir. 1999) (upholding exclusion of religious group from use of school facilities since the district had not opened the forum for religious worship); Bronx Household of Faith v. Cmty. Sch. Dist., 127 F.3d 207 (2d Cir. 1997) (upholding a school district's viewpoint-neutral prohibition on religious groups using the public school's limited forum for weekly worship services); Bronx Household of Faith v. Bd. of Educ., 226 F. Supp. 2d 401 (S.D.N.Y. 2002) (applying *Good News* and finding substantial likelihood that the denial of the request to use the public school for religious worship violated the First Amendment).

113. In some instances community groups have sought school access for religious advertisements. *See* DiLoreto v. Downey Unified Sch. Dist., 196 F.3d 958 (9th Cir. 1999) (holding that the school could exclude religious advertisements from the fence surrounding its baseball field, which was a nonpublic forum open only for limited purposes; finding the district's fears about violating the Establishment Clause to be reasonable and not impermissible viewpoint discrimination).

114. *See, e.g.,* Jabr v. Rapides Parish Sch. Bd., 171 F. Supp. 2d 653 (W.D. La. 2001) (finding that school principal violated the Establishment Clause by distributing New Testament Bibles to public school students).

115. *See, e.g.,* Doe v. Duncanville Indep. Sch. Dist., 70 F.3d 402 (5th Cir. 1995); Berger v. Rensselaer Cent. Sch. Corp., 982 F.2d 1160 (7th Cir. 1993).

116. Peck v. Upshur County Bd. of Educ., 155 F.3d 274 (4th Cir. 1998). *See also* Meltzer v. Bd. of Pub. Instruction, 577 F.2d 311 (5th Cir. 1978) (allowing distribution of Gideon Bibles in public schools under stringent guidelines controlling the location and means of distribution); Bacon v. Bradley-Bourbonnais High Sch. Dist. No. 307, 707 F. Supp. 1005 (C.D. Ill. 1989) (upholding right of Gideons to distribute Bibles on the school-owned sidewalk in front of a high school, because the sidewalk was considered a public forum for use by the general public).

court noted that access to the forum was available to a broad array of religious and secular groups and that the displays included a disclaimer that the materials were not sponsored or endorsed by the school. But the policy was invalidated at the elementary school level because of the impressionability of younger children and their greater difficulty in distinguishing private from school-sponsored speech.

Most of the recent controversies have focused on student requests to distribute religious publications. Like meetings of student-initiated religious groups, these requests pit Free Speech Clause protections against Establishment Clause restrictions. Some courts have applied the "equal access" concept in concluding that the same legal principles govern students' distribution of religious and nonreligious literature. A federal district court in Colorado held that high school students had a free expression right to distribute a religious newsletter as long as the activity did not create a disturbance.[117] Also finding the distribution of religious literature to be protected personal speech, a Pennsylvania federal district court held that students were entitled to distribute religious material during noninstructional time.[118] In 1993, the Seventh Circuit distinguished public and private speech in holding that students in an Illinois school district could distribute a religious newspaper in the public school, a nonpublic forum, but could be restricted to specified times at a table near the school's entrance. The appeals court also upheld the part of the district's policy restricting distribution of materials prepared by nonstudents to 10 or fewer copies, reasoning that it is an important part of education for students to learn to express themselves in their own words.[119]

Even personal expression is subject to reasonable time, place, and manner regulations. For example, an Indiana federal district court supported a school policy requiring students to give the principal advance notice of the distribution and to submit a copy of the literature to the superintendent, but not for approval purposes.[120] Whereas reasonable restrictions on how material is distributed have been upheld, school districts cannot place a blanket ban on the distribution of religious literature.

In a 1995 higher education decision, the Supreme Court addressed the equal treatment of private religious and secular expression, and this ruling has implications for literature distribution in public schools. Concluding that a public university could not withhold support from a student religious group seeking to use student activity funds to publish sectarian materials, the Court majority held that religious material

117. Rivera v. E. Otero Sch. Dist. R-1, 721 F. Supp. 1189 (D. Colo. 1989). *See also* Muller v. Jefferson Lighthouse Sch., 98 F.3d 1530 (7th Cir. 1996) (applying same rules to the distribution of religious and nonreligious student literature that is not sponsored by the school).

118. Thompson v. Waynesboro Area Sch. Dist., 673 F. Supp. 1379 (M.D. Pa. 1987). *See also* Slotterback v. Interboro Sch. Dist., 766 F. Supp. 280 (E.D. Penn. 1991).

119. Hedges v. Wauconda Cmty. Unit Sch. Dist., 9 F.3d 1295 (7th Cir. 1993). *But see* Perumal v. Saddleback Valley Unified Sch. Dist., 243 Cal. Rptr. 545 (Ct. App. 1988) (holding that a student religious club was not entitled to distribute its materials on the high school campus or advertise in the school's yearbook because the school had not created a limited forum for noncurriculum student groups, and even if it had, the Establishment Clause would preclude using the prestige and authority of the school to advance religious causes).

120. Harless v. Darr, 937 F. Supp. 1351 (S.D. Ind. 1996).

must be treated like other material in student-initiated publications it subsidizes.[121] The Court reasoned that the government's equal treatment of religious and secular private expression is not only permitted by the Establishment Clause, but in some circumstances is required by the Free Speech Clause.[122]

Accommodations for Religious Beliefs

In addition to challenging sectarian influences in public schools, some students have asserted a right to accommodations so they can practice their religious beliefs. These disputes often pit free exercise and free speech protections against prohibitions on religious establishment. Conflicts have arisen over release-time programs for religious education, excusal from public schools for religious observances, and religious exemptions from secular school activities.

Release-Time Programs

Although the Supreme Court has struck down the practice of using public school classrooms for clergy to provide religious training to public school students during the instructional day,[123] the Court has recognized that the school can accommodate religion by releasing students to receive such religious training off public school grounds. Noting that the state must not be hostile toward religion, the Court declared in 1952 that "when the state encourages religious instruction or cooperates with religious authorities by adjusting the schedule of public events to sectarian needs, it follows the best of our traditions."[124]

   A release-time program was even upheld in a school district where students received an hour of religious instruction each week in a mobile unit parked at the edge of school property.[125] Courts have not been persuaded that academic instruction ceases during the period when students are released for religious instruction, and thus does not deny nonparticipating pupils their state-created right to an education.[126] Confining students to a single choice of attending religious classes or remaining in the public school has not been found to advance religion.[127]

121. Rosenberger v. Rector & Visitors, 515 U.S. 819 (1995).

122. *Id.* at 845. *See* Arval A. Morris, "Separation of Church and State?—Remarks on *Rosenberger v. University of Virginia,*" *Education Law Reporter,* vol. 103 (1995), pp. 553–571.

123. McCollum v. Bd. of Educ., 333 U.S. 203 (1948).

124. Zorach v. Clauson, 343 U.S. 306, 313–314 (1952).

125. Smith v. Smith, 523 F.2d 121 (4th Cir. 1975).

126. *See, e.g.,* Holt v. Thompson, 225 N.W.2d 678 (Wis. 1975).

127. It might appear that programs in which all students are released early from school one day a week would be easier to defend constitutionally because students would not be restricted to either remaining at the public school or attending sectarian classes.

While upholding a release-time program in Utah, the Tenth Circuit enjoined the school's practice of awarding course credit in the public high school for the secular aspects of daily instruction received at a Mormon seminary.[128] The court ruled that the award of credit for portions of the religious instruction would entangle school officials with the church because of the monitoring necessary to determine what parts of the courses were sectarian. Nevertheless, the court reasoned that time spent by students in the seminary program could be counted in satisfying compulsory school attendance and in calculating the school's eligibility for state aid.

More recently, an Indiana federal district court enjoined several features of a release-time program that was held in trailers brought on public school property, with utilities supported by the school district. In addition, nonparticipating students were required to read silently when their classmates attended the religious instruction.[129] The school district's rationale for not allowing children to do schoolwork, homework, or other activities if they remained in their classrooms was that students might be deterred from attending the nondenominational Christian release-time program if they had other options. Recognizing the legality of release-time programs, the court nonetheless found Establishment Clause violations in this school district's effort to encourage participation in the program and in the use of school property for the religious classes.

Excusal for Religious Observances

Requests for students and teachers to be excused from public schools to observe religious holidays raise particularly delicate issues, because such requests usually are made by members of minority sects; schools are closed when the majority of teachers and students are observing their religious holidays. Courts have been asked to determine how far public school authorities must go in accommodating religious holidays and how far they can go before such accommodations abridge the Establishment Clause.

Most litigation in this arena has involved claims by teachers that personnel leave policies discriminate against religious absences; such claims are addressed in Chapter 10. A few cases, however, have focused on students. To illustrate, the Fifth Circuit invalidated a school's policy that allowed students only two excused absences for religious holidays.[130] The court found that the school's interests in promoting regular attendance and protecting teachers from extra work were not sufficiently compel-

---

128. Lanner v. Wimmer, 662 F.2d 1349 (10th Cir. 1981).

129. Moore v. Metro. Sch. Dist., No. IP 00-1859-C-M/S, 2001 U.S. Dist. LEXIS 2722 (S.D. Ind. Feb. 7, 2001). *See also* Doe v. Shenandoah County Sch. Bd., 737 F. Supp. 913 (W.D. Va. 1990) (granting a temporary restraining order against Weekday Religious Education classes being held in buses—almost identical to public school buses—parked in front of the school, with instructors going into the school to recruit students).

130. Church of God v. Amarillo Indep. Sch. Dist., 511 F. Supp. 613 (N.D. Tex. 1981), *aff'd*, 670 F.2d 46 (5th Cir. 1982) (per curiam).

ling to justify requiring students to take unexcused absences to observe several holy days and a week-long convocation of the Worldwide Church of God.

The judiciary, however, has not condoned excessive student absences for religious reasons. For example, a Pennsylvania court rejected Islamic parents' request for their children to be absent every Friday, holding that the state's interest in providing continuity in instruction prevailed over the parents' free exercise rights.[131] Also, courts have not been receptive to attempts to avoid school attendance altogether for religious reasons, although parents can select private education or home schooling for their children.[132] The Virginia Supreme Court recognized that "no amount of religious fervor . . . in opposition to adequate instruction should be allowed to work a lifelong injury" to children.[133] As discussed previously, the one judicially endorsed exception to compulsory school attendance involves Amish children after completion of the eighth grade, because of the uniqueness of the Amish lifestyle.[134]

Religious Exemptions from Secular Activities

Teachers and other school employees have requested exemptions from public school activities that offend their religious beliefs, but most exemptions have been sought for students, because particular school requirements allegedly impair the practice of their religious tenets. In evaluating whether school authorities must honor such requests, courts have attempted to balance parents' interests in directing the religious upbringing of their children against the state's interest in ensuring an educated citizenry.

Courts have relied on the First Amendment in striking down required student participation in certain public school activities and observances. In the landmark case, *West Virginia State Board of Education v. Barnette,* the Supreme Court in 1943 ruled that students could not be required to salute the American flag in contravention of their religious beliefs,[135] overturning a precedent established by the Court only three years earlier.[136] In *Barnette,* the Court held that refusal to participate in the flag salute and the Pledge of Allegiance does not interfere with the rights of others to do so or threaten any type of disruption. Thus, state action to compel this observance unconstitutionally "invades the sphere of intellect and spirit" that the First Amendment is designed "to reserve from all official control."[137] Based on *Barnette,* courts subsequently have protected students' rights not only to decline to participate for religious or philosophical reasons in the flag-salute ceremony but also to register a silent protest by remaining

---

131. Commonwealth v. Bey, 70 A.2d 693 (Pa. Super. Ct. 1950).

132. *See, e.g.,* Jernigan v. State, 412 So. 2d 1242 (Ala. Crim. App. 1982); Johnson v. Charles City Cmty. Schs., 368 N.W.2d 74 (Iowa 1985). For a discussion of the legal status of home education programs, see text accompanying note 10, Chapter 3.

133. Rice v. Commonwealth, 49 S.E.2d 342, 348 (Va. 1948).

134. *See* Wisconsin v. Yoder, 406 U.S. 205 (1972); *supra* text accompanying note 13.

135. 319 U.S. 624 (1943).

136. Minersville Sch. Dist. v. Gobitis, 310 U.S. 586 (1940).

137. *Barnette,* 319 U.S. at 642.

seated during the observance.[138] Of course, if students should carry the silent protest to the point that it disrupts the classroom, such conduct could be curtailed.

The Supreme Court has not directly addressed teachers' free exercise rights in connection with patriotic observances in public schools, but several lower courts have adopted the *Barnette* rationale in concluding that teachers, like students, have a First Amendment right to refuse to pledge allegiance as a matter of personal conscience.[139] Teachers, however, cannot use their religious beliefs to deny students the opportunity to engage in this observance. If a school district requires the pledge to be recited daily, which is more prevalent since the terrorist attacks on September 11, 2001, teachers must make provisions for this observance in their classrooms.

Although individuals are entitled not to participate, it has generally been assumed that saying the Pledge of Allegiance in public schools is not vulnerable to a First Amendment challenge. The Seventh Circuit ruled that the phrase, *under God,* which was added to the pledge in 1954, does not convert this patriotic observance into a religious exercise that would abridge the Establishment Clause.[140] But in 2002, a Ninth Circuit panel attracted national attention and political responses when it declared that saying the pledge in public schools abridges the Establishment Clause by endorsing a belief in monotheism.[141] Within days, an appellate judge stayed implementation of this decision pending appeals.

Patriotic observances have not been the only source of controversy; religious exemptions also have been sought from components of the curriculum. Whereas teachers cannot assert a free exercise right to disregard aspects of the state-prescribed curriculum, the judiciary has been more receptive to students' requests for exemptions from instructional requirements. Students, unlike teachers, are compelled to attend school, and for many this means a public school. Accordingly, the judiciary has been sensitive to the fact that certain public school policies may have a coercive effect on religious practices. In balancing the interests involved, courts consider the extent to which the school requirement burdens the exercise of sincere religious beliefs, the governmental justification for the requirement, and alternative means available to meet the state's objectives. School authorities must have a compelling justification to deny students an exemption from a requirement that impairs the exercise of sincere religious beliefs.

Most requests for religious exemptions are handled at the classroom or school level and do not evoke legal controversies. But when they have generated litigation, students often have been successful in securing religious exemptions from various

---

138. *See, e.g.,* Lipp v. Morris, 579 F.2d 834 (3d Cir. 1978); Goetz v. Ansell, 477 F.2d 636 (2d Cir. 1973).

139. *See, e.g.,* Russo v. Cent. Sch. Dist. No. 1, 469 F.2d 623, 634 (2d Cir. 1972); Opinion of the Justices, 363 N.E.2d 251 (Mass. 1977).

140. Sherman v. Cmty. Consol. Sch. Dist. 21, 980 F.2d 437 (7th Cir. 1992). The court reasoned that through rote repetition some phrases have lost their sectarian meaning and can be characterized as "ceremonial deism." *Id.,* 980 F.2d at 447.

141. Newdow v. U.S. Congress, 292 F.3d 597 (9th Cir. 2002), *judgment stayed,* No. 00-16423, 2002 U.S. App. LEXIS 12826 (9th Cir. June 27, 2002).

instructional activities, such as drug education, sex education, coeducational physical education, dancing instruction, officers' training programs, and specific course assignments if alternatives can satisfy the instructional objectives.[142] The relief ordered in these cases has entailed the excusal of specific children, but the secular activities themselves have not been disturbed.[143]

Religious exemptions have not been honored if considered unnecessary to accommodate the practice of religious tenets or if the exemptions would substantially disrupt the school or students' academic progress. In an illustrative case, parents were unsuccessful in obtaining an exemption for their children from health and music courses and from classes whenever instructional media were used. The federal district court in New Hampshire declared that the requested exemption could lead to disruption of the public school's instructional program.[144] Courts also have denied religious exemptions for student athletes if an excuse from specific regulations might pose a safety hazard or interfere with the management of athletic teams.[145]

In a widely publicized 1987 case, the Sixth Circuit rejected fundamentalist Christian parents' request that their children be excused from exposure to the basal reading series used in elementary grades in a Tennessee school district.[146] Reversing the lower court's grant of the exemption, the Sixth Circuit reasoned that the readers did not burden the students' exercise of their fundamentalist religious beliefs, because the students were not required to profess a creed or perform religious exercises. More recently, a federal district court rejected a parent's request for his son to be exempted from a Connecticut school district's mandatory health curriculum.[147] The student was allowed to be excused from lessons on family life, physical growth, and AIDS instruction, but his father argued that state law entitled him to be exempt from the entire health course. The parent alleged that the subject matter of the course conflicted with his religious beliefs, but the court ruled that the health curriculum served the legitimate state interest of providing students important information. The Court was not

142. *See, e.g.,* Spence v. Bailey, 465 F.2d 797 (6th Cir. 1972); Moody v. Cronin, 484 F. Supp. 270 (C.D. Ill. 1979); S.T. v. Bd. of Educ., 552 A.2d 179 (N. J. 1988); Valent v. N. J. State Bd. of Educ., 274 A.2d 832 (N.J. Super. Ct. Ch. Div. 1971).

143. *See* Mitchell v. McCall, 143 So. 2d 629 (Ala. 1962) (holding that school authorities do not have to make special arrangements or alter programs to protect students from the embarrassment associated with nonparticipation). *See also* Smith v. Bd. of Educ., 844 F.2d 90 (2d Cir. 1988) (ruling that scheduling high school commencement exercises on a student's sabbath did not abridge the Free Exercise Clause).

144. Davis v. Page, 385 F. Supp. 395 (D.N.H. 1974). Although government interests prevailed over free exercise rights in denying the exemption from academic classes, the court recognized that offended students could be excused when audiovisual equipment was used solely for entertainment purposes. *Id.* at 401.

145. *See, e.g.,* Menora v. Ill. High Sch. Ass'n, 683 F.2d 1030 (7th Cir. 1982); Keller v. Gardner Cmty. Consol. Grade Sch. Dist. 72C, 552 F. Supp. 512 (N.D. Ill. 1982).

146. Mozert v. Hawkins County Bd. of Educ., 827 F.2d 1058 (6th Cir. 1987). This case divided civil libertarians; some felt the students had legitimate free exercise rights at stake, whereas others felt that the requested accommodation would breach the Establishment Clause.

147. Leebaert v. Harrington, 193 F. Supp. 2d 491 (D. Conn. 2002).

persuaded that the state law entitling students to be excused from a family life education program on religious grounds could be used for students to secure exemptions from the entire health curriculum.

As will be discussed in Chapter 3, conservative parents' organizations have secured federal and state laws allowing students to be excused from public school activities and components of the curriculum for religious and other reasons. Thus, parents may be able to use legislation to secure exemptions for their children,[148] even if they cannot substantiate that particular instructional activities impair free exercise rights.

Religious Challenges to the Secular Curriculum

Some parents have not been content with securing religious exemptions for their own children and have pressed for elimination of various courses, activities, and instructional materials from public schools. Although courts often have been receptive to requests for individual exemptions from specific public school activities, the judiciary has not been inclined to allow the restriction of the secular curriculum to satisfy parents' religious preferences. In 1968, the Supreme Court recognized that "the state has no legitimate interest in protecting any or all religions from views distasteful to them."[149]

Defining What Is "Religious"

These challenges to the curriculum raise complex questions involving what constitutes religious beliefs and practices that are subject to First Amendment protections and restrictions. In several cases protecting the free exercise of beliefs, the Supreme Court has adopted an expansive view toward religion,[150] but it has not yet found an Establishment Clause violation in connection with a nontheistic creed. Only one federal appellate court has ruled that a public school curricular offering (instruction in transcendental meditation) unconstitutionally advances a nontraditional religious belief (the Science of Creative Intelligence).[151] However, several other courts have suggested that secular religions should be subjected to the same standards that are applied to theistic religions in determining whether the Establishment Clause has been breached.[152]

---

148. *See* Protection of Pupil Rights Amendment to the No Child Left Behind Act of 2001, 20 U.S.C. § 1232h (2002); text accompanying note 195, Chapter 3.

149. Epperson v. Arkansas, 393 U.S. 97, 107 (1968) (quoting Joseph Burstyn, Inc. v. Wilson, 343 U.S. 495, 505 (1952)).

150. *See, e.g.,* Thomas v. Review Bd., 450 U.S. 707, 714 (1981); United States v. Seeger, 380 U.S. 163, 175 (1965).

151. Malnak v. Yogi, 592 F.2d 197 (3d Cir. 1979).

152. *See, e.g.,* Jaffree v. James, 544 F. Supp. 727, 732 (S.D. Ala. 1982); Fink v. Bd. of Educ., 442 A.2d 837, 843 (Pa. Commw. Ct. 1982). The Supreme Court also has noted that "the state may not establish a 'religion of secularism' in the sense of affirmatively opposing or showing hostility to religion, thus 'preferring those who believe in no religion.'" Sch. Dist. of Abington Township v. Schempp, 374 U.S. 203, 225 (1963). *See also* Torcaso v. Watkins, 367 U.S. 488, 495 n.11 (1961).

Allegations are being made that specific components of the public school curriculum violate the Establishment Clause because they advance "secular humanism" or "New Age theology," which critics claim disavow God and exalt humans as masters of their own destinies. Evolution, sex education, values clarification, and outcome-based education have been central targets, but few aspects of the curriculum have remained untouched by such claims. Recently, books in the *Harry Potter* series have been attacked, because they deal with wizardry and magic that allegedly advance the occult/Satanism.[153]

Even courts that have considered nontheistic creeds as "religions" for First Amendment purposes have not ruled that challenged public school courses and materials advance such creeds.[154] In a 1987 case that attracted substantial media attention, the Eleventh Circuit reversed an Alabama federal judge's conclusion that secular humanism was being unconstitutionally advanced in the Mobile County schools.[155] The judge had enjoined the school district's use of several dozen home economics, history, and social studies books found to advance secular humanism. Disagreeing, the appellate court held that the books did not promote an antitheistic creed but rather instilled "in Alabama public school children such values as independent thought, tolerance of diverse views, self-respect, maturity, self-reliance, and logical decision-making."[156] The court further rejected the contention that the mere omission of religious facts in the curriculum represented unconstitutional hostility toward theistic beliefs. The Eighth Circuit more recently ruled that a Missouri teacher's contract was not renewed for impermissible reasons after she sent a "magic rock" home with each student, with a letter indicating that the rock is "special and unique, just like you."[157] The court found community complaints that the letter and rock advanced New Ageism to be the basis for the board's action rather than the asserted concerns about the teacher's grading practices.

Challenged Curriculum Components

Sex education classes have been particularly susceptible to charges that an antitheistic faith is being advanced, but courts consistently have found that the challenged courses present public health information that furthers legitimate educational objectives and do not denounce Christianity.[158] The judiciary also has ruled that the Establishment

---

153. *See* Kathy Ishizuka, "'Harry Potter' Tops Most Challenged Books—Again," *School Library Journal,* vol. 48, no. 3 (2002), p. 29.

154. *See, e.g.,* Grove v. Mead Sch. Dist. No. 354, 753 F.2d 1528 (9th Cir. 1985) (reasoning that *The Learning Tree* does not advance an antitheistic faith).

155. Smith v. Bd. of Sch. Comm'rs, 655 F. Supp. 939 (S.D. Ala. 1987), *rev'd,* 827 F.2d 684 (11th Cir. 1987).

156. *Id.,* 827 F.2d at 692.

157. Cowan v. Strafford R-VI Sch. Dist., 140 F.3d 1153 (8th Cir. 1998); text accompanying note 113, Chapter 9.

Clause precludes the state from barring sex education simply to conform to the religious beliefs of some parents. However, the judiciary has acknowledged that students have a free exercise right to be excused from sex education classes if such instruction conflicts with their sectarian beliefs.[159]

Because conservative citizen groups have not been successful in getting sex education barred from the public school curriculum, they have lobbied for the adoption of programs that stress abstinence between unmarried people. A Louisiana appeals court agreed with plaintiffs that one of these programs, *Sex Respect: The Option of True Sexual Freedom,* promoted Christian doctrine and included some erroneous information in violation of state law.[160] The court ordered the school district to delete passages that were factually inaccurate or that dealt with the moral and spiritual implications of premarital sex, contraceptives, and sexually transmitted diseases.

Instruction pertaining to the origin of humanity also has generated continuing legal disputes. Historically, some states by law barred evolution from the curriculum, because it conflicted with the Biblical account of creation. In the famous Scopes "monkey trial" in the 1920s, the Tennessee Supreme Court upheld such a law, prohibiting the teaching of any theory that denies the Genesis version of creation or suggests "that man has descended from a lower order of animals."[161] In 1968, however, the United States Supreme Court struck down an Arkansas anti-evolution statute under the Establishment Clause, reasoning that evolution is science (not a secular religion), and a state cannot restrict student access to such information simply to satisfy religious preferences.[162]

After creationists were unable to convince the judiciary that evolution unconstitutionally advances an antitheistic faith, they focused on securing laws that require equal emphasis on the Biblical account of creation whenever evolution is taught in public schools. In 1987, the Supreme Court invalidated a Louisiana statute that mandated "equal time" for creation science and evolution and required school boards to make available curriculum guides, teaching aids, and resource materials on creation science.[163] Reasoning that creationism is not science, the Court concluded that the law was intended to discredit scientific information and advance religious beliefs in vio-

---

158. *See, e.g.,* Citizens for Parental Rights v. San Mateo County Bd. of Educ., 124 Cal. Rptr. 68 (Ct. App. 1975); Hobolth v. Greenway, 218 N.W.2d 98 (Mich. Ct. App. 1974); Smith v. Ricci, 446 A.2d 501 (N.J. 1982).

159. For a discussion of this issue, *see* Valent v. N. J. State Bd. of Educ., 274 A.2d 832, 840–841 (N.J. Super. Ct. Ch. Div. 1971).

160. Coleman v. Caddo Parish Sch. Bd., 635 So. 2d 1238 (La. Ct. App. 1994). *See also* ACLU v. Foster, No. 02-1440, 2002 U.S. Dist. LEXIS 13778 (E.D. La. July 25, 2002) (ordering state officials to ensure that federal funds are no longer used to promote religious beliefs under the Governor's Program on Abstinence).

161. Scopes v. State, 289 S.W. 363, 364 (Tenn. 1927).

162. Epperson v. Arkansas, 393 U.S. 97 (1968).

163. Edwards v. Aguillard, 482 U.S. 578 (1987). *See also* Daniel v. Waters, 515 F.2d 485 (6th Cir. 1975); McLean v. Ark. Bd. of Educ., 529 F. Supp. 1255 (E.D. Ark. 1982).

lation of the Establishment Clause. The Court did not accept the argument that the law promoted academic freedom and reasoned that it actually inhibited teachers' discretion to incorporate scientific theories about the origin of humanity into the curriculum. The Ninth Circuit subsequently ruled that school districts can mandate instruction in evolution, rejecting a teacher's claim that teaching this "antitheistic" doctrine would violate the Establishment Clause,[164] and a Minnesota appeals court upheld reassignment of a teacher who refused to teach evolution in conformance with the biology curriculum specifications.[165]

But teaching about the origin of humanity remains a volatile topic. The Kansas State Board of Education attracted national attention in 1999 when it rejected proposed science standards emphasizing evolution and adopted an alternative set eliminating the requirement that local school districts teach or test students about evolution.[166] The success of anti-evolution forces in Kansas was short lived, as a power shift created a moderate majority on the state board, which approved new science standards reinstating the study of evolution in 2000. Also, the Fifth Circuit ruled that a Louisiana school board's resolution, specifying that teachers must issue a disclaimer that the presentation of evolutionary theory is not intended to dissuade students from the Biblical version of Creation, lacked a secular purpose and conveyed a message of government approval of religion in violation of the Establishment Clause.[167] Other states, however, are considering anti-evolution measures,[168] and despite the judicial posture supporting evolution, religious challenges to such instruction may still persist when we mark the century anniversary of the Scopes trial.

Reading series also have been faulted for allegedly advancing antitheistic doctrine. For example, the Impressions reading series, published by Harcourt Brace Jovanovich, generated numerous challenges in the late 1980s and early 1990s. The series, employing the whole-language approach to reading instruction, was challenged as being morbid and depressing and promoting witchcraft based on the Wicca religion. Wicca has been recognized as a religion for the protection of free exercise rights, but the Ninth Circuit did not find that reading stories about witches or even

---

164. Peloza v. Capistrano Unified Sch. Dist., 37 F.3d 517 (9th Cir. 1994). *See also* Webster v. New Lenox Sch. Dist. No. 122, 917 F.2d 1004 (7th Cir. 1990) (upholding the school board's prohibition on teaching nonevolutionary theory).

165. LeVake v. Indep. Sch. Dist. No. 656, 625 N.W.2d 502 (Minn. Ct. App. 2001), *cert. denied,* 534 U.S. 1081 (2002). *See also supra* text accompanying note 82.

166. *See* Robert Hemenway, "The Evolution of a Controversy in Kansas Shows Why Scientists Must Defend the Search for Truth," *The Chronicle of Higher Education,* vol. 46, no. 10 (October 29, 1999), p. B7.

167. Freiler v. Tangipahoa Parish Bd. of Educ., 185 F.3d 337 (5th Cir. 1999). *See also* Moeller v. Schrenko, 554 S.E. 2d 198 (Ga. Ct. App. 2001) (using a biology text that addresses evolution does not denigrate students' religious beliefs in violation of the First Amendment); Johnson v. Chesapeake City Sch. Bd., 52 Va. Cir. 252 (Va. Cir. Ct. 2000) (rejecting challenge to use of science textbook that allegedly promoted a secular religion by teaching evolution as a scientific fact).

168. *See* David Hoff, "Debate Over Teaching of Evolution Theory Shifts to Ohio," *Education Week* (March 20, 2002), pp. 14–16.

creating poetic chants constituted the practice of witchcraft.[169] Similarly, the Seventh Circuit held that some stories in the Impressions series were scary, but that was a far cry from advancing a pagan cult.[170]

New York parents asserted that specific components of the curriculum offended their Catholic faith.[171] The Second Circuit agreed with the parents that one teacher's assignment for students to construct images of a Hindu deity abridged the First Amendment. Also, the court reasoned that making worry dolls amounted to preference of superstition over religion in violation of the Establishment Clause. But the court did not find constitutional violations in celebrating Earth Day or in role-playing as part of a drug prevention program using peer facilitators.

Although courts have not condoned parental attacks on various aspects of the public school curriculum that allegedly conflict with their religious values, more difficult legal questions are raised when policymakers support curriculum restrictions for religious reasons. Since courts show considerable deference to legislatures and school boards in educational matters, conservative parent organizations have pressed for state and federal legislation and school board policies barring certain content from public schools. There is concern among educators that neutral, nonreligious instruction is threatened by such efforts.

State Aid to Private Schools

In addition to disputes over the place of religion in public schools, government relations with private—primarily religious—schools have generated a substantial amount of First Amendment litigation. Unquestionably, parents have a legitimate interest in directing the upbringing of their children, including their education. In 1925, the Supreme Court afforded constitutional protection to private schools' rights to exist and to parents' rights to select private education as an alternative to public schooling.[172] Yet, the Court also recognized that the state has a general welfare interest in mandating school attendance and regulating private education to ensure an educated citizenry, considered essential in a democracy.[173] Some disputes have resulted from conflicts between the state's exercise of its *parens patriae* authority to protect the well-being of children and parental interests in having their children educated in settings that reinforce their religious and philosophical beliefs. If the government interferes with parents' child-rearing decisions, it must show that the intervention is necessary to protect the child or the state.[174] Although courts have upheld minimum

169. Brown v. Woodland Joint Unified Sch. Dist., 27 F.3d 1373 (9th Cir. 1994).

170. Fleischfresser v. Dirs. of Sch. Dist. 200, 15 F.3d 680 (7th Cir. 1994). This series was discontinued in 1994 because of the controversies generated.

171. Altman v. Bedford Cent. Sch. Dist., 245 F.3d 49 (2d Cir. 2001), *cert. denied,* 122 S. Ct. 68 (2001).

172. Pierce v. Society of the Sisters, 268 U.S. 510 (1925).

173. *See* text accompanying note 2, Chapter 3, for a discussion of compulsory attendance laws.

174. *See* Wisconsin v. Yoder, 406 U.S. 205, 214 (1972); *supra* text accompanying note 13.

state requirements for private schools (e.g., prescribed courses, personnel requirements),[175] the recent trend has been toward imposing outcome measures, such as
requiring private school students to participate in statewide testing programs.[176]

About 12 percent of all K–12 students in the United States are enrolled in private
schools or home education, but this ratio could change if additional government aid
flows to private education. Despite the fact that more than three-fifths of the states
specifically prohibit the use of public funds for sectarian purposes, about three-fourths
of the states provide public aid to private school students, including those attending
sectarian schools. The primary types of aid are for transportation services, the loan of
textbooks, state-required testing programs, special education for children with disabilities, and counseling services.[177] Some of the most significant Supreme Court
decisions interpreting the Establishment Clause have pertained to the use of public
funds for private, primarily sectarian, education. The following discussion focuses on
the legality of government aid for student services in parochial schools and to encourage family choice in education.

Aid for Student Services

The Supreme Court's support of religious accommodations in terms of allowing government support for parochial school students has been consistent since 1993,[178] with
some evidence of the accommodationist trend much earlier.[179] Indeed, the "child-
benefit" doctrine has been used to justify government aid for transportation and
secular textbooks for parochial school students since the mid-twentieth century.[180]
Also, the Supreme Court in 1980 upheld government support for state-required testing

175. *See e.g.,* New Life Baptist Church Acad. v. Town of E. Longmeadow, 885 F.2d 940 (1st Cir. 1989)
     (holding that a Massachusetts religious academy must allow local school district officials to review
     its curricula and operations to ensure comparability with public schools).

176. Also, the Supreme Court has ruled that private schools must conform to national antidiscrimination
     policies to receive tax exempt status. *See* Bob Jones Univ. v. United States, 461 U.S. 574, 592 (1983).
     See also Norwood v. Harrison, 413 U.S. 455 (1973) (holding that state funds could not be used to pro-
     vide textbooks for private school students attending racially discriminatory private schools).

177. Ironically, most states that provide aid to students in religious schools have state constitutional pro-
     hibitions on aid to religious institutions.

178. *See* Mitchell v. Helms, 530 U.S. 793 (2000); Agostini v. Felton, 521 U.S. 203 (1997); Rosenberger
     v. Rector & Visitors, 515 U.S. 819 (1995); Zobrest v. Catalina Foothills Sch. Dist., 509 U.S. 1 (1993);
     infra text accompanying notes 183–195. *But see* Bd. of Educ. v. Grumet, 512 U.S. 687 (1994); *infra*
     text accompanying note 198.

179. *See* Witters v. Wash. Dep't of Servs. for the Blind, 474 U.S. 481 (1986) (upholding use of federal
     vocational rehabilitation aid to support ministerial training); Mueller v. Allen, 463 U.S. 388 (1983)
     (upholding state tax benefit for educational expenses available to parents of public or private school
     students).

180. *See* Bd. of Educ. v. Allen, 392 U.S. 236 (1968) (finding no Establishment Clause violation in a state
     law requiring public school districts to loan secular textbooks to all secondary students, including
     those attending parochial schools); Everson v. Bd. of Educ., 330 U.S. 1 (1947) (rejecting an Estab-
     lishment Clause challenge to the use of public funds to provide transportation services for nonpublic
     school students).

programs in private schools,[181] even though a few years earlier it had found aid to develop and administer state-required as well as teacher-developed tests in violation of the Establishment Clause, because such tests potentially could be used to advance sectarian purposes.[182]

Then, in 1993, the Supreme Court found no Establishment Clause violation in publicly supporting sign-language interpreters in parochial schools,[183] signaling a paradigm shift toward the use of public school personnel in sectarian schools. The Court in *Zobrest v. Catalina Foothills School District* reasoned that the aid is going to the child as part of a federal government program that distributes benefits neutrally to qualifying children with disabilities under federal law. The child is the primary recipient of the aid, and the school receives only an incidental benefit. The Court reasoned that unlike a teacher or counselor, an interpreter neither adds to nor subtracts from the sectarian school's environment but merely interprets material that is presented.

Two years later, in a decision discussed previously, the Supreme Court ruled that the University of Virginia could not deny a student religious organization access to student activities funds to pay an outside contractor to print its religious publications.[184] Since other student organizations had access to such funds, the Court majority reasoned that discrimination against religious viewpoints was impermissible. Although the Supreme Court traditionally has been more receptive to governmental aid to private institutions of higher education than to elementary and secondary schools,[185] no other postsecondary decision has involved direct support for student-initiated proselytizing activities.

In the 1997 decision, *Agostini v. Felton,* the Supreme Court removed the prohibition on public school personnel providing remedial instruction in religious schools that it had announced 12 years earlier.[186] The controversy focused on Title I of the Elementary and Secondary Education Act (ESEA) of 1965, which targets educationally and economically disadvantaged students and has gone through a number of reauthorizations since enacted.[187] The law requires comparable services to be provided for

181. Comm. for Pub. Educ. & Religious Liberty v. Regan, 444 U.S. 646 (1980).

182. Levitt v. Comm. for Pub. Educ. & Religious Liberty, 413 U.S. 472 (1973); Meek v. Pittenger, 421 U.S. 349 (1975).

183. Zobrest v. Catalina Foothills Sch. Dist., 509 U.S. 1 (1993).

184. Rosenberger v. Rector & Visitors, 515 U.S. 819 (1995).

185. *See, e.g.,* Roemer v. Bd. of Pub. Works, 426 U.S. 736 (1976) (upholding noncategorical grants to private colleges and universities); Hunt v. McNair, 413 U.S. 734 (1973) (approving the use of state revenue bonds to finance private college and university construction); Tilton v. Richardson, 403 U.S. 672 (1971) (allowing federal grants for private college and university construction). *See also* Columbia Union Coll. v. Oliver, 254 F.3d 496 (4th Cir. 2001) (applying the "neutrality plus" standard, the court upheld aid to an institution of higher education because the funds were assigned in a neutral and even-handed manner and were not diverted to religious purposes).

186. 521 U.S. 203 (1997), overturning its ruling that barred the use of public school personnel to provide Title I remedial services on sectarian school premises, Aguilar v. Felton, 473 U.S. 402 (1985), and the portion of its decision that invalidated a shared-time program under which public school classes were provided for parochial school students on parochial school premises, Sch. Dist. v. Ball, 473 U.S. 373 (1985).

eligible students attending nonpublic schools. For the first time, the Court in *Agostini* held that comparability can be achieved by allowing public school personnel to provide instructional services in sectarian schools. The Court reasoned that under current Establishment Clause interpretations, the program's threat of increasing political divisiveness and requiring pervasive monitoring were insufficient to create excessive governmental entanglement with religion. The Court further recognized that in *Zobrest* it abandoned the presumption that public employees in sectarian schools would be tempted to inculcate religion.[188] In both *Zobrest* and *Agostini,* the Court rejected the notion that the Establishment Clause lays down an "absolute bar to the placing of a public employee in a sectarian school."[189]

The Supreme Court in *Mitchell v. Helms* subsequently found no Establishment Clause violation in using federal aid to purchase instructional materials and equipment for student use in sectarian schools.[190] Specifically, the ruling allows the use of public funds for computers, other instructional equipment, and library books in religious schools under Title II of the ESEA federal aid program. Those challenging the program argued that the aid was divertible for religious purposes, was direct and nonincidental, and supplanted rather than supplemented private school funds.[191]

Justice Thomas, speaking for the *Helms* plurality, found none of these contentions persuasive, rejecting a distinction between direct and indirect aid that has appeared in prior cases involving challenges to the use of government funds in religious schools.[192] The plurality reasoned that religious indoctrination or subsidization of religion could not be attributed to the government when aid, even direct aid, is distributed based on secular criteria, is available to religious and secular beneficiaries on a nondiscriminatory basis, and flows to religious schools only because of private choices of parents.[193] Justice Thomas declared, "We did not, as respondents do, think that the *use* of governmental aid to further religious indoctrination was synonymous with religious indoctrination *by* the government or that such use of aid created any improper incentives" for parents to send their children to religious schools.[194] Conceding that the equipment at issue could be diverted for sectarian uses, the plurality

---

187. The most recent reauthorization is P.L. 107-110, the No Child Left Behind Act of 2001, 20 U.S.C. § 6301 *et seq.* (2002).

188. 521 U.S. at 223–224.

189. Zobrest v. Catalina Foothills Sch. Dist., 509 U.S. 1, 13 (1993).

190. 530 U.S. 793 (2000). On remand, the Fifth Circuit changed its position regarding the federal aid program and its Louisiana counterpart to conform with the Supreme Court ruling. The appeals court also reaffirmed the constitutionality of the Louisiana school transportation and special education programs that provide public support for children attending parochial schools. Helms v. Picard, 229 F.3d 467 (5th Cir. 2000).

191. Although six justices supported the Court's holding, only Chief Justice Rehnquist and Justices Scalia and Kennedy signed Justice Thomas's plurality opinion in *Helms.* Justices O'Connor and Breyer signed a concurring opinion. 530 U.S. at 836 (O'Connor, J., joined by Breyer, J., concurring).

192. 530 U.S. at 815–816.

193. *Id.* at 809–810.

194. *Id.* at 821.

asserted that the central issue is not divertibility of the aid, because government support for secular activities always frees parochial school resources for religious purposes. Instead, the plurality emphasized that the constitutional standard is whether the aid itself would be appropriate for a public school to receive and is distributed in an even-handed manner—conditions it concluded were satisfied by the aid at issue in *Helms.* Six justices agreed that prior Supreme Court rulings barring state aid in the form of providing maps, slide projectors, and other instructional materials and equipment to sectarian schools[195] were no longer good law.

There are very few rulings left that reflect the Supreme Court's separationist stance regarding state aid to nonpublic schools. In fact, the Supreme Court seems to have dismantled most of the decisions rendered during the heyday of applying the stringent *Lemon* test in the 1970s, in which it struck down various types of public assistance to private schools.[196] The only separationist decisions of this period that have not been eroded at least in part by subsequent Supreme Court opinions involved government aid made available *solely* to private schools or their patrons, such as direct support for nonpublic school teachers' salaries in secular subjects or grants to maintain private elementary and secondary school facilities.[197] And the only separationist decision in this domain since 1990 was *Board of Education v. Grumet,* in which the Supreme Court struck down a legislative attempt to create a separate school district along religious lines to serve special-needs Satmar Hasidic children whose strict form of Judaism does not allow them to be educated with non-Satmars.[198]

195. Six justices agreed that *Helms* overturned two prior rulings: Wolman v. Walter, 433 U.S. 229 (1977) (invalidating direct government subsidies to parochial schools for remedial, guidance, and therapeutic services provided on parochial school grounds and for instructional materials and equipment, standardized tests, and field trip transportation for parochial school students); Meek v. Pittenger, 421 U.S. 349 (1975) (invalidating government aid in terms of direct loan of instructional materials and equipment and provision of auxiliary services on parochial school premises). These six justices also supported a modification of the *Lemon* test, making it explicit that excessive entanglement is simply part of consideration of the policy's primary effect.

196. This lends some support to the assertion of Justice Thomas that *Meek* and *Wolman* were simply anomalies. 530 U.S. at 807–808.

197. *See, e.g.,* Sloan v. Lemon, 413 U.S. 825 (1973) (striking down reimbursement to parents for part of tuition paid to nonpublic schools); Comm. for Pub. Educ. & Religious Liberty v. Nyquist, 413 U.S. 756 (1973) (striking down direct grants for maintenance and repair of private schools, tuition reimbursements to parents of nonpublic school children, and tax benefits restricted to parents of private school students); Lemon v. Kurtzman, 403 U.S. 602 (1971) (striking down a Rhode Island statute calling for salary supplements for teachers of secular subjects in private schools and a Pennsylvania statute calling for reimbursement to private schools of the costs of teachers' salaries, textbooks, and instructional materials in secular subjects). But even some of these decisions may be called into question by the rationale adopted by the Court in Zelman v. Simmons-Harris, 122 S. Ct. 2460 (2002). *See infra* text accompanying note 207.

198. 512 U.S. 687 (1994). *But see* Stark v. Indep. Sch. Dist. No. 640, 123 F.3d 1068 (8th Cir. 1997) (upholding a school district's decision to reopen a one-class school with a modified curriculum in response to a request from the Brethren sect); Ralph Mawdsley, "Extending the Limits of Permissible Government-Religion Interaction: *Stark v. Indep. Sch. Dist. No. 640,*" *Education Law Reporter,* vol. 124 (1998), pp. 499–519.

It must be remembered, however, that simply because courts have interpreted the Establishment Clause as allowing various types of public aid for nonpublic school students does not mean that states must use public funds for these purposes. For example, several state courts have ruled that transportation aid to private school students violates state constitutional provisions prohibiting the use of public funds for sectarian purposes.[199] Similarly, some state courts have invalidated lending textbooks to nonpublic school students under their state constitutions.[200] In 1981, the California Supreme Court called the child-benefit doctrine "logically indefensible" in striking down a state law that provided for the loan of textbooks to nonpublic school students.[201]

Aid to Encourage Educational Choice

There also has been legislation to provide indirect aid to make private schooling a viable choice for more families. Tax-relief measures for private school tuition and educational vouchers have received considerable attention in legislative forums. The primary justification for such measures is that the aid flows to religious schools only because of private choices of parents.

Tax-Relief Measures.   Tax benefits in the form of deductions or credits for private school expenses have been proposed at both the state and federal levels. Although Congress has not yet endorsed any proposals for federal income tax credits for private school tuition, a few states have enacted tax-relief provisions for educational expenses. The central constitutional question is whether such measures advance religion, in violation of the Establishment Clause, because the primary beneficiaries are the parents of parochial school children and ultimately religious institutions.

In 1983, the Supreme Court upheld a Minnesota tax-benefit program allowing parents of public or private school students to claim a limited state income tax deduction for tuition, transportation, and secular textbook expenses incurred for each elementary or secondary school dependent. The Court majority in *Mueller v. Allen* found

---

199. *See, e.g.,* Matthews v. Quinton, 362 P.2d 932 (Alaska 1961); McVey v. Hawkins, 258 S.W.2d 927 (Mo. 1953); Visser v. Nooksack Valley Sch. Dist. No. 506, 207 P.2d 198 (Wash. 1949). *See also* Healy v. Indep. Sch. Dist. No. 625, 962 F.2d 1304 (8th Cir. 1992) (terminating transportation benefits from the state for students attending a Lutheran school outside the school district did not violate students' constitutional rights).

200. *See, e.g.,* Fannin v. Williams, 655 SW.2d 480 (Ky. 1983); Bloom v. Sch. Comm., 379 N.E.2d 578 (Mass. 1978); *In re* Advisory Opinion, 228 N.W.2d 772 (Mich. 1975); Paster v. Tussey, 512 S.W.2d 97 (Mo. 1974); Gaffney v. State Dep't of Educ., 220 N.W.2d 550 (Neb. 1974); Elbe v. Yankton Indep. Sch. Dist. No. 63-3, 372 N.W.2d 113 (S.D. 1985).

201. Cal. Teachers Ass'n v. Riles, 632 P.2d 953, 962 (Cal. 1981).

the Minnesota law "vitally different" from an earlier New York provision, which violated the Establishment Clause by bestowing tax benefits only on private school patrons.[202] The majority declared that Minnesota's "decision to defray the cost of some educational expenses incurred by parents—regardless of the type of schools their children attend—evidences a purpose that is both secular and understandable."[203] The Court opined that such state assistance differs significantly from the direct transmission of public funds to parochial schools.[204]

Notwithstanding the Supreme Court ruling, only a few states provide such tax benefits. Most efforts to provide state tax relief for educational expenses have been defeated when placed before the voters, possibly because of the significant impact of such policies on state revenues.

Vouchers. For several decades, there has been debate over the merits of various voucher models under which public funds would flow to private schools because of parental choices. A number of New England states have had de facto voucher plans for years in that school districts without high schools provide a designated amount for high school tuition in neighboring public school districts or in private schools that the families select. However, very few other plans were adopted until the mid-1990s, and not until 1999 did Florida become the first state to implement a statewide voucher plan targeting students attending failing public schools. Under the Florida program, students attending schools that are rated as deficient (based on test scores, attendance, graduation rates, and other factors) are entitled to government vouchers that can be used in qualified public or private schools of their choice.[205] Also, a few urban districts have adopted state-funded voucher plans for disadvantaged youth, and privately funded scholarships are available for students to attend private schools in more than 30 major cities nationally.

In 2002, the Supreme Court rendered a significant decision, *Zelman v. Simmons-Harris,* resolving the conflict among lower courts regarding the participation of

202. 463 U.S. 388, 398 (1983) (contrasting Comm. for Pub. Educ. & Religious Liberty v. Nyquist, 413 U.S. 756 (1973)).

203. *Id.,* 463 U.S. at 395.

204. *See also* Kotterman v. Killian, 972 P.2d 606 (Ariz. 1999) (rejecting an Establishment Clause challenge to state tax credit of up to $500 for contributions to school tuition organizations to support private school tuition); Toney v. Bower, 744 N.E.2d 351 (Ill. App. Ct. 2001) (rejecting federal and state religious establishment challenge to state tax credit for a portion of K–12 education expenses at public or private schools).

205. In 2000, a Florida appeals court found no state constitutional bar to the well-delineated use of public funds for private school education. Bush v. Holmes, 767 So. 2d 668 (Fla. Cir. Ct. App. 2000), *rev. denied,* 790 So. 2d 1104 (Fla. 2001). However, two years later, a circuit court struck down the voucher plan under the explicit state constitutional prohibition on using public funds for religious purposes. Holmes v. Bush, No. CV 99-3370, 2002 WL 1809079 (Fla. Cir. Ct. Aug. 5, 2002).

religious schools in state-funded voucher programs.[206] In this five-to-four ruling, the Court upheld a scholarship program that gives choices to economically disadvantaged families in the Cleveland City School District through vouchers that can be used for up to $2,250 of the tuition at participating public or private schools.[207] No public school has elected to be involved in this voucher program, and the vast majority of the participating private schools are church related.

The Supreme Court relied heavily on the fact that parents—not the government—make the decision for the scholarship funds to flow to private schools. The Court emphasized that the aid is completely neutral with respect to religion because the government benefits are provided to a broad group of individuals defined only by their financial need and residence in the Cleveland School District. Considering the program to be one of "true private choice" among public and private options, the Court found no Establishment Clause violation. Even though 96 percent of participating students attend religious schools, the Court reasoned that the program does not provide incentives for parents to choose sectarian schooling for their children, since they must still contribute a small portion of the tuition. Similar to its reasoning in *Mueller,* the Court emphasized that the neutral program does not become unconstitutional simply because most recipients decide to use the aid in religious schools.[208]

Immediately following *Zelman,* a number of states indicated that they were seriously considering voucher programs to provide additional choices to disadvantaged students. Such programs still face state constitutional hurdles, even though the Supreme Court has rejected an Establishment Clause challenge to the use of state vouchers in religious schools. Many state constitutions contain explicit prohibitions

---

206. Prior to the Supreme Court's ruling, lower-court decisions on voucher programs had been mixed, but the two federal appellate courts addressing this issue had found Establishment Clause violations in the participation of religious schools in state-funded voucher programs. *See* Simmons-Harris v. Zelman, 234 F.3d 945 (6th Cir. 2000), *rev'd,* 122 S. Ct. 2460 (2002); Strout v. Albanese, 178 F.3d 57 (1st Cir. 1999) (upholding Maine's efforts to exclude religious schools from participating in a program under which towns with no secondary schools could provide scholarships for students to attend public or private nonreligious schools outside the district). *See also* Bagley v. Raymond Sch. Dep't, 728 A.2d 127 (Me. 1999). Striking down voucher programs on state constitutional grounds, *see* Giacomucci v. Southeast Delco Sch. Dist., 742 A.2d 1165 (Pa. Commw. Ct. 1999); Chittenden Town Sch. Dist. v. Vt. Dep't of Educ., 738 A.2d 539 (Vt. 1999). Rejecting Establishment Clause challenges to voucher plans, *see* Simmons-Harris v. Goff, 711 N.E. 2d 203 (Ohio 1999); Jackson v. Benson, 578 N.W.2d 602 (Wis. 1998). *See also supra* note 205.

207. 122 S. Ct. 2460 (2002). The voucher program is part of a larger initiative to address failing public schools by providing educational options to families, including tutorial services, theme-based magnet schools, and community schools that receive additional funding and are governed by their own boards. The scholarship program provides 90 percent of the tuition up to $2,250 for students below 200 percent of the poverty line, for whom participating private schools may not charge a parental co-payment greater than $250. If space is available for other families, the program pays 75 percent of the tuition costs up to $1,875, with no cap on the co-payment that can be charged. *See also* Davey v. Locke, 299 F.3d 748 (9th Cir. 2002) (striking down college's denial of scholarship to a qualified student solely because he chose to pursue a degree in theology).

208. The Court relied heavily on Zobrest v. Catalina Foothills Sch. Dist., 509 U.S. 1, 13 (1993); Witters v. Wash. Dep't of Servs. for the Blind, 474 U.S. 481 (1986); Mueller v. Allen, 463 U.S. 388 (1983). *See supra* note 179 and text accompanying note 189.

on the use of public funds for religious purposes.[209] And even where voucher programs that include sectarian schools satisfy state constitutions, fiscal concerns may influence whether large-scale voucher initiatives are implemented, because states currently are not supporting students attending private schools.

Conclusion

For almost a half century, church/state controversies have generated a steady stream of education litigation, and there are no signs of diminishing legal activity in this domain. The principle that the First Amendment demands wholesome governmental neutrality toward religion has been easier to assert than to apply. Although some lawsuits have involved claims under the Free Exercise Clause, most school cases have focused on interpretations of Establishment Clause prohibitions.

From the 1960s through the mid-1980s, the federal judiciary seemed more committed to enforcing Establishment Clause restrictions in elementary and secondary school settings than elsewhere. Recently, however, there seems to be greater government accommodation of religion, especially in terms of public funds flowing to religious schools. Also, the "bright line rule that public schools could never be a home for religious activity" is no longer very bright.[210] The Free Speech Clause increasingly seems to prevail over Establishment Clause restrictions in protecting religious expression in public schools. And the metaphor of separation of church and state seems to have been replaced by the concepts of equal access for and equal treatment of religious groups.

The following generalizations characterize the current status of church/state relations involving schools.

1. State-imposed devotional activities in public schools, regardless of voluntary participation, violate the Establishment Clause.
2. Students have a free exercise right to engage in silent prayer in public schools, but school officials cannot promote such silent devotionals.
3. Prayers delivered by members of the clergy in public school graduation ceremonies violate the Establishment Clause, but student-initiated devotionals during the ceremony may be permissible under certain circumstances.
4. Holidays with both secular and religious significance can be observed in an objective and prudent manner in public schools.

---

209. *See* Holmes v. Bush, No. CV 99-3370 (Fla. Cir. Ct. 2002), rendered a few months after the *Zelman* decision, *supra* note 206. However, a post-*Zelman* challenge has already been mounted to Maine's law prohibiting the participation of religious schools in its reimbursement program for districts not operating high schools. Plaintiffs are contending that the main rationale for upholding the exclusion in the past has now been rejected by the Supreme Court in *Zelman*. *See* "Suit Targets Religious Plank in Maine's Voucher Law," *School Law News* (September 27, 2002), p. 8.

210. Lupu, "The Lingering Death of Separationism," p. 246.

5. The Ten Commandments and other religious documents cannot be posted permanently in public schools.

6. The academic study of religion is legitimate in public schools, but such instruction cannot be used as a ploy to instill religious beliefs.

7. Under the Equal Access Act, if a secondary school receives federal funds and creates a limited open forum for student groups to meet during noninstructional time, religious clubs cannot be denied access to the forum.

8. Most courts have ruled that religious organizations cannot distribute their literature in public schools, but religious materials prepared and distributed by students are usually treated like other types of private student expression, subject to reasonable time, place, and manner restrictions.

9. If community groups are allowed to use public schools after school hours, groups cannot be discriminated against based on the religious content of their meetings, even groups that target children attending the schools.

10. Students can be released from public schools to receive religious instruction that is provided off public school grounds.

11. Students are entitled to excused absences to observe religious holidays if the absences do not place an undue hardship on the school.

12. Attempts to evade compulsory school attendance mandates for religious reasons have been unsuccessful, but Amish children have been excused from mandatory schooling after successfully completing the eighth grade.

13. Students can be excused from specific public school observances and activities that impede the practice of their religious beliefs as long as the management of the school or the students' academic progress is not disrupted.

14. Some courts have indicated that "secular humanism" or "New Age theology" may constitute an antitheistic religion for First Amendment purposes, but they have not ruled that public school instruction (e.g., sex education, evolution) advances this faith.

15. Laws requiring equal emphasis on the Genesis account of creation when evolution is taught violate the Establishment Clause.

16. States have a general welfare interest in mandating school attendance to ensure an educated citizenry; however, parents have the right to select private schooling for their children.

17. States can regulate private education, but unduly restrictive regulations may impair free exercise rights.

18. Direct governmental subsidies available only to religious schools violate the Establishment Clause.

19. Public aid for certain services that benefit the child and only incidentally the religious institution (e.g., transportation to school; loan of textbooks; and provision of standardized testing, sign-language interpreters, computers, and other equipment) does not violate the Establishment Clause.

20. Tax benefits for education expenses incurred in public and private schools and voucher programs that allow public funds to flow to religious schools because of the private choices of parents do not violate the Establishment Clause.

3

School Attendance and Instructional Issues

Although U.S. citizens have no federal constitutional right to a public education, each state constitution places a duty on its legislature to provide for free public schooling, thus creating a state entitlement (property right) for all children to be educated at public expense.[1] Substantial litigation has resulted from the collision of state interests in guaranteeing the general welfare with individual interests in exercising constitutional and statutory rights. This chapter focuses on legal mandates pertaining to various requirements and rights associated with school attendance and the instructional program. Other aspects of students' rights and responsibilities are explored in more detail in subsequent chapters.

Compulsory School Attendance

Presently, all 50 states compel children between specified ages, usually 6 to 16, to be educated. The legal basis for compulsory education is grounded in the common law doctrine of *parens patriae,* which means that the state, in its guardian role, has the authority to enact reasonable laws for the welfare of its citizens and the state. Parents can face criminal prosecution or civil suits for failing to meet their legal obligations under compulsory school attendance laws; furthermore, their children can be expelled for excessive truancy or judicially ordered to return to school.[2] In some instances, tru-

---

1. *See* Goss v. Lopez, 419 U.S. 565 (1975), text accompanying note 54, Chapter 7.
2. *See, e.g., In re* J. B., 58 S.W.3d 575 (Mo. Ct. App. 2001); *In re* C. S., 382 N.W.2d 381 (N.D. 1986). *See also* State *ex rel.* Estes v. Egnor, 443 S.E.2d 193 (W. Va. 1994) (emphasizing that criminal prosecution is aimed at parents; a student cannot be prosecuted for failure to attend school, regardless of the student's age). *But see* Hamilton v. Indiana, 694 N.E.2d 1171 (Ind. Ct. App. 1998) (holding that parents cannot be convicted of neglect under the compulsory attendance law if not served proper notice of their children's failure to attend school); State v. Smrekar, No. 99 CO 35, 2000 Ohio App. LEXIS 5381 (Ohio App. Ct. Nov. 17, 2000) (holding that the school district presented insufficient evidence of unexcused absences to consider a student a habitual truant and impose a fine and jail sentence on the parents).

ant children have been made wards of juvenile courts, with probation officers supervising their school attendance.[3]

Most states do not compel school attendance beyond age 16, but a number of states encourage high school graduation by conditioning a driver's license on school attendance for students under age 18. In an illustrative case, the West Virginia high court upheld such a state law as sufficiently related to the legitimate goals of keeping teenagers in school and reducing automobile accidents among children who have not exhibited responsibility.[4] School personnel must be certain, however, that they do not violate students' privacy rights in releasing information about individuals who do not meet such prerequisites to obtaining their licenses.[5]

Alternatives to Public Schooling

Although states can require schooling, it was settled in 1925 that private school attendance can satisfy such mandates. In *Pierce v. Society of Sisters,* the Supreme Court invalidated an Oregon statute requiring children between 8 and 16 years old to attend *public* schools. The Court declared that "the fundamental theory of liberty upon which all governments in this union repose excludes any general power of the state to standardize its children by forcing them to accept instruction from public teachers only."[6] In essence, parents do not have the right to determine *whether* their children are educated, but they do have some control over *where* such education takes place.[7] If divorced parents have joint custody over their children, educational decisions cannot be made unilaterally by the custodial parent.[8]

A few statutes that require attendance at a public or private school have been found unconstitutionally vague because they do not specify what constitutes a private school,[9] but most of these laws have been interpreted as permitting home education

---

3. *See, e.g., In re* Michael G., 747 P.2d 1152 (Cal. 1988).

4. Means v. Sidiropolis, 401 S.E.2d 447 (W. Va. 1990) (holding, however, that before a license is revoked, a school dropout must be provided a hearing with appropriate school officials to ascertain if the circumstances for dropping out are beyond the individual's control).

5. *See* Codell v. D. F., No.1998-CA-002895-MR, 2001 Ky. App. LEXIS 71 (Ky. Ct. App. June 22, 2001), *rev. granted,* 2002 Ky. LEXIS 205 (Ky. Oct. 9, 2002); *infra* text accompanying note 181.

6. 268 U.S. 510, 535 (1925). *See also* Troxel v. Granville, 530 U.S. 57, 66 (2000) (holding that Washington's overbroad child-visitation law as applied to grandparent visitations violated the mother's fundamental right to direct the upbringing of her child; extensive precedent leaves little doubt "that the Due Process Clause of the Fourteenth Amendment protects the fundamental right of parents to make decisions concerning the care, custody, and control of their children").

7. *See* Peterson v. Minidoka County Sch. Dist. No. 331, 118 F.3d 1351 (9th Cir. 1997) (finding no compelling state interest to justify interfering with a school principal's right to exercise his religious beliefs by home schooling his own children).

8. *See, e.g.,* Ralston v. Henley, No. M 2001–02274–COA–R9-CV, 2001 Tenn. App. LEXIS 728 (Tenn. Ct. App. Oct. 2, 2001); Anderson v. Anderson, 56 S.W.3d 5 (Tenn. Ct. App. 1999).

9. *See* Roemhild v. Georgia, 308 S.E.2d 154 (Ga. 1983); Wisconsin v. Popanz, 332 N.W.2d 750 (Wis. 1983).

programs that meet state standards.[10] Estimates indicate that home education has grown from about 15,000 children nationwide in the mid-1970s to between 850,000 and one million by 2001.[11] Courts have not spoken with a single voice regarding the constitutionality of state requirements that home instruction must be "essentially equivalent" to public school offerings.[12]

Despite states' legal authority to regulate alternatives to public education, there has been a trend since the 1980s to ease personnel and curriculum requirements and monitor the quality of private education by subjecting students to state-prescribed tests. Private schools may have to adhere to specific standards to receive state accreditation or to have their students compete interscholastically, but enrollment in nonaccredited programs generally can satisfy compulsory school attendance. However, parents educating their children at home can be convicted of violating compulsory education for failing to report their children's course of study, texts, and instructors to the local school district, and parents can be required to maintain portfolios of their children's work that are subject to review by school district personnel.[13]

10. *See, e.g., In re* D.B., 767 P.2d 801 (Colo. Ct. App. 1988); Delconte v. State, 329 S.E.2d 636 (N.C. 1985); Tex. Educ. Agency v. Leeper, 893 S.W.2d 432 (Tex. 1994). *See also* State v. Trucke, 410 N.W.2d 242 (Iowa 1987) (recognizing that unclear language in the compulsory attendance law precluded conviction of home-educating parents).

11. *Homeschooling in the United States: 1999* (Parent Survey) (Washington, DC: National Center for Education Statistics, 2000); Patricia Lines, *Homeschooling*—Eric Digest 151 (Eugene, OR: Educational Resources Information Center, 2001). Accurate estimates are difficult to obtain because some parents may not report that their children are being educated at home.

12. *Compare* Blackwelder v. Safnauer, 866 F.2d 548 (2d Cir. 1989) (rejecting a vagueness challenge to the New York requirement that home instruction be provided by competent teachers and be substantially equivalent to public school offerings); Mazanec v. N. Judson-San Pierre Sch. Corp., 798 F.2d 230 (7th Cir. 1986) (rejecting a constitutional challenge to Indiana's compulsory attendance law; the district court's finding that the home education program was essentially equivalent to public school instruction did not entitle the parents to injunctive or monetary relief); *with* Jeffery v. O'Donnell, 702 F. Supp. 516 (M.D. Pa. 1988) (finding legislation vague and in violation of parents' due process rights because it did not prescribe standards for determining who would be considered a qualified tutor and what would be considered satisfactory curricula); Minnesota v. Newstrom, 371 N.W.2d 525 (Minn. 1985) (finding the requirement that home instructors' qualifications be essentially equivalent to the minimum standard for public school teachers unconstitutionally vague). *See also* Duro v. Dist. Attorney, 712 F.2d 96, 99 (4th Cir. 1983) (interpreting the North Carolina compulsory attendance law as placing the burden on parents educating their children at home to prove that the instruction will prepare the children "to be self-sufficient participants in our modern society or enable them to participate intelligently in our political system").

13. *See, e.g.,* Battles v. Anne Arundel County Bd. of Educ., 95 F.3d 41 (4th Cir. 1996); Hartfield v. E. Grand Rapids Pub. Schs., 960 F. Supp. 1259 (W.D. Mich. 1997); State v. Skeel, 486 N.W.2d 43 (Iowa 1992); Care and Protection of Ivan, 717 N.E.2d 1020 (Mass. App. Ct. 1999). *See also* Pollard v. Goochland County Sch. Bd., No. 3:OOCV563, 2001 U.S. Dist. LEXIS 15363 (E.D. Va. Sept. 27, 2001) (holding that parents can be required to keep their children in school while their application to educate them at home is pending). *But see* Brunelle v. Lynn Pub. Schs., 702 N.E.2d 1182 (Mass. 1998) (holding that mandated home visits were not essential to the approval of a home education plan); *In re* T.M., 756 A.2d 793 (Vt. 2000) (reversing the order that the child was in need of care and supervision, because Commissioner of Education failed to order a hearing within 45 days of receipt of parents' notice of enrolling child in home schooling).

Traditionally, a number of states required home tutors to be certified teachers or to hold baccalaureate degrees, but now only a few states specify postsecondary education for such instructors, and none requires home tutors to be state licensed.[14] Indeed, since 1980, the majority of states have changed their laws to ease restrictions on home education, and no state has strengthened such regulations.[15] However, about three-fifths of the states require students educated at home to be subjected to some state-supervised form of assessment to ensure that students are mastering basic skills.[16] In a typical case, a West Virginia federal district court rejected parents' challenge to the state law making children ineligible for home schooling if they score poorly on standardized tests and do not improve after home remediation.[17]

Some legal disputes have focused on rights of children with disabilities if their parents elect to educate them at home or in private schools. As discussed in Chapter 2, the Establishment Clause does not bar states from furnishing services for children with disabilities in private schools. However, this does not necessarily mean that education agencies must provide the services on private school premises or in the children's homes as long as they make appropriate programs available elsewhere for all children with disabilities.[18]

Another controversial issue is whether private school students and those who are home schooled have an entitlement to take selected courses and participate in extracurricular activities in public schools. A few states by law authorize such participation, but statutes in most states are silent on this issue. In the absence of a state law, the Tenth Circuit upheld an Oklahoma school district's prohibition on part-time enrollment except for fifth-year seniors and special education students.[19] The court found no burden on the religious liberties or parental rights of families who educate their children at home. The school district justified its policy because it could not receive state aid for part-time students.

---

14. *See e.g.,* People v. DeJonge, 501 N.W.2d 127 (Mich. 1993) (striking down the state's certification requirement for home tutors as applied to families whose religious convictions prohibit the use of certified instructors); Lawrence v. S.C. State Bd. of Educ., 412 S.E.2d 394 (S.C. 1991) (finding unreasonable the state's requirement that home tutors with only high school diplomas must pass a basic skills test). *But see* North Dakota v. Brewer, 444 N.W.2d 923 (N.D. 1989) (upholding the requirement that home instructors without a college degree must pass an examination). Under current North Dakota law, high school graduates also can be home tutors if monitored by certified teachers during at least the first two years, N.D. Cent. Code § 15.1-23-03 (2002). For information on requirements in each state, *see* Mary Jo Dare, *The Tensions of the Home School Movement: A Legal/Political Analysis* (Ed.D dissertation, Indiana University, 2001).

15. *See* Dare, *The Tensions of the Home School Movement;* C. J. Klicka, *Home Schooling in the United States: A Legal Analysis* (Paeonian Springs, VA: Home School Legal Defense Association, 1996).

16. *See, e.g.,* Murphy v. Arkansas, 852 F.2d 1039 (8th Cir. 1988) (upholding the test requirement for home-schooled students and rejecting parents' assertion that Arkansas Home School Act impaired privacy, free exercise, and equal protection rights by treating home education differently from private schools). *See also* Dare, *The Tensions of the Home School Movement.*

17. Null v. Bd. of Educ., 815 F. Supp. 937 (S.D.W.V. 1993).

18. *See, e.g.,* Hooks v. Clark County Sch. Dist., 228 F.3d 1036 (9th Cir. 2000); Forstrom v. Byrne, 775 A.2d 65 (N.J. Super. 2001).

19. Swanson v. Guthrie Indep. Sch. Dist., 135 F.3d 694 (10th Cir. 1998).

High school activities associations in most states govern interscholastic competition for students attending qualifying public and private schools,[20] and some associations prohibit interscholastic participation of home-schooled pupils. A New York appeals court upheld a regulation under which a school district refused to allow home-schooled students to play on interscholastic sports teams, finding it reasonable to require students to be enrolled in public school and take a specified number of academic credits to participate.[21] The West Virginia athletic association rule excluding home-schooled students from interscholastic sports competition was similarly found to be a reasonable means to keep home schoolers from avoiding academic eligibility requirements that public and private school students must satisfy.[22]

States reflect wide variance in regulating alternatives to public education, but a number of states are relaxing input requirements and focusing on student outcome standards. The legal status of specific instructional programs depends on judicial interpretations of applicable state statutes and administrative regulations. With increasing interest in private schools and home-education programs, controversies seem likely to escalate over public/private relationships in connection with dual enrollment, provision of special services, and extracurricular activities.

Exceptions to Compulsory Attendance

State laws generally recognize certain exceptions to compulsory attendance mandates. The most common exemption is for married students, who are emancipated from required school attendance because they have assumed adult responsibilities. Statutes often include other exceptions, such as students serving temporarily as pages for the state legislature and children who have reached age 14 and have obtained lawful employment certificates. In addition to statutory exceptions from compulsory attendance mandates, the Supreme Court has granted an exemption on First Amendment religious grounds to Amish children who have successfully completed the eighth grade.[23]

However, most other attempts to keep children out of school on sectarian grounds[24] or for reasons beyond religious convictions have not been successful. For

---

20. The Supreme Court has ruled that where such private associations are significantly involved with state officials, they are considered state actors and subject to federal constitutional restrictions on their actions. Brentwood Acad. v. Tenn. Secondary Sch. Athletic Ass'n, 531 U.S. 288 (2001). *See* text accompanying note 142, Chapter 4.

21. Bradstreet v. Sobol, 650 N.Y.S.2d 402 (App. Div. 1996).

22. Gallery v. W. Va. Secondary Sch. Activities Comm., 518 S.E.2d 368 (W. Va. 1999) (finding the appeal moot as the student had transferred to a public school). *See also* Thomas v. Allegany County Bd. of Educ., 443 A.2d 622 (Md. Ct. App. 1982) (upholding the school district's policy limiting participation in all-county high school band program to public school students).

23. Wisconsin v. Yoder, 406 U.S. 205 (1972), text accompanying note 13, Chapter 2.

24. *See, e.g.,* Johnson v. Charles City Cmty. Schs., 368 N.W.2d 74 (Iowa 1985) (refusing to exempt fundamentalist Baptist children from compulsory education); Johnson v. Prince William County Sch. Bd., 404 S.E.2d 209 (Va. 1991) (upholding the school board's denial of parents' application for a religious exemption from the compulsory school attendance law because the parents failed to establish that their request was based on bona fide religious beliefs).

example, a North Carolina appeals court ruled that an American Indian father's refusal to send his children to school because they were not taught about Indian history and culture was an insufficient reason for defying the compulsory education law.[25] The court concluded that the children were "neglected" under state law, because they were neither permitted to attend public school nor provided an alternative education. Also, the Tenth Circuit held that the conflict between a school's grooming restrictions and Indian customs, traditions, and religious beliefs did not justify an exemption from compulsory education mandates.[26]

Health Requirements

State agencies have the power not only to mandate school attendance but also to require that students be in good health to protect the well-being of others.[27] In an early case, the Supreme Court rejected a federal constitutional challenge to a Texas law authorizing local school officials to condition public and private school attendance on vaccination against communicable diseases.[28] Numerous courts have upheld mandatory immunization, even when challenged on religious grounds, declaring that a pending epidemic is not necessary to justify such requirements.[29] Parents have been convicted for indirectly violating compulsory attendance laws by refusing to have their children vaccinated as a prerequisite to school admission.[30] Upholding such an immunization requirement, the Supreme Court of Arkansas declared that religious freedom does not mean that parents can "engage in religious practices inconsistent with the peace, safety, and health of inhabitants of [the] state."[31]

Some state statutes provide for an exemption from required immunization for members of religious sects whose teachings oppose the practice as long as the welfare of others is not endangered by the exemption.[32] Several courts have broadly inter-

25. *In re* McMillan, 226 S.E.2d 693 (N.C. Ct. App. 1976).

26. Hatch v. Goerke, 502 F.2d 1189 (10th Cir. 1974) (finding, however, that the student's expulsion without a hearing for refusing to cut his hair impaired due process rights).

27. *See, e.g.,* Kampfer v. Gokey, 955 F. Supp. 167 (N.D.N.Y. 1997) (upholding state law requiring public school students showing symptoms of a contagious disease to be sent home from school and preventing their return until checked by the school nurse).

28. Zucht v. King, 260 U.S. 174 (1922).

29. *See, e.g.,* Boone v. Boozman, 217 F. Supp. 2d 938 (E.D. Ark. 2002); Liebowitz v. Dinkins, 575 N.Y.S.2d 827 (App. Div. 1991).

30. *See, e.g.,* Maricopa County Health Dep't v. Harmon, 750 P.2d 1364 (Ariz. Ct. App. 1987); Maack v. Sch. Dist., 491 N.W.2d 341 (Neb. 1992); Lynch v. Clarkstown Cent. Sch. Dist., 590 N.Y.S.2d 687 (Sup. Ct. 1992); Calandra v. State Coll. Area Sch. Dist., 512 A.2d 809 (Pa. Commw. Ct. 1986).

31. Cude v. Arkansas, 377 S.W.2d 816, 818-819 (Ark. 1964). *See also* Mannis v. Arkansas *ex rel.* Dewitt Sch. Dist., 398 S.W.2d 206 (Ark. 1966) (holding that parents could not evade a mandatory vaccination requirement by withdrawing their child from public school and starting a parochial school that the parents asserted was not subject to the state immunization requirement).

32. *See, e.g.,* Fla. Dep't of Health v. Curry, 722 So. 2d 874 (Fla. App. 1998); Turner v. Liverpool Cent. Sch. Bd., 186 F. Supp. 2d 187 (N.D.N.Y. 2002).

preted such provisions as not requiring a prohibition against vaccination in official church doctrine or even that individuals are church members for them to qualify for the religious exemption.[33] But courts have rejected parental attempts to use statutory religious exemptions for philosophical opposition to immunization,[34] fear of health risks,[35] or their beliefs that immunization is contrary to the "genetic blueprint"[36] or "chiropractic ethics."[37] The Supreme Court of Mississippi even questioned the rationale for religious exemptions from mandatory immunization. The court concluded that a statutory exemption discriminated against parents who opposed immunization for nonreligious reasons, and further held that such an exemption defeated the purpose of an immunization requirement—to protect all students from exposure to communicable diseases.[38] Most other courts have reasoned that states are empowered to enact religious exemptions, but are not obligated to do so.

Although it is well established that school attendance can be conditioned on immunization against communicable diseases, states cannot abdicate their responsibility to educate children with such diseases. Children can be denied attendance in the regular school program if their presence poses a danger to others, but it is generally assumed that an alternative educational program (e.g., home instruction by computer) must be provided.

Some controversies have focused on school attendance by students with acquired immune deficiency syndrome (AIDS). Several states have adopted policies, modeled after guidelines issued by the National Centers for Disease Control, stipulating that students with AIDS should be allowed to attend public school unless they have open lesions, cannot control their bodily secretions, or display behavior such as biting. The Centers for Disease Control have suggested that determinations of whether individual students pose a health risk to others should be made on a case-by-case basis by a team of appropriate health and education personnel. Courts have held that AIDS-infected children are protected by federal statutes barring discrimination against individuals with disabilities[39] and consistently have ruled that

33. *See, e.g.,* Berg v. Glen Cove City Sch. Dist., 853 F. Supp. 651 (E.D.N.Y. 1994); Sherr v. Northport-E. Northport Union Free Sch. Dist., 672 F. Supp. 81 (E.D.N.Y. 1987).

34. Kleid v. Bd. of Educ., 406 F. Supp. 902 (W.D. Ky. 1976).

35. Farina v. Bd. of Educ., 116 F. Supp. 2d 503 (E.D.N.Y. 2000).

36. Mason v. Gen. Brown Cent. Sch. Dist., 851 F.2d 47 (2d Cir. 1988).

37. Hanzel v. Arter, 625 F. Supp. 1259 (S.D. Ohio 1985) (rejecting additional claims that the immunization requirement also impaired constitutional privacy and due process rights). *See also* Heard v. Payne, 665 S.W.2d 865 (Ark. 1984) (holding that a statement from chiropractor could not satisfy medical exemption from immunization).

38. Brown v. Stone, 378 So. 2d 218 (Miss. 1979).

39. *See, e.g.,* Thomas v. Atascadero Unified Sch. Dist., 662 F. Supp. 376 (C.D. Cal. 1987); Dist. 27 Cmty. Sch. Bd. v. Bd. of Educ., 502 N.Y.S.2d 325 (Sup. Ct. 1986).

public schools must enroll children with AIDS upon certification by health officials that they pose minimal danger of infecting others.[40]

Concerns about student health have caused some school boards, particularly in urban areas, to establish school-based clinics, offering services from immunization to disease diagnosis and treatment. The most controversial aspect of the clinics has been their involvement in prescribing and dispensing forms of birth control. The Supreme Court declined to review a decision in which the Massachusetts high court upheld a school board's authority to place condom machines in high school restrooms and allow junior and senior high school students to request condoms from the school nurse.[41] The Third Circuit also rejected a parental challenge to a school district's condom-distribution program, which was found within the school board's statutory powers to promote health services that prevent disease.[42]

Residency Requirements

In general, courts have ruled that public schools are obligated to educate school-age children who are bona fide residents in that they live in the district with their parents or legal guardian, are emancipated minors, or are adult students who live independently from their parents.[43] In an important 1982 decision, *Plyler v. Doe,* the Supreme Court held that school districts could not deny a free public education to resident children whose parents had entered the country illegally.[44] Recognizing the individual's significant interest in receiving an education, the Court ruled that classifications affecting access to education would have to be substantially related to an important governmental objective to satisfy the Equal Protection Clause. The Court found that

---

40. *See, e.g.,* Doe v. Dolton Elementary Sch. Dist. No. 148, 694 F. Supp. 440 (N.D. Ill. 1988); Parents of Child v. Coker, 676 F. Supp. 1072 (E.D. Okla. 1987); Phipps v. Saddleback Valley Unified Sch. Dist., 251 Cal. Rptr. 720 (Ct. App. 1988). *See also* Martinez v. Sch. Bd., 861 F.2d 1502, 1506 (11th Cir. 1988), *on remand,* 711 F. Supp. 1066 (M.D. Fla. 1989) (finding the "remote theoretical possibility" of transmitting AIDS from a child's tears, saliva, and urine did not support segregation of the child with AIDS in a separate cubicle); N.Y. Ass'n for Retarded Children v. Carey, 612 F.2d 644 (2d Cir. 1979) (holding that children with hepatitis B cannot be excluded from or segregated in public schools).

41. Curtis v. Sch. Comm., 652 N.E.2d 580 (Mass. 1995).

42. Parents United for Better Schs. v. Sch. Dist., 148 F.3d 260 (3d Cir. 1998). *See also* Decker v. Carroll Acad., No. 02A01-9709-CV-00242, 1999 Tenn. App. LEXIS 336 (Tenn Ct. App. May 26, 1999). *But see* Alfonso v. Fernandez, 606 N.Y.S.2d 259 (App. Div. 1993) (striking down a school district's program of distributing condoms without parental consent as violating parents' constitutional right to direct the upbringing of their children and their statutory right to give consent before health services are provided to their children).

43. Even students temporarily in the district because their parents are assigned to federal installations for a short period of time are considered bona fide residents. *See, e.g.,* United States v. Onslow County Bd. of Educ., 728 F.2d 628 (4th Cir. 1984).

44. 457 U.S. 202 (1982). For a discussion of standards of judicial review under the Equal Protection Clause, *see* text accompanying note 1, Chapter 5; note 1, Chapter 10.

Texas's asserted interest in deterring aliens from entering the country illegally was not important enough to deny students an opportunity to be educated.

Despite the Supreme Court precedent, California voters in 1994 supported Proposition 187, an initiative denying free education and health-care services to aliens residing in the state illegally. This law was challenged almost immediately, and the Ninth Circuit affirmed the lower court's injunction against implementation of several sections of the initiative, including the denial of free public education to children of illegal aliens.[45]

Children who are wards of the state and live in state facilities are usually considered residents of the school district where the facility is located, even if their parents live elsewhere.[46] Children with disabilities who have court-appointed guardians are entitled to support for an appropriate education where their guardians reside.[47] Courts have also held that school districts cannot deny an education to homeless children being sheltered in their districts.[48]

In contrast to the judiciary's position that school boards must provide free public schooling for resident students, courts in general have not required public schools to admit *nonresident* students tuition free.[49] The Supreme Court upheld a Texas requirement allowing local school boards to deny tuition-free schooling to any unemancipated minor who lives apart from a parent or legal guardian for the primary purpose of attending public school.[50] The court ruled that the requirement advanced the

---

45. Gregorio T. v. Wilson, 59 F.3d 1002 (9th Cir. 1995).

46. *See, e.g.,* Steven M. v. Gilhool, 700 F. Supp. 261 (E.D. Pa. 1988) (holding, however, that a state facility can charge tuition for children who are legal wards of another state).

47. *See, e.g.,* Olivas v. Ariz. Sch. for the Deaf and Blind, 743 F. Supp. 700 (D. Ariz. 1990). *But see* Catlin v. Sobol, 93 F.3d 1112 (2d Cir. 1996) (finding that a child living in a group home since infancy while receiving parental support was not entitled to free schooling in the district of the home's location); Wise v. Ohio Dep't of Educ., 80 F.3d 177 (6th Cir. 1996) (finding that Ohio officials could seek reimbursement for special education costs where parents, who were not Ohio residents, unilaterally placed their child in an Ohio private residential facility).

48. *See, e.g.,* Lampkin v. District of Columbia, 886 F. Supp. 56 (D.D.C. 1995); Orozco *ex rel.* Arroyo v. Sobol, 703 F. Supp. 1113 (S.D.N.Y. 1989). In 1987, Congress passed the Stewart B. McKinney Education for Homeless Children Act, later renamed the McKinney-Vento Homeless Assistance Act, 42 U.S.C. § 11431 (2002), providing some federal aid for the education of homeless children, including transportation to school. The most recent reauthorization in the No Child Left Behind Act of 2001, 20 U.S.C. § 6312(b)(1)(E) (2002), strengthens protections for homeless children and requires each state's plan to include a description of how services for the homeless will be coordinated and integrated with other educational services.

49. *See, e.g.,* Joshua v. Unified Sch. Dist. 259, No. 98-3248, 2000 U.S. App. LEXIS 8837 (10th Cir. May 2, 2000); Dover Town Sch. Dist. v. Simon, 650 A.2d 514 (Vt. 1994). *See also* Baerst v. State Bd. of Educ., 642 A.2d 76 (Conn. App. Ct. 1994) (holding that even though a minor portion of their home was physically located in another school district, the student was a resident of the community with which her family was primarily associated); Massie v. Lexington Local Schs., No. 00-CA-101, 2001 Ohio App. LEXIS 3269 (Ohio Ct. App. July 3, 2001) (finding resident school district to be where parents' home was located even though their property spanned two districts).

50. Martinez v. Bynum, 461 U.S. 321 (1983).

substantial state interest of assuring high-quality public education for residents (those living in a school district with the intent to remain).

Other courts similarly have upheld residency requirements, reasoning that tuition can be charged when students legally reside outside the school district, even though they may live in the district with someone other than their legal guardians.[51] The Fifth Circuit also recognized that students have no state-created right to attend public school tuition free in the school district where they formerly resided prior to changing their legal residence.[52] As will be discussed in Chapter 4, several cases involving residency disputes have involved student athletes, and courts consistently have rejected efforts to establish limited guardianships to enable students to attend school tuition free for athletic reasons.[53]

Minnesota was the first state to enact an interdistrict open enrollment plan, allowing students to apply for transfers to any public school district within the state. Transfer requests are subject to certain restrictions, such as space limitations and racial balance criteria, and participation by local districts is optional under some plans. The majority of states now allow for some type of open enrollment within districts and/or across district boundaries. Assessing a claim under an open enrollment plan, a Wisconsin appeals court found no rational basis for a school district's argument that lack of space caused it to deny a nonresident student's transfer request when it had admitted three other nonresident students who had been attending high school in the district. The court reasoned that state law required admission on a random basis when space was insufficient, so the rejection of one student while admitting three others was arbitrary and unreasonable.[54] But in the absence of authorized open enrollment plans, students do not have a right to attend school outside their resident district or even outside their attendance zone within the district.[55]

In some situations, however, courts have found that there are legitimate reasons for children to live apart from their parents, such as health concerns or the need to provide a more suitable home environment.[56] The Eighth Circuit found that an Arkan-

---

51. *See, e.g., Joshua,* 2000 U.S. App. LEXIS 8837; Hallissey v. Sch. Admin. Dist. No. 77, 755 A.2d 1068 (Me. 2000); Woodbury Heights Bd. of Educ. v. Starr, 725 A.2d 1180 (N.J. Super. Ct. App. Div. 1999); Graham v. Mock, 545 S.E.2d 263 (N.C. Ct. App. 2001).

52. Daniels v. Morris, 746 F.2d 271 (5th Cir. 1984). *See also* Clayton v. White Hall Sch. Dist., 875 F.2d 676 (8th Cir. 1989) (rejecting an equal protection challenge to an Arkansas school district's policy allowing nonresident children of certified and administrative employees, but not other employees, to attend school in the district; the policy was considered rationally related to the objective of recruiting high quality teachers and administrators).

53. *See* text with note 152, Chapter 4.

54. McMorrow v. Benson, 617 N.W.2d 247 (Wis. Ct. App. 2000).

55. *See* Mullen v. Thompson, 31 Fed. Appx. 77 (3d Cir. 2002) (rejecting assertion that students, who attended Pittsburgh public schools slated to be closed, had any constitutional interest in attending schools of their choice).

56. *See, e.g.,* Major v. Nederland Indep. Sch. Dist., 772 F. Supp. 944 (E.D. Tex. 1991); Israel *ex rel.* Owens v. Bd. of Educ., 601 N.E.2d 1264 (Ill. App. Ct. 1992); Pat v. Stanwood Sch. Dist., 705 P.2d 1236 (Wash. Ct. App. 1985).

sas school district's residency requirement, denying tuition-free enrollment to minors whose guardians were not domiciled in the district, abridged equal protection rights by discriminating against students living apart from their parents with no control over the situation.[57] The court further concluded that the policy violated due process guarantees by creating an irrebuttable presumption that a student who does not reside with a parent or guardian is not living in the school district with the intent to remain. More recently, a state appeals court ruled that a Korean student living with relatives in New Jersey was entitled to free public schooling under the hardship exception to the residency requirement because his parents in Korea could not care for him.[58]

Courts have rejected parental claims that assignment to allegedly inadequate resident school districts is detrimental to their children's welfare and impairs protected rights,[59] but such assertions may be more successful in the future. Under the federal No Child Left Behind Act of 2001, students assigned to schools that have not met annual progress goals for two consecutive years must be provided other educational options with transportation provided.[60] A number of states are enacting similar accountability legislation, including technical assistance and sanctions for schools and districts that are not meeting state academic standards and providing educational choices for students attending failing public schools. These measures may negate some of the traditional discretion enjoyed by school districts in establishing residency requirements for students.

School Fees

Public schools face mounting financial pressures due to escalating costs of facilities, supplies, insurance, and services required by students with special needs. Furthermore, intergovernmental competition for tax dollars is increasing while citizens continue to press for tax relief. Thus, it is not surprising that school officials are attempting to transfer some of the fiscal burden for public school services and materials to students and their parents. Although the law is clear that public schools cannot charge tuition as a prerequisite to school attendance, various "user fees" for transportation, books, and course materials have been controversial.

---

57. Horton v. Marshall Pub. Schs., 769 F.2d 1323 (8th Cir. 1985). Also, school districts have been required to educate students where they mistakenly enrolled nonresidents. *See, e.g.,* Cohen v. Wauconda Cmty. Unit Sch. Dist. No. 118, 779 F. Supp. 88 (N.D. Ill. 1991); Burdick v. Indep. Sch. Dist. No. 52, 702 P.2d 48 (Okla. 1985).

58. P.B.K. v. Bd. of Educ., 778 A.2d 1124 (N.J. Super. App. Div. 2001). *See also* J. A. v. Bd. of Educ., 723 A.2d 1270 (N.J. Super. Ct. App. Div. 1999) (finding documentation sufficient to entitle a student to free pubic education in her aunt's school district).

59. *See* Ramsdell v. N. River Sch. Dist. No. 200, 704 P.2d 606 (Wash. 1985) (holding that denial of parents' request for their children to transfer from an allegedly inadequate school district did not abridge their children's state constitutional right to an "ample education").

60. 20 U.S.C. § 6316 (b) (2002).

Transportation

Several courts have distinguished transportation charges from tuition charges, concluding that transportation is not an essential part of students' entitlement to free public schooling.[61] Courts have upheld policies allowing school districts to differentiate between resident and nonresident students regarding transportation fees,[62] to provide one-way transportation only,[63] to impose geographic limitations on bus services and fees charged,[64] and to charge for summer school transportation.[65]

In the only Supreme Court decision involving public school user fees, the Court in 1988 upheld a North Dakota statute permitting selected school districts to charge a transportation fee, not to exceed the school district's estimated cost of providing the service.[66] When the school district in question implemented door-to-door bus service, it assessed a fee for approximately 11 percent of the costs, with the remainder supported by state and local tax revenues. Rejecting a parental challenge, the Supreme Court concluded that the law served the legitimate purpose of encouraging school districts to provide bus services. Noting that the state is not obligated to provide school transportation services at all, the Court held that such services need not be free.

In general, it appears that as long as school officials have a rational basis for their decisions, reasonable school transportation fees can be imposed. As will be discussed in Chapter 6, however, states do not have the same discretion regarding transportation for children with disabilities. Under federal and state laws, transportation is a related service that must be provided free if necessary for a child with disabilities to participate in the educational program.

Textbooks, Courses, and Materials

The legality of charging students for the use of public school textbooks has been contested with some regularity. In 1972, the Supreme Court was asked to address the federal constitutional issue in a New York case that focused on a state law allowing school districts to decide by election whether to charge elementary school students a book rental fee. The Second Circuit concluded that the law did not violate Fourteenth

---

61. *See, e.g.,* Kadrmas v. Dickinson Pub. Schs., 487 U.S. 450 (1988); Salazar v. Eastin, 890 P.2d 43 (Cal. 1995); Arcadia Unified Sch. Dist. v. State Dep't of Educ., 825 P.2d 438 (Cal. 1992).

62. *See, e.g.,* Fenster v. Schneider, 636 F.2d 765 (D.C. Cir. 1980).

63. *See, e.g.,* Shaffer v. Bd. of Sch. Dirs., 730 F.2d 910 (3d Cir. 1984).

64. *See, e.g.,* Sch. Dist. v. Hutchinson, 508 N.W.2d 832 (Neb. 1993); State *ex rel.* Rosenberg v. Grand Coulee Dam Sch. Dist. No. 301, 536 P.2d 614 (Wash. 1975).

65. *See, e.g.,* Crim v. McWhorter, 252 S.E.2d 421 (Ga. 1979).

66. *Kadrmas,* 487 U.S. 450. The Court further concluded that the law's distinction between reorganized and nonreorganized school districts did not present an equal protection violation in the absence of proof that the statute was arbitrary and irrational. Under the law, school districts have the discretion to waive any fee for families financially unable to pay, and benefits such as diplomas and grades are not to be affected by nonpayment of fees.

Amendment equal protection rights, even though it disadvantaged children from poor families. The Supreme Court agreed to review the case, but before it had the opportunity, the issue became moot because voters in the school district decided to assess a tax to purchase all textbooks for grades 1 through 6.[67]

Because the Supreme Court has not invalidated textbook fees under federal equal protection guarantees, the legality of such fees rests on interpretations of state law. The dominant practice is for public schools to loan textbooks to students without charge, and courts in several states, such as Idaho, Michigan, North Dakota, and West Virginia, have interpreted state constitutional provisions as precluding the imposition of textbook fees.[68] However, courts in some states, such as Arizona, Colorado, Illinois, Indiana, and Wisconsin, have interpreted their constitutional provisions as permitting rental fees for public school textbooks.[69] While authorizing textbook fees, an Indiana federal district court ruled that the state student disciplinary code and federal equal protection guarantees precluded school boards from suspending students for their parents' failure to pay the fees.[70] The Ninth Circuit also recognized that students have a constitutional right not to be subjected to embarrassment, humiliation, or other penalties for failure to pay textbook fees.[71] Where textbook fees have been condoned, waivers are usually available for students who cannot afford to pay the assessed amount.[72]

In addition to fees for textbooks, fees for courses and supplies also have been challenged, generating a range of judicial opinions. The Supreme Court of Missouri ruled that the practice of charging course fees as a prerequisite to enrollment in academic classes impaired students' rights to free public schooling.[73] The Supreme Courts of Montana and New Mexico interpreted their state constitutions as prohibiting

---

67. Johnson v. N.Y. State Educ. Dep't, 449 F.2d 871 (2d Cir. 1971), *vacated and remanded,* 409 U.S. 75 (1972) (per curiam).

68. Paulson v. Minidoka County Sch. Dist. No. 331, 463 P.2d 935 (Idaho 1970); Bond v. Ann Arbor Sch. Dist., 178 N.W.2d 484 (Mich. 1970); Cardiff v. Bismarck Pub. Sch. Dist., 263 N.W.2d 105 (N.D. 1978); Randolph County Bd. of Educ. v. Adams, 467 S.E.2d 150 (W. Va. 1995).

69. Carpio v. Tucson High Sch. Dist. No. 1, 524 P.2d 948 (Ariz. 1974); Marshall v. Sch. Dist. RE No. 3, 553 P.2d 784 (Colo. 1976); Hamer v. Bd. of Educ., 265 N.E.2d 616 (Ill. 1970); Chandler v. S. Bend Cmty. Sch. Corp., 312 N.E.2d 915 (Ind. Ct. App. 1974).

70. Carder v. Mich. City Sch. Corp., 552 F. Supp. 869 (N.D. Ind. 1982).

71. Canton v. Spokane Sch. Dist. No. 81, 498 F.2d 840 (9th Cir. 1974). *But see* Ass'n for Def. v. Kiger, 537 N.E.2d 1292 (Ohio 1989) (upholding state law authorizing school districts to withhold grades or credit if students failed to pay fees for materials used in courses; however, fees could not be collected for materials used for administrative rather than instructional purposes).

72. *See* Vandevender v. Cassell, 208 S.E.2d 436 (W. Va. 1974) (interpreting the state constitution as requiring textbooks, workbooks, and other materials necessary for the state-prescribed curriculum to be provided free for students who cannot afford to purchase them). *But see Carpio,* 524 P.2d 948 (holding that an Arizona school district's failure to supply indigent high school students with textbooks did not abridge equal protection or due process rights).

73. Concerned Parents v. Caruthersville Sch. Dist. No. 18, 548 S.W.2d 554 (Mo. 1977).

fees for required courses, but allowing reasonable fees for elective courses.[74] In contrast, the Supreme Courts of Illinois, Ohio, and North Carolina have concluded that their state constitutions permit public schools to charge instructional supply fees for *any* courses.[75] In some cases, the concept of charging parents for materials and other supplies has received judicial endorsement, but the manner of fee collection (e.g., inadequate waiver provisions) has been invalidated.[76]

Currently, school districts in many states solicit fees from students for various consumable materials. The legality of such practices varies across states and depends primarily on the state judiciary's assessment of state constitutional provisions. An issue receiving increasing attention is the imposition of fees for participation in extracurricular activities, which is discussed in Chapter 4.

The School Curriculum

The public school curriculum is controlled primarily by states and local school boards. However, the federal government does influence the curriculum through funds it provides for particular initiatives. For example, under the No Child Left Behind Act of 2001, states can apply for federal aid to strengthen reading instruction in the early grades.[77] Unlike the federal government, state legislatures have broad authority to impose curriculum mandates. State legislation regarding the public school curriculum has become increasingly explicit, with some enactments challenged as violating individuals' protected rights. Also, curriculum policies of local school boards have been controversial. This section focuses on legal developments involving curriculum requirements/restrictions and instructional censorship.

---

74. Granger v. Cascade County Sch. Dist., 499 P.2d 780, 786 (Mont. 1972); Norton v. Bd. of Educ., 553 P.2d 1277 (N.M. 1976). Fees for drivers' education have generated conflicting rulings. *Compare* Cal. Ass'n for Safety Educ. v. Brown, 36 Cal. Rptr. 2d 404 (Ct. App. 1994) (charging fees for drivers' education violates the free school guarantee of the state constitution) *with* Kristin Nat'l v. Bd. of Educ., 552 S.E.2d 475 (Ga. Ct. App. 2001) (upholding a school district's policy charging students a fee for drivers' education, because it was offered after regular school hours); Messina v. Sobol, 553 N.Y.S.2d 529 (App. Div. 1990) (upholding fees because drivers' education is not a mandatory course for high school graduation).

75. Beck v. Bd. of Educ., 344 N.E.2d 440 (Ill. 1976); State *ex rel.* Massie v. Bd. of Educ., 669 N.E.2d 839 (Ohio 1996); Sneed v. Greensboro City Bd. of Educ., 264 S.E.2d 106 (N.C. 1980). *See also* Ambroiggio v. Bd. of Educ., 427 N.E.2d 1027 (Ill. App. Ct. 1981) (upholding an Illinois district's lunchroom supervision fee for students who were not provided bus transportation, lived within .7 mile of school, and ate at school).

76. *See, e.g.,* Sodus Cent. Sch. v. Rhine, 406 N.Y.S.2d 175 (App. Div. 1978); *Sneed,* 264 S.E.2d at 114; Lorenc v. Call, 789 P.2d 46 (Utah Ct. App. 1990).

77. No Child Left Behind Act of 2001 (Reading First), 20 U.S.C. § 6362 (2002).

Requirements and Restrictions

Courts have repeatedly recognized that the state retains the power to determine the public school curriculum as long as federal constitutional guarantees are respected. A few state constitutions include specific curriculum mandates, but more typically, the legislature is given responsibility for curricular determinations. States vary as to the specificity of legislative directives, but most states require instruction pertaining to the Federal Constitution, American history, English, mathematics, drug education, health, and physical education. Some state statutes specify what subjects will be taught in which grades, and many states have detailed legislation pertaining to vocational education, bilingual education, and special services for children with disabilities. State laws usually stipulate that local school boards must offer the state-mandated minimum curriculum, which they may supplement unless there is a statutory prohibition.[78] In about half of the states, local school boards (and in some instances, school-based councils) are empowered to adopt courses of study, but often they must secure approval from the state board of education.

Despite states' substantial discretion in curricular matters, some legislative attempts to impose curriculum restrictions have run afoul of federal constitutional rights. The first curriculum case to reach the Supreme Court involved a 1923 challenge to a Nebraska law that prohibited instruction in a foreign language to any public or private school students who had not successfully completed the eighth grade.[79] The state high court had upheld the dismissal of a private school teacher for teaching reading in German to elementary school students. In striking down the statute, the Supreme Court reasoned that the teacher's right to teach, the parents' right to engage him to instruct their children, and the children's right to acquire useful knowledge were protected liberties under the Due Process Clause of the Fourteenth Amendment.

The Supreme Court on occasion has ruled that other curriculum decisions violate constitutional rights. The Court held in 1968 that the First Amendment precludes states from barring public school instruction, such as teaching about evolution, simply because it conflicts with certain religious views.[80] Almost two decades later, the Supreme Court invalidated a Louisiana law requiring instruction in the Biblical account of creation whenever evolution was introduced in the curriculum, concluding that the law unconstitutionally advanced religion.[81]

If constitutional rights are not implicated, however, courts will uphold decisions of state and local education agencies in curricular matters. For example, school dis-

---

78. *See* Triplett v. Livingston County Bd. of Educ., 967 S.W.2d 25 (Ky. Ct. App. 1997) (holding that local board can go beyond state minimums in setting graduation requirements).

79. Meyer v. Nebraska, 262 U.S. 390 (1923).

80. Epperson v. Arkansas, 393 U.S. 97 (1968).

81. Edwards v. Aguillard, 482 U.S. 578 (1987). *See* text accompanying note 163, Chapter 2.

tricts increasingly have implemented community service requirements as part of the mandatory high school curriculum, and federal appellate courts have rejected allegations that such requirements represent involuntary servitude prohibited by the Thirteenth Amendment, forced expression of altruistic values in violation of the First Amendment, or impairments of parents' Fourteenth Amendment rights to direct the upbringing of their children.[82] Given the state's plenary power over education and the judiciary's lack of educational expertise, courts are reluctant to interfere with instructional decisions made by state and local education agencies, unless decisions are clearly arbitrary or impair constitutional rights.

Courts defer to school authorities not only in determining courses of study but also in establishing standards for pupil performance[83] and imposing other instructional requirements. For example, school districts can establish prerequisites and admission criteria for particular courses as long as such criteria are not arbitrary and do not disadvantage certain groups of students. The Fifth Circuit recognized that, absent a state law or other authoritative source entitling students to a particular course of study, students have no property right to be admitted to any class that is offered in the public school.[84] A New York court also rejected a student's assertion that he had a mandatory right to early graduation since he had accumulated sufficient credits, noting that the program in question required completion of the twelfth grade.[85]

In addition to having authority over the content of the public school curriculum, states also have the power to specify textbooks and to regulate the method by which such books are obtained and distributed. In most states, textbooks are prescribed by the state board of education or a textbook commission. A list of acceptable books typically is developed at the state level, and local school boards then adopt specific texts for their course offerings. However, in some states, such as Colorado, local boards are delegated almost complete authority to make textbook selections. Courts will not interfere with textbook decisions unless the established procedures are not followed or overtly biased materials are adopted.[86]

Censorship of Instructional Materials

Attempts to remove books from classrooms and libraries and to tailor curricular offerings and methodologies to particular religious and philosophical values have led to

---

82. Herndon v. Chapel Hill-Carrboro City Bd. of Educ., 89 F.3d 174 (4th Cir. 1996); Immediato v. Rye Neck Sch. Dist., 73 F.3d 454 (2d Cir. 1996); Steirer v. Bethlehem Area Sch. Dist., 987 F.2d 989 (3d Cir. 1993). *See also* Onondaga-Cortland-Madison Bd. of Coop. Educ. Servs. v. McGowan, 285 A.D.2d 36 (N.Y. App. Div. 2001) (having students perform unpaid work on a school construction project for class credit under a workforce training program did not violate New York labor law).

83. *See infra* text accompanying note 120 for a discussion of the judicial reluctance to interfere with assessments of students' academic performance.

84. Arundar v. Dekalb County Sch. Dist., 620 F.2d 493 (5th Cir. 1980).

85. Fiacco v. Santee, 421 N.Y.S.2d 431 (App. Div. 1979). *See also* Bennett v. City Sch. Dist., 497 N.Y.S.2d 72 (App. Div. 1985) (holding that students have no protected right to be admitted to a full-time program for the gifted); text with note 95, Chapter 5.

substantial litigation. Few aspects of the public school program remain untouched by censorship activities. Although most people agree that schools transmit values, there is little consensus regarding *which* values should be transmitted or *who* should make this determination.

Some challenges to public school materials and programs emanate from civil rights and consumer groups, contesting materials that allegedly promote racism, sexism, or bad health habits for students. But most of the challenges come from conservative parent groups, alleging that the use of instructional activities and materials considered immoral and anti-Christian impairs parents' rights to control their children's course of study in public schools.[87] As discussed in Chapter 2, courts have endorsed requests for specific children to be excused from selected course offerings (e.g., sex education) that offend their religious beliefs, as long as the exemptions do not impede the students' academic progress or the management of the school.[88] Challenges to the courses themselves, however, have not found a receptive judicial forum. The discussion here focuses primarily on censorship of library and classroom materials.

To date, courts have not allowed mere parental disapproval of instructional materials to dictate the public school curriculum, noting that parents' "sensibilities are not the full measure of what is proper education."[89] In an early case in Kanawha County, West Virginia, parents alleged that the adopted English materials were godless, communistic, and profane. National attention was aroused as the protests evolved into school boycotts, a coal miners' strike, shootings, a courthouse bombing, and even public prayer calling for the death of school board members. Although the federal district court upheld the board's authority to determine curricular materials and rejected the parents' contention that use of the books posed an infringement of constitutionally protected rights, a reconstituted school board eventually eliminated the series.[90] In more recent cases, federal appellate courts similarly have been unsympathetic to claims that reading series or individual novels used in public schools conflict with Christian doctrine and advance an antitheistic creed, finding the

---

86. *See* Loewen v. Turnipseed, 488 F. Supp. 1138 (N.D. Miss. 1980) (finding evidence of unlawful racial bias by a state textbook-rating committee that barred a history textbook from the approved list because of its controversial treatment of racial matters, particularly the reconstruction period and civil rights movement). *But see* Grimes v. Sobol, 832 F. Supp. 704 (S.D.N.Y. 1993) (rejecting damages suit claiming that city's public school curriculum was biased against African Americans by failing to incorporate their important contributions).

87. Some of the best-known conservative groups are the American Coalition for Traditional Values, the Christian Coalition, Citizens for Excellence in Education, Concerned Women for America, the Eagle Forum, and Focus on the Family.

88. *See* text accompanying note 142, Chapter 2.

89. Right to Read Def. Comm. v. Sch. Comm., 454 F. Supp. 703, 713 (D. Mass. 1978) (citing Keefe v. Geanakos, 418 F.2d 359, 361–362 (1st Cir. 1969)). *See also* Skipworth v. Bd. of Educ., 874 P.2d 487 (Colo. Ct. App. 1994) (rejecting parental claim that public schools must teach morality).

90. Williams v. Bd. of Educ., 530 F.2d 972 (4th Cir. 1975).

challenged materials to be religiously neutral and related to legitimate educational objectives.[91]

Many challenges have religious overtones,[92] but some simply assert parents' rights to determine their children's education. The Supreme Court declined to review a case in which the First Circuit rejected parents' claim that the school district was liable for subjecting their children to a mandatory AIDS-awareness assembly that featured a streetwise, comedic approach to the topic. The appeals court observed that "if all parents had a fundamental constitutional right to dictate individually what the schools teach their children, the schools would be forced to cater a curriculum for each student whose parents had genuine moral disagreements with the school's choice of subject matter."[93] The Ninth Circuit subsequently held that the Oregon law restructuring public schools to impose a rigorous academic program and student assessments, develop alternative learning environments, and create early childhood programs with an emphasis on work-related learning experiences did not abridge speech rights or "freedom of mind."[94] The court reasoned that nothing in the law compelled students to adopt state-approved views. And the same court dismissed African American parents' complaint that their daughter suffered psychological injuries due to being required to read two literary works that contained repeated use of the term "nigger."[95]

Although courts have not been receptive to challenges to school boards' curricular decisions simply because some materials or course content offend the sensibilities of specific students or parents, the legal issues are more complicated when policymakers themselves (e.g., legislators, school board members) support the censorship activity. Bills calling for instructional censorship have been introduced in Congress and numerous state legislatures, and policies have been proposed at the school board level to eliminate "objectionable" materials from public school classrooms and libraries.

---

91. *See, e.g.,* Monteiro v. Tempe Union High Sch. Dist., 158 F.3d 1022 (9th Cir. 1998); Fleischfresser v. Dirs. of Sch. Dist. 200, 15 F.3d 680 (7th Cir. 1994); Brown v. Woodland Joint Unified Sch. Dist., 27 F.3d 1373 (9th Cir. 1994); Smith v. Sch. Comm'rs of Mobile County, 827 F.3d 684 (11th Cir. 1987); Grove v. Mead Sch. Dist., 753 F.2d 1528 (9th Cir. 1985); text accompanying notes 153–170, Chapter 2.

92. *See* Altman v. Bedford Cent. Sch. Dist., 245 F.3d 49 (2d Cir. 2001), *cert. denied,* 122 S. Ct. 68 (2001) (finding that the celebration of Earth Day in public schools did not constitute a religious ceremony, but concluding that having students construct worry dolls and images of a Hindu deity advanced nontraditional faiths in violation of the Establishment Clause). *See* text accompanying note 171, Chapter 2 for a discussion of other claims in this case.

93. Brown v. Hot, Sexy and Safer Productions, 68 F.3d 525, 534 (1st Cir. 1995). *See also* Akshar v. Mills, 671 N.Y.S.2d 856 (App. Div. 1998) (rejecting parents' petition for a formal hearing with the state commissioner regarding the school board resolution allowing peer presentations about AIDS after school and requiring parental permission for students to participate).

94. Tennison v. Paulus, 144 F.3d 1285, 1287 (9th Cir. 1998).

95. *Monteiro,* 158 F.3d 1022 (finding, however, allegations that school personnel failed to respond to complaints of a racially hostile environment in violation of Title VI of the Civil Rights Act of 1964 warranted a remand for further proceedings on this issue).

The Supreme Court has recognized the broad discretion of school boards to make decisions that reflect the "legitimate and substantial community interest in promoting respect for authority and traditional values, be they social, moral, or political."[96] Thus, the judiciary has been reluctant to interfere with school boards' prerogatives in selecting and eliminating instructional materials. The Second Circuit on two occasions upheld a school board's right to remove particular books from public school libraries, noting that a book does not acquire tenure and can therefore be removed by the same authority that made the initial selection.[97] The court reasoned that a school board's decision to remove "vulgar" and "obscene" books and to screen future library acquisitions does not threaten to suppress ideas.[98] Similarly, the Seventh Circuit endorsed an Indiana federal district court's conclusion that "it is legitimate for school officials... to prohibit the use of texts, remove library books, and delete courses from the curriculum as a part of the effort to shape students into good citizens."[99] According to the appellate court, the judiciary should not interfere with a school board's broad discretion in making curricular determinations unless there is a "flagrant abuse" of that discretion.[100]

Although the judiciary has generally upheld school boards' authority in determining curricular materials and offerings, some specific censorship activities have been invalidated. For example, the Sixth Circuit upheld the school board's right to override faculty judgments regarding the selection of books for academic courses and the school library, but concluded that the board failed to demonstrate any compelling reason for removing books that had already been placed in the library.[101]

Other courts have intervened if the censorship of specific library selections has clearly been motivated by a desire to suppress particular viewpoints or controversial ideas in violation of the First Amendment.[102] To illustrate, the Fifth Circuit held that there were material issues of fact regarding a Louisiana school board's motivation in removing from public school libraries all copies of *Voodoo & Hoodoo,* which traces the development of African tribal religion and its evolution in African American communities in the United States. The appeals court remanded the case for a trial to deter-

96. Bd. of Educ. v. Pico, 457 U.S. 853, 864 (1982). *See also* Bethel Sch. Dist. No. 403 v. Fraser, 478 U.S. 675, 684 (1986); text accompanying note 15, Chapter 4; Zykan v. Warsaw Cmty. Sch. Corp., 631 F.2d 1300, 1306-1307 (7th Cir. 1980).

97. Bicknell v. Vergennes Union High Sch. Bd. of Dirs., 638 F.2d 438 (2d Cir. 1980); Presidents Council v. Cmty. Sch. Bd. No. 25, 457 F.2d 289 (2d Cir. 1972). See Chapter 9 for a discussion of teachers' rights to academic freedom.

98. *Bicknell,* 638 F.2d at 441.

99. *Zykan,* 631 F.2d at 1303. *See also* Cary v. Bd. of Educ., 598 F.2d 535 (10th Cir. 1979).

100. *Zykan,* 631 F.2d at 1306. *See also* Seyfried v. Walton, 668 F.2d 214 (3d Cir. 1981) (holding that the high school drama club's performances were a part of the school program and therefore the school board could prohibit performance of the musical *Pippin* because of its explicit sexual scenes).

101. Minarcini v. Strongsville City Sch. Dist., 541 F.2d 577 (6th Cir. 1976).

102. *See, e.g.,* Case v. Unified Sch. Dist. No. 233, 908 F. Supp. 864 (D. Kan. 1995) (*Annie on My Mind*); Salvail v. Nashua Bd. of Educ., 469 F. Supp. 1269 (D.N.H. 1979) (*Ms.* magazine).

mine whether removal of the book was substantially based on unconstitutional motivation to suppress ideas as suggested by the preliminary evidence (e.g., the board's
failure to consider recommendations of two committees; its vote to remove the book
even though many board members had viewed only excerpts supplied by the Christian
Coalition).[103] Likewise, the Eighth Circuit struck down a Minnesota school board's
attempt to ban certain films from school because of their ideological content.[104]

Despite substantial activity in lower courts, the Supreme Court has rendered
only one decision involving censorship in public schools. This case, *Board of Education v. Pico,*[105] unfortunately, did not provide significant clarification regarding the
scope of school boards' authority to restrict student access to particular materials. In
fact, seven of the nine Supreme Court justices wrote separate opinions, conveying a
range of viewpoints as to the governing legal principles. At issue in *Pico* was the
school board's removal of certain books from junior high and high school libraries and
the literature curriculum, in spite of the contrary recommendation of a committee
appointed to review the books.[106]

The Supreme Court narrowly affirmed the appellate court's remand of the case
for a trial because of irregularities in the removal procedures and unresolved factual
questions regarding the school board's motivation. Only three of the Supreme Court
justices endorsed the notion that students have a protected right to receive information. And even those justices recognized the broad authority of school boards to
remove materials that are vulgar or educationally unsuitable and indicated that a trial
might have been unnecessary if the school board had employed regular and unbiased
procedures in reviewing the controversial materials.[107] The *Pico* plurality also emphasized that the controversy involved *library* books, which are not required reading for
students, noting that school boards "might well defend their claim of absolute discretion in matters of *curriculum* by reliance upon their duty to inculcate community values."[108]

103. Campbell v. St. Tammany Parish Sch. Bd., 64 F.3d 184 (5th Cir. 1995).

104. Pratt v. Indep. Sch. Dist., 670 F.2d 771, 777 (8th Cir. 1982).

105. 474 F. Supp. 387 (E.D.N.Y. 1979), *rev'd and remanded,* 638 F.2d 404 (2d Cir. 1980), *aff'd,* 457 U.S.
     853 (1982).

106. After several board members received a list of "objectionable" books from a conservative parents'
     organization, the school board ordered 11 books removed from the library despite the superinten-
     dent's objection. The superintendent urged the board to follow its policy for handling such problems,
     and the board eventually did appoint a review committee, but disregarded the committee's recom-
     mendation by ordering the removal of 9 of the books.

107. Following the Supreme Court's *Pico* decision, the school board voted to return the controversial
     books to the school libraries, thus averting the need for a trial regarding the board's motivation for
     the original censorship.

108. 457 U.S. at 869 (1982). Courts are even more protective of access to materials in public libraries. *See,
     e.g.,* Sund v. City of Wichita Falls, Tex., 121 F. Supp. 2d 530 (N.D. Tex. 2000) (finding the city's res-
     olution, empowering any 300 patrons to remove objectionable materials from library's children's
     section, to entail impermissible content and viewpoint discrimination and improper delegation of
     government authority).

Further strengthening the broad discretion of school authorities in curriculum-related censorship was the landmark 1988 Supreme Court decision involving students' free speech rights, *Hazelwood School District v. Kuhlmeier.*[109] The Court declared that public school authorities can censor student expression in school-related activities to ensure that the expression is consistent with educational objectives. The Court's conclusion that expression appearing to represent the school can be restricted for educational reasons has been cited by courts in upholding school boards' censorship decisions.[110]

For example, the Eleventh Circuit upheld a Florida school board's decision to ban a humanities book because it included Aristophanes' *Lysistrata* and Chaucer's *The Miller's Tale,* which board members considered vulgar and immoral. Voicing disapproval of the board basing its decision on fundamentalist religious views, the court nonetheless relied on *Hazelwood* in deferring to the board's broad discretion in curricular matters.[111] A California appeals court similarly acknowledged that school boards can censor instructional materials for educational reasons. However, the court noted that this authority does have limits; motives of board members must be assessed to ensure that they are not banning materials for religious reasons.[112]

Specific issues may change, but controversies surrounding the selection of materials for the public school library and curriculum will likely persist, reflecting the "inherent tension" between the school board's two essential functions of "exposing young minds to the clash of ideologies in the free marketplace of ideas" and instilling basic community values in our youth.[113] School boards would be wise to establish procedures for reviewing objections to course content and library materials, and to do so *before* a controversy arises. Criteria for the acquisition and elimination of instructional materials should be clearly articulated and educationally defensible. Once a process is in place to evaluate complaints relating to the instructional program, school boards should follow it carefully, as courts will show little sympathy when a school board ignores its own established procedures.

The next wave of censorship activity is likely to focus on the electronic frontier. It was estimated in 2001 that approximately 176.5 million Americans had Internet access.[114] With schools increasingly making on-line services accessible to students, concerns are being raised about the possible transmission of sexually explicit material to minors. Several states have enacted laws or are considering measures that would prohibit sending obscene materials over the Internet. Also, the federal Child Online Protection Act (COPA) prohibits materials harmful to minors being distributed for

---

109. 484 U.S. 260 (1988). *See* text accompanying note 42, Chapter 4.

110. *See, e.g.,* Borger v. Bisciglia, 888 F. Supp. 97 (E.D. Wis.1995) (upholding the school district's ban on showing R-rated films as related to legitimate pedagogical concerns).

111. Virgil v. Sch. Bd., 862 F.2d 1517 (11th Cir. 1989).

112. McCarthy v. Fletcher, 254 Cal. Rptr. 714 (Ct. App. 1989).

113. Seyfried v. Walton, 668 F.2d 214, 219 (3d Cir. 1981) (Rosenn, J., concurring).

114. "More Americans Online," *The New York Times* (November 19, 2001), p. C7.

commercial purposes through the World Wide Web, and violators can be fined up to $50,000 and sentenced to six months in jail.[115] Congress enacted COPA after the Supreme Court in 1997 ruled that the Communications Decency Act was unconstitutionally vague and overinclusive in its criminalization of some legitimate sexually explicit speech.[116] In 2000, the Third Circuit enjoined implementation of COPA, reasoning that its use of contemporary community standards to judge harm to minors placed an impermissible burden on free speech rights because standards from the most restrictive community in the nation would have to be satisfied. However, the Supreme Court concluded that COPA's reliance on community standards was not sufficient to abridge the First Amendment, and remanded the case for additional consideration of other allegations that the law was overbroad and vague.[117]

Also, Congress enacted the Children's Internet Protection Act (CIPA), requiring libraries and school districts that receive technology funds to implement technology protection measures that safeguard students from access to harmful content and to monitor student Internet use.[118] In implementing the required Internet safety plans, most school districts are relying on filtering software and thus delegating to companies the decisions as to what materials are appropriate for their students. A Pennsylvania federal court in 2002 ruled that the CIPA library provisions violate the First Amendment by preventing library patrons from accessing some constitutionally protected speech that the four leading filtering programs block, and causing libraries to relinquish their First Amendment rights as a condition of receiving federal aid.[119] The court reasoned that there were alternatives less restrictive than software filters that would serve the government's interest in preventing the dissemination of obscenity and child pornography to library patrons, but this decision does not affect CIPA's school provisions. There are some fears that measures such as CIPA and COPA will have a chilling effect on schools using computer networks to enhance instructional experiences for students. The competing governmental and individual interests

---

115. 47 U.S.C. § 231 (2002). For intentional violations, each day is considered a separate violation. An affirmative defense can be offered that reasonable steps have been taken to restrict access by minors.

116. Reno v. ACLU, 521 U.S. 844, 877 (1997). In 2002, the Supreme Court also struck down provisions of the Child Pornography Prevention Act of 1996 that prohibit possession or distribution of virtual child pornography, reasoning that the overbroad prohibition was not sufficiently related to actual abuse of minors and that some proscribed materials may have literary value. Ashcroft v. Free Speech Coalition, 122 S. Ct. 1389 (2002), *interpreting* 18 U.S.C. § 2252A(a) (2002). *See also* PSINET v. Chapman, 167 F. Supp. 2d 878 (W.D. Va. 2000) (finding the state law, criminalizing dissemination by computer of material harmful to minors, to unduly burden interstate commerce and adult access to protected speech); Mainstream Loudon v. Bd. of Trs., 24 F. Supp. 2d 552 (E.D. Va. 1998) (finding the library's policy on Internet sexual harassment that prohibited access to certain content-based categories of publications to be an improper prior restraint on speech).

117. ACLU v. Reno, 217 F.3d 162 (3d Cir. 2000), *vacated and remanded sub nom.* Ashcroft v. ACLU, 122 S. Ct. 1700 (2002).

118. H.R. 5666 § 1721; 20 U.S.C..§ 9134(f) (2002); 47 U.S.C. § 254(h)(5) (2002).

119. American Library Ass'n v. United States, 201 F. Supp. 2d 401 (E.D. Pa. 2002), *probable jurisdiction noted,* 123 S. Ct. 551 (2002).

affected by legislative restrictions on information distributed electronically will likely generate a stream of litigation.

Student Proficiency Testing

Acknowledging the state's authority to establish academic standards, including mandatory examinations, the judiciary traditionally has been reluctant to interfere with assessments of pupil performance. In 1978, the Supreme Court distinguished an academic determination from a disciplinary action, noting that the former "judgment is by its nature more subjective and evaluative than the typical factual questions presented in the average disciplinary decision."[120] The Court emphasized that academic performance is properly assessed by professional educators who have expertise in this area. The judiciary has rejected challenges to teachers' grading practices unless they constitute extreme and outrageous conduct.[121]

Courts have recognized that assurance of an educated citizenry is an appropriate government goal and that the establishment of minimum performance standards to give value to a high school diploma is a rational means to attain that goal.[122] An Illinois federal district court noted that "local boards of education and their staffs have the right, if not a positive duty, to develop reasonable means to determine the effectiveness of their educational programs with respect to all individual students to whom they issue diplomas."[123] The concept of performance assessment is not new, but the use of proficiency tests as a condition of grade promotion or the receipt of a high school diploma has a relatively brief history. In 1976, only four states had enacted student proficiency testing legislation. Now all states have laws or administrative regulations pertaining to statewide performance testing programs, and the majority of states condition receipt of a high school diploma on passage of a test.

Recently, other forms of performance assessment, such as portfolios, have received attention, but machine-scorable tests continue to be used in most school districts and are strongly supported by the federal government. Indeed, the No Child Left Behind Act mandates annual testing in grades 3 through 8 in reading and math by 2006 and in science by 2007 at selected grades, requires high school students to take a general test in core subjects at least once, and ties federal assistance and sanctions for schools to student test scores.[124] High-stakes assessments shape the instructional program, and states increasingly are evaluating educators' performance based on their

---

120. Bd. of Curators v. Horowitz, 435 U.S. 78, 89-90 (1978). *See also* Regents v. Ewing, 474 U.S. 214 (1985).

121. *See* Barrino v. E. Baton Rouge Parish Sch. Bd., 697 So. 2d 27 (La. App. Ct. 1997).

122. Debra P. v. Turlington, 644 F.2d 397 (5th Cir. 1981).

123. Brookhart v. Ill. St. Bd. of Educ., 534 F. Supp. 725, 728 (C.D. Ill. 1982).

124. No Child Left Behind Act of 2001, 20 U.S.C. § 6301 *et seq.* (2002).

students' test scores.[125] Not surprisingly, claims are being made that teachers are limiting classroom activities to material covered on the tests and/or unfairly coaching students for the exams.[126]

Although the state's authority to evaluate student performance has not been questioned, the implementation of specific assessment programs has been legally challenged as impairing students' rights to fair and nondiscriminatory treatment. In a case still widely cited as establishing the legal standards, *Debra P. v. Turlington,* the Fifth Circuit in 1981 recognized that by making schooling mandatory, Florida created a property interest—a valid expectation that students would receive diplomas if they passed required courses. This property right necessitates sufficient notice of conditions attached to high school graduation and an opportunity to satisfy the standards before a diploma can be withheld. The court found that 13 months was insufficient notice of the test requirement and further held that the state may have administered a fundamentally unfair test covering material that had not been taught in Florida schools. The appeals court also enjoined the state from using the test as a diploma prerequisite for four years to provide time for the vestiges of prior school segregation to be removed and to ensure that all minority students subjected to the requirement started first grade under desegregated conditions.[127] However, the court held that continued use of the test to determine remediation needs was constitutionally permissible, noting that the disproportionate placement of minority students in remedial programs *per se* does not abridge the Equal Protection Clause without evidence of intentional discrimination.

On remand, the district court ruled that the injunction should be lifted, and the appeals court affirmed this decision in 1984.[128] By presenting substantial evidence, including curriculum guides and survey data, the state convinced the judiciary that the test was instructionally valid in that it covered material taught to Florida students. Also, data showed significant improvement among African American students during the six years the test had been administered, which convinced the court that the testing program could help remedy the effects of past discrimination.

125. High-stakes testing programs have been extremely controversial. The American Evaluation Association issued a statement in 2002 opposing "the use of tests as the sole or primary criterion for making decisions with serious negative consequences for students, educators, and the schools." *American Evaluation Association Position Statement on High Stakes Testing in Pre-K-12 Education,* Fairhaven, MA (February, 2002), p. 1 *(www.eval.org/hst3htm).* AEA thus joined a number of other professional associations and advocacy groups (e.g., American Educational Research Association, National Council for Teachers of English, National Council for Teachers of Mathematics, International Reading Association, National Council for the Social Studies, and National Education Association) in opposing the inappropriate use of tests to make high-stakes decisions.

126. *See* Buck v. Lowndes County Sch. Dist., 761 So. 2d 144 (Miss. 2000) (upholding nonrenewal of teachers' contracts for noncompliance with testing procedures that resulted in a reduction in the district's accreditation level).

127. Debra P. v. Turlington, 644 F.2d 397, 407 (5th Cir. 1981).

128. Debra P. v. Turlington, 564 F. Supp. 177 (M.D. Fla. 1983), *aff'd,* 730 F.2d 1405 (11th Cir. 1984). It should be noted that the Fifth Circuit was divided into the Fifth and Eleventh Circuits while this case was in progress.

Other courts have reiterated the principles established in *Debra P.*[129] A Texas federal district court in 2000 rejected challenges to the Texas Assessment of Academic Skills (TAAS) that has been administered to all Texas students since 1990.[130] Despite evidence of higher minority failure rates, the court noted that the passing-rate gap was narrowing and that the testing and remediation programs were addressing the effects of prior discrimination. The court also held that the test met curricular validity standards in that students were given a fair opportunity to learn the material on the test and that students had received adequate notice of the test requirement.

The Supreme Court in 2002 declined to review a decision in which the lower courts rejected a challenge to a Louisiana school district's policy that conditioned promotion at the fourth and eighth grades on test passage, finding no property or liberty interest in grade promotion.[131] Yet, courts have not clarified whether similar notice and due process protections required for tests used as a condition of receiving a diploma also must accompany tests used as a prerequisite to promotion. Most high-stakes testing programs include provisions for students who fail proficiency examinations to receive remediation and retake the tests.

Two Texas federal district courts reached opposite conclusions regarding individual rights at stake when students were not allowed to participate in graduation exercises because they failed the statewide proficiency examination. One court ruled that if students have been given adequate notice of the test and offered the necessary courses to prepare, they have no constitutional right to participate in the graduation ceremony that can be reserved for students meeting all requirements.[132] The other federal court granted a preliminary injunction that required a Texas school to permit students, who failed the exam but satisfied other graduation requirements, to take part in the graduation ceremony. This court found the potential for irreparable harm to the students if they were not allowed to participate in this milestone event and found no possible harm to the district from their participation, because the students would not receive diplomas until passage of the test.[133]

Most testing controversies have focused on statewide exams and usually on their use as a diploma sanction, but other test requirements also have generated some legal controversies. For example, the judiciary has upheld school district requirements that all students transferring from nonaccredited schools must take proficiency

129. *See, e.g.,* Anderson v. Banks, 540 F. Supp. 761 (S.D. Ga. 1982); Bd. of Educ. v. Ambach, 457 N.E.2d 775 (N.Y. 1983). *See also* Rankins v. La. State Bd. of Elementary and Secondary Educ., 637 So. 2d 548 (La. Ct. App. 1994) (finding no equal protection violation in requiring public, but not private, school students to pass a high school exit examination).

130. GI Forum v. Tex. Educ. Agency, 87 F. Supp. 2d 667 (W.D. Tex. 2000).

131. Parents Against Testing Before Teaching v. Orleans Parish Sch. Bd., 273 F.3d 1107 (5th Cir. 2001), *cert. denied,* 534 U.S. 1162 (2002). Other courts have upheld the practice of conditioning grade promotion on test scores. *See* Bester v. Tuscaloosa City Bd. of Educ., 722 F.2d 1514 (11th Cir. 1984); Sandlin v. Johnson, 643 F.2d 1027 (4th Cir. 1981); Erik V. v. Causby, 977 F. Supp. 384 (E.D.N.C. 1997).

132. Williams v. Austin Indep. Sch. Dist., 796 F. Supp. 251 (W.D. Tex. 1992).

133. Crump v. Gilmer Indep. Sch. Dist., 797 F. Supp. 552 (E.D. Tex. 1992).

tests at their own expense.[134] In a Kentucky case, the Sixth Circuit ruled that requiring a high school student to pass equivalency exams to gain public school credit for a religious home study program did not violate equal protection or free exercise rights.[135] Local school districts also can impose test requirements beyond those mandated by the state.[136]

Given the high stakes attached to some exams, parents have requested access to questions on previously administered versions of the tests. The Ohio Supreme Court ruled that the statewide proficiency test fell under the definition of a public record, so previously administered exams must be disclosed to parents, except for portions owned and developed by a private nonprofit corporation.[137] But a Kentucky appeals court held that parents were not entitled to view the statewide proficiency exam because indiscriminate viewing by the public could jeopardize the test's reliability.[138]

Administering proficiency tests to children with disabilities has been controversial. Courts in general have ruled that the state does not have to alter its academic standards for students with disabilities; they can be denied grade promotion or a diploma if they do not meet the specified standards.[139] Such children, however, cannot be denied the *opportunity* to satisfy requirements (including tests) for promotion or a diploma.

A child with mental disabilities may be given the option of not taking a proficiency examination if the team charged with planning the individualized education program (IEP) concludes that there is little likelihood of the child mastering the material covered on the test. Children excused from the test requirement usually are awarded certificates of school attendance instead of diplomas. If children with disabilities were awarded regular diplomas based on successful completion of their IEPs, this might implicate equal protection rights of nonhandicapped students who failed the test and were denied diplomas.

The Seventh Circuit has suggested that children with disabilities may need earlier notice of a proficiency test requirement than other students to ensure an adequate opportunity for the material on the test to be incorporated into their IEPs.[140] However, an Indiana appeals court subsequently reasoned that three years was sufficient notice before diplomas for children with disabilities were conditioned on test passage.[141] In

---

134. *See* Hubbard v. Buffalo Indep. Sch. Dist., 20 F. Supp. 2d 1012 (W.D. Tex. 1998).

135. Vandiver v. Hardin County Bd. of Educ., 925 F.2d 927 (6th Cir. 1991).

136. *See* Triplett v. Livingston County Bd. of Educ., 967 S.W.2d 25 (Ky. Ct. App. 1997).

137. Rea v. Ohio Dep't of Educ., 692 N.E.2d 596 (Ohio 1998).

138. *Triplett,* 967 S.W.2d 25. *See also* Gabrilson v. Flynn, 554 N.W.2d 267 (Iowa 1996) (holding that under state law school board members can review confidential school records as they are charged with handling the district's affairs).

139. *See, e.g.,* Brookhart v. Ill. State Bd. of Educ., 697 F.2d 179 (7th Cir. 1983); Anderson v. Banks, 540 F. Supp. 761 (S.D. Ga. 1982); Bd. of Educ. v. Ambach, 457 N.E.2d 775 (N.Y. 1983).

140. *Brookhart,* 697 F.2d at 187. *See* Chapter 6 for a discussion of federal and state protections of children with disabilities.

141. Rene v. Reed, 751 N.E.2d 736 (Ind. Ct. App. 2001), *transfer denied,* 774 N.E. 2d 506 (Ind. 2002).

upholding the statewide testing requirement, the court also noted that there were ample opportunities to receive remediation and retake the exam and that the plaintiff student's IEP sufficiently covered material on the test.

Students with disabilities are entitled to special accommodations in the administration of examinations to ensure that their knowledge, rather than their disability, is being assessed, but the nature of the required accommodations remains controversial. In the Indiana case cited above, the court rejected accommodations that would jeopardize the validity of the graduation test, such as reading to the student a test measuring reading comprehension, even though such accommodations were part of the student's IEP.[142] A federal court conversely held that students with disabilities were entitled to all accommodations in their IEPs when taking California's graduation test, but the Ninth Circuit found parts of the order overboard and not ripe for adjudication.[143]

Specific proficiency testing programs will likely generate additional litigation on constitutional and statutory grounds. Educators can take steps to defeat legal challenges by ensuring that (1) students have the opportunity to be adequately prepared for the tests (2) students are advised upon entrance into high school of test requirements as a prerequisite to graduation, (3) tests are not intentionally discriminatory and do not perpetuate the effects of past school segregation, (4) students who fail are provided remedial opportunities and the chance to retake the examinations, and (5) children with disabilities receive appropriate accommodations.

Educational Malpractice and Instructional Negligence

A topic prompting litigation since the mid-1970s is instructional negligence, commonly referred to as *educational malpractice*.[144] Initial suits focused on whether students have a right to attain a predetermined level of achievement in return for state-mandated school attendance; parents asserted a right to expect their children to be functionally literate upon high school graduation. More recent cases have involved allegations that school authorities have breached their duty to diagnose students' deficiencies and place them in appropriate instructional programs. This section includes an overview of claims in which parents have sought damages from school districts for instructional negligence.

In the first educational malpractice suit to receive substantial attention, *Peter W. v. San Francisco Unified School District,* a student asserted that the school district was negligent in teaching, promoting, and graduating him from high school with the ability

---

142. *Id.* The Office for Civil Rights in the U.S. Department of Education has also reasoned that states can deny use of reading devices to accommodate children with disabilities on graduation exams, even though their IEPs allow use of such devices. *See* Alabama Dep't of Educ., 29 IDELR 249 (1998).

143. Smiley v. Cal. Dep't of Educ., No. 02-1552, 2002 U.S. App. LEXIS 26516 (9th Cir. Dec. 19, 2002) (dissolving the parts of the lower court's injunction pertaining to required test waivers and alternative assessments for children with disabilities).

144. *See* Chapter 13 for an overview of tort law pertaining to negligence suits.

to read only at the fifth-grade level.[145] He also claimed that his performance and progress had been misrepresented to his parents, who testified that they were unaware of his deficiencies until he was tested by a private agency after high school graduation. Concluding that the school district was not negligent, a California appeals court reasoned that the complexities of the teaching/learning process made it impossible to place the entire burden on the school to ensure that all students, with their varying abilities to learn, attain a specified reading level before high school graduation. The court declared that to hold the school district liable would expose all educational agencies to countless "real or imagined" tort claims of "disaffected students and parents."[146]

The New York high court in 1979 dismissed what had appeared to be a successful educational malpractice suit. A state appellate court had awarded a former public school student $500,000 in damages after concluding that the New York City Board of Education had negligently diagnosed his needs and erroneously instructed him for 12 years in a program for the mentally retarded.[147] The thrust of the negligence claim was that the school psychologist's report, recommending reassessment of the child within two years of the original evaluation, was ignored for over a decade—even though the student scored in the 90th percentile on reading readiness tests at ages 8 and 9. Distinguishing this case from previous educational malpractice suits, the lower court noted that school personnel committed affirmative acts of negligence (i.e., ignoring the psychologist's report) that placed crippling burdens on the student. Nonetheless, the New York high court by a narrow margin reversed the lower court's ruling and held that it was not the role of the judiciary to make such educational policy determinations. The court emphasized that instructional negligence claims should instead be handled through the state educational system's administrative appeals. The same court subsequently ruled that a student who was incorrectly diagnosed at age 10, after having been tested in English although he understood only Spanish, was not entitled to damages from the child-care agency for its alleged failure to obtain suitable instruction for him to learn to read.[148] The court determined that the issue involved educational policy matters regarding which instructional programs might have been preferable and was not actionable in a negligence suit.

---

145. 131 Cal. Rptr. 854 (Ct. App. 1976).

146. *Id.* at 861.

147. Hoffman v. Bd. of Educ., 410 N.Y.S.2d 99 (App. Div. 1978), *rev'd,* 424 N.Y.S.2d 376 (1979). *See also* Donohue v. Copiague Union Free Schs., 391 N.E.2d 1352 (N.Y. 1979) (dismissing an educational malpractice suit brought by a learning-disabled high school graduate who claimed that because of the school district's negligence he was unable to complete job applications and cope with the problems of everyday life).

148. Torres v. Little Flower Children's Servs., 485 N.Y.S.2d 15 (1984). But on the same day, the court awarded damages in a medical malpractice suit although the impact of the malpractice was educational. Snow v. New York, 469 N.Y.S.2d 959, 964 (App. Div. 1983), *aff'd,* 485 N.Y.S.2d 987 (1984) (awarding damages to an individual diagnosed by a state school as mentally deficient, when actually deaf, and instructed in classes for the retarded for nine years; failure to reassess the student upon learning that he was deaf was a "discernible act of medical malpractice on the part of the state," rather than a mere mistake in judgment pertaining to the student's educational program).

Other courts also have indicated a reluctance to intervene in such educational policy decisions by recognizing instructional malpractice claims.[149] For example, a California appellate court dismissed a negligence suit in which parents sought damages for the school district's alleged breach of its duty under state and federal statutes to evaluate and develop an individualized education plan for their child with multiple disabilities.[150] Similarly, the Supreme Court of Alaska refused to allow damages against a school district for the alleged misclassification of a student with dyslexia,[151] and a New Jersey superior court ruled that a school district's failure to provide remedial instruction for a student was not actionable in a tort suit for damages.[152] More recently, a Colorado appeals court rejected a suit for damages alleging that the Denver Public Schools' failure to provide students with a quality education resulted in intellectual and emotional harm and diminished their future educational and career opportunities.[153]

Although educational malpractice claims have not yet been successful, some courts have recognized circumstances under which plaintiffs possibly could recover damages in an instructional tort action. In a Maryland case, parents were not able to establish instructional malpractice for unintentional negligent acts in evaluating a child's learning disabilities and inappropriately instructing the child, but the state high court held that parents could maintain an action to prove that the defendants intentionally engaged in acts that injured a child placed in their educational care.[154] The Supreme Court of Montana went further, ruling that unintentional acts might result in

---

149. *See, e.g.,* Brantley v. District of Columbia, 640 A.2d 181 (D.C. App. 1994); Vogel v. Maimonides Acad., 754 A.2d 824 (Conn. App. Ct. 2000); Brodsky v. Mead Sch. of Human Dev., No. X05CV 970156788S, 1999 Conn. Super. LEXIS 1459 (Conn. Super. Ct. June 4, 1999); Page v. Klein Tools, 610 N.W.2d 900 (Mich. 2000); Suriano v. Hyde Park Cent. Sch. Dist., 611 N.Y.S.2d 20 (App. Div. 1994); Poe v. Hamilton, 565 N.E.2d 887 (Ohio Ct. App. 1990).

150. Keech v. Berkeley Unified Sch. Dist., 210 Cal. Rptr. 7 (Ct. App. 1984). *See also* Smith v. Alameda County Soc. Servs. Agency, 153 Cal. Rptr. 712 (Ct. App. 1979) (rejecting a damages claim for alleged inappropriate placement in a class for the mentally retarded).

151. D.S.W. v. Fairbanks N. Star Borough Sch. Dist., 628 P.2d 554 (Alaska 1981). *See also* Doe v. Bd. of Educ., 453 A.2d 814 (Md. 1982); Johnson v. Clark, 418 N.W.2d 466 (Mich. Ct. App. 1987).

152. Myers v. Medford Lakes Bd. of Educ., 489 A.2d 1240 (N.J. Super. Ct. App. Div. 1985). *See also* Camer v. Seattle Sch. Dist. No. 1, 762 P.2d 356 (Wash. Ct. App. 1988) (finding frivolous a suit alleging that the district was not respecting state laws as to student discipline, course content, and student assessment practices, thus denying children their entitlement to a basic education guaranteed by the state constitution), *supra* text accompanying note 59; Bishop v. Ind. Technical Vocational Coll., 742 F. Supp. 524, 525 (N.D. Ind. 1990) (finding frivolous an allegation that college's provision of inferior educational experience interfered with the federal right to pursuit of happiness; "educational malpractice is a matter of state law that does not, by itself, deprive its victims of their constitutional rights").

153. Denver Parents Ass'n v. Denver Bd. of Educ., 10 P.3d 662 (Colo. Ct. App. 2000). *But see* Bell v. Bd. of Educ., 739 A.2d 321 (Conn. App. Ct. 1999) (remanding case for a determination as to whether the school district's adoption of the teaching method, "responsive classroom method," met the minimal standards for creating intentional infliction of emotional distress).

154. Hunter v. Bd. of Educ., 439 A.2d 582 (Md. 1982). *See also* Squires v. Sierra Nev. Educ. Found., 823 P.2d 256 (Nev. 1991) (declining to address the educational malpractice claim, the court did find that parents presented a triable case of breach of contract and misrepresentation against the private school where their child had been enrolled for four years and allegedly received inappropriate instruction).

liability where school authorities violate mandatory statutes pertaining to special education placements.[155] Declaring that school districts have a duty to exercise reasonable care in testing and placing exceptional students in appropriate programs, the court concluded that damages could be assessed for injuries resulting from a breach of that duty. On remand, however, the trial court held that the plaintiff failed to present evidence substantiating that the child was erroneously placed in a segregated special education class, and the state high court affirmed this ruling. The Third Circuit, though not awarding monetary damages, held that a student with severe disabilities who had not progressed over the past decade was entitled to compensatory services from a New Jersey school district, because school authorities should have known that the child's individualized education program was inadequate.[156]

The increasing specificity of legislation pertaining to student proficiency standards and special education placements may strengthen the grounds for tort suits involving *placement negligence*.[157] Also, state and federal legislation making school districts accountable for ensuring student mastery of state standards may increase school districts' potential liability. Even though it seems unlikely that public schools in the near future will be held responsible for a specified quantum of student achievement, it is conceivable that schools will be held legally accountable for diagnosing pupils' needs, placing them in appropriate instructional programs, reporting their progress to parents, and providing other educational options if they are not progressing in their current placements.

Instructional Privacy Rights

The protection of students' privacy rights has become an increasingly volatile issue in political forums. State and federal laws place dual duties on the government—to protect the public's First Amendment right to be informed about government activities and to protect the personal privacy of individuals. In addition, laws have been enacted to protect students from mandatory participation in research projects or instructional activities designed to reveal personal information in sensitive areas. This section provides an overview of legal developments pertaining to students' privacy rights in instructional matters.

155. B.M. v. Montana, 649 P.2d 425 (Mont. 1982), *after remand,* 698 P.2d 399 (Mont. 1985). *See also* Savino v. Bd. of Educ., 506 N.Y.S.2d 210 (App. Div. 1986) (recognizing that parents could recover damages if school personnel knew that a student's psychological problems could worsen if untreated and did not notify the student's mother; the court distinguished such a claim from a nonactionable assertion of malpractice in properly educating students).

156. M.C. v. Cent. Reg'l Sch. Dist., 81 F.3d 389 (3d Cir. 1996).

157. *See* Richard Fossey and Perry A. Zirkel, "Educational Malpractice and Students with Disabilities: 'Special' Cases of Liability?" *Journal of Law & Education,* vol. 23 (1995), pp. 25–45.

Student Records

The Supreme Court has recognized that the Constitution protects a zone of personal privacy.[158] Thus, there must be a compelling justification for governmental action that impairs privacy rights, including the right to have personal information kept confidential. Because of this right, questions about who has access to public school students' permanent files and the contents of such files have been the source of controversy. Legal challenges to school record-keeping procedures have resulted in courts ordering school officials to expunge irrelevant information from students' permanent folders. In some situations, students have brought successful libel suits for damages against school authorities who allegedly recorded and communicated defamatory information about them.[159]

Because of widespread dissatisfaction with educators' efforts to ameliorate abuses associated with student record-keeping practices, Congress enacted the Family Educational Rights and Privacy Act (FERPA) in 1974.[160] This law stipulates that federal funds may be withdrawn from any educational agency or institution that (1) fails to provide parents access to their child's educational records or (2) disseminates such information (with some exceptions) to third parties without parental permission. Upon reaching age 18, students may exercise the rights guaranteed to parents under this law.[161]

Education officials may assume that a parent is entitled to exercise rights under FERPA unless state law or a court order bars a parent's access to his or her child's records under specific circumstances and the education agency has been instructed accordingly.[162] The Second Circuit recognized that joint custodial parents must have equal access to education information about their child.[163] If copies of juvenile court proceedings are maintained by the school, these records are subject to FERPA in terms of confidentiality and accessibility to parents.[164]

After reviewing a student's permanent file, the parent or eligible student can request amendments in any information thought to be inaccurate, misleading, or in violation of the student's protected rights. If school authorities decide that an amendment is not warranted, the parent or eligible student must be advised of the right to a hearing. The hearing officer may be an employee of the school district, but may not

---

158. *See* Griswold v. Connecticut, 381 U.S. 479 (1965); text accompanying note 167, Chapter 9.

159. *See, e.g.,* Elder v. Anderson, 23 Cal. Rptr. 48 (Ct. App. 1962). *See also* Chapter 13 for a discussion of tort law.

160. 20 U.S.C. § 1232g (2002); 34 C.F.R. § 99 *et seq.* (2002).

161. The Family Policy Compliance Office was created to investigate alleged FERPA violations, 20 U.S.C. § 1232g(g) (2002). This office reviews complaints and responses from accused agencies and submits written findings with steps the agency must take to comply, 34 C.F.R. 99.65(a)(2), 99.66(b), 99.66(c)(1) (2002).

162. *See* Cherry v. LeDeoni, No. 99 CV 6860 (SJ), 2002 U.S. Dist. LEXIS 6701 (E.D.N.Y. April 8, 2002).

163. Fay v. S. Colonie Cent. Sch. Dist., 802 F.2d 21 (2d Cir. 1986).

164. *See, e.g.,* Belanger v. Nashua, N.H. Sch. Dist., 856 F. Supp. 40 (D.N.H. 1994).

be an individual with a direct interest in the outcome of the hearing. Either party may be represented by counsel at the hearing, and the hearing officer must issue a written decision summarizing the evidence presented and the rationale for the ruling. If the hearing officer concludes that the records should not be amended, the parent or eligible student has the right to place in the file a personal statement specifying objections.[165]

Individuals can file a complaint with the U.S. Department of Education if they believe a school district displays a custom or practice of violating FERPA provisions. The remedy for FERPA violations is the withdrawal of federal funds, and the Department of Education has enforcement authority. Some school districts have been advised to remedy their practices to conform to FERPA, but no district to date has lost federal funds for noncompliance.

The Department of Education functioned without direction from the Supreme Court until 2002, when the Court rendered two FERPA decisions. In one case, *Gonzaga University v. Doe,* the Court ruled that individuals cannot bring damages suits for FERPA violations.[166] The Court held that FERPA's nondisclosure provisions do not create privately enforceable rights, which Congress must do in unambiguous terms. Resolving the conflict among lower courts, the Supreme Court further held that since FERPA contains no rights-creating language, the law cannot be enforced through suits under 42 U.S.C., Section 1983, which provides individuals a damages remedy for the deprivation of federal rights.[167]

In *Gonzaga,* the Supreme Court overturned the Washington Supreme Court's award of damages to a student for a FERPA violation in connection with a private university's release to the state education department an unsubstantiated allegation of sexual misconduct involving the student. The disclosure resulted in the student being denied an affidavit of good moral character required of all new teachers. The Supreme Court reiterated that FERPA has an aggregate rather than individual focus and the remedy for violations is the denial of federal funds to schools that exhibit a policy or practice of noncompliance. School personnel were relieved that the Court did not authorize private suits for damages to enforce FERPA, as such a ruling would have provided a significant incentive for parents to challenge student record-keeping practices in court.

In the second 2002 Supreme Court ruling, *Owasso Independent School District v. Falvo,* the Court reversed the Tenth Circuit's conclusion that peer grading practices violate FERPA.[168] The Supreme Court concluded that peer graders are not "maintain-

165. *See* Meury v. Eagle-Union Cmty. Sch. Corp., 714 N.E.2d 233 (Ind. Ct. App. 1999), *transfer denied,* 735 N.E.2d 224 (Ind. 2000) (upholding school district in sending parents' letter, urging that certain disciplinary notations in their child's file not be disclosed, with the student's transcript requested by various colleges and scholarship-granting organizations; the letter did not contain substantive private information that would abridge FERPA or state law).

166. 536 U.S. 273 (2002).

167. Civil Rights Act of 1871, § 1, codified as 42 U.S.C. § 1983 (2002).

168. 233 F.3d 1203 (10th Cir. 2000), *rev'd and remanded,* 534 U.S. 426 (2002), *on remand,* 288 F.3d 1236 (10th Cir. 2002) (granting summary judgment in favor of defendant school district and administrators).

ing" student records under FERPA, and even though they may call out the scores in class, they are not "acting for" the educational institution.[169] There may be educational reasons for not having students grade each others' work, but given the *Falvo* ruling, there is no legal barrier under FERPA. The Court also hinted that teachers' grade books may not be subject to FERPA, mentioning that records covered by the act are usually kept in a central repository, but it specifically declined to resolve this issue.

A student's records can be released to officials of a school where the student is transferring if the parents or eligible student are notified, or if the sending institution has given prior notice that it routinely transfers such records. A Maryland appeals court rejected a claim that a school's release of a student's records, including psychological reports, to the school where the student was transferring represented an invasion of privacy.[170] There was no evidence that any unauthorized individuals had access to the information in the records or that any unwarranted publicity resulted from the release of the records.

Similarly, students' privacy rights do not preclude federal and state authorities from having access to data needed to audit and evaluate federally supported education programs. These data, however, are to be collected in a way that prevents the disclosure of personally identifiable information. Also, composite information on pupil achievement can be released to the public as long as individual students are not personally identified.[171] In a typical case, a Louisiana appeals court found that the release of composite achievement data did not violate students' privacy rights, declaring that the public had the right to examine the rankings of schools participating in a school effectiveness study conducted by the state department of education.[172]

The Tenth Circuit addressed what constitutes an educational record in connection with notification of parents about how disciplinary incidents involving an aggressive student were handled. The appeals court concluded that school personnel could alert parents of harassment victims how they dealt with the perpetrator. The court concluded that a second disclosure to parents of children who were assaulted by the same student on the playground or who witnessed the assault also did not comprise an edu-

---

169. *Id.,* 534 U.S. at 433. Although peers can call out scores, students' grades cannot be posted or disseminated in any manner that allows individual students to be identified (e.g., by name or listed in alphabetical order). LeRoy S. Rooker, Director, Family Policy Compliance Office, letter dated July 15, 1993.

170. Klipa v. Bd. of Educ., 460 A.2d 601 (Md. Ct. Spec. App. 1983). *See also* Norris v. Bd. of Educ., 797 F. Supp. 1452 (S.D. Ind. 1992) (finding no FERPA violation in school authorities giving confidential information on a child with disabilities to a local coordinating committee that was challenging the parents' request for a residential placement for the child); Phillips v. Village of Carey, 2000 Ohio 1733 (Ohio Ct. App. 2000) (upholding release of former student's transcript to police department, resulting in dismissal of the individual for falsifying his academic record).

171. *See, e.g.,* Bowie v. Evanston Cmty. Consol. Dist. 65, 538 N.E.2d 557 (Ill. 1989); Human Rights Auth. v. Miller, 464 N.E.2d 833 (Ill. App. Ct. 1984); Kryston v. Bd. of Educ., 430 N.Y.S.2d 688 (App. Div. 1980).

172. Laplante v. Stewart, 470 So. 2d 1018 (La. Ct. App. 1985). *But see* W. Servs. v. Sargent Sch. Dist. No. RE-33J, 751 P.2d 56 (Colo. 1988) (holding that student scholastic data were exempt from disclosure under the state's open records law).

cational record that would implicate FERPA.[173] In an Alabama case, no FERPA violation was found where a school secretary's daughter without permission gained access to a classmate's file and divulged that he was adopted. Such unauthorized access to the records without the knowledge of school personnel was considered an isolated, single occurrence that did not constitute a custom or practice of releasing information.[174] But a Louisiana federal court held that release to the media of a letter written by a political candidate to her son's teacher presented a FERPA claim precluding summary judgment.[175]

A Pennsylvania court held that parents of elementary students were entitled under FERPA to have access to notes taken by the school psychologist during interviews with the students. The interviews pertained to allegations that a teacher had physically and emotionally abused the students.[176] However, FERPA cannot be used by parents to assert a right to review faculty evaluations used to determine which students will be given academic honors, such as membership in the National Honor Society.[177] Also, students cannot rely on FERPA to challenge teachers' grading procedures, other than whether grades were accurately recorded.[178] The Fourth Circuit ruled that FERPA does not entitle students to see an answer key to exams to check the accuracy of their grades, because the key is not part of students' educational records.[179]

Under FERPA, certain public directory information, such as students' names, addresses, dates and places of birth, major fields of study, e-mail addresses, pictures, and degrees and awards received, can be released without parental consent.[180] Any educational agency releasing such data must give public notice of the specific categories it has designated as "directory" and must allow a reasonable period of time for parents to inform the agency that any or all of this information on their child should not be released without their prior consent.

173. Jensen v. Reeves, 3 Fed. Appx. 905 (10th Cir. 2001). *See also* Cudjoe v. Edmond Pub. Schs., 297 F.3d 1058 (10th Cir. 2002) (finding a teacher's comments about a student during a residents' meeting at her condominium complex did not rise to the level of invading privacy rights protected by FERPA or the Federal Constitution); Lewin v. Cooke, 28 Fed. Appx. 186 (4th Cir. 2002) (holding that answer key for an exam is not an educational record under FERPA and thus is not subject to access by an eligible student).

174. Appelberg v. Devilbiss, No. 00–0202 BH–C, 2001 U.S. Dist. LEXIS 1456 (S.D. Ala. Jan. 30, 2001).

175. Warner v. St. Bernard Parish Sch. Bd., 99 F. Supp. 2d 748 (E.D. La. 2000).

176. Parents Against Abuse in Schs. v. Williamsport Area Sch. Dist., 594 A.2d 796 (Pa. Commonw. Ct. 1991).

177. *See, e,g.,* Moore v. Hyche, 761 F. Supp. 112 (N.D. Ala. 1991); Price v. Young, 580 F. Supp. 1 (E.D. Ark. 1983); Becky v. Butte-Silver Bow Sch. Dist. 1, 906 P.2d 193 (Mont. 1995).

178. *See, e.g.,* Tarka v. Cunningham, 917 F.2d 890 (5th Cir. 1990).

179. Lewin v. Cooke, 28 Fed. Appx. 186 (4th Cir. 2002).

180. For a complete list of directory items, *see* 34 C.F.R. § 99.3(b) (2002).

Directory data about a student cannot be released if accompanied by other personally identifiable information unless it is among the specified exceptions to the general rule against nonconsensual disclosure. A Kentucky appeals court ruled that disclosure of personally identifiable information under the state's "no pass, no drive" statute did not fall within the FERPA exceptions.[181] Thus, the court ruled that the regulation requiring transmission of a student's directory information to the Transportation Cabinet along with the notation that the student had dropped out of school or was academically deficient violated FERPA. The regulation subsequently was amended so that the notice indicates only that students are not in compliance with state law. Identifiable information can be disclosed to appropriate authorities, however, if necessary to protect the health or safety of the student or others.[182]

Other federal laws provide additional protections regarding the confidentiality and accessibility of student records. For example, the Individuals with Disabilities Education Act (IDEA) stipulates that records of children with disabilities must be accessible to their parents or guardians.[183] Furthermore, the school must hire interpreters, if necessary to translate the contents of students' files for parents, and must obtain parental consent before such records can be disclosed to third parties.

Many states also have enacted legislation addressing the maintenance and disclosure of student records. Both state and federal privacy laws recognize certain exceptions to "access and disclosure" provisions. For example, a teacher's daily notes pertaining to pupil progress that are shared only with a substitute teacher are exempt from the laws. Private notes, however, become education records and are subject to legal specifications once they are shared, even among educators who have a legitimate need for access to such information.

At times there are conflicts between "freedom of information" or "right to know" provisions and federal and state laws protecting privacy rights. In general, FERPA protections of personally identifiable educational records prevail over state open records provisions. The Virginia Supreme Court denied a student editor's request for individual vote totals in a student election, reasoning that such information was exempt from public disclosure by the law granting custodians discretion concerning disclosure of identifiable scholastic records.[184] In a subsequent case, the University of Vermont was ordered to disclose documents that detailed its response to a formal complaint pertaining to student hazing on the hockey team, but all identifying

---

181. Codell v. D.F., No. 1998-CA-002895-MR, 2001 Ky. App. LEXIS 71 (Ky. Ct. App. June 22, 2001), *rev. granted,* 2002 Ky. LEXIS 205 (Ky. Oct. 9, 2002).

182. *See, e.g.,* Doe v. Woodford County Bd. of Educ., 213 F.3d 921 (6th Cir. 2000) (upholding disclosure to coach of information that student was a hemophiliac and carrier of hepatitis B); 34 C.F. R. § 99.36 (2002).

183. 20 U.S.C. § 1415 (b)(1) (2002).

184. Wall v. Fairfax County Sch. Bd., 475 S.E.2d 803 (Va. 1996). *See also* Lett v. Klein Indep. Sch. Dist., 917 S.W.2d 455 (Tex. Ct. App. 1996) (holding that the Texas Open Records Act did not exempt from disclosure to a student all records relating to his complaint about a conduct grade in a music class).

information about team members had to be withheld from the media to protect the students' privacy rights under FERPA.[185]

Courts have ruled that student disciplinary records can be released to school employees authorized to review such information[186] and to law-enforcement agencies under certain circumstances. The Supreme Court declined to review a decision in which the Massachusetts high court held that a school district did not violate a student's rights under state privacy law when it shared samples of the student's school work with police to compare his handwriting with graffiti on school property in connection with criminal charges.[187] Also, disciplinary information (number of occurrences and when) must be released to the media under some state open records laws as long as specific students cannot be identified.[188] But the Sixth Circuit ruled in 2002 that universities could not release to the media personally identifiable disciplinary records, which are educational records under FERPA.[189]

Students' records must be disclosed if subpoenaed by a court. In compelling a school district to reveal records of individual pupils, a New York federal district court held that FERPA does not preclude the disclosure of student records where a genuine need for the information outweighs the students' privacy interests. In this case, data on the performance of individual students were needed to substantiate charges that inadequate instructional programs were being provided for children with English language deficiencies.[190] Also, a New York appeals court ruled that the records of students in a teacher's class would have to be disclosed (obliterating identifying data) for use by the teacher in defending charges pertaining to his reputation and competence.[191]

Since Congress, state legislatures, and the judiciary have indicated a continuing interest in safeguarding students' privacy rights in connection with school records, school boards would be wise to reassess their policies to ensure that they are adhering to federal and state laws. School personnel should use some restraint, however, before purging information from student files. Pertinent material that is necessary to provide continuity in a student's instructional program *should* be included in a permanent record and be available for use by authorized personnel. It is unfortunate that school personnel, fearing federal sanctions under FERPA, have deleted useful information— along with material that should be removed—from student records.

185. Burlington Free Press v. Univ. of Vt., 779 A.2d 60 (Vt. 2001).

186. Achman v. Chisago Lakes Indep. Sch. Dist. No. 2144, 45 F. Supp. 2d 664 (D. Minn. 1999).

187. Commonwealth v. Buccella, 751 N.E.2d 373 (Mass. 2001), *cert. denied,* 122 S. Ct. 810 (2002).

188. *See, e.g.,* Hardin County Schs. v. Foster, 40 S.W.3d 865 (Ky. 2001).

189. United States v. Miami Univ., 294 F.3d 797 (6th Cir. 2002).

190. Rios v. Read, 480 F. Supp. 14 (E.D.N.Y. 1978). *See also* Zaal v. Maryland, 602 A.2d 1247 (Md. 1992).

191. Bd. of Educ. v. Butcher, 402 N.Y.S.2d 626 (App. Div. 1978). *See also* People v. Owens, 727 N.Y.S.2d 266 (Sup. Ct. 2001) (finding no FERPA violation in prosecution based in part on records subpoenaed from educational institutions).

The mere fact that information in a student's file is negative does not imply that the material is inappropriate. Courts have held that school authorities have an obligation to record relevant data pertaining to students' activities as long as such information is accurate. In an illustrative Pennsylvania case, a federal court upheld school officials in objectively noting in permanent records and communicating to institutions of higher education that the students had participated in a demonstration during graduation ceremonies.[192] The court held that school officials have a *duty* to record and communicate true, factual information about students to institutions of higher learning in order to present an accurate picture of applicants for admission.

Pupil Protection and Parental Rights Laws

Congress and state legislatures have enacted laws to protect family privacy in connection with school research activities and treatment programs. Under federal law, human subjects are protected in research projects supported by federal grants and contracts in any private or public institution or agency.[193] Informed consent must be obtained before placing subjects at risk of being exposed to physical, psychological, or social injury as a result of participating in research, development, or related activities. All education agencies are required to establish review committees to ensure that the rights and welfare of all subjects are adequately protected.

In 1974, two amendments to the General Education Provisions Act required, among other things, that all instructional materials in federally assisted research or experimentation projects (designed to explore new or unproven teaching methods or techniques) be made available for inspection by parents of participating students. The amendments also stipulated that children could not be required to participate in such research or experimentation projects if their parents objected in writing. In 1978, Congress enacted the Hatch Amendment, which retained the protection of parents' rights to examine instructional materials in experimental programs and further required parental consent before students could participate in federally supported programs involving psychiatric or psychological examination, testing, or treatment designed to reveal information in specified sensitive areas pertaining to personal beliefs, behaviors, and family relationships.[194]

Several amendments have extended federal privacy protections for students and their families. Parents must be allowed to review in advance all instructional materials in programs administered by the Department of Education, and federally assisted education programs cannot require students, without prior written parental consent, to be subjected to surveys or evaluations administered by the Department of Education that

---

192. Einhorn v. Maus, 300 F. Supp. 1169 (E.D. Pa. 1969).

193. 42 U.S.C. § 201 *et seq.* (2002); 45 C.F.R. § 46.101 *et seq.* (2002).

194. 20 U.S.C. § 1232h (2002); 34 C.F.R. §§ 75.740, 76.740, and 98.4 (2002).

reveal sensitive information about students or their families.[195] The department is charged with reviewing complaints under this law; if an educational institution is found in violation and does not comply within a reasonable period, federal funds can be withheld.

Some conservative citizen groups have pressed for a broad interpretation of the federal law, but courts usually have not agreed. The Sixth Circuit affirmed without an opinion a Michigan federal district court's ruling that a school district's decision to have a child see a school counselor (because of his problems interacting with class-mates) without securing his parents' consent did not violate the parents' rights under the Hatch Amendment.[196] A Kentucky court rejected a Hatch Amendment challenge to the use of certain questions used in the statewide student assessment program.[197] Also, a federal district court rejected New Jersey parents' claim that a voluntary survey asking students sensitive questions about their attitudes and behavior violated federal privacy protections because written parental permission was not secured for their chil-dren to participate.[198] But the Third Circuit reversed the summary judgment for the school board, remanding the case for consideration of whether the survey was pur-chased with federal funds and whether students knew that participation was voluntary.

There is considerable concern that the federal requirements and similar provi-sions being enacted or considered by many states will cause certain instructional activities to be dropped even before legally challenged. Although these measures are couched in terms of protecting students' privacy rights by granting them *exemptions* from particular instructional activities, if a substantial number of exemptions are requested, the instructional activity itself may be eliminated from the curriculum.

Conclusion

The state and its agents enjoy considerable latitude in regulating various aspects of public education, but any requirements that restrict students' activities must be rea-

195. *See* the Grassley and Tiahrt Protection of Pupil Rights Amendments, 20 U.S.C. § 1232h (2002). The sensitive areas specified in the most recent amendment are political affiliations; mental or psycholog-ical problems of students or families; sexual behavior and attitudes; illegal, antisocial, self-incrimi-nating, and demeaning behavior; critical appraisals of individuals with whom respondents have close family relationships; legally recognized, privileged relationships; religious practices, affiliations, or beliefs of the student or parents; or income (other than that required to determine eligibility for finan-cial assistance programs). Parents must be notified at least annually of their rights under this law.

196. Newkirk v. E. Lansing Pub. Schs., No. 91-00563 (W.D. Mich. 1993), *aff'd mem.,* 57 F.3d 1070 (6th Cir. 1995). After the Hatch Amendment's regulations became effective in 1984, this previously obscure provision became extremely controversial, pitting conservative parents' groups against pro-fessional education associations. *See* Hatch Amendment Coalition and American Educational Research Association, *The Hatch Amendment Regulations: A Guidelines Document* (Washington, DC: AERA, 1985).

197. Triplett v. Livingston County Bd. of Educ., 967 S.W.2d 25 (Ky. Ct. App. 1997).

198. C.N. v. Ridgewood Bd. of Educ., 146 F. Supp. 2d 528 (D.N.J. 2001), *aff'd in part, rev'd in part, and remanded,* 281F.3d 219 (3d Cir. 2001).

sonable and necessary to carry out legitimate educational objectives. When students' or parents' protected rights are impaired, school authorities must be able to substantiate that there is an overriding public interest to be served. From an analysis of court cases and legislation pertaining to general requirements and rights associated with school attendance and the instructional program, the following generalizations seem warranted.

1. The state can compel children between specified ages to attend school.[199]
2. Students can satisfy compulsory attendance mandates by attending private schools and, in most states, by receiving equivalent instruction (e.g., home tutoring) that is comparable to the public school program.
3. School officials can require immunization against diseases as a condition of school attendance and can allow religious exemptions to such requirements.
4. Students cannot be excluded from public school because of particular health conditions, unless school attendance would endanger the health of others.
5. Public school districts must provide an education for bona fide resident children (even those whose parents entered the country illegally), but children who live apart from their parents for educational purposes are not entitled to tuition-free schooling.
6. Fees can be charged for public school transportation as long as the fees are rationally related to legitimate state objectives.
7. Fees can be charged for the use of public school textbooks and for supplies associated with courses unless such fees are prohibited by state constitutional or statutory provisions.
8. The state and its agencies have the authority to determine public school course offerings and instructional materials, and such curricular determinations will be upheld by courts unless clearly arbitrary or in violation of constitutional or statutory rights.
9. School boards can eliminate instructional materials considered educationally unsuitable if objective procedures are followed in making such determinations.
10. Courts defer to school authorities in assessing student performance, in the absence of evidence of arbitrary or discriminatory academic decisions.
11. Proficiency examinations can be used to determine pupil remedial needs and as a prerequisite to high school graduation if students are given sufficient notice prior to implementation of the test requirements and are provided adequate preparation for the examinations.
12. Public schools do not owe students a duty to ensure that a specified level of achievement is attained.
13. Parents and 18-year-old students must be granted access to the student's school records and an opportunity to contest the contents.

---

199. The notable exception to compulsory attendance pertains to Amish children who have successfully completed eighth grade. *See* Wisconsin v. Yoder, 406 U.S. 205 (1972); text accompanying note 13, Chapter 2.

14. Individuals do not have a private right to bring suits for damages under the Family Educational Rights and Privacy Act; the remedy for violations is the withdrawal of federal aid from the noncomplying agency.

15. School personnel must ensure the accuracy of information contained in student records and maintain the confidentiality of such records.

16. Parents have the right to inspect materials used in federally funded experimental projects or surveys, and students have a right to be excused from participation in such programs or activities involving psychiatric or psychological testing or treatment designed to reveal information in specified sensitive areas pertaining to personal beliefs, behaviors, and family relationships.

4

Students' Rights in Noninstructional Matters

Students continue to test the limits of their personal freedoms in public schools, frequently colliding with educators' efforts to maintain an appropriate school environment. When controversies cannot be resolved locally, courts often are called on to address the legal issues involved. For example, what types of student expression are constitutionally protected? Under what circumstances must student-initiated groups be allowed to meet in public schools? What restrictions can be placed on student appearance? What conditions can be attached to participation in school-related activities? This chapter addresses these and other questions regarding students' rights in connection with selected noninstructional issues with an emphasis on First Amendment freedoms of speech and press and closely related association rights.

Freedom of Speech and Press

The First Amendment, as applied to the states through the Fourteenth Amendment, restricts *governmental* interference with citizens' free expression rights. The government, including public school boards, must have a compelling justification to curtail citizens' expression. The First Amendment also shields the individual's right to remain silent when confronted with an illegitimate government demand for expression, such as mandatory participation in the salute to the American flag in public schools.[1] In short, the First Amendment protects decisions regarding what to say and what not to say; "the difference between compelled speech and compelled silence is without constitutional significance."[2]

---

1. *See* W. Va. State Bd. of Educ. v. Barnette, 319 U.S. 624 (1943); text with note 135, Chapter 2.
2. Parate v. Isibor, 868 F.2d 821, 828 (6th Cir. 1989).

In our nation, free expression rights are perhaps the most preciously guarded individual liberties[3] and are often relied on to protect unpopular viewpoints. For example, the Supreme Court has used the First Amendment to protect political pro- testers' right to burn the American flag[4] and the Ku Klux Klan's right to place a cross on public property that is available to citizens for speech purposes.[5] In 2002, the Ninth Circuit observed:

> The First Amendment judicial scrutiny should now be at its height, whether the individ- ual before us is a troubled schoolboy, a right-to-life-activist, an outraged environmental- ist, a Taliban sympathizer, or any other person who disapproves of one or more of our nation's officials or policies for any reason whatsoever.[6]

Although public school authorities traditionally were allowed to restrict student expression for almost any reason, the Supreme Court has recognized since the mid-twentieth century that students do not shed their constitutional rights as a condi- tion of public school attendance and that public education is an appropriate setting in which to instill a respect for these rights. The Court has acknowledged that First Amendment freedoms must receive "scrupulous protection" in schools "if we are not to strangle the free mind at its source and teach youth to discount important principles of our government as mere platitudes."[7] The Court has further noted that schools func- tion as "a marketplace of ideas" and that the "robust exchange of ideas" is "a special concern of the First Amendment."[8]

However, the Supreme Court has also stated that "the constitutional rights of students in public school are not automatically coextensive with the rights of adults in other settings," and may be limited by reasonable policies designed to take into account the special circumstances of the educational environment.[9] Particularly sen- sitive constitutional issues are being raised in connection with the national surge of patriotism following the terrorist attacks on September 11, 2001. Many school dis- tricts have reinstated the daily Pledge of Allegiance to the American flag, and some schools are displaying banners with "God Bless America" or "In God We Trust."[10]

---

3. Despite their fundamental significance, free expression rights can be restricted. As Justice Holmes noted, freedom of speech does not allow an individual to yell "fire" in a crowded theater when there is no fire. Schenck v. United States, 249 U.S. 47, 52 (1919).

4. Texas v. Johnson, 491 U.S. 397 (1989).

5. Capitol Square Review & Advisory Bd. v. Pinette, 515 U.S. 753 (1995).

6. Lavine v. Blaine Sch. Dist., 279 F.3d 719, 720 (9th Cir. 2002), *cert. denied,* 122 S. Ct. 2663 (2002).

7. W. Va. State Bd. of Educ. v. Barnette, 319 U.S. 624, 637 (1943). *See also* Shelton v. Tucker, 364 U.S. 479, 487 (1960); Sweezy v. New Hampshire, 354 U.S. 234, 250 (1957).

8. Keyishian v. Bd. of Regents, 385 U.S. 589, 603 (1967) (quoting in part, United States v. Associated Press, 52 F. Supp. 362, 372 (S.D.N.Y. 1943), *aff'd,* 326 U.S. 1 (1945)).

9. Bethel Sch. Dist. No. 403 v. Fraser, 478 U.S. 675, 682 (1986). *See also* Tinker v. Des Moines Indep. Sch. Dist., 393 U.S. 503, 506–507 (1969).

10. *See* John Gehring, "States Weigh Bills to Stoke Students' Patriotism," *Education Week* (March 27, 2002), pp. 19, 22; Mark Walsh, "Patriotism and Prayer: Constitutional Questions Are Muted," *Educa- tion Week* (October 10, 2001), p. 14.

These activities have placed new strains on the exercise of First Amendment rights to abstain from patriotic observances, to criticize government policies, or to raise church/state questions in connection with patriotic displays in public schools.

Unprotected Conduct and Expression

A threshold question before applying First Amendment standards is whether the behavior at issue constitutes expression *at all*. Only where conduct is meant to communicate an idea that is likely to be understood by the intended audience is it considered expression for First Amendment purposes.[11] Even if specific conduct qualifies as expression, it is not assured constitutional protection; the judiciary has recognized that defamatory, obscene, and inflammatory communications are outside the protective arm of the First Amendment. In addition, lewd and vulgar expression is not protected in the public school context.

Defamatory Expression.   Defamation includes spoken (slander) and written (libel) statements that are false, expose another to public shame or ridicule, and are communicated to someone other than the person defamed. Courts have upheld school authorities in banning libelous content from publications distributed at school and imposing sanctions on students responsible for such material, but regulations cannot be vague or grant school officials complete discretion to censor materials considered potentially libelous.

Fair comment on the actions of public figures, unlike defamatory expression, is constitutionally protected. Public figures can establish that they have been defamed only with evidence that the comment was false and the speaker acted recklessly or with actual malice.[12] As will be discussed in Chapter 13, school board members and superintendents are generally considered public figures for defamation purposes, but courts have rendered conflicting opinions regarding whether teachers, principals, and coaches have assumed the risk of nonmalicious defamation.[13]

Obscene, Lewd, or Vulgar Expression.   The judiciary has held that individuals cannot claim a First Amendment right to voice or publish obscenities, but school authorities do not have to prove that student expression is obscene for it to be curtailed.[14] In a significant 1986 decision, *Bethel School District No. 403 v. Fraser,* the Supreme Court granted school authorities considerable latitude in censoring lewd, vulgar, and indecent student expression. Overturning the lower courts, the Supreme Court upheld disciplinary action against a student for using a sexual metaphor in a nominating

---

11. *See, e.g.,* Jarman v. Williams, 753 F.2d 76 (8th Cir. 1985) (holding that social and recreational dancing in public schools does not enjoy First Amendment protection).
12. *See, e.g.,* Hustler Magazine v. Falwell, 485 U.S. 46 (1988).
13. *See* text with note 78, Chapter 13, for a discussion of the principles of tort law governing defamation suits for damages.

speech during a student government assembly.[15] Concluding that the sexual innuendos were offensive to both teachers and students, the majority held that the school's legitimate interest in protecting the captive student audience from exposure to lewd, vulgar, and offensive speech justified the disciplinary action. The Court reiterated that speech protected by the First Amendment for adults is not necessarily protected for children, reasoning that in the public school context the sensibilities of fellow students must be considered. The majority recognized that an important objective of public schools is the inculcation of fundamental values of civility and that the school board has the authority to determine what manner of speech is appropriate in classes or assemblies.[16] The majority further rejected the contention that the student had no way of knowing that his expression would evoke disciplinary action, concluding that the school rule barring obscene and disruptive expression and teachers' admonitions that his planned speech was inappropriate provided adequate warning of the consequences of the expression.[17]

Noting that *Fraser* had altered the expression rights of students in public schools, the Eleventh Circuit dismissed a claim against school officials who disciplined a student for displaying a Confederate flag to classmates during a school lunch break.[18] The student was suspended and recommended for expulsion for displaying a racist symbol. Concluding that the disciplinary action did not violate the student's clearly established constitutional rights, the appeals court adopted the flexible reasonableness test from *Fraser* and found that the student's display of the Confederate flag interfered with the school's objectives of promoting civility.

14. Miller v. California, 413 U.S. 15, 24 (1973) (identifying the following test to distinguish obscene material from constitutionally protected material: "(a) whether 'the average person, applying contemporary community standards' would find that the work, taken as a whole, appeals to the prurient interests; ... (b) whether the work depicts or describes, in a patently offensive way, sexual conduct specifically defined by the applicable state law; and (c) whether the work, taken as a whole, lacks serious literary, artistic, political or scientific value"). On several occasions, the Supreme Court has recognized the government's authority to adjust the definition of *obscenity* as applied to minors. *See, e.g.,* Ginsberg v. New York, 390 U.S. 629, 636–637 (1968) (upholding a state law prohibiting the sale to minors of magazines depicting female nudity, noting that the state may accord minors "a more restricted right than that assured to adults to judge and determine for themselves what sex material they may read or see").

15. 478 U.S. 675 (1986).

16. *Id.* at 683. *See also* Lopez v. Tulare Joint Union High Sch. Bd. of Trs., 40 Cal. Rptr. 2d 762 (Ct. App. 1995) (requiring students to delete profanity from a film they prepared for a class did not violate their First Amendment rights); Hinze v. Superior Court of Marin County, 174 Cal. Rptr. 403 (Ct. App. 1981) (holding that a badge stating "Fuck the Draft" was vulgar and not protected expression; a student who persistently refused to remove the button could be disciplined).

17. Fraser was suspended for two days and disqualified as a candidate for commencement speaker. However, he did eventually deliver a commencement speech, so his claim that the disqualification violated due process rights was not reviewed by the appellate court.

18. Denno v. Sch. Bd., 218 F.3d 1267 (11th Cir. 2000). *See also* Melton v. Young, 465 F.2d 1332 (6th Cir. 1972) (upholding a student's suspension for persisting to wear a Confederate flag sleeve patch in a racially tense, newly integrated Tennessee school); *infra* text accompanying note 85.

More recently, the South Dakota federal district court upheld punishment of a student for saying the word *shit* within earshot of the school secretary in the school's office.[19] Under the school's zero tolerance rule prohibiting profane or inappropriate language on school property, the student received an in-school suspension resulting in a grade reduction for classes missed. The court recognized that promoting proper decorum and complying with school rules are legitimate educational concerns justifying such a rule.

Inflammatory Expression. The judiciary also has sanctioned regulations banning the use of inflammatory expression in public schools. Courts have differentiated expression that agitates, threatens, or incites an immediate breach of peace (fighting words),[20] from speech that is "a mere doctrinal justification of a thought or idea," leaving an opportunity for calm and reasonable discussion.[21] Although inflammatory student expression at school is not constitutionally protected, courts have not spoken in unison regarding whether such expression off school grounds can be the basis for school sanctions.[22]

A growing body of First Amendment litigation involves alleged threats made by students toward classmates or school personnel. For example, the Ninth Circuit upheld suspension of a student for threatening a teacher, despite conflicting testimony regarding what was actually said.[23] The appeals court emphasized that threats of physical violence are not shielded by the First Amendment.

In determining if a true threat has been made, courts can consider a number of factors, such as reactions of the recipient and other listeners, whether the maker of the alleged threat had made similar statements to the victim in the past, if the utterance was conditional and communicated directly to the victim, and whether the victim had reason to believe that the speaker would engage in violence.[24] In an illustrative case, the Arkansas Supreme Court held that a rap song did not entail fighting words but was a true threat, as it contained an unconditional threat to the life of a classmate and was delivered to the targeted student who perceived it as unequivocally threatening.[25] Also finding a true threat, the Eighth Circuit reversed the court below and upheld expulsion

---

19. Anderson v. Milbank Sch. Dist., 197 F.R.D. 682 (D.S.D. 2000). *See also* Pangle v. Bend-Lapine Sch. Dist., 10 P.3d 275 (Or. App. 2000), *review denied,* 34 P.3d 1176 (Or. 2001) (upholding punishment of a student who distributed an underground newspaper that used vulgar and threatening language).

20. Gooding v. Wilson, 405 U. S. 518, 524 (1972).

21. Stacy v. Williams, 306 F. Supp. 963, 972 (N.D. Miss. 1969).

22. *See* text with note 14, Chapter 7.

23. Lovell v. Poway Unified Sch. Dist., 90 F.3d 367 (9th Cir. 1996).

24. United States v. Dinwiddie, 76 F.3d 913 (8th Cir. 1996). *See also* Shoemaker v. State, 343 Ark. 727 (2001) (finding a state law unconstitutionally vague that criminalized student conduct or expression abusing or insulting a teacher; a student could not be charged with a misdemeanor for calling her teacher "a bitch" because this utterance did not entail fighting words).

25. Jones v. State, 347 Ark. 409 (2002). *See also* United States v. Morales, 272 F.3d 284 (5th Cir. 2001), *cert. denied,* 122 S. Ct. 2624 (2002), *infra* text accompanying note 93.

of a student for writing a letter threatening to rape and murder his former girlfriend. The Court was convinced that the writer intended to communicate the threat, as he shared the letter with a friend whom he assumed would give it to his former girl-friend.[26]

Utterances can be considered inflammatory, and thus unprotected, even if not found to be true threats or fighting words. A Ninth Circuit panel ruled that a student could be subject to emergency expulsion, with a hearing occurring afterwards, for writing a poem about someone who committed multiple murders two years earlier and decided to kill himself for fear of murdering others.[27] The poem was not considered a true threat or to contain fighting words. A circuit judge who dissented from the denial of rehearing *en banc* asserted that the panel created a new First Amendment principle in that school officials "may punish school children whose speech gives rise to a con-cern that they may be dangerous to themselves or others, even though the speech is not a threat, disruptive, defamatory, sexual, or otherwise within any previously recog-nized category of constitutionally unprotected speech."[28]

The Wisconsin Supreme Court also held that school authorities had more than enough reason to suspend a student for his creative writing assignment, describing a student removed from class for being disruptive (as the writer had been), who returned the next day to behead his teacher.[29] But the court found no true threat that would jus-tify prosecution as disorderly conduct. The Supreme Court of New Hampshire simi-larly overruled a disorderly conduct conviction of a student who said he might "shoot up the school" if a teacher did not give him a hug. The court found no evidence that the expression caused a school disruption to justify the conviction.[30] Courts generally seem more inclined to uphold school disciplinary action, in contrast to criminal pros-ecution, for students' alleged threats.[31]

26. Doe v. Pulaski County Special Dist., 306 F.3d 616 (8th Cir. 2002).

27. The school board wanted the student's file to note that the action was for safety rather than disciplinary reasons, and the student was readmitted to school after three psychiatric visits. Lavine v. Blaine Sch. Dist., 279 F.3d 719 (9th Cir. 2002), *cert. denied*, 122 S. Ct. 2663 (2002). *See also* Cuesta v. Miami-Dade County Sch. Bd., 285 F.3d 962 (11th Cir. 2002) (upholding principal's compliance with the school's zero tolerance policy by reporting to the police a student's distribution of a threatening pam-phlet).

28. *Lavine,* 279 F.3d at 724 (Reinhardt, Cir. J., dissenting from rehearing *en banc*) (agreeing with the lower court that the student should have been suspended, pending psychological evaluation, rather than expelled). If a student posts a threat on the Internet that would be accessible to individuals in other states, the expression might violate 18 U.S.C. § 875 (2002) that makes the posting of interstate threats a misdemeanor.

29. *In re* Douglas D., 626 N.W.2d 725 (Wis. 2001). *See also In re* C.C.H., 651 N.W.2d 702 (S.D. 2002).

30. State v. McCooey, 802 A.2d 1216 (N.H. 2002). *See also* D. G. & C. G. v. Indep. Sch. Dist. No. 11, No. 00-C-0614-E, 2000 U.S. Dist. LEXIS 12197 (N.D. Okla. Aug. 21, 2000) (granting injunction to rein-state a student in her regular high school, since the poem she wrote about killing her teacher, which was left in the classroom, was not a true threat).

31. *But see In re* A.S., 626 N.W.2d 712 (Wis. 2001) (finding students' comments that he intended to kill everyone at his middle school to represent an intent to inflict harm in violation of the disorderly con-duct law).

Commercial Expression

Unlike obscene, lewd, inflammatory, or defamatory expression, commercial speech enjoys some measure of constitutional protection. However, expression with economic motives has not been afforded the same level of First Amendment protection as has speech intended to convey a particular point of view.[32] In 1989, the Supreme Court recognized that governmental restrictions on commercial speech do not have to be the least restrictive means to achieve the desired end; rather, there only needs to be a reasonable "fit" between the restrictions and the governmental goal.[33] In several cases involving school newspapers, courts have upheld school authorities in rejecting advertisements that conflict with educational objectives.[34]

Courts generally have upheld regulations prohibiting sales and fund-raising activities in public schools as justified to preserve schools for their educational function and to prevent commercial exploitation of students. For example, the Second Circuit declined to enjoin the implementation of a public school rule prohibiting students from soliciting funds from their classmates.[35] The students sought the injunction so they could distribute leaflets to solicit funds for the legal defense of persons on trial for anti-war demonstrations. In denying the injunction, the court asserted that it was unlikely that a court would find the school's rule overbroad.

Some controversies focus on students' rights *not* to be exposed to commercial expression in public schools, rather than on their rights to engage in commercial activity. For example, a number of school districts nationwide subscribe to Channel One; in return for students watching a 10-minute news program and 2 minutes of commercials each day, the schools receive free equipment. Although the judiciary has recognized the legal authority of school boards to enter into contracts for supplementary instructional materials that include commercials,[36] some courts have required school

32. *See, e.g.,* Bolger v. Youngs Drug Prods. Corp., 463 U.S. 60, 64-75 (1983) (holding that unsolicited mailings concern commercial speech, which is afforded less constitutional protection than other forms of expression).

33. Bd. of Trs. v. Fox, 492 U.S. 469 (1989).

34. *See, e.g.,* Planned Parenthood v. Clark County Sch. Dist., 887 F.2d 935 (9th Cir. 1989), *infra* text accompanying note 48; Williams v. Spencer, 622 F.2d 1200 (4th Cir. 1980), *infra* text accompanying note 72.

35. Katz v. McAulay, 438 F.2d 1058 (2d Cir. 1971). *See also* Bernard v. United Township High Sch. Dist. No. 30, 5 F.3d 1090 (7th Cir. 1993) (rejecting student's claim against school district for alleged interference with his sale of a print he had made).

36. *See, e.g.,* Wallace v. Knox County Bd. of Educ., No. 92-6195, 1993 U.S. App. LEXIS 20477 (6th Cir. Aug. 10, 1993) (finding no violation of students' rights in school's broadcast of news program with commercials, since students could be excused from the broadcasts); Dawson v. E. Side Union High Sch. Dist., 34 Cal. Rptr.2d 108 (Ct. App. 1994) (holding that school boards have the discretion to permit commercial broadcasting in schools); State v. Whittle Communications, 402 S.E.2d 556 (N.C. 1991) (dismissing complaint that contracts between school districts and private company to air broadcasts at school violated state law).

boards to excuse students who are offended by the commercial activities.[37] With an increasing number of companies offering monetary enticements for school boards to air commercials over public address systems and display advertisements on scoreboards,[38] such commercial activities in public schools seem destined to generate additional legal challenges.

School-Sponsored (Governmental) Expression

In contrast to defamatory, obscene, vulgar, and inflammatory expression, students' airing of political or ideological views in public schools *is* protected by the First Amendment. Since the latter 1980s, the Supreme Court has emphasized the distinction between student expression that appears to represent the school and *private* student expression of ideological views that merely occurs at school. The latter commands substantial constitutional protection, but student expression appearing to bear the school's imprimatur can be restricted to ensure that it is consistent with educational objectives. The Court's expansive interpretation of what constitutes school-sponsored expression has narrowed the circumstances under which students can prevail in First Amendment claims.

Type of Forum.   In recent Free Speech Clause litigation, an assessment of the type of forum the government has created for expressive activities has been important in determining whether expression can be restricted. The Supreme Court has recognized that public places, such as streets and parks, are traditional public forums for assembly and communication where content-based restrictions cannot be imposed unless justified by a compelling government interest.[39] In contrast, expression can be confined to the governmental purpose of the property in a nonpublic forum, such as a public school. Content-based restrictions are permissible in a nonpublic forum to assure that expression is compatible with the intended governmental purpose, provided that regulations are reasonable and do not entail viewpoint discrimination.

The government, however, can create a limited public forum for expression on public property that otherwise would be considered a nonpublic forum and reserved for its governmental function.[40] For example, a student activities program held after school might be established as a limited forum for student expression. A limited forum can be restricted to a certain class of speakers (e.g., students) and/or to specific cate-

---

37. *See, e.g., Dawson,* 34 Cal. Rptr. 2d 108. *See also* DiLoreto v. Downey Unified Sch. Dist. Bd. of Educ., 196 F.3d 958 (9th Cir. 1999) (holding that the school could exclude certain subjects from advertisements allowed on the fence surrounding the school's baseball field, which was a nonpublic forum available only for limited purposes).

38. *See* Martha McCarthy, "Privatization of Education: Marketplace Models," in Bruce Jones (Ed.), *Educational Leadership: Policy Dimensions in the 21st Century* (Stamford, CT: Ablex, 2000), pp. 21–39.

39. Cornelius v. NAACP Legal Def. & Educ. Fund, 473 U.S. 788 (1985); Perry Educ. Ass'n v. Perry Local Educators' Ass'n, 460 U.S. 37 (1983).

40. *See* Kincaid v. Gibson, 236 F.3d 342 (6th Cir. 2001) (holding that the university's yearbook was created as a limited public forum for student expression; the university's actions in confiscating copies because of objections violated the editors' First Amendment rights).

gories of expression (e.g., noncommercial speech). Otherwise, expression in a limited forum is subject to the same protections that govern a traditional public forum.

During the 1970s and early 1980s, a number of courts broadly interpreted the circumstances under which limited forums for student expression were created in public schools. School-sponsored newspapers often were considered such a forum, and accordingly, courts held that articles on controversial subjects such as the Vietnam War, abortion, and birth control could not be barred from these publications.[41] Courts scrutinized policies requiring prior administrative review of the content of school-sponsored as well as nonsponsored literature and placed the burden on school authorities to justify such prior review schemes.

Hazelwood and Its Progeny.   In 1988, the Supreme Court delivered a significant decision, *Hazelwood School District v. Kuhlmeier,* holding that school authorities can censor student expression in school publications and other school-related activities as long as the censorship decisions are based on legitimate pedagogical concerns.[42] At issue in *Hazelwood* was a high school principal's deletion of two pages from the school newspaper because of the content of articles on divorce and teenage pregnancy and fears that individuals could be identified in the articles. The Court ruled that the principal's actions were based on legitimate educational concerns. Rejecting the assertion that the school newspaper had been established as a public forum for student expression, the Court declared that only with school authorities' clear *intent* do school activities become a public forum.[43] The Court drew a distinction between a public school's *toleration* of private student expression, which is constitutionally required under some circumstances, and its *promotion* of student speech that represents the school. Reasoning that student expression appearing to bear the school's imprimatur can be censored, the Court acknowledged school authorities' broad discretion to ensure that such expression occurring in school publications and all school-sponsored activities (including extracurricular) is consistent with educational objectives.[44] The Court reiterated the sentiment voiced in *Fraser* two years earlier that school boards can determine for themselves what expression is consistent with pedagogical objectives.[45]

---

41. *See, e.g.,* Gambino v. Fairfax County Sch. Bd., 564 F.2d 157 (4th Cir. 1977) (holding that school-sponsored newspaper was established as a forum for student expression).

42. 484 U.S. 260 (1988), *on remand,* 840 F.2d 596 (8th Cir. 1988).

43. *Id.,* 484 U.S. at 267.

44. In response to this decision, several state legislatures have enacted laws granting student editors of school-sponsored papers specific rights in determining the content of those publications. *See, e.g.,* Cal. Ed. Code § 48907 (2002); Colo. Rev. Stat. Ann. § 22-1-120 (2001); Iowa Code § 280.22 (2002); Kan. Stat. Ann. § 72-1506 (2002); Mass. Gen. Laws Ann. ch. 71, § 82 (2002). *See also* Pyle v. Sch. Comm. of S. Hadley, 667 N.E.2d 869 (Mass. 1996) (finding the state law more protective than the First Amendment in that it allows students to engage in vulgar, private expression in public schools as long as the expression is not disruptive).

45. 484 U.S. at 267. The Court in *Fraser* recognized that a voluntary student government assembly is not a public forum for student expression, but noted that school authorities' broad discretion to curtail lewd and vulgar student expression is not confined to school-sponsored events. Bethel Sch. Dist. No. 403 v. Fraser, 478 U.S. 675 (1986); *supra* text accompanying note 15.

Relying on *Hazelwood,* the Sixth Circuit in 1989 held that a student could be disqualified from running for student council president because his candidacy speech at a school-sponsored assembly was discourteous. Noting that civility is a legitimate pedagogical concern, the court emphasized that "limitations on speech that would be unconstitutional outside the schoolhouse are not necessarily unconstitutional within it."[46] The court acknowledged that decisions regarding whether specific comments are rude are "best left to the locally elected school board, not to a distant, life-tenured judiciary."[47]

Also echoing the *Hazelwood* rationale, the Ninth Circuit rejected Planned Parenthood's claim that a school district's denial of its request to advertise in school newspapers, yearbooks, and programs for athletic events violated free speech rights. The court concluded that the district could reject advertisements that were inconsistent with its educational mission or might interfere with the "proper function of education."[48] Similarly reflecting the broad discretion granted to school authorities, the Fourth Circuit upheld a high school principal's decision to bar the school's use of the Johnny Reb symbol following complaints that it offended African American students.[49] The court reasoned that the school can disassociate itself from controversial expression at odds with its objectives.

The Eighth Circuit in 1998 found no impairment of a student's First Amendment rights in her suspension and ultimate expulsion for defying school personnel and repeatedly reposting a letter on the divider around her workspace.[50] The letter was from a classmate's parents asking her not to use information gathered from the classmate for an article on frogs that she was writing for publication on the Internet. Evidence indicated that the classmate and his brother felt harassed by her posting of the letter and that their schoolwork was severely affected. The appeals court rejected the assertion that the display boards were limited public forums for student expression.

The following year, the Eighth Circuit again relied on *Hazelwood* in upholding a principal's decision to disqualify a student council candidate who handed out condoms with stickers bearing his campaign slogan.[51] The court approved the requirement that students must obtain administrative approval before distributing materials at school, noting that *Hazelwood* grants school authorities considerable discretion to control student expression in school-sponsored activities. Also, a Missouri federal district court upheld school authorities in prohibiting the marching band's performance of a song they feared would be construed as advocating drug use.[52] The court

46. Poling v. Murphy, 872 F.2d 757, 762 (6th Cir. 1989).

47. *Id.,* 872 F.2d at 761. *See also* Guidry v. Broussard, 897 F.2d 181 (5th Cir. 1990) (upholding censorship of a student's valedictory speech).

48. Planned Parenthood v. Clark County Sch. Dist., 887 F.2d 935, 942 (9th Cir. 1989) (quoting Burch v. Barker, 861 F.2d 1149, 1158 (9th Cir. 1988)), *rehearing en banc,* 941 F.2d 817 (9th Cir. 1991).

49. Crosby v. Holsinger, 852 F.2d 801 (4th Cir. 1988) (noting also that the one-day delay in posting students' notices of the upcoming board meeting constituted a minimal impairment of expression rights).

50. Fister v. Minn. New Country Sch., 149 F.3d 1187 (8th Cir. 1998).

51. Henerey v. City of St. Charles Sch. Dist., 200 F.3d 1128 (8th Cir. 1999).

52. McCann v. Ft. Zumwalt Sch. Dist., 50 F. Supp. 2d 918 (E.D. Mo. 1999).

found band performances to be school-sponsored expression over which the school exercises broad control.

There are limits, however, on school authorities' wide latitude to censor student expression that bears the public school's imprimatur. Blatant viewpoint discrimination, even in a nonpublic forum, abridges the First Amendment.[53] For example, the Ninth Circuit held that a school board violated students' First Amendment rights, because it failed to produce a compelling justification for excluding an anti-draft organization's advertisement from the school newspaper, while allowing military recruitment advertisements.[54] Similarly, the Eleventh Circuit placed the burden on school authorities to justify viewpoint discrimination against a peace activist group that was excluded from the public school's career day and not allowed to display its literature on school bulletin boards and in counselors' offices, when military recruiters were allowed such access.[55] The court found no compelling justification for censoring specific views that the board found distasteful.

Even if viewpoint discrimination is not involved, censorship actions in a nonpublic forum still must be based on legitimate pedagogical concerns. The New Jersey Supreme Court held that the exclusion of a student's reviews of R-rated movies violated First Amendment rights, even though the junior high school newspaper was not a public forum.[56] Noting that R-rated movies were discussed in class and available in the school library, the court concluded that school authorities did not produce legitimate educational reasons for the censorship action.

Protected Private Expression

Student expression that does not fall within one of the categories of unprotected expression or bear the school's imprimatur is governed by the landmark Supreme Court decision, *Tinker v. Des Moines Independent School District*, rendered in 1969. In *Tinker,* three students were suspended from school for wearing armbands to protest the Vietnam War. School officials did not attempt to prohibit the wearing of all symbols, but instead prohibited the expression of one particular opinion. Concluding that school authorities punished the students for expression that was not accompanied by any disorder or disturbance, the Supreme Court ruled that "undifferentiated fear or apprehension of disturbance is not enough to overcome the right to freedom of expres-

---

53. *See* Bd. of Regents v. Southworth, 529 U.S. 217 (2000) (upholding a university's mandatory student activities fees used to facilitate the free and open exchange of ideas among students as long as the institution operated in a viewpoint-neutral manner, but striking down the use of a student referendum to determine what clubs would be subsidized, because the referendum disenfranchised minority viewpoints).

54. San Diego Comm. Against Registration & the Draft v. Governing Bd. of Grossmont Union High Sch. Dist., 790 F.2d 1471 (9th Cir. 1986). *See also* Clergy & Laity Concerned v. Chi. Bd. of Educ., 586 F. Supp. 1408 (N.D. Ill. 1984) (striking down the school board's practice of allowing military recruiters access to schools while denying anti-war activists such access to provide information about alternatives to military service).

55. Searcey v. Harris, 888 F.2d 1314 (11th Cir. 1989).

56. Desilets v. Clearview Reg'l Bd. of Educ., 647 A.2d 150 (N.J. 1994).

sion."[57] Furthermore, the Court declared that school officials must have "more than a mere desire to avoid discomfort and unpleasantness that always accompany an unpopular viewpoint" in order to justify curtailment of student expression.[58] The Court emphasized that "students in school as well as out of school are 'persons' under our Constitution. They are possessed of fundamental rights which the state must respect."[59]

In *Tinker,* the Supreme Court echoed statements made in an earlier federal appellate ruling: A student may express opinions on controversial issues in the classroom, cafeteria, playing field, or any other place, as long as the exercise of such rights does not "materially and substantially interfere with the requirements of appropriate discipline in the operation of the school" or collide with the rights of others.[60] The Supreme Court emphasized that educators have the authority and duty to maintain discipline in schools, but they must consider students' constitutional rights as they exert control.

Because school authorities can censor school-sponsored student expression for educational reasons,[61] the *Tinker* standard now applies *only* to protected expression that does not give the appearance of representing the school. Ironically, since *Hazelwood,* student expression in underground student papers distributed at school enjoys greater constitutional protection than does expression in school-sponsored publications. The former is considered private expression governed by the *Tinker* principle, whereas the latter is subject to censorship under *Hazelwood.* As discussed in Chapter 2, most courts have treated students' distribution of religious literature like the distribution of other material that is not sponsored by the school.[62]

But even a school-sponsored publication might be considered a forum for student expression under certain circumstances. In a Massachusetts case, school authorities had given students editorial control of school publications, so independent decisions of the students could not be attributed to school officials. In this situation, the student editors of the school newspaper and yearbook rejected advertisements from a parent who was a leading opponent of the district's condom-distribution policy. The First Circuit concluded that school officials, who had recommended that the students publish the ads, could not be held liable for the students' decisions, because the student editors were not state actors.[63]

57. 393 U.S. 503, 508 (1969).

58. *Id.* at 509.

59. *Id.* at 511.

60. *Id.* at 513 (quoting Burnside v. Byars, 363 F.2d 744, 749 (5th Cir. 1966)). *Compare with* Blackwell v. Issaquena County Bd. of Educ., 363 F.2d 749 (5th Cir. 1966); *infra* text accompanying note 65.

61. *See* Hazelwood Sch. Dist. v. Kuhlmeier, 484 U.S. 260 (1988), *supra* text accompanying note 42; Bethel Sch. Dist. No. 403 v. Fraser, 478 U.S. 675 (1986), *supra* text accompanying note 15.

62. *See* text accompanying note 117, Chapter 2. Of course, proselytizing materials in *school-sponsored* publications would be barred by the Establishment Clause.

63. Yeo v. Town of Lexington, 131 F.3d 241 (1st Cir. 1997).

Prior Restraints.   When determined that protected private expression is at issue, courts then are faced with the difficult task of assessing whether restrictions are justified in particular circumstances. Under the *Tinker* principle, private expression can be curtailed if it is likely to disrupt the educational process. The Sixth Circuit concluded that a rule banning the wearing of freedom buttons was lawful in a situation where the learning environment would be disrupted if pupils were allowed to wear the "badges of their respective disagreements."[64] Also, bans on wearing buttons have been upheld where student button-wearers have created disturbances within the school by harassing students without buttons.[65]

The law clearly allows students to be punished after the fact if they cause a disruption, but school authorities have a greater burden of justification when they impose prior restraints on such expression. The Supreme Court has recognized that "a free society prefers to punish the few who abuse rights of speech after they break the law [rather] than to throttle them and all others beforehand."[66] The imposition of prior restraints on student speech must bear a substantial relationship to an important government interest, "lest students' imaginations, intellects, and wills be unduly stifled or chilled."[67] In addition, any regulation must contain narrow, objective, and unambiguous criteria for determining what material is prohibited and procedures that allow a speedy determination of whether materials meet those criteria.[68]

The burden is on school authorities to justify policies requiring administrative approval of unofficial (underground) student publications, but such prior review is not unconstitutional per se. In 1987, the Eighth Circuit rejected a vagueness challenge to a school board's policy requiring administrative review of unofficial student papers distributed at school and barring the distribution of material that advertises something unlawful or is disruptive, obscene, libelous, or pervasively indecent.[69] However, the court invalidated the part of the policy proscribing material that invades others' privacy, reasoning that such expression could not be curtailed unless it would subject the school to a libel suit under state law.

64. Guzick v. Drebus, 431 F.2d 594, 600 (6th Cir. 1970).

65. *See Blackwell,* 363 F.2d 749.

66. Southeastern Promotions v. Conrad, 420 U.S. 546, 559 (1975).

67. Scoville v. Bd. of Educ., 425 F.2d 10, 14 (7th Cir. 1970).

68. *See, e.g.,* Fujishima v. Bd. of Educ., 460 F.2d 1355 (7th Cir. 1972); Riseman v. Sch. Comm., 439 F.2d 148 (1st Cir. 1971).

69. Bystrom v. Fridley High Sch. Indep. Sch. Dist. No. 14, 822 F.2d 747 (8th Cir. 1987). Subsequently, disciplinary action was upheld against the students for distributing another unauthorized edition of their underground paper containing material that was disruptive, vulgar, and advocated violence against a teacher. Bystrom v. Fridley High Sch., 686 F. Supp. 1387 (D. Minn. 1987), *aff'd mem.,* 855 F.2d 855 (8th Cir. 1988). *See also* Muller v. Jefferson Lighthouse Sch., 98 F.3d 1530 (7th Cir. 1996) (upholding school district policy requiring copies of nonschool student literature to be given to the principal at least one day before distribution and allowing censorship of material that encourages disruption or illegal acts or is libelous, obscene, or insulting).

Several other courts have approved the *concept* of prior review of nonschool publications, but have found challenged policies constitutionally defective.[70] In decisions since *Hazelwood,* courts have continued to scrutinize prior review regulations applied to unofficial student publications, recognizing that the Constitution requires a high degree of specificity when imposing restraints on private expression. For example, the Ninth Circuit held that school authorities in a Washington school district could not bar distribution of a student paper produced off campus and could not subject the paper's content to prior review. Noting that "prior restraints are permissible in only the rarest of circumstances," the Ninth Circuit considered the policy subjecting *all* nonschool publications to prior review for the purpose of censorship to be overbroad.[71] Suspension of students for distributing the unauthorized paper at a school function was found to impair First Amendment rights.

Postexpression Discipline.   Although prior restraints on private expression may be legally vulnerable, courts are inclined to support disciplinary action and confiscation of materials *after* the expression has occurred, if it is considered unprotected (e.g., libelous or vulgar comments), fosters a disruption of the educational process, or encourages others to engage in dangerous or unlawful activity. For example, the Fourth Circuit upheld school administrators in impounding copies of a student publication that contained an advertisement for drug paraphernalia and in banning further distribution on school property.[72] The court emphasized that the literature was not subjected to predistribution approval; copies were impounded only after distribution began. The court held that the regulation authorizing the principal to halt the distribution of any publication encouraging actions that endanger students' health or safety was not unconstitutionally vague, and further ruled that school officials were not required to demonstrate that the harmful activity would lead to a substantial disruption.

Students often have been disciplined after the fact for distributing material that is abusive toward classmates or teachers. To illustrate, the Eighth Circuit found no impairment of speech rights in requiring a student, who distributed a letter that criticized the girl's varsity basketball coach, to apologize to the coach and teammates as a

---

70. *See, e.g.,* Quarterman v. Byrd, 453 F.2d 54 (4th Cir. 1971) (invalidating regulation that lacked criteria to assess the materials and procedural safeguards to ensure an expeditious review); Eisner v. Stamford Bd. of Educ., 440 F.2d 803 (2d Cir. 1971) (finding the challenged policy constitutionally defective in its lack of a definite time frame for the review and procedures as to how and to whom written materials were to be submitted).

71. Burch v. Barker, 861 F.2d 1149, 1155 (9th Cir. 1988). *See also* Romano v. Harrington, 725 F. Supp. 687 (E.D.N.Y. 1989) (holding that the First Amendment precludes school authorities from exercising editorial control over student newspapers that are not part of the curriculum).

72. Williams v. Spencer, 622 F.2d 1200 (4th Cir. 1980). The court further ruled that the school district's appeals procedures for students to contest the confiscation of literature were adequate and not unduly lengthy and noted that commercial speech is not entitled to the same protection as other types of speech. For a discussion of commercial expression, *see supra* text accompanying note 32.

condition of returning to the team.[73] The student's comments violated provisions of the student conduct handbook and the basketball handbook prohibiting disrespectful and insubordinate behavior.

Students also can be disciplined for advocating the destruction of school property in publications they distribute at school.[74] The Seventh Circuit recognized that a "reason to believe" or "reasonable forecast" standard can be applied to punish a student for such expression, even though the anticipated destruction of school property never materializes.[75] In this case, the student was expelled for one year for publishing and distributing at school an article in an underground paper that contained information about how to disable the school's computer system.

Courts consistently have condoned disciplinary action against students who have engaged in walkouts, boycotts, sit-ins, or other protests involving conduct that blocks hallways, damages property, causes students to miss class, or in other ways interferes with essential school activities.[76] An Indiana federal district court upheld disciplinary action against several students who attempted to incite a student walkout by distributing leaflets, although no disruption occurred.[77] But the Ninth Circuit overturned the suspension of students for wearing buttons containing the word *scab* in connection with a teachers' strike.[78] Recognizing that such expression is governed by *Tinker,* the court reasoned that students could not be disciplined for nondisruptive, private expression that was merely critical of school personnel or policies. However,

73. Wildman v. Marshalltown Sch. Dist., 249 F.3d 768 (8th Cir. 2001). *See also* Kicklighter v. Evans County Sch. Dist., 968 F. Supp. 712 (S.D. Ga. 1997), *aff'd mem.,* 140 F.3d 1043 (11th Cir. 1998) (finding no impairment of First Amendment rights in requiring student to apologize to the class for her truculent and disruptive behavior or face a 5-day suspension); Donovan v. Ritchie, 68 F.3d 14 (1st Cir. 1995) (upholding a student's 10-day suspension from school and exclusion from various extracurricular activities for distributing an abusive and vulgar document about classmates).

74. *See, e.g.,* Bd. of Educ. v. Comm'r of Educ., 690 N.E.2d 480 (N.Y. 1997) (upholding suspension of student for producing a publication that advocated various acts of insubordination including the destruction of school property).

75. Boucher v. Sch. Bd., 134 F.3d 821, 828 (7th Cir. 1997).

76. *See, e.g.,* Tate v. Bd. of Educ., 453 F.2d 975 (8th Cir. 1972); Farrell v. Joel, 437 F.2d 160 (2d Cir. 1971); Walker-Serrano v. Leonard, 168 F. Supp. 2d 332 (M.D. Penn. 2001). *But see* Boyd v. Bd. of Dirs., 612 F. Supp. 86 (E.D. Ark. 1985) (holding that students who walked out of school pep rally to protest the coach's alleged manipulation of the homecoming queen election were engaging in protected expression).

77. Dodd v. Rambis, 535 F. Supp. 23 (S.D. Ind. 1981). *See also* Wiemerslage v. Me. Township High Sch. Dist. 207, 29 F.3d 1149 (7th Cir. 1994) (upholding disciplinary action against a high school student who violated an anti-loitering rule; rejecting assertion that the rule was vague and impaired First Amendment rights of free speech and assembly).

78. Chandler v. McNinnville Sch. Dist., 978 F.2d 524 (9th Cir. 1992). *See also* Local Org. Comm., Million Man March v. Cook, 922 F. Supp. 1494, 1497 (D. Colo. 1996) (finding an unconstitutional prior restraint in a Denver school's denial of a permit for African American students to hold a rally at the high school after school hours as there was no evidence that the rally would threaten unlawful action; the prior restraint served as a "content-based colander," giving unfettered discretion to school authorities to determine what is in the best interests of the community).

the court acknowledged that vulgar, lewd, obscene, or plainly offensive buttons could be banned *even if* considered private expression.[79]

Students cannot be disciplined for materials distributed off school grounds unless the off-campus activity threatens the educational process. The Second Circuit found that school officials overstepped their authority by disciplining high school students who published a satirical magazine in their homes and sold it at a local store.[80] Although not addressing the question of whether distribution of the "vulgar" publication at school was permissible, the court enjoined school officials from punishing the student publishers for off-campus distribution of their magazine in the absence of evidence that the activity had an adverse impact on the school. The court concluded that to rule otherwise could subject students to school-imposed punishments for such behavior as watching X-rated movies on cable television in their own homes.

Anti-Harassment Policies.   A number of school districts have adopted policies prohibiting expression that constitutes verbal or physical harassment based on race, religion, color, national origin, gender, sexual orientation, disability, or other personal characteristics.[81] Until recently, these public school policies have not appeared vulnerable to First Amendment challenges, whereas "hate speech" policies have been struck down in municipalities and public higher education.[82] Public schools have been considered a special environment in terms of government restrictions on private expression, because of their purpose in educating America's youth and inculcating basic values, such as civility and respect for others with different backgrounds and beliefs.[83]

To illustrate, the Tenth Circuit upheld disciplinary action against a Kansas middle school student for drawing a Confederate flag during math class in violation of the school district's anti-harassment policy.[84] The student had been disciplined numerous times during the school year and had been accused of using racial slurs. The court was persuaded that the school district had reason to believe that the display of the Confed-

79. *See also* Karp v. Becken, 477 F.2d 171 (9th Cir. 1973) (upholding the confiscation of signs, protesting the nonrenewal of a teacher's contract, that were brought to school by students who intended to distribute them, but invalidating a student's suspension for engaging in this form of pure speech).

80. Thomas v. Bd. of Educ., 607 F.2d 1043 (2d Cir. 1979). *See also* the discussion of censorship of electronic student expression, *infra* text accompanying note 90.

81. *See, e.g.,* Fister v. Minn. New Country Sch., 149 F.3d 1187 (8th Cir. 1998) (upholding policy specifying that fighting, threatening language, other endangerment, or harassment would be grounds for suspension or expulsion); *supra* text accompanying note 50.

82. *See, e.g.,* R. A. V. v. St. Paul, 505 U.S. 377 (1992) (invalidating a St. Paul ordinance barring expression that could arouse anger or resentment on the basis of race, color, creed, religion, or gender); Dambrot v. Cent. Mich. Univ., 55 F.3d 1177 (6th Cir. 1995) (striking down the university's policy prohibiting harassing speech as overbroad and vague, but holding that the coach's use of the term "nigger" during locker-room talk was not protected by the First Amendment).

83. *See, e.g.,* Bethel Sch. Dist. v. Fraser, 478 U.S. 675 (1986); West v. Derby Unified Sch. Dist., 206 F.3d 1358 (10th Cir. 2000); Poling v. Murphy, 872 F.2d 757 (6th Cir. 1989).

84. *West,* 206 F.3d 1358.

erate flag might cause a disruption and interfere with the rights of others, as the school district had experienced some racial incidents related to the Confederate flag. In a case mentioned previously, the Eleventh Circuit applied a "flexible reasonableness standard," instead of the *Tinker* disruption standard, to assess student expression that intruded on the school's legitimate function of inculcating manners and habits of civility.[85] Holding that school authorities were not liable for disciplining a student who displayed a small Confederate flag to a group of friends during an outdoor lunch break, the court observed, "Racist and other hateful views can be expressed in a public forum. But an elementary school under its custodial responsibilities may restrict such speech that could crush a child's sense of self-worth."[86]

However, in 2001, the Third Circuit struck down a Pennsylvania school district's anti-harassment policy.[87] The controversy arose because the plaintiffs feared reprisals under the policy for voicing their religious views about moral issues, including the harmful effects of homosexuality. The policy defined the term *harassment,* provided specific examples of what would be considered unacceptable behavior (e.g., demeaning comments, graffiti, gestures), and set forth punishments for any member of the school community who violated the policy.[88] Finding the policy unconstitutionally overbroad, the Third Circuit reviewed existing anti-discrimination laws to refute the district court's conclusion that the policy simply curtailed expression already prohibited under such federal and state laws. The court found no evidence that the policy was necessary to advance the recognized compelling government interests in maintaining an orderly, nondisruptive school environment and protecting the rights of others, reasoning that the overbroad policy went beyond expression that could be curtailed under the *Tinker* disruption standard.

The same court in 2002 upheld a district's anti-harassment policy that was enacted to respond to incidents of race-based conflicts and was narrowly designed to reduce "racially divisive" expression. But, the court ordered the phrase banning speech that "creates ill will or hatred" to be eliminated as it reaches some protected expression.[89] The Third Circuit rulings have raised significant questions about the legal vulnerability of school districts' anti-harassment policies.

Electronic Expression. Another topic generating volatile controversies pertains to students' expression rights involving the Internet. These cases are particularly troublesome because students often prepare and disseminate the materials from their

---

85. Denno v. Sch. Bd., 218 F.3d 1267, 1272 (11th Cir. 2000), *supra* text accompanying note 18.

86. *Id.* at 1273.

87. Saxe v. State Coll. Area Sch. Dist. (SCASD), 240 F.3d 200 (3d Cir. 2001).

88. *SCASD Anti-Harassment Policy* (approved August 9, 1999), quoted in *Saxe,* 240 F.3d at 218, 220, 222. The court faulted the school district for addressing what constitutes prohibited expression in separate passages of the policy, which arguably provide different definitions of the banned speech. *Id.,* 240 F.3d at 215. Since the Third Circuit found the SCASD policy overbroad, it did not have to evaluate the plaintiffs' claim that the policy was also unconstitutionally vague. *Id.* at 214.

89. Sypniewski v. Warren Hills Reg'l Bd. of Educ., 307 F. 3d 243 (3d Cir. 2002).

homes, but their expression is immediately available to the entire school population and beyond. Courts have not spoken with a single voice on the First Amendment issues raised in these cases.

Students have prevailed in several challenges to disciplinary actions for web pages they have created at home. For example, a high school senior created a web site where he posted mock obituaries of students and allowed visitors to the site to vote as to who would "die" next.[90] After a television news story called it a "hit list" of people who would be killed at the school, the student removed the web site. The next day, the student was placed on emergency expulsion, which was modified to a five-day suspension. The student challenged the suspension, and the federal district court granted a preliminary injunction, reasoning that the student was likely to succeed on the merits of his claim. The court noted that the student's web site was not produced in connection with any class or school activity, and school personnel failed to substantiate that the material threatened or intended harm to anyone. Another student received a preliminary injunction blocking his suspension for using his home computer to create a home page criticizing school administrators, given the lack of evidence of any interference with school discipline.[91] And a Pennsylvania federal district court invalidated the suspension of a student for sending an e-mail message to friends that included a discourteous and rude "top 10 list" about the school's athletic director.[92] The student did not print the list or bring copies to school, although a friend who received his e-mail message did so.

In contrast, the Fifth Circuit in a case mentioned previously upheld a student's conviction for his Internet communication threatening to shoot and kill students at his high school. Finding that only general intent was required to constitute a threat in violation of federal law, the court upheld the student's conviction of knowingly and intentionally transmitting in interstate commerce a threat to injure another.[93] Also, the Pennsylvania Supreme Court upheld a student's expulsion because he created a web site ("Teacher Sux") on his home computer that contained derogatory comments about teachers and administrators and a graphic depiction of the algebra teacher's death. In this case, the court reasoned that the off-campus activities substantially disrupted the school, noting that the algebra teacher was so upset by the material that she had to take a leave of absence.[94] The key determinant in these cases appears to be whether the material created off campus has a direct and detrimental impact on the school.

Time, Place, and Manner Regulations.   Although private expression enjoys greater constitutional protection than does school-sponsored expression, the judiciary consistently has upheld reasonable policies regulating the time, place, and manner of private

90. Emmett v. Kent Sch. Dist. No. 415, 92 F. Supp. 2d 1088 (W.D. Wa. 2000).

91. Beussink v. Woodland R-IV Sch. Dist., 30 F. Supp. 2d 1175 (E.D. Mo. 1998).

92. Killion v. Franklin Reg'l Sch. Dist., 136 F. Supp. 2d 446 (W.D. Pa. 2001).

93. United States v. Morales, 272 F.3d 284 (5th Cir. 2001), *cert. denied,* 122 S. Ct. 2624 (2002).

94. J.S. v. Bethlehem Area Sch. Dist., 807 A.2d 847 (Pa. 2002).

expression. For example, students can be prohibited from voicing political and ideological views and distributing literature during instructional time. Also, school authorities can ban literature distribution near the doors of classrooms while class is in session, near building exits during fire drills, and on stairways when classes are changing, to ensure that the distribution of student publications does not impinge on other school activities.

Time, place, and manner regulations, however, must be reasonable, content neutral, and uniformly applied to expressive activities. School officials must provide students with specific guidelines as to when and where they can express their ideas and distribute materials. Moreover, literature distribution cannot be relegated to remote times or places either inside or outside the school building, and regulations must not inhibit any person's right to accept or reject literature that is distributed in accordance with the rules. Policies governing demonstrations should convey to students that they have the right to gather, distribute petitions, and express their ideas under nondisruptive circumstances.[95] If regulations do not precisely inform demonstrators of what behavior is prohibited, the judiciary may conclude that punishment cannot be imposed.

Future Directions. It appears likely that courts will continue to be called on to balance students' rights to express views and receive information with educators' duty to maintain an appropriate educational environment. Since the mid-1980s, the Supreme Court has broadened the category of unprotected student expression to include lewd, vulgar, and indecent expression and has given school authorities latitude to determine what belongs in these categories. The Supreme Court also has granted school authorities broad discretion to censor student expression that appears to represent the school, which further restricts the application of *Tinker*. Nonetheless, courts continue to rely on the *Tinker* disruption standard in evaluating student expression rights in connection with underground publications, anti-harassment policies, and postings on personal web pages.

Student-Initiated Clubs

Free expression and related association rights have arisen in connection with the formation and recognition of student clubs. Freedom of association is not specifically included among First Amendment protections, but the Supreme Court has held that associational rights are "implicit in the freedoms of speech, assembly, and petition."[96]

---

95. *See, e.g.,* Orin v. Barclay, 272 F.3d 1207 (9th Cir. 2001) (upholding the community college in granting permits for protests on the condition that students would not create a disturbance or interfere with campus activities, but striking down condition barring religious activities during protests); Godwin v. E. Baton Rouge Parish Sch. Bd., 408 So. 2d 1214 (La. 1981) (holding that prohibition on carrying signs, placards, or posters in the school board office building is a reasonable restriction on the place and manner of communication).

96. Healy v. James, 408 U.S. 169, 181 (1972).

The term *association* refers to the medium through which individuals seek to join with others to make the expression of their own views more meaningful.[97]

Public school pupils have not prevailed in asserting that free expression and association rights shield student-initiated social organizations or secret societies with exclusive membership usually determined by a vote of the clubs' members.[98] Courts have upheld public school officials in denying recognition of and prohibiting student membership in such secret societies.

In contrast, prohibitions on student-initiated organizations with *open* membership are vulnerable to First Amendment challenge. Even before Congress enacted the Equal Access Act (EAA), several courts had recognized that public school access policies for student meetings must be content neutral.[99] The EAA, enacted in 1984, codified these rulings by stipulating that if federally assisted secondary schools provide a limited open forum for noncurricular student groups to meet during noninstructional time, access cannot be denied based on the religious, political, philosophical, or other content of the groups' meetings.[100] The EAA was championed by the Religious Right, but its protection encompasses far more than student-initiated religious expression.[101]

As discussed in Chapter 2, the Supreme Court in 1990 rejected an Establishment Clause challenge to the EAA in *Board of Education of the Westside Community Schools v. Mergens.*[102] The Court reasoned that religious expression initiated by students during noninstructional time does not give the impression that the school endorses religion. The Court further held that if a federally assisted high school allows even one noncurricular group to use school facilities during noninstructional time, the EAA guarantees equal access for other noncurricular student groups. Of course, meetings that threaten a disruption can be barred.

Moreover, school authorities can decline to establish a limited forum for student-initiated meetings and thus confine school access to student organizations that are an extension of the curriculum, such as drama groups, language clubs, and athletic

---

97. *See* Griswold v. Connecticut, 381 U.S. 479, 483 (1965).

98. *See* Robinson v. Sacramento Unified Sch. Dist., 53 Cal. Rptr. 781 (Ct. App. 1966); Passel v. Fort Worth Indep. Sch. Dist., 453 S.W.2d 888 (Tex. Civ. App. 1970).

99. *See, e.g.,* Dixon v. Beresh, 361 F. Supp. 253 (E.D. Mich. 1973) (holding that school authorities would have to present clear evidence that particular clubs would produce a disruption of the educational process in order to deny recognition to *selected* student organizations).

100. 20 U.S.C. § 4071 (2002). *See* text accompanying note 97, Chapter 2.

101. A limited forum is defined more broadly under the EAA than under the First Amendment. The Supreme Court emphasized in *Hazelwood,* 484 U.S. 260, 267 (1988), that a public school activity becomes a limited forum for First Amendment purposes only through the *express intent* of school authorities, but such intent is not necessary to trigger the EAA.

102. 496 U.S. 226 (1990). The Court rejected the contention that only noncurricular, *advocacy* groups are protected under the EAA. *See also* Student Coalition for Peace v. Lower Merion Sch. Dist., 776 F.2d 431 (3d Cir. 1985), *on remand,* 633 F. Supp. 1040 (E.D. Pa. 1986) (finding that the Student Coalition for Peace had to be granted access to the school's limited forum during noninstructional time to hold its peace exposition; also recognizing students' private right to initiate suits to compel EAA compliance).

teams. Controversies have surfaced over what constitutes a curriculum-related group since the EAA is triggered only if noncurriculum student groups are allowed school access during noninstructional time. For example, a California federal district court ruled that a school board had established a limited forum by allowing some noncurriculum student groups to meet during noninstructional time and thus could not discriminate against the Gay-Straight Alliance.[103] The board raised a novel argument, claiming that the club at issue was not protected under the EAA because it was related to the sex education curriculum, which is governed by district instructional guidelines. Rejecting this argument, the court held that the board cannot foreclose access to its limited forum "merely by labeling a group curriculum-related."[104]

Even if agreed that a secondary school has *not* established a limited forum, it still cannot exert viewpoint discrimination against particular curriculum-related groups. After the Salt Lake City School Board adopted a policy denying school access to all noncurriculum student groups, the federal district court rejected the Gay-Straight Alliance's EAA petition to hold meetings in a public high school.[105] The court concluded that the school no longer had a forum for noncurriculum student groups to meet. However, this did not end the controversy, as the alliance asserted that it was related to the curriculum and should be treated like other curriculum-related groups. In 1999, the federal court held that there were genuine issues regarding whether the school had an unwritten policy excluding all gay-positive viewpoints from student club meetings.[106] The court subsequently enjoined school authorities from denying access to a student club designed to address issues related to the school's history and sociology courses, even though the club's major focus was on the rights of gay, lesbian, bisexual, and transgendered persons.[107]

Controversies over school access for community groups focus on the Free Speech Clause rather than the EAA, as the latter provision pertains only to student groups in secondary schools. The Supreme Court has delivered several significant decisions holding that schools cannot exert viewpoint discrimination when they open facilities to meetings of community groups, even groups that might target students.[108] School access for Boy Scouts has been controversial following the Supreme Court's

---

103. Colin v. Orange Unified Sch. Dist., 83 F. Supp. 2d 1135 (C.D. Cal. 2000).

104. *Id.* at 1146.

105. E. High Gay/Straight Alliance v. Bd. of Educ., 30 F. Supp. 2d 1356 (D. Utah 1998).

106. E. High Gay/Straight Alliance v. Bd. of Educ., 81 F. Supp. 2d 1166 (D. Utah 1999).

107. The school district argued that it denied the club's application because its subject matter was narrowed to a particular group, but the court reasoned that the district's "no narrowing of viewpoints" policy had been inconsistently applied in assessing curriculum-related student clubs. E. High Sch. Prism Club v. Seidel, 95 F. Supp. 2d 1239 (D. Utah 2000). *See also* Schoick v. Saddleback Valley Unified Sch. Dist., 104 Cal. Rptr.2d 562 (Ct. App. 2001) (finding triable issues pertaining to whether all clubs meeting at a high school were curriculum related, which would preclude meetings of the Fellowship of Christian Athletes during noninstructional time); text accompanying note 103, Chapter 2.

108. *See, e.g.,* Good News Club v. Milford Cent. Sch., 533 U.S. 98 (2001); Lamb's Chapel v. Ctr. Moriches Union Free Sch. Dist., 508 U.S. 384 (1993); text accompanying notes 106–111, Chapter 2.

decision that allows this organization to deny homosexuals the opportunity to be group leaders,[109] because such discrimination based on sexual orientation conflicts with some school districts' policies. A Florida federal district court held that a school board's prohibition on the Boy Scouts using school facilities entailed unconstitutional viewpoint discrimination.[110] The court reasoned that the school's anti-discrimination policy applied to members of the school community and not to private organizations using the school during a limited forum for expression after school hours.

Student Appearance

Fads and fashions in hairstyles and clothing have regularly evoked litigation as educators have attempted to exert some control over pupil appearance. Courts have been called on to weigh students' interests in selecting their attire and hairstyle against school authorities' interests in preventing disruptions and promoting school objectives.

Hairstyle

Substantial judicial activity in the 1970s focused on school regulations governing the length of male students' hair. The Supreme Court, however, refused to hear appeals of these cases, and federal circuit courts of appeal reached different conclusions in determining the legality of policies governing student hairstyle. In the First, Fourth, Seventh, and Eighth Circuits, appellate courts declared that hairstyle regulations impaired students' First Amendment freedom of symbolic expression, the Fourteenth Amendment right to personal liberty, or the right to privacy included in the Ninth Amendment's unenumerated rights.[111] In contrast, appellate courts in the Third, Fifth, Sixth, Ninth, and Tenth Circuits upheld grooming policies pertaining to pupil hairstyle, finding no constitutional rights at stake.[112] In sanctioning a hair-length restriction, the Fifth Circuit concluded that it constituted a "reasonable means of furthering the school board's undeniable interest in teaching hygiene, instilling discipline, asserting authority, and compelling uniformity."[113]

---

109. Boy Scouts of Am. v. Dale, 530 U.S. 640 (2000) (upholding restriction barring homosexuals from being Boy Scouts group leaders as constitutionally protected freedom of association).

110. Boy Scouts of Am. v. Till, 136 F. Supp. 2d 1295 (S.D. Fla. 2001). *See supra* text accompanying note 81 for a discussion of controversies over school districts' anti-harassment policies.

111. *See* Massie v. Henry, 455 F.2d 779 (4th Cir. 1972); Bishop v. Colaw, 450 F.2d 1069 (8th Cir. 1971); Richards v. Thurston, 424 F.2d 1281 (1st Cir. 1970); Breen v. Kahl, 419 F.2d 1034 (7th Cir. 1969).

112. *See* Zeller v. Donegal Sch. Dist., 517 F.2d 600 (3d Cir. 1975), *overruling* Stull v. Sch. Bd. of W. Beaver Jr.-Sr. High Sch., 459 F.2d 339 (3d Cir. 1972); King v. Saddleback Jr. Coll. Dist., 445 F.2d 932 (9th Cir. 1971); Freeman v. Flake, 448 F.2d 258 (10th Cir. 1971); Jackson v. Dorrier, 424 F.2d 213 (6th Cir. 1970); Ferrell v. Dallas Indep. Sch. Dist., 392 F.2d 697 (5th Cir. 1968).

113. Domico v. Rapides Parish Sch. Bd., 675 F.2d 100, 102 (5th Cir. 1982). *See also* Stevenson v. Bd. of Educ., 426 F.2d 1154 (5th Cir. 1970) (upholding the school board's "good grooming" policy requiring students to be clean shaven).

If school officials have offered health or safety reasons for grooming regulations, such as requiring hair nets, shower caps, and other hair restraints intended to protect students from injury or to promote sanitation, the policies typically have been upheld. For instance, the Third Circuit ruled that a school board acted properly when it required a student to cut his hair because the student's long, unclean hair was a health hazard in the school cafeteria.[114] Furthermore, restrictions on male students' hairstyles at vocational schools have been upheld to create a positive image for potential employers visiting the school for recruitment purposes.[115] Special grooming regulations have been endorsed as conditions of participation in extracurricular activities for legitimate health or safety reasons,[116] and, in some instances, to enhance the school's image.[117] Of course, students can be disciplined for hairstyles that cause a disruption, such as hair groomed or dyed in a manner that distracts classmates from educational activities.

But hairstyle regulations cannot be arbitrary or devoid of an educational rationale. For example, the Fifth Circuit affirmed a lower court's ruling that enjoined a school district's restriction on male students' hair length because school officials failed to show that the restriction was a valid means to maintain discipline, foster respect for authority, or project an appropriate public image.[118] The court concluded that long hair worn by Native American students was protected expression that did not disrupt the educational process.

Whether different hair-length restrictions can be applied to male and female students has not been judicially clarified. In two cases, the Texas Supreme Court rejected claims that restrictions applied only to the length of male students' hair constituted gender discrimination, refusing to use the state constitution to micro-manage public schools.[119] Also, a Mississippi federal court rejected a gender discrimination challenge to a hair-length restriction, noting that federal law does not require all gender distinctions to be erased.[120] However, an Ohio federal court reasoned that long-haired

114. Gere v. Stanley, 453 F.2d 205 (3d Cir. 1971).

115. *See, e.g.,* Bishop v. Cermenaro, 355 F. Supp. 1269 (D. Mass. 1973); Farrell v. Smith, 310 F. Supp. 732 (D. Me. 1970).

116. *See, e.g.,* Long v. Zopp, 476 F.2d 180 (4th Cir. 1973) (recognizing that legitimate health and safety concerns might justify a restriction on hair length during football season, but finding no justification for denying a letter to a student who violated such a restriction after football season ended); Menora v. Ill. High Sch. Ass'n, 683 F.2d 1030 (7th Cir. 1982) (holding that Jewish basketball players had no First Amendment right to wear yarmulkes fastened by bobby pins in violation of the state high school association rule forbidding players from wearing hats or other headgear during games for safety reasons).

117. *See, e.g.,* Davenport v. Randolph County Bd. of Educ., 730 F.2d 1395 (11th Cir. 1984) (finding neither arbitrary nor unreasonable a coach's requirement that student athletes, as representatives of the school, must be clean shaven).

118. Ala. and Coushatta Tribes v. Trs., 817 F. Supp. 1319 (E.D. Tex. 1993), *remanded,* 20 F.3d 469 (5th Cir. 1994).

119. Bd. of Trs. v. Toungate, 958 S.W.2d 365 (Tex. 1997); Barber v. Colo. Indep. Sch. Dist., 901 S.W.2d 447 (Tex. 1995); *infra* note 126.

120. Trent v. Perritt, 391 F. Supp. 171 (S.D. Miss. 1975).

male students could not be denied band participation if long-haired female students were not excluded.[121]

Attire

Although public school students' hair length has subsided as a major subject of litigation, other appearance fads have become controversial as students have asserted a First Amendment right to express themselves through their attire at school. Some courts have distinguished attire restrictions from hair regulations because clothes, unlike hair length, can be changed after school. Even in situations where students' rights to govern their appearance have been recognized, the judiciary has noted that attire can be regulated if immodest, disruptive, unsanitary, or contrary to the school's objectives.

Dress Codes.   Under the principle established in *Fraser,* lewd and vulgar expression is outside the protective arm of the First Amendment. Thus, indecent attire can be curtailed applying *Fraser,* regardless of whether the attire would meet the *Tinker* test of threatening a disruption. For example, an Idaho federal district court held that a school could prevent a student from wearing a t-shirt that depicted three high school administrators drunk on school grounds.[122] In finding the shirt intolerable, the court noted that the student had no free expression right to portray administrators in a fashion that would undermine their authority and compromise the school's efforts to educate students about the harmful effects of alcohol.

A Virginia middle school student was unsuccessful in challenging her one-day suspension for refusing to change her shirt printed with the words *Drugs Suck.* [123] The court reasoned that regardless of whether *suck* has a sexual meaning, its use is offensive and vulgar to many people, including some middle school students. Citing *Fraser,* the court found the disciplinary action permissible "to regulate middle school children's language and channel their expression into socially appropriate speech."[124] More recently, a Georgia federal district court upheld the suspension of a student who wore a t-shirt with the phrases *kids have civil rights too* and *even adults lie.*[125] The court ruled that wearing the shirt was the last incident in a series of disruptions justifying the student's suspension.

---

121. Cordova v. Chonko, 315 F. Supp. 953 (N.D. Ohio 1970). *See also* Sims v. Colfax Cmty. Sch. Dist., 307 F. Supp. 485 (S.D. Iowa 1970) (ruling in favor of a female student who challenged a school rule prohibiting both males and females from wearing their hair longer than one finger width above the eyebrow).

122. Gano v. Sch. Dist. 411, 674 F. Supp. 796 (D. Idaho 1987).

123. Broussard v. Sch. Bd., 801 F. Supp. 1526 (E.D. Va. 1992) (rejecting also the student's due process claim, because sufficient notice was given that wearing inappropriate attire would result in suspension).

124. *Id.* at 1537.

125. Smith v. Greene County Sch. Dist., 100 F. Supp. 2d 1354 (M.D. Ga. 2000).

Several courts have upheld dress codes that prohibit male students from wearing earrings, rejecting the assertion that jewelry restrictions must be applied equally to male and female students. In an illustrative case, an Illinois federal district court found the school district's ban on male students' wearing earrings rationally related to the school's legitimate objective of inhibiting the influence of gangs, as earrings were used to convey gang-related messages.[126] Also, an Indiana appeals court upheld a school district's ban on male students' wearing earrings.[127] Finding no gang-related justification for the ban applied to elementary students, the appeals court nonetheless upheld the policy as advancing legitimate educational objectives and community values supporting different attire standards for males and females.

In a New Mexico case, the federal district court upheld a student's suspension for wearing "sagging" pants in violation of the school's dress code.[128] The student did not convince the court that his attire conveyed an African American cultural message. Instead, the court noted that "sagging" pants could as easily be associated with gang affiliation or gang "wannabes," or it simply could reflect a fashion trend among adolescents. Also, an Ohio federal court upheld the removal of two students from the high school prom for dressing in clothing of the opposite sex. The court reasoned that the school board's dress regulations were "reasonably related to the valid educational purposes of teaching community values and maintaining school discipline."[129]

More recently, the Sixth Circuit upheld a school district's decision to prohibit students from wearing Marilyn Manson t-shirts. The appeals court agreed with school authorities that the shirts were offensive, promoted destructive conduct, and were counter to the school's efforts to denounce drugs and promote human dignity and democratic ideals.[130] The court reiterated that schools can prohibit student expression that is inconsistent with its basic educational mission, even though such speech might be protected by the First Amendment outside the school environment.

The same court in 2001 upheld a restrictive student dress code devised by a Kentucky school-based council. The code limited the colors, materials, and type of clothing that could be worn, and barred logos, shorts, cargo pants, jeans, and other specific items. The council justified the restrictions based on evidence of gang symbols in the school and student conflicts over clothing. Finding no intent to suppress free speech, the Sixth Circuit affirmed the lower court's acceptance of the school's safety justifi-

126. Olesen v. Bd. of Educ., 676 F. Supp. 820 (N.D. Ill. 1987). *See also* Barber v. Colo. Indep. Sch. Dist., 901 S.W.2d 447 (Tex. 1995) (upholding earring and hair-length restrictions applied only to male students).

127. Hines v. Caston Sch. Corp., 651 N.E.2d 330 (Ind. App. Ct. 1995), *petition to transfer denied,* No. 25A05-9401-CV-22 (Ind. Feb. 21, 1996). *See also* Jones v. W. T. Henning Elem. Sch., 721 So. 2d 530 (La. App. 1998) (upholding prohibition on male students wearing earrings as reasonable to reflect prevailing community values and avoid disruption).

128. Bivens *ex rel.* Green v. Albuquerque Pub. Schs., 899 F. Supp. 556 (D.N.M. 1995), *aff'd mem.,* 131 F.3d 151 (10th Cir. 1997).

129. Harper v. Edgewood Bd. of Educ., 655 F. Supp. 1353, 1355 (S.D. Ohio 1987).

130. Boroff v. Van Wert City Bd. of Educ., 220 F.3d 465 (6th Cir. 2000), *cert. denied,* 532 U.S. 920 (2001).

cations for the dress code.[131] An Illinois court also upheld a restrictive dress code that confined student clothing to all black, all white, or a combination of the two, and prohibited logos, patches, imprinted words, and designs on clothing.[132] Noting the opportunity to opt out of the dress code for religious reasons, the court held that the restriction on student expression in the school's nonpublic forum is justified by pedagogical concerns that include maintaining an orderly environment and inculcating civility and traditional moral, social, and political norms.

However, as with hairstyle regulations, school authorities must have an educational rationale for attire restrictions, such as preventing class disruptions or curtailing gang behavior. The Third Circuit struck down a prohibition on wearing t-shirts with the comedian Jeff Foxworthy's "red-neck sayings," as not sufficiently linked to racial harassment or other disruptive activity.[133] A California federal district court found that a dress code prohibiting clothing identifying any college or professional sports team violated free speech rights of elementary and middle school students, as the rule was not tied to an educational rationale.[134] Also, a Texas federal district court found overly broad a dress code prohibiting students from wearing gang-related apparel. Two students who wore rosaries outside their shirts were advised that they were in violation of the policy, and the court held that wearing rosaries was a well-recognized form of religious expression protected by the First Amendment. Since the term *gang related* was ambiguous and not defined, the policy was also held to be void for vagueness.[135]

In addition, dress codes must not discriminate on the content of students' messages or be discriminatorily enforced. The Sixth Circuit ordered a school district to reconsider suspensions of two students who wore t-shirts with a country singer on the front and the Confederate flag on the back and who refused to turn the shirts inside out or to go home and change.[136] School authorities asserted that the shirts violated the school's dress code prohibiting clothing or emblems that contain slogans or words depicting alcohol or tobacco or have illegal, immoral, or racist implications. Finding evidence that the dress code had been selectively enforced, the court reasoned that any restriction on private expression cannot be enforced in a content-specific manner.

131. Long v. Bd. of Educ., 121 F. Supp. 2d 621 (W.D. Ky. 2000), *aff'd mem.,* 21 Fed. Appx. 252 (6th Cir. 2001). *See also* Byars v. City of Waterbury, 795 A.2d 630 (Conn. Super. Ct. 2001) (finding restrictive school dress code rationally related to reducing disruptions and loss of instructional time).

132. Vines v. Zion Sch. Dist., No. O1 C 7455, 2002 U.S. Dist. LEXIS 382 (N.D. Ill. Jan. 10, 2002).

133. Sypniewski v. Warren Hills Reg'l Bd. of Educ., 307 F.3d 243 (3d Cir. 2002); *supra* text accompanying note 89.

134. Jeglin v. San Jacinto Unified Sch. Dist., 827 F. Supp. 1459 (C.D. Cal. 1993) (finding insufficient gang influence at the elementary and middle school levels, but holding that the evidence of high school gangs, although not conclusive, satisfied the school's burden in justifying the restriction at the high school level).

135. Chalifoux v. New Caney Indep. Sch. Dist., 976 F. Supp. 659 (S.D. Tex. 1997).

136. Castorina v. Madison County Sch. Bd., 246 F.3d 536 (6th Cir. 2001). *See also* Chambers v. Babbitt, 145 F. Supp. 2d 1068 (D. Minn. 2001) (granting a temporary order allowing a student to wear a sweatshirt bearing the message "straight pride" in the absence of any disruption). For a discussion of challenges to anti-harassment policies, *see supra* text accompanying note 81.

Thus, the case was remanded to determine if the students' First Amendment rights had been violated.

Student Uniforms. Some student attire controversies since the 1990s have focused on school board policies specifying uniforms for students, and the line is not always clear between restrictive dress codes and student uniforms.[137] Voluntary as well as mandatory student uniforms are gaining popularity in large-city school districts, including Baltimore, Chicago, Houston, Los Angeles, Miami, New Orleans, New York City, and Philadelphia.[138] Advocates assert that student uniforms eliminate gang-related attire, reduce violence and socioeconomic distinctions, and improve school climate by placing the emphasis on academics rather than fashion fads.

The Fifth Circuit has rejected challenges to uniform policies in Louisiana and Texas school districts. In both cases the court recognized that attire can communicate a message and thus may be entitled to First Amendment protection. Nonetheless, the appellate court reasoned that the student uniform policies were justified by substantial government interests unrelated to suppressing expression. In the Louisiana case, evidence was presented that test scores increased and disciplinary problems decreased after the uniform policy was adopted. The court rejected the parents' claim that the uniforms posed a financial burden, noting that the uniforms were inexpensive and a donation program was available for those who could not afford them.[139] In the Texas case, the school district required students to wear specified types and colors of shirts or blouses with blue or khaki pants, shorts, skirts, or jumpers.[140] Parents could apply for their children to be exempt from wearing the uniform based on philosophical or religious objections or medical necessity. The court found only a minimal intrusion on students' rights and concluded that the uniform policy served the legitimate educational purposes of improving safety, decreasing socioeconomic tensions, increasing attendance, and reducing dropout rates. The court rejected the parents' assertion that the policy violates their Fourteenth Amendment right to direct the upbringing of their children and found no impairment of the religion clauses as the policy includes a procedure for granting religious exemptions.

After the New York City school board adopted a citywide uniform policy for children in elementary schools, a father brought suit claiming that if his child took advantage of the "opt out" provision, the child would "stick out" in violation of the child's rights.[141] But the Second Circuit affirmed the federal district court's conclu-

137. *See supra* text accompanying notes 131, 132, as these dress codes might be viewed as prescribing student uniforms.

138. *See* National Association of Elementary School Principals, *Backgrounder on Public School Uniforms* (Alexandria, VA: NAESP, 1998).

139. Canady v. Bossier Parish Sch. Bd., 240 F.3d 437 (5th Cir. 2001).

140. Littlefield v. Forney Indep. Sch. Dist., 268 F.3d 275 (5th Cir. 2001) (also prohibiting clothing made of specific materials, certain types of shoes, and any clothing suggesting gang affiliation).

141. Lipsman v. New York City Bd. of Educ., No. 98 Civ. 2008 (SHS), 1999 U.S. Dist. LEXIS 10591, *11 (S.D.N.Y. July 14, 1999), *aff'd,* 13 Fed. Appx. 13 (2d Cir. 2000). *See also* Mitchell v. McCall, 143 So. 2d 629, 632 (Ala. 1962) (finding no impairment of rights because the exempted child appears as a "speckled bird" to classmates; exercising the right to be treated differently is subject to such inconveniences).

sion that the opt-out provision adequately addressed parents' rights to direct the upbringing of their children. Courts have not been persuaded that any rights are violated because a stigma is associated with exercising the First Amendment right to be exempt from certain requirements.

Although federal appellate courts have differed in their interpretations of constitutional protections regarding appearance regulations, school officials would be wise to ensure that they have a legitimate educational justification for any grooming or dress code. Policies designed to protect students' health and safety, reduce violence and discipline problems, and enhance learning usually will be endorsed. Given the current student interest in tatoos, body piercing, and other fashion fads and school authorities' concerns about attire linked to gangs and violence, continued legal controversies over student appearance in public schools seem assured.

Extracurricular Activities

School-sponsored activities that are not part of the regular academic program have generated considerable litigation. Almost every secondary school offers some extracurricular activities, and about 80 percent of high school students participate in at least one activity. In most states, a not-for-profit private organization regulates interscholastic sports and often has jurisdiction over other competitive activities among private and public schools. The Supreme Court ruled in 2001 that where such associations are extensively entwined with state school officials, they are considered state actors.[142] Thus, they are subject to constitutional restrictions on their activities and can be liable for constitutional violations.

It is clear that once a state provides public education, students cannot be denied attendance without due process of law,[143] but this state-created property right to attend school does not extend to extracurricular activities. The prevailing view is that conditions can be attached to extracurricular participation, because such participation is a privilege rather than a right.[144] Even though school authorities may not be required by

---

142. Brentwood Acad. v. Tenn. Secondary Sch. Athletic Ass'n, 531 U.S. 288 (2001).

143. *See* Goss v. Lopez, 419 U.S. 565 (1975); text with note 54, Chapter 7.

144. *See, e.g.,* James v. Tallahassee High Sch., 104 F.3d 372 (11th Cir. 1996) (recognizing that students do not have a property right to participate in extracurricular activities, the court dismissed a cheerleader's challenge to the sponsor's decision to choose head cheerleaders even though the student handbook indicated that the respective squads would select their leaders); Angstadt v. Midd-West Sch. Dist., 182 F. Supp. 2d 435 (M.D. Pa. 2002) (holding that a cyber student had no property right to participate in the school district's interscholastic basketball program); Ryan v. Cal. Interscholastic Fed'n, 114 Cal. Rptr. 2d 798 (Ct. App. 2001), *review denied,* No. S104111, 2002 Cal. LEXIS 2480 (Cal. April 10, 2002) (finding participation in interscholastic athletics a privilege, not a right, in upholding eight-semester rule). *But see* Butler v. Oak Creek-Franklin Sch. Dist., 172 F. Supp. 2d 1102 (E.D. Wis. 2001) (finding reasonable likelihood that there was a property interest to continue athletic participation, necessitating procedural due process before imposing a one-year suspension on a student's eligibility).

the Fourteenth Amendment to provide due process when denying students extracurricular participation, a hearing for the students to defend their actions is always advisable. And if school boards have established rules for suspending or expelling students from extracurricular activities, courts will require compliance.[145]

The remainder of this section focuses on various features of extracurricular activities that have generated legal activity. Allegations of discrimination based on disabilities, gender, and marital status in connection with such activities are discussed in Chapters 5 and 6.

Attendance, Training, and Recruitment Regulations

Schools frequently condition extracurricular participation on students attending practice sessions and games or performances. For example, the Fourth Circuit rejected a parent's challenge to her son's removal from the high school band for missing a required band trip.[146] Courts also have recognized that school officials should be given latitude in establishing training and conduct standards for high school athletes to foster discipline. The judiciary has upheld the suspension of students from interscholastic athletic competition for violating regulations prohibiting smoking and drinking, even if the regulations apply to athletes' off-campus, off-season conduct. In an illustrative case, an Illinois court rejected a student's challenge to his suspension from participating in the entire football season because of a violation of the school's zero-tolerance policy pertaining to alcohol use.[147] In general, courts will not interfere with attendance requirements or training regulations simply because they appear harsh; students voluntarily subject themselves to the regulations as a condition of participation. The judiciary is reluctant to invalidate disciplinary action for rule violations unless the rules are clearly arbitrary, discriminatory, or excessive.

State athletic associations place various restrictions on member schools in terms of recruiting athletes. The Sixth Circuit in 2001 upheld the Tennessee Secondary School Athletic Association's regulation of member schools' communication with prospective athletes from feeder schools. The court found no impairment of a private school's expression rights in the imposition of penalties for the school's violation of the regulation. The court reasoned that the content-neutral regulation

---

145. *See, e.g.,* Ferguson v. Phoenix-Talent Sch. Dist., 19 P.3d 943 (Or. Ct. App. 2001) (recognizing that disciplinary rules pertaining to extracurricular activities must be uniformly applied, but finding that the rule placing a four-week limit on suspensions from extracurricular participation for drug offenses did not apply to the removal of a student as class president for drug possession).

146. Bernstein v. Menard, 728 F.2d 252 (4th Cir. 1984) (finding the band director's conduct reasonable, the court held that the lawsuit was frivolous and awarded attorneys' fees to the defendant school district). *See also* Keller v. Gardner Cmty. Consol. Grade Sch. Dist. 72C, 552 F. Supp. 512 (N.D. Ill. 1982) (upholding regulation that students missing a practice session cannot play in the next game; the court noted that catechism classes were available at a different locale that did not conflict with practice sessions).

147. Jordan v. O'Fallon Township High Sch. Dist., 706 N.E.2d 137 (Ill. App. Ct. 1999).

and penalties were justified to guard against schools using undue influence to attract athletes.[148]

Restrictions on Eligibility

Courts have also allowed school authorities flexibility in formulating eligibility rules for extracurricular activities. Schools can impose conditions such as skill prerequisites for athletic teams, academic and leadership criteria for honor societies, and musical proficiency for band and choral groups. Members of athletic teams and other extra-curricular groups often are selected through a competitive process, and students have no inherent right to be chosen. Selection can be based on subjective judgments, and as long as fair procedures are uniformly applied, courts will not disturb such decisions.[149]

One of the most obvious conditions is that students can be required to have physical examinations and be in good physical health to participate on athletic teams. The Supreme Court also has upheld policies requiring student athletes and those par-ticipating in other extracurricular activities to submit to random urinalysis as a condi-tion of participation.[150] As addressed in Chapter 6, the imposition of additional health restrictions on athletes with disabilities has generated litigation. Given federal and state protections of such children, school authorities would be wise to have evidence of legitimate health or safety risks before excluding specific children with disabilities from athletic teams.[151]

Courts generally approve residency requirements as conditions of interscholas-tic competition. To prevent schools, including private schools,[152] from recruiting stu-dent athletes, most state athletic associations prohibit involvement in interscholastic competition for one year after a change in a student's school without a change in the

---

148. Brentwood Acad. v. Tenn. Secondary Sch. Athletic Ass'n, 262 F.3d 543 (6th Cir. 2001), *cert. denied,* 122 S. Ct. 1439 (2002) (remanding the case to the district court to determine if the recruiting rule is narrowly tailored to the athletic association's interests). *See also* NCAA v. Lasege, 53 S.W.3d 77 (Ky. 2001) (holding that high school and collegiate athletic association rules will not be invalidated unless the associations act arbitrarily and capriciously toward student athletes).

149. *See, e.g.,* Pfeiffer v. Marion Ctr. Area Sch. Dist., 917 F.2d 779 (3d Cir. 1990) (holding that a pregnant student could be dismissed from the National Honor Society for engaging in premarital sex in viola-tion of the Society's standards); Bull v. Dardanelle Pub. Sch. Dist. No. 15, 745 F. Supp. 1455 (E.D. Ark. 1990) (holding that students have no constitutional right to run for student council; the require-ment that teachers approve council candidates was not vague); Karnstein v. Pewaukee Sch. Bd., 557 F. Supp. 565 (E.D. Wis. 1983) (ruling that students do not have a property right to be selected for the National Honor Society).

150. Bd. of Educ. v. Earls, 122 S. Ct. 2559 (2002); Vernonia Sch. Dist. 47J v. Acton, 515 U.S. 646 (1995). For a discussion of this topic, *see* text accompanying note 191, Chapter 7.

151. *See, e.g.,* Doe v. Woodford County Bd. of Educ., 213 F.3d 921 (6th Cir. 2000) (upholding exclusion of a student with hemophilia and hepatitis B from athletic participation that would put him at increased risk of physical injury). *See* text accompanying note 103, Chapter 6.

152. *See* Zeiler v. Ohio High Sch. Athletic Ass'n, 755 F.2d 934 (6th Cir. 1985) (upholding the associa-tion's rule barring from interscholastic competition those students whose parents live in another state as not impairing rights of Michigan residents who attended private high schools in the Toledo area).

parents' address. Several federal appellate courts have ruled that such residency requirements are rationally related to legitimate government interests and do not place an impermissible burden on students' rights to travel or on their freedom of family association.[153]

Some courts, however, have ordered exceptions where a student's welfare has necessitated the move. For example, the Seventh Circuit concluded that the state athletic association acted arbitrarily and capriciously when it declared a student ineligible for athletic competition for one year after he moved from his divorced father's home to his mother's home in another school district.[154] An Indiana court similarly found that a student qualified for a hardship exception where a change in financial circumstances caused him to transfer from a private to a public school.[155] Furthermore, if there are compelling medical reasons necessitating a student's change of residence or the change is necessitated for the student to receive special education services, courts will order exceptions to transfer restrictions.[156] A few courts have even questioned whether such residency requirements for transfer students serve their intended purpose (i.e., deterring the recruitment of high school athletes), and they have recognized the negative consequences for students whose moves are not athletically motivated.[157] Nonetheless, most residency requirements continue to receive judicial endorsement.

Courts also usually uphold age restrictions on extracurricular participation in order to equalize competitive conditions. In a typical case, the Supreme Court of Oklahoma upheld a rule barring students who reach their nineteenth birthday by September 1 from participating in interscholastic athletics as fair and reasonably related to legitimate state interests. The court agreed with the state defendants that older and more mature athletes could pose a threat to the health and safety of younger students and

153. *See, e.g.,* Niles v. Univ. Interscholastic League, 715 F.2d 1027 (5th Cir. 1983); *In re* United States *ex rel.* Mo. State High Sch. Activities Ass'n, 682 F.2d 147 (8th Cir. 1982). *See also* Ryan v. Cal. Interscholastic Fed'n, 114 Cal. Rptr. 2d 798 (Ct. App. 2001) (upholding residency requirement for student transferring from another country).

154. Crane v. Ind. High Sch. Athletic Ass'n, 975 F.2d 1315 (7th Cir. 1992). *See also* Crocker v. Tenn. Secondary Sch. Athletic Ass'n, 735 F. Supp. 753 (M.D. Tenn. 1990) (holding that a student with learning disabilities who transferred from a private school to a public school to receive special education could not be denied extracurricular participation for one year).

155. Ind. High Sch. Athletic Ass'n v. Durham, 748 N.E.2d 404 (Ind. Ct. App. 2001).

156. *See, e.g.,* Doe v. Marshall, 459 F. Supp. 1190 (S.D. Tex. 1978), *vacated as moot,* 622 F.2d 118 (5th Cir. 1980) (granting an injunction to halt enforcement of the interscholastic league's transfer policy against a student with severe psychiatric difficulties who was taken out of his family home and placed with his maternal grandparents in another school district on his therapist's recommendation, but ruling on appeal that the case was moot because the student had continued to play football throughout high school and had graduated).

157. *See, e.g.,* Ind. High Sch. Athletic Ass'n v. Carlberg, 661 N.E.2d 833 (Ind. Ct. App. 1996) (enjoining application of transfer rule to student who transferred for academic and financial reasons); Sullivan v. Univ. Interscholastic League, 616 S.W.2d 170 (Tex. 1981) (invalidating transfer rule because it did not provide a means to rebut the presumption of recruiting athletes).

that the rule eliminated the possibility of "red shirting" athletes.[158] Similarly, a number of courts have endorsed rules limiting athletic eligibility to eight consecutive semesters or four years after completion of eighth grade.[159] However, several courts have enjoined state athletic associations from enforcing maximum age and eight-semester requirements where the students in question had been required to repeat courses or withdraw from school for a term because of extensive illnesses.[160] Also, as discussed in Chapter 6, the application of such eligibility requirements to students with disabilities has been controversial.[161]

A nationwide trend among school districts is to condition extracurricular participation on satisfactory academic performance. Several states through legislation or administrative rules have adopted statewide "no pass, no play" provisions, and these measures consistently have been upheld. A Texas provision requiring students, with some exceptions, to maintain a 70 average in all classes to be eligible for extracurricular participation has survived legal challenges.[162] The Texas high court reasoned that the law was rationally related to the state's legitimate interest in providing quality education to all students. Despite the law's exemption for students with disabilities and for those enrolled in honors or advanced courses, the court found no equal protection violation. Rejecting the due process claim as well, the court held that the regulation did not violate the principles of fundamental fairness.

The West Virginia high court also endorsed academic standards for extracurricular participation, holding that the state board of education's rule, requiring students to maintain a 2.0 grade-point average (GPA) to participate, was a legitimate exercise of its supervisory power and advanced the goal of educational excellence. Moreover, the court upheld a county school board's regulation that went beyond the state policy by requiring students to maintain a passing grade in all classes as a prerequisite to

---

158. Mahan v. Agee, 652 P.2d 765 (Okla. 1982). *See also* Ark. Activities Ass'n v. Meyer, 805 S.W.2d 58 (Ark. 1991) (finding rational basis for athletic association's age limitation); Thomas v. Greencastle Cmty. Sch. Corp., 603 N.E.2d 190 (Ind. Ct. App. 1992) (finding age restriction on participation neither under nor over inclusive).

159. *See, e.g.,* Grabow v. Mont. High Sch. Ass'n, 312 Mont. 92 (2002); Ala. High Sch. Athletic Ass'n v. Medders, 456 So. 2d 284 (Ala. 1984); J.M., Jr. v. Mont. High Sch. Ass'n, 875 P.2d 1026 (Mont. 1994).

160. *See, e.g.,* Clay v. Ariz. Interscholastic Ass'n, 779 P.2d 349 (Ariz. 1989) (holding that the interscholastic association had arbitrarily refused to consider an exception to the eight-consecutive-semester eligibility rule for a student who was unable to attend school while being rehabilitated for drug use and incarcerated for theft related to his drug problems). *See also* Jordan v. Ind. High Sch. Athletic Ass'n, 813 F. Supp. 1372 (N.D. Ind. 1993), *vacated,* 16 F.3d 785 (7th Cir. 1994) (allowing a student to play his senior year because his move from Illinois to Indiana, where he repeated his junior year, was not athletically motivated and he had not been redshirted).

161. *See, e.g.,* Washington v. Ind. High Sch. Athletic Ass'n, 181 F.3d 840 (7th Cir. 1999) (affirming preliminary injunction for learning-disabled student to receive a waiver from the eight-semester rule to accommodate his disability); text accompanying note 98, Chapter 6.

162. Spring Branch Indep. Sch. Dist. v. Stamos, 695 S.W.2d 556 (Tex. 1985).

extracurricular participation.[163] A Kentucky appeals court similarly upheld a school board's policy requiring students to maintain a 2.0 GPA in five of six subjects as a condition of participating in extracurricular activities.[164]

In view of the nationwide concern about achieving educational excellence, school boards and state legislatures are apt to place additional academic conditions on extracurricular participation. Only if academic standards are not uniformly applied are they likely to be struck down.[165]

Fees for Participation

Several courts have ruled that public schools can condition extracurricular participation on the payment of fees. For example, the Supreme Court of Idaho rejected a state constitutional challenge to a school district's policy requiring students to pay fees for extracurricular participation, concluding that such activities "are not necessary elements of a high-school career."[166] The Wisconsin and Montana Supreme Courts reached similar conclusions regarding the legality of charging fees for activities that are optional or elective.[167] In upholding fees for playing on interscholastic athletic teams, a Michigan appeals court noted the confidential waiver process available for students who could not afford the fees. The court recognized that no student had been denied participation because of inability to pay, and further declared that interscholastic athletics are not considered an integral, fundamental part of the educational program, which would necessitate providing them at no cost to students.[168]

However, individual state mandates may preclude charging students for extracurricular activities. In 1984, the California Supreme Court struck down a school district's decision to adapt to its reduced budget by charging students fees for participation in dramatic productions, musical performances, and athletic events. The court reasoned that extracurricular activities are an integral part of the educational program and thus encompassed within the state constitution's guarantee of a free public education. The court further held that the fee violated the state administrative code

---

163. Truby v. Broadwater, 332 S.E.2d 284 (W. Va. 1985). *See also* Mont. v. Bd. of Trs., 726 P.2d 801 (Mont. 1986) (holding that the state's interest in classification based on academic grades was more important than students' interest in participating in extracurricular activities).

164. Thompson v. Fayette County Pub. Schs., 786 S.W.2d 879 (Ky. Ct. App. 1990). *See also* Rousselle v. Plaquemines Parish Sch. Bd., 527 So. 2d 376 (La. Ct. App. 1988) (upholding a school rule requiring a specified GPA to try out for the cheerleader squad).

165. *See, e.g.,* Fontes v. Irvine Unified Sch. Dist., 30 Cal. Rptr. 2d 521 (Ct. App. 1994) (striking down a policy imposing a higher GPA for eligibility for the pep and cheerleading squads than for interscholastic sports as not rationally related to a realistically conceivable purpose).

166. Paulson v. Minidoka County Sch. Dist. No. 331, 463 P.2d 935, 938 (Idaho 1970).

167. Bd. of Educ. v. Sinclair, 222 N.W.2d 143 (Wis. 1974); Granger v. Cascade County Sch. Dist., 499 P.2d 780 (Mont. 1972).

168. Attorney Gen. v. E. Jackson Pub. Schs., 372 N.W.2d 638 (Mich. Ct. App. 1985).

stipulating that students shall not be required to pay any fees or deposits.[169] Given the fiscal constraints faced by school districts, an increasing number of school boards are likely to consider charging fees for extracurricular activities. The legality of such programs will depend on judicial interpretations of state law.

Other Conditions

A number of other conditions have been attached to extracurricular participation. Some courts, for example, have upheld limitations on student participation in out-of-school athletic competition as a condition of varsity participation to protect students from overtaxing themselves and to make interscholastic athletics more competitive and fair.[170] Restrictions on the number of team members allowed to participate in championships also have been upheld as rationally related to the legitimate state objectives of reducing costs of play-off contests and promoting fair play in championship games.[171] Additionally, requirements specifying that athletes must have participated in a certain portion of season contests to be eligible for tournament play have been upheld.[172]

Although extracurricular activities remain a heavily contested aspect of public school offerings, courts generally have allowed school authorities discretion in attaching a variety of conditions to student participation. Educators should ensure, however, that all policies pertaining to extracurricular activities are reasonable, clearly stated, related to an educational purpose, publicized to parents and students, and applied without discrimination.

Conclusion

Noninstructional issues have generated a substantial amount of school litigation. Many cases have focused on students' First Amendment freedoms of speech and

---

169. Hartzell v. Connell, 679 P.2d 35, 44 (Cal. 1984).

170. *See, e.g.,* Burrows v. Ohio High Sch. Athletic Ass'n, 891 F.2d 122 (6th Cir. 1989) (prohibiting soccer squad members from participating in spring independent soccer if they play fall interscholastic soccer; rule was rationally related to the association's legitimate interest of promoting fairness in competition). *See also* Kite v. Marshall, 661 F.2d 1027 (5th Cir. 1981) (upholding rational basis for interscholastic league's rule restricting participation by students who attended summer camps).

171. *See, e.g.,* The Fla. High Sch. Activities Ass'n v. Thomas, 434 So. 2d 306 (Fla. 1983). *See also* Graham v. Tenn. Secondary Sch. Athletic Ass'n, No. 1:95-cv-044, 1995 U.S. Dist. LEXIS 3211 (E.D. Tenn. Feb. 20, 1995), *appeal dismissed per curiam,* 107 F.3d 870 (6th Cir. 1997) (upholding the association's "quota rule" that limits the number of students who play varsity sports and receive financial aid, to prevent private schools from using aid to recruit athletes).

172. *See, e.g.,* Pearson v. Ind. High Sch. Athletic Ass'n, No. IP 99 1857-C-T/G, 2000 U.S. Dist. LEXIS 10501 (S.D. Ind. Feb. 22, 2000) (upholding the requirement that tennis players participate in a minimum of 50 percent of the season's contests in the number-one doubles position to qualify for the doubles tournament).

press, but other constitutional rights, such as due process and equal protection guarantees, also have been asserted in challenging restrictions on students' noninstructional activities. In the latter 1960s and early 1970s, the federal judiciary expanded constitutional protections afforded to students in noninstructional matters. It appeared that the reach of the *Tinker* standard was narrowing after the Supreme Court ruled that lewd or vulgar speech and attire are not protected by the First Amendment and that school authorities can censor school-sponsored expression. Yet, the *Tinker* principle is being revitalized in emerging First Amendment challenges to anti-harassment policies and electronic censorship. Concerns over student violence coupled with restrictions imposed on expression in response to terrorism have placed new strains on First Amendment freedoms in public schools. Tensions are exacerbated by students' ability to distribute materials to broad audiences through the Internet.

Moreover, students do not need to rely solely on constitutional protections, as federal and state laws, most notably the Equal Access Act, also protect students' expression and association rights and afford protections in noninstructional matters. Although judicial criteria applied in weighing the competing interests of students and school authorities continue to be refined, the following generalizations characterize the current posture of the courts.

1. Students do not have a First Amendment right to engage in defamatory, obscene, lewd, or inflammatory expression in public schools.
2. School boards can ban commercial solicitation on school premises, but they also have the authority to contract with companies to advertise in public schools unless there is a state prohibition.
3. Student expression that represents the school is subject to restrictions; school authorities have broad discretion to censor such expression, provided the decisions are based on pedagogical concerns and do not entail viewpoint discrimination.
4. Student-initiated expression of ideological views that merely occurs at school (in contrast to representing the school) cannot be curtailed unless a material interference with or substantial disruption of the educational process can reasonably be forecast from the expression.
5. School authorities cannot bar controversial or critical content from nonschool student publications; policies requiring prior administrative review of such publications must specify the procedures for review and the types of material that are prohibited.
6. School authorities cannot punish students for the content of materials that are published and distributed off school grounds, including material posted from home on the Internet, unless such distribution substantially interferes with the operation of the school.
7. Most courts have justified school districts' anti-harassment policies that prohibit uncivil and disrespectful expression as necessary to promote legitimate school objectives, even though similar policies could not be imposed outside school settings.

8. Any regulation imposing time, place, and manner restrictions on student expression must be specific, publicized to students and parents, and applied without discrimination.
9. Under the Equal Access Act, if a federally assisted secondary school establishes a limited open forum for student-initiated clubs to meet during noninstructional time, the access policy must be content neutral; however, public schools are not required to create such a forum for noncurriculum student groups to meet.
10. School authorities can restrict student hairstyles and attire that are vulgar, jeopardize health and safety, threaten to disrupt the educational process, or interfere with the attainment of educational objectives.
11. Restrictive student dress codes and uniforms can be imposed in public schools if justified by legitimate educational objectives, such as reducing violence and improving achievement, and not designed to suppress expression.
12. Students do not have an inherent right to participate in extracurricular activities.
13. Nonprofit, private associations that regulate interscholastic sports and other competitive activities among private and public schools within states are considered state actors and subject to constitutional restrictions on their actions.
14. School authorities possess considerable latitude in attaching reasonable conditions to extracurricular participation (e.g., skill criteria, attendance and training regulations, residency rules, academic standards, age and length of eligibility requirements).
15. Restrictions can be imposed on student participation in extracurricular activities based on legitimate health and safety considerations, and student athletes can be subjected to drug testing.
16. Whether public schools can charge fees for extracurricular participation depends on the judiciary's interpretation of a state's constitutional and statutory provisions.

5

Student Classifications

It might appear from a literal translation of "equality" that once a state establishes an educational system, all students must be treated in the same manner. Courts, however, have recognized that individuals are different and that equal treatment of unequals can have negative consequences. Accordingly, valid classification practices, designed to enhance the educational experiences of children by recognizing their unique needs, generally have been accepted as a legitimate prerogative of educators. Indeed, all schools classify students in some fashion, and state laws often specifically authorize or even require school boards to group students by academic levels, gender, age, and other distinguishing traits.

Although educators' authority to classify students has not been contested, the bases for certain classifications and the procedures used to make distinctions among students have been the focus of substantial litigation. To the extent that school classifications determine a student's access to educational resources, courts and legislatures have looked closely at the practices. Under no circumstances is it permissible for public schools to impose student classifications based on race. Under certain circumstances, however, other student classifications have been upheld. This chapter explores differential treatment of students based on race, native language, ability and achievement, age, and gender. Classifications based on disability are discussed in Chapter 6.

Legal Context

The Fourteenth Amendment to the United States Constitution states in part that no state shall deny to any person within its jurisdiction equal protection of the laws. This applies to subdivisions of states, including school districts. Given this explicit provision, there has been considerable litigation regarding what constitutes "equal protection." Facial discrimination (e.g., gender-segregated schools mandated by local board policy) will be scrutinized through one of three prevailing tests: strict, intermediate, or rational basis scrutiny (see Figure 5.1).

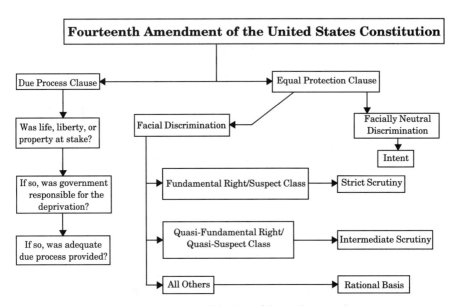

FIGURE 5.1   *Fourteenth Amendment of the United States Constitution*
Source: Stephen B. Thomas, *Student, Colleges, and Disability Law* (Dayton, OH: Education Law Association, 2002), p. 17. Reprinted with permission.

Identifying the appropriate standard of review requires a determination of whether a *suspect class* is involved or whether a *fundamental right* allegedly has been infringed. If either is present, *strict scrutiny* is applied and a compelling state interest must be shown to justify the action. If neither is involved, rational basis scrutiny is used, and the state must show only a rational relationship between its actions and its goals or objectives. Legislation rarely withstands analysis under the strict scrutiny test but nearly always is found to have some rational basis.

To date, only alienage, race, and national origin have been identified by the Supreme Court as suspect classes.[1] Accordingly, any grouping based on these characteristics would be scrutinized closely by courts and upheld only if the justification is found compelling. Whether the intended grouping is for a laudable reason is irrelevant without more to justify its use. For example, the good faith effort to segregate African American males in order to better address their unique educational needs would violate the Fourteenth Amendment unless a compelling interest can be shown.

Fundamental rights are either explicitly identified in the Constitution (e.g., freedom of speech, press, assembly) or are "fundamental" by implication (e.g., interstate travel, procreation[2]). Education is not mentioned in the Constitution, and although the

---

1. *See* Graham v. Richardson, 403 U.S. 365 (1971) (alienage); Hunter v. Erickson, 393 U.S. 385 (1969) (race); Korematsu v. United States, 323 U.S. 214 (1944) (national origin).
2. *See* Shapiro v. Thompson, 394 U.S. 618 (1969) (interstate travel); Skinner v. Oklahoma, 316 U.S. 535, 541 (1942) (procreation).

Supreme Court has referred to it as being important to maintaining a democratic society,[3] it has not been identified as an implied fundamental right.[4] Nevertheless, if the state were to adversely affect fundamental rights that were express or implied, it would once again be required to produce a compelling reason. Such a showing goes well beyond the production of any rational basis; the government basically would have to show why it is absolutely necessary to deprive the individual of a constitutionally protected right.

Supplementing these two primary standards is *intermediate scrutiny.* This standard is used in comparatively narrow circumstances where strict scrutiny is considered too demanding and rational basis too lenient. To date, the Supreme Court has applied this intermediate standard only where children were totally excluded from school,[5] or where illegitimacy or gender issues[6] were raised. It requires governmental actions to be substantially related to advancing significant governmental objectives. Moreover, the classification must be necessary, not merely convenient, and will not be upheld if there are reasonable, less restrictive means of reaching the same goal.

A fourth level of review is applied where acts of the state have the outward appearance of being neutral but result in a disproportionate adverse affect on a particular class of persons; when this occurs, the plaintiff must prove that the state intended to discriminate. For example, if standardized test scores provide the basis for assigning students to various programs (e.g., gifted, remedial) and result in disproportionate placement according to gender, the plaintiff bears the burden of demonstrating that school personnel intended to discriminate in their selection and use of the tests. This standard is difficult to meet and generally results in a verdict for the government, even if disparate impact results.

In addition to the constitutional protections reviewed here, equal educational opportunities are guaranteed through various federal and state laws. In many instances, the statutes create new substantive rights that are more extensive than constitutional guarantees. Among the more significant federal laws discussed in this chapter are Title VI of the Civil Rights Act of 1964 (barring discrimination on the basis of race, color, or national origin by recipients of federal financial assistance), the Equal Educational Opportunities Act of 1974 (guaranteeing public school children

---

3. Specifically, the Court noted, "Today, education is perhaps the most important function of state and local governments. Compulsory school attendance laws and the great expenditures for education both demonstrate our recognition of the importance of education to our democratic society. It is required in the performance of our most basic public responsibilities. . . . It is the very foundation of good citizenship. Today it is a principal instrument in awakening the child to cultural values, in preparing him for later professional training, and in helping him to adjust normally to his environment. In these days, it is doubtful that any child may reasonably be expected to succeed in life if he is denied the opportunity of an education. Such an opportunity, where the state has undertaken to provide it, is a right [that] must be made available to all on equal terms." Brown v. Bd. of Educ., 347 U.S. 483, 493 (1954).

4. San Antonio Indep. Sch. Dist. v. Rodriguez, 411 U.S. 1, 35-36 (1973).

5. Plyler v. Doe, 457 U.S. 202 (1982).

6. *See, e.g.,* Clark v. Jeter, 486 U.S. 456 (1988) (illegitimacy); Miss. Univ. for Women v. Hogan, 458 U.S. 718 (1982) (gender discrimination).

equal educational opportunity without regard to race, color, gender, or national origin), Title IX of the Education Amendments of 1972 (prohibiting gender discrimination in institutions with federally assisted educational programs), and the Age Discrimination Act of 1975 (prohibiting recipients from discriminating based on age).

Classifications Based on Race

The most prevalent reason for classifying students according to race has been to establish or perpetuate racially segregated schools. Widespread racial segregation in educational institutions existed in this country from the colonial period well into the twentieth century. Even after the adoption of the Fourteenth Amendment in 1868, most schools remained segregated either by state constitution or statute, local ordinance, district policy or practice, or court interpretation, but seldom were they equal. When such practices were challenged, courts generally mandated only that children be provided with access to public education. They did not require equal access to integrated schools or to equal school facilities, the provision of equal curricular or extracurricular opportunities, instruction by equally trained professionals, or instruction of equal duration (i.e., an equivalent school year or school day).

Today, most former de jure segregated schools (i.e., those where the separation of the races was required by law or the result of other action by the state or its agents) are already, or are in the process of becoming, integrated. In some instances, costs have exceeded $200 million, and court supervision has lasted 20 to 30 or more years. No other area of school law has involved such volatile debate, obligated such a large percentage of a school district's budget, or resulted in greater political and social turmoil than desegregation.

Most lawsuits challenging school segregation claim a violation of the Fourteenth Amendment, which provides in pertinent part that no state shall "deny to any person within its jurisdiction the equal protection of the laws." Because race qualifies as a suspect class, the state or local school district must demonstrate a compelling interest in its use of facially discriminatory racial classifications and show that its procedures are narrowly tailored if it uses race as a basis to segregate school children, to deny equal educational opportunity, or to advantage one student over another.

Pre-*Brown* Litigation

The first published school segregation case was *Roberts v. City of Boston* in 1849, 19 years prior to the passage of the Fourteenth Amendment.[7] In that case, the city had established separate primary schools for minority children but had staffed them with teachers receiving the same compensation and having the same qualifications as other teachers in the system. When a minority child was denied admission to the Caucasian school nearest her home due to her race, she filed unsuccessful administrative appeals.

---

7. 59 Mass. (5 Cush.) 198 (1849).

The parents contended that the separation of the races was a violation of the state constitution; that segregation was offensive and illegal since the school committee did not have the authority to discriminate on the basis of race; that segregation inflicted on minority children a stigma of caste; and that a school exclusively devoted to any single racial group was not equal to one where all groups met together (i.e., the argument that separate schools are inherently unequal).

The parents sought both an injunction to require admission and damages, as permitted under an 1845 state statute when *any* child was unlawfully excluded from public school instruction. Upholding the school committee, the state supreme court reasoned that the child had not been excluded from all public schools of the city (i.e., two schools reserved exclusively for minority children were open to the child). The court asserted that although equality is a broad principle, it did not warrant the conclusion that all individuals have the same legal rights (e.g., men and women, as well as adults and children, possess different powers and rights).

The *Roberts* case set the stage for 105 years of case law that generally supported the concept of separate but equal public schools. Between 1849 and 1868, cases dealt with state laws requiring school attendance, mandating equal protection, or prohibiting discrimination. After 1868 and the passage of the Fourteenth Amendment, most cases leading up to *Brown v. Board of Education* in 1954 alleged a federal constitutional violation.

Perhaps the most infamous case supporting the "separate but equal" interpretation was *Plessy v. Ferguson* in 1896, where the Supreme Court upheld racial segregation of passengers in railroad coaches as required by Louisiana law.[8] Violation of the statute resulted in a fine of $25 or imprisonment for 20 days. Such a penalty could be imposed against either the individual who attempted to occupy the coach or compartment reserved for members of another race or the officer of any railroad who refused to make the proper assignment. The only identified exemption to this requirement was a nurse who was attending a child of another race. Although "separate but equal" case law and state statutes were common 75 to 100 years before *Plessy,* it nevertheless is *Plessy* that most often is mentioned today when the standard is discussed.

Three years following *Plessy,* the Supreme Court was asked to review its first school case dealing with the "equal" treatment of school children. In *Cumming v. Richmond County Board of Education* in 1899, the Court held that the temporary cessation of services at a high school reserved for minority children did not violate equal protection, even though services continued at the high school for Caucasian students.[9] The action of the board in closing the school was held to be based on economic considerations and was not found to represent bad faith or an abuse of discretion. The Court concluded that although all must share the burdens and receive the benefits of taxation, school finance was a matter belonging to the respective states; federal interference without a clear and unmistakable disregard for constitutional rights would be inappropriate.

8. 163 U.S. 537 (1896).
9. 175 U.S. 528 (1899).

Following *Plessy* and *Cumming,* the separate but equal standard thrived, notwithstanding challenges in both state and federal courts.[10] Individuals, groups, and organizations wishing to equalize educational opportunities or to integrate schools made little progress during the nineteenth and early twentieth centuries. Then, in the late 1930s and 1940s, courts began looking more closely at "separate" facilities and programs and occasionally concluded that they were not "equal." Several of these cases involved the National Association for the Advancement of Colored People (NAACP) under the leadership of Charles Houston and Thurgood Marshall (a future United States Supreme Court justice).

The approach that Houston and Marshall took was based on the premise that if they could successfully attack the "equal" standard, the "separate" standard would be susceptible to challenge. They also reasoned that the social, political, and judicial climates were such that cases in higher education were more likely to succeed initially than were cases at the K–12 level. Four key higher education appeals reached the Supreme Court between 1938 and 1950. Houston and/or Marshall were among counsel for the plaintiffs in each. These cases included claims from minority students alleging that there were no separate but equal programs available (two cases), that the separate program was inferior, or that the education received within a previously all-Caucasian institution was unequal due to the student's separation from the rest of the student body.[11] The plaintiffs in each case prevailed.

Given the success of the higher education plaintiffs, the time appeared ripe to attack the K-12 "separate but equal" standard directly. This occurred in 1954 when the Supreme Court combined cases from four states—Kansas, South Carolina, Virginia, and Delaware.[12] Once again, Marshall served as lead attorney for the plaintiffs. Although these cases differed regarding conditions and facts, minority children in

10. *See, e.g.,* Gong Lum v. Rice, 275 U.S. 78 (1927) (finding that a 9-year-old Chinese student was not entitled to attend the school reserved for Caucasian majority students and that she was properly assigned to the school for minorities; it was irrelevant that there was no school for her particular group, as all nonmajority children could be grouped together).

11. Missouri *ex rel.* Gaines v. Canada, 305 U.S. 337 (1938) (ruling that a minority applicant was entitled to be admitted to the university in the absence of comparable legal training within the state; it was not enough for the state to pay for reasonable tuition for minority applicants at law schools located in adjacent states); Sipuel v. Bd. of Regents, 332 U.S. 631 (1948) (per curiam) (upholding the right of a minority female to attend the state's only law school); Sweatt v. Painter, 339 U.S. 629 (1950) (ordering the admission of a minority student to law school for Caucasian students; separate law school for minorities was unequal in the number of faculty, courses, opportunities for specialization, students with whom to study and interact, library books, law review, prestige, and influence of alumni); McLaurin v. Okla. State Regents for Higher Educ., 339 U.S. 637 (1950) (finding an Equal Protection Clause violation where a minority applicant was admitted to an education doctoral program, but was required to eat at different times than other students and had a sign "Reserved for Colored" used to identify his assigned areas in the library, cafeteria, and classrooms).

12. Brown v. Bd. of Educ., 98 F. Supp. 797 (D. Kan. 1951); Briggs v. Elliott, 98 F. Supp. 529 (E.D.S.C. 1951), *vacated and remanded,* 342 U.S. 350 (1952), *on remand,* 103 F. Supp. 920 (E.D.S.C. 1952); Davis v. County Sch. Bd., 103 F. Supp. 337 (E.D. Va. 1952); Gebhart v. Belton, 87 A.2d 862, *aff'd,* 91 A.2d 137 (Del. 1952).

each state sought the assistance of the courts under the Fourteenth Amendment to obtain admission to public schools on a nonsegregated basis. In the landmark decision, collectively called *Brown v. Board of Education,* Chief Justice Warren, writing for a unanimous Court, declared education to be "perhaps the most important function of state and local governments"[13] and repudiated the separate but equal doctrine, stipulating that racially segregated public schools were "inherently unequal."[14]

Because of the significant impact of this decision and the difficulty in fashioning an immediate remedy, the Supreme Court delayed an implementation decree for one year, soliciting friend-of-the-court briefs[15] regarding strategies to convert de jure segregated dual school districts into integrated unitary districts. Then, in *Brown II,* the Court in 1955 concluded that the conversion from dual to unitary must occur "with all deliberate speed,"[16] although it gave little guidance as to what specific time frame was required or to what extent integration was mandated. As a result, states varied widely in their efforts to comply.

De Jure Segregation in the South

Despite the *Brown* mandate to end segregation, during the next decade the Supreme Court was forced to react to a number of blatant violations, such as state officials' efforts to physically block the desegregation of schools in Little Rock,[17] and an attempt to avoid integration by closing public schools in one Virginia county, while maintaining public schools in other counties in the state.[18] The Court also invalidated provisions in Knoxville that allowed students to transfer back to their former schools if, after rezoning, they would be assigned to a school where their race would be in the minority,[19] and found unconstitutional a one-grade-per-year plan[20] that had been adopted in Fort Smith, Arkansas.[21] Such a practice was not an overt violation of *Brown,* but it certainly represented an effort to strain the "all deliberate speed" mandate.

Even where violations were found, however, many courts hesitated to require anything more than the removal of barriers to integration, given the dearth of guidance regarding compliance.[22] Then, in a trilogy of cases in 1968, the Supreme Court

13. Brown v. Bd. of Educ. (Brown I), 347 U.S. 483, 493 (1954).

14. *Id.* at 495.

15. Friend-of-the-court (amicus curiae) briefs, are provided by nonparties to inform or perhaps persuade the court.

16. Brown v. Bd. of Educ. (Brown II), 349 U.S. 294, 301 (1955).

17. Cooper v. Aaron, 358 U.S. 1 (1958).

18. Griffin v. County Sch. Bd., 377 U.S. 218 (1964).

19. Goss v. Bd. of Educ., 373 U.S. 683 (1963).

20. A one-grade-per-year plan requires the integration of one grade each fall term until the system is unitary and all grades are integrated.

21. Rogers v. Paul, 382 U.S. 198 (1965) (per curiam).

22. *See, e.g.,* Briggs v. Elliott, 132 F. Supp. 776, 777 (E.D.S.C. 1955) (declaring that the Constitution "does not require integration" but "merely forbids discrimination").

announced that school officials in systems that were segregated by law in 1954 had an affirmative duty to take whatever steps were necessary to convert to unitary school systems and to eliminate the effects of past discrimination.[23] Furthermore, the Court declared that desegregation remedies would be evaluated based on their effectiveness in dismantling dual school systems. Thus, the notion of state neutrality was transformed into a requirement of affirmative state action to desegregate; the mere removal of barriers to school integration was not sufficient.

In one of these 1968 cases, *Green v. County School Board,* the Court reviewed a freedom-of-choice plan adopted by a small district in Virginia. The district historically operated only two schools, both kindergarten through twelfth grade: one for African Americans, the other for Caucasians. To eliminate race-based assignments within the district, the local board implemented a plan to allow children to attend the school of their choice. During the three-year period immediately following implementation, no Caucasian children enrolled in the historically African American school, and only a few African American children enrolled in the historically Caucasian school. The district contended that any resulting segregation was due to the choices of individuals, not to government action, and was therefore permissible; but the Supreme Court disagreed. The problem with this plan was not that it was unconstitutional per se, but that it simply was not working to integrate schools. As a result, the district was ordered to come forward with a new plan that promised "realistically to work and to work now."[24] In addition, the Court ruled that school authorities must eliminate the racial identification of schools in terms of the *composition of the student body, faculty, and staff; transportation; extracurricular activities; and facilities.* These six elements still are used today and are referred to in the aggregate simply as the *Green* criteria.

In 1971, additional direction was provided when the Supreme Court ruled in *Swann v. Charlotte-Mecklenburg Board of Education* that the elimination of invidious racial distinctions may be sufficient in connection with transportation, support personnel, and extracurricular activities, but that more was necessary in terms of constructing facilities and making faculty and student assignments.[25] The Court endorsed the practice of assigning teachers on the basis of race until faculties were integrated and declared that new schools must be located so that the dual school system would not be perpetuated or reestablished.

Correcting racial imbalance among student populations, however, was more difficult. For the vestiges of segregation to be eliminated, the school district had to achieve racial balance in a sufficient number of schools, although every school did not have to reflect the racial composition of the school district as a whole. The continued presence of a small number of predominantly one-race schools in the district did not necessarily mean that it continued to practice state-imposed segregation, but the bur-

23. Green v. County Sch. Bd., 391 U.S. 430 (1968); Raney v. Bd. of Educ., 391 U.S. 443 (1968); Monroe v. Bd. of Comm'rs, 391 U.S. 450 (1968).

24. *Green, 391* U.S. at 439.

25. 402 U.S. 1 (1971).

den of proof was placed on school officials to establish that such schools were not the result of present or past discriminatory action. To achieve the desired racial balance, the Court suggested pairing or consolidating schools, altering attendance zones, and using racial quotas, but rejected the practice of assigning students to the schools nearest their homes if it failed to eliminate de jure segregation. The Court also endorsed the use of reasonable busing as a means to integrate schools, yet qualified that endorsement by noting that the soundness of any transportation plan must be evaluated based on the time involved, distance traveled, and age of students.

By applying the criteria established in *Green* and *Swann,* substantial desegregation was attained in southern states during the 1970s. Where unconstitutional segregation was found, federal courts exercised broad power in ordering remedies affecting student and staff assignments, curriculum, school construction, personnel practices, and budgetary allocations. Judicial activity was augmented by threats from the former Department of Health, Education, and Welfare to terminate federal funds to school districts not complying with Title VI of the Civil Rights Act of 1964.[26] Title VI, like the Fourteenth Amendment, requires the integration only of de jure segregated school districts.

Distinguishing between De Jure and De Facto Segregation

Since the Supreme Court carefully limited its early decisions to states and school districts with a long history of school segregation by official policy, questions remained regarding what type of evidence—other than explicit legislation requiring school segregation—was necessary to establish unconstitutional de jure segregation.[27] That is, what factors would distinguish de jure segregation from permissible de facto segregation? The answer to this question began to evolve in *Keyes v. School District No. 1, Denver* where the Supreme Court in 1973 held that if "no statutory dual system has ever existed, plaintiffs must prove not only that segregated schooling exists but also that it was brought about or maintained by intentional state action."[28] Some federal courts have found that a presumption of unlawful purpose can be established if the natural, probable, and foreseeable result of public officials' acts perpetuate segregated conditions,[29] whereas others have required evidence that policymakers actually harbored a desire to segregate.[30] Although courts vary in the processes they use to determine whether school districts are guilty of discriminatory intent, they often consider the impact of the disputed governmental act, the history of discriminatory official action, procedural and substantive departures from norms generally followed, and dis-

---

26. 42 U.S.C. §§ 2000d–2000d–7 (2002).

27. In the 1960s, some courts reasoned that school segregation did not warrant remedial action in school districts where segregation was not imposed by law in 1954. *See, e.g.,* Deal v. Cincinnati Bd. of Educ., 369 F.2d 55 (6th Cir. 1966).

28. 413 U.S. 189, 198 (1973).

29. *See, e.g.,* Arthur v. Nyquist, 573 F.2d 134 (2d Cir. 1978).

30. *See, e.g.,* Vill. of Arlington Heights v. Metro. Hous. Dev. Corp., 429 U.S. 252 (1977).

criminatory statements made publicly or in legislative or administrative sessions. If intent is proven, courts then are responsible for fashioning appropriate remedies; but when allegations of discriminatory intent are not supported, no action on the part of the district is required.[31]

School districts that either have no history of unlawful segregation or have become unitary while under court supervision will not be responsible for correcting any future racial imbalance they have not created. In 1976, the Supreme Court in *Pasadena City Board of Education v. Spangler* held that the school district, having implemented a student reassignment plan to comply with a court order, did not have an affirmative duty to revise remedial efforts annually when demographic shifts resulted in some schools becoming more than 50 percent minority.[32] The district court had made a lifetime commitment to the "no majority of any minority" rule. To comply with this provision, the school district was responsible for annually readjusting its attendance zones, even after the former constitutional violation was corrected. The Supreme Court held that although the original lower court decision was justified to correct de jure segregation, the continuation of the order exceeded the court's authority.

Fashioning Appropriate Remedies

Because each desegregation case involves a combination of unique circumstances and violations, it is not surprising that each remedy also is unique and at times requires rezoning; providing thematic magnet schools; developing new curricular offerings; closing, reopening, renovating, or constructing schools; busing students; transfering and/or retraining current staff; or hiring additional staff. Basically, courts can require nearly anything of districts and states that would result in fulfillment of the primary objective—the integration of American public schools. "All deliberate speed" in many instances has taken decades, while costs often have seemed irrelevant.

Rezoning and the Closing, Reopening, or Construction of Schools.   Although at times politically unpopular, the rezoning of schools often was the fastest, least expensive, and simplest way to integrate students. Because of a long history of gerrymandering boundary lines with the intent to segregate, many school boundaries during the 1950s and 1960s had little to do with geographic barriers (e.g., rivers, hills); safety issues (e.g., location of busy roads, highways, factories); or the size, location, or dispersion of the student population. As a result, significant integration often has resulted through the simple use of good-faith redistricting and/or, in fairly narrow circumstances, the creation of new or consolidated school districts.[33]

31. *See, e.g.,* Price v. Austin Indep. Sch. Dist., 945 F.2d 1307 (5th Cir. 1991).

32. 427 U.S. 424 (1976).

33. Newburg Area Council v. Bd. of Educ., 510 F.2d 1358 (6th Cir. 1974) (merging a city district with the surrounding county district due to both having been involved in de jure segregation). *See also* Lee v. Chambers County Bd. of Educ., 849 F. Supp. 1474 (M.D. Ala. 1994) (prohibiting the division of a district that was engaged in integration where such separation would have resulted in further school segregation).

In addition, early in the twentieth century many school districts were able to remain or become segregated by strategically locating new schools, down-sizing or closing existing buildings, or operating other schools that were overenrolled (often requiring the use of mobile units or temporary classrooms). Just as these methods were used to segregate, they also have been used to integrate.

Busing. Contributing to the cost and controversy was the use of busing to accomplish integration when other alternatives had not succeeded. Although busing is admittedly effective at achieving student integration, it also represents a significant expense; is inefficient in the use of student time; and is an unpopular option with many students, parents, taxpayers, and voters of all races. Consequently, several bills to limit the authority of federal courts to order the busing of students have been introduced in Congress. Foremost among these were provisions included in Title IV of the Civil Rights Act of 1964[34] and the Equal Educational Opportunities Act (EEOA) of 1974.[35] Title IV provides technical assistance in the preparation, adoption, and implementation of desegregation plans; gives direction in the operation of training institutes to improve the ability of educators to deal effectively with special education problems occasioned by desegregation; and places limitations on court-ordered busing.

Furthermore, the EEOA prohibits public schools[36] from denying equal educational opportunities to students based on their race, color, sex, or national origin; purports that the neighborhood is the appropriate basis for determining public school assignment; and stipulates that busing may be used only in situations where the intent to segregate is established. The EEOA explicitly forbids deliberate segregation and, where it was formerly practiced, requires educational agencies to remove the vestiges of the dual school system. The discriminatory assignment of faculty and staff and the transfer of students (voluntary or otherwise) from one school to another, when the purpose and effect are to increase segregation, also violate the EEOA. Neither Title IV nor the EEOA, however, places a limitation on judicial authority to order pupil reassignment where constitutional violations are found; a federal constitutional amendment would be required to limit such authority.

State busing limitation measures also have generated litigation. In 1971, the Supreme Court in *North Carolina State Board of Education v. Swann* struck down a state law forbidding the busing of students to create racially balanced schools. The Court concluded that the provision unconstitutionally restricted the discretion of local school authorities to formulate plans to eliminate dual school systems.[37] Accordingly, busing as an option to achieve integration could not be banned.

---

34. 42 U.S.C. §§ 2000c–2000c-9 (2002).

35. 20 U.S.C. § 1701 *et seq.* (2002).

36. The EEOA does not apply to college students who are experiencing language difficulties or are required to pass the Test of English as a Foreign Language. Khan v. Educ. Comm'n for Foreign Med. Graduates, No. 00-1701, 2000 U.S. Dist. LEXIS 17227 (E.D. Pa. Nov. 30, 2000).

37. 402 U.S. 43 (1971).

Additional guidance was provided in 1982, when the Court in *Crawford v. Board of Education* upheld a state constitutional amendment in California that permitted busing only when the Fourteenth Amendment was violated (i.e., when de jure segregation was present).[38] Prior to the adoption of the amendment, the state constitution prohibited de facto as well as de jure school segregation, thus requiring remedial plans to ensure racial balance in all school districts, including those where the separation of the races was caused by housing patterns rather than official action. This objective became both expensive and unpopular to the majority of state residents and was eventually discontinued. When the amendment was challenged, the Court concluded that California was legally obligated to integrate only de jure segregated school districts.

Programmatic Options.   Since the early 1980s, the federal judiciary has become less aggressive in requiring massive student reassignment plans to integrate schools. In the alternative, compensatory education programs, bilingual/bicultural programs, and counseling and career guidance services, among others, have been included in desegregation plans to help overcome the effects of prior racial isolation.[39] Most plans include magnet schools that offer theme-oriented instructional programs (e.g., performing arts, math and science; agriculture) or an expanded curriculum (e.g., advanced coursework in science or technology, classical guitar, horseback riding) in an effort to attract a racially balanced student body and to limit the use of busing.[40] Others provide specialized learning centers to improve remediation for underachieving pupils.[41] As with other types of freedom of choice or transfer plans, courts will uphold the use of these program and curricular options to integrate schools, but only if the plans succeed in achieving the desired level of integration within a reasonable period of time. Where they have failed, other options have been required.

Interdistrict Remedies.   Another controversial approach to integration has been the use of remedies that cross school district boundaries. Many city school districts have experienced both real and percentage increases in minority populations due to a variety of reasons, including "white flight" and "zone jumping."[42] Integration in these areas then becomes problematic, given the presence of primarily one race. As a result, several courts have reasoned that if racial integration in a predominantly one-race district is to be achieved, adjacent districts must be involved in student transfer and busing provisions.

In *Milliken v. Bradley,* the Sixth Circuit had ordered a metropolitan desegregation remedy for Detroit and 53 suburban school districts, reasoning that intentional

---

38. 458 U.S. 527 (1982).

39. *See, e.g.,* Keyes v. Sch. Dist. No. 1, 895 F.2d 659 (10th Cir. 1990); Little Rock Sch. Dist. v. Pulaski County Special Dist., 716 F. Supp. 1162 (E.D. Ark. 1989).

40. *See, e.g.,* Bradley v. Pinellas County Sch. Bd., 165 F.R.D. 676 (M.D. Fla. 1994).

41. Tasby v. Black Coalition to Maximize Educ., 771 F.2d 849 (5th Cir. 1985).

42. *See, e.g.,* Elston v. Talladega County Bd. of Educ., 997 F.2d 1394 (11th Cir. 1993). Zone jumping is transferring from the assigned attendance zone to an adjacent zone.

school segregation implicated the entire metropolitan area. The Supreme Court disagreed in 1974, however, and held that the plaintiffs did not carry their burden of proof in substantiating purposeful discrimination on the part of the suburban districts.[43] Moreover, the Court emphasized that a remedy must not be broader in scope than warranted by the constitutional violation. Since intentional school segregation was proven only in the Detroit system, the case was remanded for the formulation of a remedy within that district.

Three years later, in *Milliken II,* the Court articulated a three-part framework to guide district courts in the exercise of their authority. This framework requires that the desegregation remedy (1) be determined by the nature and scope of the constitutional violation, (2) be remedial so as to restore the victims of discriminatory conduct to the position they would have occupied in the absence of such conduct, and (3) take into account the interests of state and local authorities in managing their own affairs.[44] Accordingly, an interdistrict remedy may include only those districts that were involved in de jure segregation; courts are not authorized to include districts that were not segregated or were segregated only due to de facto circumstances.[45]

In a 1995 decision involving interdistrict remedies, *Missouri v. Jenkins,* the Supreme Court evaluated Kansas City's 18-year history of desegregation orders. Over this period, the district court ordered approximately $1.5 billion in program improvements, comprehensive magnet schools, transportation, extensive capital improvements, and salary assistance.[46] By 1994, the average annual costs were over $200 million, thereby earning the reputation as the "most ambitious and expensive remedial program in the history of school desegregation."[47] Of particular importance in the Kansas City case were the lower court's orders (1) to further increase the salaries of teachers and staff and (2) to continue to fund a wide variety of expensive programs— many of which were available nowhere else in the state or nation. The district court reasoned that these expenditures were needed if educational opportunities were to be improved to the degree necessary to attract nonminority students to the Kansas City public schools.

The Supreme Court disagreed, noting that racial imbalance within a school district, without more, did not violate the Constitution and that the lower court's plan to attract nonresident, nonminority students represented an interdistrict remedy and was therefore beyond the court's authority. Furthermore, the lower court's order requiring the continued funding of the costly educational programs clearly exceeded its authority. The district court attempted to justify its decision by noting that student achievement levels still were at or below national norms and that students had not yet reached their maximum potential. The Supreme Court admonished that instead of a "maxi-

43. 418 U.S. 717 (1974) (Milliken I).

44. Milliken v. Bradley, 433 U.S. 267, 280-281 (1977) (Milliken II).

45. *See, e.g.,* Edgerson v. Clinton, 86 F.3d 833 (8th Cir. 1996); Lauderdale County Sch. Dist. v. Enter. Consol. Sch. Dist., 24 F.3d 671 (5th Cir. 1994).

46. 515 U.S. 70 (1995).

47. *Id.* at 78.

mum potential" standard, the court should have determined whether the lower achievement of minority students was attributable to prior de jure segregation and, if so, whether it had been remedied to the extent practicable. Once this had been accomplished, control of the schools was ordered to be returned to state and local school officials.

Notwithstanding the limitations on courts to order interdistrict remedies, unitary districts have at times voluntarily entered into such agreements. In a South Carolina case, a federal district court addressed the legality of a transfer provision involving a county school district and each of its integrated constituent districts. The districts had agreed to a plan allowing for voluntary interdistrict student transfers, assuming that the reasons for the requests were nondiscriminatory. The court acknowledged that local educators were authorized to set transfer policies, but nonetheless identified for the record several specific constitutional bases for transfers (e.g., to receive instruction in courses not available in the home district; to attend school with a sibling in a special program or where the child's parent is a teacher).[48] Also, where interdistrict transfers would result in greater racial balance in a particular school or district, the court encouraged the sending districts to consider that fact in evaluating the student's proposal. On the other hand, if a valid request (i.e., one with a legitimate nondiscriminatory basis) were denied solely because it had an adverse effect on the desired racial balance, such an act by a unitary district would violate the transferring student's equal protection rights.

Staff Desegregation Remedies.   The Supreme Court has emphasized that integration of the school staff is an essential component of an effective desegregation remedy.[49] Ideally, school children will be exposed to faculty of their own race as well as to faculty of other races. This often is accomplished through the use of race-based faculty assignment and transfer procedures with the goal of achieving diversity and providing role models.

Under very narrow circumstances where race is permissibly used as a criterion to hire additional underrepresented faculty, courts will compare the racial composition of the faculty with that of the qualified relevant labor market, rather than with that of the surrounding community or the student body, in determining the targeted number. Even then, however, only where a compelling interest is present (e.g., to remedy prior de jure segregation), and the remedy has been narrowly tailored, may temporary race-based hiring be ordered by the court. It is important to note that neither societal discrimination, racial imbalance, nor the need for role models will justify imposing racial quotas.

48. United States v. Charleston County Sch. Dist., 960 F.2d 1227 (4th Cir. 1992), *on remand,* 856 F. Supp. 1060, 1063–1065 (D.S.C. 1994).

49. *See, e.g.,* Swann v. Charlotte-Mecklenburg Bd. of Educ., 402 U.S. 1, 19 (1971); United States v. Montgomery County Bd. of Educ., 395 U.S. 225, 232 (1969). *See also* Lee v. Lee County Bd. of Educ., No. 70-T-845-E, 2002 U.S. Dist. LEXIS 10277 (M.D. Ala., May 29, 2002) (declaring the district unitary except for faculty assignments to two schools).

Even when the race ratio of the faculty reflects that of the available labor market, courts often require that building assignments result in relative racial balance within each district. The Supreme Court addressed this issue in 1969 in *United States v. Montgomery County Board of Education,* where it approved a desegregation plan that included faculty reassignment provisions.[50] The plan required the district to have approximately the same ratio of minority and majority teachers in each school as existed in the district. This approach has been used often by lower courts.[51]

The racial balance of a school faculty also can be affected when it is necessary to downsize the staff. This can occur when either fewer schools are used (e.g., when two de jure districts are combined and fewer schools of larger size are operated) or fewer students are educated (e.g., when students move from the district or enroll in private schools). Although there may be exceptional circumstances where preference in hiring is permitted, that is not the case when determining whom to lay off. As a result, the diversity gained through the use of goals, court-ordered quotas, or affirmative action may be lost during a reduction-in-force (RIF) as the consideration of race in identifying the persons to be released is not permitted. The Supreme Court in *Wygant v. Jackson Board of Education* struck down a school district's negotiated agreement that gave preferential protection to minority teachers from layoffs to maintain the percentage of minority teachers employed prior to a RIF.[52] Finding that the justification for the contested staff reduction policy (i.e., the need for minority role models) failed to qualify as a compelling interest and that the preferential layoff procedures were not narrowly tailored, the Court held that the practice violated the Fourteenth Amendment. Although *Wygant* did not involve a school district engaged in court-ordered integration, there is no reason to believe that the use of racial preferences would be permitted in such districts. Race-based relief may perhaps help remedy one constitutional violation, but it would create another.

Fiscal Responsibilities. Numerous school districts have spent over $200 million to integrate their schools. The funds often were used to provide equal educational opportunity for students in existing programs and facilities. At other times, courts have required not only that there be integration, but that districts also construct or renovate facilities; purchase new furnishings, equipment, and technology; improve or expand curricular offerings; establish magnet schools; or increase staff salaries. Related costs almost always exceeded the local district's budget, if not also its tax-generating ability. Nevertheless, courts have shown little sympathy when the lack of sufficient funds has been proposed as a defense for maintaining dual school systems.[53]

Due to the extensive and seemingly endless costs associated with desegregation, balancing school budgets has been challenging. In theory, the solution appears

---

50. 395 U.S. 225 (1969).

51. *See, e.g.* Singleton v. Jackson Mun. Separate Sch. Dist., 419 F.2d 1211 (5th Cir. 1970).

52. 476 U.S. 267 (1986). *See also* Crumpton v. Bridgeport Educ. Ass'n, 993 F.2d 1023, 1031 (2d Cir. 1993) (finding that racial preference during a RIF was not narrowly tailored).

53. *See, e.g., In re* Little Rock Sch. Dist., 949 F.2d 253 (8th Cir. 1991).

clear: Reduce expenditures and/or increase revenues. In practice, however, barriers often exist to accomplishing either (e.g., the inability to further reduce staff, declines in state support during periods of recession, voter resistance to increased taxes). Among the more viable options to lower expenditures is the closing of schools. This results in lower maintenance and operation costs and the need for fewer faculty and staff. However, the option to close schools is available only where there has been consolidation, where enrollments have declined, or where new schools have opened. If decisions to close schools are motivated by legitimate budgetary or pedagogical concerns and do not adversely affect integration, they will be allowed. But where desegregation is impeded, school closings will not generally be permitted.

Another approach to balancing the budget is to reduce the number of faculty and staff, even when school closings are not feasible. Given that 85 percent or more of a district's operating budget is typically needed to compensate personnel, engaging in a RIF may at times help balance an otherwise deficit budget. Without consolidation, however, it is unlikely that districts will be able to significantly trim the number of staff, as many already operate with only essential personnel. Moreover, if the number of staff is reduced further, districts in some states will receive less state aid, as it is common for states to penalize districts that operate with too few teachers, counselors, or other support staff. Such a reduction in state dollars would in whole or in part offset any budgetary advantage the district may have experienced as a result of downsizing.

When lowering expenditures is not possible, or the amount of reduction is insufficient to meet budgetary needs, increasing revenues becomes paramount. This may be accomplished by increasing, extending, or creating local taxes. In a significant 1990 decision, *Missouri v. Jenkins,* the Supreme Court held that federal courts may order school districts to impose tax increases to fund desegregation remedies but that courts may not impose such increases directly.[54] However, if the state or district is unable to further increase its taxes due to existing state laws, courts have the authority to override such provisions as they apply to the de jure district.

In addition, courts at times have held states responsible for all or part of desegregation costs, depending on the extent to which the state was found culpable in causing or perpetuating the segregation.[55] Such was the case in Michigan in 1977 when the Supreme Court ordered the state to underwrite half of the costs of remedial programs, in-service training, guidance and counseling services, and community relations programs in Detroit because of the role the state played in creating the dual system.[56] In contrast, numerous other school districts have received no state assistance. In 1985, Tennessee initially was assessed 60 percent of the Nashville desegregation plan costs but later was relieved of any fiscal responsibility in the absence of evidence that it had

54. 495 U.S. 33 (1990).

55. *See, e.g.,* Jenkins *ex rel.* Agyei v. Missouri, 13 F.3d 1170 (8th Cir. 1994). *But see* DeKalb County Sch. Dist. v. Schrenko, 109 F.3d 680 (11th Cir. 1997) (concluding that the state need not reimburse the school district for costs associated with desegregation-related transportation, majority-to-minority transfer initiative, and magnet school program).

56. Milliken v. Bradley, 433 U.S. 267 (1977) (Milliken II).

contributed to the segregation.[57] Also, in St. Louis, the Eighth Circuit held that the state was not responsible either for sharing the costs of school construction beyond those mandated by the previous districtwide improvement plan or for financing the increase in the costs associated with the delay in selecting a site for a new magnet school.[58]

Achieving Unitary Status

Federal courts have found numerous school systems guilty of having engaged in de jure segregation and have fashioned a variety of remedies. Some orders required only a few years to demonstrate compliance, whereas others continue to exist today, even though the original decisions may have been rendered in the 1950s, 1960s, or 1970s. Such lengthy supervision has usurped the traditional roles of school administrators, elected school boards, and state legislatures regarding funding, facilities, personnel, and curriculum. Although federal judges lack the knowledge and expertise to administer schools properly or to make curricular or instructional decisions, on occasion they assumed control of these matters and then retained it for decades. With key decisions in 1991 and 1992, however, the Supreme Court provided complying districts with a means to an end.

In *Board of Education v. Dowell,* the school district had been operating since 1972 under a court-ordered plan that entailed substantial student busing to achieve integration. Five years after the initial decision, the federal district court ruled that the board had complied with the order in good faith and was entitled to pursue its legitimate policies without further court supervision. At that time, judicial monitoring was removed, but the 1972 decree was not dissolved. Later, after demographic changes led to greater burdens on minority students in continuing the student busing program, the school board in 1984 adopted a neighborhood school assignment policy for kindergarten through grade 4. The new plan was challenged because it would result in about half of the elementary schools becoming 90 percent minority or 90 percent Caucasian. The lower court upheld the plan, but the Tenth Circuit reversed. The appeals court reasoned that the district's circumstances had not changed enough to justify modifying the 1972 decree.[59] The court conjectured that compliance alone could not be the basis for dissolving an injunction and concluded that the school board failed to meet its burden of proof.

On appeal, the Supreme Court held that the appellate court's standard for dissolving the original decree was too stringent and emphasized that federal supervision of local school systems was intended only as a temporary measure to remedy past discrimination. The Court reasoned that the intent of a desegregation plan is met upon finding—as the district court had done—that the school system was operating in com-

---

57. Kelley v. Metro. County Bd. of Educ., 615 F. Supp. 1139 (M.D. Tenn. 1985).

58. Liddell v. Bd. of Educ., 20 F.3d 326 (8th Cir. 1994) (school site); Liddell v. Bd. of Educ., 988 F.2d 844 (8th Cir. 1993) (construction).

59. 890 F.2d 1483 (10th Cir. 1989).

pliance with the Equal Protection Clause and was not likely to return to its former ways. Furthermore, the Court concluded that the federal judiciary should terminate supervision of school districts where school boards have complied with desegregation mandates in good faith and have eliminated vestiges of past discrimination "to the extent practicable."[60] In making this determination, the district court on remand was directed to assess the six factors identified 23 years earlier in *Green* (i.e., student, faculty, and staff assignments; transportation; extracurricular activities; and facilities). The lower court also was instructed to reconsider whether current residential segregation in Oklahoma City was the result of private decision making and economics or a vestige of prior school segregation.

Although the *Dowell* decision gave districts the means to eventually end judicial supervision, many have had difficulty proving that they were unitary.[61] Courts have not agreed as to how long a district must be in compliance prior to ending court supervision and whether all *Green* criteria had to be met simultaneously. Then, in 1992, the Supreme Court clarified several related issues in a Georgia case, *Freeman v. Pitts.* In *Freeman,* the Court purported that a district court must relinquish its supervision and control over those aspects of a school system in which there has been compliance with a desegregation decree even if other aspects of the decree have not been met. Through this approach, the Court sought to restore to state and local authorities control over public schools at the earliest possible date and noted that "partial relinquishment of judicial control . . . can be an important and significant step in fulfilling the district court's duty to return the operations and control of schools to local authorities."[62] To guide lower courts in determining whether supervision should be removed, the Court identified three questions: Has there been full and satisfactory compliance with the decree in those aspects of the system where supervision is to be withdrawn? Is the retention of judicial control necessary or practicable to achieve compliance with the decree in other facets of the school system? Has the district demonstrated good faith commitment to the court's entire decree and relevant provisions of federal law?

With this guidance, numerous districts have been able to show that they have achieved a unitary operation. In 2001, the Seventh Circuit released the Rockford, Illinois, school district from an extensive lower court order requiring the expenditure of over $238 million. The schools were found to be desegregated, and although advanced elective courses enrolled proportionately more majority than minority students, there was no proof that such imbalance was caused by discrimination, past or present.[63]

60. 498 U.S. 237, 249–250 (1991).

61. *See, e.g.,* Lee v. Talladega County Bd. of Educ., 963 F.2d 1426 (11th Cir. 1992) (ending judicial supervision). *But see* Lee v. Etowah County Bd. of Educ., 963 F.2d 1416 (11th Cir. 1992) (continuing judicial supervision).

62. 503 U.S. 467, 489 (1992). *See also* Mills v. Freeman, 942 F. Supp. 1449 (N.D. Ga. 1996) (holding that the district had achieved unitary status in regard to faculty assignment, resource allocation, and quality of education); Arthur v. Nyquist, 904 F. Supp. 112 (W.D.N.Y. 1995) (ending 21 years of judicial supervision of the Buffalo School District and observing that control should be returned to local school authorities at the earliest practicable date given the achievement of unitary status).

63. People Who Care v. Rockford Bd. of Educ., 246 F.3d 1073 (7th Cir. 2001).

Similarly, the Eleventh Circuit supported the position that Hillsborough County, Florida, schools were unitary notwithstanding the current demographic imbalance, which the court reasoned could not be assumed to be due to prior de jure segregation.[64] Unitary status also was recognized in a number of additional cases, including those from Duval County, Florida; Charlotte-Mecklenburg, North Carolina; Muscogee County, Georgia; Russell County, Alabama; and Auburn, Alabama.[65]

Postunitary Transfer and School Assignment

Litigation will not end simply because the school district has achieved unitary status and has initially been relieved of judicial control and supervision. Any decision that may even potentially result in racial imbalance, whether de jure or de facto, is likely to be challenged. Accordingly, it is foreseeable that the placement of a new school or the creation of a new school district will be scrutinized.[66] Moreover, policies regarding school transfer, initial school assignment, open enrollment, or charter schools will be reviewed closely.

Students also have challenged presumably good faith district policies that were designed and administered to maintain racial balance or to achieve the goal of a diverse student body.[67] In such instances, students generally were permitted to enroll in or transfer to schools where their race was a minority or otherwise underrepresented (e.g., a Caucasian student would be permitted to transfer from a predominantly Caucasian school to a predominantly African American school, but not vice versa). In a Fourth Circuit case, a Caucasian student was denied the right to transfer to a magnet school with an enriched curriculum. His transfer would have adversely affected the racial diversity of the district and was therefore denied. The transfer policy applied equally to all races and was administered uniformly, unless the student could demon-

---

64. Manning v. Sch. Bd., 244 F.3d 927 (11th Cir. 2001), *cert. denied,* 534 U. S. 824 (2001).

65. NAACP, Jacksonville Branch v. Duval County Sch., 273 F.3d 960 (11th Cir. 2001); Belk v. Charlotte-Mecklenburg Bd. of Educ., 269 F.3d 305 (4th Cir. 2001); Lockett v. Bd. of Educ., 111 F.3d 839 (11th Cir. 1997); Lee v. Russell County Bd. of Educ., No. 70-T-848-E, 2002 U.S. Dist. LEXIS 4075 (M.D. Ala. Feb. 25, 2002); Lee v. Auburn City Bd. of Educ., No. 70-T-851-E, 2002 U.S. Dist. LEXIS 2527 (M.D. Ala. Feb. 14, 2002). Others, however, were not released from judicial supervision. *See, e.g.,* Jenkins v. Missouri, 216 F.3d 720 (8th Cir. 2000); Liddell v. Special Sch. Louis County, 149 F.3d 862 (8th Cir. 1998); Brown v. Bd. of Educ., 978 F.2d 585, 590 (10th Cir. 1992), *vacated and remanded,* 503 U.S. 978 (1992).

66. *See, e.g.,* Anderson v. Canton Mun. Separate Sch. Dist., 232 F.3d 450 (5th Cir. 2000); Valley v. United States, 173 F.3d 944 (5th Cir. 1999).

67. *See, e.g.,* Parents Involved in Cmty. Schs. v. Seattle Sch. Dist. No. 1, 285 F.3d 1236 (9th Cir. 2002) (concluding that under state law race may not be used as a factor in determining school assignment in an open enrollment district); Tuttle v. Arlington County Sch. Bd., 195 F.3d 698 (4th Cir. 1999) (concluding that it was unconstitutional for a board to use a weighted lottery for admission to its schools to promote racial and ethnic diversity; the goal was not to remedy past discrimination but to promote racial, ethnic, and socioeconomic diversity and was not narrowly tailored). *But see* Brewer v. W. Irondequoit Cent. Sch. Dist., 212 F.3d 738 (2d Cir. 2000) (denying a Caucasian student the right to transfer from a district where she was a minority to a district where she would be among the majority).

strate "unique hardship circumstances." The court noted that the practice was voluntary on the part of the district, rather than court ordered, and that the district had never been found guilty of segregation. In ruling for the student, the court observed that even if majority and nonmajority students were treated the same, they still were subjected to racial classification and discriminated against solely because of their race. Since race was used as the primary qualifying criterion, strict scrutiny was applied. The court argued that if it were to assume that diversity qualified as a compelling state interest (which it did not decide), the action of the board still was not narrowly tailored and was therefore unconstitutional.[68]

A similar ruling was rendered by the First Circuit in a Boston case where the assignment of students to its three renowned "examination schools," including the prestigious Boston Latin School (BLS), was based in part on race.[69] Unlike the aforementioned Fourth Circuit case, Boston had been found guilty of operating a dual school system.[70] At that time, the district court ordered integration of the public schools and stated that at least 35 percent of the enrollment at BLS be composed of African American and Hispanic students. This was done to ameliorate pervasive and persistent constitutional infirmities throughout the public school system. In 1987, the district was declared unitary in regard to student assignment, given the racial balance of the student body and the good faith efforts of school administrators. The practice of considering race when admitting students to the "examination" schools continued, however, with the intent to provide racial balance and diversity. For the purpose of resolving the case, the court assumed, without deciding, that both diversity and the desire to cure vestiges of prior discrimination qualified as compelling interests. The district's practice achieved racial balancing (i.e., a predetermined percentage of specific races), but did not result in diversity per se, as only five racial classifications (i.e., African Americans, Caucasians, Hispanics, Asians, Native Americans) were considered in making admissions decisions. The court reasoned that to achieve the goal of diversity, a far greater array of qualifications and characteristics needed to be considered and that although race and ethnic origin were important, they represented only two of potentially many factors that would contribute toward a diverse student body. In fact, the court noted that such a narrow focus of diversity would hinder rather than further the attainment of genuine diversity.

Moreover, the efforts to address past discrimination at BLS were ineffectual in that the use of racial preference advantaged some individuals who were not previously or currently victims of discrimination (e.g., African American students who had previously attended private schools, Asian students who were preferred over Caucasian students but were not considered part of the class that had been injured) to the disadvantage of others. Accordingly, the practice of admitting students in part based on race neither served a purported compelling interest nor was sufficiently narrowly tailored and was therefore unconstitutional.

68. Eisenberg v. Montgomery County Pub. Schs., 197 F.3d 123 (4th Cir. 1999).

69. Wessmann v. Gittens, 160 F.3d 790 (1st Cir. 1998).

70. Morgan v. Hennigan, 379 F. Supp. 410 (D. Mass. 1974).

The next decade should continue to provide ample desegregation case law as districts will continue to request to be relieved from judicial supervision and will be defending current policy decisions that affect racial balance. Nonetheless, the stage appears set for a significant reduction in judicial control and a long-awaited return of school operations to school administrators, teachers, and boards.

Classifications Based on Native Language

Among the numerous identifiable "classes" of students in U.S. schools are "linguistic minorities," some of whom have been denied an adequate education due to the failure of the school district to address their language barriers through appropriate instruction. Although programs that are designed to meet the educational needs of linguistic minorities are largely financed through state and local funds, the federal government provides modest funding for research regarding how students learn a second language, how to train instructors, and the effectiveness of alternative teaching methodologies and programs.[71] The Office of English Language Acquisition, Language Enhancement, and Academic Achievement for Limited English Proficient Students administers the grant programs, provides leadership and technical assistance, coordinates services, promotes best practice, and assesses outcomes. Through efforts such as these, many students today are provided with English language instruction that allows them to benefit from the public school curriculum. However, when access to school is denied or when language barriers are not removed,[72] students often turn to federal courts for protection. The rights of linguistic minorities are protected by the Fourteenth Amendment,[73] Title VI of the Civil Rights Act of 1964, and the Equal Educational Opportunities Act of 1974 (EEOA).

Title VI stipulates that "no person in the United States shall, on the ground of race, color, or national origin, be excluded from participation in, be denied the benefits of, or be subjected to discrimination under any program or activity receiving [f]ederal financial assistance from the Department of Education."[74] Moreover, this statute requires compliance throughout a school district if *any* activity is supported by federal funds (e.g., the federal lunch program). Discrimination against linguistic minorities is

---

71. 20 U.S.C. §§ 3420, 3423d, 6931, 6932 (2002).

72. Most bilingual and ESL programs are intended to eliminate foreign language barriers. As a result, there have been times when students speaking minority English dialects (e.g., black English) or American Sign Language have been denied specialized language services. *See, e.g.,* Martin Luther King Junior Elementary Sch. Children v. Ann Arbor Sch. Dist. Bd., 473 F. Supp. 1371 (E.D. Mich. 1979) (black English); Kielbus v. New York City Bd. of Educ., 140 F. Supp. 2d 284 (E.D.N.Y. 2001) (sign language).

73. *Strict scrutiny* is applied when the acts are facially discriminatory; *intent* is required when the acts are facially neutral (e.g., when tests administered only in English are used to determine enrollment in gifted programs).

74. 42 U.S.C. § 2000d *et seq.* (2002). Regulations may be found at 34 C.F.R. § 100 *et seq.* (2002).

considered a form of national origin discrimination and is therefore prohibited by Title VI.

In addition, the EEOA requires public school systems to develop appropriate programs for limited English proficient (LEP) students.[75] The act mandates in part that "no state shall deny equal educational opportunity to an individual on account of his or her race, color, sex, or national origin, by . . . the failure by an educational agency to take appropriate action to overcome language barriers that impede equal participation by its students in its instructional program."[76] The EEOA does not impose any specific type of instruction or teaching methodology on education agencies but rather requires "appropriate action."[77]

In the only United States Supreme Court decision involving the rights of LEP students, *Lau v. Nichols,* Chinese children asserted that the San Francisco public schools failed to provide for the needs of non-English-speaking students. The Supreme Court agreed with the students and held that the lack of sufficient remedial English instruction violated Title VI. The Court reasoned that equality of treatment was not realized merely by providing students with the same facilities, textbooks, teachers, and curriculum, and that requiring children to acquire English skills on their own before they could hope to make any progress in school made "a mockery of public education."[78] The Court emphasized that "basic English skills are at the very core of what these public schools teach;" therefore, "students who do not understand English are effectively foreclosed from any meaningful education."[79]

As a rule, courts acknowledge that there are numerous legitimate educational theories and practices that may be used to eliminate language barriers; courts do not typically require one method (e.g., bilingual education) over another. In fact, they tend to order the use of bilingual education (often the method preferred by plaintiffs) only when less expensive and less cumbersome options have proven ineffective.[80] In making such determinations, courts will examine the level of resources committed to the various programs, the competency and training of the instructors, the methods of classifying students for instruction, and the procedures for evaluating student progress.

A Colorado federal district court, in assessing compliance of the Denver Public Schools, concluded that the law does not require a full bilingual education program for every LEP student but does place a duty on the district to take action to eliminate barriers that prevent LEP children from participating in the educational program. According to the court, good faith effort is inadequate; what is required, according to the court,

75. 20 U.S.C. § 1701 *et seq.* (2002).

76. 20 U.S.C. § 1703(f) (2002).

77. Flores v. Arizona, 172 F. Supp. 2d 1225 (D. Ariz. 2000) (finding that the state failed to take appropriate action to remedy language barriers).

78. Lau v. Nichols, 414 U.S. 563, 566 (1974).

79. *Id.*

80. Guadalupe Org. v. Tempe Elementary Sch. Dist. No. 3, 587 F.2d 1022 (9th Cir. 1978); Castaneda v. Pickard, 648 F.2d 989 (5th Cir. 1981).

is an effort that "will be reasonably effective in producing intended results."[81] Such an effort was not found in the Denver public schools. Although a transitional bilingual program was selected by district personnel, it was not being implemented effectively, primarily due to poor teacher training, selection, and assignment. Accordingly, an EEOA violation was found. Likewise, the Seventh Circuit, in examining Illinois's compliance, argued that "appropriate action" under the law certainly means more than "no action."[82] Once again, the court found that the selection of transitional bilingual education was appropriate, but that it had not been effectively implemented. The court identified both an EEOA violation and a violation of Title VI regulations.

In contrast, a California school district's Spanish bilingual program and three forms of English as a second language were judicially endorsed. District teachers were found to be proficient, qualified, and experienced; native-language academic support was available for 38 languages in all subjects; and a cultural enrichment program was operating for grades K through 3. Plaintiffs claimed a violation of the EEOA and Title VI and requested instruction in the students' native tongue. The court disagreed and found that the program was based on sound theory, implemented consistent with that theory, and produced satisfactory results (i.e., area LEP students were learning at rates equal to or higher than their English-speaking counterparts.)[83]

In recent years, California has generated a significant amount of case law involving the instruction of non- and limited-English-speaking students. Most suits attack Proposition 227, which requires that all children within public schools be taught English through "sheltered English immersion" (SEI) (i.e., specially designed materials and procedures where "nearly all" classroom instruction is in English). In most instances, the law requires school districts to abandon their use of bilingual education. Notwithstanding the prior use of bilingual programming, immigrant children within the state had experienced a high dropout rate and were low in English literacy. Only those children who already possess good English language skills or those for whom an alternate course of study would be better suited may be excused from the SEI initiative. Even then, 20 or more exempted students per grade level are required before an alternative program such as bilingual education needs to be provided.

To ensure that the SEI approach is used, the state legislature included a *parental enforcement provision* in the law that gives parents the right to sue to receive SEI instruction, as well as for actual damages and attorneys' fees. Any educator who willfully and repeatedly refuses to teach "overwhelmingly" in English may be held personally liable. The state teachers' association attacked this provision as being unconstitutionally vague. But, the Ninth Circuit found terms such as *nearly all* and *overwhelmingly* to be no more vague than other descriptive terms used in the writing of statutes and reasoned that such language was likely to deter only a negligible amount of non-English speech, if any.[84]

---

81. Keyes v. Sch. Dist. No. 1, Denver, Colo., 576 F. Supp. 1503, 1520 (D. Colo. 1983).

82. Gomez v. Ill. State Bd. of Educ., 811 F.2d 1030, 1043 (7th Cir. 1987).

83. Teresa P. v. Berkeley Unified Sch. Dist., 724 F. Supp. 698 (N.D. Cal. 1989).

For decades, educators have disagreed as to which method is best for instructing LEP students. The "best," however, is not legally required. What is required is the elimination of language barriers that will allow LEP students the opportunity to participate in the programs and activities offered in public school.

Classifications Based on Ability or Achievement

Courts have generally upheld decisions related to grade placement, denial of promotion, and assignment to instructional groups. Ability grouping purportedly permits more effective and efficient teaching by allowing teachers to concentrate their efforts on students with similar needs. Grouping according to ability or achievement is permissible, although there have been challenges concerning the use of standardized intelligence and achievement tests for determining pupil placements in regular classes and special education programs. These suits have alleged that such tests are racially and culturally biased and that their use to classify or track pupils results in erroneous placements that stigmatize children. Other challenges have arisen regarding the rights of gifted and talented students to an appropriate education.

Tracking Schemes

In the most widely publicized case pertaining to ability grouping, *Hobson v. Hansen,* the use of standardized intelligence test scores to place elementary and secondary students in various ability tracks in Washington, D.C., was attacked as unconstitutional.[85] Plaintiffs contended that some children were erroneously assigned to lower tracks and had very little chance of advancing to higher ones because of the limited curriculum and lack of remedial instruction. The federal district court examined the test scores used to track students, analyzed the accuracy of the test measurements, and concluded that mistakes often resulted from placing pupils on this basis. For the first time, a federal court evaluated testing methods and held that they discriminated against minority children. In prohibiting the continued use of such test scores, the court emphasized that it was *not* abolishing the use of tracking systems per se and reasoned that "what is at issue here is not whether defendants are entitled to provide different kinds of students with different kinds of education."[86] The court noted that

---

84. Cal. Teachers Ass'n v. State Bd. of Educ., 271 F.3d 1141 (9th Cir. 2001). *See also* Doe v. L.A. Unified Sch. Dist., 48 F. Supp. 2d 1233 (C.D. Cal. 1999) (certifying a class action to challenge Proposition 227).

85. 269 F. Supp. 401 (D.D.C. 1967), *aff'd sub nom.* Smuck v. Hobson, 408 F.2d 175 (D.C. Cir. 1969). Many of the cases addressing the use of ability grouping are based on the Fourteenth Amendment. Because ability grouping based on various forms of assessment (usually testing) is facially neutral, the appropriate Fourteenth Amendment standard is *intent.* Meeting this standard of review has been difficult, particularly when cases also do not involve de jure segregation.

86. *Hobson,* 269 F. Supp. at 511.

classifications reasonably related to educational purposes are constitutionally permissible unless they result in discrimination against identifiable groups of children.

The Fifth Circuit agreed with this latter point in its evaluation of a tracking scheme in Jackson, Mississippi.[87] Although the court had previously struck down the plan given its impact on integration efforts, it later noted that "as a general rule, school systems are free to employ ability grouping, even when such a policy has a segregative effect, so long . . . as such a practice is genuinely motivated by educational concerns and not discriminatory motives."[88]

Based on evidence indicating that ability grouping provided better educational opportunities for African American students, the Eleventh Circuit in 1985 upheld grouping practices in several Georgia school districts even though they had not achieved desegregated status.[89] Ability grouping allowed resources to be targeted toward low-achieving students and resulted in both gains on statewide tests and the reassignment of many students to higher-level achievement groups. The court further noted that, unlike students in earlier cases, these students had not attended inferior segregated schools. School systems undergoing desegregation may be subjected to closer judicial review when implementing ability grouping, but such plans will be prohibited only if found to be a ploy to resegregate students.[90]

When children are evaluated and provided with appropriate programs or grouped by ability, it is essential that all testing instruments be reliable, valid, and unbiased to the extent practical and possible. Although a few courts have found some tests to include specific questions that are racially biased[91] or administered in discriminatory ways (e.g., not in the student's native language or other mode of communication), such cases occur far less often today. Test developers have made extensive efforts to improve the reliability and validity of their instruments and to remove known forms of cultural, ethnic, and racial bias. As a result, it is unlikely that a nationally normed and marketed test used to measure ability or aptitude will be found racially biased. Nonetheless, prudent educators should take every precaution to ensure that accurate assessments are employed. Moreover, only qualified and certified school psychologists and others should be hired who are capable of nondiscriminatory administration, use multiple criteria in determining an appropriate track or placement, and evaluate test results in good faith. Care also should be taken to ensure that teachers do not discriminate against students assigned to lower tracks or develop stereotypes about their abilities or potential.[92]

87. Singleton v. Jackson Mun. Separate Sch. Dist., 419 F.2d 1211 (5th Cir. 1969).

88. Castaneda v. Pickard, 648 F.2d 989, 996 (5th Cir. 1981). On appeal of remand, the court affirmed the district court's finding that ability grouping did not discriminate on the basis of race, 781 F.2d 456 (5th Cir. 1986).

89. Ga. State Conference of Branches of NAACP v. Georgia, 775 F.2d 1403 (11th Cir. 1985).

90. *See, e.g.,* Bester v. Tuscaloosa City Bd. of Educ., 722 F.2d 1514 (11th Cir. 1984).

91. *See* Larry P. v. Riles, 495 F. Supp. 926 (N.D. Cal. 1979), *aff'd,* 793 F.2d 969 (9th Cir. 1984).

92. *See, e.g.,* United States v. City of Yonkers, 197 F.3d 41 (2d Cir. 1999).

Gifted and Talented Students

Often overlooked when identifying unique needs and providing appropriate programs are those students labeled as "gifted" or "talented." Over the years, the federal government has provided only limited aid for gifted education, and there is no federal law specifying substantive rights for the gifted as there is for children with disabilities, although the Equal Protection Clause provides general protection for this class as well as for others.

A federal effort to support gifted programs is the Jacob K. Javits Gifted and Talented Students Education Act.[93] This act supports the No Child Left Behind Act of 2001[94] by providing a coordinated program to enhance the ability of elementary and secondary schools to meet the educational needs of gifted and talented students, particularly those from disadvantaged or underrepresented groups. Under this law, gifted students are those who give evidence of high performance capability in areas such as intellectual, creative, artistic, or leadership capacity, or in specific academic fields, and who require services or activities not ordinarily provided by the school in order to fully develop such capabilities. Funds available under the act may be used toward establishing preservice and in-service training for personnel; developing and operating model projects and exemplary programs, including summer programs and cooperative programs involving business, industry, and education; strengthening the capability of state educational agencies and institutions of higher education to provide leadership and assistance; providing technical assistance and information dissemination; and carrying out research or conducting evaluations.

Any additional rights for gifted and talented students are based on state law or local school board policy. A few states meet the needs of gifted and talented children in much the same way that the Individuals with Disabilities Education Act requires the needs of children with disabilities to be met—that is, through an individualized education program or other instructional plan. Others provide a spattering of programs throughout the state or at least offer accelerated courses. Some states, however, have not even counted the number of gifted students residing in their service areas, nor have they agreed on definitions for identifying qualified youth; the appropriate instruments or cut-off scores to be used in assessment; the depth, duration, or delivery of an appropriate curriculum; or the procedures used to regulate admissions in light of court ordered integration mandates.[95]

Pennsylvania, one of the leading states in mandating programs for the gifted, includes gifted and talented students under its designation of "exceptional children" who "deviate from the average in physical, mental, emotional or social characteristics

---

93. Pub. Law 107-110, Title V, Part D, Subpart 6 of the Elementary and Secondary Education Act (1992).

94. No Child Left Behind Act of 2001, 20 U.S.C. 6301 et seq. (2002).

95. *See, e.g.,* Jacksonville Branch, NAACP v. Duval County Sch. Bd., No. 85-316-Civ-J-10C, 1999 U.S. Dist. LEXIS 15711 (M.D. Fla. May 27, 1999); Manning v. Sch. Bd., 24 F. Supp. 2d 1277 (M.D. Fla. 1998).

to such an extent that they require special educational facilities or services."[96] The Pennsylvania Supreme Court interpreted this law as placing a mandatory obligation on school districts to establish individualized programs for gifted students beyond the general enrichment program.[97] However, the court qualified its interpretation of state statute by observing that the law does not require "exclusive individual programs outside or beyond the district's existing, regular, and special education curricular offerings"[98] and does not impose a duty to maximize a child's potential. Given this precedent, when the parents of a gifted child demanded reimbursement for college tuition, the board was within its authority to deny the request.[99] The board had never agreed to pay for the courses and had provided the student with advanced programming, permission to be away from school during his college courses, and independent study.

In Connecticut, a gifted student claimed to have the right to a special, individualized education under state statute, given that gifted children were included within the state definition of exceptional children (i.e., those who do not progress effectively in a regular school program without special education). The local school board refused to provide the program and the student filed suit. The Supreme Court of Connecticut disagreed with the student's claim, however, and held that he was not entitled to a special education, that the state never intended to extend such a right, and that special education must be provided only for students with disabilities. No equal protection violation was proved because the state's action of serving individuals with disabilities, but not the gifted, met rational basis scrutiny.[100]

Along these same lines, New York law stipulates that school districts *should* develop programs to assist gifted students in achieving their full potential. However, an appellate court found that the use of the word *should* indicated that the development of gifted programs was optional, not mandatory.[101] Consequently, the court held that a district was permitted to serve only a portion of the students identified as gifted and to select those students through a lottery system. Although use of a lottery may seem illogical, it provides an equal opportunity for each qualified youth to participate and does not illegally discriminate.

The procedures used to select students who are to participate in gifted courses or programs continue to be challenged. Obviously, this is a problem only in those programs where space is limited and enrollments are capped. Criteria such as IQ, test

---

96. Pa. Stat. Ann. tit. 24 § 13-1371(1) (Purdon, West Supp. 2002).

97. Centennial Sch. Dist. v. Commonwealth Dep't of Educ, 539 A.2d 785 (Pa. 1988).

98. *Centennial Sch. Dist.,* 539 A.2d at 791.

99. New Brighton Area Sch. Dist. v. Matthew Z., 697 A.2d 1056 (Pa. Commw. Ct. 1997). *See also* Brownsville Area Sch. Dist. v. Student X, 729 A.2d 198 (Pa. Commw. Ct. 1999) (determining that college courses and other education beyond the current offerings of the district did not have to be provided to a gifted student).

100. Broadley v. Bd. of Educ., 639 A.2d 502 (Conn. 1994).

101. Bennett v. City Sch. Dist., 497 N.Y.S.2d 72 (App. Div. 1985).

scores, grade-point average, and teacher evaluations are used in the selection process. Although age under certain circumstances may be a permissible criterion for admission (as discussed below), gender and race will seldom be permitted unless court ordered.[102] Even then, the court must perceive the preference and current act of discrimination to be narrowly tailored and to last only long enough to address prior discrimination.

Classifications Based on Age

Age is one of the factors most commonly used to classify individuals, not only in schools but also in society. For example, a specified age is used as a prerequisite to obtaining a driver's license, buying alcoholic beverages, viewing certain movies, and receiving federal benefits. The two primary federal grounds used by students when they claim age-based violations are the Fourteenth Amendment[103] and the Age Discrimination Act of 1975.[104] The Age Discrimination Act applies to recipients of federal financial assistance, has a statute of limitations of 180 days, requires the exhaustion of administrative remedies prior to the filing of suit,[105] and prohibits some forms of age discrimination. This law is seldom used today, and when a violation is claimed, it generally is directed toward a college or university rather than a K–12 school or district (e.g., a claim that age was used as a basis to deny admission to a law school or medical school[106]). But age discrimination also has been litigated at the K–12 level, particularly in regard to early school admission or to eligibility for particular programs or activities.

Ranges vary, but within most states, students *must* attend school between the ages of 6 and 16 and *may* attend between the ages of 3 and 21. Students below or above state-established age limits have neither a state property right nor a federal constitutional right to public school attendance. Nevertheless, parents have challenged state and local decisions denying admission or services. In a Texas case, a policy was challenged that excluded children under the age of 6 as of September 1 of the current year

---

102. Rosenfeld v. Montgomery County Pub. Schs., 25 Fed. Appx. 123 (4th Cir. 2001) (affirming dismissal of case as the plaintiff eventually was admitted to the gifted program; the court acknowledged, however, that if different, less stringent selection criteria had been used for minority students, the plaintiff would have had a basis for seeking damages).

103. Under the Fourteenth Amendment, rational basis scrutiny is required in age cases where the policy or practice is facially discriminatory and intent must be shown where the act is facially neutral.

104. 42 U.S.C. §§ 6101 *et seq.* (2002).

105. 42 U.S.C. § 6104(e)(2)(B) (2002). *See also* Simmons v. Middle Tenn. State Univ., No. 95-6111, 1997 U.S. App. LEXIS 17751 (6th Cir. July 11, 1997).

106. *See, e.g.,* Homola v. S. Ill. Univ. at Carbondale, Sch. of Law, No. 93-1940, 1993 U.S. App. LEXIS 34465 (7th Cir. Dec. 16, 1993).

from admission to the first grade.[107] The plaintiff had completed kindergarten in a private accredited school and had scored well on a standardized test, but was two months too young to qualify. The district had uniformly adhered to the state statute and local policy, refusing all requests for early admission. Noting this uniform application, the Texas Court of Appeals upheld the school district's action. Similar decisions have been reached by other courts in denying students admission to kindergarten and other programs.[108] Rationales used to justify the consideration of age include the state's right to limit the benefit of public education and related curricular and extracurricular opportunities to children between specific ages, the administrative need to project enrollment, the costs of assessing learning readiness and meeting a wide range of individual needs, and the desire for children to develop emotionally, socially, and physiologically prior to admission.

In addition to admissions decisions, age can be used as one of several criteria to determine eligibility for special courses or programs (e.g., college credit courses; gifted programs), selected activities (e.g., interscholastic sports[109]), or specialized services (e.g., those available under the Individuals with Disabilities Education Act). As discussed in Chapter 6, the IDEA mandates that services must be available for all children with disabilities between the ages of 3 and 21, although school districts are not required to provide programs for children with disabilities under the state's minimum school age unless programs are being provided for other children in that age group. Concomitantly, if services are provided for other students beyond 18 years of age, students with disabilities are entitled to similar opportunities.

With few exceptions (e.g., when interscholastic sports participation has been written into an overage student's individualized educational program), it is unlikely that schools will be restricted in their uniform application of legitimate age requirements. Where exceptions are made, school personnel must document a legal and permissible basis.

Classifications Based on Gender

Gender classifications and discriminatory treatment based on gender in public education are as old as public education itself, as the first public schools and colleges primarily served males. When women were eventually allowed to enroll, programs were typically segregated and inferior. Over the years, gender equality in public schools has

---

107. Wright v. Ector County Indep. Sch. Dist., 867 S.W.2d 863 (Tex. Ct. App. 1993). *See also* Morrison v. Chic. Bd. of Educ., 544 N.E.2d 1099 (Ill. App. Ct. 1989) (holding that local board had discretion whether to assess a child to determine readiness to attend kindergarten).

108. *See, e.g.,* Zweifel v. Joint Dist. No. 1, Belleville, 251 N.W.2d 822 (Wis. 1977); O'Leary v. Wisecup, 364 A.2d 770 (Pa. Commw. Ct. 1976).

109. *See, e.g.,* Cruz v. Pa. Interscholastic Athletic Ass'n, 157 F. Supp. 2d 485 (E.D. Pa. 2001).

improved, but at times gender classifications have limited both academic as well as extracurricular activities for females.

Aggrieved parties often have turned to federal courts to vindicate their rights. In most cases, plaintiffs allege a violation of either the Fourteenth Amendment[110] or Title IX of the Education Amendments of 1972.[111] Under Title IX, educational recipients of federal financial assistance are prohibited from discriminating, excluding, or denying benefits because of gender.[112] Interestingly, Title IX applies in some situations where the Fourteenth Amendment does not (e.g., when the recipient institution is a private school), and conversely the Fourteenth Amendment applies at times when Title IX does not (e.g., in the rare instance that a public school district does not receive federal funds).

Interscholastic Sports

Gender discrimination litigation involving interscholastic sports has focused on two primary themes: the integration of single-gender teams and the unequal treatment of males and females (e.g., the number of athletic opportunities available for males and females, the use of facilities, the selection of "seasons," and the development of different rules for competition). Although courts will issue injunctions to correct discriminatory conduct where it is found, they will not award monetary damages unless the school receives actual notice of the violation and then is shown to be deliberately indifferent to the claim.[113]

Single-Gender Teams.   One of the more controversial issues involving high school athletics is the participation of males and females together in contact sports (i.e., boxing, wrestling, rugby, ice hockey, football, basketball, and other sports that involve bodily contact). A Title IX regulation allows recipients to

> operate or sponsor separate teams for members of each sex where selection for such teams is based upon competitive skill or the activity involved is a contact sport. However, where a recipient operates or sponsors a team in a particular sport for members of one sex but operates or sponsors no such team for members of the other sex, and athletic opportunities for members of that sex have previously been limited, members of the excluded sex must be allowed to try out for the team offered unless the sport involved is a contact sport.[114]

---

110. Under the Fourteenth Amendment, *intermediate scrutiny* is applied in gender cases where facial discrimination exists, whereas *intent* is used when facially neutral practices result in alleged discrimination.

111. 20 U.S.C. § 1681 (2002).

112. Furthermore, if aid is received by any program or activity within the school system, compliance must be demonstrated district wide.

113. Grandson v. Univ., 272 F.3d 568 (8th Cir. 2001), *cert. denied,* 122 S. Ct. 1910 (2002).

114. 34 C.F.R. § 106.41(b) (2002).

Accordingly, Title IX permits, but does not require, gender segregation in contact sports. Because Title IX does not explicitly proscribe female participation on contact teams, it has been interpreted to allow each school the flexibility of determining whether to meet the goal of equal athletic opportunity through single-gender or coeducational teams. However, in many instances, athletic association rules have limited the options available to school districts by prohibiting coeducational competition.

The Sixth Circuit reviewed an Ohio High School Athletic Association rule that prohibited coeducational participation in all contact sports in grades 7 through 12.[115] In this case, the school system wanted to establish coeducational interscholastic basketball teams at the middle school level. The appeals court, noting that compliance with Title IX rests with individual schools and not with athletic associations, concluded that the rule impermissibly restricted the discretion of school systems to provide equal athletic opportunities for female students. The court emphasized, however, that its ruling did not mean that all teams must be coeducational or that Title IX's regulations were unconstitutional because they permitted separate teams.[116]

In a Fourteenth Amendment case, a federal district court in New York reviewed a female student's request to try out for the junior varsity football squad.[117] The school district was unable to show that its policy of prohibiting mixed competition served an important governmental objective. In rejecting the district's assertion that its policy was necessary to ensure the health and safety of female students, the court noted that no female student was given the opportunity to show that she was as fit, or more fit, than the weakest male member of the team.

A Wisconsin federal district court similarly ruled that female students have the right to compete for positions on traditionally male contact teams, declaring that once a state provides interscholastic competition, such opportunities must be provided to all students on equal terms.[118] The court reasoned that the objective of preventing injury to female athletes was not sufficient to justify the prohibition of coeducational teams in contact sports. In preventing the school district from denying female students the opportunity to participate in varsity interscholastic competition in certain contact sports, the court noted that school officials had options available other than establishing coeducational teams: Interscholastic competition in these sports could be eliminated for all students or separate teams for females could be established. The court also recognized that if comparable gender-segregated programs were provided,

---

115. Yellow Springs Exempted Vill. Sch. Dist. Bd. of Educ. v. Ohio High Sch. Athletic Ass'n, 647 F.2d 651 (6th Cir. 1981).

116. It is unlikely that state athletic associations will be subjected to Title IX suits in the future as the Supreme Court has ruled that the receipt of dues from member institutions that are recipients of federal aid does not make the association an indirect recipient. NCAA v. Smith, 525 U.S. 459 (1999).

117. Lantz v. Ambach, 620 F. Supp. 663 (S.D.N.Y. 1985). *See also* Adams v. Baker, 919 F. Supp. 1496 (D. Kan. 1996) (upholding female student's right under the Fourteenth Amendment to participate in wrestling).

118. Leffel v. Wis. Interscholastic Athletic Ass'n, 444 F. Supp. 1117 (E.D. Wis. 1978).

female athletes could not assert the right to try out for the male team simply because of its higher level of competition.

Where integration is either permitted or required in a contact sport, each athlete must receive a fair, nondiscriminatory opportunity to participate. In a 1999 case from North Carolina, a female kicker made the football team but was later dropped; she also was given only limited opportunities to participate or to condition. The Fourth Circuit concluded that where integration is permitted, it may not be accompanied by gender discrimination; the court then remanded for a determination of whether the restrictions placed on the kicker were based on gender.[119]

In addition to the controversies regarding coeducational participation in contact sports, there have been numerous challenges to policies denying gender integration of noncontact sports. Females filed the majority of these suits and prevailed in nearly every instance.[120] As noted, Title IX regulations explicitly require recipient districts to allow coeducational participation in those sports that are available only to one gender, presuming that athletic opportunities for that gender have been historically limited. Thus, females tend to succeed in their claims, whereas males tend to fail,[121] notwithstanding the fact that the same laws and standards[122] apply to both genders. As a rule, school districts have been able to show an important governmental interest (e.g., redressing disparate athletic opportunities for females) in support of their decisions to exclude males from participating on teams traditionally reserved for females,[123] whereas males have had difficulty supporting the claim that their athletic opportunities have been historically limited.

Fewer Sports Opportunities for Females.   Although athletic opportunities for females have significantly increased since passage of Title IX in 1972, equal opportunity has not been achieved within all school districts. State efforts to provide a greater number of opportunities for girls have been weakened significantly by public education budgetary problems. Expenditures for special education, literacy, the elimination of language barriers, school safety, and the like have been given priority when dividing a shrinking public purse. As a result, in recent years equality of athletic opportunities for males and females often has been achieved either by reducing the

---

119. Mercer v. Duke Univ., 190 F.3d 643 (4th Cir. 1999).

120. *See, e.g.,* Croteau v. Fair, 686 F. Supp. 552 (E.D. Va. 1988); Israel v. W. Va. Secondary Sch. Activities Comm'n, 388 S.E.2d 480 (W. Va. 1989).

121. *See, e.g.,* Williams v. Sch. Dist., 998 F.2d 168 (3d Cir. 1993) (remanding to determine whether the "real" opportunities for females exceeded those for males and whether the opportunities available to males were limited); B.C. v. Bd. of Educ., Cumberland Reg'l Sch. Dist., 531 A.2d 1059 (N.J. Super. Ct. App. Div. 1987) (excluding a male from the field hockey team was permitted because allowing his participation would result in unequal opportunities for males and females).

122. *See, e.g.,* Clark v. Arizona, 695 F.2d 1126 (9th Cir. 1982) (excluding a male from the volleyball team was upheld under intermediate scrutiny).

123. *See, e.g.,* Rowley v. Members of the Bd. of Educ., 863 F.2d 39 (10th Cir. 1988) (denying a male the opportunity to participate in volleyball).

number of sports traditionally available for males,[124] or by lowering the number of participants on boys teams (e.g., football) to provide generally equal opportunities for boys and girls.[125]

Additionally, at times female athletes have expressed an insufficient interest in a given sport to have it approved by the state athletic association. In a Kentucky case, female high school athletes claimed a Title IX violation when the state athletic association refused to approve females' interscholastic fast-pitch softball. The association's decision was based on its policy of not sanctioning a sport unless at least 25 percent of its member institutions demonstrated an interest in participation. Since only 17 percent indicated an interest, approval was denied. In the original hearing on this controversy in 1994, the Sixth Circuit had held that the 25 percent requirement did not violate the Equal Protection Clause (i.e., the facially neutral policy was not proven to entail intentional discrimination).[126] The case then was remanded and later appealed in 2000. The court again found no Title IX violation and further concluded that grouping sports by gender did not violate federal law. Moreover, the court resolved that the plaintiffs did not qualify for attorneys' fees because they did not prevail.[127] Plaintiffs had argued that since fast-pitch softball is now available in the state, they ultimately were the winning party. The court noted, however, that such relief was not court ordered and plaintiffs could not show that they were responsible for the change in state law directing the association to offer the requested sport.

In a higher education case, Brown University responded to budget cuts in 1991 by eliminating two interscholastic teams for men and two for women. At the time of the reductions, only 37 percent of the participants in varsity sports, compared to 48 percent of the institution's students, were women. By 1994, the ratio had not changed. The First Circuit found a Title IX violation, concurring with the Office for Civil Rights' policy interpretation that for schools to be in compliance, they should (1) provide interscholastic sports opportunities for both genders in terms of numbers of participants that are substantially proportionate to the respective enrollments of male and female students, (2) show a history of expanding sports programs for the underrepresented gender, or (3) provide enough opportunities to match the sports interests and abilities of the underrepresented gender.[128] The court rejected the university's unproven assertion that female students were less interested in sports and viewed the comment as being based on a stereotypical view of women.

---

124. *See, e.g.,* Chalenor v. Univ. of N.D., No. 00-3379ND, 2002 U.S. App. LEXIS 14404 (8th Cir. May 30, 2002); Boulahanis v. Bd. of Regents, Ill. State Univ., 198 F.3d 633 (7th Cir. 1999); Miami Univ. Wrestling Club v. Miami Univ., 195 F. Supp. 2d 1010 (S.D. Ohio 2001).

125. Neal v. Bd. of Trs., 198 F.3d 763 (9th Cir. 1999) (concluding that a board may limit the size of its men's teams, rather than eliminate some teams altogether, to reduce the number of scholarships provided men).

126. Horner v. Ky. High Sch. Athletic Ass'n, 43 F.3d 265 (6th Cir. 1994).

127. Horner v. Ky. High Sch. Athletic Ass'n, 206 F.3d 685 (6th Cir. 2000). *See also* Kelley v. Bd. of Trs., 35 F.3d 265 (7th Cir. 1994) (permitting the termination of men's swimming while retaining women's swimming).

Modified Sports and Separate Seasons for Females.   Among the equity claims initiated by female athletes are those contesting the use of gender-based modifications in sports. Although federal courts historically have permitted different rules for boys and girls (e.g., split-court rules for women's basketball), unfounded and unsupported stereotypes about either gender regarding strength, endurance, or ability will no longer justify differential treatment of male and female athletes.[129]

Also, maintaining separate playing seasons for female and male teams has been challenged as a violation of the equal protection clauses of both federal and state constitutions. In some instances, separate seasons have been upheld due to a lack of adequate facilities and general comparability of programs;[130] in other instances, separate playing seasons have been found to violate equal protection rights. This was the case in Michigan in 2001, where a federal district court ruled that the difficulty in finding facilities, coaches, and officials did not justify the use of separate seasons for boys and girls where the girls bore the burden of off-season participation.[131] The court opined that if single-sexed seasons were in fact necessary, the burden must be shared. For example, the court suggested that junior varsity teams of both sexes could be placed into the disadvantageous season and that the varsity teams then could compete during the preferred season. This plan would result in the same utilization of facilities and staff, yet the advantages and disadvantages of off-season play would be equally divided between the sexes.

This position also was subscribed to by the West Virginia high court when it held that the scheduling of the girls' basketball season outside the traditional season violated the state Equal Protection Clause.[132] Such a practice did not serve an important governmental interest and effectively excluded female athletes from interstate competition, disadvantaged them with regard to gaining access to college recruiters, limited their time in the gym to hot summer months, and resulted in reduced interest by the public and the media. The simple solution to this problem was to have both teams share facilities and play during the "regular" season when at all possible. When that was not possible, alternating the season among male and female teams was found permissible, assuming that the burden was shouldered equally by both genders.

128. Cohen v. Brown Univ., 101 F.3d 155 (1st Cir. 1996). *See also* Pederson v. La. State Univ., 213 F.3d 858 (5th Cir. 2000) (concluding that the university had violated Title IX by failing to accommodate effectively the interests and abilities of certain female athletes); Boucher v. Syracuse Univ., 164 F.3d 113 (2d Cir. 1999) (reviewing class certification claims by female students who were claiming discrimination based on the unequal participation opportunities and scholarships available to male and female athletes).

129. Cape v. Tenn. Secondary Sch. Athletic Ass'n, 563 F.2d 793 (6th Cir. 1977) (permitting the use of split-court rules as they reflected physical differences between males and females). *But see* Dodson v. Ark. Activities Ass'n, 468 F. Supp. 394 (E.D. Ark. 1979) (invalidating the use of separate basketball rules for males and females).

130. *See, e.g.,* Ridgeway v. Mont. High Sch. Ass'n, 749 F. Supp. 1544 (D. Mont. 1990); Striebel v. Minn. State High Sch. League, 321 N.W.2d 400 (Minn. 1982).

131. Cmtys. for Equity v. Mich. High Sch. Athletic Ass'n, 178 F. Supp. 2d 805 (W.D. Mich. 2001).

132. State *ex rel.* Lambert v. W. Va. State Bd. of Educ., 447 S.E.2d 901 (W. Va. 1994).

Academic Programs

Allegations of gender bias in public schools have not been confined to athletic programs. Differential treatment of males and females in academic courses and schools also has generated litigation.[133] Although the "separate but equal" principle has been applied in this area, as it has in athletics, rulings indicate that public school officials must bear the burden of showing a substantial justification for classifications based on gender in academic programs. Moreover, where the programs are separate, they must be proven equal.

Single-Gender Schools. In a Third Circuit case, the court held that the operation of gender-segregated public high schools, in which enrollment is voluntary and educational offerings are essentially equal, is permissible under the Equal Protection Clause and the Equal Educational Opportunities Act of 1974.[134] Noting that Philadelphia's gender-segregated college preparatory schools offered functionally equivalent programs, the court concluded that the separation of males and females was justified because adolescents might study more effectively in gender-segregated high schools. The court emphasized that the female plaintiff was not compelled to attend the gender-segregated academic school; she had the option of enrolling in a coeducational school within her attendance zone. Furthermore, the court stated that her petition to attend the male academic high school was based on personal preference rather than on an objective evaluation of the offerings available in the two schools. Subsequently, an equally divided United States Supreme Court affirmed this decision without delivering an opinion.

In contrast, Detroit school officials did not prevail in their attempt to segregate inner-city, African American male students to address more effectively these students' unique educational needs. Three African American male academies (preschool to fifth grade, sixth to eighth grade, and high school) were proposed. The three-year experimental academies were to offer an Afrocentric, pluralistic curriculum, including a futuristic course on preparation for the twenty-first century. The programs were to emphasize male responsibility, provide mentors, offer Saturday classes and extended classroom hours, provide individual counseling, and require student uniforms. No comparable program existed for females, although school authorities indicated that one would be forthcoming. The district court issued a preliminary injunction prohibiting the board from opening the academies, given the likelihood that the practice violated the Equal Protection Clause, Title IX, and state law. Additionally, the court reasoned that failing to provide the injunction could result in irreparable injury to the female students and cause great disruption if the schools were allowed to

---

133. Gossett v. Oklahoma, 245 F.3d 1172 (10th Cir. 2001) (remanding for a factual determination of whether a male nursing student was discriminated against by female instructors by failing to provide help, counseling, and opportunities to improve his performance).

134. Vorchheimer v. Sch. Dist., 532 F.2d 880 (3d Cir. 1976), *aff'd by equally divided court,* 430 U.S. 703 (1977).

open and then were forced to close.[135] The court noted that Title IX does not permit the opening of new public single-gender schools, and that the district failed to show a substantial justification for its actions, as is required under the Fourteenth Amendment for facially discriminatory acts involving gender.

In a higher education case, the Supreme Court in 1982 struck down a nursing school's admission policy that restricted admission in degree programs to females without providing comparable opportunities for men.[136] Although the Court acknowledged that gender-based classifications may be justified in limited circumstances when a particular gender has been disproportionately burdened, it rejected the university's contention that its admission policy was necessary to compensate for past discrimination against women. The Court found no evidence that women had ever been denied opportunities in the field of nursing that would justify remedial action by the state. In applying intermediate scrutiny, the Court concluded that the university failed its burden of showing that the facially discriminatory gender classification served an important governmental objective, or that its discriminatory means were substantially related to the achievement of those objectives.

More recently, the Fourth Circuit addressed male-only admissions policies in Virginia and South Carolina. The court found such a policy at the Virginia Military Institute (VMI) to be in violation of the Equal Protection Clause (applying intermediate scrutiny) because there were no comparable opportunities for women.[137] The appellate court held that VMI's claims that its male-only program provided needed diversity in higher education did not justify exclusion of women. The state was given three options: admit women, establish a parallel institution for women, or abandon state support for VMI. The state chose to establish a parallel program for women at Mary Baldwin College, a small private women-only institution; that decision was initially upheld.[138] On appeal in *United States v. Virginia*, however, the Supreme Court reversed the lower courts and held that the state had violated the Fourteenth Amendment by its failure to provide equal opportunities for women in the area of military training.[139] The Court refuted the reasons given by VMI for its refusal to admit women. The exclusion of women from VMI failed to further the institution's purported purpose of providing diversity in higher education; VMI's distinctive teaching methods and techniques could be used unchanged in many instances or slightly modified in the instruction of women; and privacy issues were resolvable.

In South Carolina, a woman sued for admission to the all-male cadet corps.[140] With the state unable to show a substantial justification for the discrimination, the appellate court again found that the institution's admission policy violated the Four-

---

135. Garrett v. Bd. of Educ., 775 F. Supp. 1004 (E.D. Mich. 1991).

136. Miss. Univ. for Women v. Hogan, 458 U.S. 718 (1982).

137. United States v. Virginia, 976 F.2d 890 (4th Cir. 1992).

138. United States v. Virginia, 852 F. Supp. 471 (W.D. Va. 1994), *aff'd,* 44 F.3d 1229 (4th Cir. 1995).

139. 518 U.S. 515 (1996).

140. Faulkner v. Jones, 51 F.3d 440 (4th Cir. 1995).

teenth Amendment. The court also reasoned that establishing a comparable parallel all-female cadet corps (assuming that was even possible) would not address the female student's interest in a timely manner. Moreover, relinquishing state control was not feasible for both political and economic reasons. Accordingly, the court ordered that the female student be admitted to the existing male academy.[141]

Gender-Segregated Courses and Programs.   Unequal educational opportunities for males and females will not be permitted by courts. Although most cases challenging the exclusion of one gender from specific curricular offerings have been settled on constitutional grounds, Title IX regulations prohibit gender-segregated health, industrial arts, business, vocational-technical, home economics, music (although requirements based on vocal range that result in disparate impact are permissible), and adult education classes. These regulations also prohibit gender discrimination in counseling and bar gender-based course requirements for graduation (e.g., home economics for females and industrial arts for males). Moreover, Title IX prohibits separate physical education classes, although students may be grouped by skill levels.[142]

Gender-Based Admission Criteria.   At times, two sets of admission standards have been used, one for males the other for females. Without a substantial justification, this facially discriminatory practice will not satisfy constitutional scrutiny or provisions of Title IX.[143] For example, the admission practices of two Boston schools were found to have discriminated against female applicants and were therefore invalidated.[144] Due to the different seating capacities of the two schools, the Latin School for males required a lower score on the entrance examination than did the school for females. Although permitting the operation of gender-segregated schools, the federal district court was unsympathetic to the school's alleged physical plant problems and ruled that the same entrance requirements had to be applied to both genders. Similarly, the Ninth Circuit concluded that a school district's plan to admit an equal number of male and female students to a high school with an advanced college preparatory curriculum violated equal protection guarantees because it resulted in unequal admission criteria.[145] The court found the district's admission policy to be an illegitimate means of reaching its goal of balancing the number of male and female students enrolled in the school.

   If the district uses reliable, valid, and bias-free forms of assessment to admit students to special programs or to grant awards or scholarships, decisions will be upheld even if a disparate impact occurs. Moreover, it is recommended that multiple

141. Neither of these cases involved allegations of a Title IX violation. That law does not apply to education institutions whose primary purpose is the training of individuals for the military or to public undergraduate institutions that have admitted students of only one gender since they were established. *See* 20 U.S.C. § 1681(a)(4),(5) (2002).

142. 34 C.F.R. § 106.34(b) (2002).

143. 45 C.F.R. § 86.35(b) (2002).

144. Bray v. Lee, 337 F. Supp. 934 (D. Mass. 1972).

145. Berkelman v. S.F. Unified Sch. Dist., 501 F.2d 1264 (9th Cir. 1974).

forms of assessment be used and that all personnel involved in assessment have appropriate credentials and training.

Sexual Harassment of Students

Title IX and the Fourteenth Amendment also have been applied in gender-based claims of sexual harassment and abuse of students. Note, however, that Title IX does not apply when the harassment is due to sexual preference, transvestism, transsexualism, or other behaviors that are sexual in nature; it applies only when the harassment is due to gender (i.e., being male or being female). For example, in a Tenth Circuit case, Title IX was held not to apply where a male high school football player was hazed by his teammates, duct-taped while nude to a towel rack, and then subjected to viewing by his former girlfriend, who had been invited into the locker room. He reported the incident, resulting in the eventual cancellation of the final game of the season. Following this altercation, he was subjected to great animosity and verbal threats and harassment from numerous students until he eventually transferred schools. Because the plaintiff was unable to show that his harassment was gender related, however, the Title IX portion of his suit was dismissed.[146]

Historically, charges of sexual harassment against school districts generally were dismissed.[147] In 1992, however, the Supreme Court reviewed a case in which a female student alleged that a coach initiated sexual conversations, engaged in inappropriate touching, and had coercive intercourse with her on school grounds on several occasions. In this case, *Franklin v. Gwinnett County Public Schools,* the Court held that Title IX prohibited the sexual harassment of students and that damages could be awarded where appropriate.[148] Since *Gwinnett,* numerous other cases with mixed results have been filed by current and former students under Title IX, the Fourteenth Amendment, and state tort law. They have alleged student-to-student harassment,[149] sexual involvement and abuse of students by school staff,[150] off-campus harassment that resulted in an on-campus hostile environment,[151] harassment by a student teacher,[152] and same-sex and opposite-sex harassment.[153] With *Gwinnett* as a starting

146. Seamons v. Snow, 84 F.3d 1226 (10th Cir. 1996).

147. *See, e.g.,* D.R. v. Middle Bucks Area Vocational Technical Sch., 972 F.2d 1364 (3d Cir. 1992); J.O. v. Alton Cmty. Unit Sch. Dist. 11, 909 F.2d 267 (7th Cir. 1990).

148. 503 U.S. 60 (1992).

149. *See, e.g.,* Doe v. Dallas Indep. Sch. Dist., No. 3:01-CV-1092-R, 2002 U.S. Dist. LEXIS 13014 (N.D. Tex. July 16, 2002); Rowinsky v. Bryan Indep. Sch. Dist., 80 F.3d 1006 (5th Cir. 1996).

150. *See, e.g.,* Canutillo Indep. Sch. Dist. v. Leija, 101 F.3d 393 (5th Cir. 1996).

151. *See, e.g.,* Patricia H. v. Berkeley Unified Sch. Dist., 830 F. Supp. 1288 (N.D. Cal. 1993).

152. *See, e.g.,* Oona R.-S. v. Santa Rosa City Schs., 890 F. Supp. 1452 (N.D. Cal. 1995).

153. *See, e.g.,* Shrum v. Kluck, 249 F.3d 773 (8th Cir. 2001) (male-to-male); M.H.D. v. Westminster Schs., 172 F.3d 797 (11th Cir. 1999) (male-to-female); Kinman v. Omaha Pub. Sch. Dist., 171 F.3d 607 (8th Cir. 1999) (female-to-female); Nabozny v. Podlesny, 92 F.3d 446 (7th Cir. 1996) (male-to-male). *See also* Oncale v. Sundowner Offshore Servs., 523 U.S. 75 (1998) (permitting same-sex sexual harassment cases under Title VII of the Civil Rights Act of 1964).

point, two similar but slightly different standards have evolved: one for employee-to-student harassment and the other for student-to-student harassment.

Employee-to-Student Harassment.   In 1998, the Supreme Court provided further guidance in *Gebser v. Lago Vista Independent School District* regarding the liability of school districts when students are harassed by school employees.[154] In this case, a high school student and a teacher had a relationship that had not been reported to the administration until the couple was discovered having sex and the teacher was arrested. The district then terminated the teacher's employment and the parents sued under Title IX. On appeal, the Supreme Court held that to be liable, the district had to have *actual notice* of the harassment. The Court reasoned that allowing recovery of damages based on either *respondeat superior* or *constructive notice* (i.e., notice that is inferred or implied) would be inconsistent with the objective of Title IX, as liability would attach even though the district had no actual knowledge of the conduct or an opportunity to take action to end the harassment.[155] For there to be an award of damages, an official who has the authority to address the alleged discrimination must have actual knowledge of the inappropriate conduct and then fail to ameliorate the problem.[156] Moreover, the failure to respond must amount to deliberate indifference to the discrimination. In the instant case, the plaintiff did not argue that actual notice had been provided. Moreover, the district's failure to promulgate a related policy and grievance procedure failed to qualify as deliberate indifference.

Also of relevance in hostile environment cases where school personnel are allegedly involved is the fact that, at least for younger children, the behavior does not have to be "unwelcome," as in employment cases under Title VII of the Civil Rights Act of 1964. The Seventh Circuit in 1997 reviewed a case where a 21-year-old male kitchen worker had a consensual sexual relationship with a 13-year-old middle school girl.[157] The court noted that under Indiana criminal law, a person under the age of 16

154. 524 U.S. 274 (1998).

155. *See also* Baynard v. Malone, 268 F.3d 228 (4th Cir. 2001) (noting that actual notice may be established where an appropriate person is notified that a teacher is abusing a student; the identity of the particular child is unnecessary), *cert. denied sub nom.* Baynard v. Alexandria City Sch. Bd., 122 S. Ct. 1357 (2002); Davis v. DeKalb County Sch. Dist., 233 F.3d 1367 (11th Cir. 2000) (finding no actual notice or deliberate indifference on the part of the board in a case where a middle school coach molested several school children); Smith v. Metro. Sch. Dist. Perry Township, 128 F.3d 1014 (7th Cir. 1997) (determining that no actual notice had been provided to school officials of the consensual sexual relationship between a female student and male teacher and awarding summary judgment to the defendant).

156. *See also* Warren v. Reading Sch. Dist., 278 F.3d 163 (3d. Cir. 2002) (remanding for a determination of whom may qualify as an "appropriate person" to receive actual notice under the *Gebser* standard; a criminally prosecuted male teacher was fired due to his sexual involvement with male students); Vance v. Spencer County Pub. Sch. Dist., 231 F.3d 253 (6th Cir. 2000) (denying the school district's posttrial motion for judgment as a matter of law; the jury had awarded the plaintiff $220,000 for student-to-student harassment—numerous officials were aware of the harassment); Oona v. McCaffrey, 143 F.3d 473 (9th Cir. 1998) (concluding that liability may result when school officials with actual knowledge of sexual abuse fail to prevent its recurrence).

157. Mary M. v. N. Lawrence Cmty. Sch. Corp., 131 F.3d 1220 (7th Cir. 1997).

cannot consent to sexual intercourse and that children may not even understand that they are being harassed. To rule that only behavior that is unwelcome is actionable would permit violators to take advantage of young, impressionable youth who voluntarily participate in requested conduct. Moreover, if welcomeness were an issue properly before the court, the children bringing the suits would be subject to intense scrutiny regarding their degree of fault.

Student-to-Student Harassment. Educators must be in control of the school environment, including student conduct, and eliminate known dangers and harassment. Not all harassment will be known, however, and not all behavior that is offensive will be so severe as to violate Title IX. Also, for student-to-student harassment to be actionable, the behavior must be unwelcome.

Further clarification regarding liability associated with student-to-student harassment was provided in 1999 when the Supreme Court in *Davis v. Monroe County Board of Education*[158] proposed a two-part test: (1) whether the board acted with deliberate indifference to known acts of harassment[159] and (2) whether the harassment was so severe, pervasive, and objectively offensive that it effectively barred the victim's access to an educational opportunity or benefit.[160] The Court remanded the case to determine whether these standards were met. The plaintiff's daughter had allegedly been subjected to unwelcome sexual touching and rubbing, as well as sexual talk. On one occasion, the violating student purportedly put a doorstop in his pants and acted in a sexually suggestive manner toward the plaintiff. Ultimately, the youth was charged with and pled guilty to sexual battery for his misconduct. The student or the mother notified several teachers, the coach, and the principal of these incidences. No disciplinary action was ever taken other than to threaten the violating student with possible action.

Neither Eleventh Amendment immunity[161] nor the claim that the violator was engaged in First Amendment protected free speech may be used as defenses to Title IX actions.[162] As a result, damage awards[163] are available from educational institu-

158. 526 U.S. 629 (1999).

159. *See also* Oden v. N. Marianas Coll., 284 F.3d 1058 (9th Cir. 2002) (concluding that administrative sluggishness did not equate to deliberate indifference in a case where a student's initial hearing was slightly delayed).

160. *See also* Bruneau v. S. Kortright Cent. Sch. Dist., 163 F.3d 749 (2d Cir. 1998) (affirming lower court which had determined that offensive behavior of male students against a female student did not qualify as harassment or adversely affect her education).

161. Franks v. Ky. Sch. for the Deaf, 142 F.3d 360 (6th Cir. 1998) (holding that the Eleventh Amendment did not bar a Title IX suit; remanding a case where a male student raped a female student following warnings by the rape victim's mother to school officials that the rapist was dangerous and had threatened her daughter).

162. Cohen v. San Bernardino Valley Coll., 883 F. Supp. 1407 (C.D. Cal. 1995), *aff'd in part, rev'd in part, remanded,* 92 F.3d 968 (9th Cir. 1996).

163. However, it is unlikely that punitive awards are available under Title IX. Schultzen v. Woodbury Cent. Cmty. Sch. Dist., 187 F. Supp. 2d 1099 (N.D. 2002).

tions receiving federal funds, although not from those persons who were directly responsible for the harassment.[164] "Individuals" are not "recipients" and therefore cannot be held liable under this particular law. However, they can be sued under state tort law for sexual battery or intentional infliction of emotional distress,[165] and criminal charges (e.g., rape, sodomy) may be filed against perpetrators where force is used or minors are involved. Moreover, being found guilty of sexual harassment can justify demotion, suspension, or termination, even for tenured educators.

The volume of sexual harassment litigation will likely continue to increase. This is due in part to the widespread occurrence of qualifying behaviors and the relative ineptitude some administrators have displayed in dealing with such sensitive matters. Even when administrators eventually learn to deal with claims of sexual harassment in timely and effective ways, parents still are likely to file suit. They will be understandably angry that their child has been subjected to inappropriate behavior and will be looking for someone to blame, if not pay.

Marriage and Pregnancy

Legal principles governing the rights of married and pregnant students have changed dramatically since 1960. The evolution of the law in this area is indicative of the judicial commitment to protect students from unjustified classifications that limit educational opportunities. When public school students are discriminated against because they are married, both the Fourteenth Amendment and Title IX may be violated. Strict scrutiny is used in evaluating claims under the Equal Protection Clause because marriage qualifies as an implied fundamental right.[166] Accordingly, states will have to show a compelling interest in their differential treatment of married students to satisfy the Constitution.

Title IX regulations explicitly prohibit a recipient from applying "any rules concerning a student's actual or potential parental, family, or marital status which treats students differently on the basis of sex."[167] Discrimination based on pregnancy, childbirth, false pregnancy, termination of pregnancy, or recovery therefrom is prohibited. Where separate programs for pregnant students are available, the student may volunteer to participate but may not be automatically enrolled or coerced. However, the school district may require the student to obtain a physician's statement attesting that she is physically and emotionally able to continue in general education, assuming that students with other physical or emotional conditions also are required to provide such

---

164. *See, e.g.,* Hartley v. Parnell, 193 F.3d 1263 (11th Cir. 1999); Floyd v. Waiters, 133 F.3d 786 (11th Cir. 1998). *But see* Mennone v. Gordon, 889 F. Supp. 53 (D. Conn. 1995) (concluding that individuals can be sued under Title IX as long as they have a sufficient level of control over the program or activity).

165. *See, e.g.,* Johnson v. Elk Lake Sch. Dist., 283 F.3d 138 (3d Cir. 2002).

166. Loving v. Virginia, 388 U.S. 1, 12 (1967).

167. 34 C.F.R. § 106.40 (2002). *See also* Wort v. Vierling, 778 F.2d 1233 (7th Cir. 1985) (prohibiting the expulsion of a student from the National Honor Society based on her pregnant unwed status).

documentation. Where programs are provided separately, they must be comparable to those offered nonpregnant students.

In Massachusetts, a federal district court held that school authorities could not exclude a pregnant, unmarried student from regular high school classes.[168] School officials had proposed that the pregnant student be allowed to use all school facilities, attend school functions, participate in senior activities, and receive assistance from teachers in continuing her studies. The district also stipulated, however, that she was not to attend school during regular school hours. Since there was no evidence of any educational or medical reason for this special treatment, the court held that the pregnant student had a constitutional right to attend classes with other pupils. Similarly, a Texas civil appeals court invalidated a public school rule that prohibited mothers from attending regular classes.[169] The only alternative available to the excluded students was to attend adult education classes, which required them to be at least 21 years of age. The court ruled that such a policy violated pregnant students' entitlement to free public schooling. Other courts also have invalidated the exclusion of married students from extracurricular activities, reasoning that public schools cannot discriminate against them without showing a compelling state interest.[170]

Conclusion

A basic purpose of public education is to enhance life opportunities for all students, regardless of their innate characteristics. Accordingly, courts and legislatures have become increasingly assertive in guaranteeing that students have the chance to realize their capabilities while in school. Arbitrary classification practices that disadvantage certain groups are not tolerated. On the other hand, valid classifications, applied in the best interests of students, are generally supported. Indeed, some legal mandates *require* the classification of certain students to ensure that they receive instruction appropriate to their needs, as will be explored in detail in Chapter 6. In exercising professional judgment pertaining to the classification of students, educators should be cognizant of the following generalizations drawn from judicial and legislative mandates.

1. School segregation resulting from state laws or other intentional state action (e.g., gerrymandering school attendance zones) violates the Equal Protection Clause of the Fourteenth Amendment.
2. Where a school district has not achieved unitary status, school officials have an affirmative duty to eliminate the vestiges of past intentional discrimination;

---

168. Ordway v. Hargraves, 323 F. Supp. 1155 (D. Mass. 1971).

169. Alvin Indep. Sch. Dist. v. Cooper, 404 S.W.2d 76 (Tex. Civ. App. 1966).

170. *See, e.g.,* Beeson v. Kiowa County Sch. Dist. RE-1, 567 P.2d 801 (Colo. Ct. App. 1977); Bell v. Lone Oak Indep. Sch. Dist., 507 S.W.2d 636, 641-642 (Tex. Civ. App. 1974).

under such a duty, official action (or inaction) is assessed in terms of its effect on reducing segregation.

3. Segregatory effect alone does not establish unconstitutional intent; however, the consequences of official actions can be considered in substantiating discriminatory motive.

4. The scope of a desegregation remedy cannot exceed the scope of the constitutional violation.

5. States can, but are not obligated to, go beyond the requirements of the Fourteenth Amendment in remedying school segregation; such additional state mandates can subsequently be repealed without violating the United States Constitution.

6. Interdistrict desegregation remedies cannot be judicially imposed unless there is evidence of intentional discrimination with substantial effect across district lines.

7. School districts cannot plead "lack of funds" as a defense for failing to remedy unconstitutional school segregation; a state can be required to share the costs of remedial plans if it played a role in creating or maintaining the segregated system.

8. Courts can set aside state limitations on local taxing authority and can order school boards to raise sufficient funds to support remedial plans, but courts cannot impose tax increases.

9. Judicial supervision can be terminated, in whole or in part, where school districts have complied with desegregation mandates in good faith and have eliminated the vestiges of past discrimination as far as practicable.

10. In determining whether a school district has eliminated the vestiges of school segregation, courts assess racial equality in student, faculty, and staff assignments; transportation; extracurricular activities; and facilities.

11. Once a school district has eliminated the vestiges of its prior discriminatory conduct to the court's satisfaction, future acts must represent purposeful discrimination to violate the Fourteenth Amendment; school districts are not obligated to continue remedies after unitary status is attained and resegregation occurs through no fault of school officials.

12. Children who are deficient in English are entitled to compensatory instruction designed to overcome English language barriers.

13. Students can be classified by age, but such classifications must be substantiated as necessary to advance legitimate educational objectives.

14. Ability-tracking schemes are permissible; pupil assignments should be based on multiple criteria.

15. Students cannot be segregated by gender in public academic programs or schools unless there is a legitimate educational reason for maintaining gender segregation, and then only if comparable programs are available to both males and females.

16. Criteria for admission to public programs or schools cannot be gender based.

17. If a school district establishes an interscholastic athletic program, opportunities must be made available to male and female athletes on an equal basis (i.e., either mixed-gender teams or comparable gender-segregated teams).
18. Sexual harassment of students, by either employees or other students, can result in liability against the school district when an official with the authority to correct the situation has received actual notice of the harassment and has failed to correct it or shown deliberate indifference toward the action.
19. Students cannot be disadvantaged based on marital status or pregnancy.

6

Rights of Students with Disabilities

Since children with disabilities represent a vulnerable minority group, their treatment has aroused considerable judicial and legislative concern. Courts have addressed the constitutional rights of such children to attend school and to be classified accurately and instructed appropriately. Federal and state statutes have further delineated the rights of students with disabilities and have provided funds to assist school districts in meeting their special needs.

Legal Context

The first significant court case to impact children with disabilities dealt with racial segregation rather than special education, and was filed under the Fourteenth Amendment to the Constitution rather than a narrowly tailored disability statute. Nevertheless, the Court's 1954 pronouncement in *Brown v. Board of Education* that "education must be made available to all on equal terms"[1] ultimately served as a basis for the admission to public schools of a number of previously limited or excluded populations, including those classified by race, gender, national origin, and disability. Related court cases, ... interests, and changes in state laws eventually helped pave the way ... eral laws specially designed to protect and enhance the ... ilities—the Rehabilitation Act, the Americans with ... ls with Disabilities Education Act (see Table 6.1).

TABLE 6.1   *Applicability of Selected Federal Laws Related to Disability*

Federal Law	Public Recipient Required to Comply	Public Nonrecipient Required to Comply	Private Recipient Required to Comply	Private Nonrecipient Required to Comply
Fourteenth Amendment Equal Protection Clause	yes	yes	no	no
Fourteenth Amendment Due Process Clause	yes	yes	no	no
Section 1983	yes	yes	no	no
Section 504	yes	no	yes	no
ADA Title II	yes	yes	no	no
ADA Title III	no	no	yes	yes

Source: From "College Students and Disability Law" by S. B. Thomas, Winter 2000, *The Journal of Special Education, 33, 4,* p. 249. Copyright 2000 by PRO-ED, Inc. Reprinted with permission.

Rehabilitation Act

Section 504 of the Rehabilitation Act of 1973 applies to both public and private recipients of federal financial assistance and is enforced in large part by the Office for Civil Rights. Section 504 stipulates that "no otherwise qualified individual with a disability in the United States . . . shall, solely by reason of her or his disability, be excluded from the participation in, be denied the benefits of, or be subjected to discrimination under any program or activity receiving federal financial assistance."[2] Furthermore, if any program or activity operated by a recipient (e.g., school district) receives federal funds from the Department of Education, all operations of the entity must comply with the act's provisions. Compliance requires the recipient to file an *assurance of compliance* (i.e., a written guarantee that it will not discriminate based on disability), remediate violations of the act, correct those circumstances that historically limited the participation of persons with disabilities in the recipient's program, conduct a self-evaluation to determine the level of compliance, identify a compliance coordinator, adopt grievance procedures, and provide notice to participants that the recipient's program does not discriminate based on disability.[3]

2. 29 U.S.C. § 794(a) (2002).

3. 34 C.F.R. §§ 104.5–104.8 (2002).

Under the Rehabilitation Act, an individual with a disability is one who has a *physical or mental impairment*[4] (with consideration of mitigating measures) that substantially limits one or more major life activities, has a *record of impairment,* or is *regarded as having an impairment.*[5] These latter two definitions (i.e., "record of" and "regarded as") apply when a person has been subjected to discrimination (e.g., terminated as a teacher due to having a record of hospitalization for tuberculosis;[6] excluded from school for being HIV positive[7]). However, only those children who meet the first definition (i.e., have an impairment that is substantially limiting) will be eligible for individualized instruction and services. Students with only a record of past impairment are not currently in need of accommodation, whereas students who are only regarded as having such an impairment have no actual limitation to accommodate.

In assessing whether a person qualifies as disabled and is therefore eligible for services under Section 504, consideration will be given to the results of *mitigating or corrective measures* (both positive and negative).[8] *Positive results* can be seen when a student with impaired vision has a visual acuity of 20/20 with glasses or contact lenses or when a child with impaired hearing has average hearing when wearing a hearing aid. *Negative results* can be observed when a student is medicated for a health problem, but as a result has difficulty focusing or staying alert in class. Consideration of such positive and negative factors provides a clearer understanding of whether a limitation qualifies as a disability and provides important information regarding the impairment's nature and extent.

In addition, the limitation must *substantially limit* a *major life activity.*[9] In making this determination, courts compare the performance difficulties of the student with those of the theoretical "average person" (or in this discussion, "average student") in the general population. To qualify, the student will have to be either incapable of performing the designated activity or significantly restricted (i.e., functioning merely below average will be insufficient). This assessment requires a case-by-case evaluation, as impairments will vary in severity, affect people differently, and may or may not be restricting, given the nature of the life activity. As a result, some students with physical or mental impairments will be substantially limited and others will not, with

---

4. 34 C.F.R. § 104.3(j)(2(i)) (2002) (defining physical or mental impairments as including "any physiological disorder or condition, cosmetic disfigurement, or anatomical loss affecting one or more of the following body systems: neurological; musculoskeletal; special sense organs; respiratory, including speech organs; cardiovascular; reproductive, digestive, genito-urinary; hemic and lymphatic; skin; and endocrine; or any mental or psychological disorder, such as mental retardation, organic brain syndrome, emotional or mental illness, and specific learning disorders."

5. 34 C.F.R. § 104.3(j)(1) (2002).

6. Sch. Bd. v. Arline, 480 U.S. 273 (1987) (concluding that a teacher suffering from the contagious disease of tuberculosis qualified as an individual with a disability because she had a record of physical impairment that limited a major life activity—working).

7. Ray v. Sch. Dist., 666 F. Supp. 1524 (M.D. Fla. 1987).

8. Sutton v. United Airlines, 527 U.S. 471 (1999); Murphy v. United Parcel Serv., 527 U.S. 516 (1999).

9. Major life activities include caring for oneself, performing manual tasks, walking, seeing, hearing, speaking, breathing, *learning,* working. 34 C.F.R. § 104.3(j)(2)(ii) (2002).

only the former qualifying for special instruction, services, and accommodations.[10] Failure to recognize the fact that Section 504 provides enhanced rights only for persons who are disabled but not for those who are merely impaired, can lead to the over-classification of students under Section 504. This, then, could possibly result in increased instruction and services costs, additional hurdles and limitations in regard to discipline, greater parental expectations for programming, and the increased likelihood of litigation and liability.

When a student's limitation qualifies as a disability, it still is necessary to determine whether he or she is *otherwise qualified.* For preK–12 education purposes, children may qualify if they are of school age, or if they are eligible for services for the disabled under either state law or the IDEA.[11] Students who qualify under Section 504, but not under the IDEA (e.g., "regular" education children who are wheelchair confined),[12] need to be provided with accommodation plans that will include regular and special education as appropriate, as well as any individualized aids and services that will allow participation in the recipient's program. The programs must be delivered in accessible facilities,[13] and programming must be designed and selected to meet the needs of students with disabilities as adequately as the needs of their nondisabled peers are met. Furthermore, children with disabilities should not be segregated from other children unless an appropriate program cannot otherwise be provided. Where such segregation exists, programs must be comparable in materials, facilities, teacher quality, length of school term, and daily hours of instruction.

When the recipient and the parents disagree as to whether a free appropriate public education (FAPE) has been provided, the parents should have the opportunity

---

10. *See, e.g.,* Costello v. Mitchell Pub. Sch. Dist 79, 266 F.3d 916 (8th Cir. 2001) (concluding that the plaintiff's health impairment was not substantially limiting in her effort to learn); Bercovitch v. Baldwin Sch., 133 F.3d 141 (1st Cir. 1998) (determining that student's Attention Deficit Hyperactivity Disorder was not substantially limiting in regard to learning, as his achievement remained constantly above average); Ballard v. Kinkaid Sch., 147 F. Supp. 2d 603 (S.D. Tex. 2000) (concluding that a student with a visual perceptual disorder was not substantially limited in learning, given his academic success in the seventh and eighth grades with the use of overlay filters to assist him in dealing with light and sensitivity).

11. 34 C.F.R. § 104.3(l)(2) (2002). In contrast, in higher education the student must be able to meet all the academic and technical standards of the program in spite of his or her disability, although accommodations may at times be necessary. *See* 34 C.F.R. § 104.3(l)(3) (2002).

12. It is the position of the Office for Civil Rights that a student who qualifies under the IDEA is not entitled also to receive a plan formulated consistent with the provisions of § 504. *See* Response to McKethan, 25 IDELR 295 (OCR 1996). Also, if a local education agency fails to provide an IEP to a child who qualifies for services under the IDEA and instead proffers only a § 504 plan, it can be required to reimburse the parents for any expenses they may incur in purchasing appropriate instruction or services for their child. *See* Muller v. Comm. on Special Educ., 145 F.3d 95 (2d Cir. 1998).

13. 34 C.F.R. § 104.22 (2002). To comply, a recipient need not make each existing facility or every part of a facility accessible, but must operate its programs so that they are accessible to individuals with disabilities. Accessibility can be achieved through redesign of equipment, reassignment of classes to accessible buildings, delivery of services to alternate sites, alteration of existing facilities, and construction of new facilities. A recipient is not required to renovate or construct when other less expensive but effective methods are available.

to review records, participate in an impartial hearing, and be represented by counsel. Section 504 is not specific as to the procedures that must be followed, but it does acknowledge that providing notice and hearing rights comparable to those mandated under the IDEA would suffice.[14] In addition, parents also have the right to file a complaint with the Office for Civil Rights within 180 days of the alleged discrimination.[15] Officials are responsible for investigating the claim and for reviewing pertinent practices and policies. Where violations exist, federal regulations support the use of informal negotiations and voluntary action on the part of the recipient to gain compliance.[16] If the recipient fails to correct its discriminatory practices, federal funds may be terminated.

Moreover, there is a private right of action under Section 504, although IDEA exhaustion requirements[17] have to be met if the relief sought also is available under the IDEA. Where suits are filed, immunity defenses under the Eleventh Amendment are unlikely to be accepted,[18] attorneys' fees may be awarded to prevailing plaintiffs, and damage awards may be granted if claims of bad faith or gross misjudgment are supported in cases regarding a FAPE.[19]

Americans with Disabilities Act

In addition to the Rehabilitation Act, in 1990, Congress passed the Americans with Disabilities Act (ADA).[20] Two titles of that act are of particular importance to students with disabilities: Title II applies to public schools and Title III applies to those that are private. Like Section 504, these titles prohibit discrimination against persons (birth to death) who are disabled. However, unlike Section 504, the ADA requires compliance of schools that do not receive federal aid and were not heretofore federally regulated. Complaints must be filed within 180 days of an alleged violation with the Department of Justice or other responsible agency.

Upon completion of a formal Title II complaint, the Department of Justice investigates and attempts informal resolution. If a violation is identified, but a settlement is not reached, the department sends a letter to the complainant and the school that identifies each violation and proposed remedy, as well as information regarding additional ADA rights. When agreement is reached, the parties are required to sign a written document specifying time lines and any corrective action to be taken for each infraction, and provide assurance that discrimination will not recur. Where voluntary compliance

14. *See* text accompanying notes 114–128, infra.

15. Although § 504 does not have its own complaint procedures, it has adopted those outlined in Title VI of the Civil Rights Act of 1964. *See* 34 C.F.R. § 104.61 (2002).

16. 34 C.F.R. § 100.7(c),(d) (2002).

17. *See* text accompanying note 127, infra.

18. Jim C. v. United States, 235 F.3d 1079 (8th Cir. 2000).

19. Smith v. Special Sch. Dist. No. 1, 184 F.3d 764 (8th Cir. 1999) (concluding that to collect damages, the plaintiff must show gross negligence or bad faith on the part of the district).

20. 42 U.S.C. §§ 12101–12213 (2002).

is not acquired, the agency will recommend to the Attorney General that specific actions be taken (e.g., further efforts to acquire voluntary compliance, lawsuit).

The Attorney General is responsible for investigating alleged violations filed against private schools under Title III. If there is reason to believe that an infraction has occurred, the private school can be required to submit to a compliance review. Where a pattern or practice of discrimination exists, or where perceived discrimination is so significant as to represent an issue of general public importance, a civil action may be initiated. Courts are authorized to require private schools to provide auxiliary aids or services; modify policies, practices, procedures, or methods; make facilities readily accessible to and usable by individuals with disabilities; or require other relief courts consider appropriate.

Private schools, however, are not required to provide auxiliary aids and services that would either fundamentally alter the nature of the goods, services, facilities, privileges, advantages, or accommodations it provides or result in undue burden.[21] Furthermore, even though private schools also are expected to remove barriers in existing facilities that restrict or deny access, this mandate is limited to those tasks that are "readily achievable," "easily accomplished," and "without much difficulty or expense."[22]

Individuals with Disabilities Education Act

Two years after the passage of the Rehabilitation Act, and 15 years before the passage of the ADA, Part B of the Education of the Handicapped Act was amended by Public Law 94-142. This law, now known as the Individuals with Disabilities Education Act (IDEA),[23] is enforced by the Office of Special Education Programs. Recipients of IDEA funds are required to provide qualifying children a FAPE that is made available in the least restrictive environment. States, but not local education agencies (e.g., public school districts), have the option of declining IDEA funds and thereby avoiding the myriad compliance requirements, but they still must address the needs of students with disabilities as stipulated in Section 504. All states currently participate in the IDEA financial assistance program.

To qualify for services, a child must be mentally retarded, hard of hearing, deaf, speech or language impaired, visually impaired, blind, seriously emotionally disturbed, orthopedically impaired, autistic, other health impaired, learning disabled, or suffer from traumatic brain injury, *and,* as a result, be in need of special education and related services.[24] Accordingly, it is possible to have a disability (e.g., quadriplegia)

21. 28 C.F.R. § 36.303(a) (2002). Undue burden in this context is similar to that under Section 504 (but unavailable under the IDEA) and includes both administrative feasibility and cost.

22. 28 C.F.R. § 36.304(a) (2002).

23. 20 U.S.C. § 1400 *et seq.* (2002).

24. 20 U.S.C. § 1401(3)(A) (2002). Not all children will possess qualifying disabilities. *See, e.g.,* Bd. of Educ. v. J.D., No. 99-2180, 2000 U.S. App. LEXIS 26902 (4th Cir. Oct. 26, 2000) (upholding a district court ruling that the drug-using student was socially maladjusted and did not have a qualifying educational disability).

but not be in need of special education and therefore not qualify for services under the IDEA. Note also that although a child needs to qualify as "disabled" under one or more of the preceding categories for the state and district to receive federal funding, it is not necessary to "label" the child as such on the individualized education program.[25] It is important, however, for the child's needs to be correctly identified and for those needs to be properly addressed.

In the following sections, several of the more important and litigated areas of the IDEA are reviewed. The IDEA remains the primary law under which a FAPE is challenged and as a result generates most of the student-disability case law.

Free Appropriate Public Education

Under the Individuals with Disabilities Education Act, states must ensure that all children ages 3 through 21 with disabilities are provided a free appropriate public education (FAPE) that is made available in the least restrictive environment.[26] The FAPE must be provided at public expense and under public supervision and direction (even if the school district selects a private school placement); meet the standards of the state educational agency;[27] include an appropriate preschool, elementary school, or secondary school education; and be provided in conformity with the individualized education program (IEP). An "appropriate" education is one that is designed to meet the unique needs of each child and includes special education and related services (i.e., those services that are necessary for a child to benefit from special education).[28]

As needed, students also must be provided supplementary aids and services (to enable the child with a disability to be educated with nondisabled children to the maximum extent appropriate), transition services (to assist in transitioning from school to postschool activities such as postsecondary education, vocational training, integrated employment, continuing and adult education, adult services, independent living, or community participation), and assistive technology devices and services (to enable the child to increase, maintain, or improve functional capabilities).[29] When services are provided, they must be made available as close to the child's home as possible, and

25. 34 C.F.R. § 300.125(d) (2002). *See* Cronkite v. Long Beach Unified Sch. Dist., No. 97-55544, 1999 U.S. App. LEXIS 4733 (9th Cir. March 18, 1999) (concluding that the district had provided the student with a FAPE and that the IDEA does not require the district to use a specific term—e.g., *dyslexia*—provided the IEP properly identifies and addresses the disability).

26. This is true unless students ages 3 to 5 and 18 through 21 are not served within the state. *See* 34 C.F.R. § 300.300(b)(5)(i) (2002). Also, for children ages 3 to 9, a state may, at its discretion, include those who are experiencing developmental delays in physical, cognitive, communication, social or emotional, or adaptive development and are in need of special education and related services. *See* 20 U.S.C. § 1401(3)(B) (2002).

27. T.R. v. Kingwood Township Bd. of Educ., 205 F.3d 572 (3d Cir. 2000) (concluding that a private school that was not accredited by the state need not be considered as a possible placement).

28. 20 U.S.C. § 1401(22) (2002).

29. 20 U.S.C. §1401(1), (2), (29), (30) (2002).

preferably in the school the child would have attended if not disabled. But, it is not realistic to assume that all programs can be made available in every neighborhood school.

Even though IEPs must be "appropriate," they need not be "the best" available or represent "optimum" programs that will maximize learning potential.[30] This issue was addressed in *Board of Education v. Rowley,*[31] where parents had requested that the school district provide a sign-language interpreter for their daughter in her academic classes, given her minimal residual hearing. The child's IEP specified a regular first-grade placement with special instruction from a tutor one hour per day and a speech therapist three hours per week, but did not include interpreter services. An interpreter had been provided during a two-week period when she was in kindergarten, but the practice was discontinued based on recommendations by the interpreter and other educators working with the child. Due to this omission, the parents were dissatisfied with the IEP and, after unsuccessful administrative review, filed suit.

On appeal, the Supreme Court rejected the standard proposed by the lower court (i.e., maximization of the potential of children with disabilities commensurate with the opportunity provided to other children[32]) and reasoned that "the intent of the act was more to open the door of public education to [children with disabilities] on appropriate terms than to guarantee any particular level of education once inside."[33] The act was found to guarantee a "basic floor of opportunity,"[34] consisting of access to specialized instruction and related services that are individually designed to provide educational benefit. Applying these principles, the Court held that the plaintiff was receiving an appropriate education—that is, the child was incurring educational benefit from individualized instruction and related services, as evidenced by her better-than-average performance in class, promotion from grade to grade, and positive interpersonal relationships with educators and peers.

The Court also made clear that lower courts are not to define an appropriate education. Rather, their review is limited to two questions. First, has the state complied with the procedures identified in the act? Second, is the IEP as developed through

30. *See, e.g.,* D.B. v. Craven County Bd. of Educ., No. 99-1326, 2000 U.S. App. LEXIS 6176 (4th Cir. April 3, 2000) (concluding that the district had provided the plaintiff with a FAPE and that even if his writing skills were not as good as his parents would have liked, the IDEA requires that schools provide educational opportunities, not that they guarantee that every child will attain full potential; the student's poor achievement appeared to be more related to lack of effort and the failure to turn in assignments than to writing skill). However, state laws often have been interpreted to require the "maximization" of potential. *See, e.g.,* B.G. v. Cranford Bd. of Educ., 882 F.2d 510 (3d Cir. 1989) (finding that the student's academic progress met the minimum federal standards under *Rowley,* but that a year-round residential placement was necessary to meet New Jersey's assurance that students have the fullest opportunity to develop).

31. 458 U.S. 176 (1982).

32. 483 F. Supp. 528, 534 (S.D.N.Y. 1980).

33. 458 U.S. 176, 192 (1982).

34. *Id.* at 200.

these procedures reasonably calculated to enable the child to receive educational benefit?[35] Lower courts have interpreted this latter requirement to mandate educational programs that provide more than "trivial advancement."[36]

These two questions were addressed in an Eleventh Circuit case where a student with a learning disability had been provided special instruction, classes, and services, including a portable classroom. The student did not make significant progress early in the year, as she was refusing to complete work assignments and had engaged in assaultive behavior that resulted in suspension. She had threatened other students with a nail, stuck a teacher in the finger, and hit and kicked several staff members. Following this incident, she called her mother to report that her teachers were trying to "murder" her. She was suspended for seven days for her conduct. Upon her return, the child was even less compliant than before and her mother attended class with her on a regular basis. The mother helped her daughter complete in-class independent work assignments, was disrespectful to teachers, and took over her daughter's classroom instruction. Eventually, the mother removed her daughter from school and filed suit. On appeal, the Eleventh Circuit held that although there were some minor procedural deficiencies, a FAPE had been provided.[37] The IEP was prepared in a coordinated and collaborative manner and was designed to provide benefit, even if the degree of actual benefit was difficult to assess, given the involvement of the mother.

Courts often defer to state and local educators and administrative review officials regarding the nature of IEPs and matters of pedagogy,[38] but still will not uphold proposed placements that are clearly inappropriate. In such situations, courts have not been reluctant to approve a private placement or to direct the development of an appropriate public one. For example, the Ninth Circuit concluded that a California district failed to provide an appropriate education. Placement of an autistic child in a program for the "communicatively handicapped" was inappropriate, the program was not individualized, the student's needs were not being met, and the teacher was not trained to work with autistic children.[39] The district was required to reimburse the parents for the costs of an out-of-district placement, including costs associated with commuting, lodging, and tuition, as well as attorneys' fees.

---

35. *Id.* at 207.

36. *See, e.g.,* Ridgewood Bd. of Educ. v. N.E. *ex rel.* M.E., 172 F.3d 238 (3d Cir. 1999) (finding that the IDEA requires something more than a trivial educational benefit).

37. Sch. Bd. v. K.C., 286 F.3d 977 (11th Cir. 2002).

38. *See, e.g.,* Logue v. Unified Sch. Dist. No. 512, Nos. 97-3087, 97-3112, 1998 U.S. App. LEXIS 16280 (10th Cir. July 16, 1998) (upholding the district's placement of the child as the use of total communication method resulted in benefits that exceeded the *Rowley* standard; the oral communication method available in the private school and preferred by the parents was not necessary to provide the child with a FAPE).

39. Union Sch. Dist. v. Smith, 15 F.3d 1519 (9th Cir. 1994).

Individualized Education Programs

The process of preparing and delivering an appropriate program begins when a child with a disability is identified and ends only when the child withdraws or graduates[40] from the school, fails to qualify for services, or reaches the age of 21. To begin this process, the child is identified and evaluated; then an individualized education program (IEP) is written and a placement is selected.

Initial Identification

Under the Individuals with Disabilities Education Act's (IDEA's) "child find" mandate, states and school districts are required to identify, locate, and evaluate *all* resident children with disabilities, regardless of the severity of their disability or whether they attend public or private schools. No child with a disability is to be denied an appropriate program ("zero reject"[41]). Although federal law requires that children with disabilities be identified, it does not dictate how this is to occur. Nevertheless, courts give deference to districts when their efforts appear substantial and in good faith.[42] Consequently, state practices vary widely and include census taking; community surveys; public awareness activities; referrals by parents, teachers, and medical doctors; and the screening of kindergarten and preschool children. The screening process may necessitate the use of tests that are administered to all children, not simply those suspected of having disabilities. Prior to testing, parents must be given notice that identifies the tests to be used and provides a general explanation of their intended purpose. Educators, however, need not acquire consent at this time, unless consent for all children is required. When these initial referral and screening efforts have been completed, all children *potentially in need* of special education ideally will be identified.

Next, school districts are responsible for evaluating further those children residing in their respective service areas who are initially perceived to be in need of special

---

40. T.S. v. Indep. Sch. Dist. No. 54, Stroud, Okla., 265 F.3d 1090 (10th Cir. 2001) (finding the case moot, as the student had already graduated—he had filed for a due process hearing the last day of classes his senior year, claiming that the district had failed to process his graduation properly; he was not contesting the propriety of graduation although he did question the services that had been provided).

41. 34 C.F.R. § 300.304 (2002). There has been some debate as to whether children with severe disabilities (i.e., those who seemingly cannot benefit or can benefit only marginally from instruction) actually qualify for services. The First Circuit concluded that Congress intended for *all* children with disabilities to be educated and noted that the word *all* permeates the statute. The court reasoned that there should be "zero-rejects" and that the IDEA is explicit in granting priority to children who are the most severely disabled. *See* Timothy W. v. Rochester, N.H., Sch. Dist., 875 F.2d 954 (1st Cir. 1989).

42. Doe v. Metro. Nashville Pub. Schs., 9 Fed Appx. 453 (6th Cir. 2001) (holding that the district had effectively participated in "child-find," given its dissemination of information to schools, day-care centers, nursery schools, hospitals, and medical personnel; public service announcements through the local media; participation in PTA meetings; and implementation of an outreach program).

education. Although state residency laws vary, generally children who physically live in the district's service area with a custodial parent,[43] legal guardian, or foster parent; are emancipated minors; or have reached the age of majority and live apart from their parents will qualify as "residents."[44]

Evaluation

Prior to placement of a child with disabilities, the IDEA requires a multifactored evaluation using a variety of technically sound assessment tools and strategies to gather information related to the child's health, vision, hearing, social and emotional status, general intelligence, academic performance, communicative status, and motor abilities. No single criterion or procedure may be used to determine a child's placement. Standardized tests must be validated for the purposes for which they are used, administered by qualified personnel, selected and administered in ways that neither racially nor culturally discriminate, and be available in the child's native language or other mode of communication. Furthermore, assessments must accurately reflect aptitude or achievement rather than the child's impaired sensory, manual, or speaking skills, unless those skills are the ones being measured.[45]

Notice must be provided to the parents that the district intends to test the student. It must describe any assessments the district proposes to conduct (including each evaluation procedure, test, record, or report that will be used), as well as any other information relevant to the matter. Generally, informed parental consent[46] must be acquired prior to individualized testing for either an initial evaluation or reevaluation. However, consent is not required where the parents fail to respond to requests for reevaluation, assuming that the school district can demonstrate that it took reasonable measures to obtain consent and the child's parent failed to respond. In this effort, the

---

43. Joshua v. U.S.D. 259 Bd. of Educ., No. 98-3248, 2000 U.S. App. LEXIS 8837 (10th Cir. May 2, 2000) (denying reimbursement for tuition paid to a private school and concluding that the child was not entitled to services, as neither parent continued to live in the district; staying with his sister did not qualify as a "person acting as a parent" under state law). *But see* Navin v. Park Ridge Sch. Dist. 64, 270 F.3d 1147 (7th Cir. 2001) (concluding that a father retained rights in regard to his son's education consistent with his divorce decree and that only if the custodian mother disagreed could the father's position be devalued; the father had concerns that tutorial services were being provided by a crossing-guard supervisor with no certification in educating dyslexic youth).

44. *See* text accompanying note 43, Chapter 3.

45. 34 C.F.R. § 300.532(a)(1),(c)(1),(e),(f),(g) (2002).

46. However, all IDEA rights, including the right to provide consent, transfer to the student upon reaching the age of majority (generally 18) as specified within state statute. Moreover, one year prior to reaching majority age, the student's IEP must include a statement that the student has been informed of his pending rights. *See* 34 C.F.R. § 300.347(c) (2002).

district must provide documentation such as detailed telephone records, copies of correspondence, and records of visits made to the home or the parents' place of work.[47]

If the parents refuse consent, the district may seek authority to evaluate the student by initiating due process procedures.[48] Assuming the school district succeeds, the parents then have three options: permit the child to be evaluated, seek a court order to prohibit the assessment, or remove the child from public schools. If the latter action is taken, the parent must comply with state compulsory attendance requirements by enrolling the child in another school or by providing home schooling. If the child is to remain in public schools, the parents may not impede the assessment process by failing to make the child available for testing or by temporarily removing him or her from the state to evade school officials.

As part of an initial evaluation or as part of any reevaluation, the IEP team and other qualified professionals are responsible for reviewing existing evaluation data on the child, including evaluations and information provided by the parents, current classroom-based assessments, and observations by teachers and related services providers. The IEP team then can identify what additional data, if any, are needed. Once this is accomplished, the team must identify the child's educational needs and present level of performance; whether the child requires special education and related services; and whether any additions or modifications to the instruction or services are necessary to enable the child to meet measurable annual goals and to participate, as appropriate, in the regular curriculum.

Parents have the right to request an independent evaluation if they disagree with the district's evaluation or placement decision. The public school pays for the additional evaluation, unless officials contest the need for reassessment or the evaluation already obtained by the parent did not meet district criteria.[49] This would be accomplished by requesting an impartial hearing and demonstrating that all procedures and appropriate professional practices were followed. If the impartial hearing officer rules in favor of the district, and that decision is not appealed, the parents still may acquire a second, independent evaluation but must pay for it themselves. School personnel are required to *consider* the results of the independent evaluation but are not required to *follow* them.[50]

---

47. 34 C.F.R. § 300. 505(c) (2002); 34 C.F.R. § 300.345(d) (2002).

48. *See* text accompanying notes 114–128, infra.

49. 34 C.F.R. § 300.502(a)(1),(b) (2002). Also, it may be necessary under atypical circumstances for a hearing officer to request that a third evaluation be performed. When this occurs, the district bears all costs. *See* 34 C.F.R. § 300.502(d) (2002).

50. 34 C.F.R. § 300.502(c)(1) (2002). *See also* T.S. v. Bd. of Educ., 10 F.3d 87 (2d Cir. 1993) (holding that an independent evaluation had been "considered," even though only two members of the placement committee read the report, limited discussion ensued, and a placement contrary to that recommended was selected).

IEP Preparation

The school district, through its IEP teams, is responsible for determining whether children qualify under the IDEA for services and, if so, for designing appropriate, least restrictive placements. Each team should include the parents of the child with a disability; the child, when appropriate; at least one regular education teacher; at least one special education teacher; a representative of the district who is qualified to provide and/or supervise specially designed instruction to meet the unique needs of the child; and other individuals (including related services personnel) who have knowledge about the child's needs or have special expertise. The team also must include an individual who can interpret the evaluation results and identify instructional implications, assuming that no existing member of the team has such abilities. If the team decides that the child will not be placed in the regular education classroom, the regular educator then may be dropped from the committee.

Parents must agree to the IEP meeting time and location, and the district must ensure that the parents have the opportunity to participate fully (e.g., by hiring foreign-language translators or sign-language interpreters).[51] If neither parent is available or willing to attend, school officials should document each of their efforts to encourage parental involvement. Where no parent can be identified or located, a surrogate parent must be appointed. The surrogate possesses all of the IDEA rights and responsibilities of the parent (e.g., receive notice, provide consent, request a hearing). The surrogate may not be an employee of the district or have interests that conflict with those of the child and must have the knowledge and skills needed to ensure adequate representation.

Once developed, the IEP should identify (1) the child's current level of educational performance; (2) annual and short-term goals and objectives; (3) special education, related services, supplementary aids and services, and transition services to be provided; (4) program modifications or supports for school personnel that will be applied; (5) the extent, if any, to which the child will not be included in regular education program activities; (6) any modifications that will be made in performing state or district assessments of student achievement; (7) the date to initiate services; (8) the projected frequency, location, and duration of services; (9) appropriate evaluation procedures; (10) methods to inform parents of their child's progress; and (11) interagency responsibilities and linkages. The program must be reviewed annually, or more often as appropriate, and a reevaluation must be performed every three years if the IEP team determines that conditions warrant, or if requested by the child's parent or teacher.

---

51. However, this right to participate does not extend to preparatory meetings conducted by the local school district to generate proposals to be discussed with the parents at a later IEP meeting. *In re* D., 32 IDELR 103 (SEA CT, 2000).

Public and Private Placement

After agreement has been reached as to the elements of an individualized education program, an appropriate placement must be made available at public expense. Alternative placements may include a regular education classroom with various support services, a regular classroom with or without itinerant teachers or resource rooms, self-contained special classes, special schools, home instruction, or instruction in hospitals or residential institutions.[52] Within this continuum of placements, the IDEA requires that the child be educated in the least restrictive environment (LRE).

Least Restrictive Environment.   Children with disabilities are to be educated with children who are not disabled to the *maximum extent appropriate.* Special classes, separate schooling, or other removal of a child from regular education may occur only if the nature or severity of the disability is such that education cannot be achieved satisfactorily.[53] In making LRE decisions, school districts should determine within which types of placements the IEP may be delivered (along the continuum of alternative placements) and then select the option that is least restrictive. Educational and noneducational benefits for each placement should be assessed. The LRE for one child (in fact most children) may be regular education with supplemental aids and services, whereas it may be residential placement for another.[54] First and foremost is the provision of an appropriate program; only then should consideration be given to identifying a placement that also is least restrictive. This is true for both initial as well as subsequent placement decisions.

It is important that children not be placed experimentally in the regular classroom under the guise of full inclusion,[55] and then provided appropriate placements

---

52. 34 C.F.R. § 300.551(b) (2002).

53. 34 C.F.R. § 300.550(b) (2002). Interestingly, the Fourth Circuit has ruled that the LRE requirement mandates compliance only of school districts and not parents. *See* Jaynes v. Newport News Sch. Bd., 13 Fed. Appx. 166 (4th Cir. 2001).

54. *See, e.g.,* Beth B. v. Clay, 282 F.3d 493 (7th Cir. 2002) (supporting selection of a placement that was more restrictive than regular education as the child's academic progress was virtually nonexistent and her developmental progress was limited within regular education); Indep. Sch. Dist. No. 284 v. A.C., 258 F.3d 769 (8th Cir. 2001) (concluding that a segregated, possibly even residential, placement was appropriate for a truant misbehaving student who otherwise had no learning difficulties; she had a conduct disorder with explosive and oppositional behavior); Doe v. Arlington County Sch. Bd., No. 99-1426, 2000 U.S. App. LEXIS 4287 (4th Cir. March 20, 2000) (determining that the full-inclusion program promoted by the parents would not meet their child's educational needs for core academic subjects, given her significant cognitive limitations and distractibility); Blackmon v. Springfield R-XII Sch. Dist., 198 F.3d 648 (8th Cir. 1999) (finding that the district proposed school placement in a "reverse mainstream" classroom, where a few regular education students are educated with a larger number of special needs students, was appropriate and that the home schooling sought by the parents was not least restrictive, because it did not permit the opportunity for the child to interact with peers).

55. The term *full inclusion* is used here to refer to placement in regular education where the child's educational needs are appropriately addressed through the use of supplemental aides and services.

only after they fail to meet short-term objectives or acquire educational benefit. Inappropriate placements may require the unnecessary expenditure of thousands of dollars and delay the provision of appropriate and beneficial education.

Note, however, that the IEP team need not select a placement that is entirely in regular education or entirely segregated. In some instances, it is appropriate to deliver the child's program within a range of LRE settings (e.g., a segregated program to assist in the development of lip reading, but a regular education setting for other instructional and noninstructional activities). Where integration to any degree is feasible and appropriate, states are responsible for ensuring that teachers and administrators are fully informed about their LRE responsibilities and for providing them with technical assistance and training.[56]

Public Placement of a Child in a Private School. When a child is capable of working within regular education, but the school district does not operate a school or pre-school program that would be age appropriate (e.g., in a rural area where only a few families reside), the IDEA does not require that the district create such a program or school.[57] In the alternative, placement may be made in other public schools or in private facilities, including those that are residential. Although the fiscal obligation placed on school systems can be substantial, the district will be held financially responsible for residential placements that are required to provide a free appropriate public education. In such instances, the district must cover all nonmedical costs, including room and board. The IDEA's provision for residential care, however, is not intended to compensate for a poor home environment[58] or to serve as a means of delivering social, medical, or incarceration services.[59] Accordingly, if a residential placement is sought by the parents for reasons other than the education of the child with a disability (e.g., the risk the child poses in the home, the inability to shelter or feed the youth, the student being the target of a parent's abuse), the request may be denied.

When the public school system selects a private placement, a representative of the private school should participate in IEP placement meetings. If attendance is not possible, participation must be achieved through individual or conference calls. Subsequent meetings to review and revise the IEP may be initiated and conducted by private school personnel, if approved by district officials. Where this occurs, both the

---

56. 34 C.F.R. § 300.555 (2002). *See also* Asbury v. Mo. Dep't of Elementary and Secondary Educ., 248 F.3d 1163 (8th Cir. 2001) (affirming summary judgment for defendant where the plaintiff claimed that the district had failed to properly train its personnel to educate children with autism), *cert. denied,* 534 U.S. 890 (2001).

57. *See* T.R. *ex rel.* N.R. v. Kingwood Township Bd. of Educ., 205 F.3d 572 (3d Cir. 2000).

58. Gonzalez v. P.R. Dep't of Educ., 254 F.3d 350 (1st Cir. 2001) (determining that the child had been offered a FAPE, notwithstanding parental arguments to the contrary or their concern for their daughter's safety if their son were to return home), *cert. denied,* 525 U.S. 815 (2001).

59. Dale M. v. Bd. of Educ., 237 F.3d 813 (7th Cir. 2001) (concluding that the district is not required to pay the cost of confinement of an incorrigible youth with a lengthy criminal record; his problems were not primarily educational—they were based on his lack of proper socialization), *cert. denied,* 534 U.S. 1020 (2001).

parents and a public school representative must be involved in any decision about the child's IEP, and the district must authorize any change prior to implementation. Notwithstanding the above, the state education agency and local school district remain responsible for compliance with the IDEA, even if the child is being served in a private school. Importantly, private schools are not required to implement special programs or to lower their academic standards to permit placement of children with disabilities.[60] Applicants who cannot participate effectively in the private school's regular education curriculum, assuming the availability of "minor adjustments," may be denied admission.

Unilateral Parental Placement of Child in a Private School.   In some instances, parents elect to place their children in private schools, either initially or when they perceive public programs to be inappropriate. Parents always have the option of selecting an alternative program, but such placements will be at parental expense, unless the parents can show that the public placement is inappropriate and that their selected placement is appropriate.

The Supreme Court first addressed this issue in 1985 in *Burlington School Committee v. Massachusetts Department of Education.*[61] In that case, a father had disagreed with the school district's proposed educational placement of his child with learning disablilities and, after seeking an independent evaluation from medical experts and initiating the appeals process, enrolled the child in a private school. The Court rejected the school district's argument that a change in placement without district consent waived all rights to reimbursement. In the Court's opinion, denying relief would defeat the IDEA's major objective of providing an appropriate program. When the school district's proposed placement is ultimately found to be inappropriate, reimbursement is considered necessary, since the review process can be quite lengthy (eight years in this case). The Court reasoned that children should not be educationally disadvantaged by an inappropriate placement and that parents should not be economically penalized for removing their children.

The Supreme Court, however, issued one caveat: Parents who unilaterally seek private placements do so at their own financial risk. If the public school placement is found to be proper, reimbursement will be denied, even if the parentally selected program is shown to be appropriate, better, or even cheaper.[62] Furthermore, reimbursement will be denied when both the public and private placements are shown to be

---

60. St. Johnsbury Acad. v. D.H., 240 F.3d 163 (2d Cir. 2001).

61. 471 U.S. 359 (1985). *See also* Houston Indep. Sch. Dist. v. Bobby R., 200 F.3d 341 (5th Cir. 2000) (denying reimbursement for a placement unilaterally selected by the parent, given that the district had provided the student with a FAPE that was reasonably calculated to provide educational benefit as evidenced by increased test scores in a range of areas).

62. Dong v. Bd. of Educ., 197 F.3d 793 (6th Cir. 1999) (concluding that the proffered placement was appropriate and denying reimbursement for a placement the parents perceived to be better).

inappropriate.[63] Thus, relief can be acquired only if the public placement is inappropriate and the private placement is appropriate.[64]

A subsequent Supreme Court decision, *Florence County School District Four v. Carter,* gave additional support to parents seeking reimbursement for private placements.[65] In that case, a child with a learning disability was removed by her parents from what was proven to be an inappropriate public placement and enrolled in an appropriate private program. Controversy developed when the parents sought reimbursement but were denied because the private school was not included on the state-approved list—a list that was not made available to the public as the state preferred to evaluate each case individually. The Court held that reimbursement could not be denied simply because the school was not state approved. The touchstone was that the public program was inappropriate, and the unilaterally selected program was appropriate. As a result, the reimbursement of "reasonable costs" was required.

Parental requests are not always reasonable, however, and therefore are not always funded. For example, the Eleventh Circuit upheld a lower court decision denying reimbursement as the student had been provided an IEP that was reasonably calculated to confer an appropriate education. The requested residential placement was found to be both unnecessary and not the least restrictive. The court also rejected the opinion of an expert hired by the parents who had indicated that the family needed respite care (i.e., someone to take care of their son in their home), as family members had responsibilities other than caregiver and teacher.[66] In another case, the parents sued a school district for failure to provide a FAPE, notwithstanding the out-of-state placement of the child in a private residential facility and payment for three round-trips home for the child to visit. Additionally, the parents were demanding that the district also pay transportation costs (including airfare for both parents and two siblings), hotel, food, and rental car expenses so they could visit the child. The court

---

63. M.S. v. Bd. of Educ., 231 F.3d 96 (2d Cir. 2000).

64. *Compare* Knable v. Bexley City Sch. Dist., 238 F.3d 755 (6th Cir. 2001) (providing reimbursement to parents of child with oppositional defiant disorder, given the lack of due process provided by the district; a proper IEP meeting was not conducted, so an appropriate IEP was never in place); Walker County Sch. Dist. v. Bennett, 203 F.3d 1293 (11th Cir. 2000) (requiring reimbursement to parents for one year of private education; the proffered public placement was found inappropriate); Bd. of Educ. v. Ill. State Bd. of Educ., 184 F.3d 912 (7th Cir. 1999) (awarding tuition costs as both public placement options were found inappropriate) *with* J.D. v. Pawlet Sch. Dist., 224 F.3d 60 (2d Cir. 2000) (denying reimbursement to parents who had enrolled their gifted son in an out-of-state boarding school—post-secondary college—for academically gifted youth following an erroneous § 504 committee decision that he was a "qualified individual with a disability" given his frustration, boredom, alienation, apathy, and hopelessness due to the absence of intellectual peers at the public high school); Burilovich v. Bd. of Educ., 208 F.3d 560 (6th Cir. 2000) (upholding lower court judgment that reimbursement was unnecessary, as plaintiff failed to show that the IEP was inappropriate); Renner v. Bd. of Educ., 185 F.3d 635 (6th Cir. 1999) (concluding that an autistic child was provided with a FAPE and need not be provided a 40-hour per week program as sought by the parents and supported by their expert).

65. 510 U.S. 7 (1993).

66. Devine v. Indian River County Sch. Bd., 249 F.3d 1289 (11th Cir. 2001).

acknowledged that the IEP encouraged the development of family relations, but ruled that the district was not required to "foot the bill for family gatherings."[67]

In an effort to limit district liability for private placements selected by parents, the IDEA permits reduction or denial of reimbursement if the parents fail to provide public officials with notification of their intent or if a court finds their conduct unreasonable.[68] Proper notification can be accomplished either by discussing the matter with the IEP team during a formal meeting or by providing the district with written notice, including an explanation of the reasons for the decision, at least 10 days prior to the projected removal of the child. At that point, if the district elects to perform additional student evaluations, the parent needs to make the child available.[69]

Services Available to Children in Private Schools.   Students enrolled by their parents in private schools have no *individual right* to receive special education and related services provided by the school district.[70] Instead, public officials are responsible for meeting with representatives of the children to decide who is to receive services; what, where, and how services are to be provided; and how services are to be evaluated. In selecting a site for the delivery of services, officials will consider available alternative delivery systems as well as whether provision on campus (e.g., at a religious school) violates state law.[71] If off-campus delivery is selected, eligible children must be transported from the school to the site and back (or to home). Funding for private school children services is provided in the IDEA at a per-pupil prorated amount. This amount is modest, however, when compared to the dollars contributed by state and local governments. As a result, services that are made available will tend

67. Cohen v. Sch. Bd., 450 So. 2d 1238, 1240 (Fla. Dist. Ct. App. 1984).

68. Pollowitz v. Weast, No. 00-1690, 2001 U.S. App. LEXIS 6729(4th Cir. April 17, 2001) (determining that reimbursement was unnecessary, as the parents failed to provide the district with notice of withdrawal); Sandler v. Hickey, 5 Fed. Appx. 233 (4th Cir. 2001) (observing that parents who enroll their children in nonpublic schools without affording the local school system an opportunity to provide a FAPE in a timely fashion will not be entitled to reimbursement). However, reimbursement will not be reduced or denied (1) if the parent is illiterate and cannot write in English, (2) if by staying within the IEP for the 10-day period the child would suffer physical or emotional harm, or (3) if the district prevented the parents from providing the notice or had failed to notify them of the notice requirement.

69. Patricia P. v. Bd. of Educ., 203 F.3d 462 (7th Cir. 2000) (denying reimbursement to parents who failed to cooperate by allowing the district a reasonable opportunity to evaluate their child; the extent of their cooperation was to allow their child to be tested if Illinois personnel were willing to travel to a unilaterally selected private school in Maine).

70. 34 C.F.R. § 300.454(a)(1) (2002). *See also* Foley v. Special Sch. Dist., 153 F.3d 863 (8th Cir. 1998). *But see* John T. v. Marion Indep. Sch. Dist., 173 F.3d 684 (8th Cir. 1999) (concluding that the district should have provided the plaintiff with an assistant while enrolled in a private school, as was required under state law).

71. K.D.M. v. Reedsport Sch. Dist., 196 F.3d 1046 (9th Cir. 1999) (upholding Oregon administrative regulation stipulating that if a district decides to provide services to children in private schools, such appropriate special education and services must be provided in a religiously neutral setting).

to be fewer in number or in less duration than those available in IEPs provided by the local school district.[72]

Change of Placement.   Following an appropriate initial placement in a public or private school, adjustments to a child's IEP may be necessary due to the results of an annual review or reevaluation; discontinuation of a school, program, or service; violent or disruptive behavior; or graduation. Before changing a substantive aspect of a student's program, written notice must be given to the parents of their right to review the proposed alteration, although consent is not required at this time. In the alternative, parents have the right to discuss the matter with the rest of the IEP team and, if dissatisfied, challenge the decision through either mediation or an impartial hearing.

Related Services

As noted previously, a free appropriate public education may include related services in addition to special education. *Related services* are defined as transportation and such developmental, corrective, and other supportive services (including speech pathology and audiology, psychological services, physical and occupational therapy, recreation, social work services, early identification and assessment, orientation and mobility services, school health services, counseling services,[73] medical services for diagnostic and evaluation purposes, and parent counseling and training) that are necessary for a child with a disability to benefit from special education.[74] Services such as physical therapy, occupational therapy,[75] and speech therapy also may qualify as related services. The areas of transportation, psychological, and health services have been subject to comparatively high levels of litigation and are summarized briefly here.

---

72. 34 C.F.R. § 300.455(a)(2),(3) (2002). *See also* Jasa v. Millard Pub. Sch. Dist. No. 17, 206 F.3d 813 (8th Cir. 2000) (concluding that the district had provided the child with a FAPE and need not fund the same services in a private school unilaterally selected by the parents); Hooks v. Clark County Sch. Dist., 228 F.3d 1036 (9th Cir. 2000) (affirming lower court ruling denying reimbursement for speech therapy services, attorneys' fees, and declaratory relief for a child who was home schooled but wanted the school district to pay for speech therapy).

73. *But see* M.C. v. Voluntown Bd. of Educ., 226 F.3d 60 (2d Cir. 2000) (denying reimbursement for counseling services, as the parents failed to raise the issue in a timely fashion; had the complaint been timely, they may have obviated the need for related expenditures).

74. 20 U.S.C. § 1401(a)(17) (2002).

75. Erickson v. Albuquerque Pub. Schs., 199 F.3d 1116 (10th Cir. 1999) (concluding that the reduction of occupational therapy from two hours per week to one, as agreed to by the parents, was not a change of placement; furthermore, the elimination of hippotherapy—occupational therapy involving horses—was not a change of placement, as other forms of occupational therapy were continued).

Transportation

Federal regulations require the provision of transportation as a related service for qualified children to and from school, within school buildings, and on school grounds. The child qualifies for transportation if such a service is provided for other children (e.g., all children residing more than two miles from school), or if it is included within an individualized education program or Section 504 plan. Failure to provide the service to qualified students has resulted in courts requiring districts to reimburse parents for transportation costs, time, effort, baby-sitting services, and interest on their expenses.[76] However, other courts have concluded that where alternative transportation was provided, the district was not required to reimburse parents who wanted to transport their own child;[77] that a child's hearing impairment did not qualify her for special transportation;[78] and that transportation did not have to be provided following involvement in a privately funded after-school program unrelated to the IEP.[79]

Psychological Services

Psychological services are explicitly identified in federal statutes as related services to be included within IEPs, as appropriate. Such services include the administration and interpretation of psychological and educational tests as well as other assessment procedures; obtaining, integrating, and interpreting information about the child's behavior and condition; consulting with staff in planning IEPs; planning and managing a program of psychological services; and assisting in the development of positive behavioral intervention strategies.[80] When psychological services are needed to assist the child to benefit from instruction and are provided by a psychologist or other qualified individual, the services should be included within the IEP. However, if parents request psychiatric and other medical services, such requests may be denied.[81]

In an Illinois case, psychotherapy qualified as an appropriate related service but had not been provided by the district. As a result, the parents hired a psychiatrist to provide the therapy. The court was aware that the IDEA specifically excludes medical services, but reasoned that the services provided in this case were not medical, even though they were provided by a physician.[82] In supporting its decision, the court con-

---

76. *See, e.g.,* Hurry v. Jones, 734 F.2d 879 (1st Cir. 1984); Taylor v. Bd. of Educ., 649 F. Supp. 1253 (N.D.N.Y. 1986).

77. *See, e.g.,* DeLeon v. Susquehanna Cmty. Sch. Dist., 747 F.2d 149 (3d Cir. 1984).

78. McNair v. Oak Hills Local Sch. Dist., 872 F.2d 153 (6th Cir. 1989).

79. Roslyn Union Free Sch. Dist. v. Univ. of N.Y., 711 N.Y.S.2d 582 (App. Div. 2000).

80. 34 C.F.R. § 300.24(b)(9) (2002).

81. Butler v. Evans, 225 F.3d 887 (7th Cir. 2000) (concluding that the district was not responsible for paying for psychiatric placement or related medical expenses; the child was schizo-affective, paranoid, suicidal, and satanical and represented a danger to self and others).

jectured that the "intent" of the statute required courts to look at the nature of the service in addition to the credentials of the provider. Accordingly, because psychotherapy was an appropriate service for the child and had not been provided, reimbursement was required.

Health Services

Courts also have been asked to differentiate between medical and health services. As indicated, the Individuals with Disabilities Education Act (IDEA) excludes medical services except for diagnostic and evaluative purposes and defines both medical (i.e., those provided by a licensed physician) and health services (i.e., those provided by a school nurse or other qualified person). The Supreme Court began its review of school health-care issues in *Irving Independent School District v. Tatro*.[83] In that case, a child required clean intermittent catheterization every three to four hours. The Court found that catheterization was essential in that it would enable the child to attend school and thereby benefit from instruction, and that it could be performed by either a nurse or a trained layperson. Accordingly, the service clearly did not qualify as a medical service and could not be excluded from consideration for the child's IEP.

In post-*Tatro* years, the issue of health care has been a volatile one, given the growing number of medically fragile children now in public schools and the escalating costs of health care. This growth is due in part to the number of seriously ill children who now live to school age (e.g., children who are HIV positive, have AIDS, or are addicted to crack) and to the desire of many parents to have their children educated in regular education facilities whenever possible. Over the years, some courts adopted a "bright-line" test requiring the provision of all health-care services provided by anyone other than a physician, if required to enable the child to attend school. Other courts aggregated the health-care services a child received and then determined whether they collectively qualified as medical or resulted in an undue financial hardship. In such cases, the challenged services often were extensive (one-to-one care), varied, time consuming, and/or expensive.

The Supreme Court resolved the division among the lower courts in 1999 in *Cedar Rapids Community School District v. Garret F.*[84] In this case, the child had a severed spinal column and was paralyzed from the neck down. To remain in school, he required full-time nursing care (e.g., catheterization, suctioning, ambu bagging, ventilator assistance, emergency aid). The district argued that the services collectively should be viewed as medical, even if individually they qualified as health services, and asserted that it would incur an undue financial burden if required to provide the

---

82. Max M. v. Thompson, 592 F. Supp. 1437 (N.D. Ill. 1984). *See also* Max M. v. Ill. State Bd. of Educ., 629 F. Supp. 1504 (N.D. Ill. 1986) (ordering full reimbursement of the physician-provided care since the school district did not offer proof that the services could be provided for less cost).

83. 468 U.S. 883 (1984).

84. 526 U.S. 66 (1999).

services. The Court acknowledged the legitimate financial concerns of the district, but noted that the law as currently constructed required the court to reject the undue burden claim.[85] Moreover, by applying the bright-line test, the Court made clear the position that any health service (i.e., one provided by qualified staff other than a physician) that a student may need to participate in a school setting[86] had to be provided, regardless of cost.

Tangential to this controversy is the issue of who is to pay for required health services. As a rule, services that are included within the IEP are the responsibility of the local school district. However, some financial assistance may be available from Medicaid. Due to a 1988 Supreme Court decision, *Bowen v. Massachusetts,*[87] and an amendment to Title XIX of the Social Security Act (Medicaid),[88] health services included on the state-approved list can no longer be excluded from reimbursement solely because they are provided at school. Medicaid-eligible individuals include those who are receiving aid to families with dependent children, qualified low-income pregnant women and their children, low-income people age 65 or older, and others who are blind or disabled and are receiving Supplemental Security Income. The use of Medicaid is limited, however, as not all children are Medicaid eligible and not all health services are included on state-approved lists that vary by state.

Extended School Year

Federal statutes require that programs be both appropriate and designed to provide educational benefit. In meeting these mandates, it may be necessary for a particular child to receive services beyond the traditional nine-month school year. Although school districts can prescribe a fixed number of instructional days for students without disabilities, such a determination must be made on an individual basis for children with disabilities. Nonetheless, when extended school year (ESY) services are found "beneficial" or even "maximizing," but are not "essential" to the provision of an appropriate program, they are not required under the Individuals with Disabilities Education Act.[89]

---

85. Although unavailable under the IDEA, the undue burden defense is available under both Section 504 and the ADA.

86. Note, however, that some health-care services do not have to be provided when the child is home bound. *See, e.g.,* Daniel O. v. Mo. State Bd. of Educ., No. 99-2792, 2000 U.S. App. LEXIS 7032 (8th Cir. April 19, 2000).

87. 487 U.S. 879 (1988). *See also* Detsel v. Sullivan, 895 F.2d 58 (2d Cir. 1990) (ruling that the student was entitled to Medicaid payment for private-duty nursing services during the school day).

88. 42 U.S.C. § 1396 (2002).

89. Cordrey v. Euckert, 917 F.2d 1460 (6th Cir. 1990) (holding that a school district was not required to pay for a summer program for an autistic teenager because the summer break in his program would not substantially impede his progress).

When ESY services are provided, programs will vary widely with some mandating the extension of the full individualized education program (IEP) for one, two, or three additional months; others providing new or different services; and yet others utilizing all or some of the same services, but in different amounts. Furthermore, in fairly narrow circumstances an ESY program may include the delivery of only related services (e.g., when a child needs physical therapy during the summer to remain sufficiently flexible or mobile to participate within the IEP in the fall). The IEP team is responsible for making individualized decisions regarding eligibility for ESY services and for selecting appropriate services, including their amount and duration.[90]

Eligibility decisions should be made annually during the IEP review and be based on information in addition to regression-recoupment.[91] Consideration also should be given to individual need, the nature and severity of the disability, self-sufficiency and independence, whether educational benefit can be incurred without such services, whether short-term goals and objectives are being met, and whether progress is being made toward the accomplishment of long-term goals. The child's receipt of ESY services in previous years is not a factor to consider in making the eligibility decision for the current year.

Participation in Sports

Children with disabilities, like many children without disabilities, often are interested in participating in interscholastic sports. But the requests of these student-athletes to participate have at times been denied because either they failed to meet eligibility requirements or their participation represented too great a risk either to themselves or to others. A few cases have been filed under the Individuals with Disabilities Education Act, but most disputes are based either on Section 504 of the Rehabilitation Act or the Americans with Disabilities Act.

The IDEA has been involved in two types of sports-related disability cases: (1) where parents wanted to include sports in the individualized education program and (2) where the IEP team included sports in the IEP and the state athletic association penalized the school for allowing an ineligible student to participate. Because sports participation is seldom considered *essential* for students to incur educational benefit,

---

90. Adams v. Oregon, 195 F.3d 1141 (9th Cir. 1999) (ruling that parents were entitled to reimbursement for a private placement and tutoring if such services were found on remand to be appropriate and reasonable; school officials had agreed to 12.5 hours of weekly instruction, but reduced that amount to 7.5 because of staff summer vacations).

91. In this context, *regression* refers to the loss of knowledge, ability, or skill a student may experience during a break in instruction, whereas *recoupment* refers to the time it takes to regain the knowledge, ability, or skill that was lost once instruction is resumed. *See* Johnson v. Indep. Sch. Dist. No. 4, 921 F.2d 1022 (10th Cir. 1990) (holding that this analysis must include not only retrospective data related to regression but also predictive data). *But see* Reusch v. Fountain, 872 F. Supp. 1421 (D. Md. 1994) (finding that the district violated the IDEA by determining eligibility for an extended year program on a single factor: regression-recoupment analysis).

it typically is not included in IEPs.[92] Furthermore, from the school district's perspective, it generally is not prudent to include sports, or any other extracurricular activity, in individualized programs. Such a practice establishes an entitlement to team membership (not to participation per se, however) and enables sports to become a right that can be withdrawn only through due process.

In the second scenario (i.e., where the team is penalized), state athletic associations do not receive IDEA funds or any other type of federal financial assistance and consequently are not required to comply with either the IDEA or Section 504. Accordingly, if the IEP team were to include sports in the IEP and thereby allow an otherwise ineligible student to participate in an interscholastic contest, school officials may have created a situation that will result in rules violations and penalties. The Montana Supreme Court "strongly encouraged" educators to be prudent in including sports in IEPs and warned that they might be "making a promise [they] simply cannot keep."[93] Given this situation, the district will have to sue the athletic association possibly under the Fourteenth Amendment[94] or the ADA to terminate whatever remedial actions have been taken against it. In the end, even if the district were to prevail, which is unlikely, it will have incurred substantial expense and dedicated considerable personnel time to a problem that could have easily been avoided by not including sports in IEPs and by uniformly applying eligibility regulations.

Unlike the IDEA, there are a myriad related scenarios and cases regarding athletic participation under Section 504, and more recently under the ADA. Most claims have alleged discrimination due to facially neutral regulations that disproportionately affect students with disabilities, such as age limitations,[95] grade-point average restrictions,[96] one-year residency and transfer requirements,[97] and eight-semester/four-season limitations.[98]

92. *But see* Kling v. Mentor Pub. Sch. Dist., 136 F. Supp. 2d 744 (N.D. Ohio 2001) (granting preliminary injunction to require the participation of an overage athlete who was likely to receive educational benefits only with the inclusion of sports on his IEP; this decision was made following a determination of whether the intent of the age policy would be fulfilled notwithstanding the student's involvement).

93. J.M. v. Mont. High Sch. Ass'n, 875 P.2d 1026, 1032 (Mont. 1994).

94. Such suits are more likely today, given the Supreme Court's ruling in Brentwood Acad. v. Tenn. Secondary Sch. Athletic Ass'n., 122 S. Ct. 1439 (2002) where the state athletic association was declared a state actor, notwithstanding the fact that it was a private corporation. *See* text accompanying note 142, Chapter 4.

95. *See, e.g.,* Sandison v. Mich. High Sch. Athletic Ass'n, 64 F.3d 1026 (6th Cir. 1995); Reaves v. Mills, 904 F. Supp. 120 (W.D.N.Y. 1995); Pottgen v. Mo. State High Sch. Activities Ass'n, 857 F. Supp. 654 (E.D. Mo. 1994), *rev'd and remanded,* 40 F.3d 926 (8th Cir. 1994). *But see* Dennin v. Conn. Interscholastic Athletic Conference, 913 F. Supp. 663 (D. Conn. 1996) (granting motion for preliminary injunction where student athlete with a disability alleged § 504, ADA, and Fourteenth Amendment violations when he was refused the opportunity to participate in sports due to age).

96. *See, e.g.,* Hoot v. Milan Area Sch., 853 F. Supp. 243 (E.D. Mich. 1994).

97. *See, e.g.,* Crocker v. Tenn. Secondary Sch. Athletic Ass'n, 980 F.2d 382 (6th Cir. 1992).

98. *See, e.g.,* J. M. v. Mont. High Sch. Ass'n, 875 P.2d 1026 (Mont. 1994); Clay v. Ariz. Interscholastic Ass'n, 779 P.2d 349 (Ariz. 1989). *See* text accompanying note 159 in Chapter 4 for a related discussion.

Historically, all students were required to meet eligibility criteria and were allowed to play only when they were otherwise qualified to participate *and* if they made the team. Most courts still permit the uniform application of such rules, but that approach may be changing. A related issue reviewed by the Supreme Court in a professional sport context may affect interscholastic and all other organized sports. In *PGA Tour v. Martin,* the Court supported a professional golfer's effort to be permitted to ride a cart rather than walk the course, as the event rules required.[99] Walking caused him pain that resulted in fatigue and anxiety that could lead to hemorrhaging and the development of blood clots or fractures. The Court reasoned that "shot making" was the essence of golf and that walking was neither an essential attribute nor an indispensable feature of the sport, notwithstanding contradictory testimony from golf legends Arnold Palmer, Jack Nicklaus, and Ken Venturi. This decision will have implications for all sports. It does not require lowering the basket, widening the goal, or bringing in the fences in basketball, soccer, and baseball, respectively, but it does require the evaluation of any rule that disqualifies an otherwise qualified participant with a disability. Review of such rules should reveal whether they qualify as essential features of the sport or are peripheral and therefore subject to alteration or elimination.

Given the Supreme Court majority opinion in *PGA Tour,* state athletic associations need to follow a four-step process in the development and application of their policies and rules: (1) identify those rules that potentially disqualify students with disabilities due to the limitations posed by their disabilities; (2) determine whether each identified rule supports a necessary and valid purpose; (3) assess whether the requested modification or adjustment is reasonable and necessary for the individual to participate in the activity; and (4) ascertain whether provision of the modification or adjustment would fundamentally alter the nature of the competition, adversely affect the demonstrated valid purpose of the rule, or result in an unfair advantage.[100]

The Seventh Circuit examined such a case where a student with above average intelligence had dropped out of school at least in part due to his poor performance that was related to a learning disability.[101] He later reentered school and participated in basketball. Eventually, he was declared ineligible under the rule limiting participation during the first eight semesters following commencement of the ninth grade. The student argued that the period he was not enrolled in school should not count against his eligibility, notwithstanding explicit wording in the bylaw to the contrary. The court reasoned that waiver of the rule in *this* instance involving *this* student would not rep-

---

99. 532 U.S. 661 (2001).

100. *See, e.g.,* Cruz v. Penn. Interscholastic Athletic Ass'n, 157 F. Supp. 2d 485 (E.D. Pa. 2001) (applying *PGA Tour* criteria and granting a preliminary injunction where a student with a disability was denied the opportunity to participate in sport due to being over age).

101. Washington v. Ind. High Sch. Athletic Ass'n, 181 F.3d 840 (7th Cir. 1999).

resent a fundamental alteration to the rule or create an undue financial burden for the association.[102]

Another type of sports-related case involves athletes with physically limiting conditions but who are otherwise qualified to participate. In many of these situations, the athlete is willing to assume the risks of participation, to sign a waiver of liability if injured in the normal occurrence of the game, and to provide affidavits signed by physicians both indicating that participation is safe and identifying any necessary safety wear. Since the mid-to-late 1970s, the majority of courts has supported the right of student athletes to participate, even with the absence of organs, limbs, vision, and the like.[103] More recently, however, two courts addressing claims of discrimination filed by college athletes have sided with the educational institutions.[104] Both courts indicated that they were not in a position to determine which "experts" were correct as to the degree of risk that would be present if the athlete were to participate. Instead, it was their view that deference should be given to the institution's experts as long as their professional judgment was reasonable, rational, and supported by substantial, competent evidence. This reasoning is consistent with recent trends in disability law and may signal a return to providing deference to school experts in such matters.

Discipline

Students with disabilities are not exempt from reasonable disciplinary measures, although due process exceeding that provided to regular education students is required at times, and penalties are capped on occasion. In 1988, the Supreme Court in *Honig v. Doe* reviewed its only IDEA discipline case to date. In that case, the Court held that an indefinite suspension of two students pending the outcome of expulsion proceedings was a prohibited change in placement and violated the stay-put provision of the IDEA.[105] The state superintendent of public instruction had urged the Supreme Court to recognize a "dangerousness" exception to the stay-put requirement. The superin-

---

102. *But see* McPherson v. Mich. High Sch. Athletic Ass'n, 119 F.3d 453 (6th Cir. 1997) (upholding application of an eight-semester rule against a student with ADHD and seizure disorder and concluding that its waiver would represent a fundamental alteration of the sports program and create an immense and undue financial burden for the state association).

103. *See, e.g.,* Grube v. Bethlehem Area Sch. Dist., 550 F. Supp. 418 (E.D. Penn. 1982) (loss of kidney); Suemnick v. Mich. High Sch. Athletic Ass'n, No. 4-70592 (E.D. Mich. 1974) (loss of leg); Kampmeier v. Harris, 411 N.Y.S.2d 744 (App. Div. 1978) (impaired vision).

104. Knapp v. Northwestern Univ., 101 F.3d 473 (7th Cir. 1996) (determining that participation in basketball could be denied to an athlete who had previously experienced sudden cardiac death but was revived and had an internal cardioverter-defibrillator implanted in his abdomen—designed to enable his heart to restart if it were to stop again); Pahulu v. Univ. of Kan., 897 F. Supp. 1387 (D. Kan. 1995) (denying right to play football to an athlete who suffered a hit to the head, resulting in an extremely high risk of permanent severe neurological injury if he were again to engage in contact such as that found in football).

105. 484 U.S. 305 (1988).

tendent also contended that Congress could not have intended that school officials return violent or dangerous students to the classroom during the lengthy administrative proceedings. Disagreeing, the Supreme Court stated that Congress deliberately stripped schools of the unilateral authority to exclude students with disabilities. The history of exclusion of such students prior to passage of the IDEA and the early litigation that guided the development of the law convinced the Court that the conspicuous absence of an emergency exception was intentional.

The Supreme Court, however, emphasized that school officials are not without options when confronted with a dangerous student. They can use a range of normal procedures (e.g., suspension of up to 10 days, detention, time-out[106]). In addition, the Court indicated that if other forms of discipline are not successful, and the student already has been suspended for the maximum 10-day period but continues to pose a threat, school officials may seek injunctive relief if the parents refuse to agree to a change in placement.[107]

Among the disciplinary options available to school officials, suspension and expulsion have resulted in considerable judicial action. Each is reviewed here in greater detail.[108]

Suspension

Suspension is the removal of a student from the educational setting for 10 or fewer days, and it may result in either an in-school placement (e.g., in-school suspension room) or complete removal from the school setting. Students with disabilities generally may not be suspended for more than 10 consecutive days or receive repetitive brief suspensions that aggregate to more than 10 days during the school year. Successive suspensions exceeding the 10-day limit are theoretically possible, but only where they do not represent a pattern of removal and are based on separate incidents of misconduct.[109] In the comparatively exceptional circumstance where removal justifiably exceeds the 10-day limit, services consistent with the individualized education pro-

---

106. Not all assignments to time-out will be found legal, however. *See, e.g.,* Covington v. Knox County Sch. Sys., 205 F.3d 912 (6th Cir. 2000) (concluding that the exhaustion of administrative remedies would have been futile given that the plaintiff sought a damage award that was not available under the IDEA; the child had been routinely locked in a small time-out room for up to several hours at a time, denied lunch, required to disrobe on one occasion, and forced to remain in the room following urination that resulted when the confinement period was lengthy).

107. *See also* Tex. City Indep. Sch. Dist. v. Jorstad, 752 F. Supp. 231 (S.D. Tex. 1990) (issuing a preliminary injunction prohibiting an emotionally disturbed child from attending regular classes consistent with his IEP; in the alternative he could attend a behavioral management class or have home instruction); E. Islip Union Free Sch. Dist. v. Andersen, 615 N.Y.2d 852 (Sup. Ct. 1994) (granting a preliminary injunction continuing a student's suspension pending review and revision of his IEP given the student's threats against certain students and teachers).

108. *See* text accompanying notes 25–67, Chapter 7.

109. For example, a pattern of removal would be present where a student receives three five-day suspensions for smoking cigarettes while on school grounds.

gram must be provided beginning on the eleventh day.[110] The key in determining whether a day of suspension applies toward the total is to assess whether the child has been removed from the IEP, not whether the child has received an in-school or out-of-school suspension.

If a student is assigned to a time-out room, rather than an in-school suspension room, and instruction and/or services identified within the IEP continue to be delivered by a properly credentialed individual, it is unlikely that the time removed from the regular education classroom will contribute to the 10-day limit. To reduce the likelihood of litigation, however, it is recommended that assignment to time-out be included within the IEPs of students who are likely to require such assignments as a form of behavior modification or intervention. Once the parent has agreed to such a provision, assignment to time-out will be *consistent with* the IEP and not be viewed as *removal from* the IEP.

Expulsion

Expulsion is the removal of a student from the IEP for more than 10 consecutive days, and it qualifies as a change of placement. In such instances, the student will either be at home or assigned to an appropriate interim alternative educational setting for up to 45 days. Assignment to an alternative setting is possible when the student carries a weapon or *knowingly* possesses, uses, sells, or solicits illegal drugs while at school or at a school function. If this occurs, the school district is responsible for conducting a functional behavioral assessment and for preparing a behavioral intervention plan, if one has not already been prepared. Interventions should be appropriately implemented to address the conduct that resulted in the disciplinary action, and modified when needed.[111]

A hearing officer, in an expedited hearing, is authorized to assign a student to an alternative setting if the claims are supported by *substantial evidence* (i.e., something greater than preponderance of evidence, but less than proof beyond a reasonable doubt) that maintaining the student in the current placement is likely to result in injury to the student or to others. The hearing officer will consider the appropriateness of the student's current placement, whether supplementary aids and services were used to minimize the risks in the current placement, and whether the alternative setting will permit the student to make progress within the IEP.

No later than 10 days following a student's removal, a review must be conducted to assess the relationship between the student's disability and the behavior that is subject to the disciplinary action. This *manifestation determination* must be conducted by the IEP team and other qualified personnel and entails reviewing evaluations, diagnostic results, information supplied by the parents, the IEP, observations, and the like. The team must determine whether, at the time of the disruption, the student was being provided with a free appropriate public education in the least restric-

110. 34 C.F.R. § 300.520(a)(1)(ii) (2002).

111. 34 C.F.R. § 300.519–300.520(a)(2), (b), (c) (2002).

tive environment, whether intervention strategies were provided consistent with the IEP, and whether the disability impaired the student's ability to understand the impact and consequences of the conduct or to control the behavior. If the placement and services were improper or if the disability impaired the ability to "understand" or "control," the conduct must be considered disability related.[112] When this occurs, the student cannot be expelled, although a change of placement to a more restrictive setting may be necessary if the student's prior conduct is likely to be repeated within the current placement, in spite of behavioral interventions and supervision.

If the behavior is not found to be disability related, the student may be subjected to the same punishment that would have been administered had the student not been disabled. At this time, officials need to transmit the records of the student to those making the final disciplinary decision. If removal for more than 10 days is supported, services consistent with the IEP need to be delivered in the home or other environment that will enable the student to make progress toward achieving the goals identified in the IEP.

When expulsion is permissible and appropriate, the parents have the right to challenge the manifestation determination and resulting decision. In such instances, federal law once again requires that an expedited hearing be conducted. During the appeals process, the "then-current placement" is the alternative setting, not the former placement where the disruption occurred, unless the expulsion has been served by the time a hearing can be provided. Even then, however, if school personnel can document that the student would represent a danger in the former placement, a new, more restrictive placement can be provided. The parents also have the right to challenge this change-of-placement decision.

Interestingly, even students who are not yet identified as disabled may be protected by the Individuals with Disabilities Education Act if district officials had knowledge that such students *may be* disabled. "Knowledge" exists where a parent or educator either expresses concern that the student may be disabled given the behavior or performance *or* requests an evaluation. The student is not entitled to protection if he or she is found not to qualify following an evaluation, or if school officials determine that assessment is not necessary. Where an evaluation is requested and appears justified, it should be expedited.[113] If the student does not qualify as both disabled and in need of special education and related services, instruction during the removal

112. Doe v. Bd. of Educ., 115 F.3d 1273 (7th Cir. 1997) (noting that the committee unanimously determined that plaintiff's drug use was not related to his learning disability); Randy M. v. Texas City I.S.D., 93 F. Supp. 2d 1310 (S.D. Tex. 2000) (concluding that ripping the break-away pants off a female student, thereby exposing her underwear was not related to the student's learning disability). *But see* Richland Sch. Dist. v. Thomas P., No. 00-C-0139-X, 2000 U.S. Dist. LEXIS 15162 (W.D. Wis. May 24, 2000) (concluding that although the student's vandalism was not related to his learning disability, it was related to his newly discovered attention deficit disorder and dysthymia, given uncontradicted testimony from the parent's expert).

113. *But see* Colvin v. Lowndes County, Miss. Sch. Dist., 114 F. Supp. 2d 504 (N.D. Miss. 2000) (determining that the district failed to properly assess a student who was being expelled for one year under a zero-tolerance policy for bringing a Swiss army knife on campus).

period need not be provided, unless available to regular education students who have been similarly withdrawn. In contrast, if the student does qualify as disabled, special education and related services need to be provided.

It should be recognized, however, that the IDEA does not prohibit personnel from reporting any crime a student may have committed to law-enforcement authorities. Law-enforcement officials are not bound by the IDEA and may require an unruly or delinquent student to submit to treatment, home detention, or incarceration, in addition to any penalty the district may provide.

Procedural Safeguards

School officials generally make good faith efforts to meet the needs of children with disabilities, yet there will be times when the parents disagree with evaluation, placement, and program decisions. Disagreement may come about early in the process (e.g., failure to provide consent for initial evaluation) or later (e.g., termination of services allegedly due to graduation). Understandably, many parents seek the best possible education for their children. Alternatively, it is not uncommon for school districts to offer a minimally appropriate program (i.e., one that provides for some educational benefit and is based on student needs, but is not "the best"). Moreover, on occasion, districts wittingly (based on current program availability, staffing, or limited funding), unwittingly (because of ambiguity of assessment results), or through incompetency or neglect proffer something other than an appropriate placement.[114] If disagreement and an eventual impasse occurs, either party may initiate the due process procedures identified in the Individuals with Disabilities Education Act. Parents should be provided a comprehensive copy of procedural safeguards upon initial referral for evaluation, and again upon each notification of an individualized education program meeting, reevaluation, or hearing. These procedures are reviewed next and presented in Figure 6.1.

Stay-Put

During IDEA administrative and judicial appeals, the student is assigned to the "then-current educational placement" or a placement agreed to by the parents and the public officials.[115] This stay-put provision applies in cases where any change of placement

114. Everett v. Santa Barbara High Sch. Dist., 28 Fed. Appx. 683 (9th Cir. 2002) (concluding that the district failed to provide a FAPE when all parties agreed that the child was improperly placed in a class for seriously emotionally disturbed; was placed in home instruction without an instructor; and later, when two different teachers were used, only one was properly credentialed).

115. 34 C.F.R. § 300.514(a) (2002).

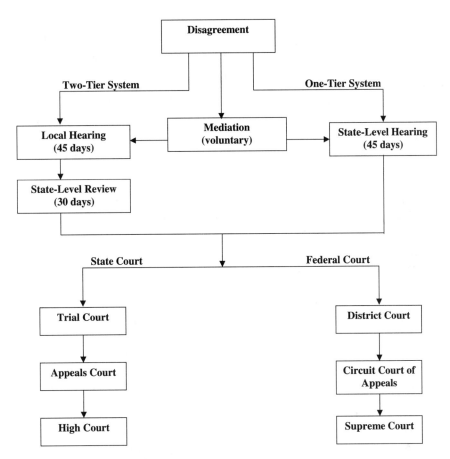

FIGURE 6.1 *IDEA Due Process*

is to occur,[116] including those where the content of the placement remains the same, but the least restrictive environment (LRE) has been altered.[117] The current placement may be anywhere along the continuum of alternative public or private placements. If the complaint deals with the initial placement of the child, the regular classroom represents the current placement, although additional services may be agreed to by the

116. However, where a child transitions from an individualized family service plan to an IEP, changing the personnel to provide the services (e.g., tutors) was not found to be a violation of the stay-put provision. *See* Johnson v. Special Educ. Hearing Office, 287 F.3d 1176 (9th Cir. 2002).

117. Hale v. Poplar Bluff R-1 Sch. Dist., 280 F.3d 831 (8th Cir. 2002) (requiring the provision of compensatory education during the summer, as the district had violated the stay-put provision by changing the student's placement from home bound to school without going through due process; the school had argued that it need not provide due process, because the services remained the same, only the location of service changed).

parties. The placement remains the same until all administrative hearings have been completed, unless the child is unilaterally removed by the parent and placed in an alternative setting. Once administrative appeals have been exhausted, the current placement may change, depending on the position taken by the state hearing officer or state review official.

Also, according to Office of Special Education Programs, stay-put requirements apply even when a child changes school districts within the same state, given that the placement has already been determined in accordance with state procedures and with the consent of the child's parents.[118] However, the office does not expect public school systems to maintain the current placements of children moving into their service areas from out of state,[119] or to maintain a private placement unilaterally selected by the parent, but not supported at the conclusion of administrative hearings.[120] Due process may begin with either mediation or an impartial hearing.

Mediation

Mediation sessions are designed to be nonadversarial and involve only the parents, essential educators, and the mediator. The mediation process may be initiated any time the public agency proposes or refuses to initiate or change the identification, evaluation, placement, or provision of a free appropriate public education for a child with a disability. Participation in the process must be voluntary and may not be used to deny or delay a parent's right to a due process hearing or other IDEA rights. When parents elect to mediate, sessions must be provided in a timely manner and held in a convenient location. Any discussions that occur during the process must remain confidential and may not be used as evidence in any subsequent due process hearing or civil proceeding. To accomplish this purpose, the parties may be required to sign a confidentiality pledge prior to the commencement of the process. This pledge is not intended, however, to exclude in subsequent due process hearings and civil proceedings any information that otherwise would have been subject to discovery;[121] it is intended to protect only those "discussions" that occur during mediation.

Mediators and hearing officers[122] must have no personal or professional conflict of interest in the dispute or otherwise be employees of the state or local district. Such persons must be knowledgeable of applicable laws and regulations and trained in effective mediation techniques. Mediators do not "rule," as would a court, nor do they make IEP decisions—that responsibility remains with the IEP team. The mediator is

118. Inquiry of Rieser, OSEP Policy Letter, July 17, 1986 (U.S. Dep't Educ. 1986).

119. OSEP Policy Memorandum 96-5. *See also* Michael C. *ex rel.* Stephen C. v. Radnor Township Sch. Dist., 202 F.3d 642 (3d Cir. 2000) (concluding that the stay-put provision did not apply when a child moved from one state to another).

120. Tucker v. Calloway County Bd. of Educ., 136 F.3d 495 (6th Cir. 1998) (denying reimbursement and noting that the stay-put provision does not require the district to pay for a unilaterally selected private placement during the course of litigation).

121. *Discovery* is a pretrial procedure where a party gains information about the case that is held by the other party (e.g., depositions, interrogatories).

122. *See* text accompanying notes 123–125, infra.

responsible for conducting the meeting, facilitating discussion, helping the parties make mutually beneficial decisions, and preparing written copies of any agreement the parties may have reached. Even when total agreement is not achieved, mediators often help the parties identify points of agreement and disagreement, clarify available options, and narrow the dispute, thereby reducing the complexity and cost of administrative and judicial proceedings.

Impartial Due Process Hearing

If mediation is not undertaken or proves unsuccessful, either party may request that an impartial due process hearing be conducted. Although the public school system is not obligated to provide counsel for the plaintiff,[123] it is required at this time to inform the parents of free or low-cost legal services available in the community. In a one-tier state, the impartial hearing will be conducted by a state official, with no further administrative appeal available. In a two-tier state, the first hearing is conducted locally by an impartial hearing officer; any resulting decision then may be appealed to a second-tier state review official.

If parents elect to initiate the due process procedures, they must notify the public agency. This notice should include the child's name, address, school of attendance, a description of the problem to be addressed at the hearing, and a proposed resolution.[124] To encourage compliance with this provision, fees for the parents' attorney may be reduced if the attorney fails to provide the public agency with the required information. Additionally, the IDEA stipulates that all parties to the initial administrative hearing disclose to all other parties at least *five business days* prior to a hearing all evaluations, recommendations, and evidence that the party intends to use. If disclosure is not provided, the hearing officer is empowered to prohibit the introduction of information, unless consent of the other party is provided. The parties may be accompanied and advised by counsel as well as other persons with special knowledge or training relevant to the child; present evidence; and confront, cross-examine, and compel the attendance of witnesses.[125] Furthermore, parents have the discretion to involve their child in the proceedings and to have the hearing either closed or open to the public. Once the proceedings have been completed, the parents may obtain at no cost a written *or* an electronic verbatim record of such hearing, findings of facts, and decisions.

Hearing officer opinions must be available no later than 45 days following the receipt of a request for a hearing. Such opinions must be based only on evidence presented by the parties. Under certain conditions, evidence that may be inadmissible in a court of law may be admissible in a special education due process hearing. For example, *hearsay evidence* (i.e., evidence that is not based on the personal knowledge of the witness, but rather from the repetition of what he or she has heard others say) is

---

123. Daniel B. v. Wis. Dep't of Pub. Instruction, 581 F. Supp. 585 (E.D. Wis. 1984), *aff'd*, 776 F.2d 1051 (7th Cir. 1985).

124. 34 C.F.R. § 300.507(c)(2) (2002).

125. 34 C.F.R. § 300.509(a) (2002).

typically admissible in IDEA hearings, but may be given less weight than *direct evidence* (i.e., testimony from firsthand witnesses).

State Review

If the school district conducts the impartial hearing (signifying a two-tier state), either party aggrieved by the findings and decision may appeal to the state. At the state level, the review official is responsible for ensuring that the hearing officer followed appropriate procedures, impartially reviewing the record in its entirety, and seeking additional evidence, if necessary. Additionally, the review official may permit the parties the opportunity for oral and/or written argument. Following the completion of these procedures, the reviewer must make an independent decision and provide the parties with written findings no later than 30 days following the request for review.

Civil Action

Either party to an IEP dispute may bring a civil action in a state trial court or federal district court. Most courts place the burden of proof on the party challenging the results of the final administrative hearing. When an action is filed, the court receives the records of the administrative proceedings; hears additional evidence at the request of a party; bases its decision on the preponderance of the evidence; and grants such relief as it determines to be appropriate. In reaching their own independent decisions, courts most often provide deference to the findings reached in the administrative proceedings, unless such findings are determined to be arbitrary or clearly erroneous. Furthermore, they generally view the decision of the state-level review official as controlling, except when the credibility of the witness is concerned,[126] given that the state reviewer would have no direct knowledge of a witness's demeanor, trustworthiness, confidence, or professionalism.

Prior to filing an IDEA suit, the plaintiff is required to exhaust administrative remedies (i.e., an impartial hearing and state review),[127] unless such remedies would prove futile or fail to provide the required relief, or where emergency conditions exist that could result in severe or irreparable harm to the child. Such mandatory administrative remedies cannot be avoided by filing under the Constitution, the Americans with Disabilities Act, the Rehabilitation Act, or any other applicable federal law, if the

---

126. Amanda J. v. Clark County Sch. Dist., 267 F.3d 877 (9th Cir. 2001) (concluding that deference should be given to the hearing officer rather than a state review official when it comes to determining the credibility of witnesses).

127. Frazier v. Fairhaven Sch. Comm., 276 F.3d 52 (1st Cir. 2002); Rose v. Yeaw, 214 F.3d 206 (1st Cir. 2000); Weber v. Cranston Sch. Comm., 212 F.3d 41 (1st Cir. 2000). *But see* Iascone v. Conejo Valley Unified Sch. Dist., 15 Fed. Appx. 401 (9th Cir. 2001) (reversing lower court decision dismissing a case for failure to exhaust administrative remedies; the court noted that the plaintiff had alleged facts that, if proven, would establish the futility of the administrative proceedings); Covington v. Knox County Sch. Sys., 205 F.3d 912 (6th Cir. 2000) (noting that exhaustion would have been futile, as the plaintiff had graduated from school and the only award that could make him whole was money damages, which was not available under the IDEA).

requested relief also is available under the IDEA. Such a practice helps reduce the caseload for courts, limits expenditures associated with litigation, and ensures that recipients and states have the opportunity to resolve matters in ways that ideally are less adversarial and more child focused than a law suit (e.g., through IEP meetings or mediation). Where administrative remedies have been exhausted or would prove futile, suits must be filed within the statutory limitation period. Courts are responsible for selecting a limitations period, as none is identified within the IDEA or its regulations. The limitations period is typically taken from state disability or tort statutes and most often is set at two years, but can range from 30 days to three or more years.[128]

Remedies and Attorneys' Fees

In IDEA cases, courts have awarded declaratory relief, injunctive relief, compensatory education, and reimbursement for evaluations, tuition, transportation, and related services. However, most courts have concluded that damage awards are not available under the IDEA, even in conjunction with 42 U.S.C. Section 1983 (i.e., a statute providing the right to sue a state actor for conduct that deprives selected federal rights).[129] The Supreme Court has drawn a sharp distinction between awarding damages and requiring tuition reimbursement; the latter has been viewed simply as the recovery of justified costs that should have been initially incurred by the public school system.[130] Similarly, numerous lower courts have held that awards of compensatory education were necessary when districts failed to provide an appropriate program, committed gross procedural violations that delayed instruction, or prematurely terminated services by offering a diploma.[131] The Eighth Circuit found an award of compensatory educational services to be analogous to the granting of retroactive tuition reimbursement.[132]

---

128. Cory D. v. Burke County Sch. Dist., 285 F.3d 1294 (11th Cir. 2002) (30 days); S.V. v. Sherwood Sch. Dist., 254 F.3d 877 (9th Cir. 2001) (two years); C.M. v. Bd. of Educ., 241 F.3d 374 (4th Cir. 2001) (60 days); Birmingham v. Omaha Sch. Dist., 220 F.3d 850 (8th Cir. 2000) (three years).

129. *See, e.g.,* Wolverton v. Doniphan R-1 Sch. Dist., 16 Fed. Appx. 523 (8th Cir. 2001) (determining that the IDEA does not allow the recovery of damages in a case where a student assigned to a classroom for behaviorally disadvantaged students was sprayed with mace by a security guard for behavior that could have been attributed to his mental illness); Sellers v. Sch. Bd., 141 F.3d 524 (4th Cir. 1998) (concluding that the IDEA does not provide for compensatory or punitive damages and that a plaintiff may not sue under § 1983 for an IDEA violation). For a discussion of § 1983 liability, *see* text accompanying note 189, Chapter 11.

130. Sch. Comm. v. Dep't of Educ., 471 U.S. 359 (1985).

131. *See, e.g.,* Parents of Student W. v. Puyallup Sch. Dist. No. 3, 31 F.3d 1489 (9th Cir. 1994); Murphy v. Timberlane Reg'l Sch. Dist., 22 F.3d 1186 (1st Cir. 1994); Pihl v. Mass. Dep't of Educ., 9 F.3d 184 (1st Cir. 1993).

132. Miener v. Missouri, 800 F.2d 749 (8th Cir. 1986). *See also* Strawn v. Mo. State Bd. of Educ., 210 F.3d 954 (8th Cir. 2000) (finding that the plaintiff had been denied a FAPE and remanded to determine the amount of compensatory education that would be appropriate). *But see* Wenger v. Canastota Cent. Sch. Dist., No. 97-9441, 2000 U.S. App. LEXIS 4647 (2d Cir. March 22, 2000) (determining that plaintiff was not entitled to compensatory education beyond the twenty-first birthday, money damages, reimbursement for administrative and legal costs, or lost income).

In addition, attorneys' fees also may be available to parents who prevail in special education cases. To qualify as a prevailing party, the parents must succeed on a key or primary issue and not simply on a minor, procedural, or tactical issue.[133] Fees are based on the actual time needed to represent the client during both administrative and judicial proceedings, but the hourly rate must be within the range charged by attorneys practicing in the community. Fees have been reduced when time was spent pursuing unsuccessful claims, when proceedings were unnecessarily protracted by the plaintiffs, and when the relief acquired was no greater than that provided in a settlement offer made prior to the proceedings.[134] Moreover, fees need not be paid for time spent at IEP meetings (unless they are held as a result of an administrative hearing or litigation[135]) or to compensate parents who serve as their own attorney.[136]

Conclusion

The rights of students with disabilities have expanded significantly since 1975 and include rights to access programs and facilities, appropriate programs, and least restrictive placements. Several of the more significant points regarding disability law are summarized briefly here.

1. All impairments do not necessarily qualify as disabilities requiring accommodation.

133. J.C. v. Reg'l Sch. Dist. 10, Bd. of Educ., 278 F.3d 119 (2d Cir. 2002) (denying summary judgment under both the IDEA and § 504, as the plaintiff failed to qualify as a prevailing party); Doe v. Eagle-Union Cmty. Sch. Corp., 2 Fed. Appx. 567 (7th Cir. 2001) (denying attorneys' fees as the plaintiff only won a small tactical victory, but lost on the main issues), *cert. denied*, 122 S. Ct. 619 (2001); Bd. of Educ. v. Nathan R., 199 F.3d 377 (7th Cir. 2000) (concluding that parents receiving stay-put order were not the prevailing party and therefore not entitled to attorneys' fees); Linda W. v. Ind. Dep't of Educ., 200 F.3d 504 (7th Cir. 1999) (concluding that the plaintiffs were not the prevailing party, as they won only tactical victories in interlocutory skirmishes).

134. 34 C.F.R. § 300.513(c)(1), (c)(2)(C). *See also* Holmes v. Millcreek Township Sch. Dist., 205 F.3d 583 (3d Cir. 2000) (reducing attorneys' fees to one-fourth the original requested amount; the attorney did not prevail on the primary claim, litigation was needlessly protracted, the hourly rate did not reflect experience, and the number of hours billed was excessive).

135. 34 C.F.R. § 300.513(c)(2)(C)(ii). *See also* Lucht v. Molalla River Sch. Dist., 225 F.3d 1023 (9th Cir. 2000) (upholding lower court award of attorneys' fees resulting from participation in IEP meetings following a successful administrative appeal of an improper IEP; the award was necessary, given that the IEP meetings were "convened as a result of an administrative proceeding"); Daniel S. v. Scranton Sch. Dist., 230 F.3d 90 (3d Cir. 2000) (providing attorneys' fees for involvement during an IEP team meeting conducted prior to, but because of, a pending administrative hearing).

136. Woodside v. Sch. Dist., 248 F.3d 129 (3d Cir. 2001) (concluding that a parent-attorney cannot receive attorneys' fees for work representing his child in proceedings under the IDEA). *See also* Collinsgru v. Palmyra Bd. of Educ., 161 F.3d 225 (3d Cir. 1998) (concluding that a nonattorney parent may not represent his or her child in IDEA litigation).

2. Under Section 504 of the Rehabilitation Act and the Americans with Disabilities Act, the appropriate standard for whether an impairment is substantially limiting is to compare one's performance with that of the average person in the general population; mitigating or corrective measures must be considered in determining whether a student qualifies as disabled.

3. The local school district is responsible for identifying all children with disabilities that live within its service area.

4. Children with disabilities are entitled to a free appropriate public education in the least restrictive environment.

5. Assessments are to be administered by properly trained personnel; instruments must be validated for their intended purpose and administered in the child's native language or other mode of communication.

6. An appropriate program for a child with a disability must be specially designed to meet his or her unique needs and provide meaningful access to an individualized education program that confers some educational benefit; the best program or one that maximizes the child's potential is not required.

7. Under the Individuals with Disabilities Education Act an individualized education program (including goals and objectives, specification of the services to be provided, and an education plan) must be developed for each eligible child; under Section 504, an accommodation plan must be developed and implemented.

8. School district placements may be in either public or private (including religious) schools that are capable of providing the student with an appropriate education.

9. Due process procedures must be followed in identifying, evaluating, or changing the educational placement of children with disabilities.

10. Parents may recover tuition and other costs for a unilateral private placement only if the private placement is determined to be appropriate and the placement proposed or provided by the local school district is found to be inappropriate.

11. Related services necessary to support the specially designed instruction for children with disabilities are required, regardless of cost; school districts are not obligated to provide medical services, but must provide health services if needed for the child to attend school and benefit from instruction.

12. School districts may not impose arbitrary limits on the number of school days for children with disabilities, because certain children may require an extended school year in order to receive "some educational benefit."

13. Students with physical impairments may be denied the opportunity to participate in interscholastic sports if school officials, after consultation with medical experts, determine that it is not safe for the student-athlete to participate on the school's team.

14. During administrative or judicial proceedings regarding a free appropriate public education, the student should remain in the then-current educational placement.

15. Students with and without disabilities may be suspended using the same hearing procedures.
16. Students with disabilities may be expelled only if the misbehavior is not related to their disability; even then, services consistent with the IEP must be provided.
17. When time-out has been incorporated into a student's IEP, the time that a student is assigned to time-out will not count toward the 10-day limit on suspensions.

7

Student Discipline

Student misconduct continues to be one of the most persistent and troublesome problems confronting educators. With the increased incidence of drug and alcohol abuse and violence among teenagers, greater public attention has focused on school disciplinary problems. Schools have devoted more attention to violence prevention strategies including not only stringent security measures but also modification of the curricula to strengthen students' social skills and the training of teachers and administrators to monitor the school climate. Some states and local school districts have enacted restrictive laws or policies that call for *zero tolerance* of weapons, drugs, and violence on campus.[1] The efficacy of legislating tougher approaches to create safe schools has evoked volatile debates, particularly in light of the higher rates of suspension and expulsion for African American and Hispanic students.[2] The range of strategies employed by educators to maintain a safe and secure learning environment is examined in this chapter from a legal perspective; no attempt is made to debate the merits of particular strategies. The analyses focus on the development of conduct regulations, the imposition of sanctions for noncompliance, and the procedures required in the administration of student punishments.

The law clearly authorizes the state and its agencies to establish and enforce reasonable conduct codes to protect the rights of students and school districts and to ensure that school environments are conducive to learning. Historically, courts exercised limited review of student disciplinary regulations, and pupils seldom were successful in challenging policies governing their behavior. In 1923, the Arkansas

1. A study conducted jointly by the Centers for Disease Control, U.S. Department of Education, and U.S. Department of Justice reported that 253 violent deaths occurred on school campuses or en route to and from school between 1994 and 1999. In over half the incidents, there was some warning from the offender, such as a note, journal entry, or threat. Mark Anderson, Joanne Kaufman, Thomas Simon, Lisa Barrios, Len Paulozzi, George Ryan, Rodney Hammond, William Modezeleski, Tomas Feuct, and Lloyd Potter, "School-Associated Violent Deaths in the United States, 1994–1999," *Journal of the American Medical Association,* vol. 286 (2001). pp. 2695–2702.

2. Robert C. Johnston, "Federal Data Highlight Disparities in Discipline," *Education Week* (June 21, 2000), p. 3.

Supreme Court upheld the expulsion of a student who wore talcum powder on her face in violation of a school rule forbidding pupils to wear transparent hosiery, low-necked dresses, face paint, or cosmetics.[3] In another early case, the Michigan Supreme Court endorsed the suspension of a female high school student for smoking and riding in a car with a young man.[4] In these and similar cases, courts were reluctant to interfere with the judgment of school officials because public education was considered to be a privilege bestowed by the state.

There has been a quantum leap from this early judicial posture to the active protection of students' rights in the late 1960s and early 1970s,[5] but judicial developments have not eroded educators' rights or their responsibilities.[6] The Seventh Circuit noted that the Supreme Court "has repeatedly emphasized the need for affirming the comprehensive authority of the states and of school officials, consistent with fundamental constitutional safeguards, to prescribe and control conduct in the schools."[7] Reasonable disciplinary regulations, even those impairing students' protected liberties, have been upheld if justified by a legitimate educational interest. Educators not only have the authority but also the duty to maintain discipline in public schools. Although rules made at any level (e.g., classroom, building, school board) cannot conflict with higher authorities (e.g., constitutional and statutory provisions), building administrators and teachers retain substantial latitude in establishing and enforcing conduct codes that are necessary for instructional activities to take place. In the subsequent sections of this chapter, educators' prerogatives and students' rights are explored in connection with conduct regulations, expulsions and suspensions, corporal punishment, academic sanctions, search and seizure, and remedies for unlawful disciplinary actions.

Conduct Regulations

School boards are granted considerable latitude in establishing and interpreting their own disciplinary rules and regulations. The Supreme Court has held that the interpretation of a school regulation resides with the body that adopted it and is charged with its enforcement.[8] Disciplinary policies, however, have been struck down if unconstitutionally vague. Policies prohibiting "improper conduct" and behavior "inimical to the best interests of the school" have been invalidated because they have not specified

---

3. Pugsley v. Sellmeyer, 250 S.W. 538 (Ark. 1923). *See also* Jones v. Day, 89 So. 906 (Miss. 1921).

4. Tanton v. McKenney, 197 N.W. 510 (Mich. 1924).

5. *See, e.g.,* Tinker v. Des Moines Indep. Sch. Dist., 393 U.S. 503 (1969); text accompanying note 57, Chapter 4.

6. *See, e.g.,* Hazelwood Sch. Dist. v. Kuhlmeier, 484 U.S. 260 (1988); Bethel Sch. Dist. No. 403 v. Fraser, 478 U.S. 675 (1986); New Jersey v. T.L.O., 469 U.S. 325 (1985).

7. Boucher v. Sch. Bd., 134 F.3d 821, 827 (7th Cir. 1998).

8. *See* Bd. of Educ. v. McCluskey, 458 U.S. 966 (1982); Wood v. Strickland, 420 U.S. 308 (1975).

the precise nature of the impermissible conduct.[9] A vague school district discipline policy prohibiting the consumption of alcohol prior to the school day or a school event was found to be overly broad in an Arkansas case; it could be arbitrarily interpreted as minutes, hours, or even days before attending a school activity.[10] Although policies should be precise, courts have recognized that disciplinary regulations do not have to satisfy the stringent criteria or level of specificity required in criminal statutes.[11] The Eighth Circuit noted that the determining factor is whether a regulation's wording is precise enough to notify an individual that specific behavior is clearly unacceptable.[12]

In addition to reviewing the validity of the conduct regulation on which a specific punishment is based, courts evaluate the nature and extent of the penalty imposed in relation to the gravity of the offense. Courts also consider the age, gender, mental condition, and past behavior of the student in deciding whether a given punishment is appropriate. The judiciary has sanctioned punishments such as the denial of privileges, suspension, expulsion, corporal punishment, and detention after school. Any of these punishments, however, could be considered unreasonable under a specific set of circumstances. Consequently, courts study each unique factual situation; they do not evaluate the validity of student punishments in the abstract.

9. *See, e.g.,* Killion v. Franklin Reg'l Sch. Dist., 136 F. Supp. 2d 446, 459 (W.D. Pa. 2001) (finding school district's retaliatory policy against verbal or other abuse of teachers unconstitutionally vague—"devoid of any detail"); Wilson v. S. Cent. Local Sch. Dist., 669 N.E.2d 277 (Ohio Ct. App. 1995) (holding that a student could not be suspended for possession of tobacco under a conduct code specifying that suspension would be for "very serious offenses," because state law required the board of education to specify the type of misconduct for which a student may be suspended). *But see* Fuller v. Decatur Pub. Sch. Bd. of Educ., 252 F.3d 662 (7th Cir. 2001) (concluding that a prohibition of gang-like behavior was not overly vague when the students' conduct clearly violated the regulation).

10. Caliborne v. Beebe Sch. Dist., 687 F. Supp. 1358 (E.D. Ark. 1988). *See also* Martinez v. Sch. Dist. No. 60, 852 P.2d 1275 (Colo. Ct. App. 1992) (finding that "affected by" the consumption of alcohol was vague but meant more than mere consumption prior to attending school or a school-sponsored event); Warren County Bd. of Educ. v. Wilkinson, 500 So. 2d 455 (Miss. 1986) (concluding that in the absence of a board rule prohibiting the consumption of beer at home, a school board could not impose loss of credit for the semester when a student drank a few sips of beer at her home before going to school the last day of the semester).

11. *See* Bethel Sch. Dist. No. 403 v. Fraser, 478 U.S. 675 (1986); text accompanying note 15, Chapter 4.

12. Woodis v. Westark Cmty. College, 160 F.3d 435 (8th Cir. 1998). *See also* West v. Derby Unified Sch. Dist., 206 F.3d 1358 (10th Cir. 2000) (holding that the student knew the written school harassment and intimidation policy clearly prohibited him from drawing a confederate flag); Hammock v. Keys, 93 F. Supp. 2d 1222 (S.D. Ala. 2000) (finding that a school board regulation regarding discipline for drug possession was not impermissibly vague when applied to a student who was expelled after marijuana residue was found in her car); Busch v. Omaha Pub. Sch. Dist., 623 N.W.2d 672 (Neb. 2001) (ruling that school district rule regarding expulsion of a student for injury to a school employee who is attempting to break up a fight was clear and definite whether injury was accidental or intentional); Schmader v. Warren County Sch. Dist., 808 A.2d 596, 600 (Pa. Commw. Ct. 2002) (ruling that the Miscellaneous Inappropriate Behavior section of the school district's disciplinary code was not unconstitutionally vague as applied to a third-grade student's failure to report a planned assault on another student; language that referred to "behavior that may be harmful to others" gave clear notice to the student that he had a duty to report his classmate's threat).

Litigation challenging disciplinary practices often has focused on the procedures followed in administering punishments rather than on the substance of disciplinary rules or the nature of the sanctions imposed. Implicit in all judicial declarations
regarding school discipline is the notion that severe penalties require more formal procedures, whereas minor punishments necessitate only minimal due process. Nonetheless, any disciplinary action should be accompanied by some procedure to ensure the
rudiments of fundamental fairness and to prevent mistakes in the disciplinary process.
The Fifth Circuit noted that "the quantum and quality of procedural due process to be
afforded a student varies with the seriousness of the punishment to be imposed."[13]

The judiciary has recognized that punishment for student conduct off school
grounds must be supported by evidence that the behavior has a detrimental impact on
other pupils, teachers, or school activities.[14] In an early case, the Connecticut Supreme
Court held that school officials could regulate student conduct outside school hours
and off school property if such conduct affected the management of the school.[15]
Courts have upheld sanctions imposed on students for engaging in assault or criminal
acts off school grounds,[16] compiling a "shit list" of other students noting derogatory
characteristics,[17] making threatening, harassing remarks on a web site created at
home,[18] writing a threatening letter over the summer break to a former girl friend,[19]
and stealing automobile parts.[20] Courts, however, have prohibited school authorities
from punishing students for misbehavior off school grounds if pupils had not been
informed that such conduct would result in sanctions[21] or if the misbehavior had no
direct relationship to the welfare of the school.[22]

School personnel must be careful not to place unnecessary constraints on student behavior. In developing disciplinary policies, all possible means of achieving the

13. Pervis v. LaMarque Indep. Dist., 466 F.2d 1054, 1057 (5th Cir. 1972).

14. For a synthesis of applicable case law on conduct off school grounds, *see* Perry A. Zirkel, "Disciplining Students for Off-Campus Misconduct," *Education Law Reporter,* vol. 163 (2002), pp. 551–553.

15. O'Rourke v. Walker, 102 Conn. 130 (1925).

16. Pollnow v. Glennon, 757 F.2d 496 (2d Cir. 1985); Nicholas v. Sch. Comm. 587 N.E.2d 211 (Mass. 1992).

17. Donovan v. Ritchie, 68 F.3d 14 (1st Cir. 1995).

18. J. S. v. Bethlehem Area Sch. Dist., 807 A.2d 847 (Pa. 2002). *See also* text accompanying note 94, Chapter 4. *But see* Beussink v. Woodland R-IV Sch. Dist., 30 F. Supp. 2d 1175 (E.D. Mo. 1998) (con-cluding that a web site created off campus did not materially and substantially interfere with the edu-cational process).

19. Doe v. Pulaski County Special Sch. Dist., 306 F.3d 616 (8th Cir. 2002). The junior high school student did not send the letter, but its contents were communicated to the former girlfriend by another student who read the letter.

20. Felton v. Fayette Sch. Dist., 875 F.2d 191 (8th Cir. 1989).

21. Galveston Indep. Sch. Dist. v. Boothe, 590 S.W.2d 553 (Tex. Civ. App. 1979). *But see Howard v. Colonial,* 621 A.2d 362 (Del. Super. Ct. 1992) (holding that school board's determination that a 17-year-old drug dealer posed a potential harm to the safety and welfare of students was not arbitrary or capricious in spite of the fact that the student discipline code did not prohibit drug dealing off school grounds).

desired outcomes should be explored, and means that are least restrictive of students' personal freedoms should be selected. Once it is determined that a specific conduct regulation is necessary, the rule should be clearly written so that it is not open to multiple interpretations. Each regulation should include the rationale for enacting the rule as well as the penalties for infractions. Considerable discretion exists in determining that certain actions deserve harsher penalties (i.e., imposing a more severe punishment for the sale of drugs as opposed to the possession or use of drugs).[23] To ensure that students are knowledgeable of the conduct rules, it is advisable to require students to sign a form indicating that they have read the conduct regulations.[24] With such documentation, pupils would be unable to plead ignorance of the rules as a defense for their misconduct.

In general, educators would be wise to adhere to the following guidelines:

- Rules must have an explicit purpose and be clearly written to accomplish that purpose.
- Any conduct regulation adopted should be necessary in order to carry out the school's educational mission; rules should not be designed merely to satisfy the preferences of school board members, administrators, or teachers.
- Rules should be publicized to students and their parents.
- Rules should be specific and clearly stated so that students know what behaviors are expected and what behaviors are prohibited.
- Student handbooks that incorporate references to specific state laws also should include the law or paraphrase the statutory language.
- Regulations should not impair constitutionally protected rights unless there is an overriding public interest, such as a threat to the safety of others.
- A rule should not be "ex post facto"; it should not be adopted to prevent a specific activity that school officials know is being planned or has already occurred.
- Regulations should be consistently enforced and uniformly applied to all students without discrimination.
- Punishments should be appropriate to the offense, taking into consideration the child's age, gender, disability, and past behavior.
- Some procedural safeguards should accompany the administration of all punishments; the formality of the procedures should be in accord with the severity of the punishment.

---

22. *See, e.g.,* Killion v. Franklin Reg'l Sch. Dist., 136 F. Supp. 2d 446 (W.D. Pa. 2001): Klein v. Smith, 635 F. Supp. 1440 (D. Me. 1986); Packer v. Bd. of Educ., 717 A.2d 117 (Conn. 1998); M. T. v. Sch. Bd., 779 So. 2d 328 (Fla. Dist. Ct. App. 1999).

23. *See, e.g.,* Morgan v. Girard City Sch. Dist., 630 N.E.2d 71 (Ohio Ct. App. 1993).

24. An Alabama federal district court found students' claim that they were not knowledgeable of the school rule against fighting to be frivolous. The court expressed doubt that any student in the United States is not aware that fighting is a serious infraction. Craig v. Selma City Sch. Bd., 801 F. Supp. 585 (S.D. Ala. 1992).

- A process for periodic review of the student handbook should be established that involves students and school staff members in the revisions and refinement.

In designing and enforcing pupil conduct codes, it is important that school personnel bear in mind the distinction between students' substantive and procedural rights. If a disciplinary regulation or the administration of punishment violates substantive rights (e.g., restricts protected speech), the regulation cannot be enforced nor the punishment imposed. When only procedural rights are impaired, however, the punishment eventually can be administered if determined at an appropriate hearing that the punishment is warranted.

Expulsions and Suspensions

Expulsions and suspensions are among the most widely used disciplinary measures. Courts uniformly have upheld educators' authority to use such measures as punishments, but due process is required to ensure that students are afforded fair and impartial treatment. Although most states have recognized that students have a property right to an education, this right may be lost for violation of school rules. This section focuses on disciplinary action in which students are removed from the regular instructional program; suspensions and expulsions from extracurricular activities are addressed in Chapter 4.

Expulsions

State laws and school board regulations are usually quite specific regarding the grounds for expulsions—that is, the removal of students from school for a lengthy period of time (usually in excess of 10 days). Such grounds are not limited to occurrences during school hours and can include infractions on school property immediately before or after school or at any time the school is being used for a school-related activity. Expulsions also can result from infractions occurring en route to or from school or during school functions held off school premises. Although specific grounds vary from state to state, infractions typically considered legitimate grounds for expulsion include violence, stealing or vandalizing school or private property, causing or attempting to cause physical injury to others, possessing a weapon, possessing or using drugs or alcohol, and engaging in criminal activity or other behavior forbidden by state laws.

Procedural Requirements.   State statutes specify procedures for expulsion and the limitations on their length. Except for the possession of weapons, a student generally cannot be expelled beyond the end of the current academic year unless the expulsion takes place near the close of the term.[25] A teacher or administrator may initiate expul-

25. *See, e.g.,* S. Gibson Sch. Bd. v. Sollman, 768 N.E.2d 437 (Ind. 2002).

sion proceedings, but usually only the school board can expel a student. Prior to expulsion, students must be provided procedural protections guaranteed by the U.S. Constitution; however, school officials can remove students immediately if they pose a danger or threat to themselves or others.[26] No duty exists to provide an educational alternative for a properly expelled student unless the school board policies or state mandates specify that alternative programs must be provided or the student is receiving special education services.[27]

Although the details of required procedures must be gleaned from state statutes and school board regulations, courts have held that students facing expulsion from public school are guaranteed at least minimum due process under the Fourteenth Amendment.[28] It is advisable to provide the following safeguards:

- Written notice of the charges;[29] the intention to expel; the place, time, and circumstances of the hearing;[30] and sufficient time for a defense to be prepared[31]
- A full and fair hearing before an impartial adjudicator[32]
- The right to legal counsel or some other adult representation[33]

---

26. *See, e.g.,* Lavine v. Blaine Sch. Dist., 257 F.3d 981 (9th Cir. 2001), *cert. denied,* 122 S.Ct. 2663 (2002).

27. *See* Gun-Free Schools Act, 20 U.S.C. 8921 (2002) (allows school officials to place students expelled for gun possession in alternative instructional programs). *See also* text accompanying note 111, Chapter 6, for a discussion of the expulsion of children with disabilities.

28. Courts have cautioned that expulsion hearings do not have to conform to the judicial requirements of a trial. *See, e.g.,* Linwood v. Bd. of Educ. 463 F.2d 763 (7th Cir. 1972); Baxter v. Round Lake Area Schs., 856 F. Supp. 438 (N.D. Ill. 1994). *See also* Trujillo v. Taos Mun. Schs., 91 F. 3d 160 (10th Cir. 1997) (concluding that school officials were not required to provide a second hearing to a student who had been permanently expelled).

29. *See, e.g.,* Adrovet v. Brunswick City Sch. Dist., 735 N.E.2d 995 (Ohio Com. Pl. 1999) (holding that the statute required written notice to the student, not the parent; the court relied on the "express wording" of the statute). *But see* Watson v. Beckel, 242 F.3d 1237 (10th Cir. 2001) (concluding that failure to specify charges in written notice did not violate due process when the student had constructive notice—clearly knew the allegations under investigation).

30. *See, e.g.,* Hill v. Rankin County, Miss. Sch. Dist., 843 F. Supp. 1112 (S.D. Miss. 1993) (finding that a hearing should be held as soon as practicable when it is evident that a suspension will be lengthy).

31. *See, e.g.,* Brian A. v. Stroudsburg Area Sch. Dist., 141 F. Supp. 2d 502 (M.D. Pa. 2001) (ruling that a 5-day notice was adequate when for weeks the student and parent had been aware of the pending expulsion); Bivens v. Albuquerque Pub. Schs., 899 F. Supp. 556 (D.N.M. 1995) (holding that a 10-day notice prior to expulsion hearing was adequate notwithstanding lack of receipt by the parent).

32. *See, e.g.,* Remer v. Burlington Area Sch. Dist., 286 F.3d 1007 (7th Cir. 2002) (finding that a student who declined to attend a scheduled expulsion hearing waived his right to present his case).

33. *See, e.g., In re* Roberts, 563 S.E.2d 37 (N.C. Ct. App. 2002) (finding the school board's denial of student's request to be represented by counsel when faced with expulsion violated his due process rights). Several courts have recognized students' right to seek advice of legal counsel but have not held that a right exists for students' attorneys to participate in a disciplinary proceeding in the role of trial counsel. *See, e.g.,* Osteen v. Henley, 13 F.3d 221 (7th Cir. 1993); Newsome v. Batavia Local Sch. Dist., 842 F.2d 920 (6th Cir. 1988); Lake Cent. Sch. Corp. v. Scartozzi, 759 N.E.2d 1185 (Ind. Ct. App. 2001).

- The right to be fully apprised of the proof or evidence[34]
- The opportunity to present witnesses or evidence[35]
- The opportunity to cross-examine opposing witnesses[36]
- Some type of written record demonstrating that the decision was based on the evidence presented at the hearing.[37]

Procedural safeguards required, however, may vary depending on the circumstances of a particular situation. In a Mississippi case, a student and his parents claimed that prior to an expulsion hearing they should have been given a list of the witnesses and a summary of their testimony.[38] Recognizing that such procedural protections generally should be afforded prior to a long-term expulsion, the Fifth Circuit nonetheless held that they were not requisite in this case. The parents had been fully apprised of the charges, the facts supporting the charges, and the nature of the hearing. Consequently, the court concluded that the student suffered no material prejudice from the school board's failure to supply a list of witnesses; the witnesses provided no surprises or interference with the student's ability to present his case. In a later case involving expulsion for possession of drugs, the same court found no impairment of a student's rights when he was denied an opportunity to confront and rebut witnesses who accused him of selling drugs.[39] The names of student witnesses had been withheld to prevent retaliation against them.

Similarly, the Sixth Circuit noted that it is critical to protect the anonymity of students who "blow the whistle" on classmates involved in serious offenses such as drug dealing.[40] Although the right to cross-examine witnesses did not constitute a denial of due process in this case, the court held that the superintendent's disclosure

34. *See, e.g.,* Ruef v. Jordan, 605 N.Y.S.2d 530 (App. Div. 1993).

35. *See, e.g.,* Fuller v. Decatur Pub. Sch. Bd. of Educ., 251 F.3d 662 (7th Cir. 2001).

36. *See, e.g.,* Dillon v. Pulaski County Special Sch. Dist., 594 F.2d 699 (8th Cir. 1979); *In re* E. J. W., 632 N.W.2d 775 (Minn. Ct. App. 2001). *But see Newsome,* 842 F.2d 920 (holding that denial of cross-examination to protect anonymity of student drug informants did not violate due process); Brewer v. Austin Indep. Sch. Dist., 779 F.2d 260 (5th Cir. 1985) (holding that names of witnesses could be withheld to prevent retaliation).

37. *See, e.g., Ruef,* 605 N.Y.S.2d 530 (concluding that board members listening to two separate disciplinary hearings [Ruef and another student] involving the same incident violated Ruef's right to have the disciplinary decision based solely on the record at his hearing).

38. Keough v. Tate County Bd. of Educ., 748 F.2d 1077 (5th Cir. 1984). *See also* Snyder v. Farnsworth, 896 F. Supp. 96 (N.D.N.Y. 1995) (finding no evidence that failure to provide the list of witnesses and their testimony resulted in prejudice to the student); Covington County v. G.W., 767 So. 2d 187 (Miss. 2000) (ruling that school officials' failure to provide a list of witnesses did not violate a student's due process rights).

39. *Brewer,* 779 F.2d 260. *See also* Nash v. Auburn Univ., 812 F.2d 655 (11th Cir. 1987) (holding that where basic fairness is provided in a university disciplinary case, cross-examination of witnesses and a full adversarial proceeding are not required).

40. Newsome v. Batavia Local Sch. Dist., 842 F.2d 920 (6th Cir. 1988). *See also* Dornes v. Lindsey, 18 F. Supp. 2d 1086 (C.D. Cal. 1998).

of evidence in the school board's closed deliberations that was not introduced during the open hearing violated the student's procedural rights. Given this violation, the appellate court remanded the case to determine if the student was entitled to injunctive and compensatory relief.

State laws and school board policies often provide students facing expulsion with more elaborate procedural safeguards than the constitutional protections noted earlier. Once such expulsion procedures are established, courts will require that they be followed.[41] Under Ohio law, a student's expulsion hearing two weeks after he received the notice was found to violate a statutory requirement that hearings be held no later than five school days after notification.[42] A Washington appellate court held that a student's due process rights were violated when he was not allowed to question witnesses at his expulsion hearing;[43] Washington law specifically provides students the right to confront witnesses. A Louisiana appeals court ruled that a student's possession of marijuana off school property did not justify expulsion under a state law proscribing the possession of controlled substances on school property.[44]

Expulsions often are challenged as excessive for certain offenses. Unless actions are arbitrary, capricious, or oppressive, school officials have broad discretionary powers in establishing disciplinary penalties. An Illinois student, expelled for the remainder of the school year for possession of caffeine pills, challenged the punishment as too harsh for a first offense.[45] The trial court agreed that the punishment far outweighed the crime, but the appellate court found the action reasonable and justified in light of the dangers posed by unauthorized drugs in the schools. An Alabama court did not find the permanent expulsion of a high school senior to be excessive based on the student's extensive history of behavioral problems that included threats to a teacher and a physical attack on a classmate.[46] A Pennsylvania federal district court noted that a rational relationship should exist between a student's punishment and offense. Such a relationship was found when a student was permanently expelled for

---

41. The failure to enact required state rules or to follow them, however, would violate state law rather than the Federal Constitution. *See* White v. Salisbury Township Sch. Dist., 588 F. Supp. 608 (E.D. Pa. 1984). *See also* Rogers v. Gooding Pub. Joint Sch. Dist., 20 P.3d 16 (Idaho 2001) (holding that charging a student under the wrong policy does not violate due process when the student receives notice of the factual circumstances).

42. Kresser v. Sandusky Bd. of Educ., 748 N.E.2d 620 (Ohio Ct. App. 2001).

43. Stone v. Prosser Consol. Sch. Dist. No. 116, 971 P.2d 125 (Wash. Ct. App. 1999). *See also In re* Expulsion of E.J.W., 632 N.W.2d 775 (Minn. Ct. App. 2001) (finding violation of state law when a student accused of involvement in a bomb threat was not given the witnesses' names nor provided an opportunity to confront and cross-examine them).

44. Labrosse v. St. Bernard Parish Sch. Bd., 483 So. 2d 1253 (La. Ct. App. 1986).

45. Wilson v. Cmty. Comm. Unit Sch. Dist., 451 N.E.2d 939 (Ill. App. Ct. 1983). *But see* McEntire v. Brevard County Sch. Bd., 471 So. 2d 1287 (Fla. Dist. Ct. App. 1985) (overturning expulsion of student for selling caffeine pills because evidence did not support that the student represented the pills as speed; school board policy prohibited the selling of counterfeit pills only if represented as speed).

46. Scoggins v. Henry County Bd. of Educ., 549 So. 2d 99 (Ala. Civ. App. 1989).

leaving a written note behind in a classroom that claimed there was a bomb in the school.[47]

Zero-Tolerance Policies.   The growing concern about school safety has led to specific federal and state laws directed at the discipline of students who bring weapons onto school campuses. Under the Gun-Free Schools Act of 1994, all states were mandated to enact legislation requiring at least a one-year expulsion for students who bring firearms to school.[48] In expanding the scope of the law, states have added to the list of prohibitions weapons such as knives, explosive devices, hand chains, and other offensive weapons as well as drugs and violent acts. The federal law also requires state provisions to permit the local school superintendent to modify the expulsion requirement on a case-by-case basis.[49]

Severe criticism has been directed at zero-tolerance policies when school officials fail to exercise discretion and flexibility. The American Bar Association and others have called for an end to such policies that require automatic penalties without assessing the circumstances.[50] Recent cases underscore the harsh consequences when students encounter inflexible policies. In a Virginia case, a 13-year-old student, attempting to save a suicidal friend's life, took a binder containing a knife and placed it in his locker. Upon hearing about the knife, the assistant principal asked him to retrieve it from his locker. Although the assistant principal felt that the student was acting in the best interest of his friend and at no time posed a threat to anyone, he was expelled from school for four months. The Fourth Circuit, in upholding the expulsion, noted its harshness but found no violation of the student's due process rights. In a concurring opinion, one justice commented: "The panic over school violence and the intent to stop it has caused school officials to jettison the common sense idea that a person's punishment should fit his crime in favor of a single harsh punishment, namely, mandatory school suspension."[51]

Invoking mandatory expulsion policies may implicate constitutional rights if administrators fail to take into consideration the individual student's history and the circumstances surrounding the conduct. The Sixth Circuit noted that expelling a stu-

---

47. Brian A. v. Stroudsburg Area Sch. Dist., 141 F. Supp. 2d 502 (M.D. Pa. 2001).

48. 20 U.S.C. 8921 (2002). Additionally, most states have enacted gun-free or weapons-free school zone laws restricting possession of firearms in or near schools.

49. *See, e.g.,* Lyons v. Penn Hills Sch. Dist., 723 A.2d 1073 (Pa. Commw. Ct. 1999) (concluding that the school board exceeded its authority in adopting a zero-tolerance policy for weapons possession that failed to provide the superintendent with discretion to modify mandatory expulsion on a case-by-case basis as required by state law). *See also* J.M. v. Webster County Bd. of Educ., 534 S. E. 2d 50 (W. Va. 2000) (holding that state law and the local school board policy provided students several opportunities for exoneration in the review process).

50. Report to the ABA House of Delegates, February 19, 2001, American Bar Association, Chicago, IL.

51. Ratner v. Loudoun County Pub. Schs., 16 Fed. Appx. 140, 143 (4th Cir. July 30, 2001), *cert. denied,* 534 U.S.1114 (2002). *See also* S. Gibson Sch. Bd. v. Sollman, 768 N.E.2d 437 (Ind. 2002) (ruling that the judiciary's role is to determine whether a school board acted arbitrarily or capriciously and not to assess the harshness of zero-tolerance policies).

dent for weapons possession when the student did not know that the weapon was in his car could not survive a due process challenge.[52] Other courts, however, have been reluctant to impose the *knowing possession* standard that would require the determination of a student's intent.[53]

Suspensions

Suspensions are frequently used to punish students for violating school rules and standards of behavior when the infractions are not of sufficient magnitude to warrant expulsion. Suspensions include the short-term denial of school attendance as well as the denial of participation in regular courses and activities (in-school suspension). Most legal controversies have focused on out-of-school suspensions, but it is advisable to apply the same legal principles to any disciplinary action that separates the student from the regular instructional program even for a short period of time.

In contrast to expulsions, historically state laws and judicial decisions differed widely in identifying and interpreting procedural safeguards for suspensions. In 1975, however, the Supreme Court provided substantial clarification regarding the constitutional rights of students confronting short-term suspensions. The Court majority in *Goss v. Lopez* held that minimum due process must be provided before a student is suspended for even a brief period of time.[54] Recognizing that a student's state-created property right to an education is protected by the Fourteenth Amendment, the Court ruled that such a right cannot be impaired unless the student is afforded notice of the charges and an opportunity to refute them.[55] The Supreme Court also emphasized that suspensions implicate students' constitutionally protected liberty interests because of the potentially damaging effects that the disciplinary process can have on a student's reputation and permanent record.

The *Goss* majority strongly suggested that its holding applied to all short-term suspensions, including those of only one class period. Consequently, many school boards have instituted policies that require informal procedures for every brief sus-

---

52. Seal v. Morgan, 229 F.3d 567 (6th Cir. 2000). *See also* Colvin v. Lowndes County, Miss. Sch. Dist., 114 F. Supp. 2d 504 (N.D. Miss. 1999) (holding that expulsion under the school board's zero-tolerance policy violated due process rights where the school board did not consider facts and circumstances of the student's case).

53. *See, e.g.,* Bundick v. Bay City Indep. Sch. Dist., 140 F. Supp. 2d 735, 740 (S.D. Tex. 2001) (holding that knowledge "can be imputed from the fact of possession").

54. 419 U.S. 565 (1975). Individuals posing a danger or threat may be removed immediately with notice and a hearing following as soon as possible. *See, e.g.,* Willis v. Anderson Cmty. Sch. Corp., 158 F.3d 415 (7th Cir. 1998); C.B. v. Driscoll, 82 F.3d 383 (11th Cir. 1996); Craig v. Selma City Sch. Bd., 801 F. Supp. 585 (S.D. Ala. 1992).

55. *See, e.g.,* Meyer v. Austin Indep. Sch. Dist., 167 F.3d 887 (5th Cir. 1999) (noting that school officials' speaking with a student's parents does not necessarily provide a meaningful opportunity for the student to be heard). *But see* Achman v. Chi. Lakes Indep. Sch. Dist., 45 F. Supp. 2d 664 (D. Minn. 1999) (finding that parents' exclusion of their son from a suspension hearing did not deny him an opportunity to be heard, specifically when the principal had witnessed the misconduct).

pension and more formal procedures for longer suspensions. In the absence of greater specificity in state statutes or administrative regulations, students have a constitutional right to the following protections prior to suspension:

- Oral or written notification of the nature of the violation and the intended punishment
- An opportunity to refute the charges before an objective decision maker (such a discussion may immediately follow the alleged rule infraction)
- An explanation of the evidence on which the disciplinarian is relying

The requirement of an impartial decision maker does not infer that an administrator or teacher who is familiar with the facts cannot serve in this capacity. The decision maker simply must judge the situation fairly and on the basis of valid evidence.[56]

The Supreme Court's *Goss* decision established the rudimentary procedural requirements for short-term suspensions, but students continue to seek expansion of their procedural rights. The Supreme Court specifically noted that such formal procedures as the right to secure counsel, to confront and cross-examine witnesses, and to call witnesses are not constitutionally required. The Court reiterated this stance in a later case by noting that a two-day suspension "does not rise to the level of a penal sanction calling for the full panoply of procedural due process protections applicable to a criminal prosecution."[57] Decisions by lower state and federal courts indicate a reluctance to impose these additional requirements unless mandated by state law. In a Maine case, a student claimed a violation of procedural due process because the school administrator denied him permission to leave during questioning and failed to advise him of his right to remain silent or to have his parents present during the interrogation.[58] The court rejected all claims, noting that there was no legal authority to

56. *See, e.g.,* Kubany v. Sch. Bd. of Pinellas County, 839 F. Supp. 1544 (M.D. Fla. 1993) (finding that a provision of the student code that stated the school board and administrators shall support the disciplinary decisions of the principal raised genuine issue as to adequacy of due process); Riggan v. Midland Indep. Sch. Dist., 86 F. Supp. 2d 647 (W.D. Tex. 2000) (finding that the principal was not an unbiased decision maker when he also was the aggrieved party).

57. Bethel Sch. Dist. No. 403 v. Fraser, 478 U.S. 675, 686 (1986). *See also* Covington County v. G.W., 767 So. 2d 187 (Miss. 2000).

58. Boynton v. Casey, 543 F. Supp. 995 (D. Me. 1982). The "right to remain silent" also has been advanced in other cases, with students arguing that school disciplinary proceedings should be governed by the principle established by the Supreme Court in Miranda v. Arizona, 384 U.S. 436 (1966) (holding that persons subjected to custodial interrogation must be advised of their right to remain silent, that any statement made may be used against them, and that they have the right to legal counsel). Courts have readily dismissed these claims, finding that discussions with school administrators are noncustodial. Clearly, in the *Miranda* decision, the Supreme Court was interpreting an individual's Fifth Amendment right against self-incrimination when first subjected to police questioning in connection with criminal charges. *See, e.g.,* Cason v. Cook, 810 F.2d 188 (8th Cir. 1987); Pollnow v. Glennon, 757 F.2d 496 (2d Cir. 1985); Brian A. v. Stroudsburg Area Sch. Dist., 141 F. Supp. 2d 502 (M.D. Pa. 2001); G.J. v. State, 716 N.E.2d 475 (Ind. Ct. App. 1999); *In re* Harold S., 731 A.2d 265 (R.I. 1999). *But see In re* R.H., 791 A.2d 331 (Pa. 2002) (holding that school police officers were required to give a student *Miranda* warnings prior to interrogation since they exercised the same powers as municipal police and the interrogation led to charges by the police, not punishment by school officials).

substantiate any of the asserted rights. The court reasoned that to rule otherwise would, in fact, contradict the informal procedures outlined in *Goss* allowing for immediate questioning and disciplinary action. Also relying on *Goss,* the Tenth Circuit held that the removal of a student from class for 20 minutes for questioning did not constitute the denial of a property right to an education without due process.[59]

Although the Supreme Court in *Goss* recognized the possibility of "unusual situations" that would require more formal procedures than those outlined, little guidance was given as to what these circumstances might be. The only suggestion offered in *Goss* was that a disciplinarian should adopt more extensive procedures in instances involving factual disputes "and arguments about cause and effect."[60] Courts have declined to expand on this brief listing. The Sixth Circuit rejected a student's contention that drug charges constituted such an "unusual situation" because of the stigmatizing effect on his reputation. The court did not believe that an eighth-grade student suspended for 10 days for possessing a substance that resembled an illegal drug was "forever faced with a tarnished reputation and restricted employment opportunities."[61] More extensive procedures also were found unnecessary when a student was barred from interscholastic athletics and other activities in addition to a 10-day suspension.[62]

Students also have asserted that suspensions involving loss of course credit or occurring during exam periods require greater due process than outlined in *Goss*. The Fifth Circuit, however, did not find persuasive the argument that the loss incurred for a 10-day suspension during final examinations required more than a mere give-and-take discussion between the principal and the student. In refusing to require more formal proceedings, the court noted that *Goss* makes no distinction as to when a short-term suspension occurs, and a contrary ruling would "significantly undermine, if not nullify, its definitive holding."[63] Similarly, the Seventh Circuit rejected a student's claim that additional procedures were required because a suspension occurred at the end of the school year and precluded the student from taking his final exams and graduating.[64]

State laws, however, may require additional procedural protections for suspensions. For example, the Ohio statute, earlier found to be constitutionally defective in *Goss,* now requires that prior to suspension each student must be provided written notice of the intent to suspend and the reasons for the intended suspension.[65] Pennsylvania law also mandates written notification to parents prior to the informal hearing.[66]

59. Edwards v. Rees, 883 F.2d 882 (10th Cir. 1989).

60. Goss v. Lopez, 419 U.S. 565, 583–584 (1975).

61. Paredes v. Curtis, 864 F.2d 426, 429 (6th Cir. 1988).

62. Palmer v. Merluzzi, 868 F.2d 90 (3d Cir. 1989). *See also* Donovan v. Ritchie, 68 F.3d 14 (1st Cir. 1995) (ruling that a bar to interscholastic athletics and other activities in addition to a 10-day suspension did not necessitate the provision of more formal procedures).

63. Keough v. Tate County Bd. of Educ., 748 F.2d 1077, 1081 (5th Cir. 1984).

64. Lamb v. Panhandle Comm. Unit Sch. Dist. No. 2, 826 F.2d 526 (7th Cir. 1987).

65. Ohio Rev. Code § 3313.66 (2002).

66. 24 Pa. Stat. Ann. § 13–1318 (2002).

A Pennsylvania commonwealth court declared that a 7-day suspension violated a student's due process rights because the parents received only oral notification of the reasons for suspension.[67]

In-school suspensions or isolation may be equivalent to an out-of-school suspension, thereby necessitating minimal due process procedures. A Mississippi federal district court noted that whether procedural due process is required depends on the extent to which the student is deprived of instruction or the opportunity to learn.[68] The physical presence of a student at school does not conclusively relieve school officials of their duty to provide due process for disciplinary measures that exclude a student from the learning process. However, a Tennessee federal district court found that a student's placement in a classroom "time-out box" did not require due process because he continued to work on class assignments and could hear and see the teacher from the confined area.[69] The court emphasized that teachers must be free to administer minor forms of classroom discipline such as time-out, denial of privileges, and special assignments.

Courts have continued to resist attempts to elaborate or formalize the minimal due process requirements outlined in *Goss* for short-term suspensions. As the Supreme Court noted, "Further formalizing the suspension process and escalating its formality and adversary nature may not only make it too costly as a regular discipline tool but also destroy its effectiveness as part of the teaching process."[70]

Closely related to suspensions are *involuntary transfers of students* to alternative educational placements for disciplinary reasons. Such transfers generally do not involve denial of public education, but they might implicate protected liberty or property interests.[71] Legal challenges to the use of disciplinary transfers have addressed primarily the adequacy of the procedures followed. Recognizing that students do not have an inherent right to attend a given school, some courts nonetheless have held that pupils facing involuntary reassignment are entitled to minimal due process if such transfers are occasioned by misbehavior.[72]

67. Mifflin County Sch. Dist. v. Steward, 503 A.2d 1012 (Pa. Commw. Ct. 1986).

68. Cole v. Newton Special Mun. Separate Sch. Dist., 676 F. Supp. 749 (S.D. Miss. 1987), *aff'd,* 853 F.2d 924 (5th Cir. 1988).

69. Dickens v. Johnson County Bd. of Educ., 661 F. Supp. 155 (E.D. Tenn. 1987). *See also* Rasmus v. Arizona, 939 F. Supp. 709 (D. Ariz. 1996) (holding that denying a student the ability to work on class assignments during a 10-minute time-out was *de minimis* and did not violate a property right).

70. Goss v. Lopez, 419 U.S. 565, 583 (1975). *See, e.g.,* Hammock v. Keys, 93 F. Supp. 2d 1222 (S.D. Ala. 2000) (finding that informal give and take immediately following search of the student's car satisfied due process requirements prior to suspension).

71. Courts also have held that students do not have an inherent entitlement to specific aspects of a public education program. For example, the Rhode Island federal district court ruled that a student was not deprived of an education because he was removed from a science class the last five weeks of the school year and received individual instruction from a former science teacher. Casey v. Newport Sch. Comm., 13 F. Supp. 2d 242 (D.R.I. 1998).

72. *See, e.g.,* McCall v. Bossier Parish Sch. Bd., 785 So. 2d 57 (La. Ct. App. 2001). *But see* Martinez v. School Dist. No. 60, 852 P.2d 1275 (Colo. Ct. App. 1992) (rejecting students' argument that a disciplinary transfer for 90 days required a hearing because education was not interrupted).

For example, a New Jersey superior court ruled that a hearing was required before a student could be assigned to home instruction because of misconduct occurring off school premises after school hours.[73] The court noted that school officials had the authority to suspend the student and place him in homebound instruction, if determined at a proper hearing that he was dangerous to himself or others. The court declared, however, that the student could not be denied the right to attend school without first being given an opportunity to present a full defense regarding the incident precipitating the disciplinary action. Similarly, a New York court held that a student could not be assigned to homebound instruction for disruptive behavior and truancy without procedural due process.[74] The court rejected the assertion that the student was merely being afforded alternative education, and equated the assignment to homebound instruction with a suspension from school.

A Pennsylvania federal district court also ruled that "lateral transfers" for disciplinary reasons affected personal liberty and property interests of sufficient magnitude to require procedural due process. Even though such transfers involved comparable schools, the court reasoned that a disciplinary transfer carried with it a stigma and thus implicated a protected liberty right. Noting that a transfer of a student "during a school year from a familiar school to a strange and possibly more distant school would be a terrifying experience for many children of normal sensibilities," the court concluded that such transfers were more drastic punishments than suspensions, and thus necessitated due process.[75] As to the nature of the procedures required, the court held that the student and parents must be given notice of the proposed transfer, and that a prompt informal hearing before the school principal must be provided. The court stipulated that if parents were still dissatisfied with the arrangement after the informal meeting, they had the right to contest the transfer recommendation at a more formal hearing, with the option of being represented by legal counsel.

The Fifth Circuit, however, declined to find a federally protected property or liberty interest when a student arrested for aggravated assault was reassigned to an alternative education program under a Texas statute. According to the court, the student was not denied, even temporarily, a public education. In dismissing the case, the court did note that to ensure fairness, the state and local school districts should provide students and parents an opportunity to explain why a disciplinary transfer may not be warranted; however, failure to do so does not infringe constitutional rights.[76]

---

73. R.R. v. Bd. of Educ. 263 A.2d 180 (N.J. Super. Ct. App. Div. 1970).

74. Johnson, v. Bd. of Educ, 393 N.Y.S.2d 510 (Sup. Ct. 1977).

75. Everett v. Marcase, 426 F. Supp. 397, 400 (E.D. Pa. 1977). *See also* Riggan v. Midland Indep. Sch. Dist., 86 F. Supp. 2d 647 (W.D. Tex. 2000) (holding that extensive punishment—including a five-day assignment to an alternative school, a three-day suspension, exclusion from graduation, and two letters of apology—implicated property interests requiring at least minimum due process protections).

76. Nevares v. San Marcos Consol. Indep. Sch. Dist., 111 F.3d 25 (5th Cir. 1997). *See also* Stafford Mun. Sch. Dist. v. L.P., 64 S.W.3d 559 (Tex. App. 2001) (ruling that the assignment of a student charged with a felony to an alternative education program under the Texas statute did not involve a constitutionally protected property or liberty right).

Fundamental fairness necessitates at least minimal due process procedures when students are denied school attendance or removed from the regular instructional program. Severity of the separation dictates the amount of process due under the United States Constitution and state laws. Permanent expulsion from school triggers the most extensive process, whereas minor infractions may involve a brief give and take between school officials and students. Simply providing students the opportunity to be heard can preserve trust in the school system.

Corporal Punishment

Although a number of states permit educators to administer corporal punishment, a growing number have banned the practice either by law or state regulation. In 1971, only one state prohibited corporal punishment; today, more than half proscribe its use.[77] Generally, where state law permits corporal punishment, courts have upheld its reasonable application and have placed the burden on the aggrieved students to prove otherwise. In evaluating the reasonableness of a teacher's actions in a given situation, courts have assessed the child's age, maturity, and past behavior; the nature of the offense; the instrument used; any evidence of lasting harm to the child; and the motivation of the person inflicting the punishment.[78] This section provides an overview of the constitutional and state law issues raised in the administration of corporal punishment.

Constitutional Issues

In 1977, the Supreme Court addressed the constitutionality of corporal punishment that resulted in the severe injury of two students. The Court held in *Ingraham v. Wright* that the use of corporal punishment in public schools does not violate either the Eighth Amendment's prohibition against the government's infliction of cruel and unusual punishment or the Fourteenth Amendment's procedural due process guarantees.[79] While recognizing that corporal punishment implicates students' constitutionally protected liberty interests, the Court emphasized that state remedies are available, such as assault and battery suits, if students are excessively or arbitrarily punished by

77. American Academy of Pediatrics, "Corporal Punishment in Schools," *Pediatrics,* vol. 106 (August 2000), p. 343. *See* http://www.aap.org/advocacy/corpchrt.htm for the status of corporal punishment laws in each state. The American Academy of Pediatrics has recommended that corporal punishment be abolished in all states because of its detrimental affect on students' self-image and achievement as well as possible contribution to disruptive and violent behavior.

78. *See, e.g.,* LeBoyd v. Jenkins, 381 So. 2d 1290 (La. Ct. App. 1980); Gaspershon v. Harnett County Bd. of Educ., 330 S.E.2d 489 (N.C. Ct. App. 1985); Burton v. Kirby, 775 S.W.2d 834 (Tex. Civ. App. 1989).

79. 430 U.S. 651 (1977). *See also* Cunningham v. Beavers, 858 F.2d 269 (5th Cir. 1988) (concluding that Texas law permitting corporal punishment does not violate the Equal Protection Clause of the Constitution).

school personnel. In essence, the Court majority concluded that state courts under provisions of state laws should handle cases dealing with corporal punishment. The majority distinguished corporal punishment from a suspension by noting that the denial of school attendance is a more severe penalty that deprives students of a property right and thus necessitates procedural safeguards. Furthermore, the majority reasoned that the purpose of corporal punishment would be diluted if elaborate procedures had to be followed prior to its use.[80]

The Supreme Court's ruling in *Ingraham,* however, does not foreclose a successful constitutional challenge to the use of *unreasonable* corporal punishment. Most federal appellate courts have held that students' substantive due process right to be free of brutal and egregious threats to bodily security might be impaired by the use of shockingly, excessive corporal punishment.[81] The Fourth Circuit concluded that although *Ingraham* bars federal litigation on procedural due process issues, excessive or cruel corporal punishment may violate students' substantive due process rights, which protect individuals from arbitrary and unreasonable governmental action. According to the appellate court, the standard for determining if such a violation has occurred is "whether the force applied caused injury so severe, was so disproportionate to the need presented, and was so inspired by malice or sadism rather than a merely careless or unwise excess of zeal that it amounted to a brutal and inhumane abuse of official power literally shocking to the conscience."[82] Clearly, student challenges to the reasonable use of ordinary corporal punishment are precluded by this standard. Substantive due process claims generally are evaluated by examining the need for administering corporal punishment, the relationship between the need and the amount of punishment administered, whether force was applied to maintain or restore discipline or used maliciously with the intent of causing harm, and the extent of a student's injury.[83] The Fifth and Seventh Circuits, disagreeing with the stance of the majority of the appellate courts, concluded that substantive due process claims cannot be raised if states prohibit unreasonable student discipline and provide adequate postpunishment civil or criminal remedies for abuse.[84]

Other courts have allowed such claims but have found the threshold for recovery for the violation of a student's substantive due process rights to be high. Minor pain, embarrassment, and hurt feelings do not rise to this level; actions must literally

---

80. The Court noted that procedures outlined earlier by a federal district court, although desirable, were not required under the United States Constitution. *See* Baker v. Owen, 395 F. Supp. 294 (M.D.N.C. 1975), *aff'd,* 430 U.S. 651 (1977).

81. Johnson v. Newburgh Enlarged Sch. Dist., 239 F.3d 246 (2d Cir. 2001); Neal v. Fulton County Bd. of Educ., 229 F.3d 1069 (11th Cir. 2000); P.B. v. Koch, 96 F.3d 1298 (9th Cir. 1996); Metzger v. Osbeck, 841 F.2d 518 (3d Cir. 1988); Wise v. Pea Ridge Sch. Dist., 855 F.2d 560 (8th Cir. 1988); Garcia v. Miera, 817 F.2d 650 (10th Cir. 1987); Webb v. McCullough, 828 F.2d 1151 (6th Cir. 1987); Hall v. Tawney, 621 F.2d 607 (4th Cir. 1980). *But see infra* text accompanying note 84.

82. *Hall,* 621 F.2d at 613.

83. *See, e.g., Neal,* 229 F.3d 1069; *Wise,* 855 F.2d 560.

84. Moore v. Willis Indep. Sch. Dist., 233 F.3d 871 (5th Cir. 2000); Wallace v. Batavia Sch. Dist. 101, 68 F.3d 1010 (7th Cir. 1995).

be *"shocking to the conscience."*[85] Actions courts have found *not* to rise to this level include requiring a 10-year-old boy to clean out a stopped-up toilet with his bare hands,[86] two licks with a paddle that resulted in bruises to a sixth-grade boy,[87] a push to a student's shoulder causing her to fall against a door jam,[88] and the piercing of a student's upper arm with a straight pin.[89] In contrast, the Tenth Circuit ruled that substantive due process rights were implicated where a 9-year-old girl was paddled with a split paddle while she was held upside down by another teacher, resulting in severe bruises, cuts, and permanent scarring.[90] Similarly, other conscience-shocking behavior involved a coach knocking a student's eye out of the socket with a metal weight lock[91] and a teacher physically restraining a student until he lost consciousness and fell to the floor, suffering significant injuries.[92]

State Law

Although the Supreme Court has ruled that the United States Constitution does not prohibit corporal punishment in public schools, its use may conflict with state constitutional provisions or local administrative regulations. As noted, the majority of states now prohibit corporal punishment,[93] and others have established procedures or conditions for its use. Teachers can be disciplined or discharged for violating these state and local provisions regulating corporal punishment. Courts have upheld dismissals based on insubordination for failure to comply with reasonable school board requirements in administering corporal punishment.[94] In a typical case, a Michigan teacher was dismissed because he violated board policy by using corporal punishment after having been warned repeatedly to cease.[95] Teachers also have been dismissed under

85. *Wise,* 855 F.2d at 564. *See also Garcia,* 817 F.2d 650; Woodard v. Los Fresnos Indep. Sch. Dist., 732 F.2d 1243 (5th Cir. 1984).
86. Harris v. Robinson, 273 F.3d 927 (10th Cir. 2001).
87. *Wise,* 855 F.2d 560. *See also* Bisignano v. Harrison Cent. Sch. Dist., 113 F. Supp. 2d 591 (S.D.N.Y. 2000) (finding that physical force resulting in red marks on the arm of an eighth-grade girl did not violate substantive due process).
88. Gottlieb v. Laurel Highlands Sch. Dist., 272 F.3d 168 (3d Cir. 2001).
89. Brooks v. Sch. Bd., 569 F. Supp. 1534 (E.D. Va. 1983). *See also* Smith v. Half Hollow Hills Cent. Sch. Dist., 298 F.3d 168 (2d Cir. 2002) (concluding that a single slap did not violate student's substantive due process rights but refusing to rule that a single slap could never be sufficiently brutal to invoke due process protections); Lilliard v. Shelby County Bd. of Educ., 76 F.3d 716 (6th Cir. 1996) (holding that a single slap did not rise to the level of a constitutional violation).
90. Garcia v. Miera, 817 F.2d 650 (10th Cir. 1987).
91. Neal v. Fulton County Bd. of Educ., 229 F.3d 1069 (11th Cir. 2000).
92. Metzger v. Osbeck, 841 F.2d 518 (3d Cir. 1988).
93. *See supra* text accompanying note 77.
94. *See, e.g.,* Sch. Dist. v. Geller, 755 N.E.2d 1241 (Mass. 2001); Burton v. Kirby, 775 S.W.2d 834 (Tex. Civ. App. 1989); Simmons v. Vancouver Sch. Dist., 704 P.2d 648 (Wash. Ct. App. 1985).
95. Tomczik v. State Tenure Comm'n, 438 N.W.2d 642 (Mich. Ct. App. 1989).

the statutory grounds of "cruelty" for improper use of physical force with students. In Illinois, a tenured teacher was dismissed on this ground for using a cattle prod in punishing students.[96] Other disciplinary measures also may be taken against teachers. A Nebraska teacher who "tapped" a student on the head was suspended without pay for 30 days under a state law that prohibits the use of corporal punishment.[97]

Beyond statutory or board restrictions, other legal means exist to challenge the use of unreasonable corporal punishment in public schools. Teachers can be charged with criminal assault and battery, which might result in fines and/or imprisonment. Civil assault and battery suits for monetary damages also can be initiated against school personnel.

When allowed, educators should use caution in administering corporal punishment, since improper administration can result in dismissal, monetary damages, and even imprisonment. Corporal punishment should never be administered with malice, and the use of excessive force should be avoided. Teachers would be wise to keep a record of incidents involving corporal punishment and to adhere to minimum procedural safeguards, such as notifying students of behavior that will result in a paddling, asking another staff member to witness the act, and providing parents on request written reasons for the punishment. Moreover, teachers should become familiar with relevant state laws and school board policies before attempting to use corporal punishment in their classrooms.

Academic Sanctions

It is indisputable that school authorities have the right to use academic sanctions for poor academic performance. Consistently, courts have been reluctant to substitute their own judgment for that of educators in assessing students' academic accomplishments. Failing grades, denial of credit, academic probation, retention, and expulsion from particular programs have been upheld as legitimate means of dealing with poor academic performance. The Supreme Court stated:

> When judges are asked to review the substance of a genuinely academic decision, . . . they should show great respect for the faculty's professional judgment. Plainly, they may not override it unless it is such a substantial departure from accepted academic norms as to demonstrate that the person or committee responsible did not actually exercise professional judgment.[98]

96. Rolando v. Sch. Dirs. 358 N.E.2d 945 (Ill. App. Ct. 1976).
97. Daily v. Bd. of Educ., 588 N.W.2d 813 (Neb. 1999).
98. Regents of Univ. of Mich. v. Ewing, 474 U.S. 214, 225 (1985).

Courts usually have granted broad discretionary powers to school personnel in establishing academic standards,[99] but there has been less agreement regarding the use of grade reductions or academic sanctions as punishments for student absences and misbehavior. More complex legal issues are raised when academic penalties are imposed for nonacademic reasons. These issues are explored next in connection with grade reductions for absences and misconduct.

Absences

Excessive student absenteeism is a growing concern and has led many school boards to impose academic sanctions for absences. These practices have generated legal challenges related to students' substantive due process rights. To meet the due process requirements, the sanction must be reasonable—that is, rationally related to a valid educational purpose. Since students must attend class to benefit from the educational program, most courts have found that academic penalties for absenteeism serve a valid educational goal.

In an Illinois case, a student claimed that a school regulation stipulating that grades would be lowered one letter grade per class for an unexcused absence impaired protected rights.[100] In defending the rule, school officials asserted that it was the most appropriate punishment for the serious problem of truancy. They argued that students could not perform satisfactorily in their class work if they were absent, since grades reflected class participation in addition to other standards of performance. The appeals court was not persuaded by the student's argument that grades should reflect only scholastic achievement, and therefore concluded that the regulation was reasonable.

The Supreme Court of Connecticut upheld a schoolwide policy that provided for a five-point reduction in course grades for each unapproved absence and that denied course credit for such absences in excess of 24. The court drew a sharp distinction between academic and disciplinary sanctions, noting that the school board's policy was academic, rather than disciplinary, in intent and effect. Specifically, the court found that a board's determination that grades should reflect more than examinations and papers "constitutes an academic judgment about academic requirements."[101] The Supreme Court of Missouri drew a similar distinction between academic and disciplinary sanctions but concluded that a school district's policy providing for loss of credit for previously earned academic work was punishment for unsatisfactory attendance rather than deductions for academic performance. Therefore, the court ruled that the student was entitled to a due process hearing prior to imposition of the penalty.[102]

---

99. In Bd. of Curators v. Horowitz, 435 U.S. 78 (1978), the Supreme Court reiterated that school authorities can establish and enforce academic standards. In this case, a medical student who was dismissed without notice of the charges or a formal hearing alleged that her constitutional rights were violated. The high court, however, concluded that neither the student's liberty nor property interests were impaired by the academic dismissal without a hearing.

100. Knight v. Bd. of Educ., 348 N.E.2d 299 (Ill. App. Ct. 1976).

101. Campbell v. Bd. of Educ., 475 A.2d 289, 294 (Conn. 1984).

102. State v. McHenry, 915 S.W.2d 325 (Mo. 1995).

Even policies that do not differentiate between excused and unexcused absences in imposing academic penalties have been upheld by some courts. For example, the Supreme Court of Arkansas upheld a board policy that disallowed course credit and permitted expulsion of students who accumulated more than 12 absences per semester.[103] The court, in refusing to substitute its judgment for the school board's, concluded that under state law, this action was within the board's power to make reasonable rules and regulations for the administration of the schools. A Michigan appellate court upheld a school board's authority to require students with more than three days of excused absences to attend after-school study sessions or have their letter grades reduced.[104] Similarly, a New York appellate court found that a policy denying course credit for absences in excess of 9 classes for semester courses and 18 absences for full-year courses was rational; students were permitted and encouraged to make up the classes before they exceeded the limit.[105]

To ensure procedural fairness, however, students must be informed that absences will result in academic penalties. In a Missouri case, a student received a failing grade for half of a semester in a music course for missing the last two performances of the semester.[106] The court upheld the grade reduction because students were informed the first day of class that attendance at all performances was required to complete the course and that unexcused absences would result in a failing grade. Where grade reductions are part of academic evaluations, courts generally do not require additional procedural safeguards beyond notice. An Indiana appellate court found that sufficient procedural protections were provided to a student who was removed from a geometry class under the school's chronic tardiness policy when he had received a prior warning from the teacher, a detention for absences, and a conference with his parents and teacher.[107]

Given the serious truancy problem confronting many school districts, it seems likely that school boards will continue to consider the imposition of academic sanctions. The legality of such policies will depend primarily on judicial interpretation of applicable state law.

Misconduct

Academic sanctions imposed for student misconduct also have been challenged. It is generally accepted that students can be denied credit for work missed while suspended from school. In fact, if students could make up such work without penalty, a suspension might be viewed as a vacation rather than a punishment. More controversy has surrounded policies that impose an additional grade reduction for suspension days, and courts have not agreed regarding the legality of this practice.

103. Williams v. Bd. of Educ., 626 S.W.2d 361 (Ark. 1982).

104. Slocum v. Holton Bd. of Educ., 429 N.W.2d 607 (Mich. Ct. App. 1988).

105. Bitting v. Lee, 564 N.Y.S.2d 791 (App. Div. 1990).

106. R.J.J. *ex rel.* Johnson v. Shineman, 658 S.W.2d 910 (Mo. Ct. App. 1983).

107. M.S. v. Eagle-Union Cmty. Sch. Corp., 717 N.E.2d 1255 (Ind. Ct. App. 1999).

For example, a Kentucky appeals court voided a regulation whereby grades were reduced because of unexcused absences resulting from student suspensions.[108] The school board policy stated that work missed because of unexcused absences could not be made up, and that five points would be deducted for every unexcused absence from each class during the grading period. The court held that the use of suspensions or expulsions for misconduct was permissible, but the additional lowering of grades as a punitive measure was not. A Pennsylvania court also agreed with this reasoning and found grade reductions for suspensions to be beyond a school board's authority.[109] In the court's opinion, it was a clear misrepresentation of students' scholastic achievement; the penalty went beyond the five-day suspension and downgraded achievement for a full grading period. The Mississippi Supreme Court, relying on a state law mandating the maintenance of alternative schools for suspended students, concluded that students attending these schools are not absent from school.[110] Under this law, a school board cannot count suspension days as unexcused for grading purposes unless the student fails to attend the alternative school.

In contrast, the Supreme Court of Indiana upheld the denial of course credit for a high school junior expelled three days before the end of a semester after the discovery of a small amount of marijuana in his truck. The court noted that although state law did not mandate loss of credit, the board could impose such a penalty.[111] A Texas appellate court upheld a school system's right to lower course grades for suspension days imposed for misconduct in addition to giving zeros on graded class work during the suspension.[112] Relying on a state attorney general's opinion approving grade reductions, the court found the pivotal question to be whether the board had actually adopted a policy that would authorize grade reductions. According to the court, oral announcements in school assemblies explaining grade penalties constituted a valid policy. Moreover, the court noted that the grade reduction did not impair constitutionally protected property or liberty rights.

Similar to some corporal punishment claims, students have asserted that drastic academic sanctions for disciplinary incidents violate their substantive due process rights.[113] The Seventh Circuit determined that the removal of two students from a band class for playing two unauthorized music pieces at a school concert did not meet the required constitutional threshold.[114] Exclusion of the students from the class

---

108. Dorsey v. Bale, 521 S.W.2d 76 (Ky. Ct. App. 1975).

109. Katzman v. Cumberland Valley Sch. Dist., 479 A.2d 671 (Pa. Commw. Ct. 1984). *See also In re Angela*, 340 S.E.2d 544 (S.C. 1986) (ruling that under state law, suspension absences could not be counted as unexcused for determining delinquency).

110. Bd. of Trs. v. T.H., 681 So. 2d 110 (Miss. 1996).

111. S. Gibson Sch. Bd. v. Sollman, 768 N.E.2d 437 (Ind. 2002).

112. New Braunfels Indep. Sch. Dist. v. Armke, 658 S.W.2d 330 (Tex. Civ. App. 1983).

113. *See supra* text accompanying note 81, for a discussion of substantive due process rights.

114. Dunn v. Fairfield Cmty. High Sch. Dist., 158 F.3d 962 (7th Cir. 1998), *appeal denied*, 782 A.2d 551 (Pa. 2001). *See also* Zellman v. Indep. Sch. Dist. No. 2758, 594 N.W.2d 216 (Minn. Ct. App. 1999) (holding that a zero grade for plagiarizing a history project did not involve a protected property or liberty interest).

resulted in a grade of F for the term and prevented one of the students from graduating with honors. The court said that although the school might have overreacted, its action was certainly not an extraordinary departure from established norms to substantiate a constitutional violation.

Generally, courts have ruled that academic course credit or high school diplomas cannot be withheld solely for disciplinary reasons. As early as 1921, the Supreme Court of Iowa held that students who had completed all academic requirements had the right to receive a high school diploma even though they refused to wear graduation caps during the ceremony.[115] The court ruled that the school board was obligated to issue a diploma to a pupil who had satisfactorily completed the prescribed course of study and who was otherwise qualified to graduate from high school. More recently, a Pennsylvania court held that a student who completed all coursework and final exams while expulsion proceedings were pending could not be denied a diploma, because state law specifies that a diploma must be issued once all requirements are met.[116]

Courts have issued conflicting decisions regarding the legality of denying a student the right to participate in graduation ceremonies as a disciplinary measure. A New York appeals court held that a student could not be denied such participation on disciplinary grounds unless conduct was related to a threatened disruption of the graduation ceremony,[117] whereas a North Carolina federal district court held that a student could be denied the privilege of participating in the graduation ceremony as a penalty for misconduct.[118] In the latter case, the federal court concluded that the student was not deprived of any property right, since he received his high school diploma even though he was not allowed to take part in the ceremony. A Pennsylvania appellate court reversed a trial court order permitting a student to participate in the graduation ceremony after he was suspended for violating the district's alcohol policy.[119] No arbitrary, capricious, or prejudicial actions were found on the part of the school board to justify judicial interference with the school's decision.

Although the use of academic sanctions for student misconduct and truancy is prevalent, students will likely continue to challenge such practices. To ensure fairness, any regulation stipulating that grades will be lowered for nonacademic reasons should be reasonable, related to absences from class, and serve a legitimate school

115. Valentine v. Indep. Sch. Dist. 183 N.W. 434 (Iowa 1921).

116. Ream v. Centennial Sch. Dist., 765 A.2d 1195 (Pa. Commw. Ct. 2001); 24 P.S. § 16-1613 (2002).

117. Ladson v. Bd. of Educ., 323 N.Y.S.2d 545 (App. Div. 1971).

118. Fowler v. Williamson, 448 F. Supp. 497 (W.D.N.C. 1978). *See also* Reese v. Jefferson Sch. Dist. No. 14J, 208 F.3d 736 (9th Cir. 2000) (holding that exclusion of four female students from graduation ceremony for throwing water balloons at boys in the boys' restroom did not violate Equal Protection Clause when the school did not punish the boys for alleged misconduct that had not been reported before the incident); Bundick v. Bay City Indep. Sch. Dist., 140 F. Supp. 2d 735 (S.D. Tex. 2001) (concluding that participation in graduation ceremony did not constitute a liberty or property interest).

119. Flynn-Scarcella v. Pocono Mountain Sch. Dist., 745 A.2d 117 (Pa. Commw. Ct. 2000).

purpose. Furthermore, students must be informed of these rules through the school's official student handbook or similar means.

Search and Seizure

Search and seizure cases involving public schools have increased in recent years, with the majority resulting from the confiscation of either illegal drugs or weapons. Students have asserted that warrantless searches conducted by school officials impair their rights under the Fourth Amendment of the Constitution. Through an extensive line of decisions, the United States Supreme Court has affirmed that the basic purpose of the Fourth Amendment is to "safeguard the privacy and security of individuals against arbitrary invasions by governmental officials."[120] This amendment protects individuals against unreasonable searches by requiring state agents to obtain a warrant based on probable cause prior to conducting a search. Under the *probable cause standard,* a governmental official must have reasonable grounds of suspicion, supported by sufficient evidence, to cause a cautious person to believe that the suspected individual is guilty of the alleged offense and that the search will produce evidence of the crime committed. Governmental officials violating Fourth Amendment rights may be subject to criminal or civil liability, but the most important remedy for the aggrieved individual is the exclusionary rule.[121] This rule renders evidence of an illegal search inadmissible in criminal prosecutions.[122] Also, under the "fruit of the poisonous tree" doctrine, additional evidence obtained later, resulting from the events set in motion by the illegal search, may be excluded.

Significant Fourth Amendment questions have been raised in the public school setting. Since Fourth Amendment protections apply only to searches conducted by agents of the state, a fundamental issue in education cases is whether school authorities function as private individuals or as state agents. Most courts have found the Fourth Amendment applicable to public schools, but it was not until 1985 in *New Jersey v. T.L.O.* that the Supreme Court finally held that the amendment's prohibition of unreasonable searches applies to school authorities.[123] The Court concluded that school officials are state agents, and all governmental actions—not merely those of law-enforcement officers—come within the constraints of the Fourth Amendment.[124]

---

120. Camara v. Mun. Ct. of S.F., 387 U.S. 523, 528 (1967).

121. *See* Mapp v. Ohio, 367 U.S. 643 (1961).

122. Evidence seized by a private person, however, is admissible since the exclusionary rule does not apply. *See, e.g.,* People v. Stewart, 313 N.Y.S.2d 253 (1970).

123. 469 U.S. 325 (1985).

124. *Id.* at 336. Although the Supreme Court rejected the *in loco parentis* (in place of parent) doctrine, the Sixth Circuit found it applicable in a search that occurred on a class trip. Recognizing school officials' supervisory duties away from the school, the court concluded that they must be given the authority necessary to intervene in a range of activities and to protect students from harm. Webb v. McCullough, 828 F.2d 1151 (6th Cir. 1987).

Although finding the Fourth Amendment applicable, the Court in *T.L.O.* concluded that educators' substantial interest in maintaining discipline required "easing" the warrant and probable cause requirements imposed on police officers. The Court reasoned that "requiring a teacher to obtain a warrant before searching a child suspected of an infraction of school rules (or of the criminal law) would unduly interfere with the maintenance of the swift and informal disciplinary procedures needed in the schools."[125] In modifying the level of suspicion required to conduct a search, the Court found the public interest was best served in the school setting with a standard less than probable cause. Accordingly, the Court held that the legality of a search should depend "simply on the reasonableness, under all the circumstances, of the search."[126]

The Court in *T.L.O.* advanced two tests for determining reasonableness. First, is the search justified at its inception? That is, are there "reasonable grounds for suspecting that the search will turn up evidence that the student has violated or is violating either the law or the rules of the school?"[127] Second, is the scope of the search reasonable? In the Court's words, are "the measures adopted reasonably related to the objectives of the search and not excessively intrusive in light of the age and sex of the student and the nature of the infraction?"[128]

The "reasonableness" standard allows courts substantial latitude in interpreting Fourth Amendment rights.[129] Among factors courts have considered in assessing reasonable grounds for a search are the child's age, history, and record in the school; prevalence and seriousness of the problem in the school to which the search is directed; exigency to make the search without delay and further investigation; probative value and reliability of the information used as a justification for the search; the school officials' experience with the student and with the type of problem to which the search is directed; and the type of search.[130] Clearly, reasonable suspicion requires more than a hunch, good intentions, or good faith. The Supreme Court, in upholding an exception to the warrant requirement for a "stop and frisk" search for weapons by police officers, concluded that to justify the intrusion, the police officer must be able to point to "specific and articulable facts."[131] In recognizing an exception for school

125. *T.L.O.*, 469 U.S. at 340.

126. *Id.* at 341.

127. *Id.* at 342.

128. *Id.*

129. As Justice Brennan noted in his dissent in *T.L.O.*, the "only definite content [of reasonableness] is that it is not the same test as the 'probable cause' standard." He argued that the departure from probable cause was unclear and unnecessary, creating an "amorphous" standard that will promote more litigation and uncertainty among school officials. *Id.* at 354.

130. *See, e.g.,* Vernonia Sch. Dist. 47J v. Acton, 515 U.S. 646 (1995); *T.L.O.*, 469 U.S. 325; Cornfield v. Consol. High Sch. Dist. No. 230, 991 F.2d 1316 (7th Cir. 1993); *In re* Angelia D.B., 564 N.W.2d 682 (Wis. 1997).

131. Terry v. Ohio, 392 U.S. 1, 21 (1968).

searches, it appears that, at a minimum, the judiciary will require searches of students to be supported by objective facts.[132]

Informants often play an important role in establishing the "specific and articulable facts" necessary to justify a search. Reliability of informants can be assumed unless school officials have reason to doubt the motives of the reporting student, teacher, parent, citizen, or anonymous caller.[133] The amount of detail given by an informant adds to the veracity of the report—that is, identifying a specific student by name, what the student is wearing, and the specific contraband and where it is located will support a decision to search.[134] Additionally, even with limited information, the level of danger presented by an informant's tip may require an immediate response. A California appellate court commented that "the gravity of the danger posed by possession of a firearm or other weapon on campus was great compared to the relatively minor intrusion involved in investigating" the accused students.[135]

A further requirement of reasonableness appears to be individualized suspicion. The Supreme Court in *T.L.O.* did not address individualized suspicion, but the Court did state that "exceptions to the requirement of individualized suspicion are generally appropriate only where the privacy interests implicated by a search are minimal and where 'other safeguards' are available 'to assure that the individual's reasonable expectation' of privacy is not subject to the discretion of the official in the field.' "[136] In the absence of exigency requiring an immediate search, courts have been reluctant to support personal searches lacking individualized suspicion.[137]

In assessing the constitutionality of searches in public schools, two questions are central: What constitutes a search, and what types of searches are reasonable? What constitutes a search must be appraised in the context of the Supreme Court's statement that "the Fourth Amendment protects people, not places. What a person knowingly exposes to the public, even in his own home or office, is not a subject of Fourth Amendment protection. But what he seeks to preserve as private, even in an area accessible to the public, may be constitutionally protected."[138] According to the Court's rulings, essential considerations in determining whether an action is a search are an individual's reasonable expectation of privacy (reasonable in the sense that

---

132. *See, e.g., Cornfield,* 991 F.2d 1316; People v. Taylor, 625 N.E.2d 785 (Ill. App. Ct. 1993); State v. Finch, 925 P.2d 913 (Or. Ct. App. 1996).

133. *See, e.g.,* C.B. v. Driscoll, 82 F.3d 383 (11th Cir. 1996); *In re* L.A., 21 P.3d 952 (Kan. 2001) (finding that a student's tip to the Crime Stoppers organizer established reasonable suspicion). The Supreme Court in *T.L.O.* noted that because the expectation of privacy is diminished in school settings, officials do not have to show the reliability level required of police officers. For a discussion of the higher standards for law enforcement, *see* Florida v. J.L., 529 U.S. 266 (2000).

134. *See, e.g.,* S.D. v. State, 650 So. 2d 198 (Fla. Dist. Ct. App. 1995).

135. *In re* Alexander B., 270 Cal. Rptr. 342, 344 (Ct. App. 1990).

136. New Jersey v. T.L.O., 469 U.S. 325, 342 n.8 (1985).

137. *See, e.g.,* Bell v. Marseilles Elementary Sch., 160 F. Supp. 2d 883 (N.D. Ill. 2001); Kennedy v. Dexter Consol. Schs., 10 P. 3d 115 (N.M. 2000).

138. Katz v. United States, 389 U.S. 347, 351–352 (1967).

society is prepared to recognize the privacy)[139] and the extent of governmental intrusion.[140]

The reasonableness of a specific type of search must be evaluated in terms of all the circumstances surrounding the search.[141] This would include variables such as who initiated the search, who conducted the search, need for the search, purpose of the search, information or factors prompting the search, what or who was searched, and use of the evidence. In the following sections, various types of school searches are examined within this context.

Lockers

In concluding that students have some legitimate expectation of privacy in their lockers, the Mississippi high court relied on the United States Supreme Court's statement that "schoolchildren may find it necessary to carry with them a variety of legitimate, noncontraband items, and there is no reason to conclude that they have necessarily waived all rights to privacy in such items merely by bringing them onto school grounds."[142] Courts, however, have singled out school lockers as generating a *lower* expectation of privacy, frequently distinguishing locker searches on the basis that a locker is school property, and students do not retain exclusive possession, particularly when they have signed a form acknowledging that the locker is school property and subject to inspection. Under the view of joint control, school officials have been allowed to inspect lockers or even to consent to searches by law-enforcement officers.[143]

A Kansas case illustrates the general judicial view toward locker searches. The Supreme Court of Kansas held that the right of inspection is inherent in the authority granted to school officials to manage schools.[144] The court maintained that it is a proper function of school personnel to inspect the lockers under their control and to prevent the use of lockers in illicit ways or for illegal purposes. The Tenth Circuit also concluded that "school authorities have, on behalf of the public, an interest in these lockers and a duty to police the school, particularly where possible serious violations of the criminal laws exist."[145] An important point in both of these cases, however, is that school officials retained a list of the combinations and had occasionally inspected the lockers. These points have been emphasized in other cases to support the nonexclusive nature of lockers.[146]

---

139. *Id.* at 361 (Harlan, J., concurring).

140. United States v. Chadwick, 433 U.S. 1, 7 (1977).

141. Terry v. Ohio, 392 U.S. 1, 9 (1968). *See also* State v. Drake, 662 A.2d 265 (N.H. 1995).

142. *In re* S.C., 583 So. 2d 188 (Miss. 1991) (quoting New Jersey v. T.L.O., 469 U.S. 325, 339 (1985)).

143. *But see infra* text accompanying note 199, for cases addressing the involvement of law enforcement personnel.

144. State v. Stein, 456 P.2d 1, 2 (Kan. 1969).

145. Zamora v. Pomeroy, 639 F.2d 662, 670 (10th Cir. 1981).

146. *See, e.g., In re* Patrick Y., 746 A.2d 405 (Md. 2000); Commonwealth v. Cass, 709 A.2d 350 (Pa. 1998); *In re* Isiah B., 500 N.W.2d 637 (Wis. 1993). *See also In re* S.C., 583 So. 2d 188 (holding that the existence of a master key did not lower the expectation of privacy, but that a policy of regularly inspecting the students' lockers might have that effect).

Applying the *T.L.O.* standard for reasonableness, the Supreme Court of Mississippi concluded that a student informant's tip indicating another student had a gun on the school premises reasonably suggested that school officials "search out the truth of the matter."[147] Similarly, a California appellate court reasoned that an anonymous parent informant reporting that a student had been seen at an evening school event with a gun substantiated reasonable suspicion to inspect the student's locker several days later.[148] The court commented that the locker search represented minimal intrusion in the context of the threat firearms pose to the safety of all students. The Massachusetts high court also concluded that a student eyewitness to an attempted sale of marijuana not only provided reasonable suspicion but probable cause to search the suspected student's locker.[149]

Most student conduct codes and some state laws specify guidelines for locker searches. These code or laws may establish that reasonable suspicion is required prior to conducting a search. In a Pennsylvania case, the state supreme court relied on the *T.L.O.* decision and the student code in establishing a legitimate expectation of privacy in lockers. The code specified: "Prior to a locker search a student shall be notified and given an opportunity to be present. However, where school authorities have a *reasonable suspicion* that the locker contains materials which pose a threat to the health, welfare, and safety of students in the school, students' lockers may be searched without prior warning [emphasis added]."[150] Although the court held that students possessed a reasonable expectation of privacy in their lockers, it was minimal. In balancing students' privacy interests and school officials' concerns, the court found the schoolwide blanket search reasonable based on the heightened awareness of drug activity that permeated the entire school and the compelling concern about drug use.

Due to recent incidents of school violence, some states have enacted broad laws eliminating any presumption of privacy in school lockers. For example, a Michigan law states: "A pupil who uses a locker that is the property of a school district... is presumed to have no expectation of privacy in that locker or that locker's content."[151] Furthermore, school officials can search the lockers at any time and can request the assistance of the local law-enforcement agency. Based on judicial interpretations of students' privacy rights, it is likely that statutes such as these will be challenged

---

147. *In re* S.C., 583 So. 2d at 192. *See also* State v. Joseph T., 336 S.E.2d 728 (W.Va. 1985) (concluding that the discovery of drugs in a jacket found in a locker was reasonably related to the search for alcoholic beverages where reasonable suspicion existed at the inception of the search).

148. *In re* Joseph G., 38 Cal. Rptr. 2d 902 (Ct. App. 1995). *See also* Commonwealth v. Carey, 554 N.E.2d 1199 (Mass. 1990) (upholding the search of locker for a gun based on report by two student informants).

149. Commonwealth v. Snyder, 597 N.E.2d 1363 (Mass. 1992). *See also* People v. Taylor, 625 N.E.2d 785 (Ill. App. Ct. 1993); S.A. v. State, 654 N.E.2d 791 (Ind. Ct. App. 1995).

150. Commonwealth v. Cass, 709 A.2d 350, 353 (Pa. 1998). *See also* Snyder, 597 N.E.2d 1363 (finding expectation of privacy of lockers based on the student handbook). *But see In re* Patrick Y., 746 A.2d 405 (Md. 2000) (holding that a local policy specifying probable cause to search lockers did not establish a reasonable expectation of privacy because state law provided that lockers were school property and could be searched without even reasonable suspicion).

regarding the expectation of privacy in the contents of the lockers as well as the use of law-enforcement personnel.

Search of Personal Possessions: Purses, Book Bags, and Other Property

Students have a greater expectation of privacy in their personal property or effects than in their school lockers. In the Supreme Court's *T.L.O.* decision, a teacher had reported that a student was smoking in the restroom. Upon questioning by the assistant principal, the student denied smoking and, in fact, denied that she even smoked. The assistant principal then opened the student's purse, seeking evidence to substantiate that she did smoke. In the process of removing a package of cigarettes, he spotted rolling papers and subsequently found marijuana and other evidence implicating her in drug dealing. Using the "reasonable suspicion" test, the Supreme Court found that the search in *T.L.O.* was reasonable. The school official had a basis for suspecting that the student had cigarettes in her purse. Although possession was not a violation of a school rule, it was not irrelevant; discovery of cigarettes provided evidence to corroborate that she had been smoking and challenged her credibility. No direct evidence existed that the student's purse contained cigarettes, but, based on a teacher's report that the student had been smoking, it was logical to suspect that she might have cigarettes in her purse. Characterizing this as a "commonsense" conclusion, the Court noted that "the requirement of reasonable suspicion is not a requirement of absolute certainty: 'sufficient probability, not certainty, is the touchstone of reasonableness under the Fourth Amendment.' "[152]

Other courts have noted that searches of students' personal possessions—such as wallets, purses, and book bags—do violate students' subjective expectations of privacy and, as such, require individualized suspicion that a violation of a law or school rule has occurred. The Supreme Court of Hawaii found that individualized suspicion existed when two students' purses were searched for marijuana.[153] The students, who were not authorized to leave campus, were discovered during the school day across the street from the school in the "tunnel" (known to be an area where students gathered to smoke cigarettes and marijuana) with the strong odor of burning marijuana in the air; a search of their purses was found to be reasonable in light of these circumstances.

Similarly, the New York high court concluded that a security officer's investigation of a student's book bag was reasonable based on hearing an "unusual metallic

---

151. MCLS § 380.1306 (2001). *See also* Ohio Rev. Code § 3313.20 (specifying that a locker can be searched when reasonable suspicion exists that it contains evidence of the violation of a school rule or the law, or can be subject to random search if the board of education posts notice in a conspicuous place in each school building to that affect). One Ohio appellate court concluded that this aspect of the law violates the Ohio and federal constitutions. *In re* Adam, 697 N.E.2d 1100 (Ohio Ct. App. 1997).

152. New Jersey v. T.L.O., 469 U.S. 325, 346 (1985).

153. *In re* Doe, 887 P.2d 645 (Haw. 1994).

thud" when the student tossed the bag on a metal shelf. Following the sound, the security officer ran his fingers over the outside of the book bag and detected the outline of a gun. The court noted that the sound alone was insufficient to justify searching the bag, but the discovery of the presence of a gun-like shape established reasonable suspicion to open the bag.[154] The Supreme Court of California, however, declined to uphold the search of a student's calculator case in the absence of articulable facts to support individualized suspicion.[155] The vice principal's search was based on the student's tardiness for class, his "furtive gestures" to hide the calculator, and his comment that the principal needed a warrant. These actions alone did not point to the possible violation of any specific rule or law.

In a Massachusetts case, the state high court assessed whether a student had a legitimate expectation of privacy in his handwriting.[156] The charges against the student grew out of several incidents of graffiti on school property containing obscenities and racial slurs, some directed toward one teacher. Because prior occurrences made the student a potential suspect, several of his homework assignments, along with two other students' papers, were analyzed to determine if they matched the graffiti. Based on a match with the student's writing, he was charged with malicious destruction of property and violation of the targeted teacher's civil rights. The court refused to suppress the handwriting analyses and samples, finding that it was reasonable for school authorities to suspect the student and that the inspection of the papers involved minimal intrusion.

A student's car, like other personal possessions, may be searched if reasonable suspicion can be established. A Texas federal district court, however, declined to uphold a general dragnet search of a school parking lot.[157] The school's interest in the contents of the cars was viewed as minimal, since students did not have access to their cars during the school day. Furthermore, the search was indiscriminate, lacking any evidence of individualized suspicion. In contrast, a Florida district court upheld the search of a student's car after a school aide observed in plain view a water pipe, commonly used to smoke marijuana.[158] The aide regularly patrolled the school parking lot to ensure enforcement of school regulations and to supervise students during their

---

154. *In re* Gregory M., 606 N.Y.S.2d 579 (1993). *See also* DesRoches v. Caprio, 156 F.3d 571 (4th Cir. 1998) (concluding that the student had a legitimate expectation of privacy in his backpack, necessitating individualized suspicion to search); S.A. v. State, 654 N.E.2d 791 (Ind. Ct. App. 1995) (finding that the search of a book bag was justified by an informant's tip related to a stolen book of school locker combinations); *In re* Murray, 525 S.E.2d 496 (N.C. App. 2000) (holding that a tip from a student established reasonable suspicion to search a book bag).

155. *In re* William G., 709 P.2d 1287 (Cal. 1985). *But see* People v. Dilworth, 661 N.E.2d 310 (Ill. 1996) (upholding the search of a student's flashlight based on a report that he was selling drugs).

156. Commonweatlh v. Buccella, 751 N.E.2d 373 (Mass. 2001).

157. Jones v. Latexo Indep. Sch. Dist., 499 F. Supp. 223 (E.D. Tex. 1980). *See also* Burnham v. West, 681 F. Supp. 1160 (E.D. Va. 1987).

158. State v. D.T.W., 425 So. 2d 1383 (Fla. Civ. App. 1983). *See also* Covington County v. G.W., 767 So. 2d 187 (Miss. 2000) (holding that a report of student drinking beer in the school parking lot justified search of his truck; no warrant was required).

lunch break. In the court's opinion, patrolling the lot fell within the school's duty to maintain order and discipline and did not constitute a search.

Personal Search of a Student

Warrantless searches of a student's person raise significant legal questions. Unlike locker searches, it cannot be asserted that there is a lower expectation of privacy. Students have a legitimate expectation of privacy in the contents of their pockets and their person.[159] The Fifth Circuit noted that "the Fourth Amendment applies with its fullest vigor against any intrusion on the human body."[160] In personal searches, not only is it necessary to have reasonable cause to search, but also the search itself must be reasonable. Reasonableness is assessed in terms of the specific facts and circumstances of a case.

A New Mexico appellate court found the search of a student's pockets reasonable under the *T.L.O.* standard.[161] In this case, an assistant principal and a police officer assigned full time to the school asked a student to empty his pockets based on his evasive behavior, smell of burnt marijuana, and a large bulge in his right pocket. When the student refused to remove his hand from his pocket, the school official felt that the incident had become a safety issue. She then asked the resource officer to search the student. The officer removed the student's hand from his right pocket and reached in and pulled out a .38 caliber handgun. The court held that the search was justified on the basis of suspicious behavior and that the scope of the search was not excessive or intrusive. Similarly, the Alabama Supreme Court found the search of two fifth-grade students for the alleged theft of nine dollars reasonable based on the fact that they had been alone in the classroom at the time the money disappeared.[162] A Washington appellate court, however, declined to support the search of a student's pockets because he was in the school parking lot during the school day, a violation of the closed campus policy. The court emphasized that "there must be a nexus between the item sought and the infraction under investigation."[163] In the absence of other sus-

159. *See, e.g.,* Brousseau v. Town of Westerly, 11 F. Supp. 2d 177 (D.R.I. 1998).

160. Horton v. Goose Creek Indep. Sch. Dist., 690 F.2d 470, 478 (5th Cir. 1982).

161. *In re* Josue T., 989 P.2d 431 (N.M. App. 2000). *See also* Greenleaf v. Cote, 77 F. Supp. 2d 168 (D. Me. 1999) (holding that information from student informant justified personal search of student for evidence of beer drinking); Wilcher v. State, 876 S.W.2d 466 (Tex. Ct. App. 1994) (concluding that reasonable suspicion existed to search a student who was not in class based on information that he possessed a gun).

162. Wynn v. Bd. of Educ., 508 So. 2d 1170 (Ala. 1987). *See also* Bridgman v. New Trier High Sch. Dist. No. 203, 128 F.3d 1146 (7th Cir. 1997) (holding that a student's unruly behavior, bloodshot eyes, and dilated pupils established reasonable suspicion to conduct search); D.B. v. State, 728 N.E.2d 179 (Ind. Ct. App. 2000) (finding that the smell of cigarette smoke coming from a bathroom stall and the student's unresponsiveness to questioning justified search).

163. State v. B. A. S., 13 P.3d 244, 246 (Wash. App. 2000). *See also* D.I.R. v. State, 683 N.E.2d 251 (Ind. Ct. App. 1997) (concluding that the search of a student's pocket because she arrived late to school was not justified); Commonwealth v. Damian D., 752 N.E.2d 679 (Mass. 2001) (finding that a student's truancy did not establish reasonable suspicion to support school officials' search).

picious factors about the student, violation of the school's closed campus rule did not justify the automatic search that led to the discovery of marijuana.

Although personal searches are permitted, strip searches usually cannot be justified on the basis of reasonable suspicion. The Second Circuit noted that "as the intrusiveness of the search intensifies, the standard of Fourth Amendment 'reasonableness' approaches probable cause, even in the school context."[164] The Seventh Circuit, in a strongly worded statement, proclaimed in an Indiana case: "It does not require a constitutional scholar to conclude that a nude search of a thirteen-year-old child is an invasion of constitutional rights of some magnitude. More than that: it is a violation of any known principle of human decency."[165]

The Ninth Circuit found a pat-down search and subsequent strip search to be unlawful.[166] Such an invasion of privacy could not be justified on the basis that a bus driver saw the student exchange "what appeared to be money" for an unidentified object. Similarly, the West Virginia high court found the strip search of a 14-year-old eighth-grader suspected of stealing $100 excessively intrusive, and thus unreasonable in scope.[167] The court concluded that unless exigent circumstances necessitate an immediate search to protect the safety of other students, a warrantless strip search is impermissible. In another strip search to locate stolen money, an Illinois federal district court found the lack of individualized suspicion and the level of intrusion pivotal in finding a search of 30 students unconstitutional.[168]

A few strip searches have been upheld with sufficient evidence of individualized suspicion, specifically related to drug use. The Sixth Circuit upheld the strip search of a female high school student suspected of possessing drugs.[169] Among the significant facts establishing reasonable suspicion were a call from another student's mother who described a glass vial containing a white powdery substance, a student informant's tip, a teacher's report of strange behavior, and an incriminating letter detailing drug use. Although the court recognized that the scope of this search was personally intrusive, it was held to be reasonable, considering the size of the vial and the suspected nature of the powdery substance. Similarly, the Seventh Circuit found that substantial evidence existed to search a high school student with an "unusual

164. M.M. v. Anker, 607 F.2d 588, 589 (2d Cir. 1979).

165. Doe v. Renfrow, 631 F.2d 91, 92–93 (7th Cir. 1980).

166. Bilbrey v. Brown, 738 F.2d 1462 (9th Cir. 1984).

167. State *ex rel.* Galford v. Mark Anthony B., 433 S.E.2d 41 (W.Va. 1993). *See also* Fewless v. Bd. of Educ., 208 F. Supp. 2d 806 (W.D. Mich. 2002) (ruling that a strip search of a 14-year-old student based on the report of two hostile classmates did not constitute reasonable suspicion to justify the search); Konop v. Northwestern Sch. Dist., 26 F. Supp. 2d 1189 (D.S.D. 1998) (holding that the strip search of eighth-grade girls was unreasonable and violated clearly established law); Kennedy v. Dexter Consol. Schs., 10 P.3d 115 (N.M. 2000) (concluding that the strip search of two high school students without individualized suspicion to find a missing ring violated clearly established law).

168. Bell v. Marseilles Elementary Sch., 160 F. Supp. 2d 883 (N.D. Ill. 2001).

169. Williams v. Ellington, 936 F.2d 881 (6th Cir. 1991). *See also* Rone v. Daviess County Bd. of Educ., 655 S.W.2d 28 (Ky. Ct. App. 1983).

bulge" in his sweatpants.[170] Acknowledging that the potential impact of a strip search is substantial, the court, however, emphasized that with the administrators' suspicion that the student was "crotching drugs," a strip search was the least intrusive way to proceed. Both circuit courts considered the nature of the contraband sought and the likelihood of it being hidden on the body in determining that the scope of the searches was reasonable.

Although courts have not prohibited strip searches of students, enough caveats exist to alert school officials of the inherent risks of such intrusive personal searches. The judicial trend indicates that reasonable suspicion alone may be inadequate to justify most strip searches; rather, the required standard approaches probable cause necessitating specific evidence linked to an individual student. Except for emergency situations posing immediate danger to the safety of students, few circumstances appear to necessitate such intrusions.

An individual may waive entitlement to Fourth Amendment protection by consenting to a search or volunteering requested evidence. The consent, however, is valid only if voluntarily given in the absence of coercion. Serious questions arise as to whether a student's consent is actually voluntary. Did the student have a free choice? Was the student aware of his or her Fourth Amendment rights? A Texas federal district court reasoned that the very nature of the school setting diminishes the presumption of consent.[171] Students are accustomed to receiving and following orders of school officials; refusal to obey a request is considered insubordination. In this case, the threat to call the students' parents and the police if they did not cooperate further substantiated a coercive atmosphere. In another case, the Sixth Circuit stated that there is "a presumption against the waiver of constitutional rights," placing the burden on school officials to show that students knowingly and intelligently waived their Fourth Amendment rights.[172] Although some courts have found student consent valid,[173] the inherent pitfalls of pursuing such a search in the absence of reasonable suspicion must be duly considered.

Use of Metal Detectors

With the increased concern about the high rate of violence in schools, metal detectors have become more commonplace as school officials seek to maintain a safe educational environment. Moreover, the use of metal detectors is no longer limited to secondary schools. In 2000, the Chicago chief education officer approved metal detectors

---

170. Cornfield v. Consol. High Sch. Dist. No. 230, 991 F.2d 1316 (7th Cir. 1993). *See also* Jenkins v. Talladega City Bd. of Educ., 115 F.3d 821 (11th Cir. 1997) (holding that a teacher and a principal had qualified immunity in conducting a strip search of three second-grade students in 1992 to find a missing $7.00 because of the lack of settled legal authority at that time).

171. Jones v. Latexo Indep. Sch. Dist., 499 F. Supp. 223 (E.D. Tex. 1980).

172. Tarter v. Raybuck, 742 F.2d 977, 980 (6th Cir. 1984).

173. *See, e.g.,* Rone v. Daviess County Bd. of Educ., 655 S.W.2d 28 (Ky. Ct. App. 1983); Commonwealth v. Carey, 554 N.E.2d 1199 (Mass. 1990).

for all the district's 489 elementary schools.[174] Although metal detectors have become standard equipment in airports and many public buildings, their use does constitute a search for Fourth Amendment purposes. Such public searches have been found to be reasonable in balancing the threat of violence against the minimally intrusive nature of the search. As challenges have been raised about the use of metal detectors in schools, similar reasoning is applied.

The Pennsylvania high court upheld a general, uniform search of all students for weapons as they entered the high school building; each student's personal belongings were searched, and then a security officer scanned each student with a metal detector.[175] Individualized suspicion was not required in light of the high rate of violence in the school district. The court concluded that the search involved a greater intrusion on students' privacy interests than the search of a locker, but with the nonintrusive nature of the search, it remained a minimal intrusion. Similarly, the Eighth Circuit found a search of all male students from grades 6 to 12 for dangerous weapons to be minimally intrusive based on reasonable suspicion that weapons had been brought to school that day.[176] Students were scanned with a metal detector after they removed their shoes and the contents of their pockets. If the metal detector sounded, a subsequent pat-down search was conducted.

An Illinois appellate court assessed the reasonableness of the use of metal detectors from the perspective of schools' "special needs."[177] In the first year of using the detectors, Chicago school officials confiscated over 300 weapons (including 15 guns) from the high schools. With continued use of these devices, they showed a reduction of about 85 percent in weapons confiscated. The court, in concluding that individualized suspicion was not required to use metal detectors, noted that the purpose of the screening was to ensure a safe school environment for all students, not to secure evidence of a crime.

In each of the cases litigated, courts pointed to the violent context that led school officials to use metal detectors and the minimally intrusive nature of these devices. With increasing use, it can be expected that courts will continue to review the constitutional issues raised by metal detectors in school searches.

Drug-Detecting Canines

The use of drug-detecting dogs in searches raises a number of controversial questions regarding Fourth Amendment rights. Does the presence of a dog sniffing students constitute a search? Must reasonable suspicion exist to justify the use of dogs? Does the alert of a dog establish reasonable suspicion? A few courts have addressed these issues.

174. Jessica Portner, "Girl's Slaying Elicits Calls for Metal Detectors," *Education Week* (March 15, 2000), p. 3.

175. *In re* F.B., 726 A.2d 361 (Pa. 1999).

176. Thompson v. Carthage Sch. Dist., 87 F.3d 979 (8th Cir. 1996).

177. People v. Pruitt, 662 N.E.2d 540 (Ill. App. Ct. 1996). *See also In re* Latasha, 70 Cal. Rptr. 2d 886 (Cal. Ct. App. 1998) (holding that "special needs" administrative searches without individualized suspicion, such as use of metal detectors, involve minimal intrusion).

The Tenth Circuit upheld the use of trained police dogs in the sniffing of lockers but did not directly address the constitutional issues presented by the canine searches. Rather, the court discussed generally the school administrator's duty to inspect, even to the point that an inspection may violate Fourth Amendment rights. Under this broad grant of authority, the alert of a dog three times at a locker established reasonable suspicion to conduct a search.[178]

The Fifth Circuit, on the other hand, confronted the question of whether sniffing by a dog is a search in terms of an individual's reasonable expectation of privacy.[179] The appellate court noted that most courts, including the United States Supreme Court, have held that law-enforcement use of canines for sniffing objects does not constitute a search.[180] Specifically, the court referenced cases involving checked luggage, shipped packages, public lockers, and cars on public streets. According to the court, a reasonable expectation of privacy does not extend to the airspace surrounding these objects. The court maintained that what has evolved is a doctrine of "public smell," equivalent to the "plain view" theory (that is, an object in plain view can be seized under certain circumstances). This point was illustrated by the example of a police officer detecting the odor of marijuana from an object or property. No search is involved because the odor is considered to be in public view and thus unprotected.

From this line of reasoning, the Fifth Circuit noted that the use of canines has been viewed as merely enhancing the ability to detect an odor, as the use of a flashlight improves vision. Accordingly, the court concluded that sniffing of student lockers and cars in public view was not a search, and therefore the Fourth Amendment did not apply. Although permitting the use of dogs to detect drugs, the court held that reasonable suspicion is required for a further search of a locker or car by school officials, and that such suspicion can be established only on showing that the dogs are reasonably reliable in detecting the actual presence of contraband.[181]

---

178. Zamora v. Pomeroy, 639 F.2d 662, 670 (10th Cir. 1981). *See also* Bundick v. Bay City Indep. Sch. Dist., 40 F. Supp. 2d 735 (S.D. Tex. 2001) (finding that the alert of a trained and certified dog provided sufficient cause to search a student's truck without a warrant).

179. Horton v. Goose Creek Indep. Sch. Dist., 690 F.2d 470 (5th Cir. 1982). *See also* Jennings v. Joshua Indep. Sch. Dist., 877 F.2d 313 (5th Cir. 1989); Jones v. Latexo Indep. Sch. Dist., 499 F. Supp. 223 (E.D. Tex. 1980).

180. The Supreme Court concluded that the brief detention of a passenger's luggage at an airport for the purpose of subjecting it to a "sniff" test by a trained narcotics detection dog did not constitute a search under the Fourth Amendment. Use of canines was characterized as unique, involving a very limited investigation and minimal disclosure. United States v. Place, 462 U.S. 696 (1983). *See also Horton,* 690 F.2d at 477, for citations to other law-enforcement cases.

181. Subsequently, in denying a rehearing, the court clarified the issue of the dogs' reliability. According to the court, a school district does not have to establish with "reasonable certainty that contraband is present . . . or even that there is probable cause to believe that contraband will be found." Rather, there must be some evidence to indicate that the dogs' performance is reliable enough to give rise to a reasonable suspicion. *Horton,* 693 F.2d 524, 525. *See also* Commonwealth v. Cass, 709 A.2d 350 (Pa. 1998) (holding canine sniff is not a search under the Fourth Amendment).

In most instances, judicial support for the use of dogs has been limited to the sniffing of objects. The Seventh Circuit, however, concluded that the presence of dogs in a classroom was not a search.[182] In this well-publicized Indiana case, school officials with the assistance of police officers conducted a schoolwide inspection for drugs in which trained dogs were brought into each classroom for approximately five minutes. When a dog alerted beside a student, school officials requested that the student remove the contents of his or her pockets or purse. A continued alert by the dog resulted in a strip search. The appellate court, in weighing the minimal intrusion of the dogs against the school's desire to eliminate a significant drug problem, concluded that sniffing of the students by the dogs did not constitute a search invoking Fourth Amendment protections. Search of pockets and purses, however, did involve an invasion of privacy but was justified because the dog's alert constituted reasonable cause to believe that the student possessed drugs. However, as discussed previously, the court drew the line at conducting a strip search based on a dog's alert.

In contrast to the reasoning of the Seventh Circuit, a Texas federal district court concluded that the use of dogs in a blanket "sniffing" (or inspection) of students did constitute a search. The court noted that drug-detecting dogs posed a greater intrusion on personal privacy than electronic surveillance devices, which have not required individualized suspicion. According to the court, "The dog's inspection was virtually equivalent to a physical entry into the students' pockets and personal possessions."[183] In finding the dog's sniffing to be a search, the court further held that for school authorities to use dogs in a search, they must have prior individualized suspicion that a student possesses contraband that will disrupt the educational process.[184] In essence, a dog alert cannot be used to establish such suspicion.

Similarly, the Fifth Circuit held that sniffing of students by dogs significantly intrudes on an individual's privacy, thereby constituting a search.[185] Although recognizing that the sniffing of a person is a search, the court did not prohibit such searches but held that their intrusiveness must be weighed against the school's need to conduct the search. The court concluded that even with a significant need to search, individualized suspicion is required prior to the use of dogs because of the degree of intrusion on personal dignity and security. The Ninth Circuit concurred, noting that the significant intrusion on a student's expectation of privacy posed by dogs requires individualized suspicion.[186]

Given the scope of the drug problem in public schools, it seems likely that school districts will continue to consider the use of drug-detecting canine units. Until the Supreme Court addresses whether such a practice constitutes a search in schools

182. Doe v. Renfrow, 631 F.2d 91 (7th Cir. 1980).

183. *Jones,* 499 F. Supp. at 233.

184. *Id. See also* Kuehn v. Renton Sch. Dist. No. 403, 694 P.2d 1078, 1081 (Wash. 1985), in which the state high court declared: "The Fourth Amendment demands more than a generalized probability; it requires that the suspicion be particularized with respect to each individual searched."

185. *Horton,* 690 F.2d 470.

186. B.C. v. Plumas Unified Sch. Dist., 192 F.3d 1260 (9th Cir. 1999).

(requiring individualized suspicion) or whether a dog alert can establish reasonable grounds for a personal search, different interpretations among lower courts seem destined to persist.

Drug Testing

In an effort to control drug use among students,[187] some districts have considered schoolwide drug-testing programs. Such programs raise serious questions about students' privacy rights. In 1989, the Supreme Court held that urinalysis, the most frequently used means for drug testing, is a search under the Fourth Amendment.[188] Although the Court upheld the testing of government employees for drug use in two separate decisions, the holdings were narrowly drawn and based on a compelling governmental interest. In one case, the Court upheld the testing of railroad employees who are involved in certain types of accidents, emphasizing the highly regulated nature of the industry and the need to ensure the safety of the public.[189] In the second case, drug testing of customs employees seeking promotion to positions involving the interdiction of illegal drugs or requiring the use of firearms was justified based on safety and security concerns.[190] Individualized suspicion was not a precondition for conducting the urinalysis in these cases, but the narrow circumstances justifying the testing programs minimized the discretion of supervisors and the potential for arbitrariness.

The Supreme Court has rendered two decisions regarding the drug testing of students. In 1995, the Court in *Vernonia School District 47J v. Acton* upheld a school district's drug policy authorizing random urinalysis drug testing of students participating in athletic programs.[191] Emphasizing the district's "custodial and tutelary" responsibility for children, the Court recognized that school personnel can exercise a degree of supervision and control over children that would not be permitted over adults. This relationship was held to be pivotal in assessing the reasonableness of the district's drug policy—a policy undertaken "in furtherance of the government's responsibilities, under a public school system, as guardian and tutor of children entrusted to its care."[192] Addressing students' legitimate privacy expectations, the

---

187. Based on a six-year study of 12- to 17-year olds in 2001, the National Center on Addiction and Substance Abuse concluded that 60 percent of high school students and 30 percent of middle school students would return that fall to schools where drugs were used, kept, or sold. Their study revealed that 76.4 percent of the students who had tried marijuana (over 1.5 million students) were still using it in the twelfth grade. *See Malignant Neglect: Substance Abuse and America's Schools,* National Center on Addiction and Substance Abuse, September 2001, http://casacolumbia.org/usr_doc/malignant.pdf

188. Skinner v. Ry. Labor Executives' Ass'n, 489 U.S. 602 (1989); Nat'l Treasury Employees Union v. Von Raab, 489 U.S. 656 (1989). *See also* Juran v. Independence, Or. Sch. Dist., 898 F. Supp. 728 (D. Or. 1995) (finding that breathalyzer tests also implicate Fourth Amendment protections).

189. *Skinner,* 489 U.S. 602.

190. *Nat'l Treasury Employees Union,* 489 U.S. 656.

191. 515 U.S. 646 (1995).

192. *Id.* at 665.

court noted that the lower privacy expectations within the school environment are reduced even further when a student elects to participate in sports. In concluding that students had a decreased expectation of privacy, the Court specifically identified the communal undress in locker rooms and showers and the highly regulated nature of athletics, involving physical examinations, conduct rules related to training and dress, and minimum grade-point averages.

In examining the intrusiveness of the search, the Supreme Court found that the manner in which the urine samples were collected and monitored was not overly intrusive. Also, the Court stressed that the urinalysis report—which could reveal significant information about one's body, including not only drug use but also various medical conditions—was disclosed only to a limited number of individuals and was not reported to law-enforcement authorities. Furthermore, the Court emphasized that the search was directed narrowly at athletes, where drug use had been high and the risk for harm to themselves and others was significant.

In 2002, the Supreme Court in *Board of Education v. Earls* again reviewed a drug-testing policy but one that applied to students in all extracurricular activities, including athletics.[193] The policy required students to take a drug test prior to participation, to submit to random drug testing while involved in the activity, and to agree to be tested at any time when reasonable suspicion existed. Acknowledging that athletes' lower expectation of privacy was noted in *Vernonia,* the Court emphasized that the critical element in upholding the earlier policy was the school context. In sustaining the drug-testing policy in *Earls,* the Court reasoned that the collection procedures, like *Vernonia,* were minimally intrusive, information was kept in confidential files with limited access, and test results were not given to law-enforcement authorities. Based on these factors, the Court concluded that the drug-testing policy was not a significant invasion of students' privacy rights. Although the students had argued that no pervasive drug problem existed to justify an intrusive measure like drug-testing, the Court responded that it had never required such evidence before allowing the government to conduct suspicionless drug testing. Moreover, in light of the widespread use of drugs nationally and some evidence of increased use in this school, the Court found it "entirely reasonable" to enact this "particular drug testing policy."[194]

Similar drug tests of students have been upheld under state constitutions. For example, the Supreme Court of Indiana, adhering to reasoning analogous to the Supreme Court's decision in *Earls,* found a school's policy of random drug testing of students participating in athletics, extracurricular, and cocurricular activities permissible under state law.[195] Moreover, the court indicated that the fact the test was preventive and rehabilitative rather than punitive was an important factor under the Indiana Constitution.

Although it is clear that specific subgroups of students, such as athletes and participants in extracurricular activities, can be subjected to drug testing, courts have not

193. 122 S. Ct. 2559 (2002).

194. *Id.* at 2568.

195. Linke v. Northwestern Sch. Corp., 763 N.E.2d 972 (Ind. 2002).

permitted blanket testing of *all* students.[196] A Texas federal district court did not find exigent circumstances or other demonstrated compelling interests to justify a mandatory testing program of all students in grades 6 through 12.[197] Accordingly, the federal court held the program unreasonable and unconstitutional under the Fourth Amendment. The Seventh Circuit rejected a school district's policy requiring drug and alcohol testing of all students suspended for three or more days for violating any school rule.[198] In this case, the student was suspended for fighting, and upon his return to school was informed that he was required to submit to a test for drug and alcohol use. When he refused, school officials suspended him again; refusal to take the test was treated as admission of unlawful drug use. In ruling that the policy violated the Fourth Amendment, the court did not find a connection between fighting and use of drugs. Furthermore, the suspension procedures in Indiana require school officials to meet with students prior to suspension. At that point, it is possible to determine if individualized suspicion exists to support testing a particular student for drugs or alcohol.

Although blanket or random drug testing of all students is not likely to withstand judicial challenge, many schools subject students to urinalysis based on individualized suspicion, and such practices have not been invalidated by courts. Any drug-testing program, however, must be carefully constructed to avoid impairing students' Fourth Amendment privacy rights. The policy must be clearly developed, specifically identifying reasons for testing. Data collection procedures must be precise and well defined. Students and parents should be informed of the policy, and it is advisable to request students' consent prior to testing. If the test indicates drug use, the student must be given an opportunity to explain the results. Providing for the rehabilitation of the student rather than punishment strengthens the policy.

Police Involvement

A "reasonable suspicion" or a "reasonable cause to believe" standard is invoked in assessing the legality of school searches, but a higher standard generally is required when police officers are involved. The nature and extent of such involvement are important considerations in determining whether a search is reasonable. If the police role is one of finding evidence of a crime, probable cause would be required.[199]

---

196. With the vast majority of students participating in extracurricular activities, school districts appear to be moving toward testing all students.

197. Tannahill *ex rel.* Tannahill v. Lockney Indep. Sch. Dist., 133 F. Supp. 2d 919 (N.D. Tex. 2001).

198. Willis v. Anderson Cmty. Sch., 158 F.3d 415 (7th Cir. 1998). *See also* Joy v. Penn-Harris-Madison Sch. Corp., 212 F.3d 1052 (7th Cir. 2000) (upholding random drug and alcohol testing of students involved in extracurricular activities and students driving to school; court rejected testing students for nicotine to determine tobacco use); Penn-Harris-Madison Sch. Corp. v. Joy, 768 N.E.2d 940 (Ind. Ct. App. 2002) (finding, under state constitution, drug and alcohol testing permissible for students participating in extracurricular activities and students driving to school; nicotine testing violated students' liberty interests).

199. *See, e.g.,* Picha v. Wielgos, 410 F. Supp. 1214 (N.D. Ill. 1976); *In re* A. J. M., 617 So. 2d 1137 (Fla. Dist. Ct. App. 1993).

Whereas early decisions generally supported police participation in searches initiated and conducted by school officials, more recent decisions have tended to draw a sharp distinction between searches with and without police assistance.[200]

The more stringent judicial posture is represented in an Illinois decision.[201] In that case, the school principal received a call that led him to suspect that three girls possessed illegal drugs. On the superintendent's advice, he called the police to assist in the investigation. After the police arrived, the school nurse and the school psychologist searched each girl; however, no drugs were discovered. Subsequently, the students filed suit alleging that their civil rights had been violated. The court found that the police were not called merely to assist in maintaining school discipline but to search for evidence of a crime. Under the circumstances, the court concluded that the students had a constitutional right not to be searched unless the police had a warrant based on probable cause.

In contrast, the same Illinois court held that a police officer's involvement in persuading a student to relinquish the contents of his pockets did not violate Fourth Amendment rights under the *T.L.O.* standard.[202] The police officer's role was quite limited in this case. He was in the school building on another matter, and his role in the search was restricted simply to asking the student to empty his pockets. There was no police involvement in the investigation that led to detaining the student, nor was the evidence used for criminal prosecution. Furthermore, the facts did not indicate that the school and the police officer were attempting to avoid the warrant and probable cause requirements.

Similarly, the Eighth Circuit held that the assistance of a police officer assigned as a liaison officer in a high school did not subject a search for stolen property to the Fourth Amendment's probable cause standard.[203] Relying on *T.L.O.*, the court found no evidence that the search activities were at the behest of a police official. Rather, the vice principal had initiated and conducted the investigation with limited assistance from the police officer. Although the police officer had participated in a pat-down search, it occurred only after the vice principal had discovered evidence of drug-related activity in a student's purse. The court found this search by a school official working in conjunction with a police officer to be permissible. Other courts have recognized the special role of school liaison or resource officers, noting that the "reason-

---

200. Searches by trained police officers employed by, or assigned to, a school district generally are governed by the *T.L.O.* reasonable suspicion standard rather than the probable cause standard. *See, e.g.,* State v. Serna, 860 P.2d 1320 (Ariz. Ct. App. 1993); S.A. v. State, 654 N.E.2d 791 (Ind. Ct. App. 1995); *In re* Angelia D.B., 564 N.W.2d 682 (Wis. 1997).

201. *Picha,* 410 F. Supp. 1214.

202. Martens v. Dist. No. 220, 620 F. Supp. 29 (N.D. Ill. 1985). *See also* Commonwealth v. Carey, 554 N.E.2d 1199 (Mass. 1990).

203. Cason v. Cook 810 F.2d 188 (8th Cir. 1987). *See also* Shade v. City of Farmington, 309 F.3d 1054 (8th Cir. 2002) (holding a police officer's search of a student at the request of school officials permissible even though it occurred en route to a body shop class away from school grounds); *In re* P.E.A., 754 P.2d 382 (Colo. 1988).

able under the circumstances" standard applies when officers are working with school officials to maintain a safe school environment.[204]

The Washington Supreme Court ruled that a call from the chief of police informing a principal that two high school students were selling speed did not constitute "police action" or "joint action."[205] The court emphasized that the chief of police did not initiate the search or request that the principal search the students. Furthermore, the court noted that there would have been a duty to search the students and to report the results to the police regardless of the source of the information. In a strongly worded dissent, one justice argued that the standard in this case should have been probable cause, since the search was used for criminal prosecution, not for school disciplinary action. In a similar case, the Superior Court of Pennsylvania agreed that a student's Fourth Amendment rights were not violated when the principal conducted an investigation based on a report from the police.[206] Although the police informed the principal about an anonymous tip indicating that the student had brought a gun to school, school officials were not acting as agents of the police or at the behest of the police. Rather, they were carrying out their duty to protect the safety and welfare of the student body.

In a number of decisions applying the reasonable suspicion standard to school searches, courts have specifically noted or implied that this lower standard is not applicable if law-enforcement officials are involved. A Florida district court stated, "The reasonable suspicion standard does not apply in cases involving a search directed or participated in by a police officer."[207] Similarly, a Kentucky appellate court found the lower standard appropriate for searches in school settings in the absence of police participation.[208]

In a Fifth Circuit case, students claimed violation of their constitutional rights when police officers called them out of class for questioning about a rumored after-school fight that was going to occur later that day.[209] Reviewing the case in the context

---

204. *See, e.g., In re* Randy G., 110 Cal. Rptr. 2d 516 (2001); *In re* Josue T., 989 P.2d 431 (N.M. App. 1999); *In re* Angelia, 564 N.W.2d 682 (Wis. 1997). *But see* Commonwealth v. Williams, 749 A.2d 957 (Pa. Super. Ct. 2000), *appeal denied,* 764 A.2d 1069 (Pa. 2001) (holding that school district police officers did not have authority to search a student's car parked off school property).

205. State v. McKinnon, 558 P.2d 781 (Wash. 1977).

206. *In re* D.E.M., 727 A.2d 570 (Pa. Super. Ct. 1999).

207. State v. D.T.W., 425 So. 2d 1838, 1385 (Fla. Civ. App. 1983). *See also In re* A.J.M., 617 So. 2d 1137 (Fla. Dist. Ct. App. 1993).

208. Rone v. Daviess County Bd. of Educ., 655 S.W.2d 28 (Ky. Ct. App. 1983). *See also* D.R.C. v. State, 646 P.2d 252 (Alaska Ct. App. 1982) (recognizing the implicit assumption that police involvement would require probable cause).

209. Milligan v. City of Slidell, 226 F.3d 652 (5th Cir. 2000). *See also In re* Randy G., 110 Cal. Rptr. 516 (2001) (finding that brief detention and questioning by school security officers did not violate student's Fourth Amendment rights). *But see In re* R.H., 791 A.2d 331 (Pa. 2002) (holding that school police officers were authorized to exercise the same powers as municipal police on school property and thus required to provide a student *Miranda* warnings prior to an interrogation that led to criminal charges).

of the special needs of the school environment, the court found the temporary "sei-zure" reasonable and constitutional. Recognizing that students can be detained and questioned about school discipline issues by school officials, the court concluded that the police officers did no more than the school officials could have done themselves to deter the fight.

Troubling questions are raised when the fruits of warrantless searches result in the criminal prosecution of students.[210] Classifying searches on the basis of who con-ducts the search and for what purpose is inadequate. Searches cannot be discreetly classified as either administrative (school related) or criminal. A search may be clearly criminal when the purpose is to find evidence of a crime, thereby necessitating probable cause prior to the search. But administrative searches undertaken strictly for disciplinary or safety purposes may result in prosecution of students if evidence of a crime is uncovered and reported to the police. In fact, school authorities have a duty to alert the police if evidence of a crime is discovered, even though the search was initiated for school purposes.

Although many legal issues involving search and seizure in schools still are controversial, school personnel can generally protect themselves by adhering to a few basic guidelines. First, students and parents should be informed at the beginning of the school term of the procedures for conducting locker and personal searches. Second, any personal search conducted should be based on "reasonable suspicion" that the stu-dent possesses contraband that may be disruptive to the educational process. Third, the authorized person conducting a search should have another staff member present who can verify the procedures used in the search. Furthermore, school personnel should refrain from using strip searches or mass searches of groups of students. And, finally, if police officials conduct a search in the school, either with or without the school's involvement, it is advisable to ensure that they first obtain a search warrant.

Remedies for Unlawful Disciplinary Actions

Several remedies are available to students who are unlawfully disciplined by school authorities. When physical punishment is involved, students can seek damages through assault and battery suits against those who inflicted the harm.[211] For unwar-ranted suspensions or expulsions, students are entitled to reinstatement without pen-alty to grades and to have their school records expunged of any reference to the illegal disciplinary action.[212] Remedies for violation of procedural due process rights may include reversal of a school board's decision rather than remand for further proceed-ings.[213] If academic penalties are unlawfully imposed, grades must be restored and

210. Even if evidence is declared inadmissible in criminal proceedings, it can be used by school personnel in a suspension or expulsion hearing.
211. *See* Ingraham v. Wright, 430 U.S. 651 (1977).
212. *See, e.g.,* John A. v. San Bernardino City Unified Sch. Dist., 654 P.2d 242 (Cal. 1982); McEntire v. Brevard County Sch. Bd., 471 So. 2d 1287 (Fla. Civ. App. 1985); Ruef v. Jordan, 605 N.Y.S.2d 530 (App. Div. 1993).
213. *See, e.g., In re* Roberts, 563 S.E.2d 37 (N.C. Ct. App. 2002).

transcripts altered accordingly.[214] For unconstitutional searches, illegally seized evidence may be suppressed, school records may be expunged, and damages may be awarded if the unlawful search results in substantial injury to the student.[215] Courts also may award court costs when students successfully challenge disciplinary actions.

The Supreme Court has held that school officials can be sued for monetary damages in state courts as well as in federal courts under 42 U.S.C. Section 1983 if they arbitrarily violate students' federally protected rights in disciplinary proceedings.[216] In *Wood v. Strickland,* the Court declared that ignorance of the law is not a valid defense to shield school officials from liability if they should have known that their actions would impair students' clearly established federal rights.[217] Under *Wood,* a showing of malice is not always required to prove that the actions of school officials were taken in bad faith, but a mere mistake in carrying out duties does not render school authorities liable. The Court also recognized in *Wood* that educators are not charged with predicting the future direction of constitutional law. Other courts have reiterated school officials' potential liability in connection with student disciplinary proceedings, but to date, students have not been as successful as teachers in obtaining monetary awards for constitutional violations. Courts have been reluctant to delineate students' "clearly established" rights, the impairment of which would warrant compensatory damages.

In 1978, the Supreme Court placed restrictions on the amount of damages that could be awarded to students in instances involving the impairment of procedural due process rights. In *Carey v. Piphus,* the Court declared that students who were suspended without a hearing, but were not otherwise injured, could recover only nominal damages (not to exceed one dollar).[218] This case involved two Chicago students who had been suspended without hearings for allegedly violating school regulations. They brought suit against the school district, claiming an abridgment of their constitutional rights. The Supreme Court ruled that substantial damages could be recovered only if the suspensions were unjustified. Accordingly, the case was remanded for the district court to determine whether the students would have been suspended if correct procedures had been followed.

This decision may appear to have strengthened the position of school boards in exercising discretion in disciplinary proceedings, but the Supreme Court indicated that students might be entitled to substantial damages if suspensions are proven to be

---

214. *See, e.g.,* Shuman v. Cumberland Valley Sch. Dist. Bd. of Dirs., 536 A.2d 490 (Pa. Commw. Ct. 1988); Katzman v. Cumberland Valley Sch. Dist., 479 A.2d 671 (Pa. Commw. Ct. 1984).

215. *See, e.g.,* Anable v. Ford, 663 F. Supp. 149 (W.D. Ark. 1985); Commonwealth v. Cass, 666 A.2d 313 (Pa. Super. Ct. 1995); Coronada v. State, 835 S.W.2d 636 (Tex. Crim. App. 1992).

216. Howlett v. Rose, 496 U.S. 356 (1990), *on remand,* 571 So. 2d 29 (Fla. Dist. Ct. App. 1990); Wood v. Strickland, 420 U.S. 308 (1975). 42 U.S.C. § 1983 provides a damages remedy for deprivations of federally protected rights under color of state law. *See also* Logiodice v. Trs., 296 F.3d 22 (1st Cir. 2002) (holding that private school receiving tuition payments for high school students from several public school districts was not a state actor requiring it to provide a student procedural due process prior to suspension); text accompanying note 209, Chapter 11.

217. 420 U.S. 308 (1975).

218. 435 U.S. 247 (1978).

unwarranted. To illustrate, an Arkansas federal district court assessed punitive damages against a high school coach for intentionally impairing students' free speech rights in a disciplinary action.[219] Students also have received damages when subjected to unlawful searches. For example, the Seventh Circuit assessed damages against school officials for an intrusive body search.[220] The New Mexico Supreme Court affirmed substantial compensatory and punitive damages to two high school students subjected to an unconstitutional strip search.[221] In addition to damages, students also may be awarded attorneys' fees.

Educators should take every precaution to afford fair and impartial treatment to students. School personnel would be wise to provide at least an informal hearing if in doubt as to whether a particular situation necessitates due process. Liability never results from the provision of too much due process, but damages can be assessed if violations of procedural rights result in unjustified suspensions, expulsions, or other disciplinary actions. Although constitutional and statutory due process requirements do not mandate that a specific procedure be followed in every situation, courts will carefully study the record to ensure that any procedural deficiencies do not impede the student's efforts to present a full defense.

Also, school authorities should ensure that constraints placed on student conduct are necessary for the proper functioning of the school. Educators have considerable latitude in controlling student behavior to maintain an appropriate educational environment and should not feel that the judiciary has curtailed their authority to discipline students. As noted in *Goss,* courts "have imposed requirements which are, if anything, less than a fair-minded principal would impose."[222]

Conclusion

In 1969, Justice Black noted that "school discipline, like parental discipline, is an integral and important part of training our children to be good citizens—to be better citizens."[223] Accordingly, school personnel have been empowered with the authority and duty to regulate pupil behavior in order to protect the interests of the student body and the school. Reasonable sanctions can be imposed if students do not adhere to legitimate conduct regulations. Courts, however, will intervene if disciplinary procedures are arbitrary or impair students' protected rights. Although the law pertaining to certain aspects of student discipline remains in a state of flux, judicial decisions support the following generalizations.

219. Boyd v. Bd. of Dirs., 612 F. Supp. 86 (E.D. Ark. 1985).

220. Doe v. Renfrow, 631 F.2d 91 (7th Cir. 1980).

221. Kennedy v. Dexter Consol. Schs., 10 P.3d 115 (N.M. 2000).

222. Goss v. Lopez, 419 U.S. 565, 583 (1975).

223. Tinker v. Des Moines Indep. Sch. Dist., 393 U.S. 503, 524 (1969) (Black, J., dissenting).

1. School authorities must be able to substantiate that any disciplinary regulation enacted is reasonable and necessary for the management of the school or for the welfare of pupils and school employees.

2. All regulations should be stated in precise terms and disseminated to students and parents.

3. Punishments for rule infractions should be appropriate for the offense and the characteristics of the offender (e.g., age, mental condition, and prior behavior).

4. Some type of procedural due process should be afforded to students prior to the imposition of punishments. For minor penalties, an informal hearing suffices; for serious punishments, more formal procedures are required (e.g., notification of parents, representation by counsel, opportunity to cross-examine witnesses).

5. Students can be punished for misbehavior occurring off school grounds if the conduct directly relates to the welfare of the school.

6. Suspensions and expulsions are legitimate punishments if accompanied by appropriate procedural safeguards and not arbitrarily imposed.

7. The transfer of students to different classes, programs, or schools for disciplinary reasons should be accompanied by procedural due process.

8. If not prohibited by state law or school board policy, reasonable corporal punishment can be used as a disciplinary technique.

9. Use of excessive force in administering corporal punishment that rises to the level of *shocking to the conscience* may violate a student's substantive due process rights.

10. Academic sanctions for nonacademic reasons should be reasonable, related to absences from class, and serve a legitimate school purpose.

11. School personnel can search students' lockers or personal effects on reasonable suspicion that the students possess contraband that is either illegal or in violation of school policy.

12. Strip searches should be avoided unless evidence substantiates that there is probable cause to search or an emergency exists.

13. General scanning of students with metal detectors is only minimally intrusive on students' Fourth Amendment rights when weighed against school officials' interest in providing a safe school environment.

14. The use of canines to sniff objects is generally not viewed as a search, but courts are not in agreement regarding whether their use with students is a search that would require individualized suspicion.

15. Students who voluntarily elect to participate in athletics and extracurricular activities may be subjected to random drug testing; others are required to submit to urinalysis based on individualized suspicion.

16. When law-enforcement officials are involved in the search of a student, it is advisable to secure a search warrant.

17. If students are unlawfully punished, they are entitled to be restored (without penalty) to their status prior to the imposition of the punishment and to have their records expunged of any reference to the illegal punishment.

18. School officials can be held liable for compensatory damages if unlawful punishments result in substantial injury to students (e.g., unwarranted suspensions from school); however, only nominal damages, not to exceed one dollar, can be assessed against school officials for the abridgment of students' procedural rights (e.g., the denial of an adequate hearing).

8

Terms and Conditions of Employment

Maintenance of a uniform system of public schools is one of the preeminent functions of the state, with the responsibility for the governance of education being vested with the legislature. The judiciary has clearly recognized the plenary power of the legislature in establishing, conducting, and regulating all public education functions. The legislature, through statutory law, establishes the boundaries within which educational systems operate; however, the actual administration of school systems is delegated to state boards of education, state departments of education, and local boards of education. These agencies enact rules and regulations pursuant to legislative policy for the operation of public schools.

Although state statutes and regulations are prominent in defining school personnel's employment rights, they cannot be viewed independently of state and federal constitutional provisions, civil rights laws, and negotiated agreements between school boards and teacher unions. These provisions may restrict or modify options available under the state school code. For example, the authority to transfer teachers may be vested in the school board, but the board cannot use this power to discipline a teacher for exercising protected constitutional rights. The board's discretion may be further limited if it has agreed in the master contract with the teachers' union to follow certain procedures prior to transferring an employee.

Among the areas affected by state statutory and regulatory provisions are the terms and conditions of educators' employment. With the intense public pressure to improve students' academic performance, most states have enacted education reform legislation demanding greater accountability from public schools. These efforts have had an impact not only on the curriculum and operation of schools but also on expectations for educators. Local school boards must ensure that the new demands are met, and courts have recognized their expansive authority to fulfill these responsibilities. This chapter presents an overview of state requirements pertaining to certification, employment, contracts, tenure, and related conditions of employment. Also, two topics of increasing interest to educators, using copyrighted materials and reporting child abuse, are addressed. Specific job requirements that implicate constitutional rights or antidiscrimination mandates are reviewed in subsequent chapters.

Licensure or Certification

To qualify for a teaching position in public schools, prospective teachers must acquire a valid license or certificate (terms used interchangeably) from their states. Licenses are issued according to each state's statutory provisions. States have not only the right but also the duty to establish minimum qualifications and to ensure that teachers meet these standards. Although the responsibility for licensing resides with state legislatures, administration of the process has been delegated to state boards of education and departments of education.

Licenses are granted primarily on the basis of professional preparation. In most states, educational requirements include a college degree, with minimum credit hours or courses in various curricular areas. Other prerequisites to certification may include a minimum age, U.S. citizenship, signing of a loyalty oath, and passage of an academic examination. Additionally, an applicant for certification may be required to have "good moral character." The definition of what constitutes good character often is elusive, with a number of factors entering into the determination.[1] Courts generally will not rule on the wisdom of a certifying agency's assessment of character; they will intervene only if statutory or constitutional rights are abridged.

Certification of teachers by examination was common prior to the expansion of teacher education programs in colleges and universities. Then, for many years, only a few southern states required passage of an exam. With the emphasis on improving the quality of teachers and the strong movement toward standards-based licensure, most states now require some type of standardized test or performance-based assessment for teacher education programs, initial license, and/or license renewal.[2] If a state establishes a test or assessment process as an essential eligibility requirement, it can deny a license to individuals who do not pass.[3] States using standardized tests prima-

1. *See, e.g.,* Arrocha v. Bd. of Educ., 690 N.Y.S.2d 503 (1999) (concluding that an individual's conviction for selling cocaine affected his ability to serve as a role model for high school students); Bay v. State Bd. of Educ., 378 P.2d 558, 561 (Or. 1963) (finding that conviction for burglary eight years prior to application for a teaching certificate was pertinent in assessing character; court noted that character embraced all "qualities and deficiencies regarding traits of personality, behavior, integrity, temperament, consideration, sportsmanship, altruism, etc.").

2. Almost half the states have set up professional standards boards to govern and regulate standards-based criteria and assessment for licenses. The principal purpose of these boards, whose membership is comprised primarily of teachers, is to address issues of educator preparation, licensure, and relicensure.

3. *See, e.g.,* Ass'n of Mexican-American Educators v. California, 231 F.3d 572 (9th Cir. 2000); Jacobsen v. Tillman, 17 F. Supp. 2d 1018 (D. Minn. 1998); Feldman v. Bd. of Educ., 686 N.Y.S.2d 842 (App. Div. 1999). *See also* Mass. Fed'n of Teachers v. Bd. of Educ., 767 N.E.2d 549 (Mass. 2002) (finding the imposition of a math assessment test for recertification of teachers in certain schools to be within the state board's authority).

rily employ the National Teachers Examination. The U.S. Supreme Court has upheld its use, even though the test has been shown to disproportionately disqualify minority applicants.[4] (Constitutional and statutory challenges to employment tests are discussed in Chapter 10.)

Signing a loyalty oath may be a condition of obtaining a teaching license, but such oaths cannot be used to restrict association rights guaranteed under the United States Constitution. The Supreme Court has invalidated oaths that require teacher applicants to swear that they are not members of subversive organizations;[5] however, teachers can be required to sign an oath pledging faithful performance of duties and support for the Federal Constitution and an individual state's constitution.[6] According to the Supreme Court, these oaths must be narrowly limited to affirmation of support for the government and a pledge not to act forcibly to overthrow the government.[7]

As a condition of licensure, a teacher may be required to be a citizen of the United States. In 1979, the Supreme Court addressed whether such a New York statutory requirement violated the Equal Protection Clause of the Fourteenth Amendment.[8] Under the New York education laws, a teacher who is eligible for citizenship but refuses to apply for naturalization cannot be certified. Although the Supreme Court has placed restrictions on the states' ability to exclude aliens from governmental employment, it has recognized that certain functions are "so bound up with the operation of the state as a governmental entity as to permit the exclusion from those functions of all persons who have not become part of the process of self-government."[9] Applying this principle, the Court held that teaching is an integral "governmental function"; thus, a state must show only a rational relationship between a citizenship requirement and a legitimate state interest. The Court concluded that New York's interest in furthering its educational goals justified the citizenship mandate for teachers.

Some litigation has focused on legislative efforts to alter licensure standards by imposing new or additional requirements as prerequisites to renew a license. The Supreme Court of Texas held that teachers possessing life certificates could be required to pass an examination as a condition of continued employment.[10] Since the certificate was found to be a "license" rather than a "contract," the court held that new

---

4. United States v. South Carolina, 445 F. Supp. 1094 (D.S.C. 1977), *aff'd sub nom.* Nat'l Educ. Ass'n v. South Carolina, 434 U.S. 1026 (1978). *See also* text accompanying note 33, Chapter 10. In challenges alleging discrimination, consent decrees between states and plaintiffs have contained agreements for the development of tests that reduce the discriminatory impact on minority candidates. *See, e.g.,* Allen v. Ala. State Bd. of Educ., 164 F.3d 1347 (11th Cir. 1999), *on remand,* Allen v. Ala. State Bd. of Educ., 190 F.R.D. 602 (M.D. Ala. 2000).

5. Keyishian v. Bd. of Regents, 385 U.S. 589 (1967).

6. Ohlson v. Phillips, 397 U.S. 317 (1970).

7. Cole v. Richardson, 405 U.S. 676 (1972); Connell v. Higginbotham, 403 U.S. 207 (1971).

8. Ambach v. Norwick, 441 U.S. 68 (1979).

9. *Id.* at 73–74.

10. State v. Project Principle, 724 S.W.2d 387 (Tex. 1987). *See also* Fields v. Hallsville Indep. Sch. Dist., 906 F.2d 1017 (5th Cir. 1990): Mass. Fed'n of Teachers v. Bd. of Educ., 767 N.E.2d 549 (Mass. 2002).

conditions for retention of the certificate could be imposed. The Supreme Court of Connecticut, recognizing teaching certificates as contracts, still upheld the state's authority to replace permanent certificates with five-year certificates renewable upon the completion of continuing education requirements.[11] Holding that this change was constitutionally acceptable, the court found only a minimal impairment of contractual rights, which could be justified by the state's significant interest in improving public education. Under statutory law, however, the Supreme Court of Rhode Island found that the State Board of Regents for Elementary and Secondary Education could not revoke valid five-year certificates for teachers' failure to meet new agency requirements.[12] Since state law provided that certificates were valid for a specified period of time and could be revoked only for cause, teachers could not be required to meet a state agency's new requirements until their certificates expired.

Licenses are issued for designated periods of time under various classifications, such as emergency, temporary, provisional, professional, and permanent. Renewing or upgrading a license may require additional university coursework, other continuing education activities, or passage of an examination. Licenses also specify professional position (e.g., teacher, administrator, librarian), subject areas (e.g., history, English, math), and grade levels (e.g., elementary, high school). Where licensure subject areas have been established, a teacher must possess a valid license to teach a specific subject. A school district's failure to employ licensed teachers may result in the loss of state accreditation and financial support.

A certificate or license indicates only that a teacher has satisfied minimum state requirements; no absolute right exists to acquire a position. It does not entitle an individual to employment in a particular district or guarantee employment in the state, nor does it prevent a local school board from attaching additional prerequisites for employment. For example, an Iowa appellate court upheld a local school board's authority to require physical education teachers to complete training in cardiopulmonary resuscitation and water-safety instruction.[13] If a local board imposes additional standards, however, the requirements must be uniformly applied.

Teaching credentials must be in proper order to ensure full employment rights.[14] Under most state laws, teachers must file their certificates with the district of employment.[15] Failure to renew a license prior to expiration or to meet educational require-

11. Conn. Educ. Ass'n v. Tirozzi, 554 A.2d 1065 (Conn. 1989).
12. Reback v. R.I. Bd. of Regents for Elementary and Secondary Educ., 560 A.2d 357 (R.I. 1989).
13. Pleasant Valley Educ. Ass'n v. Pleasant Valley Cmty. Sch. Dist., 449 N.W.2d 894 (Iowa Ct. App. 1989).
14. See, e.g., Keatley v. Mercer County Bd. of Educ., 490 S.E.2d 306 (W. Va. 1997) (ruling that an applicant who does not physically possess a certificate can be hired if all requirements will have been met for certification at the time of appointment).
15. See, e.g., Lucio v. Sch. Bd. of Indep. Sch. Dist. No. 625, 574 N.W.2d 737 (Minn. Ct. App. 1998) (ruling that the school district has a duty to determine the licensure status of teachers). See also Woodrum v. Rolling Hills Bd. of Educ., 421 N.E.2d 859 (Ohio 1981) (holding that failure to file a renewal certificate with the board did not result in a loss of tenure rights where the board had been notified of the renewal by the state).

ments necessary to maintain or acquire a higher-grade license can result in loss of employment. Without proper licensure, a teaching contract is unenforceable.[16]

The state is empowered not only to license teachers but also to suspend[17] or revoke licenses. Although a local board may initiate charges against a teacher, only the state can alter the status of a teacher's license. Revocation is a harsh penalty, generally foreclosing future employment as a teacher. As such, it must be based on statutory cause with full procedural rights provided to the teacher.[18] The most frequently cited grounds for revoking licenses are immorality, incompetency, contract violation, and neglect of duty. Examples of actions justifying revocation include misrepresenting experience and credentials in a job application and altering one's license (immorality);[19] theft of drugs and money (conduct unbecoming a teacher);[20] assault on a minor female (lack of good moral character);[21] and harassment of other teachers, removal of confidential files, and inappropriate discussion of sex life (unprofessional conduct).[22]

When revocation or suspension of a license is being considered, assessment of a teacher's competency encompasses not only classroom performance but also actions outside the school setting that may impair his or her effectiveness. The California Supreme Court found that a teacher's participation in a "swingers' club" and disguised appearance on television discussing nonconventional sexual behavior justified revocation of license on grounds of unfitness to teach.[23] An Ohio appellate court ruled that a teacher's involvement in welfare fraud constituted conduct unbecoming a teacher, justifying revocation of her license.[24] The Supreme Court of Kansas concluded that an act of burglary was sufficiently related to a teacher's fitness to teach to warrant suspension of the license for such a crime.[25] Courts will not overturn the judg-

---

16. *See, e.g.,* Maasjo v. McLaughlin Sch. Dist., 489 N.W.2d 618 (S.D. 1992) (holding that a school board could terminate a superintendent because he lacked proper administrative endorsement).

17. *See, e.g.,* Prof'l Standards Comm'n v. Denham, 556 S.E.2d 920 (Ga. Ct. App. 2001) (upholding suspension of teacher's certificate for six months for changing a student's answers on a standardized test).

18. *See, e.g.,* Joyell v. Comm'r of Educ., 696 A.2d 1039 (Conn. App. Ct. 1997); Gee v. Prof'l Practices Comm'n, 491 S.E.2d 375 (Ga. 1997); Petron v. Dep't of Educ., 726 A.2d 1091 (Pa. Commw. Ct. 1999). *See also* text accompanying note 61, Chapter 11, for details of procedural due process.

19. Nanko v. Dep't of Educ., 663 A.2d 312 (Pa. Commw. Ct. 1995). *See also* Patterson v. Superintendent of Pub. Instruction, 887 P.2d 411 (Wash. Ct. App. 1995) (supporting six-month suspension of certificate for falsifying and omitting information from application).

20. Crumpler v. State Bd. of Educ., 594 N.E.2d 1071 (Ohio Ct. App. 1991).

21. *In re* Morrill, 765 A.2d 699 (N.H. 2001).

22. Bills v. Ariz. State Bd. of Educ., 819 P.2d 952 (Ariz. Ct. App. 1991).

23. Pettit v. State Bd. of Educ., 513 P.2d 889 (Cal. 1973). In an earlier case, however, the same court held that an isolated incident of private homosexuality did not justify license revocation; no connection was shown between the teacher's activity and effectiveness to teach. Morrison v. State Bd. of Educ., 461 P.2d 375 (Cal. 1969). *See also* Ulrich v. State, 555 N.E.2d 172 (Ind. Ct. App. 1990) (ruling that the rape of a student warranted revocation of teacher's license).

24. Stelzer v. State Bd. of Educ., 595 N.E.2d 489 (Ohio Ct. App. 1991).

25. Hainline v. Bond, 824 P.2d 959 (Kan. 1992).

ment of state boards regarding an educator's fitness to teach unless evidence clearly establishes that the decision is unreasonable or unlawful.[26]

Employment by Local School Boards

As noted, a certificate or license does not guarantee employment in a state; it attests only that educators have met minimum state requirements. The decision to employ a certified teacher or administrator is among the discretionary powers of local school boards.[27] Although such powers are broad, school board actions may not be arbitrary, be capricious, or violate an individual's statutory or constitutional rights.[28] Furthermore, boards must comply with mandated statutory procedures as well as locally adopted procedures.[29] Employment decisions also must be neutral as to race, religion, national origin, and gender.[30] Unless protected individual rights are abridged, courts will not review the wisdom of a local school board's judgment in employment decisions made in good faith.

The responsibility for hiring teachers and administrators is vested in the school board as a collective body and cannot be delegated to the superintendent or board members individually.[31] In most states, binding employment agreements between a teacher or an administrator and the school board must be approved at legally scheduled board meetings. A number of state laws specify that the superintendent must make employment recommendations to the board; however, the board is not compelled to follow these recommendations unless mandated to do so by law.

---

26. *See, e.g.,* Epstein v. Benson, 618 N.W.2d 224 (Wis. Ct. App. 2000) (concluding that carrying a concealed weapon is a crime but did not constitute immoral conduct to justify revocation of teaching certificate).

27. *See, e.g.,* Carter County Bd. of Educ. v. Carter County Educ. Ass'n, 56 S.W.3d 1 (Tenn. Ct. App. 1996) (holding that selection of principals is a discretionary right of school board; appointment is not subject to collective bargaining). In some instances, this discretionary power may be vested in local school-based councils. For example, under the Chicago School Reform Act, the local school council is authorized to appoint a principal without school board approval, 105 ILCS 5/34-2.2(c) (2001). Massachusetts' Education Reform Act lodges the responsibility for hiring and firing of teachers and other building personnel with school principals under the supervision of the superintendent. Mass. Gen. Laws ch. 71 § 59B (2002).

28. *See generally* Chapter 9 for a discussion of teachers' constitutional rights.

29. *See, e.g.,* Mingo County Bd. of Educ. v. Jones, 512 S.E.2d 597 (W. Va. 1998).

30. *See generally* Chapter 10 for a discussion of discriminatory employment practices. Under limited circumstances, gender may be a bona fide occupational qualification (e.g., supervision of the girls' locker room).

31. *See, e.g.,* Crawford v. Bd. of Educ., 453 N.E.2d 627 (Ohio 1983); Fortney v. Sch. Dist., 321 N.W.2d 225 (Wis. 1982).

School boards possess extensive authority in establishing job requirements and conditions of employment for school personnel.[32] The following sections examine the school board's power to impose specific conditions on employment and to assign personnel.

Employment Requirements

The state's establishment of minimum certification standards for educators does not preclude the local school board from requiring higher professional or academic standards as long as they are applied in a uniform and nondiscriminatory manner.[33] For example, school boards often establish continuing education requirements for teachers, and a board's right to dismiss teachers for failing to satisfy such requirements has been upheld by the Supreme Court.[34] The Court concluded that school officials merely had to establish that the requirement was rationally related to a legitimate state objective, which in this case was to provide competent, well-trained teachers.

School boards can adopt reasonable health and physical requirements for school personnel. Courts have recognized that such standards are necessary to safeguard the health and welfare of students and other employees. The First Circuit held that a school board could compel an administrator to submit to a psychiatric examination as a condition of continued employment because a reasonable basis existed for the board members to believe that the administrator might jeopardize the safety of students.[35] Similarly, the Sixth Circuit ruled that a school board could justifiably order a teacher to submit to mental and physical examinations when his aberrant behavior affected job performance.[36]

Health and physical requirements imposed on school personnel, however, must not be applied in an arbitrary manner. The Second Circuit found arbitrary and unreasonable a New York school board's insistence that a female teacher on extended sick leave for a back ailment be examined by the district's male physician rather than a female physician (to be selected by the board).[37] School board standards for physical fitness also must be rationally related to ability to perform teaching duties. A New

32. *See, e.g.,* Butcher v. Gilmer County Bd. of Educ., 429 S.E.2d 903 (W. Va. 1993). *See also* Eide v. Oldham-Ramona Sch. Dist. No. 39-5, 516 N.W.2d 322 (S.D. 1994) (finding that school district must follow its own established hiring policy); Bolyard v. Kanawha County Bd. of Educ., 459 S.E.2d 411 (W. Va. 1995) (concluding that the board had reasonably exercised its hiring discretion in accordance with statutory requirements).

33. *See, e.g.,* Dennery v. Bd. of Educ., 622 A.2d 858 (N.J. 1993).

34. Harrah Indep. Sch. Dist. v. Martin, 440 U.S. 194 (1979) (upholding policy requiring teachers to earn an additional five semester hours of college credit every three years while employed).

35. Daury v. Smith, 842 F.2d 9 (1st Cir. 1988).

36. Sullivan v. River Valley Sch. Dist., 197 F.3d 804 (6th Cir. 1999). *See also* Moore v. Bd. of Educ., 134 F.3d 781 (6th Cir. 1998) (upholding a finding of insubordination for refusing to submit to mental and physical examinations).

37. Gargiul v. Tompkins, 704 F.2d 661 (2d Cir. 1983), *vacated and remanded,* 465 U.S. 1016 (1984). *See also* Harris v. Bd. of Educ., 798 F. Supp. 1331 (S.D. Ohio 1992).

York appellate court found that obesity per se was not reasonably related to ability to teach or maintain discipline.[38]

In addition, regulations must not contravene various state and federal laws designed to protect the rights of persons with disabilities. For example, in a Pennsylvania case, the Third Circuit ruled that school officials could not refuse to consider blind individuals as teachers for sighted students.[39] The United States Supreme Court ruled that tuberculosis, a contagious disease, is a disability under federal antidiscrimination provisions that protect otherwise qualified individuals with disabilities from adverse employment consequences. Accordingly, a school district could not dismiss a teacher for chronic recurrency of tuberculosis without evidence that the teacher was otherwise unqualified to perform her job or that accommodations would place undue hardships on the school district.[40]

Under state laws, most school boards are required to conduct criminal records checks of all employees prior to employment. The screening process may require individuals to consent to fingerprinting. Concern for students' safety also has led some school districts to require teacher applicants to submit to drug testing. The Sixth Circuit upheld such testing, noting that teachers occupy safety-sensitive positions in a highly regulated environment with diminished privacy expectations.[41]

School boards also may require school personnel to live within the school district as a condition of employment. Typically, residency requirements have been imposed in urban communities and encompass all city employees including educators. Proponents contend that the policy builds stronger community relationships and stabilizes the city tax base. Such requirements, however, have been challenged as impairing equal protection rights under the United States Constitution by interfering with interstate and intrastate travel. The Supreme Court has upheld a municipal regulation requiring all employees hired after a specified date in Philadelphia to be residents of the city.[42] Those already employed were not required to alter their residence. A fire department employee who was terminated when he moved to New Jersey challenged the requirement as unconstitutionally interfering with interstate travel. In upholding the regulation, the Court distinguished a requirement of residency of a given duration prior to employment (which violates the right to interstate travel) from a continuing residency requirement applied after employment. The Court concluded that a continuing residency requirement, if "appropriately defined and uniformly

38. Parolisi v. Bd. of Exam'rs, 285 N.Y.S.2d 936 (Sup. Ct. 1967).

39. Gurmankin v. Costanzo, 556 F.2d 184 (3d Cir. 1977).

40. Sch. Bd. of Nassau County, Fla. v. Arline, 480 U.S. 273 (1987). *See also* Chapter 10 for discussion of discrimination based on disabilities.

41. Knox County Educ. Ass'n v. Knox County Bd. of Educ., 158 F.3d 361 (6th Cir. 1998). *But see* Chandler v. Miller, 520 U.S. 305 (1997) (holding that a statute requiring all political candidates to submit to a drug test is unconstitutional; context did not justify suspicionless testing; Warren v. Bd. of Educ., 200 F. Supp. 2d 1053 (E.D. Mo. 2001) (denying the school board's motion for summary judgment when a teacher was required to submit to a drug test without evidence of individualized suspicion of wrong-doing). For further discussion of Fourth Amendment rights of employees, *see* text accompanying note 191, Chapter 9.

42. McCarthy v. Phila. Civil Serv. Comm'n, 424 U.S. 645 (1976).

applied," does not violate an individual's constitutional rights.[43] Lower courts have applied similar reasoning in upholding residency requirements for public educators.[44] Although residency requirements after employment do not violate the Constitution, they may be impermissible under state law.[45]

Unlike residency requirements, school board policies requiring employees to send their children to public schools have been declared unconstitutional. Parents have a constitutionally protected right to direct the upbringing of their children that cannot be restricted without a compelling state interest. The Eleventh Circuit held that a school board policy requiring employees to enroll their children in public schools could not be justified to promote an integrated public school system and good relationships among teachers when weighed against the right of parents to direct the education of their children.[46]

Assignment of Personnel and Duties

The authority to assign teachers to schools within a district resides with the board of education.[47] As with employment, in general, these decisions must not be arbitrary, made in bad faith, or in retaliation for the exercise of protected rights.[48] Within the limits of a license, a teacher can be assigned to teach in any school at any grade level.[49] Assignments designated in the teacher's contract, however, cannot be changed during a contractual period without the teacher's consent.[50] That is, a board cannot reassign a teacher to a first-grade class if the contract specifies a fifth-grade assignment. If the

43. *Id.* at 647. In several later cases, the Supreme Court reiterated that policies requiring residence prior to employment for conferring certain benefits or employment preference violate the Equal Protection Clause and the constitutional right to travel. *See* Attorney Gen. of N.Y. v. Soto-Lopez, 476 U.S. 898 (1986); Hooper v. Bernalillo County Assessor, 472 U.S. 612 (1985); Zobel v. Williams, 457 U.S. 55 (1982).

44. *See, e.g.,* Wardwell v. Bd. of Educ., 529 F.2d 625 (6th Cir. 1976).

45. *See, e.g.,* Ind. Code Ann. 20 & 6.1-6-12 (2002); Mass. Gen. Laws ch. 71 § 38 (2002). As urban school systems face difficulty in recruiting teachers, some have abolished their residency requirements, such as Philadelphia, Pittsburgh, and Providence, R.I. *See* Jeff Archer, "City Districts Lifting Rules on Residency," *Education Week* (January 16, 2002), pp. 1, 13.

46. Stough v. Crenshaw County Bd. of Educ., 744 F.2d 1479 (11th Cir. 1984). *See also* Peterson v. Minidoka County Sch. Dist. No. 331, 118 F.3d 1351 (9th Cir. 1997); Curlee v. Fyfe, 902 F.2d 401 (5th Cir. 1990); Brantley v. Surles, 804 F.2d 321 (5th Cir. 1986).

47. *See, e.g.,* Thomas v. Smith, 897 F.2d 154 (5th Cir. 1989); Sekor v. Bd. of Educ., 689 A.2d 1112 (Conn. 1997). *See also* Lazuk v. Denver Sch. Dist. No. 1, 22 P.3d 548 (Colo. Ct. App. 2000) (ruling that state law permitted a school board to delegate the power to transfer a teacher; state statute limited the transfer to positions the teacher is qualified to teach).

48. *See, e.g.,* Hinson v. Clinch County, Ga. Bd. of Educ., 231 F.3d 821 (11th Cir. 2000); Harris v. Victoria Indep. Sch. Dist., 168 F.3d 216 (5th Cir. 1999); LeVake v. Indep. Sch. Dist., 625 N.W.2d 502 (Minn. Ct. App. 2001), *review denied,* C8-00-1613, 2001 Minn. LEXIS 434 (Minn. July 24, 2001).

49. *See, e.g.,* Gordon v. Nicoletti, 84 F. Supp. 2d 304 (D. Conn. 2000); Wells v. Del Norte Sch. Dist. C-7, 753 P.2d 770 (Colo. Ct. App. 1987); Adlerstein v. Bd. of Educ., 485 N.Y.S.2d 1 (1984). *See also* Kelleher v. Flawn, 761 F.2d 1079 (5th Cir. 1985) (finding no entitlement to teach specific courses).

50. The collective bargaining agreement also may limit a school board's discretion in transferring teachers. *See, e.g.,* Leary v. Daeschner, 228 F.3d 729 (6th Cir. 2000).

contract designates only a teaching assignment within the district, the assignment still must be in the teacher's area of certification. Also, objective, nondiscriminatory standards must be used in any employment or assignment decision.[51] Assignments to achieve racial balance may be permitted in school districts that have not eliminated the effects of school segregation. Any racial classification, however, must be temporary and necessary to eradicate the effects of prior discrimination.[52]

School boards retain the authority to assign or transfer teachers, but such decisions often are challenged as demotions requiring procedural due process. Depending on statutory law, factors considered in determining whether a reassignment is a demotion may include reduction in salary, responsibility, and stature of position.[53] A Pennsylvania teacher contested a transfer from a ninth-grade to a sixth-grade class as a demotion. The court, noting the equivalency of the positions, stated that "there is no less importance, dignity, responsibility, authority, prestige, or compensation in the elementary grades than in secondary."[54] The reassignment of an Ohio classroom teacher as a permanent substitute or floating teacher, however, was found to be a demotion in violation of the state tenure law.[55] The court recognized the pervasive authority of the superintendent and board to make teaching assignments, but noted that other statutory provisions, such as the state tenure law, may limit this power. This reduction in status without notice and a hearing was found to deprive the teacher of due process guarantees.

Administrative reassignments frequently are challenged as demotions because of reductions in salary, responsibility, and status of the position. Again, as in the assignment of teachers, statutory law defines an individual employee's rights. The South Carolina appellate court concluded that the reassignment of an assistant superintendent to a principal position was within the school board's discretion when it did not involve a reduction in salary or violate the district's regulations.[56] Similarly, the Seventh Circuit found that the reassignment of a principal to a central office position did not involve an economic loss requiring an opportunity for a hearing.[57] A Pennsyl-

---

51. *See, e.g.,* Moore v. Bd. of Educ., 448 F.2d 709 (8th Cir. 1971); Singleton v. Jackson Mun. Separate Sch. Dist., 419 F.2d 1211 (5th Cir. 1970); Bolin v. San Bernardino City Unified Sch. Dist., 202 Cal. Rptr. 416 (Ct. App. 1984).

52. *See, e.g.,* Wygant v. Jackson Bd. of Educ., 476 U.S. 267 (1986) (staff reductions). *See also* text accompanying note 45, Chapter 10.

53. *See, e.g.,* Manila Sch. Dist. No. 15 v. White, 992 S.W.2d 125 (Ark. 1999) (ruling that the elimination of a teacher's coaching duties and assigning him as a director/teacher of an alternative school was non-renewal of contract, not reassignment); Hamilton v. Telfair County Sch. Dist., 455 S.E.2d 23 (Ga. 1995) (holding that one must show an adverse effect on salary, responsibility, and prestige).

54. *In re* Santee, 156 A.2d 830, 832 (Pa. 1959). *See also* Hood v. Ala. State Tenure Comm'n, 418 So. 2d 131 (Ala. Civ. App. 1982).

55. Mroczek v. Bd. of Educ., 400 N.E.2d 1362 (Ohio C.P. 1979).

56. Barr v. Bd. of Trs. 462 S.E.2d 316 (S.C. Ct. App. 1995). *See also* Johnson v. Spartanburg County Sch. Dist. No. 7, 444 S.E.2d 501 (S.C. 1994) (holding that the transfer of an assistant principal to a teaching position at a lower salary violated procedural protections of state law).

57. Bordelon v. Chi. Sch. Reform Bd. of Trs., 233 F.3d 524 (7th Cir. 2000).

vania school district increased administrative salaries, but a simultaneous increase in the number of workdays resulted in a reduction in compensation per day. Under state law, however, this did not constitute a demotion, since the annual salary was not reduced.[58] A reassignment from an administrative to a teaching position because of financial constraints or good faith reorganization is not a demotion requiring due process unless procedural protections are specified in state law.[59] A Wisconsin principal was not removed from her position, but the school board reassigned many of her duties and responsibilities. She resigned her position and claimed that violation of her property interests in the position precipitated the resignation. The Seventh Circuit concluded that under Wisconsin law, no right existed to performing specific duties as a principal.[60]

A transfer may violate federal rights even if it is not considered a demotion under state law. The Eleventh Circuit noted that a transfer might establish an adverse employment action if it involves a reduction of *either* pay, prestige, or responsibility. Under Georgia law, an individual must show a loss of all three to suffer a demotion. In remanding a case for trial under Title VII, the appellate court noted that a female principal had presented sufficient evidence for a jury to conclude that she had suffered an adverse employment action when transferred to another administrative position.[61]

Statutory procedures and agency regulations established for transferring or demoting employees must be strictly followed.[62] For example, under a West Virginia State Board of Education policy, school boards cannot initiate a disciplinary transfer unless there has been a prior evaluation informing the individual that specific conduct can result in a transfer.[63] Furthermore, there must be an opportunity for employees to improve their performance. Under Pennsylvania law, demotions related to declining enrollment involve a realignment of staff, and to assure proper realignment of positions, procedural protections are required.[64]

The assignment of noninstructional duties often is defined in a teacher's contract or the master contract negotiated between the school board and the teachers' union. In the absence of such specification, it is generally held that school officials can

---

58. Ahern v. Chester-Upland Sch. Dist., 582 A.2d 741 (Pa. Commw. Ct. 1990).

59. *See, e.g.,* Breslin v. Sch. Comm., 478 N.E.2d 149 (Mass. Ct. App. 1985). *See also* Phila. Ass'n of Sch. Adm'rs v. Sch. Dist., 471 A.2d 581 (Pa. Commw. Ct. 1984) (holding that temporary reassignment of administrators to teaching assignments during a teachers' strike was not a demotion in rank or salary requiring due process).

60. Ulichny v. Merton Cmty. Sch. Dist., 249 F.3d 686 (7th Cir. 2001).

61. Hinson v. Clinch County, Ga. Bd. of Educ., 231 F.3d 821 (11th Cir. 2000).

62. *See, e.g., Ex parte* Ezell, 545 So. 2d 52 (Ala. 1989); Powers v. Freetown-Lakeville Reg'l Sch. Dist. Comm., 467 N.E.2d 203 (Mass. 1984); Perry v. Houston Indep. Sch. Dist., 902 S.W.2d 544 (Tex. Ct. App. 1995).

63. Hosaflook v. Nestor, 346 S.E.2d 798 (W. Va. 1986). *See also* Hahn v. Bd. of Educ., 252 Cal. Rptr. 471 (Ct. App. 1988).

64. Fry v. Commonwealth, 485 A.2d 508 (Pa. Commw. Ct. 1984).

make reasonable and appropriate assignments.[65] Courts usually restrict assignments to activities that are an integral part of the school program and, in some situations, to duties related to the employee's teaching responsibilities.[66] A California teacher claimed that being required to supervise six athletic events during the school year was both unprofessional and beyond the scope of his duties.[67] The court determined that the assignment was within the scope of the contract and reasonable, since it was impartially distributed and did not place an onerous time burden on the teacher. An Illinois appellate court concluded that requiring teachers to submit typed copies of class examinations for duplication was not demeaning or detrimental to a teacher's professional standing; the board has the right to assign nonclassroom duties.[68] A New Jersey appellate court stated that the reasonableness of an assignment should be evaluated in terms of time involvement, teachers' interests and abilities, benefits to students, and the professional nature of the duty.[69] Refusal to accept assigned duties can result in dismissal.[70]

Contracts

The employment contract defines the rights and responsibilities of the teacher and the school board in the employment relationship. The general principles of contract law apply to this contractual relationship. Like all other legal contracts, it must contain the basic elements of (1) offer and acceptance, (2) competent parties, (3) consideration,

---

65. *See, e.g.,* Lewis v. Bd. of Educ., 537 N.E.2d 435 (Ill. App. Ct. 1989) (holding that assignments cannot be unreasonable, onerous, or burdensome); Pleasant Valley Educ. Ass'n v. Pleasant Valley Cmty. Sch. Dist., 449 N.W.2d 894 (Iowa Ct. App. 1989) (finding that school boards have extensive authority in assigning personnel); Ballard v. Bd. of Educ., 469 N.E.2d 951 (Ohio Ct. App. 1984) (concluding that additional duties can be assigned to teachers without providing supplemental pay). *See also* Griffin-Spalding County v. Daniel, 451 S.E.2d 480 (Ga. Ct. App. 1994) (concluding that a state statute prohibiting the assignment of instructional, administrative, and supervisory responsibilities during teachers' duty-free lunch period did conflict with a principal's decision to require teachers to remain on campus during lunch).

66. *See, e.g.,* Wolf v. Cuyahoga Falls City Sch. Dist., 556 N.E.2d 511 (Ohio 1990) (holding that supervision of the student newspaper was related to teaching journalism, but supplemental contract was required for the newspaper sponsor because other teachers who performed similar class-related duties were paid).

67. McGrath v. Burkhard, 280 P.2d 864 (Cal. Ct. App. 1955).

68. Thomas v. Bd. of Educ., 453 N.E.2d 150 (Ill. App. Ct. 1983). *See also* Penns Grove-Carneys Point Educ. Ass'n v. Bd. of Educ., 506 A.2d 1289 (N.J. Super. Ct. App. Div. 1986) (holding that band instructor could be assigned extra duties on weekends).

69. Bd. of Educ. v. Asbury Park Educ. Ass'n, 368 A.2d 396 (N.J. Super. Ct. Ch. Div. 1976).

70. *See, e.g.,* Howell v. Ala. State Tenure Comm'n, 402 So. 2d 1041 (Ala. 1981) (holding that a teacher's refusal to participate in a program to improve classroom management justified dismissal); Jones v. Ala. State Tenure Comm'n, 408 So. 2d 145 (Ala. 1981) (holding that a counselor's refusal to supervise students before school hours could result in dismissal).

(4) legal subject matter, and (5) proper form.[71] Beyond these basic elements, it also must meet the requirements specified in state law and administrative regulations.

The authority to contract with teachers is an exclusive right of the board. The school board's offer of a position to a teacher—including (1) designated salary, (2) specified period of time, and (3) identified duties and responsibilities—creates a binding contract when accepted by the teacher. In most states, only the board can make an offer, and this action must be approved by a majority of the board members in a properly called meeting. In a Washington case, the coordinator of special services extended a teacher an offer of employment at the beginning of the school year, pending a check of references from past employers. The recommendations were negative, and the teacher was not recommended to the board even though she had been teaching for several weeks. The state appellate court held that no enforceable contract existed; under state law, hiring authority resides with the board.[72]

Contracts also can be invalidated because of lack of competent parties. To form a valid, binding contract, both parties must have the legal capacity to enter into an agreement. The school board has been recognized as a legally competent party with the capacity to contract. A teacher who lacks certification or is under the statutorily required age for certification is not considered a competent party for contractual purposes. Consequently, a contract made with such an individual is not enforceable.[73]

Consideration is another essential element of a valid contract. Consideration is something of value that one party pays in return for the other party's performance. Teachers' monetary compensation and benefits are established in the salary schedule adopted by the school board or negotiated between the school board and the teachers' association.[74] The contract also must involve a legal subject matter and follow the proper form required by law. Most states prescribe that a teacher's contract must be in

---

71. For a discussion of contract elements, *see* Kern Alexander & M. David Alexander, *American Public School Law,* 5th Ed. (Belmont, CA: West/Thomson Learning, 2001), pp. 667–669. *See, e.g.,* Drain v. Bd. of Educ., 508 N.W.2d 255 (Neb. 1993).

72. McCormick v. Lake Wash. Sch. Dist., 992 P.2d 511 (Wash. Ct. App. 2000). *See also* Branch v. Greene County Bd. of Educ., 533 So. 2d 248 (Ala. Civ. App. 1988) (holding that a superintendent's promise of a contract made without concurrence of the school board does not create a contract); Brown v. Caldwell Sch. Dist. No. 132, 898 P.2d 43 (Idaho 1995) (holding that an assistant superintendent's offer of employment to a teacher could not bind the school board).

73. *See, e.g.,* Guthrie v. Indep. Sch. Dist. No. I-30, 958 P.2d 802 (Okla. Civ. App. 1997); Nelson v. Doland Bd. of Educ., 380 N.W.2d 665 (S.D. 1986).

74. Increasingly, legal challenges are being brought to secure health, retirement, and other benefits for domestic partners of gay and lesbian employees. Rights may exist under state constitutional and statutory provisions or institutional policies. Some courts have held that the denial of benefits discriminates on the basis of marital status. *See, e.g.,* Univ. of Alaska v. Tumeo, 933 P.2d 1147 (Alaska 1998); Tanner v. Oregon Health Sciences Univ., 971 P.2d 435 (Or. Ct. App. 1998); Baker v. State, 744 A.2d 864 (Vt. 1999). *But see* Rutgers Council of AAUP Chapters v. Rutgers State Univ., 689 A.2d 828 (N.J. Super Ct. App. Div. 1997); Funderburke v. Uniondale Union Free Sch. Dist. No. 15, 660 N.Y.S.2d 659 (Sup. Ct. 1997). *See also* Donna Euben, *Domestic Partnership Benefits on Campus: A Litigation Update* (Washington, DC: American Association of University Professors, 2002).

writing to be enforceable,[75] but if there is no statutory specification, an oral agreement is legally binding on both parties.

In addition to employment rights derived from the teaching contract, provisions of any collective bargaining agreement (master contract) are part of the employment contract.[76] Statutory provisions and school board rules and regulations also may be considered part of the terms and conditions of the contract.[77] If not included directly, the provisions existing at the time of the contract may be implied. Moreover, the contract cannot be used as a means of waiving teachers' statutory or constitutional rights.[78]

Term and Tenure Contracts

Two basic types of employment contracts are issued to teachers: term contracts and tenure contracts. *Term contracts* are valid for a fixed period of time (e.g., one or two years). At the end of the contract period, renewal is at the discretion of the school board; nonrenewal requires no explanation unless mandated by statute. Generally, a school board is required only to provide notice prior to the expiration of the contract that employment will not be renewed.[79] *Tenure contracts,* created through state legislative action, ensure teachers that employment will be terminated only for adequate cause and that procedural due process will be provided. After the award of tenure or during a term contract, school boards cannot unilaterally abrogate teachers' contracts. At a minimum, the teacher must be provided with notice of the dismissal charges and a hearing.[80]

Since tenure contracts involve statutory rights, specific procedures and protections vary among the states. Consequently, judicial interpretations in one state provide little guidance in understanding another state's law. Most tenure statutes specify requirements and procedures for obtaining tenure and identify causes and procedures

75. *See, e.g.,* Bradley v. W. Sioux Cmty. Sch. Bd. of Educ., 510 N.W.2d 881 (Iowa 1994); Bd. of Educ. v. Jones, 823 S.W.2d 457 (Ky. 1992); Jones v. Houston Indep. Sch. Dist., 805 F. Supp. 476 (S.D. Tex. 1991), *aff'd,* 979 F.2d 1004 (1992).

76. *See, e.g.,* LaSorsa v. UNUM Life Ins. Co., 955 F.2d 140 (1st Cir. 1992).

77. *See, e.g.,* Mifflinburg Area Educ. Ass'n v. Mifflinburg Area Sch. Dist., 724 A.2d 339 (Pa. 1999); Stone v. Mayflower Sch. Dist., 894 S.W.2d 881 (Ark. 1995).

78. *See, e.g.,* Denuis v. Dunlap, 209 F.3d 944 (7th Cir. 2000) (holding that the teacher was not required to relinquish constitutional privacy rights regarding medical or financial records for an employment background check); Parker v. Indep. Sch. Dist. No. I-003 Okmulgee County, Okla., 82 F.3d 952 (10th Cir. 1996) (ruling that a school board could not evade procedural protections of the Oklahoma Teacher Due Process Act by having a teacher sign a contract permitting summary removal as a teacher if her supplemental coaching position was terminated).

79. *See, e.g.,* Rhoades v. Idaho Falls Sch. Dist. No. 91, 965 P.2d 187 (Idaho 1998).

80. *See also* Trimble v. W. Va. Bd. of Dirs., 549 S.E.2d 294 (W. Va. 2001) (concluding that a teacher's property interest in continued employment required progressive disciplinary measures before resorting to termination for one incident of insubordination in light of his unblemished record). *See also* text accompanying note 61, Chapter 11, for discussion of procedural due process requirements.

for dismissing a tenured teacher. In interpreting tenure laws, courts have attempted to protect teachers' rights while simultaneously preserving school officials' flexibility in personnel management.

Prior to a school board awarding a tenure contract to a teacher, most states require a probationary period of approximately three years to assess a teacher's ability and competence. During this probationary period, teachers receive term contracts, and there is no guarantee of employment beyond each contract. Tenure statutes generally require regular and continuous service to complete the probationary period. For example, the Massachusetts tenure law requires three consecutive school years of teaching service immediately prior to the award of tenure. Interpreting this mandate, a Massachusetts appellate court held that a teacher who taught for approximately three-fourths of a school term could not count such teaching service toward tenure because it was less than a year.[81] However, part-time employment of a continuous and regular nature was interpreted as meeting probationary requirements under the Massachusetts statute, because the law required only continuous service and did not designate a separate classification for part-time service.[82]

The authority to grant a tenure contract is a discretionary power of the local school board that cannot be delegated.[83] Although the school board confers tenure, it cannot alter the tenure terms established by the legislature; the legislature determines the basis for tenure, eligibility requirements, and the procedures for acquiring tenure status.[84] Thus, if a statute requires a probationary period, this term of service must be completed prior to the school board awarding tenure. When teachers meet the statutory requirements, the school board cannot refuse to carry out its obligation to award tenure[85] nor can the board require new teachers to waive tenure rights as a precondition to employment.[86] Moreover, a board may be compelled to award tenure if a teacher completes the statutory requirements and the school board does not take action

---

81. Brodie v. Sch. Comm., 324 N.E.2d 922 (Mass. Ct. App. 1975). *See also* Corns v. Russell County Va. Sch. Bd., 52 F.3d 56 (4th Cir. 1995), *certifying question to* 454 S.E.2d 728 (Va. 1995) (holding that a statutory provision providing for "a probationary term of service of three years" required three consecutive years of employment); Fairbanks N. Star Borough Sch. Dist. v. NEA-Alaska, 817 P.2d 923, 925 (Alaska 1991) (finding part-time employment totaling two years did not meet state statutory requirement of employment "continuously for two full school years"); Burns v. State Bd. of Elementary and Secondary Educ., 529 So. 2d 398 (La. Ct. App. 1988) (holding that time spent in a federally funded teaching position did not apply to probationary period).

82. *See also* State *ex rel.* Williams v. Belpre City Sch. Dist., 534 N.E.2d 96 (Ohio Ct. App. 1987) (finding that regular and substantial part-time employment rendered a teacher eligible for tenure).

83. *See, e.g.,* Bd. of Educ. v. Carroll County Educ. Ass'n, 452 A.2d 1316 (Md. Ct. App. 1982) (holding that the school board cannot enter a negotiated agreement delegating tenure-granting authority to another party).

84. *See, e.g.,* State *ex rel.* Cohn v. Shaker Heights City Sch. Dist., 678 N.E.2d 1385 (Ohio 1997); Scheer v. Indep. Sch. Dist. No. I-26, 948 P.2d 275 (Okla. 1997).

85. *See, e.g.,* Conetta v. Bd. of Educ., 629 N.Y.S.2d 640 (Sup. Ct. 1995).

86. *See, e.g.,* Lambert v. Bd. of Educ., 664 N.Y.S.2d 422 (Sup. Ct. 1997).

to grant or deny tenure.[87] Unless specified in statute, however, tenure is not transferable from one school district to another.[88] This ensures that school officials are provided an opportunity to evaluate teachers before granting tenure.

A tenure contract provides a certain amount of job security, but it does not guarantee permanent employment, nor does it convey the right to teach in a particular school, grade, or subject area. Teachers may be reassigned to positions for which they are certified as well as dismissed for the causes specified in the tenure law.[89]

In establishing tenure, a legislature may create a contractual relationship that cannot be altered without violating constitutional guarantees. The Federal Constitution, Article I, Section 10, provides that the obligation of a contract cannot be impaired. The Supreme Court found such a contractual relationship in the 1927 Indiana Teacher Tenure Act, which prevented the state legislature from subsequently depriving teachers of rights conveyed under the act.[90] A statutory relationship that does not have the elements of a contract, however, can be altered or repealed at the legislature's discretion.[91] Some state tenure laws are clearly noncontractual, containing provisos that the law may be altered, whereas other state laws are silent on revisions. The Seventh Circuit noted that there is a general presumption that statutes do not create contract rights. Relying on this presumption, the appellate court held that there was no impairment of the state's contractual obligations when principals' tenure was repealed in the Chicago School Reform Act.[92] If a tenure law is asserted to be contractual, the language of the act is critical in the judiciary's interpretation of legislative intent.

---

87. *See, e.g.,* Speichler v. Bd. of Coop. Educ. Servs., 659 N.Y.S.2d 199 (N.Y. 1997). *But see* Bowden v. Memphis Bd. of Educ., 29 S.W.3d 462 (Tenn. 2000) (ruling that a teacher did not acquire tenure upon reappointment after the probationary period when the superintendent failed to provide statutory notice to the school board that the teacher was eligible for tenure).

88. *See, e.g.,* Washington v. Indep. Sch. Dist., 590 N.W.2d 655 (Minn. Ct. App. 1999). *See also* Nelson v. Bd. of Educ., 689 A.2d 1342 (N.J. 1997) (holding that tenure is earned in a specific position listed in state law only if the individual has served in that capacity; tenure as a supervisor did not extend to tenure as a principal or other administrative position).

89. *See* Chapter 11 for an extended discussion of termination of employment.

90. Indiana *ex rel.* Anderson v. Brand, 303 U.S. 95 (1938). Under such legislation, the status of teachers who have received tenure cannot be altered, but the legislature is not prohibited from changing the law for future employees.

91. *See, e.g.,* Krueth v. Indep. Sch. Dist. No. 38, Red Lake, Minn., 496 N.W.2d 829 (Minn. Ct. App. 1993) (ruling that a statute giving preference to American Indian teachers with less seniority in a reduction-in-force did not impermissibly impair the contract rights of teachers with greater seniority); State v. Project Principle, 724 S.W.2d 387 (Tex. 1987) (holding that a teaching certificate was a license rather than a contract and thus could be subject to future restrictions by the state).

92. Pittman v. Chi. Bd. of Educ., 64 F.3d 1098 (7th Cir. 1995). Although a Tennessee appellate court was not examining the contractual nature of the Private Tenure Act that conferred tenure upon principals in the Knox County School System, the court found that the Education Improvement Act repealed the principals' tenure. Knox County Educ. Ass'n v. Knox County Bd. of Educ., 60 S.W.3d 65 (Tenn. Ct. App. 2001).

A number of states limit the award of tenure to teaching positions, thereby excluding administrative, supervisory, and staff positions. Where tenure is available for administrative positions, probationary service and other specified statutory terms must be met. Although tenure as a teacher usually does not imply tenure as an administrator, most courts have concluded that continued service as a certified professional employee, albeit as an administrator, does not alter tenure rights acquired as a teacher.[93] The Supreme Court of Wyoming noted, "It is desirable—and even important—to have people with extensive classroom teaching experience in administrative positions. It would be difficult to fill administrative positions with experienced teachers if the teachers would have to give up tenure upon accepting administrative roles."[94] In contrast to the prevailing view, the Supreme Court of New Mexico held that an individual who voluntarily resigned a teaching position for advancement to an administrative position forfeited tenure rights.[95] According to the court, state tenure rights attach to a position rather than to an individual.

Supplemental Contracts

School boards can enter into supplement contracts with teachers for duties beyond the regular teaching assignments. As with teaching contracts, authority to employ resides with the school board.[96] Generally, these are limited contracts specifying the additional duties, compensation, and time period. Extra duties often relate to coaching, department chair responsibilities, supervision of student activities or clubs, and extended school year assignments.

Supplemental service contracts are usually considered outside the scope of tenure protections. Coaches, in particular, have asserted that supplemental contracts are an integral part of the teaching position and thereby must be afforded the procedural and substantive protections of state tenure laws. Several courts have noted that tenure rights apply only to employment in certified areas and that the lack of certification requirements for coaches in a state negates tenure claims for such positions.[97] The Supreme Court of Iowa, however, held that even a requirement that coaches must be

---

93. *See, e.g.,* Downing v. City of Lowell, 741 N.E.2d 469 (Mass. App. Ct. 2001); E. Canton Educ. Ass'n v. McIntosh, 709 N.W.2d 468 (Ohio 1999); Burke v. Lead-Deadwood Sch. Dist. No. 40-1, 347 N.W.2d 343 (S.D. 1984).

94. Spurlock v. Bd. of Trs. 699 P.2d 270, 272 (Wyo. 1985).

95. Atencio v. Bd. of Educ., 655 P.2d 1012 (N.M. 1982). *See also* Rose v. Currituck County Bd. of Educ., 350 S.E.2d 376 (N.C. Ct. App. 1986) (finding that a principal retains tenure as a teacher during the probationary period as principal).

96. *See, e.g.,* Gilmore v. Bonner County Sch. Dist. No. 82, 971 P.2d 323 (Idaho 1999). *See also* Hanlon v. Logan County Bd. of Educ., 496 S.E.2d 447 (W.Va. 1997) (holding that the school board can enter into extracurricular assignment contracts with individuals who are not employed in the school system).

97. Smith v. Bd. of Educ., 708 F.2d 258 (7th Cir. 1983); Neal v. Sch. Dist. of York, 288 N.W.2d 725 (Neb. 1980); Coles v. Glenburn Pub. Sch. Dist. 26, 436 N.W.2d 262 (N.D. 1989).

certified did not confer teachers' tenure rights on coaching positions.[98] In this case, the coaching assignment was found to be clearly an extra duty, requiring a separate contract and compensation based on an extra-duty pay scale.

Other courts also have distinguished coaching and various extra duties from teaching responsibilities based on the extracurricular nature of the assignment and supplemental compensation.[99] In denying the claim of a 10-year veteran baseball coach, the Ninth Circuit held that the coach did not have a protected interest in his coaching position, since California law specified that extra duty assignments could be terminated by the school board at any time.[100] When both classroom teaching and extra-duty assignments are covered in the same contract, however, protected property interests may be created. Accordingly, the teacher would be entitled to due process prior to the termination of the extra-duty assignment.[101]

Because coaching assignments generally require execution of a supplemental contract, a teacher can usually resign a coaching position and maintain the primary teaching position.[102] School boards having difficulty in filling coaching positions, however, may tender an offer to teach on the condition that an individual assume certain coaching responsibilities. If a single teaching and coaching contract is found to be indivisible, a teacher cannot unilaterally resign the coaching duties without relinquishing the teaching position.[103] Individual state laws must be consulted to determine the status of such contracts.

98. Slockett v. Iowa Valley Cmty. Sch. Dist., 359 N.W.2d 446 (Iowa 1984). *But see* Reid v. Huron Bd. of Educ., 449 N.W.2d 240 (S.D. 1989) (ruling that the position of head coach came under the continuing contract law since state administrative rules defined certification requirements for the job).

99. *See, e.g.,* Lancaster v. Indep. Sch. Dist. No. 5, 149 F.3d 1228 (10th Cir. 1998); Sch. Comm. v. Educ. Ass'n, 666 N.E.2d 486 (Mass. 1996); Issaquah Educ. Ass'n v. Issaquah Sch. Dist. No. 411, 706 P.2d 618 (Wash. 1985). *But see* Smith v. Bd. of Educ., 341 S.E.2d 685 (W.Va. 1985) (finding that failure of a school board to renew a coaching contract was considered a transfer, which under state law required procedural due process).

100. Lagos v. Modesto City Schs. Dist., 843 F.2d 347 (9th Cir. 1988). *But see* Kingsford v. Salt Lake City Sch. Dist., 247 F.3d 1123 (10th Cir. 2001) (remanding to determine if school officials created an "implied-in-fact" promise that coaches would only be terminated for cause; case prompted state legislature to amend law to specify that extra duty assignments are limited contracts); Vail v. Bd. of Educ., 706 F.2d 1435 (7th Cir. 1983), *aff'd by an equally divided court,* 466 U.S. 377 (1984) (holding that the school board's promise of a two-year teaching and coaching contract prevented the board from terminating employment at the end of the first year without procedural due process).

101. *See, e.g.,* Farner v. Idaho Falls Sch. Dist. No. 91, 17 P.3d 281 (Idaho 2000).

102. *See, e.g.,* Hachiya v. Bd. of Educ., 750 P.2d 383 (Kan. 1988); Lewis v. Bd. of Educ., 537 N.E.2d 435 (Ill. App. Ct. 1989); Babitzke v. Silverton Union High Sch., 695 P.2d 93 (Or. Ct. App. 1985). *See also* Parker v. Indep. Sch. Dist. No. I-003, 82 F.3d 952 (10th Cir. 1996) (holding that the school board could not circumvent a teacher's entitlement to procedural due process with the termination of her teaching position by having the teacher sign a contract that specified she would not be reemployed as a teacher if her coaching contract was not renewed; court emphasized that the school board could not amend or repeal statutory rights).

103. *See, e.g.,* Munger v. Jesup Cmty. Sch. Dist., 325 N.W.2d 377 (Iowa 1982).

Where teaching and coaching positions are combined, a qualified teaching applicant who cannot assume the coaching duties may be rejected. This practice, however, may be vulnerable to legal challenge if certain classes of applicants, such as women, are excluded from consideration. In an Arizona case, female plaintiffs successfully established that a school district was liable for gender discrimination by coupling a high school biology teaching position with a football coaching position. The school board was unable to demonstrate a business necessity for the practice that resulted in female applicants for the teaching position being eliminated from consideration.[104]

Leaves of Absence

Contracts may specify various types of leaves of absence. Within the parameters of state law, school boards have discretion in establishing requirements for these leaves. This topic often is the subject of collective negotiations, with leave provisions specified in bargained agreements. School boards, however, cannot negotiate leave policies that impair rights guaranteed by the United States Constitution and various federal and state antidiscrimination laws.[105] Similarly, where state law confers specific rights, local boards do not have the discretion to deny or alter these rights. Generally, statutes identify employees' rights related to various kinds of leaves such as sick leave, personal leave, pregnancy or child-care leave, sabbatical leave, disability leave, family leave and military leave. State laws pertaining to leaves of absence usually specify eligibility for benefits, minimum days that must be provided, whether leave must be granted with or without pay, and restrictions that may be imposed by local school boards. If a teacher meets all statutory and procedural requirements for a specific leave, a school board cannot deny the request.

Personnel Evaluation

To ensure a quality teaching staff, many states have enacted laws requiring periodic appraisal of teaching performance. Beyond the purposes of faculty improvement and remediation, results of evaluations may be used in a variety of employment decisions, including retention, tenure, dismissal, promotion, salary, reassignment, and reduction-in-force. When adverse personnel decisions are based on evaluations, legal concerns of procedural fairness arise. Were established state and local procedures followed? Did school officials employ equitable standards? Was sufficient evidence collected to support the staffing decision? Were evaluations conducted in a uniform and consistent manner?

104. Civil Rights Div. of the Ariz. Dep't of Law v. Amphitheater Unified Sch. Dist. No. 10, 706 P.2d 745 (Ariz. Ct. App. 1985).

105. Charges of discrimination in connection with leave policies pertaining to pregnancy-related absences and the observance of religious holidays are discussed in Chapter 10.

School systems have broad discretionary powers to establish teacher performance criteria, but state statutes may impose specific evaluation requirements. More than half of the states have enacted laws governing teacher evaluation.[106] Content and requirements vary substantially across states, with some states merely mandating the establishment of an appraisal system and others specifying procedures and criteria to be employed. Iowa law notes only that the local board must establish an evaluation system.[107] California, on the other hand, specifies the intent of evaluations, areas to be assessed, frequency of evaluations, notice to employees of deficiencies, and an opportunity to improve performance.[108] Florida requires the superintendent of schools to establish criteria and procedures for appraisal, including evaluation at least once a year, a written record of assessment, prior notice to teachers of criteria and procedures, and a meeting with the evaluator to discuss the results of the evaluation.[109] Although a few evaluation systems are established at the state level, state laws usually require local officials to develop evaluation criteria, often in conjunction with teachers or other professionals.[110] Unless prohibited as managerial policy, it also may be negotiable with the teachers' union.[111]

When evaluation procedures are identified in statutes, board policies, or employment contracts, courts generally require strict compliance with these provisions. A California appeals court found that the nonrenewal of a teacher's contract violated the statutory notification deadline and requirement for a written evaluation.[112] A Washington appellate court required the reinstatement of a principal because the school board had not adopted evaluation criteria and procedures as required by law.[113] The court noted that in the absence of evaluation criteria, the principal would serve at the whim of the superintendent and would be deprived of guide-

---

106. Perry A. Zirkel, *The Law of Teacher Evaluation* (Bloomington, IN: Phi Delta Kappa, 1996).

107. Iowa Code Ann. § 279.14 (2002). *See also* Ark. Code Ann. § 6-17-1504 (2002).

108. Cal. Code Ann. §§ 44660–44665 (2002). *See also* Ill. Sch. Code, 105 ILCS 5/24A (1994); Chi. Bd. of Educ. v. Smith, 664 N.E.2d 113 (Ill. App. Ct. 1996).

109. Fla. Stat. § 231.29 (2002).

110. *See, e.g.,* Ariz. Rev. Stat. Ann. § 15-537 (2002); Or. Rev. Stat. Ann. § 342.850 (2002); Conn. Gen. Stat. Ann. § 10-151b (2002).

111. *See, e.g., In re* Pittsfield Sch. Dist., 744 A.2d 594 (N.H. 1999). *See also* text accompanying note 55, Chapter 12.

112. Anderson v. San Mateo Cmty. Coll. Dist., 151 Cal. Rptr. 111 (Ct. App. 1978). *See also* Boss v. Fillmore County Sch. Dist. No. 19, 559 N.W.2d 448 (Neb. 1997). *But see* Retzlaff v. Grand Forks Pub. Sch. Dist. No. 1, 424 N.W.2d 637 (N.D. 1988) (holding that a "supervisory report" containing specific educational goals for a teacher substantially complied with state requirement of a written performance review); Baker v. Bd. of Educ., 534 S.E.2d 378 (W. Va. 2000) (finding that the lack of a "written improvement plan" was not required in the nonrenewal of a principal's contract when the superintendent in meetings and letters had fully apprised her of deficiencies and suggested a remediation plan).

113. Hyde v. Wellpinit Sch. Dist. 49, 611 P.2d 1388 (Wash. Ct. App. 1980).

lines to improve his performance. Under the Ohio statutory evaluation requirement for nontenured teachers, failure to comply with the twice-yearly evaluation mandate resulted in the reinstatement of a nontenured teacher.[114] The West Virginia Supreme Court held that a school system could not transfer an individual because the decision was not based on performance evaluations as required by state board policy.[115]

Where school boards have been attentive to evaluation requirements, courts have upheld challenged employment decisions.[116] A California appellate court found that a teacher's dismissal comported with state evaluation requirements because he received periodic appraisals noting specific instances of unsatisfactory performance.[117] The evaluation reports informed the teacher of the system's expectations, his specific teaching weaknesses, and actions needed to correct deficiencies. An Iowa court found a school district's policy requiring a formal evaluation every three years for nonprobationary teachers to be adequate under a statutory requirement that "the board shall establish evaluation criteria and shall implement evaluation procedures."[118] The court denied a teacher's claim that the law required an additional evaluation whenever termination of employment was contemplated. According to the Supreme Court of South Dakota, violation of an evaluation procedure per se does not require reinstatement of a teacher.[119] Reinstatement is justified only if the violation substantially interfered with a teacher's ability to improve deficiencies.

Courts are reluctant to interject their judgment into the teacher evaluation process. Judicial review generally is limited to the procedural issues of fairness and reasonableness. Several principles emerge from case law to guide educators in developing equitable systems: Standards for assessing teaching adequacy must be defined and communicated to teachers; criteria must be applied uniformly and consistently; an opportunity and direction for improvement must be provided; and procedures specified in state laws and school board policies must be followed.

114. Snyder v. Mendon-Union Local Sch. Dist. Bd. of Educ., 661 N.E.2d 717 (Ohio 1996). *See also* McComb v. Gahana-Jefferson City Sch. Dist. Bd. of Educ., 720 N.E.2d 984 (Ohio Ct. App. 1998) (concluding that prior to nonrenewal, the teacher was provided specific recommendations for improvement in evaluations as required by state law).

115. Holland v. Bd. of Educ., 327 S.E.2d 155 (W. Va. 1985).

116. *See, e.g.,* Tippecanoe Educ. Ass'n v. Tippecanoe Sch. Corp., 700 N.E.2d 241 (Ind. Ct. App. 1998); Thomas v. Bd. of Educ., 643 N.E.2d 132 (Ohio 1994); Kudasik v. Bd. of Dirs., 455 A.2d 261 (Pa. 1983).

117. Perez v. Comm'n on Prof'l Competence, 197 Cal. Rptr. 390 (Ct. App. 1983). *See also* Hoffner v. Bismarck Pub. Sch. Dist., 589 N.W.2d 195 (N.D. 1999) (concluding that a principal's nonrenewal complied with statute requiring that reasons be drawn from findings arising from written evaluations).

118. Johnson v. Bd. of Educ., 353 N.W.2d 883, 887 (Iowa Ct. App. 1984).

119. Schaub v. Chamberlain Bd. of Educ., 339 N.W.2d 307 (S.D. 1983). It must be emphasized that failure to follow established evaluation procedures does not necessarily result in a denial of constitutional due process rights in termination actions if the minimum notice, specification of charges, and opportunity for a hearing are provided. *See, e.g.,* Goodrich v. Newport News Sch. Bd., 743 F.2d 225 (4th Cir. 1984); Farmer v. Kelleys Island Bd. of Educ., 638 N.E.2d 79 (Ohio 1994); text accompanying note 63, Chapter 11.

Personnel Records

Because several or more statutes in each state as well as employment contracts govern school records, it is difficult to generalize as to the specific nature of teachers' privacy rights regarding personnel files. State privacy laws that place restrictions on maintenance and access to the records typically protect personnel information. Among other provisions, these laws usually require school boards to maintain only necessary and relevant information, provide individual employees access to their files,[120] inform employees of the various uses of the files, and establish a procedure for challenging the accuracy of information. Collective bargaining contracts may impose additional and more stringent requirements regarding access and dissemination of personnel information.[121]

A central issue in the confidentiality of personnel files is whether the information constitutes a public record that must be reasonably accessible to the general public. Public-record, freedom of information, or right-to-know laws that grant broad access to school records may directly conflict with privacy laws, requiring courts to balance the interests of the teacher, the school officials, and the public. The specific provisions of state laws determine the level of confidentiality granted to personnel records.[122] The federal Freedom of Information Act (FOIA),[123] which serves as a model for many state FOIAs, often is used by courts in interpreting state provisions. Unlike the federal law, however, many states do not exempt personnel records.

In the absence of a specific exemption, most courts have concluded that any doubt as to the appropriateness of disclosure should be decided in favor of public disclosure.[124] The Supreme Court of Michigan held that teachers' personnel files are open to the public because they are not specifically exempt by law.[125] The Supreme Court of Washington noted that the public disclosure act mandated disclosure of information that is of legitimate public concern.[126] As such, the state superintendent of public instruction was required to provide a newspaper publisher records specifying the rea-

---

120. *See, e.g.,* Cook v. Lisbon Sch. Comm., 682 A.2d 672 (Me. 1996) (holding that the school committee must produce documents requested by an employee within statutory time period of five working days; providing the material months after the request is inadequate); Boor v. McKenzie County Pub. Sch. Dist. No. 1, 560 N.W.2d 213 (N.D. 1997) (concluding that a principal's notations of complaints in his desk journal about a teacher did not violate state law prohibiting a secret personnel file when he had promptly brought the complaints to the teacher's attention).

121. *But see* Bradley v. Bd. of Educ., 565 N.W.2d 650 (1997) (holding that the board could not bargain away the requirements of the state Freedom of Information Act).

122. *See, e.g.,* Bangor Area Educ. Ass'n, 720 A.2d 198 (Pa. Commw. Ct. 1998), *aff'd,* 750 A.2d 282 (Pa. 2000) (per curiam) (confirming that teachers' personnel files are not public records).

123. 5 U.S.C. § 552 (2002).

124. *See, e.g.,* Kirwan v. The Diamondback, 721 A.2d 196 (Md. 1998), Brouillet v. Cowles Pub. Co., 791 P.2d 526 (Wash. 1990); Wis. Newspress v. Sch. Dist., 546 N.W.2d 143 (Wis. 1996).

125. Bradley v. Bd. of Educ., 565 N.W.2d 650 (Mich. 1997).

sons for teacher certificate revocations. The Supreme Court of Connecticut interpreted the state Freedom of Information Act exemption, prohibiting the release of information that would constitute an "invasion of personal privacy," to include employees' evaluations[127] but not their sick-leave records.[128] In general, information that must be maintained by law is a public record (i.e., personal directory information, salary, employment contracts, leave records, and teaching license) and must be released.

Educators have not been successful in asserting that privacy interests in personnel records are protected under either the Family Educational Rights and Privacy Act of 1974 (FERPA) or the United States Constitution. FERPA applies only to students and their educational records, not to employees' personnel records.[129] Similarly, employees' claims that their constitutional privacy rights bar disclosure of their personnel records have been unsuccessful. In a case where a teacher's college transcript was sought by a third party under the Texas Open Records Act, the Fifth Circuit ruled that even if a teacher had a recognizable privacy interest in her transcript, that interest "is significantly outweighed by the public's interest in evaluating the competence of its school teachers."[130]

Access to personnel files also has been controversial in situations involving allegations of employment discrimination. Personnel files must be relinquished if subpoenaed by a court. The Equal Employment Opportunity Commission (EEOC)

---

126. Brouillet v. Cowles Pub. Co., 791 P.2d 526 (Wash. 1990). *See also* S. Bend Tribune v. S. Bend Cmty. Sch. Corp., 740 N.E.2d 937 (Ind. Ct. App. 2000) (holding that a public agency must disclose designated personnel information for present or former employees but not information pertaining to applicants for positions); Cypress Media v. Hazleton Area Sch. Dist., 708 A.2d 866 (Pa. Commw. Ct. 1998) (finding that applications for employment are not public records).

127. Chairman v. Freedom of Info. Comm'n, 585 A.2d 96 (Conn. 1991). *See also* DeMichele v. Greenburgh Cent. Sch. Dist. No. 7, 167 F.3d 784 (2d Cir. 1999) (relying on New York law noted that the disposition of misconduct charges is not exempt private information); Carpenter v. Freedom of Info. Comm'n, 755 A.2d 364 (Conn. App. Ct. 2000) (ruling that record of personal misconduct was not a record of teaching performance or evaluation exempt under state law); Williams v. Bd. of Educ., 747 A.2d 809 (N.J. Super. Ct. App. Div. 2000) (holding that tenure charge documents are public record); Linzmeyer v. Forcey, 646 N.W.2d 811 (Wis. 2002) (finding that the open records law applies to the report of a police investigation; the police had investigated a high school teacher for allegedly engaging in inappropriate conduct with females students). *But see* Wakefield Teachers Ass'n v. Sch. Comm., 731 N.E.2d 63 (Mass. 2000) (concluding that a disciplinary report is personnel information that is exempt under the public records law).

128. Perkins v. Freedom of Info. Comm'n, 635 A.2d 783 (Conn. 1993). *See also* Scottsdale Unified Sch. Dist. No. 48 v. KPNX Broad. Co., 955 P.2d 534 (Ariz. 1998) (finding that the public availability of teachers' birth dates did not negate teachers' legitimate expectation of privacy). *But see* Brogan v. Sch. Comm, 516 N.E.2d 159 (Mass. 1987) (holding that individual absentee records noting dates and generic type of absences were not records of a "personal nature" exempt from Public Record Law).

129. *See, e.g.,* Klein Indep. Sch. Dist. v. Mattox, 830 F.2d 576 (5th Cir. 1987); Brouillet v. Cowles Publ'g Co., 791 P.2d 526 (Wash. 1990). *But see* Cypress Media v. Hazelton Area Sch. Dist., 708 A.2d 866 (Pa. Commw. Ct. 1998) (concluding that release of college transcripts of applicants for teaching positions would violate FERPA).

130. *Klein,* 830 F.2d at 580. *See also* Hovet v. Hebron Pub. Sch. Dist., 419 N.W.2d 189 (N.D. 1988).

also is authorized to subpoena relevant personnel files in order to investigate thoroughly allegations that a particular individual has been the victim of discriminatory treatment. Holding that confidential peer review materials used in university promotion and tenure decisions were not protected from disclosure to the EEOC, the Supreme Court ruled that under the provisions of Title VII of the Civil Rights Act of 1964, the EEOC must only show relevance, not special reasons or justifications, in demanding specific records. Regarding access to peer review materials, the Court noted that "if there is a 'smoking gun' to be found that demonstrates discrimination in tenure decisions, it is likely to be tucked away in peer review files."[131]

With respect to the maintenance of records, information clearly cannot be placed in personnel files in retaliation for the exercise of constitutional rights. Courts have ordered letters of reprimand expunged from files when they have been predicated on protected speech and association activities. Reprimands, although not a direct prohibition on protected activities, may present a constitutional violation because of their potentially chilling effect on the exercise of constitutional rights.[132]

Other Employment Issues

In addition to the terms and conditions of employment already discussed, other reasonable requirements can be attached to public employment as long as civil rights laws are respected and constitutional rights are not impaired without a compelling governmental justification. Public educators are expected to comply with such reasonable requirements as a condition of maintaining their jobs. Some requirements, such as those pertaining to the instructional program and prohibitions against proselytizing students, are discussed in other chapters. Requirements pertaining to two topics have received substantial attention since the 1980s and warrant discussion here: using copyrighted materials and reporting child abuse.

Using Copyrighted Materials

Educators' extensive use of published materials and various other media in the classroom raises issues relating to the federal copyright law. As a condition of employment, educators are expected to comply with restrictions on the use of copyrighted materials. Although the law grants the owner of a copyright exclusive control over the protected material, courts since the 1800s have recognized exceptions to this control

---

131. Univ. of Pa. v. EEOC, 493 U.S. 182, 193 (1990). *See also* EEOC v. Maryland Cup Corp., 785 F.2d 471 (4th Cir. 1986); EEOC v. Franklin & Marshall Coll., 775 F.2d 110 (3d Cir. 1985); James v. Ohio State Univ., 637 N.E.2d 911 (Ohio 1994).

132. *See, e.g.,* Aebisher v. Ryan, 622 F.2d 651 (2d Cir. 1980) (concluding that a letter of reprimand for speaking to the press about violence in the school implicated protected speech); Columbus Educ. Ass'n v. Columbus City Sch. Dist., 623 F.2d 1155 (6th Cir. 1980) (holding that a letter of reprimand issued to a union representative for zealous advocacy of a fellow teacher violated the First Amendment); Swilley v. Alexander, 629 F.2d 1018 (5th Cir. 1980) (ruling that a union president's press release was protected conduct and letter of reprimand implicated liberty interests).

under the doctrine of "fair use." The fair use doctrine cannot be precisely defined, but a definition frequently used by the judiciary is the "privilege in others than the owner of the copyright to use the copyrighted material in a reasonable manner without his consent, notwithstanding the monopoly granted to the owner."[133]

Congress incorporated the judicially created fair use concept into the 1976 revisions of the Copyright Act.[134] In identifying the purposes of the fair use exception, Congress specifically noted teaching. The exception provides needed flexibility for teachers but by no interpretation grants them exemption from copyright infringement. The law stipulates four factors to assess whether the use of specific material constitutes fair use or an infringement:

> (1) the purpose and character of the use, including whether such use is of a commercial nature or is for non-profit educational purposes; (2) the nature of the copyrighted work; (3) the amount and substantiality of the portion used in relation to the copyrighted work as a whole; and (4) the effect of the use upon the potential market for or value of the copyrighted work.[135]

To clarify fair use pertaining to photocopying from books and periodicals, the House and Senate conferees incorporated into their conference report a set of classroom guidelines developed by a group representing educators, authors, and publishers.[136] These guidelines are only part of the legislative history of the Copyright Act and do not have the force of law, but they have been widely used as persuasive authority in assessing the legality of reproducing printed materials in the educational environment. The guidelines permit making single copies of copyrighted material for teaching or research but are quite restrictive on the use of multiple copies. To use multiple copies of a work, the tests of brevity, spontaneity, and cumulative effect must be met. *Brevity* is precisely defined according to type of publication. For example, reproduction of a poem cannot exceed 250 words; copying from longer works cannot exceed 1,000 words or 10 percent of the work (whichever is less); only one chart or drawing can be reproduced from a book or an article. *Spontaneity* requires that the copying be initiated by the individual teacher (not an administrator or supervisor) and that it occur in such a manner that does not reasonably permit a timely request for permission. *Cumulative* effect restricts use of the copies to one course; limits material reproduced from the same author, book, and journal during the term; and sets a limit of nine instances of multiple copying for each course during one class term. Furthermore, the guidelines do not permit copying to substitute for anthologies or collective works or to replace consumable materials such as workbooks.

---

133. Marcus v. Rowley, 695 F.2d 1171, 1174 (9th Cir. 1983).

134. 17 U.S.C. § 101 *et seq.* (2002).

135. *Id.* at § 107.

136. For a summary of the guidelines, *see* Mark Merickel, "The Educator's Rights to Fair Use of Copyrighted Works," *Education Law Reporter*, vol. 51 (1989), pp. 711–724.

Publishers have taken legal action to ensure compliance with these guidelines. The Sixth Circuit held that Michigan Document Services, Inc., a commercial copy shop, violated the fair use doctrine in the reproduction of course packets for faculty at the University of Michigan. Three publishers (Macmillan, Princeton University Press, and St. Martin's Press) challenged the duplication of copyrighted material for commercial sale by a for-profit corporation. The copy shop owner argued that such reproduction of multiple copies for classroom use is a recognized statutory exemption. The appellate court disagreed, reasoning that the sale of multiple copies for commercial, not educational, purposes destroyed the publishers' potential licensing revenue from photocopying, contained creative material, and involved substantial portions of the copyrighted publications (as much as 30 percent for one work).[137] This ruling does not prevent faculty use of course packets or anthologies in the classroom, but it does require permission from publishers and the possible payment of fees prior to photocopying.

The fair use doctrine and congressional guidelines have been strictly construed in educational settings. Although the materials reproduced meet the first factor in determining fair use—educational purpose—the remaining factors must be met. The Ninth Circuit held that a teacher's use of a copyrighted booklet to make a learning activity packet abridged the copyright law.[138] The court concluded that fair use was not met in this case because the learning packet was used for the same purpose as the protected booklet, the nature of the work reproduced was a "creative" effort rather than "information," and one-half of the packet was verbatim copy of the copyrighted material. Furthermore, the copying was found to violate the guideline of spontaneity in that it was reproduced several times over two school years. It is important to note that the appeals court did not find the absence of personal profit on the part of the teacher to lessen the violation.

Although not using the material for teaching purposes, a Chicago teacher and editor of a newspaper called *Substance* published copyrighted tests developed to assess educational levels of Chicago public high school freshmen and sophomores. He published entire copies of a number of the subject area tests along with his criticism of the tests. The tests were clearly marked with the copyright notice and included a warning that the material could not be duplicated. The Chicago school board sued, claiming infringement of their copyright. In a ruling dismissing the teacher's affirmative defenses, an Illinois federal district court ruled that he did not possess a First Amendment right to publish the copyrighted tests; the Copyright Act limits First

137. Princeton Univ. Press v. Mich. Document Servs., 99 F.3d 1381 (6th Cir. 1996). *See also* Basic Books v. Kinko's Graphics Corp., 758 F. Supp. 1522 (S.D.N.Y. 1991) (concluding that the photocopying of copyrighted works for course packets violated fair use; awarded eight publishers $510,000 in damages); Sheldon E. Steinbach, "Photocopying Copyrighted Course Materials: Doesn't Anyone Remember the NYU Case?" *Education Law Reporter,* vol. 50 (1989), pp. 317–330.

138. Marcus v. Rowley, 695 F.2d 1171 (9th Cir. 1983).

Amendment freedoms.[139] Furthermore, the publication of the material did not fall within the fair use guidelines.

Rapid developments in instructional technology pose a new set of legal questions regarding use of videotapes and computer software. Recognizing the need for guidance related to videotaping, Congress issued guidelines for educational use in 1981.[140] These guidelines specify that taping must be made at the request of the teacher. The taped material must be used for relevant classroom activities only once within the first 10 days of taping. Additional use is limited to instructional reinforcement or evaluation purposes. After 45 calendar days, the tape must be erased. A New York federal district court held that a school system violated the fair use standards by extensive off-the-air taping and replaying of entire television programs.[141] The taping interfered with the producers' ability to market the tapes and films. In a subsequent appeal, the school system sought permission for temporary taping; however, because of the availability of these programs for rental or lease, even temporary recording and use was held to violate fair use by interfering with the marketability of the films.[142]

Taping television broadcasts on home video recorders for later classroom use may constitute copyright infringement if off-the-air taping guidelines are not followed. Under the legal principles advanced by the Supreme Court in *Sony Corporation v. Universal City Studios,* "even copying for noncommercial purposes may impair the copyright holder's ability to obtain the rewards that Congress intended him to have."[143] In this case, the Court found that personal video recording for the purpose of "time shifting" was a legitimate, unobjectionable purpose, posing minimal harm to marketability. Home taping for broader viewing by students in the classroom, however, would be beyond the purposes envisioned by the Court in *Sony* and would necessitate careful adherence to the guidelines for limited use outlined above.

Under 1980 amendments to the copyright law, software was included as protected intellectual property.[144] Established copyright principles provide guidance in analyzing fair use. It is clear from the amended law that only one duplicate or backup copy can be made of the master computer program by the owner. This is to ensure a working copy of the program if the master copy is damaged. Application of the fair use exception does not alter this restriction for educators. Although duplicating multiple copies would be clearly for educational purposes, other factors of fair use would be violated: The software is readily accessible for purchase (not impossible to obtain),

139. Chi. Sch. Reform Bd. v. Substance, Inc., 79 F. Supp. 2d 919 (N.D. Ill. 1999).

140. Guidelines for Off-the-Air Recording of Broadcast Programming for Educational Purposes, Cong. Rec. § E4751, October 14, 1981.

141. Encyclopedia Britannica Educ. Corp. v. Crooks, 542 F. Supp. 1156 (W.D.N.Y. 1982).

142. Encyclopedia Britannica Educ. Corp. v. Crooks, 558 F. Supp. 1247 (W.D.N.Y. 1983).

143. 464 U.S. 417, 450 (1984).

144. 17 U.S.C. § 117 (2002).

programs can only be duplicated in their entirety, and copying substantially reduces the potential market.

In spite of the amendments, publishers continue to be concerned about illegal copying of computer software in the school environment. Limited school budgets and high costs have led to abuse of copyrighted software. In 1999, the Los Angeles Board of Education settled what might be the worst case of software piracy discovered in public schools.[145] An investigation by a group of software companies discovered more than 1,400 copies of software, such as Microsoft Word and Adobe Photoshop, allegedly being used without authorization. The school district denied the violation but settled to avoid the costs of a trial.

A question not answered by the copyright law but plaguing schools is the legality of multiple use of a master program. That is, can a program be loaded in a number of computers in a laboratory for simultaneous use, or can a program be modified for use in a network of microcomputers? Again, application of the fair use concept would indicate that multiple use is impermissible. The most significant factor is that the market for the educational software would be greatly diminished. A number of students using the master program one at a time (serial use), however, would appear not to violate the copyright law. To acquire broad use of particular software, school systems must either purchase multiple copies or negotiate site license agreements with the publishers.

As schools are developing their capacity to take advantage of the Internet, copyright law also is evolving. Congress amended the law in 1998, passing the Digital Millennium Copyright Act.[146] The "White Paper" produced by President Clinton's Working Group on Intellectual Property Issues identified numerous and complex issues that influenced the new law.[147] Questions were raised about what constitutes distribution (traditionally interpreted as a hard copy being transferred to another individual as opposed to transmission over data lines) and publication (current definition limits protection to physical copies). The new law reinforces that an individual's copyright is secured when the work is created and "fixed in any tangible medium of expression."[148] Although critics find many ambiguities in the law, they agree that it includes a clear commitment to extending "fair use" to digital technology for educators.

---

145. "L.A. School Board Settles Software Copyright Suit," *School Law News,* vol. 27, no. 4 (March 5, 1999), p. 2. The case was settled for $300,000 plus an additional $1.5 million for a task force to monitor software usage over a three-year period.

146. 112 Stat. 2860 § 1 (2002).

147. Bruce A. Lehman, Chair, Working Group on Intellectual Property Rights, "Report on Intellectual Property and the National Information Infrastructure," Washington, DC: Information Infrastructure Task Force (1995).

148. 17 U.S.C. § 102 (2002). Recent litigation indicates that material published and distributed on the Internet will be fully protected by the basic principles of copyright law. For example, the Ninth Circuit imposed an injunction against Napster Corporation and its distribution of a file-sharing program that allowed individuals to download music files. A&M Records v. Napster, 239 F.3d 1004 (9th Cir. 2001).

Extraordinary technological advances have given teachers and their school systems the means to access a wide range of instructional materials and products, but many of them are protected by the federal copyright law that restricts unauthorized reproduction. Because violation of the law can result in school district and educator liability, school boards should adopt policies or guidelines to prohibit infringement and to alert individuals of practices that violate protected materials.[149]

Reporting Suspected Child Abuse

Child abuse and neglect are recognized as national problems, with reported cases remaining at a high level.[150] Because the majority of these children are school age, educators are in a unique role to detect signs of potential abuse. States, recognizing the daily contact teachers have with students, have imposed certain *duties* for reporting suspected abuse.

All states have enacted legislation identifying teachers among the professionals required to report signs of child abuse. Most state laws impose criminal liability for failure to report suspected abuse. Penalties may include fines ranging from $500 to $5,000, prison terms up to one year, or both. Civil suits also may be initiated against teachers for negligence in failing to make such reports.[151] Additionally, school systems may impose disciplinary measures against a teacher who does not follow the mandates of the law. The Seventh Circuit upheld the suspension and demotion of a teacher-psychologist for not promptly reporting suspected abuse.[152] The court rejected the teacher's claim to a federal right of confidentiality, noting the state's compelling interest to protect children from mistreatment.

Although specific aspects of the laws may vary from one state to another, definitions of abuse and neglect often are based on the Federal Child Abuse Prevention

---

149. *See* 17 U.S.C. § 511(a) (2002). In response to several appellate court decisions holding that under the Eleventh Amendment states and their agents were not subject to suit in federal courts for the infringement of copyrights, Congress amended the copyright law (Copyright Remedy Clarification) specifically abrogating immunity. *See also* BV Engineering v. Univ. of Cal., L.A., 858 F.2d 1394 (9th Cir. 1988); Richard Anderson Photography v. Brown, 852 F.2d 114 (4th Cir. 1988).

150. In 2000, three million referrals were made to child protection agencies with almost 900,000 children found to be victims of abuse. Children's Bureau Administration on Children, Youth, & Families, *National Child Abuse and Neglect Data System,* Washington, DC: U.S. Dep't of Health and Human Services, April 2002.

151. The Ohio Supreme Court ruled that a school system and its employees did not have sovereign immunity for damages when state law expressly imposed liability for failure to report suspected abuse. Campbell v. Burton, 750 N.E.2d 539 (Ohio 2001). *See also* Chapter 13 for discussion of the elements of negligence.

152. Pesce v. J. Sterling Morton High Sch. Dist. 201, Cook County, Ill., 830 F.2d 789 (7th Cir. 1987). *See also* State v. Grover, 437 N.W.2d 60 (Minn. 1989) (finding principal criminally negligent for failure to report child abuse by teacher).

and Treatment Act of 1974, which provides funds to identify, treat, and prevent abuse. The Act identifies *child abuse* and *neglect* as

> the physical or mental injury, sexual abuse or exploitation, negligent treatment, or mal-treatment of a child under the age of eighteen, or the age specified by the child protection law of the state in question, by a person who is responsible for the child's welfare under the circumstances which indicate that the child's health or welfare is harmed or threat-ened thereby.[153]

Several common elements are found in state child abuse statutes. The laws man-date that certain professionals such as doctors, nurses, and educators report suspected abuse. Statutes do not require that reporters have absolute knowledge, but rather "rea-sonable cause to believe" or "reason to believe" that a child has been abused or neglected.[154] Once abuse is suspected, the report must be made immediately to the designated child protection agency, department of welfare, or law-enforcement unit as specified in state law. All states grant immunity from civil and criminal liability to individuals if reports are made in good faith.[155] In Ohio, absolute immunity exists even for reports made in bad faith.[156]

School districts often establish reporting procedures that require teachers to report suspected abuse to their principal or school social worker. However, if statutory provisions specify that teachers must promptly report suspected abuse to another agency or law enforcement, teachers are not relieved of their individual obligation to report to state authorities. Furthermore, the Kentucky Supreme Court held that report-ing to a supervisor then imposes a burden on the supervisor to make a separate report.[157] Some state laws do relieve teachers of the obligation to report if someone else has already reported or will be reporting the incident. But teachers should always follow up to be sure the report was made to the appropriate agency.

State laws are explicit as to reporting requirements for suspected child abuse, but it is difficult to prove that a teacher had sufficient knowledge of abuse to trigger legal liability for failure to report. Therefore, it is desirable for school officials to

---

153. 42 U.S.C. § 5101 (2002).

154. *See, e.g.,* Kimberly S. M. v. Bradford Cent. Sch., 649 N.Y.S.2d 588 (App. Div. 1996); Morris v. State, 833 S.W.2d 624 (Tex. Ct. App. 1992). *See also* Hughes v. Stanley County Sch. Dist., 638 N.W.2d 50 (S.D. 2001) (finding that the school board lacked evidence to support its allegation that a teacher failed to report suspected abuse).

155. *See, e.g.,* Landstrom v. Ill. Dep't of Children and Family Servs., 892 F.2d 670 (7th Cir. 1990); Liedtke v. Carrington, 763 N.E.2d 213 (Ohio Ct. App. 2001); Davis v. Durham City Schs., 372 S.E.2d 318 (N.C. Ct. App. 1988).

156. Ohio Rev. Code § 2151.421 (2002); Bishop v. Ezzone, No. WD-80-63, 1981 Ohio App. LEXIS 11406 (Ohio App. June 26, 1981). While school authorities and health- and child-care professionals have absolute immunity, other persons who report abuse are entitled to immunity only if the report is made in good faith.

157. Commonwealth v. Allen, 980 S.W.2d 278 (Ky. 1998). *See also* Barber v. State, 592 So. 2d 330 (Fla. Dist. Ct. App. 1992) (noting that requiring multiple reports of the same incident of abuse demon-strates the gravity of the situation).

establish policies and procedures to encourage effective reporting. The pervasiveness of the problem and concern about the lack of reporting by teachers also indicate a need for in-service programs to assist teachers in recognizing signs of abused and neglected children.

Although sanctions have rarely been imposed on educators for failure to report abuse inflicted by parents, recent litigation has involved allegations that school employees are the abusers. These cases have received substantial publicity and raised questions regarding the duties of teachers, administrators, and school boards to report suspicions of abuse and to prevent such abuse from occurring in the school setting by employees.

Litigation has addressed whether a school district's failure to protect students from suspected abuse by school employees violates students' constitutional or statutory rights.[158] Damages can be sought under the Civil Rights Act of 1871, 42 U.S.C. Section 1983, if a claimant has been deprived of a federally protected right by an individual acting under official state policy or custom.[159] Although the Supreme Court did not find a violation of a federal right in a case involving a social worker's failure to intervene when she knew a child was being severely beaten by his father (a private individual), abuse in the school setting involves actions by public employees.[160] The Third Circuit recognized a clearly established constitutional right to bodily security—to be free from sexual abuse—and found that school districts may violate this right by maintaining a policy, practice, or custom reflecting "deliberate indifference" to this right. The court concluded that the student's evidence showing that school officials' actions in discouraging and minimizing reports of sexual misconduct by teachers and failing to take action on complaints may have established a custom or practice in violation of Section 1983.[161] If school officials have not had knowledge of abuse or acted with indifference to complaints, liability has not been assessed.[162]

In addition to Section 1983 liability, the Supreme Court in *Franklin v. Gwinnett County Public Schools* ruled that monetary damages are available under Title IX of the Education Amendments of 1972[163] if school authorities are knowledgeable of sexual abuse and harassment and fail to stop it.[164] Following *Gwinnett,* the Supreme

---

158. *See, e.g.,* Doe v. Gooden, 214 F.3d 952 (8th Cir. 2000) (ruling that failure to report suspected abuse as required by state law does not establish unconstitutional misconduct); Abeyta v. Chama Valley Indep. Sch. Dist., 77 F.3d 1253 (10th Cir. 1996) (holding that gender-specific verbal abuse by a teacher does not give rise to a constitutional violation; calling a student a prostitute is a substantial abuse of authority but not a violation of substantive due process rights).

159. See text accompanying note 210, Chapter 11.

160. DeShaney v. Winnebago County Dep't of Soc. Servs., 489 U.S. 189 (1989).

161. Stoneking v. Bradford Area Sch. Dist., 882 F.2d 720 (3d Cir. 1989). For a definition of the "deliberate indifference" standard, *see* City of Canton, Ohio v. Harris, 489 U.S. 378 (1989).

162. *See, e.g.,* P.H. v. Sch. Dist., 265 F.3d 653 (8th Cir. 2001); Canutillo Indep. Sch. Dist. v. Leija, 101 F.3d 393 (5th Cir. 1996); Gates v. Unified Sch. Dist. No. 449, 996 F.2d 1035 (10th Cir. 1993).

163. 20 U.S.C. § 1681–1688 (2002). *See t*ext accompanying note 148, Chapter 5.

164. 503 U.S. 60 (1992).

Court in *Gebser v. Lago Vista Independent School District* addressed the standard for assessing school district liability in Title IX cases involving teachers' sexual harassment of students. The Court rejected the student's argument that the district should be held liable for the misconduct of an individual teacher in the absence of school authorities' actual knowledge of the abuse. The Court ruled that a school official "who at a minimum has *authority to institute corrective* measures on the district's behalf" must have *actual knowledge* of the abuse and respond with *deliberate indifference* to the victim.[165]

In subsequent litigation, courts have assessed who is an "appropriate official" with authority, what constitutes "actual knowledge," and what substantiates "deliberate indifference." *Gebser* did not identify which individuals in the school district must have knowledge. Is this a person who can initiate an investigation, or must the individual possess the power to terminate the suspected abuser? Without deciding whether a principal possesses this authority, several courts have assumed for the purpose of analyzing claims that principals have the power to remedy abuse.[166] The Third Circuit concluded that a principal's knowledge is sufficient, noting that "if a principal is not an 'appropriate person' for purposes of Title IX, a substantial portion of the Supreme Court's analysis in *Gebser* was nothing more than a meaningless discussion."[167] The Fourth Circuit, however, specifically ruled that a principal in Virginia does not possess the requisite power to hire, fire, transfer, or suspend teachers to serve as a proxy for the school district.[168]

Questions also have arisen concerning notice of sexual harassment or abuse. Evidence indicating a potential risk has not been equated with actual knowledge. For example, the Eighth Circuit noted that sexual abuse could not be inferred simply because a teacher was spending considerable time with one student or appeared to be showing favoritism.[169] Similarly, the Eleventh Circuit did not find a student's complaint about a teacher touching her when she played center and he was quarterback during a football game in a physical education class or his attempt to touch her later at a water fountain to be adequate notice to the school district of possible sexual abuse of other students.[170] A New York federal district court, however, found that a principal had notice of a teacher's sexual harassment of a student when the student's mother reported his inappropriate sexual comments, touching, and innuendoes.[171]

165. 524 U.S. 274, 277 (1998).

166. Davis v. Dekalb County Sch. Dist., 233 F.3d 1367 (11th Cir. 2000); Doe v. Dallas Indep. Sch. Dist., 220 F.3d 380 (5th Cir. 2000). *See also* Floyd v. Waiters, 133 F.3d 786 (11th Cir. 1998) (ruling in a pre-*Gebser* case that the superintendent or school board must be aware of conduct to be liable); Flores v. Saulpaugh, 115 F. Supp. 2d 319 (N.D.N.Y. 2000) (holding that principal had the authority to address the suspected abuse and institute corrective measures).

167. Warren v. Reading Sch. Dist., 278 F.3d 163, 170 (3d Cir. 2002).

168. Baynard v. Malone, 268 F.3d 228 (4th Cir. 2001), *cert. denied,* 122 S. Ct. 1357 (2002).

169. P.H. v. Sch. Dist., 265 F.3d 653 (8th Cir. 2001). *See also Davis,* 233 F.3d 1367.

170. *Davis,* 233 F.3d 1367.

171. *Flores,* 115 F. Supp. 2d 319.

To counter claims of deliberate indifference, school officials must show that they took action on complaints. Although a principal's actions were not effective in preventing a teacher's sexual abuse of students, the Fifth Circuit commented that it could not find her response inadequate.[172] Similarly, a principal who followed up a complaint by asking the counselor to interview the student and the accused teacher as well as other possible witnesses and by taking corrective measures even though it appeared nothing had happened was not responding with indifference.[173] Although these actions did not prevent the teacher from sexually molesting students, the court found the relevant fact to be that the principal did not act with deliberate indifference.

Given the availability of damages and fewer restrictions (no cap on damage awards or requirement to exhaust administrative remedies), increased litigation can be expected under Title IX for teacher-to-student sexual harassment.[174] With the judicial recognition that sexual abuse by school employees can result in school district liability, school boards are developing and implementing policies for handling child abuse complaints and protecting teachers and other school employees from becoming the targets of false child abuse charges. It is becoming increasingly common for school boards to prohibit physical contact between teachers and students in the absence of another adult and to place restrictions on private meetings between students and teachers before or after school. Employees can face disciplinary action for failing to comply with such directives, even if they are not found guilty of actual child abuse.

Conclusion

Except for certain limitations imposed by constitutional provisions and federal civil rights laws, state statutes govern educators' employment. The state prescribes general requirements for certification, contracts, tenure, and employment. Local school boards must follow state mandates and, in addition, may impose other requirements. In general, the following terms and conditions govern teacher employment.

1. The state establishes minimum qualifications for license, which may include professional preparation, a minimum age, U.S. citizenship, good moral character, signing a loyalty oath, and passing an academic examination.
2. A teacher must acquire a valid license to teach in public schools.
3. A license does not assure employment in a state.
4. A license may be revoked for cause, generally identified in state law.
5. School boards are vested with the power to appoint teachers and to establish professional and academic employment standards above the state minimums.

172. Doe v. Dallas Indep. Sch. Dist., 220 F.3d 380 (5th Cir. 2000).

173. *Davis,* 233 F.3d 1367.

174. *See* text accompanying notes 146–157, Chapter 5, for discussion of challenges involving student-to-student harassment.

6. Courts generally have upheld school board residency requirements, reasonable health and physical standards, and background checks prior to employment if formulated on a reasonable basis.

7. A teacher may be assigned or transferred to any school or grade at the board's discretion, as long as the assignment is within the teacher's certification area and not circumscribed by contract terms.

8. School officials can make reasonable and appropriate extracurricular assignments.

9. Teacher contracts must satisfy the general principles of contract law as well as conform to any additional specifications contained in state law.

10. Tenure is a statutory right ensuring that dismissal is based on adequate cause and accompanied by procedural due process.

11. Tenure must be conferred in accordance with statutory provisions.

12. Supplemental contracts for extra-duty assignments are generally outside the scope of tenure laws.

13. A school board's broad authority to determine teacher performance standards may be restricted by state-imposed evaluation requirements.

14. Maintenance, access, and dissemination of personnel information must conform to state law and contractual agreements.

15. Personnel records can be subpoenaed to assess discrimination charges.

16. Educators must comply with the federal copyright law; copyrighted materials may be used for instructional purposes without the publisher's permission if fair use guidelines are followed.

17. All states have laws requiring teachers to report suspected child abuse and granting immunity from liability if reports are made in good faith.

18. School districts will be held liable for teacher harassment or abuse of students if someone in a position of authority to take corrective measures has actual knowledge of the abuse and responds with deliberate indifference.

9

Teachers' Substantive Constitutional Rights

Although statutory law is prominent in defining specific terms and conditions of employment, substantive rights also are conferred on public employees by the Federal Constitution. These rights cannot be abridged by legislation or school board action without an overriding governmental interest, nor can employment be conditioned on their relinquishment. The exercise of these protected rights often results in a conflict between school officials and teachers, requiring judicial resolution.

This chapter presents an overview of the scope of teachers' constitutional rights as defined by the judiciary in connection with free expression, academic freedom, freedom of association, freedom of choice in appearance, and privacy rights. Constitutional rights pertaining to equal protection, due process, and religious guarantees as well as remedies available to aggrieved individuals when their rights have been abridged are discussed in other chapters.

Freedom of Expression

Until the mid-twentieth century, it was generally accepted that public school teachers could be dismissed or disciplined for expressing views considered objectionable by the school board. The private-sector practice of firing such employees was assumed to apply to public employment as well. Since the late 1960s, however, the Supreme Court has recognized that the First Amendment limits public employers' discretion to condition employment on the expression of certain views, including those critical of governmental policies. Although it is now clearly established that free expression rights are not forfeited by accepting public school employment, courts have acknowledged that First Amendment rights must be weighed against the school district's interest in maintaining effective and efficient schools. In this section, the evolution of legal principles articulated by the Supreme Court and their application to specific school situations are reviewed.

Legal Principles

In the landmark 1968 decision, *Pickering v. Board of Education,* the Supreme Court recognized that teachers have a First Amendment right to air their views on matters of public concern.[1] Pickering wrote a letter to a local newspaper, criticizing the school board's fiscal policies, especially the allocation of funds between the education and athletic programs. The school board dismissed Pickering because of the letter, which included false statements allegedly damaging the reputations of school board members and district administrators. The Illinois courts upheld the dismissal.

Reversing the state courts, the Supreme Court first identified expression pertaining to matters of public concern as constitutionally protected and reasoned that the funding and allocation issues raised by Pickering were clearly questions of public interest requiring free and open debate. The Court then applied a balancing test, weighing the teacher's interest in expressing his views on public issues against the school board's interest in providing educational services. The Court recognized that if the exercise of protected expression jeopardized Pickering's relationship with his immediate supervisor, harmony with coworkers, classroom performance, or school operations, the school board's decision to curtail the expression would prevail. Concluding that Pickering's letter did not have a detrimental effect in any of these areas, the Court found no justification for limiting his contribution to public debate. Indeed, the Court noted that a teacher's role provides a special vantage point from which to formulate an "informed and definite opinion" on the allocation of school district funds, thus making it essential for teachers to be able to speak about public issues without fear of reprisal.[2] Furthermore, the Court held that false statements about matters of public record, without proof that they were "knowingly or recklessly" made, cannot be the basis for dismissal.

Since *Pickering,* teachers often have challenged dismissals or other disciplinary actions on grounds that their exercise of protected expression elicited the adverse employment consequences. In 1977, the Supreme Court established the principle that even if a teacher's expression is constitutionally protected, school officials are not prevented from discharging the employee if sufficient cause exists *independent* of the protected speech. In *Mt. Healthy City School District v. Doyle,* a school board voted not to renew the contract of a nontenured teacher who had made a telephone call to a local radio station concerning a proposed teacher grooming code. The teacher had been involved in several previous incidents, but in not renewing his contract the board cited "lack of tact in handling professional matters," referring only to the radio call

---

1. 391 U.S. 563 (1968). *See also* Bd. of County Comm'rs v. Umbehr, 518 U.S. 668 (1996) (holding that independent contractors are considered the same as public employees in weighing the government's interests against the contractors' free speech interests under the *Pickering* balancing test).
2. 391 U.S. at 572.

and obscene gestures made to several female students.[3] The lower courts ruled in favor of the teacher, but the Supreme Court reversed, instructing the courts below to assess whether the school board would have reached the same decision in the absence of the teacher's exercise of protected speech. The Supreme Court reasoned that protected expression should not place an employee in a better or worse position with regard to continued employment. On remand, the board clearly established that there were sufficient grounds other than the radio station call to justify the teacher's nonrenewal.[4]

Under the *Mt. Healthy* test, the burden is on the employee to show that the conduct is constitutionally protected and a substantial or motivating factor in the school board's adverse employment decision. Once established, the burden then shifts to the board to show by a preponderance of evidence that it would have reached the same decision if the protected expression had not occurred. Even if proven that the school board's decision was predicated on comments related to matters of public concern, the decision might still be upheld applying the *Pickering* balancing test, if established that the expression interfered with working relationships or disrupted school operations.

For over a decade after the *Pickering* decision, it was unclear whether public employees' *private* communications enjoyed First Amendment protection. In 1979, the Supreme Court concluded in *Givhan v. Western Line Consolidated School District* that as long as the expression pertains to matters of public concern (in contrast to personal grievances), statements made in private or through a public medium are constitutionally protected.[5] The teacher had made critical comments to her principal regarding race relations in the school, and the Court reasoned that the forum where the expression occurs does not determine whether it is of public or personal interest. Although the comments were found to be constitutionally protected, the Court did note that the balancing process may include additional considerations when private speech is involved. Whereas public expression is generally evaluated on its content and impact, private expression—because of the nature of the employer-employee relationship—also should be assessed based on the time, place, and manner of the remarks. Thus, it may be somewhat easier to establish a First Amendment impairment if the expression is made through a public medium, but the main determinant is whether the comments pertain to a matter of public concern.

In a significant 1983 decision, *Connick v. Myers,* the Supreme Court's interpretation of the *Pickering* balancing test narrowed the circumstances under which public employees can prevail in free expression cases.[6] The Court reiterated that the threshold inquiry is whether the expression involves matters of public concern, since personal grievances are not protected by the First Amendment. Of particular importance was the Court's conclusion that the *form* and *context* as well as the content of the

3. 429 U.S. 274, 282 (1977).

4. Doyle v. Mt. Healthy City Sch. Dist., 670 F.2d 59 (6th Cir. 1982).

5. 439 U.S. 410 (1979).

6. 461 U.S. 138 (1983).

expression should be considered in assessing whether it relates to public matters. Thus, the Court indicated that the factors applied under the *Pickering* balancing test to determine whether speech adversely affects governmental interests can be considered in the *initial* assessment of whether the expression informs public debate or is simply part of a personal employment grievance. For expression in the latter category, no additional constitutional scrutiny is required.

In *Connick,* an assistant district attorney was dissatisfied with her proposed transfer and circulated a questionnaire concerning office operations and morale among coworkers. She was subsequently terminated and challenged the action as violating her First Amendment rights. Reversing the lower courts, the Supreme Court ruled that the questionnaire related primarily to a personal employment grievance rather than matters of public interest. Only one question (regarding pressure to participate in political campaigns) was found to involve a public issue. The Court concluded that the employee's dismissal did not offend the First Amendment, weighing various factors—the importance of close working relationships to fulfill public responsibilities, the employee's attempt to solicit a vote of no confidence in the district attorney, distribution of the questionnaire during office hours, the district attorney's conclusion that office operations were endangered, and the questionnaire's very limited connection to a public concern.

The *Connick* majority recognized that the state's burden of justifying a given discharge varies according to the nature of the employee's expression; the employer's burden increases as the employee's speech more directly involves public issues and decreases as the expression interferes with close working relationships that are essential to fulfilling public responsibilities. The majority did concede, however, that this "particularized balancing" of competing interests is a difficult task.[7]

In 1994, the Supreme Court again addressed the scope of public employees' free speech rights in *Waters v. Churchill.*[8] Churchill, a nurse at a public hospital, was discharged for making critical comments about hospital operations to a coworker during a break. The comments were overheard by other coworkers, and although there was dispute about exactly what was said, Churchill's supervisors maintained that the expression disrupted the work environment. The Supreme Court plurality categorized Churchill's expression about the hospital's training policy and its impact on patient care as criticisms of her employer rather than comments on matters of public concern. The plurality further concluded that as long as the employer conducted an investigation and acted in good faith, it could discharge an employee for remarks it *believed* were made, regardless of what was actually said. In short, the government employer can reach its factual conclusions without being held to the evidentiary rules followed by courts, so the dispute over what was said did not have to be resolved by a jury. *Waters* and *Connick,* taken together, have made it more difficult for public employees

---

7. *Id.* at 150. *See also* Rankin v. McPherson, 483 U.S. 378 (1987) (assessing the context, form, and content of a public employee's pejorative statement to a coworker following the assassination attempt on President Reagan and finding no basis for dismissal in the absence of interference with work relationships or performance).

8. 511 U.S. 661 (1994).

to succeed in claims that adverse employment actions have impaired their First Amendment expression rights than was true in the decade following the *Pickering* decision.

Application of the Legal Principles

During the 1970s and early 1980s, courts relied on the *Pickering* guidelines in striking down a variety of restrictions on teachers' rights to express views on matters of public interest. Courts ordered reinstatement, nullified transfers, and ordered letters of reprimand expunged from records when evidence substantiated that dismissals or other disciplinary actions were based on the exercise of protected expression, such as wearing black arm bands as a symbolic protest against the Vietnam War, making public comments favoring a collective bargaining contract, and criticizing the instructional program and other school policies.[9]

Since the early 1980s, however, courts have seemed increasingly inclined to view teachers' and other public employees' expression as unprotected, finding that it relates to *private* employment disputes rather than to matters of public concern. To illustrate, federal appeals court have relied on *Connick* in concluding that the following expression pertains primarily to private grievances: communicating in letters to school officials dissatisfaction with overcrowded classrooms and other aspects of the work environment,[10] filing a grievance after being assigned a job-sharing position that meant part-time employment,[11] sending sarcastic critical memoranda to school officials,[12] and protesting unfavorable performance evaluations.[13] Federal appellate courts also have considered the following to be unprotected expression that can be grounds for dismissal or other disciplinary action: circulating a letter to colleagues about the delay in receipt of summer pay and urging teachers to participate in a "sick out" during examination week,[14] criticizing working conditions and low staff morale

---

9. *See, e.g.,* Lemons v. Morgan, 629 F.2d 1389 (8th Cir. 1980); Swilley v. Alexander, 629 F.2d 1018 (5th Cir. 1980); McGill v. Bd. of Educ., 602 F.2d 774 (7th Cir. 1979).

10. Ifill v. District of Columbia, 665 A.2d 185 (D.C. App. 1995). *See also* Ferrara v. Mills, 781 F.2d 1508 (11th Cir. 1986) (holding that complaints about class assignments, a policy allowing students to select their own courses, and the hiring of coaches to teach social studies did not pertain to public concerns).

11. Renfroe v. Kirkpatrick, 722 F.2d 714, 715 (11th Cir. 1984) *See also* Love-Lane v. Martin, 201 F. Supp. 2d 566 (M.D.N.C. 2002) (finding an assistant principal's disagreements with supervisors regarding school discipline and use of a time-out room to be private grievances).

12. Hesse v. Bd. of Educ., 848 F.2d 748 (7th Cir. 1988). *See also* Kadetsky v. Egg Harbor Township Bd. of Educ., 164 F. Supp. 2d 425 (D.N.J. 2001) (finding no link between adverse actions against a band director and his filing a grievance; his purported protected expression about a parental complaint and continuing problems with his principal and department head pertained to his own employment status rather than to public concerns).

13. Day v. S. Park Indep. Sch. Dist., 768 F.2d 696 (5th Cir. 1985). *See also* Roberts v. Van Buren Pub. Schs., 773 F.2d 949 (8th Cir. 1985) (holding that a grievance, expressing elementary teachers' dissatisfaction with the way parental complaints concerning a field trip had been handled, pertained more to the teacher/principal relationship than to a public concern).

14. Stroman v. Colleton County Sch. Dist., 981 F.2d 152 (4th Cir. 1992).

in a faculty newsletter,[15] and commenting about students' test scores after being instructed by the superintendent not to speak publicly on this topic.[16]

In post-*Connick* cases, courts have considered the *impact* of expression in the initial determination of whether it is protected, even if the expression touches on issues of public concern.[17] For example, the Tenth Circuit ruled that a school nurse's criticism of the school district's student medication policy, an issue of undeniable public interest, was not constitutionally protected because the expression disrupted the school's health service program.[18]

Applying *Waters,* disputes over what was said will not necessarily negate a dismissal based on private expression as long as the school board has conducted a reasonable investigation. And of course, employees cannot assert that they have suffered adverse employment consequences because of protected speech if they have denied making the comments at issue.[19]

Individuals involved in setting policy for a public agency relinquish some free speech rights to criticize their employers, because of the impact of their expression on how the agency functions. The Seventh Circuit found no impairment of free speech rights in the demotion of a principal to assistant principal for opposing the school district's efforts to secure approval of a program for disadvantaged students.[20] Similarly, the Sixth Circuit considered the importance of a tension-free superintendent/principal relationship in concluding that a principal's complaints about the superintendent's elimination of a dress code were not protected.[21] Also, a New York federal court held that a central office administrator's public statements criticizing the interim superintendent and district employees could be the basis for his termination. The court reasoned that the statements would likely impair discipline and relationships with superiors and coworkers and impede the administrator's performance of his duties.[22]

Although *Connick* and *Waters* have made it more difficult for public employees to establish that their expression is constitutionally protected, this burden can be satisfied. If the expression clearly relates to the welfare of students, it is afforded First Amendment protection. The First Circuit held that a teacher could not be dismissed for criticizing a cutback in the district's high school reading program and filing several

15. Sanguigni v. Pittsburgh Bd. of Educ., 968 F.2d 393 (3d Cir. 1992).

16. Partee v. Metro. Sch. Dist., 954 F.2d 454 (7th Cir. 1992).

17. Finding employees' expression unprotected because it jeopardized relationships with superiors and fulfillment of job responsibilities, *see, e.g.,* Marquez v. Turnock, 967 F.2d 1175 (7th Cir. 1992); Hall v. Ford, 856 F.2d 255 (D.C. Cir. 1988); Derrickson v. Bd. of Educ., 738 F.2d 351 (8th Cir. 1984).

18. Johnsen v. Indep. Sch. Dist. No. 3, 891 F.2d 1485 (10th Cir. 1989). *See also* Jeffries v. Harleston, 21 F.3d 1238 (2d Cir. 1994), *vacated and remanded,* 513 U.S. 996 (1994), *on remand,* 52 F.3d 9 (2d Cir. 1995) (holding that a university employee's off-campus speech on public issues that included derogatory statements about Jews threatened to interfere with government operations).

19. *See, e.g.,* Wasson v. Sonoma County Junior Coll., 203 F.3d 659 (9th Cir. 2000); Fogarty v. Boles, 121 F.3d 886 (3d Cir. 1997).

20. Vargas-Harrison v. Racine Unified Sch. Dist., 272 F.3d 964 (7th Cir. 2001), *cert. granted,* 123 S. Ct. 120 (2002).

21. Sharp v. Lindsey, 285 F.3d 479 (6th Cir. 2002).

22. McCullough v. Wyandanch Union Free Sch. Dist., 132 F. Supp. 2d 87 (E.D.N.Y. 2001).

grievances with the teachers' union.[23] Also, the Eighth Circuit held that a letter written by three teachers to the state department of education, complaining about the school district's delay in implementing programs for children with disabilities, pertained to a matter of public concern.[24] The Fifth Circuit found protected expression in teachers' protests regarding the school board's decision to cancel an art program serving predominantly minority children,[25] and in comments about efforts to raise the school's level of education.[26]

Federal appeals courts also have found teachers' expressions pertaining to bond issues or tax referenda to be constitutionally protected.[27] In addition, federal courts have considered expression about employee safety following a workplace rape[28] and criticism in the media of the school district's instructional requirements during Black History Month[29] to pertain to matters of public concern.

Educators who blow the whistle on unlawful or unethical acts are likely to find their expression protected. The Second Circuit ruled that an assistant principal's allegations of cheating on student achievement tests were protected.[30] Federal courts similarly have found impairments of employees' First Amendment rights in connection with their criticisms of employment practices based on political patronage,[31] bus driver safety and misconduct in the management of private bus contractors,[32] and unlawful activity in the school's athletic department.[33]

23. Fishman v. Clancy, 763 F.2d 485 (1st Cir. 1985). *See* text accompanying note 226, Chapter 11.

24. Southside Pub. Schs. v. Hill, 827 F.2d 270 (8th Cir. 1987).

25. Tompkins v. Vickers, 26 F.3d 603 (5th Cir. 1994).

26. Harris v. Victoria Indep. Sch. Dist. 168 F.3d 216 (5th Cir. 1999).

27. Hall v. Marion Sch. Dist., 31 F.3d 183 (4th Cir. 1994); Ware v. Unified Sch. Dist. No. 492, 902 F.2d 815 (10th Cir. 1990); Stewart v. Baldwin County Bd. of Educ., 908 F.2d 1499 (11th Cir. 1990).

28. *See, e.g.,* Kennedy v. Tangipahoa Parish Library Bd., 224 F.3d 359 (5th Cir. 2000).

29. Clark v. Bd. of Educ., 907 F. Supp. 826 (D.N.J. 1995).

30. Canary v. Osborn, 211 F.3d 324 (6th Cir. 2000). *See also* Patton v. Sch. Dist. #53, No. 99 C 1812, 2000 U.S. Dist. LEXIS 5983 (N.D. Ill. March 20, 2000) (finding administrator's speech about school board and superintendent misconduct to be protected).

31. Williams v. Kentucky, 24 F.3d 1526 (6th Cir. 1994) (finding no evidence that the criticism interfered with relationships, performance, or discipline in the public agency).

32. McHugh v. Bd. of Educ., 100 F. Supp. 2d 231 (D. Del. 2000). *See also* DePace v. Flaherty, 183 F. Supp. 2d 633 (S.D.N.Y. 2002) (holding that a principal's criticism of the superintendent for public intoxication and driving under the influence was protected expression and could not be the basis for adverse employment action); Koch-Weser v. Bd. of Educ., No. 98 C 5157, 2001 U.S. Dist. LEXIS 14044 (N.D. Ill. Sept. 6, 2001) (finding impermissible retaliation for a teacher's exercise of protected expression, including speaking on behalf of custodial and kitchen workers and expressing views on changes in the biology curriculum).

33. Morse v. Escobedo, No. 3:98-CV-0686-X, 1998 U.S. Dist. LEXIS 9027 (N.D. Tex. June 16, 1998) (finding a violation of the teacher's free speech rights, but reasoning that reassignment and loss of coaching duties did not constitute such a status change to be regarded as loss of employment). *See also* Green v. Me. Sch. Admin. Dist. #77, 52 F. Supp. 2d 98 (D. Me. 1999) (finding genuine issue of fact as to whether adverse employment action was based on a teacher's protected speech pertaining to whistleblower claim).

Political expression and union activities are clearly protected by the First Amendment.[34] The Eighth Circuit affirmed a jury's verdict that a teacher's dismissal was based on protected union-related expression rather than on using indecent language with a student.[35] Espousing similar logic, the Sixth Circuit rejected the nonrenewal of a probationary teacher, finding that the action was based on constitutionally protected union activities rather than the asserted reasons of declining teaching evaluations and a personality conflict with the principal.[36] However, an employee cannot transform private grievances about conditions of employment into matters of public concern by simply airing the personal concerns in a union forum.[37]

It must be noted that courts differ as to what expression directly relates to student or school welfare, and similar factual situations may elicit different judicial responses. The Seventh Circuit concluded that a teacher's complaints about class size and student discipline constituted a private grievance,[38] and in another case held that a teacher's expression about student discipline and classroom management focused on the personal impact on the teacher rather than on the welfare of the class.[39] In contrast, the Tenth Circuit ruled that a teacher's critical expression regarding the school district's method of disciplining students pertained to a public concern and was constitutionally protected.[40]

The Seventh Circuit recognized that incidences of sexual harassment in a school district were matters of public concern, but held that an employee's private complaints of harassment were intended to resolve a personal dispute rather than to shed light on a public issue.[41] Conversely, the Tenth Circuit held that a letter signed by most faculty members alleging sexual harassment of students and teachers related to a public concern.[42] The Eighth Circuit found a First Amendment violation in the nonrenewal of a teacher's contract for writing a letter to the newspaper protesting the school board's

---

34. *See, e.g.,* Morfin v. Albuquerque Pub. Schs., 906 F.2d 1434 (10th Cir. 1990); Saye v. St. Vrain Valley Sch. Dist., 785 F.2d 862 (10th Cir. 1986), *on remand,* 650 F. Supp. 716 (D. Colo. 1986).

35. Hinkle v. Christensen, 733 F.2d 74 (8th Cir. 1984).

36. Hickman v. Valley Local Sch. Dist. Bd. of Educ., 619 F.2d 606 (6th Cir. 1980).

37. *See, e.g.,* Hale v. Robersone, No. 96-1241-CV-W-6, 1998 U.S. Dist. LEXIS 13316 (W.D. Mo. June 25, 1998).

38. Cliff v. Bd. of Educ., 42 F.3d 403 (7th Cir. 1994) (noting that the comments were made in response to deficiencies listed on the teacher's performance evaluations). *See also* Berbas v. Bd. of Educ., No. 00 C 2734, 2000 U.S. Dist. LEXIS 11097 (N.D. Ill. June 28, 2000) (finding complaint about classroom conditions a subject of public interest, but the teacher's grievance addressed only her individual concerns as a teacher and did not meet the "public concern" standard).

39. Wales v. Bd. of Educ., 120 F.3d 82 (7th Cir. 1997).

40. Rankin v. Indep. Sch. Dist., 876 F.2d 838 (10th Cir. 1989).

41. Callaway v. Hafeman, 832 F.2d 414 (7th Cir. 1987).

42. Wren v. Spurlock, 798 F.2d 1313 (10th Cir. 1986). *See also* Seemuller v. Fairfax County Sch. Bd., 878 F.2d 1578 (4th Cir. 1989) (finding a teacher's publication of a satirical letter in the high school newspaper, regarding allegations of sex discrimination in the physical education department, to involve a matter of public concern).

decision to drop junior high school track, which he coached.[43] But, the Seventh Circuit held that a teacher's comments to the newspaper, voicing dissatisfaction with the school board's decision to replace him as the high school basketball coach, involved a personal grievance and could be the basis for cancelling the teacher's contract.[44] The *form* and *context* of the expression may determine whether its purpose is to further private interests or to air public concerns.

Even if protected speech is involved, courts have relied on *Mt. Healthy* to uphold terminations or transfers where other legitimate reasons justify the personnel actions.[45] The Fifth Circuit applied *Mt. Healthy* in upholding a teacher's dismissal based on a confrontation with the assistant coach during a basketball game and repeated threats toward the athletic director. The fact that the teacher also had criticized the athletic program did not negate the legitimate grounds for dismissal.[46] Similarly, the Eighth Circuit found that although a teacher's memo to the superintendent about improper storage of dangerous chemicals in the high school was a matter of public concern, the teacher's contract was not renewed for other legitimate reasons (e.g., criticizing the school administration in front of students, making a vulgar gesture behind the superintendent's back).[47] The First Circuit held that even though a teacher's criticism of the special education director and student placement practices at a school board meeting was the motivating factor in the board's decision not to renew her contract, the board would have taken this action for other legitimate reasons (e.g., difficulty with the special education director, unprofessional conduct in case conference meetings).[48]

More recently, the Eighth Circuit upheld the termination of a state university professor, noting that most of his speech was not protected, and even his statements on public concerns (e.g., criticisms of administrators' salaries and the growing number of nonacademic staff members) were not the substantial factor in the termination

43. McGee v. S. Pemiscot Sch. Dist. R-V, 712 F.2d 339 (8th Cir. 1983).

44. Vukadinovich v. Bartels, 853 F.2d 1387 (7th Cir. 1988). *See also* Vukadinovich v. Bd. of Sch. Trs., 278 F.3d 693 (7th Cir. 2002) (holding that the same teacher failed to show that proffered justifications—insubordination and neglect of duty—for his termination from a different job were pretextual to mask retaliation for exercising free speech rights).

45. For a description of the four-stage analysis under *Mt. Healthy, see* Johnson v. Clifton, 74 F.3d 1087, 1092 (11th Cir. 1996).

46. White v. S. Park Indep. Sch. Dist., 693 F.2d 1163 (5th Cir. 1982). *See also* Flath v. Garrison Pub. Sch. Dist., 82 F.3d 244 (8th Cir. 1996) (holding that the teacher failed to show that her contract nonrenewal was substantially motivated by her criticism of the principal).

47. Ingrum v. Nixa Reorganized Sch. Dist., 966 F.2d 1232 (8th Cir. 1992). *See also* Fowler v. Smith, 68 F.3d 124 (5th Cir. 1995) (holding that a maintenance worker was terminated for unprofessional conduct and not his opposition to privatizing school maintenance).

48. Wytrwal v. Saco Sch. Bd., 70 F.3d 165 (1st Cir. 1995). *See also* Oden v. Chi. Sch. Reform Bd. of Trs., No. 97 C 8579, 2000 U.S. Dist. LEXIS 7538 (N.D. Ill. March 31, 2000) (finding that a transferred teacher did not show that her complaints were the motivating force behind the transfer decision).

decision.[49] Also, the Seventh Circuit held that teachers were not dismissed for criticism of a specific academic program and/or the principal's interactions with teachers, but rather for legitimate reasons pertaining to their poor performance.[50] And, the Sixth Circuit ruled that involuntarily transferred teachers had engaged in protected speech pertaining to discipline and instructional strategies, but found insufficient evidence that their transfer was motivated by the protected speech.[51] A New York federal court reasoned that a teacher's dismissal for misconduct in trying to raise her pupils' test scores did not mask retaliation for her filing a notice of claim against other city officials.[52]

School authorities cannot rely on *Mt. Healthy* to justify termination or other adverse employment action if the school officials' stated reasons for personnel decisions are merely a pretext to restrict protected expression. For example, the Tenth Circuit ruled that a Wyoming teacher's termination for alleged lack of satisfactory progress, enthusiasm, and cooperation was in fact impermissibly based on protected speech involving public criticism of the new superintendent's proposed changes in teaching methods.[53] Similarly, the Seventh Circuit held that a counselor, allegedly dismissed for 14 incidents of insubordination and unprofessional misconduct, was actually fired in retaliation for protected expression, including articles he wrote for the local paper and criticisms of various school board procedures and actions.[54]

Assuming that the employee carries the difficult burden of establishing that the adverse employment action would not have occurred *but for* the protected expression, the school still might prevail applying the *Pickering* balancing test. If established that expression on matters of public concern is the motivating or even the sole basis for adverse action, the public employer still has the opportunity to establish that its interests in maintaining efficient school operations outweigh the individual's free speech rights. The Eighth Circuit found that teachers' interests in speaking about incidents with special education students was outweighed by interests in efficiently administering the middle school, given that the expression caused school upheaval.[55] The same

---

49. De Llano v. Berglund, 282 F.3d 1031 (8th Cir. 2002). *See also* Nieves v. Bd. of Educ., 297 F.3d 690 (7th Cir. 2002) (holding that an employee was terminated for legitimate budgetary reasons and not for speaking out about discrimination in the school against Hispanics); Patterson v. Masem, 774 F.2d 251 (8th Cir. 1985) (finding that the denial of promotion to a supervisory role was not in retaliation for the teacher recommending that an allegedly racially offensive play not be performed).

50. Love v. Chi. Bd. of Educ., 241 F.3d 564 (7th Cir. 2001). *See also* Settlegoode v. Portland Pub. Schs., No. CV-00-313-ST, 2002 U.S. Dist. LEXIS 2238 (D. Or. Jan. 31, 2002) (finding that the employee's nonrenewal was for her inability to write adequate individual education plans, rather than for her complaints about treatment of special education students).

51. Leary v. Daeschner, 228 F.3d 729 (6th Cir. 2000).

52. Rivera v. Cmty. Sch. Dist. Nine, 145 F. Supp. 2d 302 (S.D.N.Y. 2001).

53. Simineo v. Sch. Dist. No. 16, 594 F.2d 1353 (10th Cir. 1979).

54. Dishnow v. Sch. Dist., 77 F.3d 194 (7th Cir. 1996). *See also* Mosley v. Reynolds, 165 F.3d 28 (6th Cir. 1998) (holding that protected expression, rather than unsatisfactory performance as asserted by the board, was the basis for not renewing a teacher's contract).

55. Fales v. Garst, 235 F.3d 1122 (8th Cir. 2001).

court previously upheld the dismissal of a teacher who objected to releasing names of preschool students in a child count report. The court reasoned that the teacher's behavior impeded her ability to perform her duties and undermined the effective operation of the school.[56]

In applying the principles articulated by the Supreme Court, the threshold question is whether the speech pertains to a public issue considering the content, form, and context of the expression. During the 1970s, it was generally assumed that even educators' expression involving matters of private rather than public interest could not be the basis for adverse personnel action unless the expression posed some threat of disrupting the educational process.[57] But, post-*Connick* cases indicate that sanctions can be imposed for the expression of private concerns in the absence of any disruptive effect.[58] Thus, the threshold determination of whether the speech pertains to public or private issues has become increasingly important. Moreover, under *Waters,* the school board has considerable discretion in determining what constitutes unprotected, personal expression. As long as the board makes a reasonable effort to investigate the nature of the expression and its conclusion is not clearly arbitrary, a court will accept the board's decision.

Prior Restraint and Channel Rules

Although *reprisals* for expression have been the focus of most litigation, courts also have addressed *prior restraints* on public employees' expression and restrictions on the communication channels through which views may be aired. The judiciary has been more reluctant to condone prior restraints on expression than it has to uphold disciplinary action after the expression has occurred. A key is whether the prior restraint is content-based, which requires strict judicial scrutiny, or whether it is content neutral, thus receiving a "less rigorous examination."[59]

For example, the Tenth Circuit struck down a portion of an Oklahoma law authorizing the termination of teachers for "advocating . . . public or private homosexual activity in a manner that creates a substantial risk that such conduct will come to the attention of school children or school employees."[60] The appellate court held that such restrictions on teachers' expression could not be imposed unless shown to be

56. Porter v. Dawson Educ. Serv. Coop., 150 F.3d 887 (8th Cir. 1998). *See also* Brewster v. Bd. of Educ., 149 F.3d 971 (9th Cir. 1998) (recognizing that a probationary teacher's expression about errors in the attendance reporting process related to a public concern, but holding that consideration had to be given to the disharmony caused by the expression among coworkers and the teacher's relationship with the principal).

57. *See, e.g.,* James v. Bd. of Educ., 461 F.2d 566 (2d Cir. 1972) (finding that the teacher was dismissed arbitrarily and unjustifiably for wearing a black armband to protest the Vietnam War).

58. Prior to *Connick,* courts often relied on the principle that undifferentiated fear of disruption was not sufficient to curtail free expression rights. *See* Tinker v. Des Moines Indep. Cmty. Sch. Dist., 393 U.S. 503 (1969); text accompanying note 57, Chapter 4.

59. Eclipse Enter., Inc. v. Gulotta, 134 F.3d 63, 66 (2d Cir. 1997).

60. Nat'l Gay Task Force v. Bd. of Educ., 729 F.2d 1270, 1274 (10th Cir. 1984), *aff'd by an equally divided court,* 470 U.S. 903 (1985).

necessary to prevent "a material or substantial interference or disruption in the normal activities of the school."[61] The Supreme Court divided evenly in this case, thereby affirming the appellate court's ruling.

The Fifth Circuit also invalidated a school board policy requiring prior approval of all political, sectarian, or special-interest materials distributed in the schools. The board had invoked the policy to prevent distribution of documents that were critical of a proposed teacher testing program, whereas the school board's literature supporting the program had been distributed in the schools. The court reasoned that school authorities cannot permit only one side to promote its position.[62] The court noted, however, that the policies were not invalidated simply because they required prior approval; rather, they were unconstitutional because they did not "furnish sufficient guidance" to prohibit school administrators from exercising "unbridled discretion" in curtailing communication within the schools.[63]

In a significant 1983 decision, *Perry Education Association v. Perry Local Educators' Association,* the Supreme Court ruled that a school district is not constitutionally obligated to allow a rival teachers' union access to internal school mailboxes, although the exclusive bargaining agent is granted such access. Holding that a public school's internal mail system is not a public forum for expression, the Court declared that "the state may reserve the forum for its intended purposes, communicative or otherwise, as long as the regulation on speech is reasonable and not an effort to suppress expression merely because public officials oppose the speaker's view."[64] The Court determined that alternative communication channels were available to the rival union.

Subsequently, the Supreme Court affirmed a Fifth Circuit decision that a Texas school district had not created a public forum in either its schools or school mail facilities; therefore, the district could deny school access during school hours to representatives of teachers' organizations and could bar their use of the school mail system.[65] However, the court found a First Amendment violation in school policies that denied teachers the right to discuss employee organizations during nonclass time or to use school mail facilities for communications including any mention of employee organizations.

Under certain circumstances, a school's mail system might be considered a public forum because it has been designated as such by school officials. Applying the

---

61. *Id.,* 729 F.2d at 1274 (citing, in part, Pickering v. Bd. of Educ., 391 U.S. 563, 568 (1968) and Tinker v. Des Moines Indep. Cmty. Sch. Dist., 393 U.S. 503, 513 (1969)).

62. Hall v. Bd. of Sch. Comm'rs, 681 F.2d 965 (5th Cir. 1982).

63. *Id.* at 969.

64. Perry Educ. Ass'n v. Perry Local Educators' Ass'n, 460 U.S. 37, 46 (1983). *See* text accompanying note 94, Chapter 12.

65. Tex. State Teachers Ass'n v. Garland Indep. Sch. Dist., 777 F.2d 1046 (5th Cir. 1985), *aff'd mem.,* 479 U.S. 801 (1986) (holding that the school's selective visitation policy, under which certain groups of educators and representatives of textbook companies and civic and charitable groups were allowed to meet with teachers during school hours, did not create a public forum). *See also* Tex. State Teachers Ass'n v. Garland Indep. Sch. Dist., 489 U.S. 782 (1989) (awarding attorneys' fees for work on issues on which teachers' association prevailed); text accompanying note 96, Chapter 12.

principle articulated in *Perry,* the Fifth Circuit reasoned that although a school was not obligated to open its internal mail system to the general public or to employee organizations, in this case the school had designated its mail system a forum for all employee organizations and thus could not selectively deny access.[66] The court also found the school district's guidelines, requiring prior clearance of material distributed through the mail system, to be unconstitutionally vague.

Most controversies have focused on teachers' organizations using school facilities and mail systems, but other prior restraints on expression also have been challenged. The Seventh Circuit upheld a school board's denial of a request by a group of teachers to hold religious meetings in the public school before students arrived in the morning.[67] The court held that employees cannot assert a free speech right to use public school facilities for expressive purposes not related to school business, reasoning that the public school is not a forum for employees to hold meetings on matters of personal concern. Reflecting similar reasoning, the Fourth Circuit more recently upheld restrictions on state employees' access to sexually explicit Internet materials on computers owned or leased by the state.[68]

Policies limiting teachers' access to the school board also have generated legal disputes. Several courts have struck down policies prohibiting individual teachers from communicating with the school board. In 1976, the Supreme Court held that a nonunion teacher has a free speech right to comment on a bargaining issue at a public school board meeting.[69] Also, the Ninth Circuit awarded a teacher-coach damages for his suspension as a coach, which occurred because he did not advise the superintendent before writing a letter to school board members about an issue of public concern.[70] Similarly, the Seventh Circuit struck down a policy requiring all communication to the school board to be directed through the superintendent and ordered a reprimand for violating the policy to be removed from a teacher's personnel file.[71] A New York federal district court also denied a superintendent's motion for summary judgment in connection with an allegation that he improperly subjected a teacher's correspondence to prior review; the teacher was trying to communicate with the school board regarding possible misuse of school funds.[72]

66. Ysleta Fed'n of Teachers v. Ysleta Indep. Sch. Dist., 720 F.2d 1429 (5th Cir. 1983) (holding further that the school board had not yet produced evidence of a compelling interest for limiting employee organizations to one distribution of recruitment literature per year through the school mail system).

67. May v. Evansville-Vanderburgh Sch. Corp., 787 F.2d 1105 (7th Cir. 1986).

68. Urofsky v. Gilmore, 216 F.3d 401 (4th Cir. 2000), *cert. denied,* 531 U.S. 1070 (2001).

69. City of Madison, Joint Sch. Dist. No. 8 v. Wis. Employment Relations Comm'n, 429 U.S. 167 (1976). *See* text with note 103, Chapter 12.

70. Anderson v. Cent. Point Sch. Dist., 746 F.2d 505 (9th Cir. 1984).

71. Knapp v. Whitaker, 757 F.2d 827 (7th Cir. 1985). *See also* Unified Sch. Dist. No. 503 v. McKinney, 689 P.2d 860 (Kan. 1984) (finding the school board guilty of unconstitutional prior restraint for forbidding teachers from speaking at school board meetings or holding press conferences in school buildings).

72. Dauber v. Bd. of Educ., No. 99 Civ. 3931 (LMM), 2001 U.S. Dist. LEXIS 16768 (S.D.N.Y. Oct. 18, 2001) (finding, however, the alleged instances of retaliatory actions to be trivial and not to impact significantly the teacher's employment).

Although prior restraints on teachers' free speech rights are vulnerable to legal attack, courts have upheld reasonable time, place, and manner regulations. Such restrictions must not be based on the content of speech, and they must serve significant governmental interests and leave alternative communication channels open.[73]

Academic Freedom

From its origin in German universities, the concept of academic freedom historically was applied to postsecondary education and embodied the principle that faculty members should be free from governmental controls in conducting research and imparting knowledge to students. The concept has undergone substantial change in American universities, where faculty members have claimed a First Amendment right to academic freedom in research and teaching as well as activities away from the classroom.

Public school teachers have asserted a similar right to academic freedom, but courts have not extended the protections found in higher education to public elementary and secondary schools.[74] Teachers possess judicially recognized academic interests, but courts have refrained from establishing precise legal principles in this domain. Rather, controversies have been resolved on a case-by-case basis, involving a delicate balancing of teachers' interests in academic freedom against school boards' interests in assuring an appropriate instructional program and efficient school operations.

Controversies pertaining to censorship of public school courses and materials are addressed in Chapters 2 and 3; this section concentrates specifically on public educators' academic freedom within the classroom setting. Can a teacher determine the most appropriate materials for classroom use? Does the First Amendment protect a teacher's expression of personal ideas and philosophies? Is a teacher free to determine teaching methodologies? What topics or issues can a teacher discuss in a course?

Course Content

In contrast to some discretion enjoyed by university faculty in curriculum matters,[75] public school teachers in elementary and secondary schools do not have a right to

---

73. *See, e.g.,* Godwin v. E. Baton Rouge Parish Sch. Bd., 408 So. 2d 1214, 1216 (La. 1981) *But see* Crue v. Aiken, 204 F. Supp. 2d 1130 (C.D. Ill. 2002) (holding that a university chancellor's directive, prohibiting all speech directed toward prospective student athletes without prior permission, was an impermissible content-based restraint to keep students and faculty from discussing athletic program mascot with recruits).

74. *See, e.g.,* Bates v. Dallas Indep. Sch. Dist., 952 S.W.2d 543 (Tex. Ct. App. 1997) (holding that a teacher's refusal to assign a grade to a student, as instructed by his supervisor, is not shielded by academic freedom).

75. Even at the college level, courts recently have tended to conclude that faculty members do not have a First Amendment right to determine what is taught in the curriculum. *See, e.g.,* Edwards v. Cal. Univ. of Penn., 156 F.3d 488 (3d Cir. 1998) (upholding suspension of a tenured university professor for a semester for departing from the approved course syllabus and injecting religious teaching in his educational media course; university professors do not have a First Amendment right to choose classroom materials).

determine the content of the instructional program. As addressed in Chapter 3, state legislatures have plenary power to set the public school curriculum, and they usually grant local school boards considerable authority to establish programs of study and prescribe course content, including the scope and sequence of materials. Several courts have declared that school boards are not legally obligated to accept teachers' curricular recommendations in the absence of a board policy to that effect. The Tenth Circuit upheld a school board's rejection of a proposal from teachers for books to use in the English curriculum, "even though the decision was a political one influenced by the personal views of the [board] members."[76] The Fifth Circuit also held that teachers cannot assert a First Amendment right to substitute their own supplemental reading list for the officially adopted list without securing administrative approval.[77]

The Fourth Circuit held that a high school teacher did not have complete discretion to select the plays performed by her students. The teacher had selected a play dealing with a dysfunctional, single-parent family for some advanced acting students to perform in a statewide competition, and the principal ordered that certain material be deleted because of parents' complaints. At the end of the year, the principal requested that the teacher be transferred due to personal conflicts resulting from her failure to follow the school system's policy regarding controversial materials. Finding production of the play to be part of the curriculum rather than protected speech, the court recognized that school officials have legitimate pedagogical interests in regulating the curriculum.[78]

Teachers are not permitted to ignore or omit prescribed course content under the guise of academic freedom. To illustrate, the Seventh Circuit upheld a school board's dismissal of a kindergarten teacher who, for religious reasons, refused to teach patriotic topics.[79] The Supreme Court of Washington similarly found no First Amendment impairment in a school board prohibiting two teachers from team-teaching a history course. The court reasoned that "course content is manifestly a matter within the board's discretion," and requiring teachers to cover this content in a conventional manner does not violate their academic freedom.[80]

Other courts have rendered similar decisions regarding school board requirements for conformity in content coverage. The Eighth Circuit upheld the dismissal of a teacher who ignored her principal's warnings to cover prescribed material in her

---

76. Cary v. Bd. of Educ., 598 F.2d 535, 544 (10th Cir. 1979). *See also* LeVake v. Indep. Sch. Dist. #656, 625 N.W.2d 502 (Minn. Ct. App. 2001) (upholding reassignment of a teacher for criticizing evolution in class and refusing to teach the required course curriculum in the manner established by the school board), text accompanying note 82, Chapter 2.

77. Kirkland v. Northside Indep. Sch. Dist., 890 F.2d 794 (5th Cir. 1989).

78. Boring v. Buncombe County Bd. of Educ., 136 F.3d 364 (4th Cir. 1998).

79. Palmer v. Bd. of Educ., 603 F.2d 1271, 1274 (7th Cir. 1979). *See also* Roberts v. Madigan, 921 F.2d 1047 (10th Cir. 1990) (upholding requirement that a teacher remove religiously oriented books from his classroom library and refrain from silently reading his Bible during class did not impair his academic freedom), text accompanying note 75, Chapter 2.

80. Millikan v. Bd. of Dirs. , 611 P.2d 414, 418 (Wash. 1980).

economics course, emphasizing that academic freedom does not include the right to disregard a superior's valid instructional directives regarding appropriate course content.[81] The Colorado Supreme Court upheld a policy requiring administrative review of "controversial learning resources," noting the district's legitimate pedagogical interest in shaping its secondary school curriculum.[82] Finding the policy neither vague nor overbroad, the court upheld termination of a teacher for showing his high school class portions of a movie that included nudity, profanity, and graphic violence.

The Supreme Court of Alaska endorsed a school board's rule requiring the superintendent's approval of supplementary materials used in the classroom.[83] A teacher refused to comply with this rule in selecting materials to teach about homosexual rights in a unit on American Minorities. Acknowledging that the issue was not whether the materials selected by the teacher were appropriate, but rather where the authority to make curriculum determinations resides, the court concluded that the school board has such authority.

Teachers' instructional activities generally are governed by *Hazelwood School District v. Kuhlmeier,*[84] which allows school authorities to censor school-sponsored expression for pedagogical reasons. Recognizing that the state, as employer, has the right to control the curriculum, the Ninth Circuit rejected a vagueness challenge to California legislation holding teachers personally liable for actual damages if they willfully refuse to teach predominantly in English.[85] The court reasoned that in the vast majority of instances, it would be clear to teachers when they were dispensing instruction that would be subject to the language restriction.

Departing from the general trend of evaluating teachers' instructional expression under *Hazelwood,* the Sixth Circuit applied the *Pickering/Connick* analysis[86] to a teacher's classroom speech in a Kentucky case. The appeals court found genuine issues of material fact regarding whether the school district's proffered grounds for terminating the teacher (i.e., insubordination, conduct unbecoming a teacher, inefficiency, incompetency, and neglect of duty) were a pretext because of the notoriety surrounding the teacher's decision to invite an actor, Woody Harrelson, to her class-

81. Ahern v. Bd. of Educ., 456 F.2d 399 (8th Cir. 1972). *See also* Murray v. Pittsburgh Bd. of Educ., 919 F. Supp. 838 (W.D. Pa. 1996), *aff'd mem.,* 141 F.3d 1154 (3d Cir. 1998) (holding that a teacher could not assert a First Amendment right to disregard school board instructions and continue to use a classroom management technique, Learnball, that gave students responsibility for establishing class rules and grading procedures).

82. Bd. of Educ. v. Wilder, 960 P.2d 695, 702 (Colo. 1998) (rejecting also the teacher's due process claim, finding that sufficient notice of the policy had been provided).

83. Fisher v. Fairbanks N. Star Borough Sch. Dist., 704 P.2d 213 (Alaska 1985). *See also* Sch. Admin. Dist. No. 58 v. Mt. Abram Teachers Ass'n, 704 A.2d 349 (Me. 1997) (finding educational policy decisions about selection of novels for the tenth-grade curriculum to be within the school board's authority and not subject to grievance and arbitration procedures under the collective bargaining agreement).

84. 484 U.S. 260 (1988). *See* text accompanying note 42, Chapter 4.

85. Cal. Teachers Ass'n v. State Bd. of Educ., 271 F.3d 1141 (9th Cir. 2001).

86. *See supra* text accompanying notes 1–7.

room to give presentations on the environmental benefits of industrial hemp.[87] The court held that although the teacher was speaking as an employee when presenting the information on industrial hemp, the content of her speech involved political and social concerns of the community and not merely matters of private interest. The court held that the defendants' interests in efficient operation of the school and a harmonious workplace did not outweigh the teacher's interests in speaking about an issue of substantial concern in the state.

Expressing Personal Views in the Classroom

Public school classrooms are not public forums, and school boards can restrict teachers' discretion to air their personal views in class if the restrictions are based on legitimate pedagogical concerns.[88] As discussed in Chapter 2, teachers cannot use their classrooms to proselytize students, and school board prohibitions on religious advocacy consistently have been upheld.[89] Also, courts have upheld adverse employment action against teachers who share their views on topics after instructed not to do so.

A Louisiana appeals court found that a teacher's statements regarding the sexual behavior of African Americans lacked any pedagogical justification and thus were not protected by the First Amendment.[90] The First Circuit also held that a teacher's discussion of abortion of Down syndrome fetuses could be curtailed, noting that the school board may limit a teacher's classroom expression in the interest of promoting educational goals.[91]

87. Cockrel v. Shelby County Sch. Dist., 270 F.3d 1036 (6th Cir. 2001), *cert. denied,* 123 S. Ct. 73 (2002). *See also* Hardy v. Jefferson Cmty. Coll., 260 F.3d 671 (6th Cir. 2001), *cert. denied,* 122 S. Ct. 1436 (2002) (ruling that a state college instructor could use racial and gender epithets during a class discussion, as the expression was germane to the course topics and addressed a matter of public concern).

88. *See, e.g.,* Debro v. San Leandro Unified Sch. Dist., No. C-99-0676 VRW, 2001 U.S. Dist. LEXIS 17388 (N.D. Cal. Oct. 11, 2001) (holding that a teacher had no First Amendment right to depart from classroom instruction to discuss tolerance toward homosexuals, even though of public interest). However, school counselors may discuss controversial issues in confidence with counselees and provide factual information on topics such as the legal status of abortions, but they cannot urge or coerce students to have abortions. *See* Arnold v. Bd. of Educ., 880 F.2d 305 (11th Cir. 1989), *on remand,* 754 F. Supp. 853 (S.D. Ala. 1990).

89. *See, e.g.,* Webster v. New Lenox Sch. Dist. No. 122, 917 F.2d 1004 (7th Cir. 1990), text accompanying note 164, Chapter 2.

90. Simon v. Jefferson Davis Parish Sch. Bd., 289 So. 2d 511 (La. Ct. App. 1974). *See also* Dambrot v. Cent. Mich. Univ., 55 F.3d 1177 (6th Cir. 1995) (finding that a university coach's use of "nigger" in discussions with his players was not protected academic freedom), text accompanying note 82, Chapter 4; Elstrom v. Indep. Sch. Dist. No. 270, 533 N.W.2d 51 (Minn. Ct. App. 1995) (rejecting defamation claim by a teacher who was disciplined for making inappropriate comments in class that perpetuated negative racial stereotypes; the defamation suit centered on a letter of apology the principal sent to parents of students in the class). *But see* Scruggs v. Keen, 900 F. Supp. 821 (W.D. Va. 1995) (holding that a teacher's comments on interracial dating made in response to students' questions during study hall pertained to a public concern; the school district's request for summary judgment was denied because of questions regarding why the teacher's contract was not renewed).

91. Ward v. Hickey, 996 F.2d 448 (1st Cir. 1993).

The Tenth Circuit upheld disciplinary action against a teacher who made comments during class about rumors that two students had engaged in sexual intercourse on the school tennis court during lunch hour.[92] Relying on *Hazelwood,* the court reasoned that the ninth-grade government class was not a public forum and that the teacher's classroom expression could be regulated for legitimate pedagogical reasons.[93]

More recently, a high school teacher did not prevail in his efforts to post material outside his classroom that denounced homosexuality and extolled traditional family values. His display was intended to offset the posted materials recognizing Gay and Lesbian Awareness Month as required by the Los Angeles Unified School District.[94] Reasoning that the teacher was speaking for the school, the Ninth Circuit concluded that teachers' rights to express views off campus do not entitle them to express views in the classroom that are counter to the adopted curriculum.[95]

Espousing similar reasoning, a Virginia federal district court ruled that a teacher had no First Amendment right to post outside his classroom door the American Library Association's pamphlet listing banned books to "educate" his students and others who passed by.[96] The court reasoned that such expression was an extension of the curriculum and could be censored for educational reasons. The principal and superintendent felt that the pamphlets contained information potentially compromising the school's family life education program and other initiatives.

Teaching Strategies

State laws and school board policies establish the basic contours of the curriculum, but teachers retain some discretion in choosing *strategies* to convey prescribed content. In reviewing school board restrictions on teachers' classroom activities, the judiciary considers a number of factors, such as whether teachers have been provided adequate notice that use of specific teaching methodologies or materials will result in disciplinary action, the relevance of the method to the course of study, the threat of disruption posed by the method, and the impact of the strategy on community norms.

Adequate Notice.   Courts in general have recognized teachers' discretion to select appropriate teaching methods that serve a demonstrated educational purpose. If a par-

---

92. Miles v. Denver Pub. Schs., 944 F.2d 773 (10th Cir. 1991). *See also* Abeyta v. Chama Valley Indep. Sch. Dist. No. 19, 77 F.3d 1253 (10th Cir. 1996) (recognizing that a teacher calling a student a prostitute in class would be an abuse of authority under state law; however, such action would not give rise to the student bringing a § 1983 substantive due process claim for damages).

93. *But see* Cockrel v. Shelby County Sch. Dist., 270 F.3d 1036 (6th Cir. 2001), *cert. denied,* 123 S. Ct. 73 (2002), *supra* text accompanying note 87.

94. Downs v. L.A. Unified Sch. Dist., 228 F.3d 1003 (9th Cir. 2000), *cert. denied,* 532 U.S. 994 (2001).

95. *Id.* at 1011. The Supreme Court has recognized that when the speaker is conveying a particular message on behalf of the government, content distinctions can be imposed. *See* Rosenberger v. Rector and Visitors, 515 U.S. 828, 833 (1995); Rust v. Sullivan, 500 U.S. 173, 194-200 (1991).

96. Newton v. Slye, 116 F. Supp. 2d 677 (W.D. Va. 2000) (noting, however, that the teacher could still distribute the pamphlets in the classroom as part of the instructional program and students continued to have access to the pamphlets).

ticular method is supported by the profession, the teacher has no reason to anticipate that its use might result in disciplinary action unless there is a regulation forbidding the method. This procedural right of notice that specific methods are prohibited often is the decisive factor in academic freedom cases.

Failure to provide notice of prohibited material was questioned in a Texas case, where a high school civics teacher was dismissed for addressing controversial topics such as interracial marriages and antiwar protests in his classes.[97] The court upheld the teacher's right to select valid teaching methods and found that the lack of notice regarding prohibited subject matter denied the teacher procedural due process.

In contrast, the First Circuit more recently found no First Amendment violation in a teacher's suspension for handing a document to a student that contained indecent content. The court noted that the Massachusetts law permitting termination for "conduct unbecoming a teacher" furnishes sufficient notice that indecent speech directed toward students is impermissible.[98] Courts addressing the procedural due process issue have indicated that although teachers enjoy some measure of discretion, certain classroom conduct may be restricted by the school board if proper notice of proscribed methods is given.

Relevancy. A primary consideration in reviewing the legitimacy of classroom activities is whether instructional strategies are related to course objectives. In the absence of such a relationship, the teacher's behavior is not constitutionally protected. Relevancy applies not only to objectives but also to the age and maturity of the students; a controversial topic appropriate for high school students, for example, would not necessarily be suitable for elementary and junior high pupils. Even though a certain method may be considered relevant, if it lacks the general support of the profession, a school board still may prevail in barring its use.

The Seventh Circuit upheld the dismissal of teachers for distributing a brochure on the pleasures of drug use and sex to an eighth-grade class without explanation; the brochure was unrelated to class activities and lacked a legitimate educational purpose.[99] Relevance to course objectives has also been found lacking in several cases in which teachers have shown R-rated movies to public school students.[100] Similarly, the Eighth Circuit upheld termination of a teacher who willfully violated board policy by

97. Sterzing v. Fort Bend Indep. Sch. Dist., 376 F. Supp. 657 (S.D. Tex. 1972), *vacated and remanded,* 496 F.2d 92 (5th Cir. 1974). *See also* Mailloux v. Kiley, 448 F.2d 1242 (1st Cir. 1971) (acknowledging that use of a slang term for sexual intercourse in a high school discussion of taboo words lacks professional support and could be the basis for dismissing the teacher, but ordering reinstatement because there was no regulation prohibiting the teaching method); Keefe v. Geanakos, 418 F.2d 359 (1st Cir. 1969) (relying on inadequate notice and relevance of the materials to negate disciplinary action against a high school English teacher for using an article from the *Atlantic Monthly,* which parents asserted contained a vulgar term).

98. Conward v. Cambridge Sch. Comm., 171 F.3d 12 (1st Cir. 1999).

99. Brubaker v. Bd. of Educ., 502 F.2d 973 (7th Cir. 1974). *See also* Silano v. Sag Harbor Union Free Sch. Dist. Bd. of Educ., 42 F.3d 719 (2d Cir. 1994) (finding no First Amendment violation in the school board's censure of one of its members who showed a tenth-grade class a film clip that included nude actors; the board's action was based on legitimate pedagogical concerns).

permitting her students to use profanity in their creative writing assignments.[101] And, the Second Circuit allowed a state college to dismiss a teacher for a classroom "clustering" exercise in which students uttered sexually profane comments in a word-association exercise.[102]

However, teachers cannot be forced to discontinue instructionally relevant activities solely because of parental displeasure. The Fifth Circuit ruled that a teacher's use of a simulation to teach about post-Civil War American history was related to legitimate educational objectives; therefore, dismissal for refusing to stop using the simulation impaired the teacher's academic rights.[103] Similarly, the Sixth Circuit ordered reinstatement of a teacher who had been effectively discharged when citizens complained to the school board regarding his instruction in a life science course. The teacher was suspended and told that he would be terminated after he refused to accept a letter of reprimand. The court found the teacher's classroom behavior appropriate and relevant to the course objectives, noting that the films and text had been approved by the school board and used for several years.[104]

Threat of Disruption.   Among the factors courts examine in assessing restrictions on classroom instruction is whether a teacher's action poses a threat of disruption to the operation of the school. An Alabama federal district court singled out this factor and the age-appropriateness of instructional strategies in invalidating the dismissal of an eleventh-grade English teacher for using a Kurt Vonnegut story that allegedly encouraged "the killing off of elderly people and free sex."[105] The court found the story appropriate for high school students and held that it did not threaten a disruption. An Oregon federal district court found a school board's policy, banning all political speakers from the high school, unreasonable on several grounds, including the fact

100. *See, e.g.,* Fowler v. Bd. of Educ., 819 F.2d 657 (6th Cir. 1987); Bd. of Educ. v. Wilder, 960 P.2d 695, 712 (Colo. 1998). *But see* West v. Tangipahoa Parish Sch. Bd., 615 So. 2d 979 (La. Ct. App. 1993) (overturning dismissal of a teacher with an excellent record for showing two R-rated movies to students).

101. Lacks v. Ferguson Reorganized Sch. Dist. R-2, 147 F.3d 718 (8th Cir. 1998). *See also* Oleske v. Hilliard City Sch. Dist., 764 N.E.2d 1110 (Ohio Ct. App. 2001) (upholding dismissal of a teacher who told dirty jokes to middle school students and referred to another teacher by a derogatory name).

102. Vega v. Miller, 273 F.3d 460 (2d Cir. 2001), *cert. denied,* 122 S. Ct. 2295 (2002).

103. Kingsville Indep. Sch. Dist. v. Cooper, 611 F.2d 1109 (5th Cir. 1980).

104. Stachura v. Memphis Cmty. Sch. Dist., 763 F.2d 211 (6th Cir. 1985), *rev'd and remanded* (regarding award of compensatory damages), 477 U.S. 299 (1986). For a discussion of the damages issue, *see* text accompanying note 188, Chapter 11. *See also* Hosford v. Sch. Comm., 659 N.E.2d 1178 (Mass. 1996) (overturning suspension and subsequent nonrenewal of a teacher for her brief, pedagogically valid discussion of vulgar words in a therapy session with students).

105. Parducci v. Rutland, 316 F. Supp. 352, 353-354 (M.D. Ala. 1970). *See also* Bauer v. Sampson, 261 F.3d 775 (9th Cir. 2001) (finding that a professor's right to express insulting and uncivil views on a matter of public concern outweighed the college's interests in curtailing the expression to ensure no disruption; the college's policies prohibiting workplace violence, including "violent behavior overtones," were facially overbroad).

that no disruptions had occurred or could be anticipated from political discussions.[106] A Texas federal court found that community objections to a teacher's administration of a survey regarding sex roles did not equate to disruption of the school system.[107]

However, an Illinois federal district court recognized that a school board does not necessarily have to show that instructional materials actually caused a disruption to justify nonrenewal of a teacher's contract. Materials may be considered inappropriate for classroom use (e.g., an R-rated film with vulgarity and sexually explicit scenes), even though students "quietly acquiesce" to their use.[108] Also, the Supreme Court of Maine held that a school board's decision to cancel a Tolerance Day program did not impair First Amendment rights, as the decision was based on a legitimate concern for safety, order, and security due to bomb threats that had been received.[109]

Community Standards. Courts have been protective of school boards' authority to design the curriculum to reflect community values. The Seventh Circuit has recognized that school board members represent the community, which "has a legitimate, even a vital and compelling, interest 'in the choice [of] and adherence to a suitable curriculum for the benefit of our young citizens.'"[110] Other courts have similarly acknowledged that community standards can be considered in determining the appropriateness of teaching materials and methods and that school boards are empowered to establish the curriculum to transmit community values. For example, a New York appeals court held that a teacher who defied warnings that use of certain materials and sexual words in classroom discussions offended community mores had no First Amendment grounds to challenge his reprimand.[111]

Yet, the judiciary also has recognized that school boards cannot suppress First Amendment rights simply to placate angry citizens, especially if only selected viewpoints on a topic are suppressed. In a case discussed previously, the Sixth Circuit held that parental complaints and community protests regarding a teacher's instruction in a life science course, taught in conformance with school board directives, did not justify the school board placing restrictions on the teacher's classroom activities.[112]

---

106. Wilson v. Chancellor, 418 F. Supp. 1358 (D. Or. 1976). *See also Kingsville,* 611 F.2d 1109 (holding that complaints from parents and students about use of a simulation to teach history did not constitute a sufficient disruption to destroy the teacher's effectiveness).

107. Dean v. Timpson Indep. Sch. Dist., 486 F. Supp. 302 (E.D. Tex. 1979).

108. Krizek v. Bd. of Educ., 713 F. Supp. 1131, 1141 (N.D. Ill. 1989).

109. Solmitz v. Me. Sch. Admin. Dist. No. 59, 495 A.2d 812 (Me. 1985).

110. Zykan v. Warsaw Cmty. Sch. Corp., 631 F.2d 1300, 1304 (7th Cir. 1980) (quoting Palmer v. Bd. of Educ., 603 F.2d 1271, 1274 (7th Cir. 1979)).

111. *In re* Arbitration Between Bernstein and Norwich City Sch. Dist., 726 N.Y.S.2d 474 (App. Div. 2001). *See also* Ashcroft v. ACLU, 122 S. Ct. 1700 (2002) (finding that the Child Online Protection Act's reliance on community standards to assess materials harmful to minors on the World Wide Web does not abridge the First Amendment, but enjoining the law's implementation pending further proceedings); text accompanying note 117, Chapter 3.

112. Stachura v. Memphis Cmty. Sch. Dist., 763 F.2d 211 (6th Cir. 1985), *rev'd and remanded* (regarding award of compensatory damages), 477 U.S. 299 (1986).

More recently, the Eighth Circuit found sufficient evidence that a teacher's contract was not renewed for religious concerns that she was promoting New Age doctrine by sending a letter and a "magic" rock home with her second-graders at the end of school.[113] The letter accompanying the rock indicated that if the students rub the magic rock and think good things about themselves, they can do whatever they set their minds to do. The teacher was awarded two years of pay, but the court did not order reinstatement because of the damaged relationship between the teacher and school principal.

Given the school board's legitimate interest in advancing community mores, the judiciary has considered community standards in evaluating challenges to various teaching methods. Yet, if a particular strategy is instructionally relevant and supported by the profession, it likely will survive judicial review even though it might disturb some school patrons.

Freedom of Association

Although freedom of association is not specifically addressed in the First Amendment, the Supreme Court has recognized that associational rights are "implicit in the freedoms of speech, assembly, and petition."[114] The Court has consistently declared that infringements on the right to associate for expressive purposes can be justified only by a compelling governmental interest—unrelated to suppressing ideas—that cannot be achieved through less restrictive means.[115] Accordingly, public educators cannot be disciplined for forming or joining political, labor, religious, or social organizations.

Associational activities can be limited, however, if they disrupt school operations or interfere with teachers' professional duties. The Seventh Circuit found no violation of associational rights in the transfer of a teacher from a high school administrative position to an elementary school position, because the school district's interest in neutralizing bickering factions at the high school far outweighed the teacher's associational interests.[116] Also, a Texas federal district court ruled that a school district could restrict a school administrator's social relationships with certain public officials, specifying that the administrator refrain from discussing school district issues outside the presence of a designated legislative representative.[117]

113. Cowan v. Strafford R-VI Sch. Dist., 140 F.3d 1153 (8th Cir. 1998).

114. Healy v. James, 408 U.S. 169, 181 (1972).

115. *See, e.g.,* NAACP v. Button, 371 U.S. 415 (1963); NAACP v. Alabama *ex rel.* Patterson, 357 U.S. 449, 460–461 (1958). Although voicing support for this principle, the Supreme Court in some cases has seemed to apply something less than strict scrutiny in evaluating the impact of challenged state action on associational rights. *See, e.g.,* FEC v. Colo. Republican Fed. Campaign Comm., 533 U.S. 431 (2001), *infra* note 140; Nixon v. Shrink Mo. Gov't PAC, 528 U.S. 377 (2000) (upholding state law limiting campaign contributions for state political candidates).

116. Klug v. Chi. Sch. Reform Bd. of Trs., 197 F.3d 853 (7th Cir. 1999).

117. Ibarra v. Houston Indep. Sch. Dist., 84 F. Supp. 2d 825 (S.D. Tex. 1999).

This section presents an overview of teachers' associational rights in connection with political affiliations and activities. Public educators' rights to intimate association are discussed in the section on privacy rights (later in this chapter), and labor union issues are addressed in Chapter 12.

Political Affiliations

States have made attempts to prohibit or limit teachers' affiliations with subversive political organizations. These restrictions have been imposed to protect public schools from treasonable and seditious acts. In early cases, the Supreme Court held that associational rights could be restricted when a public employee was fully knowledgeable of an organization's subversive purpose,[118] but in the mid-1960s this stance was rejected. Although teachers can be required to affirm their support of the federal and respective state constitutions,[119] the Supreme Court has invalidated loyalty oaths requiring individuals to deny membership in subversive organizations as unduly vague or imposing sanctions for "guilt by association."[120] The Supreme Court in *Keyishian v. Board of Regents* firmly established that mere membership in an organization, such as the Communist Party, without the specific intent to further the unlawful aims of the organization could not disqualify an individual for public school employment.[121]

Thus, state statutes barring members of subversive or controversial organizations from public employment are unconstitutional.[122] The Texas Supreme Court recognized that "it is immaterial whether the beliefs sought to be advanced by association pertain to political, economic, religious or cultural matters"; state action with the effect of "curtailing the freedom of association is subject to the closest scrutiny."[123] Neither can a school system directly or indirectly impose restrictions on teachers' memberships or their lawful activities in certain organizations. As with protected speech, dismissal of a teacher will rarely be permitted if the motivating factor is the teacher's exercise of associational rights.

Governmental action need not proscribe organizational membership to abridge the Federal Constitution; courts will scrutinize challenged laws that *inhibit* associational rights unless the state can show that such measures are narrowly tailored to advance a compelling governmental interest. The Supreme Court overturned an Arkansas law that annually required all teachers to list every organization they had

118. *See, e.g.,* Adler v. Bd. of Educ., 342 U.S. 485 (1952); Wieman v. Updegraff, 344 U.S. 183 (1952).

119. *See, e.g.,* Cole v. Richardson, 405 U.S. 676 (1972); Connell v. Higginbotham, 403 U.S. 207 (1971). Employees also can be required to pledge that they will oppose the overthrow of the the government and that they will fulfill their job responsibilities. *See* text accompanying note 5, Chapter 8.

120. *See, e.g.,* Keyishian v. Bd. of Regents, 385 U.S. 589, 606 (1967); Elfbrandt v. Russell, 384 U.S. 11, 19 (1966).

121. 385 U.S. 589.

122. *See, e.g.,* NAACP v. Alabama *ex rel.* Patterson, 357 U.S. 449 (1958).

123. *In re* Bay Area Citizens Against Lawsuit Abuse, 982 S.W.2d 371 (Tex. 1998) (quoting *Patterson,* 357 U.S. at 460–461).

joined or regularly supported during the prior five years, because it constituted a "comprehensive interference with associational freedom."[124] Similarly, the Fifth Circuit struck down a Texas statute that allowed county judges to compel certain organizations engaged in activities designed to disrupt public schools to disclose their membership lists.[125] As in the Arkansas case, this law also swept too broadly by exposing to public recrimination those members who did not participate in disruptive activities.

The fact that associational rights are protected by the First Amendment, however, does not preclude school administrators from questioning a teacher about activities that may adversely affect teaching. In *Beilan v. Board of Public Education of Philadelphia,* the Supreme Court held that questions regarding a teacher's activities in the Communist Party were relevant to an assessment of his classroom activities and fitness to teach, and that refusal to answer the superintendent's inquiries could result in dismissal.[126] Although organizational membership per se is protected, a teacher must respond to queries about associational activities that are related to teaching fitness.

Conditioning public employment on partisan political affiliation also has been controversial. Historically, the patronage system governed public employment; when the controlling political party changed, noncivil service employees belonging to the defeated party lost their jobs. In 1976, the Supreme Court ruled that the patronage system in an Illinois sheriff's office placed a severe restriction on political association and belief.[127] The constant threat of replacing nonpolicymaking individuals, who cannot undermine the administration's policies, was considered detrimental to governmental effectiveness and efficiency. In 1980, the Court reiterated that the democratic process would be preserved by limiting patronage dismissals to policymaking positions where the public employer can demonstrate that party affiliation is an appropriate requirement for effective job performance.[128]

A decade later, the Court extended the principle established in the political firing cases to all aspects of public employment, ruling that party affiliation cannot influence promotion, transfer, recall, and other decisions pertaining to employees who do not establish policies.[129] The Sixth Circuit subsequently recognized four categories of positions that can be conditioned on political affiliation: (1) those named in law as having discretionary authority in carrying out policy, (2) those to which a considerable amount of discretionary authority has been delegated by persons in category one,

124. Shelton v. Tucker, 364 U.S. 479, 490 (1960).
125. Familias Unidas v. Briscoe, 619 F.2d 391 (5th Cir. 1980).
126. 357 U.S. 399 (1958).
127. Elrod v. Burns, 427 U.S. 347 (1976)
128. Branti v. Finkel, 445 U.S. 507 (1980).
129. Rutan v. Republican Party, 497 U.S. 62 (1990). *See also* Armour v. County of Beaver, 271 F.3d 417 (3d Cir. 2001), *cert. denied,* 122 S. Ct. 1963 (2002) (holding that access to confidential information alone was insufficient to establish that political affiliation was an appropriate job requirement for a secretary to the county commissioner).

(3) those who spend a significant portion of time advising position holders in category one or two, and (4) those positions filled to balance political party representation.[130]

Despite being insulated from partisan politics by state law, in some instances public educators have asserted that employment decisions have been based on party affiliation. In such cases, the school employee has the burden of substantiating that protected political affiliation was the motivating factor in the board's employment decision.[131] If an employee satisfies this burden, then the board must demonstrate by a preponderance of evidence that it would have reached the same decision in the absence of the political association. In an illustrative case, the First Circuit ordered reinstatement of a school superintendent because evidence supported that her political party affiliation was the motivating factor in the decision to demote her.[132]

Although public educators have substantial protection from politically based dismissals, courts have upheld anti-nepotism policies that prohibit teachers from reporting to their spouses or working in the same building as their spouses. The Sixth Circuit reasoned that such an anti-nepotism policy did not interfere with the fundamental right to marry, because the policy affected working conditions, not the marriage itself.[133] The fact that such policies do not apply to employees who are cohabiting or dating has not nullified anti-nepotism provisions.

Political Activity

Teachers, like all citizens, are guaranteed the right to participate in the political process. Often, however, active participation has prompted school officials to limit the exercise of this right, raising difficult legal questions. Can teachers run for political offices? What political activities are permitted in the school setting? Can certain political activities outside the school be restricted?

Campaigning for Issues and Candidates. First Amendment associational as well as free speech rights have been invoked to protect public educators in expressing political views and campaigning for candidates. Such political activity is constitutionally protected, but restrictions can be placed on educators' activities in the school setting. Making campaign speeches in the classroom is clearly prohibited; teachers cannot take advantage of their position of authority with an impressionable captive audience

---

130. McCloud v. Testa, 97 F.3d 1536 (6th Cir. 1996). *See also* Sowards v. Loudon County, 203 F.3d 426 (6th Cir. 2000).

131. *See, e.g.,* Piazza v. Aponte Roque, 909 F.2d 35 (1st Cir. 1990) (finding that nonrenewal of teachers' aides because of their political party affiliation impaired associational rights); Burris v. Willis Indep. Sch. Dist., 713 F.2d 1087 (5th Cir. 1983) (holding that nonrenewal of an administrator's contract was predicated on his relationship with previous "old-line" board members, which violated his associational rights).

132. Estrada-Izquierdo v. Aponte-Roque, 850 F.2d 10 (1st Cir. 1988).

133. Montgomery v. Carr, 101 F.3d 1117 (6th Cir. 1996).

to impose their political views. However, if campaign issues are related to the class topic, a teacher can present election issues and candidates in a nonpartisan manner.

In general, political activity that would cause divisiveness within the school district also can be restricted. The Kentucky Supreme Court addressed a statutory prohibition on school employees taking part in the management or activities of any school board campaign. Although finding the word *activities* too vague to identify prohibited involvement, the court upheld the prohibition on school employees taking part in the management of school board campaigns as reasonable to advance the state's compelling interest in running school districts efficiently.[134]

A California appeals court held that a school district could prevent its employees from wearing political buttons in instructional settings, because of the presence of students, but could not place such a restriction on expression in noninstructional settings.[135] Similarly, a New Jersey court found overbroad a restriction on employees campaigning outside the presence of students on school property, but the policy barring such activity, including wearing buttons, in front of students was upheld.[136]

Courts have tended to reject restrictions affecting teachers' political activities *outside* the school. Public employees are constitutionally protected from retaliation for participating in political affairs at the local, state, and federal levels. For example, the Fifth Circuit concluded that the motivating factor in a school board's decision not to hire certain teachers for summer positions was their support for defeated school board candidates.[137] More recently, the Sixth Circuit held that the coordinator of gifted education, which was not a policymaking position, could not be reassigned for the exercise of constitutionally protected political expression and association.[138] The superintendent did not demonstrate that political loyalty was essential to the duties of this position. Other courts also have overturned dismissals, transfers, or demotions predicated on the support of particular candidates in school board elections where established that protected political activity was a motivating or substantial factor in the adverse employment action.[139]

The Federal Constitution protects the right of political party members to champion candidates for government offices,[140] but public employees in policymaking positions may be vulnerable to adverse employment consequences for their political activities. The Fifth Circuit held that a superintendent's free speech and political asso-

---

134. State Bd. for Elementary Educ. v. Howard, 834 S.W.2d 657 (Ky. 1992).

135. Cal. Teachers Ass'n v. San Diego Unified Sch. Dist., 53 Cal. Rptr. 2d 474 (Ct. App. 1996).

136. Green Township Educ. Ass'n v. Rowe, 746 A.2d 499 (N.J. Super. Ct. 2000). *See also* Castle v. Colonial Sch. Dist., 933 F. Supp. 458 (E.D. Pa. 1996) (finding that prohibition on school employees engaging in political activities on school district property violated First Amendment rights of off-duty employees to solicit votes at official polling places on school grounds).

137. Solis v. Rio Grande City Indep. Sch., 734 F.2d 243 (5th Cir. 1984). *But see* Bello v. Lyndhurst Bd. of Educ., 781 A.2d 70 (N.J. Super. Ct. 2001) (finding that a public school employee's dismissal was not based on her family's political activities).

138. Hager v. Pike County Bd. of Educ., 286 F.3d 366 (6th Cir. 2002). *See also* Williams v. Kentucky, 24 F.3d 1526 (6th Cir. 1994); *supra* text accompanying note 31.

ciational rights were not violated when he was dismissed after he had actively campaigned against the school board's newly elected members.[141] The court reasoned that the superintendent's political activities precluded an effective working relationship with the new board. Also, the Fourth Circuit found no First Amendment impairment in demoting a community/schools coordinator with policymaking and public relations responsibilities after she campaigned for an unsuccessful school board candidate and openly criticized board members and school policies.[142]

Holding Public Office. Certain categories of public employees have been prevented from running for political office.[143] In 1973, the Supreme Court upheld the Hatch Act, a federal law that prevents *federal* employees from holding formal positions in political parties, playing substantial roles in partisan campaigns, and running for partisan office.[144] The Court recognized that legitimate reasons exist for restricting political activities of public employees, such as ensuring impartial and effective government, removing employees from political pressure, and preventing employee selection based on political factors. In a companion case, the Court upheld an Oklahoma law forbidding classified civil servants from running for paid political offices.[145]

Other courts similarly have endorsed certain restrictions on state and municipal employees running for elective office, such as prohibiting legislators from being employed by a state agency[146] and forbidding municipal employees from holding elective public office in the city or town where employed.[147] However, laws or poli-

---

139. *See, e.g.,* Kercado-Melendez v. Aponte Roque, 829 F.2d 255 (1st Cir. 1987); Banks v. Burkich, 788 F.2d 1161 (6th Cir. 1986); Alaniz v. San Isidro Indep. Sch. Dist., 742 F.2d 207 (5th Cir. 1984). *But see* Simmons v. Chi. Bd. of Educ., 289 F.3d 488 (7th Cir. 2002) (ruling that a school district employee was demoted for disobeying his supervisor's instructions and micromanaging his office rather than for his unsuccessful campaign for an alderman seat prior to being hired as treasurer of the Chicago Board of Education); Beattie v. Madison County Sch. Dist., 254 F.3d 595 (5th Cir. 2001) (finding insufficient causal link between employee's termination and her support for the nonincumbent candidate for school superintendent).

140. *See, e.g.,* FEC v. Colo. Republican Fed. Campaign Comm., 533 U.S. 431 (2001) (recognizing the important party role, but upholding limits on contributions and coordinated expenditures to avoid corruption or undue influence in producing obligated officeholders).

141. Kinsey v. Salado Indep. Sch. Dist., 950 F.2d 988 (5th Cir. 1992).

142. Dabbs v. Amos and Cabarrus County Bd. of Educ., 70 F.3d 1261 (4th Cir. 1995).

143. *See, e.g.,* Brazil-Breashears v. Bilandic, 53 F.3d 789 (7th Cir. 1995) (finding no First or Fourteenth Amendment infractions in prohibiting certain judicial branch employees from being candidates for public office or engaging in specified political activities).

144. United States Civil Serv. Comm'n v. Nat'l Ass'n of Letter Carriers, 413 U.S. 548 (1973). *See* 5 U.S.C. § 7324 (2002).

145. Broadrick v. Oklahoma, 413 U.S. 601 (1973).

146. *See, e.g.,* Galer v. Bd. of Regents, 236 S.E.2d 617 (Ga. 1977).

147. *See, e.g.,* Fletcher v. Marino, 882 F.2d 605 (2d Cir. 1989); Acevedo v. City of N. Pole, 672 P.2d 130 (Alaska 1983); Cranston Teachers Alliance, v. Miele, 495 A.2d 233 (R.I. 1985).

cies prohibiting *all* public employees from running for *any* political office have been struck down as overly broad.[148]

Several courts have held that public educators, unlike public employees who are directly involved in the operation of governmental agencies, have the right to hold public office. The Utah Supreme Court, for example, ruled that public school teachers and administrators were not disqualified from serving in the state legislature.[149] A New Mexico appeals court also ruled that service in the legislature by a teacher and administrator would not violate the constitutional separation of powers,[150] and the Ohio Supreme Court upheld a public school principal's right to serve as a county commissioner.[151]

Restrictions can be imposed, however, to protect the integrity of the educational system. Courts have recognized that certain offices are incompatible with public school employment, especially if they involve an employer/employee relationship. Common law has established that such incompatibility exists when a teacher seeks a position on the school board where employed.[152] Of course, a teacher would not be prevented from serving on the school board of another school district.[153]

Public educators can be required to take a leave of absence before running for a public office, if campaigning would interfere with job responsibilities. Some leave requirements, however, have been judicially struck down if lacking sufficient justification. A Kentucky appellate court voided a school board regulation requiring all employees who were political candidates to take a one-month leave of absence prior to the election as violating associational and expression rights; no evidence indicated that the political activities would hinder job performance.[154]

The Supreme Court also affirmed a lower court's decision striking down a Georgia school board's policy that required any school employee who became a candidate for public office to take a leave of absence without pay during the candidacy. Finding this policy to be a violation of the Federal Voting Rights Act, the Court reasoned that it created a substantial economic deterrent to seeking elective public office and was potentially discriminatory, since it was adopted after an African American

---

148. *See, e.g.,* Minielly v. State, 411 P.2d 69 (Or. 1966); *Cranston Teachers Alliance,* 495 A.2d 233.

149. Jenkins v. Bishop, 589 P.2d 770 (Utah 1978) (per curiam).

150. Stratton v. Roswell Indep. Schs., 806 P.2d 1085 (N.M. Ct. App. 1991).

151. State *ex rel.* Gretick v. Jeffrey, 465 N.E.2d 412 (Ohio 1984).

152. *See, e.g.,* Unified Sch. Dist. No. 501 v. Baker, 6 P.3d 848 (Kan. 2000) (invalidating election of teacher to school board where state legislature had not negated common law doctrine of job incompatibility by authorizing the holding of dual offices); West v. Jones, 323 S.E.2d 96 (Va. 1984) (disqualifying city council member, who also was employed as a public school principal, from voting on appointments to the school board because of the personal interest involved); Thomas v. Dremmel, 868 P.2d 263 (Wyo. 1994) (holding that a school maintenance worker could not also serve as elected member of the district's board of trustees).

153. *See* La Bosco v. Dunn, 502 N.Y.S.2d 200 (App. Div. 1986).

154. Allen v. Bd. of Educ., 584 S.W.2d 408 (Ky. Ct. App. 1979).

employee announced his candidacy for the state legislature.[155] However, the Supreme Court subsequently upheld the school board's revised policy denying special leaves of absence for political purposes.[156] The modified policy was considered a legitimate reaffirmation of the board's authority to require employees to fulfill their contracts.

Although school boards must respect employees' associational rights, they are obligated to ensure that the political activities of public school personnel do not adversely affect the school. If educators neglect instructional duties to campaign for issues or candidates, use the classroom as a political forum, or disrupt school operations because of their political activities, disciplinary actions can be imposed. But, school boards must be certain that constraints on employees' freedom of association are not based on mere disagreement with the political orientation of the activities. Personnel actions must be justified as necessary to protect the interests of students and the school.

Personal Appearance

Historically, school boards often imposed rigid grooming restrictions on teachers. In the 1970s, such attempts to regulate teachers' appearance generated considerable litigation, as did grooming standards for students.[157] Controversies have subsided somewhat, but constraints on school employees' appearance continue to be challenged. School boards have defended their efforts to regulate teacher appearance on the perceived need to set an appropriate tone in the classroom and enforce similar appearance and dress codes for students. Teachers have contested these requirements as abridgments of their constitutionally protected privacy, liberty, and free expression rights.

A few courts have declared that public employees have a fundamental constitutional right to govern their appearance that cannot be restricted unless their choices disrupt the educational process.[158] Most courts since the mid-1970s, however, have supported school officials in imposing reasonable grooming and dress restrictions on teachers.[159] The Supreme Court provided some clarification of public employers'

---

155. White v. Dougherty County Bd. of Educ., 431 F. Supp. 919 (M.D. Ga. 1977), *aff'd,* 439 U.S. 32 (1978). For more information on the Federal Voting Rights Act, *see* text with note 15, Chapter 1.

156. White v. Dougherty County Bd. of Educ., 579 F. Supp. 1480 (M.D. Ga. 1984), *aff'd,* 470 U.S. 1067 (1985).

157. For a discussion of restrictions on student appearance, *see* text accompanying note 111, Chapter 4. For a discussion of employees' wearing religious attire in public schools, *see* text accompanying note 120, Chapter 10.

158. *See, e.g.,* Conard v. Goolsby, 350 F. Supp. 713 (N.D. Miss. 1972); Braxton v. Bd. of Pub. Instruction, 303 F. Supp. 958 (M.D. Fla. 1969).

159. Finding prohibitions on teachers' wearing beards to instill discipline and compel uniformity to be a minor deprivation of protected rights, *see, e.g.,* Domico v. Rapides Parish Sch. Bd., 675 F.2d 100 (5th Cir. 1982); Ball v. Bd. of Trs., 584 F.2d 684 (5th Cir. 1978); Miller v. Sch. Dist. No. 167, 495 F.2d 658 (7th Cir. 1974).

authority regarding regulation of employee appearance in a 1976 decision upholding a hair grooming regulation for police officers.[160] The Court placed the burden on the individual to demonstrate the lack of a rational connection between the regulation and a legitimate public purpose.

The Supreme Court's justification for upholding the grooming regulation for police officers has been followed by lower courts assessing dress and appearance restrictions for teachers. For example, the Second Circuit upheld a Connecticut school board's requirement that all male teachers must wear ties as a rational means to promote respect for authority, traditional values, and classroom discipline.[161] Because of the uniquely influential role of teachers, the court noted that they may be subjected to restrictions in their professional lives that otherwise would not be acceptable. Applying similar reasoning, the First Circuit upheld a school board's dismissal of a teacher for wearing short skirts.[162] More recently, a federal court ruled that a school board did not violate a teacher's rights by instructing her to cover her t-shirt with the message "Jesus 2000-J2K" or change into another top.[163]

Restrictions will not be upheld, however, if found to be unrelated to a legitimate governmental concern. The Seventh Circuit overturned a school bus driver's suspension after he violated a rule prohibiting school bus drivers from wearing mustaches.[164] Finding no valid purpose for the policy, the court noted that its irrationality was exemplified by the fact that the bus driver was also a full-time teacher but was not suspended from his teaching position.

Although courts generally acknowledge that the right to govern personal appearance is a protected interest, it has not been declared a fundamental right requiring heightened judicial scrutiny. School officials thus can restrict employees' appearance as long as there is a legitimate basis for the regulation and the rules are not arbitrary.[165]

160. Kelley v. Johnson, 425 U.S. 238 (1976). *See also* Weaver v. Henderson, 984 F.2d 11 (1st Cir. 1993) (upholding a "no mustache" policy for Massachusetts police officers).

161. E. Hartford Educ. Ass'n v. Bd. of Educ., 562 F.2d 838 (2d Cir. 1977). *See also* Cade v. Dep't of Soc. Servs., 990 S.W.2d 32 (Mo. Ct. App. 1999) (recognizing an administrative agency's power to establish a dress code for its employees).

162. Tardif v. Quinn, 545 F.2d 761 (1st Cir. 1976). *See also* Zalewska v. County of Sullivan, 180 F. Supp. 2d 486 (S.D.N.Y. 2002) (upholding uniform policy for van drivers to project a professional appearance and ensure safety of vans with chair lifts; the policy's incidental restrictions on expression were minimal); Seabrook v. New York, No. 99 Civ. 9134 (HB), 2001 U.S. Dist. LEXIS 268 (S.D.N.Y. Jan. 16, 2001) (upholding rule that prohibited corrections officers from wearing skirts while on duty).

163. Downing v. W. Haven Bd. of Educ., 162 F. Supp. 2d 19 (D. Conn. 2001).

164. Pence v. Rosenquist, 573 F.2d 395 (7th Cir. 1978).

165. Claims of sexual harassment in the workplace have focused some attention on dress codes as one strategy to reduce potential harassment allegations. *See* Sandra Snaden, "Baring It All at the Workplace: Who Bears the Responsibility?" *Connecticut Law Review,* vol. 28 (1996), 1225–1258.

Privacy Rights

Public employees have asserted constitutional and statutory rights to be free from unwarranted governmental intrusions in their personal activities.[166] Although the Federal Constitution does not explicitly enumerate personal privacy rights, the Supreme Court has recognized that certain *implied* fundamental rights warrant constitutional protection because of their close relationship to explicit constitutional guarantees. Protected privacy rights have been interpreted as encompassing personal choices in matters such as marriage, contraception, procreation, family relations, and child rearing.[167] Employment decisions cannot be based on relinquishing such rights without a compelling justification. Litigation covered in this section focuses on constitutional privacy claims initiated under the Fourth Amendment (protection against unreasonable searches and seizures), the Ninth Amendment (personal privacy as an unenumerated right reserved to the people), and the Fourteenth Amendment (protection against state action impairing personal liberties without due process of law).

In some instances, public employees have asserted that governmental action has impaired their privacy right to intimate association related to creating and maintaining a family. To assess such claims, courts must weigh the employee's interests against the government's interests in promoting efficient public services.[168] To illustrate, public educators cannot be deprived of their jobs because of the politics or other activities of their partners or spouses. Recognizing a classified employee's First Amendment right to associate with her husband who disagreed with policies of the school system, the Sixth Circuit found an inference that the superintendent's nonrenewal recommendation was impermissibly based on the employee's marital relationship.[169] Also, a federal court held that a nontenured teacher, who received excellent ratings until subpoenaed at school to testify against her live-in fiancé in a child abuse case, could claim that her contract nonrenewal violated intimate associational rights.[170]

---

166. For a discussion of statutory privacy rights in connection with employment records, *see* text accompanying note 120, Chapter 8.

167. *See* Thornburgh v. Am. Coll. of Obstetricians and Gynecologists, 476 U.S. 747 (1986); Roe v. Wade, 410 U.S. 113 (1973); Loving v. Virginia, 388 U.S. 1 (1967); Griswold v. Connecticut, 381 U.S. 479 (1965); Skinner v. Oklahoma, 316 U.S. 535 (1942); Pierce v. Soc'y of Sisters, 268 U.S. 510 (1925).

168. *See e.g.,* Kelly v. City of Meriden, 120 F. Supp. 2d 191 (D. Conn. 2000) (upholding dismissal of a school social worker who was living with the noncustodial father of children to whom she had provided social services; the city director believed the employee may have violated the ethics code, discredited the municipal service, and hindered other school social workers in performing their work).

169. Adkins v. Bd. of Educ., 982 F.2d 952 (6th Cir. 1993). In several other cases, courts have overturned employees' terminations that were based on their spouses' protected expression. *See, e.g.,* Lewis v. Harrison Sch. Dist., 805 F.2d 310 (8th Cir. 1986); Anderson-Free v. Steptoe, 993 F. Supp. 870 (M.D. Ala. 1997).

170. LaSota v. Town of Topsfield, 979 F. Supp. 45 (D. Mass. 1997). *But see* Finnegan v. Bd. of Educ., 30 F.3d 273 (2d. Cir. 1994) (finding inadequate evidence that a probationary teacher was removed from his coaching position and denied tenure because he married a former member of his volleyball team shortly after she graduated).

The Second Circuit upheld a teacher's privacy claim in her refusal to submit to a physical examination by the school district's male physician and found support for the unreasonableness of the board's action because the teacher offered to go at her own expense to any female physician the board selected.[171] Also, the Fifth Circuit recognized that a teacher's interest in breast-feeding her child at school during noninstructional time was sufficiently close to fundamental rights regarding family relationships and child rearing to trigger constitutional privacy protection. The court acknowledged, however, that trial courts must determine whether school boards' interests in avoiding disruption of the educational process, ensuring that teachers perform their duties without distraction, and avoiding liability for potential injuries are sufficiently compelling to justify restrictions imposed on teachers' fundamental privacy interests.[172]

In 2001, the Supreme Court addressed a conflict between the interest in full dissemination of information concerning public issues and the protection of individuals' private speech. The case involved the intentional and repeated media disclosure of an illegally intercepted cell phone conversation between a union negotiator and the union president during contentious collective-bargaining negotiations. The persons who made the media disclosure did not participate in the interception but had reason to know that the interception was illegal. The Supreme Court held that despite the important privacy concerns, the disclosure was protected by the First Amendment.[173]

In some instances, courts have concluded that governmental interests in ensuring the welfare of students override teachers' privacy interests. A tenured teacher did not prevail in claiming that the school board violated her privacy rights by not allowing her to return from an extended medical absence unless she provided medical records from the treating physician and submitted to a physical examination by the school board doctor.[174] The First Circuit also held that a principal's constitutional privacy rights were not impaired when he was required to undergo a psychiatric examination before returning to work, as there was reason to believe that the welfare of students might be jeopardized.[175]

Teachers also have not succeeded in asserting that observations by superiors and other strategies used to assess teaching competence violate protected privacy rights. For example, a Texas appeals court upheld videotaping a teacher's performance for evaluative purposes, concluding that teachers' privacy rights do not shield them from legitimate performance evaluations.[176]

---

171. Gargiul v. Tompkins, 704 F.2d 661 (2d Cir. 1983), *vacated and remanded,* 465 U.S. 1016 (1984). *See* text accompanying note 37, Chapter 8.

172. Dike v. Sch. Bd., 650 F.2d 783 (5th Cir. 1981).

173. Bartnicki v. Vopper, 532 U.S. 514 (2001).

174. Strong v. Bd. of Educ., 902 F.2d 208 (2d Cir. 1990).

175. Daury v. Smith, 842 F.2d 9 (1st Cir. 1988).

176. Roberts v. Houston Indep. Sch. Dist., 788 S.W.2d 107 (Tex. Ct. App. 1990). *See also* Brannen v. Bd. of Educ., 761 N. E. 2d 84 (Ohio Ct. App. 2001) (holding that use of surveillance cameras to videotape custodians in their break room to identify unauthorized breaks was not unreasonable and did not constitute an unlawful search).

Although regulations are far less restrictive today than in the early 1900s, when some school districts prohibited female teachers from marrying or even dating, school boards still attempt to proscribe aspects of teachers' personal lives that are inimical to community values. School officials have defended some behavior constraints on the grounds that teachers serve as role models for students and therefore should conform to community norms to ensure an appropriate educational environment. Recognizing that teachers are held to a higher standard of conduct than general citizens, the judiciary has upheld dismissals for behavior that jeopardizes student welfare, even if it takes place during the summer break.[177] The remainder of this section focuses on litigation in which courts have assessed the competing governmental and individual interests in connection with employee searches and lifestyle choices.

Search and Seizure

Public educators, like all citizens, are shielded by the Fourth Amendment against unreasonable governmental invasions of their person and property. This amendment usually requires police officers and other state agents to secure a search warrant (based on probable cause that evidence of a crime will be found) before conducting personal searches. The Supreme Court has not addressed teachers' rights in connection with searches initiated by public school authorities, but it has upheld warrantless personal searches of students based on *reasonable suspicion* that contraband detrimental to the educational process is concealed.[178]

The Court also has upheld a warrantless search by state hospital supervisors of an employee physician's office.[179] The Court's conclusion that both the basis for the search and the scope of the intrusion were reasonable has implications for searches of other public workers by their employers. Acknowledging that public employees have a reasonable expectation of privacy in their desks and files, the Supreme Court nonetheless concluded that a warrant is not required for work-related searches that are necessary to carry out the business of the agency. In this case, items seized from a physician's desk and file cabinets were used in administrative proceedings that resulted in his dismissal for improprieties in managing the residency program.

Although case law in the public school context is scant, the judiciary has recognized that the reasonableness of a job-related search or seizure by a supervisor rests on whether educational interests outweigh the employee's expectation of privacy.[180] The Fourth Amendment prohibits *arbitrary* invasions of teachers' personal effects by

177. *See, e.g.,* Bd. of Educ. v. Wood, 717 S.W.2d 837 (Ky. 1986).

178. New Jersey v. T.L.O., 469 U.S. 325 (1985). *See* text accompanying note 126, Chapter 7, for a discussion of the reasonable suspicion standard.

179. O'Connor v. Ortega, 480 U.S. 709 (1987).

180. *See, e.g.,* Gillard v. Schmidt, 579 F.2d 825 (3d Cir. 1978) (invalidating search of school counselor's desk by a school board member, because the search was politically motivated and lacked sufficient work-related justification; Shaul v. Cherry Valley-Springfield Cent. Sch. Dist., 218 F. Supp. 2d 266 (N.D.N.Y. 2002) (upholding principal's search of suspended teacher's desk and files for educational materials).

school officials, but courts have recognized that in some situations the school's interests are overriding.[181]

Drug screening programs have become increasingly controversial. School boards can require employees to have physical examinations as a condition of employment, but mandatory screening for drugs has been challenged as impairing Fourth Amendment privacy rights. Teachers in a New York school district secured a restraining order prohibiting the school board from forcing probationary teachers to submit urine samples to determine whether they were using controlled substances.[182] The court held that the school board must have *individualized suspicion* of conduct detrimental to the school environment to subject employees to drug tests.

A Georgia federal district court struck down a state law that would have required all new state employees and veteran employees transferring to another school district or state agency to submit to urinalysis screening.[183] The Court reasoned that the general interest in maintaining a drug-free workplace was not a compelling governmental interest to justify the program. The Supreme Court subsequently struck down another Georgia law requiring candidates for state office to pass a drug test. The Court found no special need based on public safety to override the individual's privacy interests.[184]

In contrast to *blanket* testing, support for *limited* drug testing of public employees in safety-sensitive roles can be found in two 1989 Supreme Court decisions upholding the mandatory drug testing of railroad employees involved in accidents[185] and customs employees who carry firearms or who are involved in the interdiction of illegal drugs.[186] The Court found that the safety and security interests served by the programs outweighed employees' privacy concerns. In several rulings, the District of Columbia Circuit subsequently upheld random urinalysis testing of federal employees in safety-sensitive or security-sensitive roles.[187] The same court upheld the Wash-

181. *See, e.g.,* Alinovi v. Worcester Sch. Comm., 777 F.2d 776 (1st Cir. 1985) (rejecting teacher's expectation of privacy in withholding from the school administration a paper she had written—and shared with others—about a child with disabilities in her class; also, she had no First Amendment right to display letters of reprimand about the situation on parents' night).

182. Patchogue-Medford Congress of Teachers v. Bd. of Educ., 510 N.E.2d 325 (N.Y. 1987).

183. Ga. Ass'n of Educators v. Harris, 749 F. Supp. 1110 (N.D. Ga. 1990). *See also* Glover v. E. Neb. Cmty. Office of Retardation, 867 F.2d 461 (8th Cir. 1989) (finding county health agency's policy requiring mandatory screening of employees for hepatitis B and AIDS unreasonable under the Fourth Amendment).

184. Chandler v. Miller, 520 U.S. 305 (1997).

185. Skinner v. Ry. Labor Executives' Ass'n, 489 U.S. 602 (1989) (upholding alcohol testing of employees as well). *See also* Bennett v. Mass. Bay Transp. Auth., 8 Mass. L. Rptr. 201 (Mass. Super. Ct. 1998).

186. Nat'l Treasury Employees Union v. Von Raab, 489 U.S. 656 (1989). *See also* Wilcher v. Wilmington, 139 F.3d 366 (3d Cir. 1998) (rejecting constitutional challenge to testing fire fighters for drugs; city's interests in protecting public safety outweighed firefighters' expectations of privacy).

187. *See, e.g.,* Stigile v. Clinton, 110 F.3d 801 (D.C. Cir. 1997); Am. Fed'n of Gov't Employees, AFL-CIO v. Sanders, 926 F.2d 1215 (D.C. Cir. 1991); Nat'l Treasury Employees Union v. Yeutter, 918

ington, DC, School District's policy requiring all employees whose duties affect child safety, such as bus attendants, to submit to a drug test as part of routine medical examinations.[188] And, the Fifth Circuit ruled that a school custodian, whose performance affected almost 900 students, was in a safety-sensitive role justifying suspicionless drug testing.[189]

What constitutes safety-sensitive roles in the school context, however, remains unclear. Some courts seem more inclined than in the past to interpret expansively the positions in this category.[190] In a controversial 1998 case, the Sixth Circuit upheld a school district's policy requiring suspicionless drug testing for all individuals who apply for, transfer to, or are promoted to safety-sensitive positions, including teaching positions.[191] Although there was no evidence that teachers exhibited an apparent drug problem, the court reasoned that teachers are entrusted with the care of children and are on the "frontline" of school security. The court also upheld drug testing of any individual for whom there was reasonable suspicion of drug possession or use, but it struck down the provision calling for alcohol testing of all employees. The latter issue was remanded for the district court to determine whether the low level of alcohol impairment identified (.02) was reasonably related to the purpose of the testing program.

A year earlier, the Supreme Court of California upheld a city's policy mandating drug and alcohol screening of all new city workers as part of preemployment medical examinations. However, it struck down similar drug testing of all current employees seeking promotions, regardless of the nature of the positions.[192] Also, the Fifth Circuit struck down policies in two Louisiana school districts that required employees injured in the course of employment to submit to urinalysis, finding an insufficient nexus between such injuries and drug impairment.[193]

Of course, employees, like students, can be subjected to alcohol and drug testing where there is reasonable suspicion that the individual is under the influence of such substances. The Eleventh Circuit found legitimate grounds for terminating a teacher

F.2d 968 (D.C. Cir. 1990). In these cases the court recognized that employees not occupying such sensitive roles can be tested only with reasonable suspicion of drug use at work or drug-impaired performance. Congress passed the Drug-Free Workplace Act in 1988, 41 U.S.C. § 701 (2002), stipulating that federal grant and contract recipients could not receive federal funds from federal agencies unless they implemented policies to ensure workplaces free from the illegal use, possession, or distribution of controlled substances. *See also* 15 U.S.C. § 5110 (2002).

188. Jones v. McKenzie, 833 F.2d 335 (D.C. Cir. 1987), *vacated sub nom.* Jones v. Jenkins, 490 U.S. 1001 (1989), *on remand,* 878 F.2d 1476 (D.C. Cir. 1989).

189. Aubrey v. Sch. Bd., 148 F.3d 559 (5th Cir. 1998). *See also* English v. Talladega County Bd. of Educ., 938 F. Supp. 775 (N.D. Ala. 1996) (upholding random drug testing of school bus mechanics).

190. Advocates of drug testing of school employees have been encouraged by Supreme Court decisions expanding suspicionless drug testing of students to those participating in any extracurricular activities. *See* Bd. of Educ. v. Earls, 122 S. Ct. 2559 (2002); Vernonia Sch. Dist. 47J v. Acton, 515 U.S. 646 (1995); text accompanying note 191, Chapter 7.

191. Knox County Educ. Ass'n v. Knox County Bd. of Educ., 158 F.3d 361 (6th Cir. 1998).

192. Loder v. Glendale, 927 P.2d 1200 (Cal. 1997).

193. United Teachers of New Orleans v. Orleans Parish Sch. Bd., 142 F.3d 853 (5th Cir. 1998).

who refused to undergo urinalysis after a drug-sniffing dog detected marijuana in her car.[194] Ruling that the Fourth Amendment allows dog sniff searches of personal property in public places, the court rejected the teacher's asserted expectation of privacy in the odors emanating from her car.

Courts in some instances have found inadequate grounds for individualized suspicion. In a St. Louis case, a teacher forced to submit to a drug and alcohol test stated a valid Fourth Amendment claim, which precluded summary judgment for the school district, because there were genuine issues as to whether the teacher's behavior suggested drug use and whether she consented to the test.[195] Also, a North Carolina appeals court found no reasonable cause for a public employer to believe that certain employees were using a controlled substance, and thus their dismissal for refusing to submit to a drug test was unconstitutional.[196] The law is still evolving regarding what constitutes individualized suspicion of drug use and the circumstances under which certain public employees can be subjected to urinalysis without such suspicion.

Lifestyle Choices

In recent years, teachers frequently have challenged school officials' authority to restrict personal lifestyle choices. Although the right to such personal freedom is not an enumerated constitutional guarantee, it is a right implied in the concept of personal liberty embodied in the Fourteenth Amendment. Constitutional protection afforded to teachers' privacy rights is determined not only by the *location* of the conduct but also by the *nature* of the activity.[197] The judiciary has attempted to balance teachers' privacy interests against the school board's legitimate interests in safeguarding the welfare of students and the school. Sanctions cannot be imposed solely because school officials disapprove of teachers' personal and private conduct, but restrictions can be placed on unconventional behavior that is detrimental to job performance or harmful to students. Educators can be terminated based on evidence that would not be sufficient to support criminal charges,[198] but they cannot be dismissed for unsubstantiated rumors about their activities.[199]

194. Hearn v. Bd. of Pub. Educ., 191 F.3d 1329 (11th Cir. 1999). *See also* Armington v. Sch. Dist., 767 F. Supp. 661 (E.D. Pa. 1991) (upholding termination of bus driver for refusal to submit to a drug test after a parent's telephone complaint about the driver's behavior).

195. Warren v. Bd. of Educ., 200 F. Supp. 2d 1053 (E.D. Mo. 2001) (upholding school district's policy authorizing drug testing based on reasonable suspicion that a given employee is under the influence of alcohol or drugs; employees referred for testing are suspended pending the outcome and given back pay for the suspended days if the results are negative).

196. Best v. Dep't of Health & Human Servs., 563 S.E.2d 573 (N.C. Ct. App. 2002).

197. *See, e.g.,* Lile v. Hancock Place Sch. Dist., 701 S.W.2d 500, 508 (Mo. Ct. App. 1985).

198. *See, e.g.,* Montefusco v. Nassau County, 39 F. Supp. 2d 231 (E.D.N.Y. 1999) (holding that although the criminal investigation did not result in criminal charges, the school board could suspend the teacher with pay and remove extracurricular assignments for his possession of candid pictures of teenagers taken at the teacher's home).

199. *See, e.g.,* Peaster Indep. Sch. Dist. v. Glodfelty, 63 S.W.3d 1 (Tex. Ct. App. 2001) (holding that widespread gossip triggered by unproven allegations of sexual misconduct could not be the basis for not renewing teachers' contracts).

The precise contours of public educators' constitutional privacy rights have not been clearly delineated; constitutional claims have been decided on a case-by-case basis. Since many of these cases also are discussed in Chapter 11 in connection with dismissals based on charges of immorality, the following discussion is confined to an overview of the constitutional issues.

Recognizing that decisions pertaining to marriage and parenthood involve constitutionally protected privacy rights, courts have been reluctant to support dismissal actions based on teachers' unwed, pregnant status without evidence that the condition impairs fitness to teach. In a typical case, the Fifth Circuit found equal protection and due process violations in a Mississippi school district's rule that prohibited the employment of unwed parents to promote a "properly moral scholastic environment."[200] Compelled leaves of absence for pregnant, unmarried employees similarly have been invalidated as violating constitutional privacy rights.[201]

Most courts also have reasoned that public employees, including educators, have a privacy right to engage in consenting sexual relationships out of wedlock, and that such relationships cannot be the basis for dismissal unless teaching effectiveness is impaired. For example, the Supreme Court of Iowa held that a teacher's adulterous relationship was insufficient to justify revocation of his teaching certificate, since no harmful effect on his teaching was substantiated.[202] Likewise, a Florida court overturned a school board's termination of a teacher for lacking good moral character based on a personal romantic relationship.[203] Similarly, the Sixth Circuit ruled that a school board's nonrenewal of a teacher's contract, because of her involvement in a divorce, abridged constitutional privacy rights.[204]

Some courts, however, have upheld dismissals or other disciplinary actions based on public employees' lifestyle choices that involve adulterous or other unconventional sexual relationships. In two nonschool decisions, federal appellate courts upheld dismissals of public employees for engaging in sexual relationships outside wedlock that allegedly impaired job performance.[205] Also, the Texas Supreme Court held that public employees' private adulterous conduct was not constitutionally pro-

200. Andrews v. Drew Mun. Separate Sch. Dist., 507 F.2d 611, 614 (5th Cir. 1975). *See also* Avery v. Homewood City Bd. of Educ., 674 F.2d 337 (5th Cir. 1982); Cameron v. Bd. of Educ., 795 F. Supp. 228 (S.D. Ohio 1991).

201. *See, e.g.,* Ponton v. Newport News Sch. Bd., 632 F. Supp. 1056 (E.D. Va. 1986).

202. Erb v. Iowa State Bd. of Pub. Instruction, 216 N.W.2d 339 (Iowa 1974). *See also* Briggs v. N. Muskegon Police Dep't, 746 F.2d 1475 (6th Cir. 1984) (holding that dismissal of a married police officer for cohabitating with a married woman impaired fundamental privacy and associational rights).

203. Sherburne v. Sch. Bd., 455 So. 2d 1057 (Fla. Dist. Ct. App. 1984).

204. Littlejohn v. Rose, 768 F.2d 765 (6th Cir. 1985). *See also* Bertolini v. Whitehall City Sch. Dist. Bd. of Educ., 744 N.E.2d 1245 (Ohio Ct. App. 2000), text accompanying note 121, Chapter 11.

205. Shawgo v. Spradlin, 701 F.2d 470 (5th Cir. 1983) (upholding disciplinary action against two members of a police department for their off-duty cohabitation that allegedly violated department regulations); Hollenbaugh v. Carnegie Free Library, 545 F.2d 382 (3d Cir. 1976), *on remand,* 436 F. Supp. 1328 (W.D. Pa. 1977), *aff'd mem.,* 578 F.2d 1374 (3d Cir. 1978) (upholding public library's dismissal of cohabitating couple after it became public knowledge that the employees were expecting a child).

tected.[206] More recently, a New York federal court upheld termination of a teacher for actively participating in a group supporting consensual sexual activity between men and boys, reasoning that his activities in this organization were likely to impair teaching effectiveness and disrupt the school.[207]

Whether employment decisions can be based on a teacher's sexual orientation has become increasingly controversial. Among factors courts consider are the nature of the homosexual conduct (public or private), the notoriety surrounding the conduct, and its impact on teaching effectiveness.

The law is clear that educators can be dismissed for immorality if they engage in public sexual activity, whether heterosexual or homosexual in nature.[208] In 1984, the Tenth Circuit upheld an Oklahoma statute permitting a teacher to be discharged for engaging in public homosexual activity, finding that this provision was neither vague nor a violation of equal protection rights.[209] However, as discussed previously, the court struck down the portion of the law authorizing the dismissal or nonrenewal of teachers for *advocating* public or private homosexuality as impairing teachers' free speech rights.[210]

A Georgia law criminalizing public or private consensual sodomy resulted in a widely publicized Supreme Court decision in 1986. An individual challenged the law's constitutionality after being criminally charged for committing sodomy with an adult male in the privacy of his home. The Court found a rational basis in legislation reflecting the citizenry's view that sodomy is immoral and unacceptable.[211] Declaring that homosexuals have no constitutional right to engage in sodomy, the Court majority focused its opinion on the homosexual nature of the conduct at issue, even though the law's prohibition applies to heterosexual sodomy as well. A number of other states have laws similar to the contested Georgia statute, but criminal sanctions for private sodomy have not generally been enforced.

Dismissals of public school employees based solely on sexual orientation, in the absence of criminal charges, have evoked a widespread range of judicial interpreta-

206. City of Sherman v. Henry, 928 S.W.2d 464 (Tex. 1996) (finding no fundamental right to engage in adultery, so a patrolman's constitutional privacy rights were not violated by denying promotion based on his affair with a fellow officer's wife).

207. Melzer v. Bd. of Educ., 196 F. Supp. 2d 229 (E.D.N.Y. 2002).

208. *See, e.g.,* Morgan v. State Bd. of Educ., 2002 Ohio 2738 (Ohio Ct. App. May 30, 2002) (upholding revocation of teaching certificate for disorderly conduct conviction stemming from his participation in public sex act).

209. Nat'l Gay Task Force v. Bd. of Educ., 729 F.2d 1270 (10th Cir. 1984), *aff'd by an equally divided court,* 470 U.S. 903 (1985). *See supra* text accompanying note 60.

210. In addition to asserting protected privacy rights, some homosexual employees have claimed discrimination under the Fourteenth Amendment. *See* text accompanying note 102, Chapter 10.

211. Bowers v. Hardwick, 478 U.S. 186 (1986). See also Lawrence v. Texas, 41 S.W.3d 349 (Tex. App. 2001), *cert. granted,* 123 S. Ct. 661 (2002) (upholding conviction of two men for violating a Texas law prohibiting deviate sexual intercourse with a person of the same sex; finding no gender discrimination or violation of privacy rights).

tions.[212] In general, courts will require a nexus between private homosexuality and impaired teaching effectiveness to justify dismissal. To illustrate, the Utah Federal District Court ruled that the community's negative response to a teacher's homosexuality was not sufficient justification to remove the teacher as the girl's volleyball coach and instruct her not to mention her sexual orientation to students, parents, or staff.[213] Also, an Ohio federal court awarded a teacher reinstatement, back pay, and damages for his nonrenewal that was impermissibly based on his sexual orientation rather than on his teaching deficiencies as the board asserted.[214]

In contrast, the Eleventh Circuit upheld revocation of a public employee's job offer after her employer, the state's chief legal officer, learned of the employee's pending same-sex marriage. The employment action was based on her illegal wedding ceremony rather than on her status as a lesbian. The court found no impairment of associational rights, given the employer's interests in hiring staff to enforce state laws.[215] The plaintiff's intimate associational rights were subordinate to the employer's interest in the effective functioning of the government office.

A few courts have even upheld dismissals based on mere knowledge of a teacher's homosexuality, suggesting that such knowledge is sufficient to establish an impairment of teaching effectiveness that overrides any protected privacy interest. The Washington Supreme Court upheld a teacher's dismissal after he admitted his homosexuality to a school administrator.[216] Also, the Sixth Circuit upheld the nonrenewal of a guidance counselor who told other school personnel about her bisexuality as well as the homosexuality of two student advisees.[217] Since the Supreme Court has not recognized a constitutional privacy right to engage in homosexual conduct, a range of interpretations among lower courts regarding legal protections of gay and lesbian educators will likely persist.

212. There also has been litigation regarding the rights of homosexual employees in the private sector. *See* Boy Scouts of Am. v. Dale, 530 U.S. 640 (2000) (protecting expressive association rights in connection with the Boy Scouts' official position barring homosexuals from being troop leaders), text accompanying note 109, Chapter 4 and note 113, Chapter 10.

213. Weaver v. Nebo Sch. Dist., 29 F. Supp. 2d 1279 (D. Utah 1998). *But see* Burton v. Cascade Sch. Dist., 512 F.2d 850 (9th Cir. 1975) (finding that a teacher unconstitutionally dismissed for being a lesbian was entitled to damages and attorneys' fees, but not to reinstatement as would be true for dismissals based on protected speech or racial considerations).

214. Glover v. Williamsburg Local Sch. Dist., 20 F. Supp. 2d 1160 (S.D. Ohio 1998). *See also* Bd. of Educ. of Long Beach Unified Sch. Dist. v. Jack M., 566 P.2d 602 (Cal. 1977); text accompanying note 111, Chapter 10.

215. Shahar v. Bowers, 114 F.3d 1097 (11th Cir. 1997). *See also* Acanfora v. Bd. of Educ., 359 F. Supp. 843 (D. Md. 1973)(finding that a teacher who had been unjustifiably transferred because of his homosexuality went beyond the needs of his defense by making radio and television appearances; thus, refusal to renew his contract was not arbitrary or capricious).

216. Gaylord v. Tacoma Sch. Dist. No. 10, 559 P.2d 1340 (Wash. 1977).

217. Rowland v. Mad River Local Sch. Dist., 730 F.2d 444 (6th Cir. 1984).

Conclusion

Although public educators do not shed their constitutional rights as a condition of public employment, under certain circumstances restrictions on these freedoms are justified by overriding governmental interests. Constitutional protections afforded to educators continue to be delineated by the judiciary; the following generalizations reflect the status of the law in the substantive areas discussed in this chapter.

1. Public educators have a First Amendment right to express their views on issues of public concern; dismissal or other retaliatory personnel action—such as transfers, demotions, or written reprimands—cannot be predicated solely on protected speech.
2. Expression pertaining to personal employment disputes, attacks on supervisors, or speech intended to disrupt the school is not constitutionally protected.
3. If a public employer acts in good faith, conducts a reasonable investigation, and concludes from the evidence that the employee's offensive comments are unprotected, the employee can be dismissed for the expression.
4. The exercise of protected speech will not invalidate a dismissal action if the school board can show by a preponderance of evidence that it would have reached the same decision had the protected speech not occurred.
5. Even if expression on public issues is the sole basis for adverse employment action, the school board still might prevail if its interests in providing effective and efficient educational services outweigh the individual's free expression rights.
6. A school's internal mail system is not a traditional open forum for expression, and unless designated as such, access to the mail system can be restricted to business relating to the school's educational function as long as restrictions are not viewpoint based.
7. Reasonable time, place, and manner restrictions can be imposed on educators' expression, but arbitrary prior restraints on the content and channel of communication violate the First Amendment.
8. Public school teachers do not have the right to determine the content of the instructional program, but they do have some latitude in selecting appropriate strategies to convey the prescribed content.
9. In evaluating the appropriateness of teaching materials and strategies, courts consider relevance to course objectives, support of the profession, threat of disruption, age and maturity of students, and community standards.
10. Public employees cannot be retaliated against because of their membership in labor unions, political groups, or organizations with unlawful purposes.
11. A public educator's participation in political activities outside the classroom cannot be the basis for adverse employment decisions, unless the employee has policymaking responsibilities or such activities negatively affect work performance.

12. State laws can impose restrictions on the types of elected offices that public educators can hold (e.g., two incompatible positions cannot be held).
13. Public employees can be required to take a temporary leave from their positions to campaign for political office if campaign demands would interfere with professional responsibilities.
14. School officials can impose reasonable restrictions on educators' personal appearance if there is a rational basis for such regulations.
15. Public educators' desks and files at school can be searched based on reasonable suspicion that the search is necessary for educational reasons.
16. Public educators can be subjected to urinalysis with reasonable suspicion of drug use; employees in safety-sensitive roles can be subjected to blanket or random drug testing.
17. Public educators enjoy privacy rights in their lifestyle choices; however, adverse employment consequences may be justified if private choices break state laws or have a detrimental effect on job performance or the school.
18. Generally, there must be evidence that an educator's sexual orientation has a negative impact on teaching effectiveness to justify dismissal.

10

Discrimination in Employment

All persons and groups are potential victims of discrimination in employment. People of color and women claim discrimination in traditionally segregated job categories, whereas Caucasians and males claim that affirmative action has denied them the right to compete on equal grounds. The young argue that the old already hold the good jobs and that entry is nearly impossible, and the old contend that they often are let go when "downsizing" occurs and that reemployment at the same level and salary is unlikely. Religious minorities often are not allowed to dress the way they please, and religious majorities (particularly in private schools) have concerns about governmental intrusion into their homogeneous work environments. Likewise, persons with disabilities often complain that they are not given the opportunity to show what they can do, whereas employers fear that the costs of accommodation could be significant and never ending. Given these diverse and conflicting interests, it is not surprising that literally hundreds of employment discrimination suits are filed each year.

Legal Context

Most, but not all, forms of employment discrimination violate either federal or state law. Foremost among these mandates are the Fourteenth Amendment to the United States Constitution and Title VII of the Civil Rights Act of 1964; both are discussed here, given their broad application. Other more narrowly tailored statutes are reviewed in the respective sections addressing discrimination based on race and national origin, gender, sexual orientation, religion, age, and disability.

Fourteenth Amendment

The Fourteenth Amendment to the United States Constitution mandates that no state shall deny to any person within its jurisdiction equal protection of the laws. This applies to subdivisions of the state, including its public school districts. Under this

Equal Protection Clause, if a government policy or law facially discriminates in employment, one of three forms of scrutiny will be used to determine its constitutionality: strict, intermediate, or rational basis. *Facial discrimination* (e.g., the posting of a principal's position stipulating that it has been reserved for a female applicant) means that the government intended to discriminate, either for or against a particular class.

Where facial discrimination exists, the government employer bears the burden of justifying its policies, practices, or acts. The degree of difficulty in carrying that burden is in part determined by the level of scrutiny applied by courts. As discussed in Chapter 5, a policy or practice that discriminates based on race, national origin, or alienage is *strictly scrutinized* and can be justified only if narrowly tailored and supportive of a compelling state interest.[1] When a plaintiff claims discrimination based on gender or illegitimacy, *intermediate scrutiny* is used, requiring the classification to serve important governmental objectives and the discriminatory acts to be substantially related to the achievement of those objectives.[2] And, finally, *rational-basis scrutiny* is applied when any other plaintiff class is involved (e.g., classes based on religion, age, sexual orientation, disability). This level of scrutiny requires only that the justification not be arbitrary, capricious, or without foundation.

Whereas intent to discriminate is apparent with facial discrimination, some policies or practices are facially neutral but result in a disproportionate impact on a protected group (e.g., the use of a standardized test in hiring that results in disparate impact based on race). In such cases, to establish a constitutional violation, the plaintiff must prove that the employer intended to discriminate. To substantiate discriminatory *intent,* the court will examine criteria such as the pattern of discriminatory impact; the historical background of the act, policy, or practice that supports a discriminatory motive; the specific sequence of events leading up to the allegedly unconstitutional behavior; and departures from normal procedures.[3] Although disproportionate impact is not irrelevant in these cases, it is not "the sole touchstone of invidious discrimination forbidden by the Constitution,"[4] and without more does not prove a Fourteenth Amendment violation.

Title VII

Title VII is enforced by the Equal Employment Opportunity Commission (EEOC) and prohibits employers with 15 or more employees from discriminating on the basis of race, color, religion, gender, or national origin and covers hiring, promotion, and compensation practices as well as fringe benefits and other terms and conditions of

1. *See, e.g.,* Graham v. Richardson, 403 U.S. 365 (1971) (alienage); Hunter v. Erickson, 393 U.S. 385 (1969) (race); Korematsu v. United States, 323 U.S. 214 (1944) (nationality). *See also* text accompanying note 1, Chapter 5.
2. Clark v. Jeter, 486 U.S. 456 (1988) (illegitimacy); Miss. Univ. for Women v. Hogan, 458 U.S. 718 (1982) (gender).
3. *See, e.g.,* Vill. of Arlington Heights v. Metro. Hous. Dev. Corp., 429 U.S. 252, 265-268 (1977).
4. Washington v. Davis, 426 U.S. 229, 242 (1976).

employment.[5] However, protection against discriminatory employment practices is not absolute for individuals within these classifications, since both Congress and courts have identified exceptions.[6] In creating and amending Title VII over the years, Congress has expressly permitted employers to facially discriminate based on religion, gender, or national origin (but not on race or color) if they can show the existence of a *bona fide occupational qualification (BFOQ)* that is reasonably necessary to the normal operation of their particular enterprise. Additionally, courts have specified that employers may use facially neutral employment practices that result in disparate impact on a protected class, but only if a *business necessity* is identified in the use of that practice and there are no less discriminatory ways of meeting that need.[7]

Qualifying as an Employer.   Title VII applies to employers with 15 or more employees who work 20 or more weeks during the calendar year. Although this requirement is seemingly simple, its application has been complex. The Supreme Court resolved some of the issues in *Walters v. Metropolitan Educational Enterprises,*[8] where it adopted the "payroll method" to assess employment status. All that is necessary under this approach is to determine when the employee began employment during the year and when he or she left (if at all). The person is counted as an employee for each working day after being hired and before leaving. If 15 or more workers are on the payroll for 20 or more weeks during the year (or even preceding year), the employer is covered by Title VII. It is not relevant whether the employee worked partial days, every other day, or was on call, leave, or vacation. However, employees who begin or depart in the middle of a week do not count toward the total for that particular week.[9]

Much to the disdain of small employers, use of the payroll method has significantly increased the number of entities now covered under a variety of federal laws. *Walters* is a Title VII retaliation case, but the definition established by the Court also has been applied to Americans with Disabilities Act (ADA) cases, given the similarity of the two statutes.[10] Also, the EEOC has adopted that approach under the Age Dis-

---

5. 42 U.S.C. § 2000e *et seq.* (2002). Furthermore, when examining discrimination on various factors, it is important to consider "combinations" of protected categories. For example, it might be that an employer would discriminate against Asian women but not against all women or Asian men. *See, e.g.,* Harrington v. Cleburne County Bd. of Educ., 251 F.3d 935 (11th Cir. 2001); Lam v. Univ. of Haw., 40 F.3d 1551 (9th Cir. 1994).

6. *See, e.g.,* Killinger v. Samford Univ., 113 F.3d 196 (11th Cir. 1997) (exempting a religious institution in its reassignment of a professor due to his religious beliefs that were contrary to those of the divinity school).

7. Complaints must be filed with the EEOC within 180 days of the allegedly discriminatory practice—42 U.S.C. § 2000e-5(e). *See also* Vadie v. Miss. State Univ., 218 F.3d 365 (5th Cir. 2000) (finding that the plaintiff failed to file within the 180-day limit).

8. 519 U.S. 202 (1997).

9. *See also* Ramsey v. 801 Credit Union Corp., No. C-3-94-183, 1997 U.S. Dist. LEXIS 23750 (S.D. Ohio, Feb. 18, 1997).

10. Owens v. S. Devel. Council, 59 F. Supp. 2d 1210 (M.D. Ala. 1999) (concluding that employer and employee are defined similarly under Title VII of the Civil Rights Act of 1964 and the ADA and that the payroll method applies to both).

crimination in Employment Act of 1967,[11] a law applicable to employers with 20 or more employees. Similarly, the Department of Labor requires use of the payroll method under the Family Medical Leave Act of 1993,[12] even though the number of employees required for compliance under that law is 50.[13]

Employers with 15 or more employees must then comply with Title VII, as well as numerous additional laws, and will be subject to suit where violations occur. When evaluating Title VII claims, courts have developed two legal theories: disparate treatment and disparate impact. *Disparate treatment* is applied when the individual claims less favorable treatment when compared to other applicants or employees; *disparate impact* is used when an employer's ostensibly neutral practice has a discriminatory impact on the class the claimant represents. In addition, it also is possible for an employee to file a Title VII complaint based on retaliation.

Disparate Treatment.   In proving disparate treatment, plaintiffs usually do not have direct evidence (e.g., written policies, public statements[14]), so they must rely on circumstantial evidence to substantiate that they received less favorable treatment. The plaintiff must establish a prima facie case or an inference of discrimination, which, if otherwise unexplained, is "more likely than not based on the consideration of impermissible factors."[15] A prima facie case of hiring discrimination can be established by showing that the applicant is a member of a protected class; applied for and was qualified for the job; and was denied the position, while the employer continued to seek applicants with the plaintiff's qualifications. These criteria were articulated by the Supreme Court in 1973 in *McDonnell Douglas Corporation v. Green*[16] and are applied beyond claims of hiring discrimination to alleged disparate treatment in areas such as promotion, termination, nonrenewal, and tenure.

If a prima facie case is supported, the burden shifts to the employer to state a reason for its action that does not violate Title VII. Such a reason may be either objective (e.g., a higher-level degree), subjective (e.g., stronger interpersonal skills), or a combination in determining the best qualified applicant.[17] If the employer is unable to produce a nondiscriminatory reason for the action, a directed verdict for the plaintiff most likely would be granted. But given the comparative ease of presenting a nondiscriminatory reason, employers in nearly every instance provide a response.

---

11. 29 U.S.C. § 630(b) (2002).

12. 29 U.S.C. § 2611(4)(A)(i) (2002).

13. For a related discussion, *see* Stephen B. Thomas, *Students, Colleges, and Disability Law* (Dayton, OH: Education Law Association, 2002), pp. 245–246.

14. *See, e.g.,* Simmons v. New Pub. Sch. Dist., 251 F.3d 1210 (8th Cir. 2001); Gosche v. Calvert High Sch. 997 F. Supp. 867 (N.D. Ohio 1998).

15. Furnco Constr. Corp. v. Waters, 438 U.S. 567, 577 (1978).

16. 411 U.S. 792, 802 (1973). *See also* Young v. Pennsauken Township Sch. Dist., 47 Fed. Appx. 160 (3d Cir. 2002).

17. *See, e.g.,* Calhoun v. Riverview Gardens Sch. Dist., No. 98-3976EM, 2000 U.S. App. LEXIS 598 (8th Cir. Jan. 18, 2000).

After the employer provides a rebuttal, the plaintiff then has the additional burden of proving by a preponderance of the evidence not only that the proffered reason was false but also that it served as a pretext for prohibited intentional discrimination.[18] In most instances of alleged discrimination, the plaintiff is unable to show that the employer's purported nondiscriminatory basis was pretextual. When that occurs, it is common for the defendant to request summary judgment in an effort to end the litigation. Summary judgment will be issued only if the evidence shows that there remains no genuine issue of material fact and that the moving party is entitled to judgment as a matter of law.

Disparate Impact.   In contrast to disparate treatment claims, to establish disparate impact the plaintiff is not initially required to prove discriminatory intent but must establish that an employer's facially neutral practice had a disproportionate impact on the plaintiff's protected class. This generally is accomplished through the use of statistics. Once this type of prima facie case is established, the employer then must show that the challenged policies or practices (or its employment practices in the aggregate) are job related and justified by a business necessity. Accordingly, an employer's nondiscriminatory reason for the act is insufficient to rebut a prima facie case of discriminatory impact. Moreover, even if a business necessity is identified, a plaintiff still may prevail by showing that the employer's facially neutral practice had a discriminatory purpose.

The Supreme Court has recognized, however, that mere awareness of a policy's adverse impact on a protected class does not constitute proof of unlawful motive; a discriminatory purpose "implies that the decisionmaker . . . selected or reaffirmed a particular course of action at least in part 'because of,' not merely 'in spite of,' its adverse effects upon an identifiable group."[19] Nonetheless, foreseeably discriminatory consequences can be considered by courts in assessing intent, although more will be needed to substantiate unlawful motive. Furthermore, the employee may prevail if it is shown that the employer refused to adopt an alternative policy identified by the employee that realistically would have met the employer's business needs without resulting in disparate impact.

Retaliation.   By the time a complaint is filed with the EEOC or a state or federal court, the working relationship between the employer and the employee often is strained, sometimes beyond repair. In response to filing, an employee may be terminated, demoted, or harassed, even though such acts are prohibited by Title VII. When this occurs, the employee may file a second claim alleging retaliation. To support this type of prima facie case, the employee is required to show that he or she was engaged in statutorily protected activity (i.e., the filing of a complaint or suit), that an adverse employment action was taken by the employer, and that a causal connection existed

18. *See, e.g.,* St. Mary's Honor Ctr. v. Hicks, 509 U.S. 502, 514-515 (1993).
19. Personnel Adm'r of Mass. v. Feeney, 442 U.S. 256, 279 (1979).

between the protected activity and the adverse action.[20] If the employee can show that filing the complaint was the basis for the adverse employment decision, even if the original complaint of discrimination fails, the court will provide appropriate relief.[21] Showing that the retaliatory action followed soon after engagement in the protected activity often is critical to supporting a retaliation claim.[22] Furthermore, showing that the administrator responsible for the adverse action knew of the filing of the complaint will be critical to showing that he or she retaliated in response to the filling.[23]

Relief. If it is proven that the employee was a victim of prohibited discrimination, courts have the authority to require a *make-whole remedy* where the person is placed in the same position he or she otherwise would have been, absent discriminatory activity. In meeting this objective, courts may provide injunctive and declaratory relief; require that a person be reinstated, hired, tenured, or promoted; direct the payment of back pay, interest on back pay, or front pay;[24] assign retroactive seniority; and provide attorneys' fees, expert witness fees, and court costs. Requiring the employer to apologize for the discrimination appears to go beyond the court's authority, however.[25]

In cases where intentional discrimination is proven, a court also may provide compensatory and punitive damages. But an employer may not be held liable for the discriminatory acts of its managerial staff when its decisions are contrary to the employer's good faith efforts to comply with Title VII.[26] Jury trials are available where damages are sought.

20. *See, e.g.,* Greer v. Bd. of Educ., 267 F.3d 723 (7th Cir. 2001) (finding that the plaintiff had been denied reemployment due to the strictures of a consent decree and not as an act of retaliation); Sharma v. Ohio State Univ., 25 Fed. Appx. 241 (6th Cir. 2001) (concluding that the plaintiff failed to show that his comparatively low salary was due to filing discrimination complaints); Mohankumar v. Kan. State Univ., 60 F. Supp. 2d 1153 (D. Kan. 1999) (determining that the plaintiff was not retaliated against for filing a complaint).

21. *See, e.g.,* Saleh v. Upadhyay, 11 Fed. Appx. 241 (4th Cir. 2001).

22. Ahmed v. Amer. Red Cross, 218 F.3d 932 (8th Cir. 2000) (noting that a four-year period between the protected conduct and the allegedly retaliatory response suggests that the two events are not related).

23. *See, e.g.,* Tinsley v. First Union Nat'l Bank, 155 F.3d 435 (4th Cir. 1998) (noting that the plaintiff failed to show that the adverse action was based on filing an EPA complaint 14 years earlier or that the supervisor was even aware of the filing).

24. For example, if a teacher were denied a principalship due to race, the court may direct the district to hire the teacher for the next available position. Also, if the principalship line provided greater compensation than did the teacher line, the court could require as part of a make-whole remedy that the difference in salary be awarded to the teacher up to the time of promotion. That portion of the salary paid in the future is called *front pay,* and that portion due the teacher at the time of the judgment for the previous period is termed *back pay.*

25. *See, e.g.,* Woodruff v. Ohman, 29 Fed. Appx. (6th Cir. 2002).

26. Kolstad v. Am. Dental Ass'n, 527 U.S. 526 (1999).

In mixed-motive cases where legitimate as well as discriminatory motives influence the employer's decision (e.g., poor job performance as well as gender), an employer will be held liable for decisions based in part on impermissible consider- ations. However, if the same decision would have resulted notwithstanding the dis- criminatory factors, Title VII limits the legal remedy to ensure that employees will not be placed in better positions than they would have been absent the influence of an ille- gal motive. Accordingly, relief for these plaintiffs is limited to declaratory relief, attorneys' fees, and court costs.

Race and National-Origin Discrimination

Race and national-origin discrimination in employment continues in spite of more than 135 years of protective statutes and constitutional amendments. For most of that period, however, the relief received by plaintiffs was typically limited to a make- whole remedy and seldom penalized the employer sufficiently to discourage future discrimination. Due to changes in statutes and case law, it now is easier for plaintiffs to vindicate their rights in court and to receive substantial monetary awards well beyond a make-whole remedy. Race and national-origin lawsuits are filed under the Fourteenth Amendment,[27] Title VII, and 42 U.S.C. Section 1981.

Section 1981 originally was Section 1 of the Civil Rights Act of 1866. At one time, this statute prohibited only race discrimination in making and enforcing con- tracts, but now Section 1981 applies when either race or ethnicity discrimination is alleged in making, performing, modifying, and terminating contracts, as well as in the enjoyment of all benefits, privileges, terms, and conditions of the contractual relation- ship. Section 1981 allows for both compensatory and punitive damages.

Hiring and Promotion Practices

Unless a school district is under a narrowly tailored court order to correct prior proven acts of race discrimination, it may not advantage or disadvantage an applicant or employee because of that individual's race. When unsuccessful candidates believe that race played a role in the decision-making process, they will generally allege dis- parate treatment, requiring the heightened proof of discriminatory intent. In attempt- ing to support such a claim, many plaintiffs have difficulty overcoming employers' purported nondiscriminatory reasons for their decisions,[28] even when applicants can

---

27. The Fourteenth Amendment requires the application of strict scrutiny in cases where race or national- origin discrimination is facial and proof of intent where the alleged discrimination is facially neutral. Moreover, the Fifth Amendment has an express Due Process Clause and an implied Equal Protection Clause. It is used when a violation is claimed within the District of Columbia, because the Fourteenth Amendment limits only state action. *See, e.g.,* Washington v. Davis, 426 U.S. 229 (1976) (finding no implied Equal Protection Clause violation in the use of a written skills test as one of several require- ments for the Washington, DC, police-training program; the test was validated regarding performance in the training program).

show that a person of another race or national origin was selected or treated more favorably.[29] Notwithstanding this, at times plaintiffs are able to show that no legitimate bases supported the employer's decision and that the selection was based on impermissible factors.

In a 1997 Second Circuit case dealing with national origin discrimination, the plaintiff was a Caucasian American of Eastern European origin who had applied for the director position of the Spanish Language Program in a university. An American male of Hispanic descent ultimately was appointed to the position, satisfying a university affirmative action policy that encouraged the hiring of women and racial minorities. Supposedly, the same standards were to be used to evaluate the applicants once a diversified pool of candidates was identified. The Caucasian plaintiff was able to show that he was the only finalist who possessed a doctorate; that neither of the others had published as extensively or had as much college teaching; that he had experience in running the program (i.e., during an interim appointment for which he received glowing commendations); that the university had deviated from established procedures; and that he was the only finalist who could teach Portuguese, a requirement for the position. The court concluded that ample evidence was presented to permit a reasonable fact finder to conclude that the university's employment decision was more likely than not due to impermissible discrimination based on national origin.[30]

Testing.   Among the more controversial objective measures used in hiring and promotion (e.g., degree level, a specified number of years of experience, a specific type or level of licensure) is the use of standardized test scores. The Equal Employment Opportunity Commission (EEOC) requires employers to conduct validity studies for tests used in making employment decisions if they result in adverse impact on a pro-

28. Cooper v. Murphysboro Bd. of Educ., 6 Fed. Appx. 438 (7th Cir. 2001) (determining that the plaintiff failed to support a prima facie case because he lacked sufficient experience and certification for the position), *cert. denied* 122 S. Ct. 619 (2001); Mosby v. Norwalk Bd. of Educ., 4 Fed. Appx. 15 (2d Cir. 2001) (determining that the plaintiff failed to show that race influenced a decision in the selection of a custodian; promotion was based on seniority, as specified in the bargaining agreement, and the selected candidate had greater seniority than did the plaintiff); Carmen v. S.F. Sch. Dist., 1 Fed. Appx. 730 (9th Cir. 2001) (concluding that the plaintiff failed to support the claim of race discrimination or that the selected candidate was less well qualified).

29. The fact that the successful applicant and the plaintiff are of the same class is not always dispositive of a discrimination claim. The successful candidate may have been selected only after the employer learned that a claim or suit had been filed. Lowry v. Bedford County Sch. Bd., No. 98-1165, 1999 U.S. App. LEXIS 16770 (4th Cir. July 19, 1999). *See also* Freeman v. Madison Metro. Sch. Dist., 231 F.3d 374 (7th Cir. 2000) (reasoning that similarly situated persons of different races need not necessarily experience differential treatment at the same time—i.e., one may precede the other).

30. Stern v. Trs. of Columbia Univ., 131 F.3d 305 (2d Cir. 1997). *But see* Zainalian v. Memphis Bd. of Educ., 3 Fed. Appx. 429 (6th Cir. 2001) (noting that the plaintiff was not hired due to poor evaluations received during his previous employment at several schools and not due to his race or national origin).

tected class. *Adverse impact* exists when (1) one group succeeds at a rate that is less than four-fifths, or 80 percent, of that achieved by the group with the highest passing rate (e.g., adverse impact results if 90 percent of Caucasians pass a test, but fewer than 72 percent of African Americans do so) or (2) for small populations, the difference in scores between the two groups is statistically significant.

For tests with a disparate impact to be used, they must be reliable and valid, and qualify as a business necessity.[31] *Reliability* requires that test scores be replicable. For example, if a person were to take an intelligence test twice over a period of several years and receive significantly different scores, the results would be meaningless. When this occurs, the test lacks reliability and essentially serves no useful purpose for the employer.

Validity, on the other hand, requires the test to measure what it purports to measure. In that regard, the EEOC allows the use of criterion-related validity (predictive of or correlated with job performance), content validity (representative of important aspects of performance on the job), and construct validity (measuring the degree to which candidates have identifiable characteristics that are important to successful job performance). Tests may be administered to applicants for positions other than those for which the tests have been validated, but only if there are no significant differences in the skills, knowledge, and abilities required by the jobs.[32] Tests may not be discriminatorily administered, nor may their results be discriminatorily used (e.g., the use of different cut-off scores or adjusted scores based on race is prohibited, whether used to advantage or disadvantage a population).

A state has the right to require its current and future teachers to demonstrate their general literacy as well as their content knowledge. In an illustrative case, the Supreme Court affirmed (without a written majority opinion) a lower court's conclusion that South Carolina's use of the National Teachers Examination (NTE) for teacher certification and salary purposes satisfied the Equal Protection Clause.[33] The federal district court had held that the test was valid, since it measured knowledge of course content in teacher preparation courses, and that it was not administered with an intent to discriminate against minority applicants for teacher certification. The court also found sufficient evidence to establish a relationship between the use of the test scores in determining the placement of teachers on the salary scale and legitimate employment objectives, such as encouraging teachers to upgrade their skills. The

---

31. *See, e.g.,* Griggs v. Duke Power Co., 401 U.S. 424, 432 (1971) (holding that a private company's use of both a high school diploma requirement and a test of general intelligence as prerequisites to initial employment and a condition of transfer violated Title VII; neither requirement was shown to be related to successful job performance, and both operated to disqualify minority applicants at a higher rate than those who were Caucasian).

32. Albemarle Paper Co. v. Moody, 422 U.S. 405, 432 (1975).

33. United States v. South Carolina, 445 F. Supp. 1094 (D.S.C. 1977), *aff'd sub nom.* Nat'l Educ. Ass'n v. South Carolina, 434 U.S. 1026 (1978).

option proposed by the plaintiffs (i.e., graduation from an approved teacher preparation program) was rejected by the court as incapable of assuring minimally competent teachers because of the wide range in university admission requirements, academic standards, and grading practices.

The testing of practicing teachers also has been controversial. Several courts have upheld test requirements for relicensure and dismissal.[34] In 1993, the Fifth Circuit rejected a race discrimination claim by minority teachers who failed the Texas competency test and held that the teachers' statistical data did not support a disparate impact prima facie case. Furthermore, the teachers were unable to show that the district acted with the intent to discriminate in its use of a test that was designed to evaluate subject and grade-level knowledge.[35]

With increasing legislative interest in assuring teacher competence, it is foreseeable that states, districts, and teacher-training institutions will continue to use tests as a requirement for admission to training programs, a prerequisite to licensure and rerelicensure, and a basis for graduation, hiring, and promotion. To avoid discriminatory actions, employers should use only valid and reliable instruments, and test performance should not be the sole criterion for making personnel decisions. Also, even when multiple criteria are used, each criterion must be validated if it results in disproportionate impact (or if it is part of a process that in the aggregate results in disproportionate impact).[36] Consequently, school districts should not use the Graduate Record Examination (intended to predict success in graduate programs) for initial employment, the NTE for promotion to administrative positions, or a general intelligence test for determining meritorious performance. Other more appropriate tests and additional measures could be used in making such decisions.

Adverse Decisions

Employers cannot dismiss, decline to renew, or demote employees on the basis of race or national origin; legitimate, nondiscriminatory bases must be used.[37] In 1993, the Supreme Court rendered a significant race-based termination case, *St. Mary's Honor Center v. Hicks,*[38] where a minority employee of a halfway house was demoted and eventually fired. The Court first noted that the employee had met his initial burden of establishing a prima facie case (i.e., he was African American, he was qualified for

34. *See, e.g.,* Fields v. Hallsville Indep. Sch. Dist., 906 F.2d 1017 (5th Cir. 1990); Swanson v. Houston Indep. Sch. Dist., 800 S.W.2d 630 (Tex. Ct. App. 1990). *See also* text accompanying note 2, Chapter 8.
35. Frazier v. Garrison Indep. Sch. Dist., 980 F.2d 1514 (5th Cir. 1993).
36. *See, e.g.,* Connecticut v. Teal, 457 U.S. 440 (1982).
37. *See, e.g.,* Juniel v. Park Forest–Chi. Heights, Ill., Sch. Dist., 46 Fed. Appx. 853 (7th Cir. 2002) (concluding that nonrenewal of director was due to need to cut costs); Ticali v. Roman Catholic Diocese, 41 F. Supp. 2d 249 (E.D.N.Y. 1999) (ruling that the transfer of a teacher from first grade to prekindergarten was not a demotion nor due to being non-Hispanic).
38. 509 U.S. 502 (1993).

the position, he was demoted and later discharged, and the position remained open until ultimately filled by a Caucasian). The burden then shifted to the employer to produce an explanation to rebut the inference that the employer had engaged in prohibited discrimination. In response, the employer argued that the suspension, letter of reprimand, and demotion were necessary because of the employee's poor supervision of his subordinates, his failure to conduct a proper investigation of a brawl between inmates, and his use of threatening words with his immediate superior. Given this response, the burden shifted back to the employee to show both that the proffered reasons were not to be believed *and* that the true basis for the termination was race.

The district court had determined that the employer's reasons were untrue, noting that the plaintiff was the only supervisor disciplined for violations committed by his subordinates and that similar, and at times more severe, violations by others were either treated more leniently or disregarded. The district court noted, and the Supreme Court agreed, however, that even though the employee was able to show that the purported reasons were untrue, he failed to show that race was a factor in his termination. Because the plaintiff was unable to meet his entire burden of persuasion, he could not prove a Title VII violation.

Likewise, in a 2001 Eleventh Circuit case, an African American school district employee responsible for electric motor repair was terminated when the district learned of his conviction for child molestation and multiple counts of assault and battery. A Caucasian employee with a 1977 molestation conviction had not been terminated. Initially, the jury awarded the plaintiff approximately $140,000, which he appealed as the amount did not include a compensatory award. The school district also appealed, claiming that it had the right to terminate the employment of child molesters. In its defense, the district explained that the Caucasian employee was not terminated when the incident occurred 24 years earlier due to an agreement that was entered into with the state attorney's office and the local superintendent. The appeals court reversed the lower court and concluded that the frequency (four), recency (one case was still pending), and violent nature (use of a machete) of the plaintiff's crimes were the bases for his termination and not his race.[39] Similar decisions have been reached by other courts when adverse decisions were based on legitimate nonpretextual factors such as neglect of duty, incompetence, punctuality, insubordination, falsification of records, theft, unprofessional conduct, reduced need, and the like.[40]

---

39. Silvera v. Orange County Sch. Bd., 244 F.3d 1253 (11th Cir. 2001), *cert. denied,* 122 S. Ct. 1598 (2002). *See also* Conward v. Cambridge Sch. Comm. 171 F.3d 12 (1st Cir. 1999) (upholding termination of teacher for unbecoming conduct when he handed a female student a document entitled "Application for a Piece of Ass"; plaintiff failed to show that his treatment was race related or that persons of another race were treated differentially); Jackson v. Bd. of Educ., No. 98-1060, 1999 U.S. App. LEXIS 4818 (4th Cir. March 22, 1999) (upholding involuntary transfer of teacher to split schedule given the decline of enrollment in her business education program; plaintiff failed to show that persons of another race were treated differently).

40. *See, e.g.,* Shaw v. Monroe, 20 Fed. Appx. 563 (7th Cir. 2001) (stalking and rape); Clearwater v. Indep. Sch. Dist. No. 166, 231 F.3d 1122 (8th Cir. 2000) (tardiness); Jones v. Sch. Dist., 198 F.3d 403 (3d Cir.

Affirmative Action

Affirmative action has been defined as "steps taken to remedy the grossly disparate staffing and recruitment patterns that are the present consequences of past discrimination and to prevent the occurrence of employment discrimination in the future."[41] Correcting such imbalances requires the employer to engage in activities such as expanding its training programs, becoming actively involved in recruitment, eliminating invalid selection criteria that result in disparate impact, and modifying collective bargaining agreements that impermissibly restrict the promotion and retention of minorities. Courts will uphold most strategies that the EEOC identifies as affirmative action under both Title VII (for which the EEOC has regulatory authority) and the Fourteenth Amendment (for which the EEOC does not have regulatory authority). However, courts will prohibit the use of affirmative action plans that provide a discriminatory "preference" rather than an "equal opportunity."

In 1989, the Supreme Court began to question a variety of public-sector practices that provided racial preferences.[42] In the aggregate, these cases applied strict scrutiny to race-based affirmative action programs operated by federal, state, and local levels of government; discredited societal discrimination as a justification for such programs; required showing specific discriminatory action to impose a race-based remedy; and allowed only narrowly tailored plans that would further a compelling interest. Given this precedent, existing public-sector affirmative action plans that provide racial preferences without a proven history of discrimination or that are based only on underrepresentation are likely to be found unconstitutional.

In addition to affirmative action in hiring and promotion, there also have been efforts to protect the diversity gained through court order and voluntary affirmative action by providing a preference when an organization is downsizing. When a reduction in school staff is necessary due to financial exigency, declining enrollment, or a change in education priorities, it generally is based, at least in part, on seniority rankings. Accordingly, it is important for all employees to be in their rightful place on the

1999) (threatening students); Joseph v. New York City Bd. of Educ., 171 F.3d 87 (2d Cir. 1999) (poor performance and failure to meet timelines); Carter v. St. Louis Univ., 167 F.3d 398 (8th Cir. 1999) (poor performance during residency); Ruby v. Springfield R-12 Pub. Sch. Dist., 76 F.3d 909 (8th Cir. 1996) (falsifying reports and hostile environment); Jiminez v. Mary Washington Coll., 57 F.3d 369 (4th Cir. 1995) (failure to receive Ph.D. and poor teaching evaluations); Noland v. Lorain Bd. of Educ., 869 F. Supp. 529 (N.D. Ohio 1994), *aff'd without published opinion,* 70 F.3d 115 (6th Cir. 1995) (theft); Cliff v. Bd. of Sch. Comm'rs, 42 F.3d 403 (7th Cir. 1994) (failure to control students); Dugan v. Albemarle County Sch. Bd., 148 F. Supp. 2d 688 (W.D. Va. 2001) (nontenured and reduced need for physical education teachers).

41. United States Commission on Civil Rights, *Statement of Affirmative Action for Equal Employment Opportunities* (Washington, DC: United States Commission on Civil Rights, 1973).

42. *See, e.g.,* Adarand Constructors v. Pena, 515 U.S. 200 (1995); Northeastern Fla. Chapter of the Associated Gen. Contractors of Am. v. City of Jacksonville, 508 U.S. 656 (1993); Martin v. Wilks, 490 U.S. 755 (1989); City of Richmond v. J.A. Croson Co., 488 U.S. 469 (1989).

seniority list. Although at first blush this may appear simple and straightforward, it becomes more complex in districts that have a proven history of discrimination. To obtain their rightful place in the seniority hierarchy, employees have been awarded varying levels of retroactive seniority in addition to those years they have accrued while on the job.[43]

In some cases, plaintiffs have proposed the modification of seniority systems to give an overall preference to all minorities regarding eligibility for promotion and other job benefits or in protection from a reduction-in-force (RIF). Such affirmative action plans are similar to awards of retroactive seniority, but in contrast to seniority adjustments for individual discrimination victims, class remedies benefit class members who may not have been the victim of prior acts of discrimination. Courts will prohibit such practices, even if the employer is found guilty of a pattern or practice of racial discrimination.[44] The appropriate form of relief is to award competitive seniority to individual victims so as to restore them to their rightful place. Courts may not disregard a seniority system in fashioning a class remedy.

In 1986, the Supreme Court reviewed a school-based case involving a voluntary affirmative action plan that included a layoff quota, *Wygant v. Jackson Board of Education*.[45] In that case, the Court struck down a school district's collective bargaining agreement that protected minority teachers from layoffs to preserve the percentage of minority personnel employed prior to the RIF. The Court plurality reasoned that the quota system, which resulted in the release of some Caucasian teachers with greater seniority than minority teachers who were retained, violated the Equal Protection Clause. Societal discrimination alone was not sufficient to justify the class preference. Recognizing that racial classifications in employment must be justified by a compelling governmental purpose and that means must be narrowly tailored to accomplish that purpose, the Court concluded that the layoff provision in question did not satisfy either of these conditions. Moreover, the Court further rejected the lower courts' reliance on the "role model" theory (tying the percentage of minority teachers to the percentage of minority students), noting that the proper comparison for determining employment discrimination is between the racial composition of the teaching staff and the qualified relevant labor market.[46] The Court was concerned that the use of the role model theory would allow school boards to go far beyond legitimate remedial purposes.

Similarly, in 1996, the Third Circuit held that an affirmative action plan preferring minority teachers over equally qualified nonminority teachers violated Title VII. The plan had been adopted to promote racial diversity rather than to remedy prior race discrimination by the district. The preference was of "unlimited duration," imposed

---

43. Franks v. Bowman Trans. Co., 424 U.S. 747 (1976).

44. Firefighters Local Union No. 1784 v. Stotts, 467 U.S. 561 (1984).

45. 476 U.S. 267 (1986). *See also* text accompanying note 64, Chapter 12.

46. *Id.* at 275-276. *See also* Hazelwood Sch. Dist. v. United States, 433 U.S. 299, 308 (1977) (holding that the "qualified population in the relevant labor pool" should be used for statistical purposes and that the makeup of that pool may have little correlation to the racial composition of the pupil population or to the local community).

job loss on tenured nonminority employees, and unnecessarily trammeled the interests of nonminority employees.[47]

Gender Discrimination

Prior to 1963, there were no federal statutes prohibiting discrimination based on gender. Women were commonly denied employment if a qualified male applicant was in the pool, were offered less money for the same or similar job, or were expected to do work that would not have been asked of a man. Today, most forms of gender discrimination are prohibited, including those associated with hiring, promotion, and virtually all terms and conditions of employment. The Fourteenth Amendment,[48] Title VII of the Civil Rights Act of 1964, and other federal and state laws have played significant roles in allowing victims of gender discrimination to vindicate their rights in court.

Hiring and Promotion Practices

Gender discrimination is facial when an employer openly seeks a person of a particular gender (e.g., the posting of a position for a female guidance counselor). It becomes illegal discrimination when being male or female is unrelated to meeting job requirements (e.g., hiring only males as coaches of football). At other times, employment practices are facially neutral (e.g., requiring head coaching experience in football in order to qualify as athletic director), but nevertheless result in nearly the same level of exclusion as when the discrimination is facial. When this occurs, an action will be upheld only if found to qualify as a business necessity and other less discriminatory options do not meet the needs of the organization. Because direct evidence of discrimination is not always available, employees typically engage in the volley of establishing a prima facie case, followed by a response by the employer and the showing of pretext by the employee. Plaintiffs may support the claim that the purported reasons were pretextual by showing that they were better qualified than those selected; that proper procedures were not followed; or that nontraditional and unauthorized criteria were used as a basis for reaching the decision.

Where applicants or employees have been treated unfairly solely because of gender, a plaintiff typically files a Title VII suit alleging disparate treatment. The standards for such a claim are substantially similar to those used for race. Employees are required to present evidence of membership in a protected class, show that they applied and were qualified for the job,[49] and demonstrate that the employer denied

---

47. Taxman v. Bd. of Educ., 91 F.3d 1547 (3d Cir. 1996).

48. The Fourteenth Amendment requires the application of intermediate scrutiny in cases where gender discrimination is facial and proof of intent where the alleged discrimination is facially neutral. *See* Hundertmark v. Florida, 205 F.3d 1272 (11th Cir. 2000) (applying intermediate scrutiny).

49. *See, e.g.,* Marion v. Slaughter Co., No. 98-6286, 1999 U.S. App. LEXIS 34275 (10th Cir. Dec. 29, 1999) (concluding that plaintiff had neither applied for the position nor been turned down); Peden v. Suwannee County Sch. Bd., 837 F. Supp. 1188 (M.D. Fla. 1993) (finding that the plaintiff was not qualified for the position), *aff'd without published opinion,* 51 F.3d 1049 (11th Cir. 1995).

their applications and continued to seek additional candidates with the same qualifications until a person of the opposite sex was hired. If a person of the same sex eventually is hired, the prima facie case generally cannot be supported. But, assuming that a prima facie case is established, the employer then must identify a basis other than gender for its decision (e.g., showing that the successful applicant was equally or better qualified or that the plaintiff was unqualified).[50]

Where a nondiscriminatory basis has been proffered, applicants still may obtain relief if the reasons are shown to be pretextual. Rejected applicants have prevailed where employers based their decisions on stereotypic attitudes about the capabilities of their gender (e.g., that the turnover rate among women is higher); where job advertisements included the phrase *prefer male* or *prefer female;* and where job descriptions were specifically drafted to exclude qualified applicants of a particular gender.

One of the most significant cases involving gender-based discrimination in promotion was *Texas Department of Community Affairs v. Burdine,* a 1981 Supreme Court decision.[51] In this case, a female accounting clerk was denied promotion and later was terminated along with two other employees, although two males were retained. In response to the female's prima facie case, the public employer claimed that the three terminated employees did not work well together and that the male who was promoted to the position sought by the female employee was subjectively better qualified, although he had been her subordinate prior to the promotion. In rendering its decision, the Court emphasized that Title VII does not require the hiring or promotion of equally qualified women or the restructuring of employment practices to maximize the number of underrepresented employees. Instead, the employer has the discretion to choose among equally qualified candidates as long as the decision is not based on unlawful criteria. In this case, the female employee failed to show pretext, resulting in a decision for the employer.

In contrast, the Eighth Circuit in 1990 found that a female teacher who was passed over eight times for promotion to an administrative position was the victim of intentional gender discrimination.[52] As a result, she was entitled to back pay to the date of her first rejection and front pay until an appropriate administrative position became available. The court had concerns regarding how the superintendent assessed the leadership abilities of male and female applicants as well as his statement that he was "leery" about assigning a female as principal of a junior high school. Similarly, in Alabama a federal district court held that a Caucasian female applicant for a middle school principal position established a prima facie case and denied summary judgment to the district, notwithstanding its claim that a better-qualified male was hired for each of several previous vacancies.[53] The applicant was able to show that both gen-

---

50. *See, e.g.,* Bickerstaff v. Vassar Coll., 196 F.3d 435 (2d Cir. 1999) (finding that the plaintiff failed to meet the criteria for promotion to full professor).

51. 450 U.S. 248 (1981).

52. Willis v. Watson Chapel Sch. Dist., 899 F.2d 745 (8th Cir. 1990), *on remand,* 749 F. Supp. 923 (E.D. Ark. 1990). *But see* Belfi v. Prendergast, 191 F.3d 129 (2d Cir. 1999) (upholding summary judgment on Title VII claim as the plaintiff failed to prove intent).

53. Hicks v. Dothan City Bd. of Educ., 814 F. Supp. 1044 (M.D. Ala. 1993).

der (the need for male disciplinarians) and race (the need for minority role models) were considered in selecting Caucasian and African American males to fill the positions. The court required the district to acquire court approval prior to filling any principalship position during the course of deliberations.

Not all gender-based distinctions are prohibited, however, as Title VII explicitly allows a bona fide occupational qualification (BFOQ) exception. For a BFOQ to be upheld, it needs to be narrowly defined and applied only when necessary to achieve the employer's objectives. There have been few BFOQ school cases since the vast majority of jobs in education can be performed by either males or females. The only readily identifiable BFOQ in education would be the hiring of a female to supervise the girls' locker room and the hiring of a male to supervise the boys' locker room.

Moreover, where gender does not qualify as a BFOQ, a position may not be left vacant when qualified persons of the nonpreferred gender are available in the labor pool. In such a case, the Seventh Circuit in 1999 concluded that a reasonable jury had sufficient data to conclude that the plaintiff, a male, was discriminated against solely because of gender when the college dean refused to accept his nomination for a position that the dean hoped would be filled by a female.[54] The dean based his decision on the need to meet the affirmative action target for his college. The target was established to create a diversified staff, not to eradicate the consequences of prior discrimination.

Compensation Practices

Claims of gender-based compensation discrimination involving comparative entry salaries, raises, supplemental or overtime opportunities, or other perquisites and benefits are not uncommon within business and industry. However, because most K–12 salary decisions are based on objective criteria such as seniority, degree level, and civil service classification, the number of public school cases has been comparatively small.[55] Occasionally, however, facially neutral salary adjustments, such as "head of household" or "principal wage earner" allowances, are reviewed and are prohibited if not shown to be job related.[56]

The Fourteenth Amendment, Title VII, or the Equal Pay Act (EPA) of 1963 may be used where plaintiffs claim that their salaries are based in whole or in part on gender. The EPA applies only when the dispute involves gender-based wage discrimination claims of unequal pay for equal work.[57] As a result, the act does not apply when race-based or age-based salary differences are challenged, or when the work is unequal.

---

54. Hill v. Ross, 183 F.3d 586 (7th Cir. 1999).

55. *See, e.g.,* Buntin v. Breathitt County Bd. of Educ., 134 F.3d 796 (6th Cir. 1998) (remanding the case to see if the differential in "extended employment days" for which additional compensation is provided was due to gender).

56. *See, e.g.,* EEOC v. Fremont Christian Sch., 609 F. Supp. 344 (N.D. Cal. 1984), *aff'd,* 781 F.2d 1362 (9th Cir. 1986); Brock v. Ga. Southwestern Coll., 765 F.2d 1026 (11th Cir. 1985); EEOC v. Tree of Life Christian Sch., 751 F. Supp. 700 (S.D. Ohio 1990).

57. 29 U.S.C. § 206(d) (2002).

In a 1994 case from the Ninth Circuit, a former head coach of women's basketball sued under the EPA, claiming that she should be provided with the same pay as the head coach of men's basketball.[58] The university refused to offer an equal salary, but did counter with a contract that would have increased her salary to $100,000 over a three-year period, making her one of the best paid coaches of women's basketball in the country. She refused the contract and filed suit. In response, the university pointed out that the coach of men's basketball had significantly greater responsibilities, seniority, notoriety, and stress associated with his job, including the pressure to raise significant revenue. Consequently, the court denied the female coach's request for a preliminary injunction, for she failed to show that she had performed equal work.[59]

In determining whether the jobs in question are equal, courts look at more than position titles (e.g., *custodian* versus *cleaner; assistant principal* versus *assistant to the principal*) and will examine the comparative skills, effort, responsibilities, and working conditions associated with each job as well as the nature of required tasks. If the jobs are found substantially equal (although not identical) with unequal pay, the employer then must show by a preponderance of evidence that the different salaries were justified by one or more of the following criteria: seniority, merit, quantity or quality of production, or any factor other than gender.[60] Where the employer purports to be using a merit system, it should be uniformly applied and be based on established criteria.[61] Unlike Title VII, the plaintiff need not prove that the employer intended to discriminate; proof that the compensation is different and not based on factors other than gender will suffice. Where violations are discovered, compensatory damages may be awarded.[62] Furthermore, the law prohibits the lowering of the salaries for the higher paid group (generally men) and therefore requires the salaries for the lower paid group (generally women) to be raised. Importantly, relief under the EPA is not barred by Eleventh Amendment immunity.[63]

58. Stanley v. Univ. of S. Cal., 13 F.3d 1313 (9th Cir. 1994). *See also* Nixon v. State, 625 A.2d 404 (Md. Ct. Spec. App. 1993) (concluding that a lower-paid female professor failed to show that she had performed work that was equal to a better-paid male who taught in two departments, performed administrative duties, coordinated a research grant, and authored numerous academic publications). *But see* Hatton v. Hunt, 780 F. Supp. 1157 (W.D. Tenn. 1991) (upholding claims that a newly hired male administrative assistant received higher pay, not due to a greater degree of education or work experience, but rather because the administration believed that he would not accept the lower pay that was accorded to women holding the same job).

59. *See also* Marion v. Slaughter Co., No. 98-6286, 1999 U.S. App. LEXIS 34275 (10th Cir. Dec. 29, 1999) (concluding that the plaintiff's salary was appropriate, given her responsibilities and value to the organization, and was not gender based).

60. *See, e.g.,* Wollenburg v. Comtech Mfg. Co., 201 F.3d 973 (7th Cir. 2000) (identifying experience as a legitimate basis for pay difference); Stanziale v. Jargowsky, 200 F.3d 101 (3d Cir. 2000) (identifying overall qualifications as a legitimate basis for pay difference); Hughmanick v. County of Santa Clara, No. 98-16891, 2000 U.S. App. LEXIS 417 (9th Cir. Jan. 7, 2000) (identifying the terms of a reorganization agreement to represent a factor other than sex); Hutchins v. Int'l Bhd. of Teamsters, 177 F.3d 1076 (8th Cir. 1999) (identifying experience and education as factors other than sex).

61. *See, e.g.,* Port Auth. v. Ryduchowski, 530 U.S. 1276 (2000).

62. *See, e.g.,* West v. Gibson, 527 U.S. 212 (1999).

Because the EPA is limited to controversies dealing with equal work, its application is restricted to those circumstances where there are male and female workers performing substantially the same work but for different pay. Accordingly, if there are no male secretaries for a salary comparison, there can be no EPA violation, regardless how abysmal the salaries of female secretaries may be. However, a comparable male was found in a recent Sixth Circuit case where a poorly paid female faculty member sued, claiming gender discrimination.[64] The professor had worked at the university for over two decades, but apparently was neither a good teacher nor researcher. She had few grants during her tenure and few publications; as a result, she received a low salary. Any increases in her salary were due to across-the-board cost-of-living adjustments or extremely modest merit supplements during times when funds were plentiful. She prevailed on her sex discrimination claim, notwithstanding the fact that her coordinators, department chairs, and deans for most of her career were women. She was able to identify a male professor who the court reasoned was equally unproductive but made nearly $6,000 more.

Gender-based wage discrimination claims, however, are not confined exclusively to violations of the EPA; they also may be filed under Title VII.[65] As with race-based cases, intent will have to be proven in a disparate treatment case, whereas salary differences will have to be statistically significant for plaintiffs to prevail in a disparate impact case.[66] Within such a statistical analysis, variables that affect salary must be included (e.g., seniority, degree level, merit, administrative assignments, supplemental duty). The Fourth Circuit in 1996 ruled in favor of male faculty members who claimed Title VII and EPA violations when their university voluntarily increased the salaries of female faculty, allegedly to eliminate salary inequities.[67] The study did not include performance criteria used for merit, consider the impact of prior administrative experience on salary, or include career interruptions when measuring academic experience.

Termination, Nonrenewal, and Denial of Tenure

Title VII prohibits arbitrary termination, nonrenewal, and denial of tenure based on gender.[68] In disparate treatment cases, the employee is required to prove that the

63. *See, e.g.,* Siler-Khodr v. Univ. of Tex. Health Sci. Ctr. San Antonio, 261 F.3d 542 (5th Cir. 2001).
64. Kovacevich v. Kent State Univ., 224 F.3d 806 (6th Cir. 2000).
65. A controversial concept during the 1970s and early 1980s was called *comparable worth,* supporting the position that employees should be paid based on their comparable value to the organization, irrespective of market conditions surrounding supply and demand. Given the lack of judicially manageable standards in determining the comparable value employees have to an organization, this approach failed to gain judicial acceptance even though the Supreme Court recognized that claims beyond equal pay for equal work were actionable under Title VII. *See* Gunther v. County of Washington, 452 U.S. 161 (1981).
66. *See, e.g.,* Chance v. Rice Univ., 989 F.2d 179 (5th Cir. 1993).
67. Smith v. Va. Commonwealth Univ., 84 F.3d 672 (4th Cir. 1996).

employer elected to terminate or not renew the employee's contract due to gender rather than job performance, inappropriate conduct, interpersonal relationships, financial exigency, or other just cause.[69] As in most cases where proof of intent is required, employees claiming gender discrimination often have difficulty supporting their claims, even if true. Occasionally, however, corroborating evidence (both written and oral) will be inadvertently provided by officials responsible for making personnel decisions (e.g., school board members, superintendents).

In a 1994 Tenth Circuit decision, a female former principal was "bumped" by an associate superintendent, who assumed her position as well as his own. The district initially proposed that the reduction-in-force was necessary due to financial exigency but later claimed that the female principal had continuing difficulty with her faculty, which allegedly was the basis for her contract not being renewed. The appeals court found the evidence to be contradictory, including the superintendent's annual evaluation of the principal where she received high marks for establishing and maintaining staff cooperation and creating an environment conducive to learning. Given such discrepancies, the appeals court reversed the lower court's grant of summary judgment.[70]

In another case, a New York federal district court denied summary judgment for the school district where a former assistant superintendent was rejected for an assistant principal position after her central office job was eliminated.[71] Supporting the female applicant's claim of race and gender discrimination was a memorandum by the middle school committee responsible for interviewing the candidates, which purported that the successful candidate (an African American male) had a "broad cultural background" and would be an excellent male role model for students.

When making tenure decisions, it is important to follow all published and agreed upon procedures, to meet all time restrictions, and to provide all internal appeals. Where facial discrimination does not exist, most plaintiffs will attempt to show that persons of the opposite gender were treated differently (i.e., required to meet different standards; assessed differently in meeting the same standards). The problem with this approach is that it often is difficult to identify a comparable party or to challenge subjective judgments regarding performance or potential.[72]

68. *See, e.g.,* Weinstock v. Columbia Univ., 224 F.3d 33 (2d Cir. 2000) (upholding summary judgment when a female professor failed to show that gender rather than performance was the basis for her tenure denial).

69. *See, e.g.,* Brinson v. Chi. Bd. of Educ., No. 99-1896, 2000 U.S. App. LEXIS 31948 (7th Cir. Nov. 22, 2000); Euerle-Wehle v. United Parcel Serv., 181 F.3d 898 (8th Cir. 1999); Brinkley v. Harbour Recreation Club, 180 F.3d 598 (4th Cir. 1999).

70. Cole v. Ruidoso Mun. Sch., 43 F.3d 1373 (10th Cir. 1994). *See also* Harker v. Utica Coll., 885 F. Supp. 378 (N.D.N.Y. 1995) (granting summary judgment where a former coach failed to support a gender discrimination claim in her discharge).

71. Fairbairn v. Bd. of Educ., 876 F. Supp. 432 (E.D.N.Y. 1995).

72. *See, e.g.,* Jacklyn v. Schering-Plough Healthcare Prods. Sales Corp., 176 F.3d 921 (6th Cir. 1999); Krystek v. Univ. of S. Miss., 164 F.3d 251 (5th Cir. 1999).

Pregnancy Discrimination

Under the Pregnancy Discrimination Act (PDA),[73] an amendment to Title VII enacted in 1978, employers may not discriminate based on pregnancy, childbirth, or related medical conditions.[74] As such, pregnancy may not be used as a basis for refusing to hire an otherwise qualified applicant; denying disability, medical, or other benefits; or terminating or nonrenewing employment.[75] It is inappropriate for an employer even to ask questions regarding an employee's intent to marry or have children or how the employee plans to take care of her children if she were hired.[76] Nonetheless, it is the plaintiff's responsibility to show that pregnancy rather than some other factor was the basis of an adverse decision.[77] For example, in 1999, the Sixth Circuit remanded a case to determine whether a private religious school terminated the employment of a teacher due to having engaged in premarital sex (in violation of religious tenants) or to having become pregnant; the former is considered a permissible factor to be considered in the private sector, but not the latter.[78]

Before passage of the PDA, the Fourth Circuit relied on the Fourteenth Amendment in striking down a school board's practice of not renewing teachers' contracts where a foreseeable period of absence could be predicted for the ensuing year.[79] The policy had been applied only to pregnant employees, thus imposing a disproportionate burden on female teachers. The Supreme Court also has held that women of childbearing age cannot be denied equal access to what the employer perceives as "high risk" forms of employment, if they are otherwise qualified for the jobs (e.g., janitorial jobs requiring the use of strong chemicals).[80]

If an employer requires a doctor's statement for other conditions, it also may require one for pregnancy prior to granting leave or paying benefits.[81] And, if employees are unable to perform their jobs due to pregnancy, the employer is required to treat

---

73. 42 U.S.C. § 2000e(k) (2002).

74. The PDA was passed in response to two Supreme Court decisions where the denial of benefits for pregnancy-related conditions was found not to violate either Title VII or the Fourteenth Amendment. The Court reasoned that the classification involved (i.e., pregnancy) was not "gender," since nonpregnant employees included both men and women. *See* Gen. Elec. Co. v. Gilbert, 429 U.S. 125 (1976); Geduldig v. Aiello, 417 U.S. 484 (1974).

75. *See, e.g.,* Vigars v. Valley Christian Ctr., 805 F. Supp. 802 (N.D. Cal. 1992).

76. *See, e.g.,* Stukey v. United States Air Force, 790 F. Supp. 165 (S.D. Ohio 1992) (asking questions regarding marital status and children provided evidence of a per se violation of Title VII).

77. Piraino v. Int'l Orientation Res., 137 F.3d 987 (7th Cir. 1998).

78. Cline v. Catholic Diocese, 206 F.3d 651 (6th Cir. 1999). *See also* Parker-Bigback v. St. Labre Sch., 7 P.3d 361 (Mont. 2000) (holding that Title VII did not prohibit a religious school from terminating a teacher's employment for living with a man out of wedlock; her employment contract stipulated that she would conduct her private life consistent with church doctrine), *cert. denied,* 531 U.S. 1076 (2001).

79. Mitchell v. Bd. of Trs., 599 F.2d 582 (4th Cir. 1979).

80. Int'l Union, United Auto., Aerospace, & Agric. Implement Workers of Am. v. Johnson Controls, 499 U.S. 187 (1991).

81. *See, e.g.,* Hoeflinger v. W. Clermont Local Bd. of Educ., 478 N.E.2d 251 (Ohio Ct. App. 1984).

them the same as any other temporarily disabled person. Possible forms of accommodation may be to modify tasks, provide alternate assignments, or provide disability leave (with or without pay). If a pregnant employee takes a leave of absence, her position must be held open the same length of time that it would be if she were sick or disabled. Moreover, maternity leave cannot be considered an interruption in employment for the purposes of accumulating credit toward tenure or seniority if employees retain seniority rights when on leave for other disabilities.[82]

Mandatory pregnancy leave policies requiring teachers to take a leave of absence prior to the birth of their children and specifying a return date also violate the Due Process Clause by creating an *irrebuttable presumption* that all pregnant teachers are physically incompetent as of a specified date. [83] School boards, however, may establish maternity leave policies that are justified by a business necessity. For example, the Ninth Circuit upheld as reasonable a leave policy that required all teachers to take maternity leave at the beginning of the ninth month of pregnancy.[84] The board adequately demonstrated the business necessity of obtaining a replacement teacher.

Although employers may not treat pregnant employees less favorably, they may grant special leave and other benefits that are unavailable to nonpregnant persons. As indicated by the Ninth Circuit, the PDA was intended "to construct a floor beneath which pregnancy disability benefits may not drop" rather than "a ceiling above which they may not rise."[85] Although special benefits can be given to pregnant employees, in 1990, the Third Circuit invalidated a leave policy that permitted female employees, but not male employees, to use up to one year of combined sick leave and unpaid leave for child rearing.[86] Noting that the leave was not tied to any continuing disability related to pregnancy or childbirth, the court held that denial of a year of unpaid leave for child rearing to a male teacher constituted gender discrimination under Title VII.

The Seventh Circuit decided cases in 1993 and 1994 in which plaintiffs argued that school districts' maternity leave procedures were more restrictive than the procedures for other forms of leave (e.g., sick leave, medical leave, general leave, and parental leave) and therefore discriminated against pregnant teachers under the PDA.[87] The appeals court disagreed and concluded that the school board treated pregnant and nonpregnant teachers the same with regard to other forms of leave, plus gave pregnant teachers a further option of using maternity leave with some restrictions. This benefit went beyond that provided to nonpregnant employees of both sexes.

82. *See, e.g.,* Nashville Gas Co. v. Satty, 434 U.S. 136 (1977).

83. *See, e.g.,* Cleveland Bd. of Educ. v. LaFleur, 414 U.S. 632 (1974).

84. *See, e.g.,* deLaurier v. San Diego Unified Sch. Dist., 588 F.2d 674 (9th Cir. 1978).

85. Cal. Fed. Savings & Loan Ass'n v. Guerra, 758 F.2d 390, 396 (9th Cir. 1985), *aff'd,* 479 U.S. 272 (1987).

86. Schafer v. Bd. of Pub. Educ., 903 F.2d 243 (3d Cir. 1990).

87. United States v. Bd. of Educ., 983 F.2d 790 (7th Cir. 1993); EEOC v. Elgin Teachers Ass'n, 27 F.3d 292 (7th Cir. 1994).

Sexual Harassment

Sexual harassment generally refers to repeated and unwelcome sexual advances, sexually suggestive comments, or sexually demeaning gestures or acts.[88] Both men and women have been victims of sexual harassment from persons of the opposite or same sex.[89] The harasser may be a supervisor, an agent of the employer, a supervisor of another area, a coworker, or even a nonemployee. Critical to a successful claim is proof that the harassment is indeed based on gender, rather than sexual preference, being transsexual, transvestism, or personal dislike. For example, in a recent Eleventh Circuit case, a male teacher and female teacher had a consensual relationship, which the male eventually ended. The female then began making threatening overtures toward the wife and son of her prior lover; the wife eventually acquired a restraining order. As the teachers taught at the same school, the female also sought to embarrass her male colleague in front of other staff and students whenever possible. After unsuccessful administrative claims, the male teacher filed suit, claiming hostile environment. The court disagreed and determined that the female teacher had targeted the male teacher because he ended their relationship and not because of his gender.[90]

There are two types of harassment cognizable under Title VII:[91] quid pro quo and hostile environment. Each is reviewed briefly here.

Quid Pro Quo. *Quid pro quo harassment* literally means something for something. To establish a prima facie case of quid pro quo harassment against an employer, the employee must show that he or she was subjected to unwelcome sexual harassment in the form of sexual advances and requests for sexual favors, that the harassment was based on gender, and that submission to the unwelcome advances was an express or implied condition for either favorable actions (e.g., promotion) or avoidance of adverse actions (e.g., termination) by the employer. Although only a preponderance of evidence is required in such cases, acquiring the necessary 51 percent can be difficult, particularly given that the violator is unlikely to provide corroborating testimony. Also, the alleged behavior usually takes place behind closed doors so as to limit the opportunity for others to observe the conduct. If the employee succeeds, however, the law imposes strict liability on the employer, given the harasser's authority to alter the terms and conditions of employment.[92]

88. *See, e.g.,* Abeita v. TransAmerica Mailings, 159 F.3d 246 (6th Cir. 1998).

89. *See, e.g.,* Oncale v. Sundowner Offshore Servs., 523 U.S. 75 (1998).

90. Succar v. Dade County Sch. Bd., 229 F.3d 1343 (11th Cir. 2000).

91. In addition to filing a Title VII claim, plaintiffs may file charges under state employment law or state tort law. Tort claims may include intentional infliction of emotional distress, assault and battery, invasion of privacy, and defamation. *See, e.g.,* Helmick v. Cincinnati Word Processing, 543 N.E.2d 1212 (Ohio 1989).

92. *See, e.g.,* Highlander v. K.F.C. Nat'l Mgmt. Co., 805 F.2d 644, 648 (6th Cir. 1986). *See also* Townsend v. Ind. Univ., 995 F.2d 691 (7th Cir. 1993) (holding that under Title VII, an employee could recover wages lost due to psychological distress caused by alleged sexual assaults by her immediate supervisor).

Hostile Environment.   To prevail under this theory, the plaintiff must show that the environment in fact is hostile; it needs to be severe *or* pervasive.[93] In *Meritor Savings Bank v. Vinson,* the Supreme Court in 1986 recognized for the first time that a Title VII violation can be predicated on harassment that creates a hostile or offensive working environment in addition to harassment that involves conditioning employment benefits on sexual favors.[94] Furthermore, the Court rejected the employer's claim that the prohibition of sex discrimination was intended to prevent only tangible losses of an economic character, rather than injury from psychological aspects of the workplace. The Court noted that conduct unreasonably interfering with an individual's work performance or creating an intimidating, hostile, or offensive working environment is actionable. Furthermore, the Court proposed that determining whether the alleged sexual advances were "unwelcome" was critical to identifying a violation and reasoned that evidence regarding the victim's conduct (e.g., expression of sexual fantasies and provocative dress while at work) could be relevant in making this determination. Courts generally consider whether the victim solicited or initiated the conduct, whether the victim considered the conduct undesirable and offensive, whether the victim contributed to creating the environment,[95] and whether the victim informed the harasser that the unwelcome conduct was offensive.

Although the Supreme Court provided significant guidance in the *Meritor* case, it left unanswered questions regarding the need to prove psychological injury, particularly in the absence of tangible job losses. The Supreme Court addressed this issue in 1993 in *Harris v. Forklift Systems.*[96] A female executive was regularly exposed to hostile and abusive conduct by the company's president. Among the president's controversial behaviors was his request of female staff to get coins from his front pants pocket or for them to retrieve coins that he had tossed on the floor. Following the president's comment that the plaintiff must have promised sex to a customer to have acquired a lucrative contract, she quit her job and eventually sued. The lower court held that a reasonable victim would have found the president's conduct offensive but that it was not so egregious as to interfere with her work performance or to cause injury, and this opinion was affirmed by the Sixth Circuit.

In a rare unanimous decision, the Supreme Court reversed and identified what it perceived to be a middle path between finding any conduct that is merely offensive to violate Title VII and requiring the conduct to cause a diagnosed psychological

93. *See, e.g.,* Haugerud v. Amery Sch. Dist., 259 F.3d 678 (7th Cir. 2001) (noting that one extremely serious act of harassment could rise to an actionable level as could a series of less severe acts); Klemencic v. Ohio State Univ., 10 F. Supp. 2d 911 (S.D. Ohio 1998) (finding that plaintiff failed to show that the environment qualified as hostile).

94. 477 U.S. 57 (1986).

95. *See, e.g.,* Weinsheimer v. Rockwell Int'l Corp., 754 F. Supp. 1559 (M.D. Fla. 1990), *aff'd without published opinion,* 949 F.2d 1162 (11th Cir. 1991) (noting that there was strong evidence to support the position that the plaintiff was among the most prevalent and graphic participants in creating a vulgar environment that was replete with sexual innuendo).

96. 510 U.S. 17 (1993).

injury. The Court held that Title VII is violated if the environment would reasonably be perceived as hostile and abusive and that psychological injury need not be proven. The Court suggested the following criteria in assessing whether an environment is in fact hostile: the frequency and severity of the discriminatory conduct; whether the behavior is physically threatening or humiliating, or merely an offensive utterance; and whether the conduct unreasonably interferes with an employee's work performance.

Although employer liability in hostile environment claims is more difficult to establish than in quid pro quo harassment claims, it appears to be getting easier. In 1998, in *Burlington Industries v. Ellerth*[97] and *Faragher v. City of Boca Raton*[98] the Supreme Court proclaimed that an employer is subject to vicarious liability for the acts of its supervisors with immediate authority over an alleged victim. However, the employer may raise an affirmative defense to liability if the employee suffered no tangible employment loss. Such a defense requires that the employer exercise reasonable care to prevent or promptly correct harassing behavior *and* that the employee failed to take advantage of preventive and corrective opportunities provided by the employer. Accordingly, to guard against liability, school districts should prepare and disseminate sexual harassment policies; provide appropriate in-service training; establish appropriate grievance procedures, including at least two avenues for reporting in case one is blocked by the harasser;[99] take claims seriously and investigate promptly; take corrective action in a timely manner; and maintain thorough records of all claims and activities. Investigators should have no stake in the outcome of the proceedings, and both male and female investigators should be available. Also, resulting reports should be kept confidential.

Retirement Benefits

Although the longevity figures for men and women have narrowed over the last 20 years, it remains true that women, on average, live longer than men. Recognition of female longevity historically resulted in differential treatment of women with respect to retirement benefits since employers either required women to make a higher contribution or awarded them lower benefits upon retirement. In 1978, the Supreme Court rejected the use of gender-segregated actuarial tables in retirement benefits programs. The Court invalidated a retirement program requiring women to make a higher contribution to receive equal benefits on retirement, noting that gender was the only factor considered in predicting life expectancy.[100] Similarly, in 1983, the Court prohibited the state of Arizona from administering a deferred compensation program by contracting with insurance companies that used sex-segregated actuarial tables to determine

97. 524 U.S. 742 (1998).

98. 524 U.S. 775 (1998).

99. *See, e.g.,* Allen v. Dep't of Employment Training, 618 A.2d 1317 (Vt. 1992).

100. City of L.A. Dep't of Water & Power v. Manhart, 435 U.S. 702 (1978).

benefits.[101] In the latter case, female employees received lower monthly annuity payments than did males who contributed the same amount. The law is now clear that women and men must be treated the same when administering retirement benefits packages.

Sexual Preference Discrimination

When public employees are discriminated against due to sexual preference in hiring, promotion, termination, or any other term or condition of employment, they may file suit under the Fourteenth Amendment.[102] Private-sector employees must base related complaints on state statutes and local ordinances, where they exist.[103]

Access to Benefits

The amount of salary or level of benefits a school district provides its employees may not be determined, even in part, by an employee's sexual orientation. However, unless restricted by state law or local ordinance, school districts may limit the availability of family benefits to legal spouses and dependents. Because only heterosexual marriages are recognized across all states,[104] retirement, death, health care, eye care, and dental benefits are not generally available to same-sex partners or the children of same-sex partners, unless the employee has legally adopted the children.[105] This position was fortified by the passage of the Defense of Marriage Act in 1996.[106] That statute gives states the option of refusing to extend marriage benefits to same-sex partners who were legally married in another state, territory, or country. Nonetheless, some states and locales—through their constitutions, statutes, or ordinances—have elected to permit same-sex partners to receive marriage benefits; in other areas, courts have interpreted existing laws to require such access.[107]

---

101. Ariz. Governing Comm. for Tax Deferred Annuity & Deferred Comp. Plans v. Norris, 463 U.S. 1073 (1983).

102. Under the Fourteenth Amendment, rational-basis scrutiny is applied where facial discrimination is alleged, whereas discriminatory intent must be proven where the alleged discrimination is facially neutral.

103. *See, e.g.,* Evans v. Romer, 517 U.S. 620 (1996) (prohibiting the state from enforcing/maintaining voter-initiated constitutional amendment providing that homosexual, lesbian, or bisexual orientation, conduct, practices, or relationships could not provide the basis for protected class status).

104. *But see* Beahr v. Miike, Civil No. 91-1394 (Haw. Sup. Ct. Dec. 3, 1996) (holding that the state may not deny a marriage license to a same-sex couple).

105. *See, e.g.,* Rutgers Council of AAUP Chapters v. Rutgers, 689 A.2d 828 (N.J. Superior Ct., App. Div. 1997).

106. 28 U.S.C. § 1738C (2002).

107. *See, e.g.,* Tanner v. Or. Health Scis. Univ., 971 P.2d 435 (Or. Ct. App. 1998).

Harassment

The harassment of employees based on sexual preference also may violate state and local laws as well as the Fourteenth Amendment, assuming that the intent to discriminate can be supported. Proving intent may be difficult in situations where school district employees are not directly responsible for the harassment, however. In 2002, the Seventh Circuit was confronted with a case where a former teacher claimed that the school district failed to take reasonable measures to prevent students, parents, and colleagues from harassing him due to his sexual preference. The plaintiff demanded that the district engage in systemwide sensitivity training to condemn discrimination against homosexuals, given that a related memorandum and the disciplining of a few violating students had proved ineffectual. The principal suggested that the plaintiff try to ignore students' behavior, as getting them to stop would be difficult. The teacher sued under the Fourteenth Amendment, but was unable to prove either that the district demonstrated the intent to discriminate or was deliberately indifferent to his treatment.[108] District personnel were found to have made legitimate efforts to reduce or eliminate the harassment.

Adverse Employment Decisions

Terminating or nonrenewing a public employee solely due to sexual preference is unlikely to meet even rational basis scrutiny.[109] However, if a homosexual employee were engaged in a pedophile relationship, were sexually involved with students, or participated in public acts of indecency, appropriate adverse actions would be justified on grounds of immorality.[110] Of course, such reasons provide bases for terminating heterosexuals as well. In a related case, a first-year teacher was nonrenewed allegedly due to his inability to effectively manage student behavior and to deficiencies in his teaching skills. The court found these reasons to be pretextual, given that a fellow teacher with lower evaluations was retained; board members provided conflicting testimony on several matters; and the plaintiff's negative evaluations followed a classroom visit by his partner, which had resulted in rumors and false accusations of hand-holding. The court identified an equal protection violation and awarded compensatory damages as well as damages for emotional distress.[111]

---

108. Schroeder v. Hamilton Sch. Dist., 282 F.3d 946 (7th Cir. 2002). *But see* "California Lesbian Teacher Settles Harassment Lawsuit," *School Law News* (June 7, 2002), p. 5. A lesbian teacher received a $140,000 settlement. She had sued under the Fair Employment and Housing Act in response to alleged harassment and the failure to promote.

109. *But see* Rowland v. Mad River Local Sch. Dist., 730 F.2d 444 (6th Cir. 1984); Gaylord v. Tacoma Sch. Dist. No. 10, 559 P.2d 1340 (Wash. 1977), text accompanying note 216, Chapter 9.

110. *See* text accompanying notes 122–124, Chapter 11.

111. Glover v. Williamsburg Local Sch. Dist., 20 F. Supp. 2d 1160 (S.D. Ohio 1998).

As noted, a private-sector plaintiff must seek protection from either state law or local ordinance and must show that sexual orientation was in fact the basis of the adverse action.[112] Such state and local provisions may not violate federal constitutional rights in their application, however. In *Boy Scouts of America v. Dale,* the Supreme Court in 2000 found that the New Jersey public accommodation law, previously interpreted to require the Boy Scouts to admit a homosexual assistant scoutmaster to its ranks, violated the private nonprofit organization's expressive association rights.[113] The Court observed that the plaintiff's openness about his own sexual preference and advocacy of related rights operated against those expressed by the Scouts and that to require the Scouts to retain the plaintiff would significantly burden the organization in its effort to oppose homosexual conduct.[114]

Religious Discrimination

The United States is now more culturally and religiously diverse than at any time in its history, with most of the world's religions present somewhere within its boundaries. When discrimination occurs, or an employer fails to provide reasonable accommodations, First and Fourteenth Amendment[115] claims have been filed as well as suits under Title VII.

Hiring and Promotion Practices

Private religious organizations are exempt from First and Fourteenth Amendment claims and in large part from the religious restrictions imposed by Title VII.[116] As a result, they are not generally prohibited from establishing religion as a bona fide occupational qualification (BFOQ) (e.g., when a Methodist theological seminary requires

112. Das v. Ohio State Univ., 115 F. Supp. 2d 885 (S.D. Ohio 2000) (finding that under the Columbus city code, the fact that the plaintiff was the only lesbian in her department and that a colleague noticed the rainbow flag in her office was insufficient to establish a case of sexual orientation discrimination).

113. 530 U.S. 640 (2000).

114. *See also* Hall v. Baptist Mem. Health Care Corp., 215 F.3d 618 (6th Cir. 2000) (finding no Title VII religion violation when a lesbian student services specialist was terminated based on her expressed views and sexual preference; the court reasoned that although the entity was religious, that fact did not transform plaintiff's dismissal into one based on religion).

115. If an employee claims an Equal Protection Clause violation due to religion-based facial discrimination by government, either strict scrutiny or rational-basis scrutiny could apply, depending on the form of the discrimination. When the government infringes on the employee's First Amendment right to exercise religious beliefs (a fundamental right), strict scrutiny is applied. On the other hand, if the employee is a victim of discrimination based on religion, but the opportunity to freely practice religion is not affected, rational-basis scrutiny is applied. Intent must be proven in cases involving facially neutral discrimination. *See* Chapter 2 for a discussion of the First Amendment religion clauses as applied to schools.

116. 42 U.S.C. § 2000e-1(a) (2002).

that its instructors be Methodists). In contrast, religion will never qualify as a BFOQ in public education,[117] and public employers may not inquire as to an applicant's religious beliefs, use the interview process as an opportunity to indoctrinate, or require prospective employees to profess a belief in a particular faith or in God.[118]

A person's religious affiliation or practice, if any, should not be a consideration in making an employment decision. Proof of discriminatory motive may be difficult to acquire, however, as violating parties seldom create a paper trail corroborating the discriminatory act or inform others as to their real motives or prejudices. Instead, the applicant or employee is simply notified that he or she was not selected or that a "better qualified" candidate was chosen, often due to subjective criteria such as the interview process. Without direct evidence of discriminatory intent to support this type of disparate treatment case, it is unlikely that the plaintiff will be able to produce more than a prima facie case.[119]

Accommodation

Recommended forms of religious accommodation include activities such as accepting voluntary substitutions and assignment exchanges, using a flexible schedule, and modifying job assignments. Tests, interviews, and other selection procedures should not be scheduled at times when an applicant cannot attend for religious reasons. However, if requested accommodations would compromise the constitutional, statutory, or contractual rights of others (e.g., interfere with a bona fide seniority system) or result in undue hardship, Title VII does not require compliance. Undue hardship results when extensive changes are required in business practices or when the costs of religious accommodations are more than minimal. Some of the more often litigated controversies regarding religious accommodation in public education involve dress codes, personal leave, and job assignments.

Attire Restrictions. As a general rule, public school district restrictions on the wearing of religious apparel, even if also purportedly cultural, will be upheld where young and impressionable students would perceive the garment as religious. In an illustrative case, the Third Circuit held that a district's refusal to accommodate a Muslim substitute teacher who sought to wear religious attire in the public school classroom did not violate Title VII.[120] The district's action was pursuant to a state statute that regarded

---

117. *See, e.g.,* Beauregard v. City of St. Albans, 450 A.2d 1148 (Vt. 1982) (holding that membership on the school board could not be conditioned on religious preference).

118. *See, e.g.,* Torcaso v. Watkins, 367 U.S. 488 (1961) (holding that to require an appointee to the office of notary public to declare a belief in God before he received his commission violated the First Amendment).

119. *See, e.g.,* Mounla-Sakkal v. Youngstown Hosp. Ass'n, 25 Fed. Appx. 414 (6th Cir. 2002) (affirming summary judgment in religion discrimination claim as plaintiff failed to establish that she had been inappropriately dismissed as a hospital resident).

120. United States v. Bd. of Educ., 911 F.2d 882 (3d Cir. 1990).

the wearing of religious clothing as a significant threat to the maintenance of a religiously neutral public school system. Similar decisions have been reached by a federal court in Mississippi when it upheld the termination of a teacher aide who refused to comply with the school's dress code proscribing religious attire,[121] and by the Oregon Supreme Court when it upheld a statutory prohibition on religious attire in public schools as applied to a female Sikh who dressed in white clothes and turban.[122]

Personal Leave.   Although most public school calendars allow time off for Christmas and Easter to coincide with semester and spring breaks, it also is true that the holy days of religions other than Christianity are not so routinely accommodated. But, when a school district serves a significant number of students or employs a large number of teachers or staff of another religion (e.g., where the majority of students and staff are Jewish), it is not uncommon for schools to be closed on several of the more significant days of worship for that religion as well. The "secular purpose" of such an act is the need to operate the school efficiently. If schools were to remain open when large numbers of persons are not in attendance, they would have to hire numerous substitutes, prepare a burdensome level of make-up work, and accommodate a large number of students who are now behind in their work. For those systems that elect to remain open notwithstanding the absence of a majority of students or teachers, substitute teachers often are instructed not to present new material during the period in order to reduce the need to provide repetitive lessons.

Although the aforementioned approach may provide satisfactory results when attempting to accommodate one or two faiths, it is unrealistic to assume that public schools will be closed for the holy days of every religion. Alternatively, school districts often provide a variety of accommodations to avoid unduly burdening the religious beliefs of their employees (e.g., use of personal leave days, flexible schedules), depending on the nature of their employment.

Modest requests for religious absences are typically met, but others may result in undue hardship both for the district as well as for students. School officials often have had difficulty in determining appropriate limits and procedures. Some guidance is found in a significant 1977 case, *Trans World Airlines v. Hardison,* where a member of the Worldwide Church of God challenged his dismissal for refusing to work on Saturdays in contravention of his religious beliefs.[123] The employer asserted that the plaintiff could not be accommodated because shift assignments were based on seniority in conformance with the collective bargaining agreement. Evidence also showed that supervisors had taken appropriate steps in meeting with the plaintiff and in attempting to find other employees to exchange shifts. The Supreme Court found no Title VII violation and reasoned that an employer was not required to bear more than minimal costs in making religious accommodations or to disregard a bona fide seniority system in the absence of proof of intentional discrimination.

121. McGlothin v. Jackson Mun. Separate Sch. Dist., 829 F. Supp. 853 (S.D. Miss. 1992).

122. Cooper v. Eugene Sch. Dist. No. 4J, 723 P.2d 298 (Or. 1986).

123. 432 U.S. 63 (1977).

Similarly, in 2002, the Tenth Circuit found no Title VII violation where a member of the Worldwide Church of God was denied employment when he indicated that he would be unable to work between sundown Friday and sundown Saturday, as was required for the job.[124] In ruling for the employer, the court noted that undue hardship would result if the employer were required to make such a dramatic change in its work schedule or to permit the applicant to transfer to another job, in violation of the collective bargaining agreement and its mandatory use of seniority.

Where leave has been provided, some employees have been satisfied when allowed to have the day off without adverse impact; others have requested that leave be accompanied with full or partial pay. In *Ansonia Board of Education v. Philbrook,* a teacher asserted that the negotiated agreement violated Title VII by permitting employees to use only three days of paid leave for religious purposes, whereas three additional days of paid personal business leave could be used for specified secular activities. The plaintiff proposed either permitting the use of the paid personal business leave days for religious observances or allowing employees to receive full pay and cover the costs of substitute teachers for each additional day missed for religious reasons. The Supreme Court, in upholding the agreement, held that the employer was not required to show that each of the plaintiff's proposed alternatives would result in undue hardship, and noted that the employer could satisfy Title VII by offering a reasonable accommodation, which may or may not be the one the employee preferred.[125]

It is important to note that religious leave need not be paid, unless compensation is provided for all purposes except religious ones.[126] In a Tenth Circuit case, the court rejected a teacher's claim that the school district's leave policy violated Title VII and burdened his free exercise of religion because he occasionally had to take unpaid leave to observe Jewish holidays.[127] The policy allowed teachers two days of paid leave that could be used for religious observances and other purposes. The court concluded that the availability of unpaid leave for additional religious observances constituted a reasonable accommodation under Title VII and did not place a substantial burden on free exercise rights.

Job Assignments and Responsibilities. If an employee is hired to perform a certain job, he or she must be willing and able to perform all the essential functions of the job. In a somewhat unique case, an interpreter for the hearing impaired refused to translate or sign any cursing or bad language and used her religious beliefs as a basis for the

---

124. Graff v. Henderson, 30 Fed. Appx. 809 (10th Cir. 2002). *See also* Beadle v. Hillsborough County Sheriff's Dep't, 29 F.3d 589 (11th Cir. 1994) (finding no Title VII violation when a Seventh Day Adventist was discharged for refusing to work from sundown Friday to sundown Saturday). *But see* Abramson v. William Paterson Coll., 260 F.3d 265 (3d Cir. 2001) (reversing lower court summary judgment order for the College where an Orthodox Jew professor claimed religion discrimination and retaliation when she refused to work on holidays and the Sabbath).

125. 757 F.2d 476 (2d Cir. 1985), *aff'd,* 479 U.S. 60 (1986).

126. *See, e.g.,* Ansonia Bd. of Educ. v. Philbrook, 479 U.S. 60, 71 (1986).

127. Pinsker v. Joint Dist. No. 28J, 735 F.2d 388 (10th Cir. 1984).

refusal.[128] Given her willing violation of district policy and administrative directives, her contract was terminated. The Missouri appeals court upheld her termination under state law and concluded that the teacher could not have been accommodated without compromising the educational entitlements of her students and that requiring a literal translation of classroom dialogue was not unreasonable.

Likewise, in 2000, the Third Circuit found that a university hospital had reasonably accommodated a nurse who had refused to participate in abortions, given her Pentecostal religious beliefs. She had been permitted to trade assignments with other nurses, unless an emergency existed. When she failed to treat pregnant patients when they were experiencing life-threatening situations, the hospital gave her the option of transferring to a comparable job where her beliefs would not conflict with essential job requirements, but the nurse refused. The court upheld her subsequent termination and indicated that the public trust requires public health-care practitioners to provide treatment in the time of emergency.[129]

Adverse Employment Decisions

Employees at times have claimed religious discrimination when they have been transferred, demoted, nonrenewed, terminated, or denied tenure.[130] As with other claims of employment discrimination, the burden is on the plaintiff to prove that the adverse action was motivated by an impermissible reason—in this situation, the employee's religious beliefs, practices, or affiliation. Plaintiffs experience difficulty in winning such cases, as employers typically can identify one or more legitimate bases for the adverse action (e.g., lack of commitment,[131] excessive absenteeism[132]).

Age Discrimination

Unlike other characteristics that generate charges of discrimination, age is unique in that everyone is subject to the aging process and eventually will fall within the age-protected category. The mean age of the U.S. population has climbed steadily in recent years, and this phenomenon has been accompanied by an increase in judicial

128. Sedalia # 200 Sch. Dist. v. Mo. Comm'n on Human Rights, 843 S.W.2d 928 (Mo. Ct. App. 1992).

129. Shelton v. Univ. of Med. & Dentistry, 223 F.3d 220 (3d Cir. 2000).

130. *See, e.g.,* Habib v. NationsBank, 279 F.3d 563 (8th Cir. 2001) (upholding termination of an employee for insubordination when she refused to bring a doctor's statement supporting her need to leave work; she had claimed that the real reason for her firing was her need to pray five times per day, lasting 5 to 15 minutes each); Babbar v. Ebadi, 36 F. Supp. 2d 1269 (D. Kan. 1998) (finding that the university presented neutral reasons for denying the plaintiff tenure—e.g., deficient research, lack of collegiality).

131. *See, e.g.,* Lee v. Wise County Sch. Bd., No. 97-1471, 1998 U.S. App. LEXIS 367 (4th Cir. Jan. 12, 1998) (concluding that the plaintiff's outside interests and lack of commitment justified his replacement as a basketball coach; being Methodist was not proven to be a factor).

132. *See, e.g.,* Rosenbaum v. Bd. of Trs., No. 98-1773, 1999 U.S. App. LEXIS 4744 (4th Cir. March 19, 1999) (finding no proof that the college failed to accommodate the plaintiff's religious holidays).

activity pertaining to age discrimination in employment. Such individuals are afforded protection under the Equal Protection Clause,[133] the Age Discrimination in Employment Act (ADEA) of 1967,[134] and additional federal and state statutes. The Equal Employment Opportunity Commission is responsible for the enforcement of the ADEA.

The intent of the ADEA is to promote the employment of older persons based on their ability rather than their age, to prohibit arbitrary age discrimination in employment, and to find ways of meeting problems arising from the impact of age on employment. The ADEA specifically stipulates that "it shall be unlawful for an employer... to fail or refuse to hire or to discharge any individual or otherwise discriminate... with respect to his compensation, terms, conditions, or privileges of employment, because of such individual's age."[135]

Because the ADEA and Title VII are substantially similar in wording, judicial criteria (e.g., disparate treatment and disparate impact) applied in Title VII cases often are used to evaluate charges under the ADEA. However, the Supreme Court has evaluated only cases addressing disparate treatment and has emphasized that if the employment decision is based on any factor other than age (e.g., merit, seniority, vesting in a retirement plan), there is no violation of the ADEA. For a violation to be substantiated, age must play a role in the decision-making process *and* have a determinative influence on the outcome.[136]

The ADEA applies to most employers that have 20 or more employees for 20 or more weeks in the current or preceding calendar year. Where violations of the ADEA are found, courts may provide for injunctive relief; compel employment, reinstatement, or promotion; and provide back pay (including interest), liquidated damages, and attorneys' fees. Punitive damages, however, are not available.[137] Moreover, future application of the ADEA in public school cases may be limited, depending on whether state laws regard school districts as "subdivisions of the state" or "arms of the state." The Supreme Court in *Kimel v. Florida Board of Regents* held that Eleventh Amendment immunity may be claimed as a defense where money damages to be paid out of the state treasury are sought in federal court.[138] This ruling will limit public school ADEA suits only in exceptional circumstances where the district is viewed as an arm of the state; even then, however, expect plaintiffs simply to sue under comparable state statutes to vindicate their rights.[139]

133. Facially discriminatory procedures and practices that classify individuals on the basis of age can satisfy the Equal Protection Clause if they are rationally related to a legitimate governmental objective, whereas facially neutral criteria may be successfully challenged only with proof of discriminatory intent. *See, e.g.,* Gregory v. Ashcroft, 501 U.S. 452 (1991).

134. 29 U.S.C. § 621 *et seq.* (2002).

135. 29 U.S.C. § 623(a)(1) (2002).

136. *See, e.g.,* Hazen Paper Co. v. Biggins, 507 U.S. 604, 617 (1993).

137. 29 U.S.C. § 626(b) (2002). *See, e.g.,* Espinueva v. Garrett, 895 F.2d 1164, 1165 (7th Cir. 1990).

138. 528 U.S. 62 (2000).

139. *See* text accompanying note 214, Chapter 11.

Hiring and Promotion Practices

Under the ADEA, except in those circumstances where age qualifies as a bona fide occupational qualification, selection among applicants for hiring or promotion may be based on any factor other than age. Although a BFOQ defense in an educational setting is unlikely in cases involving staff, teachers, or administrators, claims could conceivably be made for school bus drivers and pilots.[140] Where a BFOQ is proposed, the employer carries the burden of persuasion to demonstrate that there is reasonable cause to believe that all, or substantially all, applicants beyond a certain age would be unable to perform a job safely and efficiently.

As with Title VII cases, most courts permit the plaintiff in an ADEA case to provide direct evidence of discrimination (e.g., written policies that facially discriminate) or meet *McDonnell Douglas* criteria.[141] In a Sixth Circuit case, a part-time substitute teacher was denied several full-time positions.[142] At trial, the plaintiff met the requirements for a prima facie case, while the board proffered the archetypical response (i.e., that better qualified candidates were hired). There were over 2,000 applicants, and 41 percent of those hired were over age 40. It then became the plaintiff's responsibility to show that the board's purported reasons were unworthy of credence and a pretext to age discrimination. Because the plaintiff was unable to fulfill this burden, the board's motion for summary judgment was granted.

In the effort to show pretext, a plaintiff need not discredit each and every proffered reason for the rejection, but must cast substantial doubt on many, if not most, of the purported bases so that a fact-finder then could rationally disbelieve the remaining reasons given the employer's loss of credibility.[143] In an illustrative 2001 Second Circuit case, a less experienced, unqualified, younger teacher was selected over the plaintiff. The district purported that the selected applicant performed better during the interview and was chosen largely on that basis. In ruling that pretext had been shown, the court noted that the successful candidate did not possess the specified degree and had submitted an incomplete file; that the employer had made misleading statements and destroyed relevant evidence; and that the plaintiff possessed superior credentials, except perhaps as to the interview. The fact that the previously selected applicant also was over the age of 40 was irrelevant; what mattered was that she was substantially younger (age 42) than the plaintiff (age 64).[144]

Compensation and Benefits

Few public school employees have alleged age-based salary discrimination. In large part, this is because teachers and staff primarily are paid on salary schedules based on

---

140. *See, e.g.,* Childers v. Morgan County Bd. of Educ., 817 F.2d 1556 (11th Cir. 1987) (bus driver); Iervolino v. Delta Air Lines, 796 F.2d 1408 (11th Cir. 1986) (pilot).

141. *See infra* text accompanying note 16.

142. Wooden v. Bd. of Educ., 931 F.2d 376 (6th Cir. 1991).

143. *See, e.g.,* Narin v. Lower Merion Sch. Dist., 206 F.3d 323 (3d Cir. 2000).

144. Byrnie v. Town of Cromwell, Bd. of Educ., 243 F.3d 93 (2d Cir. 2001).

seniority and/or degree level. As most school personnel become older, they concomitantly gain seniority and receive a higher scheduled salary. Consequently, claims of age-based salary discrimination are less likely to occur within public schools. Where age discrimination is alleged, the burden of proof remains with the employee to prove that age—rather than performance, longevity, or other factors—was used to determine the level of compensation.

Under the ADEA, a school district may not spend less on the benefits package of older workers than for younger employees. The cost of the benefits package must be the same, although the benefits derived from an equal expenditure may represent a lower level of benefits for an older worker (e.g., health and life insurance benefits for older workers at times are less, unless a higher premium is paid).[145]

Adverse Employment Actions

Courts often are asked to determine whether an employee's age was used as a basis to terminate, nonrenew, downsize, fail to rehire following a layoff, demote, or transfer an employee.[146] Courts generally support the employers' proffered reasons for their adverse decisions, although there are occasions when the purported reasons for making adverse decisions have been found pretextual.[147] For a plaintiff to prevail, the reason submitted by the employer must be refuted and age must be shown to have been the basis for the adverse action. To establish a prima facie case under the ADEA, the plaintiff must show that he or she was over age 40; applied for and was qualified for the position; subjected to adverse action; and replaced by a substantially younger person.[148]

Termination, Nonrenewal, Reduction-in-Force, and Constructive Discharge. The removal of an employee from the workforce is comparatively simple for at-will employees[149] (e.g., hourly workers) but requires the following specific procedures for some licensed employees (e.g., a nontenured teacher facing contract nonrenewal; teachers whose positions are eliminated). For those employees who are tenured or working within a long-term contract, a "for cause" hearing will be required to permit

---

145. 29 C.F.R. § 1625.10(a)(1) (2002).

146. *See, e.g.,* Oubre v. Entergy Operations, 522 U.S. 422 (1998) (concluding that a severance agreement failed to comply with the ADEA).

147. *See, e.g.,* Ware v. Howard Univ., 816 F. Supp. 737 (D.D.C. 1993). *But see* Rowe v. Marley Co., 233 F.3d 825 (4th Cir. 2000) (noting that the plaintiff failed to show that the former employer's reasons for downsizing were pretextual).

148. *See, e.g.,* Brennan v. Metro. Opera Ass'n, 192 F.3d 310 (2d Cir. 1999) (noting that the fact that the replacement is substantially younger than the plaintiff is a more valuable indicator of age discrimination than whether the replacement was over age 40); O'Connor v. Consol. Coin Caterers Corp., 517 U.S. 308 (1996) (concluding that it is more important to consider that one employee was replaced by another who was substantially younger than to consider whether the replacement was outside the protected class—i.e., over age 40).

149. At-will employees have no contract or job expectation and may leave or be terminated at any time.

the district to show why the removal of the employee is necessary. Although many factors may be considered in making such decisions (e.g., morality, efficiency), the employee's age may in no way be a consideration, unless age qualifies as a BFOQ. In a 2000 Supreme Court case, *Reeves v. Sanderson Plumbing Products,* a 57-year-old former employee was terminated and replaced with persons in their 30s.[150] In remanding and ruling that the company was not entitled to judgment as a matter of law, the Court noted that the plaintiff was able to establish a prima facie case, create a jury issue concerning the falsity of the employer's basis for the action, and introduce additional evidence showing that the director was motivated by age-related animus.

At times, employees allege that they were "constructively" discharged. This could occur when an individual resigns due to being harassed on the job or when the job is altered arbitrarily to ensure poor performance or nonperformance by the plaintiff.[151] To succeed, the employee must show that the conditions created by the employer were such that a reasonable person similarly situated would find the work intolerable and that the employer acted with the intent of forcing the employee to quit. In 1992, the Eighth Circuit held that a teacher had been constructively discharged (in this case, forced to retire and then refused reemployment) and was entitled to liquidated damages.[152] The school district was shown to have made the teacher's working conditions so intolerable that a reasonable person in his position would have resigned (i.e., he had been exposed to an intense and excessive pattern of classroom observation, criticism, and evaluation over a period of eight months).

Transfer.   When an employee is subjected to an involuntary transfer, he or she will be required to show that such transfer was based on age and that the new assignment was materially less prestigious, less suited to current skills and expertise, or less conducive to career advancement. The fact that the employee preferred one position over another does not establish an ADEA violation. Most courts have ruled for school districts when transfers have been challenged, as they seldom view a change of school or a change of grade level to represent a materially significant disadvantage or to be tantamount to a demotion.[153]

Retaliation.   Additionally, as with cases filed under Title VII, employers under the ADEA may not retaliate against employees when they file complaints or suits.[154] A plaintiff need not establish the validity of the original complaint in order to succeed in a case claiming retaliation, but it would be helpful to show that the person responsible

---

150. 530 U.S. 133 (2000).

151. *See, e.g.,* Schwarz v. Northwest Iowa Cmty. Coll., 881 F. Supp. 1323 (N.D. Iowa 1995).

152. Lee v. Rapid City Area Sch. Dist. No. 51-4, 981 F.2d 316 (8th Cir. 1992).

153. *See, e.g.,* Galabya v. New York City Bd. of Educ., 202 F.3d 636 (2d Cir. 2000).

154. *See, e.g.,* Passer v. Am. Chem. Soc'y, 935 F.2d 322 (D.C. Cir. 1991).

for the adverse decision at least knew of the prior charges of discrimination.[155] Furthermore, the plaintiff shoulders the burden to show that the adverse action was an act of retaliation, and not otherwise justified due to incompetence, insubordination, immorality, or the like.[156]

Retirement

Given that the mandatory retirement of school employees has been eliminated, districts have attempted to entice older employees to retire through attractive retirement benefits packages. Under the ADEA, employers can follow the terms of a bona fide retirement plan as long as the plan is not a subterfuge to evade the purposes of the act.[157] Also, employers may not reduce annual benefits or cease the accrual of benefits after employees attain a certain age as an inducement for them to retire.[158] In a 1999 Seventh Circuit case, a school district had offered early retirement to teachers aged 58 to 61. The longer one waited to retire after his or her 58th birthday, the less received in total dollars as a retirement incentive. The court found the practice to facially discriminate based on age in violation of the ADEA.[159]

There also can be legal problems when an employee is terminated prior to becoming eligible for full retirement benefits (i.e., prior to becoming vested). In a 1993 Supreme Court decision, *Hazen Paper Co. v. Biggins,* the plaintiff was fired at age 62, only a few weeks before completing 10 years of service and being vested in his pension plan.[160] Two issues before the Supreme Court were whether the employer's interference with the vesting of pension benefits violated the ADEA *and* whether the standard for liquidated damages[161] applied to informal age-based decisions by employers in addition to those that were based on formal, facially discriminatory policies.

In a unanimous opinion, the Court vacated and remanded the lower court decision for a determination of whether the jury had sufficient evidence to find an ADEA violation. The Court made it clear, however, that disparate treatment is not supported when the factor motivating the employer is something other than the employee's age, even if it is correlated with age (e.g., vesting or pension status).[162] Because age and

---

155. *See, e.g.,* Moore v. Reese, 817 F. Supp. 1290 (D. Md. 1993).

156. *See, e.g.,* Horwitz v. Bd. of Educ., 260 F.3d 602 (7th Cir. 2001) (noting that the former teacher was unable to show that the 31 reasons given for her termination were false and qualified as pretext).

157. *See, e.g.,* United Air Lines v. McMann, 434 U.S. 192 (1977).

158. 29 U.S.C. § 623(i)(1) (2002). *See, e.g.,* Karlen v. City Colls. of Chi., 837 F.2d 314 (7th Cir. 1988).

159. Solon v. Gary Cmty. Sch. Corp., 180 F.3d 844 (7th Cir. 1999).

160. 507 U.S. 604 (1993).

161. For a discussion of liquidated damages, *see* Trans World Airlines v. Thurston, 469 U.S. 111, 126 (1985).

162. In dicta, the Court observed that an employer could be in violation of § 510 of the Employee Retirement Income Security Act, 29 U.S.C. §§ 1001 to 1461 (2002), if the employer were to fire employees in order to prevent them from vesting in the retirement program.

years of service are distinctly different factors, an employer may take one into account, yet ignore the other. Moreover, reiterating that an act is willful if the employer knew or showed reckless disregard for whether its conduct would violate the ADEA, the Supreme Court was critical of lower courts for developing alternative standards for liquidated damages (i.e., that the conduct of the employer must be outrageous, that the evidence be direct rather than circumstantial, and that age be the predominant factor rather than simply a determinative one).[163]

Disability Discrimination

Federal discrimination law has focused primarily on race, national origin, gender, religion, age, and disability. Among these classifications, disability discrimination in employment was the last to be accorded full statutory protection beyond that provided by the Equal Protection Clause.[164] Although Section 504 of the Rehabilitation Act of 1973[165] was signed into law during the general period when other civil rights statutes were being passed, it applied then and now only to recipients of federal financial assistance. In 1990, however, Congress passed the Americans with Disabilities Act (ADA),[166] protecting persons with disabilities from discrimination.

The Rehabilitation Act of 1973 was the first federal civil rights law protecting the rights of the disabled. Section 504 of the act provides in pertinent part that no "otherwise qualified individual with a disability . . . shall . . . be excluded from participation in, be denied the benefits of, or be subjected to discrimination under any program or activity receiving [f]ederal financial assistance."[167] Section 504 applies to an entire school district, even if federal aid is received by only one of its programs. In regard to employment, a recipient of federal financial assistance may not discriminate concerning any term, condition, or privilege of employment. When education employers are involved, disability-related complaints are submitted to the Office for Civil Rights within the Department of Education.

In the past, when disability discrimination cases were filed in state court, it generally was due to state law providing enhanced rights, including forms and amounts of relief. With the heightened damages awards now available under the ADA, however, federal courts are reviewing a greater number of cases. The ADA definitions (e.g., individual with a disability, reasonable accommodation, undue hardship) are substantially the same as those provided under the Rehabilitation Act. The statute provides great specificity regarding preemployment activities (e.g., the limited use of medical examinations, testing, preemployment interviewing) as well as terms and

---

163. *Hazen Paper Co.,* 507 U.S. at 615.

164. The Fourteenth Amendment requires the application of rational basis scrutiny in cases where disability discrimination is facial and proof of intent where the alleged discrimination is facially neutral.

165. 29 U.S.C. § 794 (2002).

166. 42 U.S.C. § 12101 *et seq.* (2002).

167. 29 U.S.C. § 794(a) (2002).

conditions of employment, and it applies to employers with
The Equal Employment Opportunity Commission, the Dep
vate litigants have enforcement rights under the act. Howe
have limited application to public schools, given the state
ment immunity.

The issue of whether Eleventh Amendment immunity may ᵇᵉ ᵉ⁻⁻
cally in Title I, ADA suits was addressed by the Supreme Court in 2001 in *Board of
Trustees of the University of Alabama v. Garrett.*[169] In that case, two state employees
with disabilities sued the state for monetary damages when their respective employers
allegedly discriminated against them. After undergoing a lumpectomy, radiation treatment, and chemotherapy, a nurse employee returned to work, but was forced to resign
from her director position; she then applied for and received a lower-paying position
as a manager. In contrast, a guard employee claimed that he had been denied necessary
work accommodations (i.e., transfer to a daytime shift and reduced exposure to carbon
monoxide and cigarette smoke), given his chronic asthma and sleep apnea.

The primary issue on appeal to the Supreme Court was whether under Title I a
federal court could award monetary damages to be paid by a state employer or, in the
alternative, whether the Eleventh Amendment prohibited such relief. The Court
found that the award violated the Constitution and that there was no proven history or
pattern of employment discrimination by the state against the disabled. Whether this
decision will restrict Title I suits against school districts will depend on whether their
funds are considered state funds and whether courts view districts as subdivisions of
the state, for which immunity is not available, or as state agencies or arms of the state,
for which immunity is available. Although it is likely that most school districts will
be considered subdivisions,[170] it may be several years before the impact of this case is
known.

Notwithstanding the fact that the Eleventh Amendment may prohibit the awarding of monetary damages within some jurisdictions, do not assume that persons who
have been subjected to disability discrimination in employment are powerless to vindicate their rights. Title I still prescribes standards that are applicable to state employers. These standards could be enforced by the United States in federal judicial actions
for monetary damages and by employees in actions seeking injunctive relief. Furthermore, many state disability laws provide identical or at least similar coverage to that
mandated by the ADA and permit monetary damages under certain circumstances.
Moreover, because all (or nearly all) public schools are recipients of federal financial
assistance, they must meet substantially similar obligations under the Rehabilitation
Act—a law that at times permits the awarding of money damages. When cases are

168. Owens v. S. Devel. Council, 59 F. Supp. 2d 1210 (M.D. Ala. 1999).

169. 531 U.S. 356 (2001).

170. *See, e.g.,* Mt. Healthy City Sch. Dist. v. Doyle, 429 U.S. 274 (1977) (concluding that the school district was not entitled to assert Eleventh Amendment immunity since under state law the board was
more like a county or a city, rather than an arm of the state).

urts often are asked to resolve questions regarding whether the plaintiff is in
sabled and, if so, what type of accommodation is required.

Qualifying as Disabled

A person qualifies as disabled under Section 504 and the ADA if he or she (1) has a
physical or mental impairment that substantially limits one or more major life activities; (2) has a record of impairment (e.g., having been hospitalized due to tuberculosis,
alcoholism, or drug addiction); (3) is regarded as having an impairment (e.g., when
the person is discriminatorily treated for being HIV positive,[171] but does not have
AIDS or any type of current physical impairment limiting a major life activity; or (4)
is discriminatorily treated because of extensive scars from burns that do not limit
major life activities). However, more is required than simple knowledge of an impairment to establish a "regarded as having an impairment" claim.[172] Furthermore, suggesting that an employee see a psychologist before returning to work does not
establish that the employer regarded the employee as a person with a disability.[173]

Although federal regulations define physical or mental impairment broadly,[174]
persons who currently are involved in the use of illegal drugs,[175] are unable to perform
the duties of the job due to alcohol, have a contagious disease, or otherwise represent
a direct threat to the safety[176] or health of others do not qualify as disabled. Likewise,
persons claiming discrimination due to transvestism, transsexualism, pedophilia,
exhibitionism, voyeurism, gender identity disorders not resulting from physical
impairments, other sexual behavior disorders, compulsive gambling, kleptomania,
pyromania, and psychoactive substance use disorders resulting from current illegal
drug use are not protected by either the ADA or Section 504.

---

171. *Compare* Merillat v. Mich. State Univ., 523 N.W.2d 802 (Mich. Ct. App. 1994) (determining that a
     university dispatcher qualified as disabled when she was treated as though she had a mental and emo-
     tional impairment) *with* Amadio v. Ford Motor Co., 238 F.3d 919 (7th Cir. 2001) (noting that it is not
     enough for a plaintiff to show that the employer knew of his or her impairment; the plaintiff also must
     show that the employer believed that the impairment substantially limited a major life activity).

172. *See, e.g.,* Kellogg v. Union Pac. R.R. Co., 233 F.3d 1083 (8th Cir. 2000).

173. *See, e.g.,* Sullivan v. River Valley Sch. Dist., 197 F.3d 804 (6th Cir. 1999).

174. 34 C.F.R. § 104.3(j)(2)(i) (2002).

175. *See, e.g.,* Shafer v. Preston Mem. Hosp. Corp., 107 F.3d 274 (4th Cir. 1997) (upholding summary
     judgment for the employer where a nurse had been terminated for stealing drugs; she was a "current"
     user, notwithstanding the fact that she was not caught taking drugs the day of her termination).

176. *See, e.g.,* Reed v. LePage Bakeries, 244 F.3d 254 (1st Cir. 2001) (finding that a mentally ill bakery
     worker was fired for insubordination and threatening behavior rather than disability); Palesch v. Mo.
     Comm'n on Human Rights, 233 F.3d 560 (8th Cir. 2000) (dismissing ADA and other claims filed by
     a discharged female worker who had threatened to shoot a coworker); Palmer v. Circuit Court of
     Cook County, Soc. Servs. Dep't, 905 F. Supp. 499 (N.D. Ill. 1995) (concluding that an employee who
     displayed abusive and threatening conduct toward coworkers failed to be otherwise qualified for the
     position).

Qualifying as "disabled" requires a two-step process: identifying a physical or mental impairment and determining whether the impairment *substantially limits* a major life activity (e.g., working).[177] Moreover, in assessing whether an applicant or employee is disabled, the Supreme Court in 1999 required that mitigating and corrective measures (both positive and negative[178]) be considered.[179] Not all impairments limit major life activity (e.g., an employee who is hearing impaired may have average or near-average hearing due to the use of a hearing aid). Performance is substantially limited when an employee is unable to perform, or is significantly restricted in performing, a major life activity that can be accomplished by the average person in the general population. The nature, severity, duration, and long-term impact of the impairment are considered when determining whether a limitation is substantially limiting.[180] Also, an impairment that is substantially limiting for one person may not be for another.[181] Furthermore, those that do limit some activity are not necessarily substantially limiting, since they often restrict the ability to perform only one job rather than a broad range of jobs.[182] In such cases, courts will consider the geographic area to which the plaintiff has reasonable access and the nature of the job from which the individual was disqualified as well as other jobs that require similar training, knowledge, ability, or skill.[183]

In 2002, the Supreme Court reviewed a claim by an assembly line worker in *Toyota Motor Manufacturing v. Williams* that her employer failed to accommodate her bilateral carpal tunnel syndrome that seemed to be exacerbated by the use of pneumatic tools, repetitive motion, and lifting any significant weight.[184] The Court rea-

---

177. *See, e.g.,* Kelly v. Drexel Univ., 94 F.3d 102 (3d Cir. 1996) (holding that an employee who had suffered a hip injury was not substantially limited in the major life activity of walking so as to qualify as disabled under the ADA).

178. For example, corrected vision through use of contact lenses is a positive mitigating measure; side effects of medication represents a negative one. *See, e.g.,* Ozlowski v. Henderson, 237 F.3d 837 (7th Cir. 2001) (observing that the plaintiff's medication at times caused him to fall asleep while at work).

179. Sutton v. United Airlines, 527 U.S. 471 (1999); Murphy v. United Parcel Serv., 527 U.S. 516 (1999).

180. 29 C.F.R. § 1630.2(j)(1), (2) (2002).

181. *Compare* Williams v. Toyota Motor Mfg., 224 F.3d 840 (6th Cir. 2000) (denying summary judgment, for a reasonable jury might determine that the plaintiff's tendonitis substantially limited the major life activity of working) *with* Chanda v. Engelhard/ICC, 234 F.3d 1219 (11th Cir. 2000) (finding that the plaintiff's tendonitis was not substantially limiting).

182. *See, e.g.,* LeBron-Torres v. Whitehall Laboratories, 251 F.3d 236 (1st Cir. 2001) (holding that the plaintiff failed to show that she was substantially limited not only for a broad range of jobs but for the two jobs she had recently performed—i.e., manufacturing operator and hair stylist); Russell v. Clark County Sch. Dist., No. 98-17194, 2000 U.S. App. LEXIS 17460 (9th Cir. Feb. 9, 2000) (determining that a teacher's asthma did not substantially limit the major life activity of breathing); Pryor v. Trane Co., 138 F.3d 1024 (5th Cir. 1998) (finding that the plaintiff's inability to lift as well as the average person did not affect her ability to perform a broad class of jobs).

183. 29 C.F.R. § 1630.2(j)(2), (3) (2002). *See also* Mustafa v. Clark County Sch. Dist., 876 F. Supp. 1177 (D. Nev. 1995) (observing that for a disability to be substantially limiting for an individual, it must foreclose a type of employment and not merely a single job).

184. 534 U.S. 184 (2002).

soned that to be substantially limiting, a permanent or long-term impairment must prevent or severely restrict the individual from doing activities that are of central importance to most people's daily lives. This will require a case-by-case analysis, as symptoms vary widely for most impairments. Accordingly, the Court ruled that the lower court should not have considered the plaintiff's inability to do manual work in her specialized assembly line job as sufficient proof that she was substantially limited in performing manual tasks generally.

Some of the more unusual, but unsuccessful, attempts to claim protection based on disability involved a left-handed mail carrier, an acrophobic utility systems repairer, an overweight flight attendant, a teacher with a test-taking phobia, and a teacher with alleged emotional ailments caused by the need to adjust to a new instructional method.[185] In a case heard by the Maine Supreme Court in 1993, a teacher purported to have a compulsive sexual addiction that caused him to harass students and seek out the services of prostitutes. He contended that his behavior was a manifestation of his disability and that his rights under the ADA and Section 504, among others, were violated when he was fired. The court disagreed, however, and upheld his termination.[186]

Similarly, in 1996, a professor sexually harassed several female students, sexually assaulted a colleague, and provided alcohol to minors in violation of both the university's drug and alcohol policy and state criminal code. He admitted to most of the allegations against him and to being unfit to teach, but nevertheless claimed disability discrimination following his termination. He rebutted that his unfitness to teach was not his fault; rather, he purported that his conduct was due to a "disinhibitory psychological disorder" that limited his control and ability to refrain from engaging in intolerable conduct. The court concluded that his requested accommodation (i.e., that he not be required to teach) was not reasonable and that his alleged disability rendered him unqualified to teach.[187]

Otherwise Qualified

If a person qualifies as disabled, it then must be determined whether he or she is "otherwise qualified." To be an otherwise qualified individual with a disability, the applicant or employee must be able to perform the essential functions of the job in spite of the disability, although reasonable accommodation at times may be necessary.

In identifying the essential functions of the job, courts will give consideration to what the employer perceives to be essential. As long as each identified requirement

185. Pandazides v. Va. Bd. of Educ., 946 F.2d 345 (4th Cir. 1991), *on remand*, 804 F. Supp. 794 (E.D. Va. 1992) (test anxiety); Beauford v. Father Flanagan's Boys' Home, 831 F.2d 768 (8th Cir. 1987) (difficulty adjusting to precision teaching system); Forrisi v. Bowen, 794 F.2d 931 (4th Cir. 1986) (acrophobia); de la Torres v. Bolger, 781 F.2d 1134 (5th Cir. 1986) (left-handedness); Tudyman v. United Airlines, 608 F. Supp. 739 (D.C. Cal. 1984) (weight).

186. Winston v. Me. Technical Coll. Sys., 631 A.2d 70 (Me. 1993).

187. Motzkin v. Trs. of Boston Univ., 938 F. Supp. 983 (D. Mass. 1996).

for employment is either training related (for initial employment) or job related, the employer should not have difficulty in substantiating its claim of business necessity. For example, being on time to work and being at work on a regular daily basis can qualify as a business necessity for most positions in education as well as elsewhere. Employees often have claimed that their respective disabilities were the basis for their lateness or nonarrival. Although this may have been true, courts generally have not found such employees to be otherwise qualified.[188] In 1994, an instructor with an autoimmune system disorder claimed disability discrimination when she was fired for not meeting the attendance requirements of the job. In ruling for the employer, the Fourth Circuit held that the employer was not required to restructure the entire work schedule to accommodate the employee in her efforts to deal with her own needs as well as those of her son, who also was disabled.[189]

However, if attendance is generally good, with only an occasional disability-related absence, accommodation may be required. In *School Board of Nassau County, Florida v. Arline,* a teacher, who had three relapses of tuberculosis over a two-year period for which leave was given, was terminated prior to returning to work following the third leave.[190] The Supreme Court held that the teacher qualified as disabled under Section 504 due to her record of physical impairment and hospitalization, but remanded the case for the district court to determine whether risks of infection to others precluded her from being otherwise qualified and whether her condition could be reasonably accommodated without an undue burden on the district. Following remand, the teacher was found to be otherwise qualified, since she posed little risk of infecting others, and was ordered reinstated with back pay.

Reasonable Accommodation

Persons with disabilities must be able to perform all of the essential functions of the position, either with accommodation or without. Employers are responsible for providing accommodations that qualify as reasonable and do not result in undue hardship,[191] such as making necessary facilities accessible and usable, restructuring work schedules, acquiring or modifying equipment, and providing readers or interpreters. Also, when not restricted by bargaining rights or other entitlements, transfer within

---

188. *See, e.g.,* Carr v. Reno, 23 F.3d 525 (D.C. Cir. 1994); Walders v. Garrett, 765 F. Supp. 303 (E.D. Va. 1991), *aff'd,* 956 F.2d 1163 (4th Cir. 1992); Santiago v. Temple Univ., 739 F. Supp. 974 (E.D. Pa. 1990), *aff'd without published opinion,* 928 F.2d 396 (3d Cir. 1991); Bernard v. Avoyelles Parish Sch. Bd., 640 So. 2d 321 (La. Ct. App. 1994).

189. Tyndall v. Nat'l Educ. Ctrs., 31 F.3d 209 (4th Cir. 1994).

190. 480 U.S. 273 (1987), *on remand,* 692 F. Supp. 1286 (M.D. Fla. 1988).

191. *See, e.g.,* Vollmert v. Wis. Dep't of Trans., 197 F.3d 293 (7th Cir. 1999) (finding that the employer failed to accommodate a staff member with dyslexia and learning disabilities when the employer transferred her to a position with fewer opportunities for promotion; such transfer was inappropriate, for reasonable accommodations had not been provided for the previous job).

the organization can qualify as a reasonable accommodation.[192] However, federal law does not require the employer to bump a current employee to allow a person with a disability to fill the position, to fill a vacant position it did not intend to fill, or to create a new unnecessary position.[193] Moreover, an employer need not transfer the employee to a better position (i.e., promote the employee because he or she is disabled) or select a less qualified or unqualified applicant solely because of disability.[194] Such forms of accommodation may be theoretically possible but would result in undue hardship to the employer and discriminate against other employees. Courts determine whether undue hardship results after a review of the size of the program and its budget, the number of employees, the type of facilities and operation, and the type and cost of accommodation. Because there is no fixed formula for calculations, courts have differed markedly in identifying what they consider reasonable.

To support a case of failure to provide reasonable accommodation, plaintiffs must prove that their employers were even aware of their respective disabilities.[195] At other times, employees have had difficulty showing that reasonable accommodations existed that would enable them to fulfill job requirements.[196] In a 1998 case from the Sixth Circuit, an HIV positive surgical technician was laid off once it was determined that patients would be at risk during surgery if the infected technician were to participate. In addition to preparing and handling surgical instruments, he at times was required to put his hands in an incision to make room for the surgeon to work or to provide visibility. In the process, he would have regular exposure to blood and incur eventual needle pricks (or possibly even cuts). In the alternative, the medical center offered him a position as cart-instrument coordinator, allowing him to remain employed. The plaintiff refused this proposal and was terminated. In upholding the granting of summary judgment for the employer, the court held that no reasonable accommodation would eliminate the direct threat the plaintiff posed and that he therefore was not otherwise qualified for the former position.[197]

192. *See, e.g.,* Smith v. Midland Brake, 180 F.3d 1154 (10th Cir. 1999) (en banc) (concluding that the ADA requires an employer to reassign a disabled employee to a vacant position, if the employee is unable to perform the essential functions of the current position but is able to perform those of the new position); Aka v. Washington Hosp. Ctr., 156 F.3d 1284 (D.C. Cir. 1998) (en banc) (concluding that a hospital must reassign an employee to a vacant position when unable to perform the essential functions of the current job).

193. *See, e.g.,* Ozlowski v. Henderson, 237 F.3d 837 (7th Cir. 2001).

194. *See, e.g.,* EEOC v. Humiston-Keeling, 227 F.3d 1024 (7th Cir. 2000).

195. *See, e.g.,* Whitney v. Bd. of Educ., 292 F.3d 1280 (10th Cir. 2002).

196. *See, e.g.,* Merrell v. ICEE-USA Corp., No. 99-4173, 2000 U.S. App. LEXIS 33327 (10th Cir. 2000) (noting that the only accommodation that would allow a man who stocked carbonated beverage machines to meet the essential functions of his job would be for the employer to hire a second individual to accompany him and to perform all of his heavy lifting; such an accommodation was found to create an undue burden on the employer); Deas v. River West, 152 F.3d 471 (5th Cir. 1998) (finding that the employer appropriately determined that the plaintiff could not be accommodated in her current employment as an addiction technician due to her petit mal or "absence" seizures; she would become verbally unresponsive and seemingly lose awareness of her surroundings).

197. Estate of Mauro v. Borgess Med. Ctr., 137 F.3d 398 (6th Cir. 1998).

Termination and Nonrenewal

There are more individuals with disabilities in the workplace today than ever before, with many achieving leadership positions. Not all persons with disabilities have fared well, however, as some have not been selected for initial employment, not granted tenured, not been promoted, and not paid fairly. At times, such adverse decisions were due to inadequate qualifications or skills, better-qualified applicants, poor job performance, posing a risk, or criminal wrongdoing.[198] At other times, the employee's disability was found to be the basis for the adverse decision, or the environment had become so hostile that the employee was constructively discharged.[199]

To support a disparate treatment adverse action claim, employees first must establish a prima facie case by showing that they have a disability that substantially limits a major life activity as compared to the average person in the population. Then they must show that they applied for and were otherwise qualified for their respective jobs, and were denied employment or retention in employment due to disability. Employees also must show that the employer was either a recipient of federal financial assistance (Section 504) or employed 15 or more employees (ADA).

In a First Circuit 2000 case, the court determined that a nurse, who was a recovering drug addict, was justifiably terminated for excessive violation of protocols in regard to drug dispersement. On one occasion, she denied asking a new nurse to administer a drug she had drawn in violation of policy, but then equivocated and ultimately admitted to the violation but only after the administering nurse forthrightly acknowledged her own error.[200] In a 1998 case, a professor was dismissed due to unprofessional conduct, failure to attend meetings, harassment of colleagues, and poor work ethic rather than disability.[201]

The cost of many accommodations, along with the tightening of state and local budgets, should make disability accommodation cases among the more volatile in the years to come. Although comparatively few plaintiffs are likely to prevail on such claims, expect school districts to devote significant resources to showing that they have provided reasonable accommodations and had not discriminated based on disability.

---

198. *See, e.g.,* Haulbrook v. Michelin N. Am., 252 F.3d 696 (4th Cir. 2001); Borgialli v. Thunder Basin Coal Co., 235 F.3d 1284 (10th Cir. 2000); Robertson v. Neuromedical Ctr., 161 F.3d 292 (5th Cir. 1998); Metzenbaum v. John Carroll Univ., No. 1:96cv1387, 1997 U.S. Dist. LEXIS 17340 (N.D. Ohio Oct. 22, 1997). *See also* Cadelli v. Fort Smith Sch. Dist., 23 F.3d 1295 (8th Cir. 1994) (holding that a teacher with an anxiety panic disorder who was medicated to allow him to cope with most everyday life situations, but was suffering from short-term memory loss and hearing deficits due to injuries sustained in a car accident, was not forced to retire; he voluntarily resigned).

199. *See, e.g.,* Spells v. Cuyahoga Cmty. Coll., 889 F. Supp. 1023 (N.D. Ohio 1994), *aff'd without published opinion,* 51 F.3d 273 (6th Cir. 1995); Schwarz v. Northwest Iowa Cmty. Coll., 881 F. Supp. 1323 (N.D. Iowa 1995).

200. Griel v. Franklin Med. Ctr., 234 F.3d 731 (1st Cir. 2000).

201. Newberry v. E. Tex. State Univ., 161 F.3d 276 (5th Cir. 1998).

Conclusion

Federal law requires that employment decisions be based on qualifications, performance, merit, seniority, and the like, rather than factors such as race, national origin, gender, sexual orientation, religion, age, or disability. Statutes vary considerably, however, as to what they require. Moreover, federal regulations are extensive, complex, and at times confounding. As a result, courts differ in applying the law. Even though many questions remain, the following generalizations reflect the current status of the law.

1. The United States Constitution and various civil rights laws protect employees from discrimination in employment based on race, national origin, gender, sexual orientation, religion, age, and disability.
2. For Fourteenth Amendment facial discrimination cases, race and national-origin discrimination claims require the application of strict scrutiny; gender and illegitimacy discrimination receive intermediate scrutiny; and all other employment classifications need to satisfy only rational-basis scrutiny.
3. For Fourteenth Amendment facially neutral cases, regardless of the type of classification involved, the plaintiff is required to show that the employer intended to discriminate.
4. Race may never qualify as a bona fide occupational qualification, although gender, religion, national origin, and age may be used under narrowly tailored conditions.
5. Adverse impact alone of a facially neutral employment practice on a protected group does not establish a constitutional violation, but such impact can violate Title VII if the employer is unable to show that the challenged practice serves a business necessity.
6. A reliable and valid standardized test can be used to screen job applicants, even though it has a disproportionate impact on a protected class, as long as the test is used to advance legitimate job objectives.
7. In Title VII disparate treatment cases, plaintiffs initially must establish a prima facie case of discrimination; then the employer has the opportunity to rebut the inference of discrimination by articulating a legitimate nondiscriminatory basis for the practice; to prevail, the plaintiff then must prove that the proffered reasons were not to be believed and a pretext for discrimination.
8. Public employers may not engage in affirmative action plans involving preferences in hiring and promotion unless a court has determined that the institution has been involved in specific prior acts of discrimination and the affirmative action plan is narrowly tailored to attain a work force reflecting the qualified relevant labor market.
9. Under narrowly tailored circumstances, courts may order hiring and promotion preferences to remedy prior acts of intentional employment discrimination but may not impose layoff quotas.

10. Pregnancy-related conditions cannot be treated less favorably than other temporary disabilities in medical and disability insurance plans or leave policies.

11. Employees cannot be required to take maternity leave at a specified date during pregnancy unless the policy is justified as a business necessity.

12. Employers cannot make a distinction between men and women in retirement contributions and benefits.

13. Employees can gain relief under Title VII for sexual harassment that results in the loss of tangible benefits or creates a hostile working environment.

14. Title VII provides remedies for gender discrimination in compensation that extend beyond the Equal Pay Act guarantee of equal pay for equal work.

15. Persons who are victims of sexual preference discrimination may file suit under the Fourteenth Amendment (public sector) or under applicable state laws or local ordinances, where they exist (private sector).

16. School boards can establish bona fide retirement benefits programs, but the Age Discrimination in Employment Act (ADEA) precludes mandatory retirement based on age.

17. For a violation to be substantiated under the ADEA, age must play a role in the decision-making process *and* have a determinative influence on the outcome.

18. Employers must make reasonable accommodations to enable employees to practice their religious beliefs; however, Title VII does not require accommodations that result in undue hardship to the employer.

19. An otherwise qualified individual cannot be excluded from employment solely on the basis of a disability, and employers are required to provide reasonable accommodations for employees with disabilities.

11

Termination of Employment

State laws delineate the authority of school boards in terminating school personnel. Generally, these laws specify the causes for which a teacher may be terminated and the procedures that must be followed. The school board's right to determine the fitness of teachers is well established; in fact, courts have declared that school boards have a duty as well as a right to make such determinations. According to the United States Supreme Court:

> A teacher works in a sensitive area in a schoolroom. There he shapes the attitude of young minds towards the society in which they live. In this, the state has a vital concern. It must preserve the integrity of the schools. That the school authorities have *the right and the duty to screen* the officials, teachers, and employees as to their fitness to maintain the integrity of the schools as a part of ordered society, cannot be doubted.[1] (emphasis added)

This chapter addresses the procedures that must be followed in the termination of a teacher's employment and the grounds for dismissal. The first section provides an overview of due process in connection with nonrenewal and dismissal. Since due process is required only if a teacher is able to establish that a constitutionally protected property or liberty interest is at stake, this section explores the dimensions of teachers' property and liberty rights in the context of employment termination. In the next section, specific procedural requirements are identified and discussed. A survey of judicial interpretations of state laws regarding causes for dismissal is presented in the third section. The concluding section provides an overview of remedies available to teachers for violation of their protected rights.

Procedural Due Process in General

Basic due process rights are embodied in the Fourteenth Amendment, which guarantees that no state shall "deprive any person of life, liberty, or property without due

1. Adler v. Bd. of Educ., 342 U.S. 485, 493 (1952).

process of law."[2] Due process safeguards apply not only in judicial proceedings but also to acts of governmental agencies such as school boards. As discussed in Chapter 1, constitutional due process entails *substantive* protections against arbitrary governmental action and *procedural* protections when the government threatens an individual's life, liberty, or property interests. Most teacher termination cases have focused on procedural due process requirements.

The individual and governmental interests at stake and applicable state laws influence the nature of procedural due process required. Courts have established that a teacher's interest in public employment may entail significant "property" and "liberty" rights necessitating due process prior to employment termination. *A property interest* is a "legitimate claim of entitlement" to continued employment that is created by state law.[3] The granting of tenure conveys such a right to a teacher.[4] Also, a contract establishes a property right to employment within its stated terms.[5] A property interest in continued employment, however, does not mean that an individual cannot be terminated; it simply means that an employer must follow the requirements of due process and substantiate cause.[6]

The judiciary has recognized that Fourteenth Amendment liberty rights encompass fundamental constitutional guarantees, such as freedom of speech. Procedural due process always is required when a termination implicates such fundamental liberties. A liberty interest also is involved when termination creates a stigma or damages an individual's reputation in a manner that forecloses future employment opportunities. If protected liberty or property interests are implicated, the Fourteenth Amendment entitles the teacher at least to notice of the reasons for the school board's action and an opportunity for a hearing.

Employment terminations are classified as either dismissals or nonrenewals. The distinction between the two has significant implications for teachers' procedural rights. In this section, the procedural safeguards that must be provided the tenured teacher and the nontenured teacher are distinguished. Specific attention is given to the

---

2. As noted in Chapter 1, the Fourteenth Amendment restricts state, in contrast to private, action. The Supreme Court has recognized that mere regulation by the state will be insufficient to evoke constitutional protections in private school personnel matters. The Court rejected a suit for damages against a private school for allegedly unconstitutional dismissals, reasoning that there was no "symbiotic relationship" between the private school and the state. Rendell Baker v. Kohn, 457 U.S. 830 (1982). *See also* Logiodice v. Trs., 296 F.3d 22 (1st Cir. 2002) (ruling that payment of tuition for public school students to attend private school did not involve state action that would require the school to provide a student procedural due process prior to suspension).

3. *See* Bd. of Regents v. Roth, 408 U.S. 564 (1972).

4. *See, e.g.,* DeMichele v. Greenburgh Cent. Sch. Dist. No. 7, 167 F.3d 784 (2d Cir. 1999).

5. *See, e.g.,* Coggin v. Longview Indep. Sch. Dist., 289 F.3d 326 (5th Cir. 2002); Rogan v. Lewis, 975 F. Supp. 956 (S.D. Tex. 1997).

6. *See, e.g.,* Wuest v. Winner Sch. Dist. 59-2, 607 N.W.2d 912 (S.D. 2000). *See also* Carrington v. Mahan, 51 F.3d 106 (8th Cir. 1995) (holding that a tenured teacher who failed to report to a new position relinquished her property interests in continued employment and thereby was not entitled to due process prior to dismissal).

conditions that may give rise to a nontenured teacher's acquiring a protected liberty or property interest in employment, thereby establishing a claim to procedural due process.

Dismissal

The term *dismissal* refers to the termination for cause of any tenured teacher or a probationary teacher within the contract period. Both tenure statutes and employment contracts establish a property interest entitling teachers to full procedural protection.[7] Beyond the basic constitutional requirements of appropriate notice and an opportunity to be heard, state laws and school board policies often contain detailed procedures that must be followed. Failure to provide these additional procedures, however, results in a violation of state law, rather than constitutional law.[8] Statutory procedures vary as to specificity, with some states enumerating detailed steps and others identifying only broad parameters. In addition to complying with state law, a school district must abide by its own procedures, even if they exceed state law. For example, if school board policy provides for a preliminary notice of teaching inadequacies and an opportunity to correct remediable deficiencies prior to dismissal, the board must follow these steps.

A critical element in dismissal actions is a showing of justifiable cause for termination of employment. If causes are identified in state law, a school board must base dismissal on those grounds. Failure to relate the charges to statutory grounds can invalidate the termination decision. Because statutes typically list broad causes—such as incompetency, insubordination, immorality, unprofessional conduct, and neglect of duty—notice of discharge must indicate specific conduct substantiating the legal charges. Procedural safeguards ensure not only that a teacher is informed of the specific reasons and grounds for dismissal, but also that the school board bases its decision on evidence substantiating those grounds. Detailed aspects of procedural due process requirements and dismissal for cause are addressed in subsequent sections of this chapter.

Nonrenewal

Unless specified in state law, procedural protections are not accorded the probationary teacher when the employment contract is not renewed.[9] At the end of the contract

---

7. If a statute conferring specific property rights (e.g., tenure) is rescinded or amended to eliminate those rights, individuals are not entitled to procedural due process related to that deprivation; statutory benefits can be revoked without due process unless the change impairs contractual rights. *See, e.g.,* Indiana *ex rel.* Anderson v. Brand, 303 U.S.95 (1938); Pittman v. Chi. Bd. of Educ., 64 F.3d 1098 (7th Cir. 1995). However, school boards generally cannot amend, repeal, or circumvent statutory rights (e.g., entitlement to procedural due process) through the employment contract. *See, e.g.,* Parker v. Indep. Sch. Dist. No. I-003 Okmulgee County, Okla, 82 F.3d 952 (10th Cir. 1996).

8. *See, e.g.,* Goodrich v. Newport News Sch. Bd., 743 F.2d 225 (4th Cir. 1984); Atencio v. Bd. of Educ., 658 F.2d 774 (10th Cir. 1981).

9. *See, e.g.,* Lighton v. Univ. of Utah, 209 F.3d 1213 (10th Cir. 2000); Provoda v. Maxwell, 808 P.2d 28 (N.M. 1991); Tucker v. Bd. of Educ., 604 N.Y.S.2d 506 (1993).

period, employment can be terminated for any or no reason, as long as the reason is not constitutionally impermissible (e.g., denial of protected speech).[10] The most common statutory requirement is notification of nonrenewal on or before a specified date prior to the expiration of the contract. Courts strictly construe the timeliness of nonrenewal notices. When a statute designates a deadline for nonrenewal, a school board must notify a teacher on or before the established date. The fact that the school board has set in motion notification (e.g., mailed the notice) generally does not satisfy the statutory requirement; the teacher's actual receipt of the notice is critical.[11] A teacher, however, cannot avoid or deliberately thwart delivery of notice and then claim insufficiency of notice.[12] Failure of school officials to observe the notice deadline may result in a teacher's reinstatement for an additional year[13] or even the granting of tenure in some jurisdictions.

In the nonrenewal of teachers' contracts, some states require a written statement of reasons and may even provide an opportunity for a hearing at the teacher's request.[14] Unlike evidentiary hearings for dismissal of a teacher, the school board is not required to show cause for nonrenewal;[15] a teacher is simply provided the reasons underlying the nonrenewal and an opportunity to address the school board. When a school board is required to provide reasons, broad general statements, such as "the school district's interest would be best served," "the district can find a better teacher," or "the term contract has expired," will not suffice. The Arkansas high court noted that state law requires boards to give "simple but complete reasons."[16] The Mississippi high court emphasized that although a school board must show that "demonstrable reason" exists for a nonrenewal decision, the burden of proof remains with the teacher to prove that the board had no basis for the decision not to renew.[17] Where state law establishes specific requirements and procedures for nonrenewal, failure to abide by these provisions may invalidate a school board's decision. In Arizona, for example, if nonrenewal is based primarily on inadequate classroom performance, teachers must be given a preliminary notice of the school board's intent not to renew their contracts

10. *See, e.g.,* Smith v. King City Sch. Dist., 990 S.W.2d 643 (Mo. Ct. App. 1998). *See* Chapter 9 for a discussion of teachers' constitutional rights.

11. This general rule of actual receipt of notice would not apply, of course, if a statutory provision indicated other means of satisfying the deadline, such as requiring the notice to be postmarked by a certain date. *See, e.g.,* Andrews v. Howard, 291 S.E.2d 541 (Ga. 1982).

12. *See, e.g.,* Stollenwerck v. Talladega County Bd. of Educ., 420 So. 2d 21 (Ala. 1982).

13. *See, e.g.,* Kiel v. Green Local Sch. Dist. Bd. of Educ., 630 N.E.2d 716 (Ohio 1994).

14. *See, e.g.,* Kidd v. Bd. of Educ., 29 S.W.3d 374 (Ky. Ct. App. 2000) (remanding case to determine if the reasons offered for nonrenewal were true; if not, decision would be voided); Naylor v. Cardinal Local Sch. Dist. Bd. of Educ., 630 N.E.2d 725 (Ohio 1994) (holding that a "hearing" under Ohio law is more than an informal session with the school board; it includes the right to present evidence, confront and examine witnesses, and review both parties' arguments).

15. *See, e.g.,* Flath v. Garrison Pub. Sch. Dist. No. 51, 82 F.3d 244 (8th Cir. 1996); Stratton v. Austin Indep. Sch. Dist., 8 S.W.3d 26 (Tex. Ct. App. 1999).

16. Hamilton v. Pulaski County Special Sch. Dist., 900 S.W.2d 205 (Ark. 1995).

17. Buck v. Lowndes County Sch. Dist., 761 So. 2d 144 (Miss. 2000).

and allowed 90 days to remedy the inadequacies.[18] Failure to follow the prescribed statutory procedures for evaluating nontenured teachers in Ohio can result in reversal of a nonrenewal decision with reinstatement for an additional year.[19] Furthermore, a school board must follow not only state law but also must comply substantially with its own nonrenewal procedures.[20]

Although state laws may not provide the probationary teacher with specific procedural protections, a teacher's interest in continued public employment may be constitutionally protected if a liberty or property right guaranteed by the Fourteenth Amendment has been abridged. Infringement of these interests entitles a probationary teacher to due process rights similar to the rights of tenured teachers. These rights are delineated next.

Establishing Protected Property and Liberty Interests

The United States Supreme Court addressed the scope of protected interests encompassed by the Fourteenth Amendment in two significant decisions in 1972: *Board of Regents v. Roth*[21] and *Perry v. Sindermann.*[22] These decisions addressed whether the infringement of a liberty or property interest entitles a probationary teacher to due process rights similar to the rights of tenured teachers. The cases involved faculty members at the postsecondary level, but the rulings are equally applicable to public elementary and secondary school teachers.

In *Roth,* the question presented to the Court was whether a nontenured teacher had a constitutional right to a statement of reasons and a hearing prior to nonreappointment. Roth was hired on a one-year contract, and the university elected not to rehire him for a second year. Since Roth did not have tenure, there was no entitlement under Wisconsin law to an explanation of charges or a hearing; the university simply did not reemploy him for the succeeding year. Roth challenged the nonrenewal, alleging that failure to provide notice of reasons and an opportunity for a hearing impaired his due process rights.

The Supreme Court held that nonrenewal did not require procedural protection unless impairment of a protected liberty or property interest could be shown. To establish infringement of a liberty interest, the Court held that the teacher must show that the employer's action (1) resulted in damage to his or her reputation and standing in the community or (2) imposed a stigma that foreclosed other employment opportuni-

---

18. Wheeler v. Yuma Sch. Dist. No. One, 750 P.2d 860 (Ariz. 1988). *See also* Wren v. McDowell County Bd. of Educ., 327 S.E.2d 464 (W. Va. 1985) (holding that state board of education procedures required opportunity for probationary teachers to correct teaching inadequacies).

19. Snyder v. Mendon-Union Dist. Bd. of Educ., 661 N.E.2d 717 (Ohio 1996). *See also* Bowden v. Memphis Bd. of Educ., 29 S.W.3d 462 (Tenn. 2000).

20. *See, e.g.,* Struthers City Schs. Bd. of Educ. v. Struthers Educ. Ass'n, 453 N.E.2d 613 (Ohio 1983). *But see* Stratton v. Austin Indep. Sch. Dist., 8 S.W.2d 26 (Tex. Ct. App. 1999) (ruling that a board's failure to follow its own rules does not create a property interest conferring due process rights).

21. 408 U.S. 564 (1972).

22. 408 U.S. 593 (1972).

ties. The evidence presented by Roth indicated that there was no such damage to his reputation or future employment. Accordingly, the Court concluded, "It stretches the concept too far to suggest that a person is deprived of 'liberty' when he simply is not rehired in one job but remains as free as before to seek another."[23]

The Court also rejected Roth's claim that he had a protected property interest to continued employment. The Court held that in order to establish a valid property right, an individual must have more than an "abstract need or desire" for a position; there must be a "legitimate claim of entitlement."[24] Property interests are not defined by the Federal Constitution, but rather by state laws or employment contracts that secure specific benefits. An abstract desire or unilateral expectation of continued employment alone does not constitute a property right. The terms of Roth's one-year appointment and the state law precluded any claim of entitlement.

On the same day it rendered the *Roth* decision, the Supreme Court in the *Sindermann* case explained the circumstances that might create a legitimate expectation of reemployment for a nontenured teacher.[25] Sindermann was a nontenured faculty member in his fourth year of teaching when he was notified, without a statement of reasons or an opportunity for a hearing, that his contract would not be renewed. He challenged the lack of procedural due process, alleging that nonrenewal deprived him of a property interest protected by the Fourteenth Amendment and violated his First Amendment right to freedom of speech.

In advancing a protected property right, Sindermann claimed that the college, which lacked a formal tenure system, had created an informal, or *de facto,* tenure system through various practices and policies. Specifically, Sindermann cited a provision in the faculty guide stating that "the College wishes the faculty member to feel that he has permanent tenure as long as his teaching services are satisfactory."[26] The Supreme Court found that Sindermann's claim, unlike Roth's, may have been based on a legitimate expectation of reemployment promulgated by the college. According to the Court, the lack of a formal tenure system did not foreclose the possibility of an institution fostering entitlement to a position through its personnel policies.

In assessing Sindermann's free speech claim, the Supreme Court confirmed that a teacher's lack of tenure does not void a claim that nonrenewal was based on the exercise of constitutionally protected conduct. Procedural due process must be afforded when a substantive constitutional right is violated. In a later case, however, the Supreme Court held that if a constitutional right is implicated in a nonrenewal, the teacher bears the burden of showing that the protected conduct was a substantial or motivating factor in the school board's decision.[27] The establishment of this inference of a constitutional violation then shifts the burden to the school board to show by a

---

23. *Roth,* 408 U.S. at 575.

24. *Id.* at 577.

25. 408 U.S. 593 (1972).

26. *Id.* at 600.

27. Mt. Healthy City Sch. Dist. Bd. of Educ. v. Doyle, 429 U.S. 274 (1977). *See* text accompanying note 3, in Chapter 9 for a discussion of the First Amendment issue in this case.

preponderance of evidence that it would have reached the same decision in the absence of the protected activity.

The *Roth* and *Sindermann* cases are the legal precedents for assessing the procedural rights of nontenured teachers. To summarize, the Supreme Court held that a nontenured teacher does not have a constitutionally protected property right to employment requiring procedural due process before denial of reappointment. Certain actions of the school board, however, may create conditions entitling a nontenured teacher to notice and a hearing similar to the tenured teacher. Such actions would include:

- Nonrenewal decisions damaging an individual's reputation and integrity
- Nonrenewal decisions foreclosing other employment opportunities
- Policies and practices creating a valid claim to reemployment
- Nonrenewal decisions violating fundamental constitutional guarantees

Since the Supreme Court has held that impairment of a teacher's property or liberty interests triggers procedural protections, the question arises as to what constitutes a violation of these interests. Courts have purposely avoided precisely defining the concepts of liberty and property, preferring to allow experience and time to shape their meanings.[28] Since 1972, the Supreme Court and federal appellate courts have rendered a number of decisions that provide some guidance in understanding these concepts.

Property Interest.   In general, a nontenured employee does not have a property claim to reappointment unless state or local governmental action has clearly established such a right.[29] A federal district court found that a Delaware school board created a reasonable expectation of reemployment, requiring procedural protection, when it advised a principal that his contract would be renewed if his performance were satisfactory.[30] The court concluded that the principal was justified in believing that he would be reappointed after receiving a satisfactory rating. Similarly, the Seventh Circuit found that a promise of two years of employment to a coach/athletic director established a legitimate expectation of continued employment.[31] To persuade the athletic director to accept the position, the board had assured him that his one-year contract would be

28. *See, e.g., Roth,* 408 U.S. at 572.

29. *See, e.g.,* Kyle v. Morton High Sch., 144 F.3d 448 (7th Cir. 1998); Goudeau v. Indep. Sch. Dist. No. 37, 823 F.2d 1429 (10th Cir. 1987). *See also* Remus v. Bd. of Educ., 727 N.Y.S.2d 43 (2001) (holding that the granting of tenure for a future date did not create the right to procedural due process until that date; teachers were terminated as probationary teachers prior to the effective date of tenure with no entitlement to formal proceedings)

30. Schreffler v. Bd. of Educ., 506 F. Supp. 1300 (D. Del. 1981).

31. Vail v. Bd. of Educ., 706 F.2d 1435 (7th Cir. 1983), *aff'd by an equally divided court,* 466 U.S. 377 (1984). *But see* Thomas v. Bd. of Exam'rs, Chi. Pub. Schs., 866 F.2d 225 (7th Cir. 1988) (finding that entitlement to consideration for a promotion does not constitute a property right).

extended for a second year. Based on such an implied contract, the court found that unilateral termination of the contract after one year violated due process rights.

Protected property interests are not created by mere longevity in employment. Both the Fourth and Tenth Circuits found that issuing an employee a series of annual contracts did not constitute a valid claim to continued employment in the absence of a guarantee in state law, local policy, or an employment contract.[32] Similarly, a statute or collective bargaining agreement providing a teacher, upon request, a hearing and statement of reasons for nonrenewal does not confer a property interest in employment requiring legally sufficient cause for termination.[33] Such a provision simply gives the teacher an opportunity to present reasons why the contract should be renewed.[34]

Although a term contract establishes a property interest, due process generally is not required in transferring or reassigning a teacher or administrator unless an identifiable economic impact can be shown. For example, a Chicago principal who was reassigned to the central office was not entitled to a hearing since he continued to receive his regular salary and benefits; deprivations related to professional satisfaction and reputation did not constitute actionable injuries.[35] In contrast, the Sixth Circuit reasoned that a collective bargaining agreement specifying that teachers may not be transferred except for "good cause" and "extenuating circumstances" established a property interest in a particular position in a specific school.[36]

As noted, property rights are created by state laws or contracts but also may emanate from policies, regulations, or ordinances made by a governmental employer pursuant to statutory rule-making authority. Such policies or regulations must create an expectation of employment and impose a binding obligation on the employer in order to create a property interest in continued employment. The sufficiency of the claim, however, must be interpreted in light of state law, irrespective of the claim's origin. In some instances, reference to state law can narrowly restrict or limit alleged property interests. For example, the United States Supreme Court, in construing a North Carolina employee's property rights, relied on the state supreme court's opinion that "an enforceable expectation of continued public employment in that state can exist only if the employer, by *statute or contract* has actually granted some form of guarantee"[37] (emphasis added). Although, in this case, a city ordinance gave rise to an

---

32. Martin v. Unified Sch. Dist. No. 434, 728 F.2d 453 (10th Cir. 1984); Robertson v. Rogers, 679 F.2d 1090 (4th Cir. 1982).

33. *See, e.g.,* Perkins v. Bd. of Dirs., 686 F.2d 49 (1st Cir. 1982); Schaub v. Chamberlain Bd. of Educ., 339 N.W.2d 307 (S.D. 1983). *See also* Wells v. Hico Indep. Sch. Dist., 736 F.2d 243 (5th Cir. 1984) (holding that grievance policy and procedures did not create a property interest in continued employment).

34. *See, e.g., Schaub,* 339 N.W.2d 307 (holding that a hearing may be available to a nontenured teacher, but the board is not required to speak, produce evidence, or even answer questions at the hearing).

35. Bordelon v. Chi. Sch. Reform Bd. of Trs., 233 F.3d 524 (7th Cir. 2000). *See also* Ulichny v. Merton Cmty. Sch. Dist., 249 F.3d 686 (7th Cir. 2001) (finding that the reduction of a principal's duties and responsibilities did not impair property rights).

36. Leary v. Daeschner, 228 F.3d 729 (6th Cir. 2000).

37. Bishop v. Wood, 426 U.S. 341, 345 (1976).

expectancy of reemployment after the successful completion of a six-month probationary period, the Court reasoned that, in the absence of a statutory or contractual obligation, the employee worked at the will and pleasure of the city. To establish a property right, then, it is necessary to prove not only that the employer's actions create an expectation of employment but also that state law does not limit the claim.

Liberty Interest.   As noted previously, liberty interests encompass fundamental constitutional guarantees such as freedom of expression and privacy rights. If governmental action in the nonrenewal of employment threatens the exercise of these fundamental liberties, procedural due process must be afforded. Most nonrenewals, however, do not overtly implicate fundamental rights, and thus, the burden is on the aggrieved employee to prove that the proffered reason is pretextual to mask impermissible grounds. Teachers' substantive constitutional rights are discussed at length in Chapter 9.

A liberty interest also may be implicated if the nonrenewal of employment damages an individual's reputation. The Supreme Court established in *Roth* that damage to a teacher's reputation and future employability could infringe Fourteenth Amendment liberty rights. In subsequent decisions, the Court identified prerequisite conditions for establishing that a constitutionally impermissible stigma has been imposed. According to the Court, procedural protections must be afforded only if stigma or damaging statements are related to loss of employment, publicly disclosed, alleged to be false, and virtually foreclose opportunities for future employment.[38]

Under this "stigma-plus" test, governmental action damaging a teacher's reputation, standing alone, is insufficient to invoke the Fourteenth Amendment's procedural safeguards.[39] As such, a teacher who has been defamed by reassignment, transfer, suspension, or loss of a promotion cannot claim violation of a liberty interest.[40] The Fifth Circuit noted that the internal transfer of an employee, unless it is regarded essentially as a loss of employment, does not provide the loss of a tangible interest necessary to give rise to a liberty interest.[41] Similarly, the nonrenewal of coaching contracts does not involve a liberty interest when individuals retain their teaching positions.[42] While many of these employment actions may stigmatize and

---

38. *See, e.g.,* Codd v. Velger, 429 U.S. 624 (1977); Bishop v. Wood, 426 U.S. 341 (1976); Paul v. Davis, 424 U.S. 693 (1976); Bordelon v. Chi. Sch. Reform Bd. of Trs., 233 F.3d 524 (7th Cir. 2000); Lighton v. Univ. of Utah, 209 F.3d 1213 (10th Cir. 2000).

39. State constitutions, however, may provide greater protection of due process rights encompassing damage to reputation alone. *See, e.g.,* Kadetsky v. Egg Harbor Township Bd. of Educ., 82 F. Supp. 2d 327 (D.N.J. 2000).

40. *See, e.g.,* Ulichny v. Merton Cmty. Sch. Dist., 249 F.3d 686 (7th Cir. 2001); Thomas v. Smith, 897 F.2d 154 (5th Cir. 1989). *But see* Winegar v. Des Moines Indep. Cmty. Sch. Dist., 20 F.3d 895 (8th Cir. 1994) (holding that disciplinary transfer to another school because of the physical abuse of a student involved a significant liberty interest necessitating an opportunity to be heard).

41. Moore v. Otero, 557 F.2d 435, 438 (5th Cir. 1977).

42. *See, e.g.,* Lancaster v. Indep. Sch. Dist. No. 5, 149 F.3d 1228 (10th Cir. 1998); Lagos v. Modesto City Schs. Dist., 843 F.2d 347 (9th Cir. 1988).

affect a teacher's reputation, they do not constitute a deprivation of liberty in the absence of loss of employment. Furthermore, to sustain a stigmatization claim, an individual must show that a request was made for a name-clearing hearing and that the request was denied.[43]

The primary issue in these terminations is determining what charges constitute stigmatization. Nonrenewal alone is insufficient. As the Ninth Circuit noted, "Nearly any reason assigned for dismissal is likely to be to some extent a negative reflection on an individual's ability, temperament, or character," but circumstances giving rise to a liberty interest are narrow.[44] Not every comment or accusation by school officials that affects one's reputation is actionable under the Fourteenth Amendment.[45] Charges must be serious implications against character, such as immorality and dishonesty, to create a stigma of constitutional magnitude that virtually forecloses other employment. According to the Fifth Circuit, a charge must give rise to "a 'badge of infamy,' public scorn, or the like."[46] Such a liberty violation was clearly illustrated by the termination of a life-science teacher after public attacks on his teaching of human reproduction.[47] In this case, the appellate court found that the teacher was subjected to extensive, embarrassing publicity in the local, national, and even international media (e.g., being referred to as a sex maniac); incurred substantial personal harassment; and suffered permanent damage to his professional career. Termination of a New York probationary teacher implicated a liberty interest when her professional integrity and reputation were impugned by allegations that she helped students cheat on standardized tests, urged other teachers to cheat, and tried to assault another teacher who refused to participate in the scheme.[48] Allegations such as these represent serious accusations that damage an educator's standing and pose significant threats to future employability.[49]

Among other accusations that courts have found to necessitate a hearing are a serious drinking problem, emotional instability, mental illness, immoral conduct, accusation of child molestation, and extensive professional inadequacies.[50] Reasons

---

43. *See, e.g.,* Puchalski v. Sch. Dist. of Springfield, 161 F. Supp. 2d 395 (E.D. Pa. 2001).

44. Gray v. Union County Intermediate Educ. Dist., 520 F.2d 803, 806 (9th Cir. 1975). *See also* Hedrich v. Bd. of Regents, 274 F.3d 1174 (7th Cir. 2001); Brammer-Hoelter v. Twin Peaks Charter Acad., 81 F. Supp. 2d 1090 (D. Colo. 2000); Gordon v. Nicoletti, 84 F. Supp. 2d 304 (D. Conn. 2000).

45. *See, e.g.,* Ulichny v. Merton Cmty. Sch. Dist., 249 F.3d 686 (7th Cir. 2001); Merkle v. Upper Dublin Sch. Dist., 211 F.3d 782 (3d Cir. 2000). *See also* Santiago v. Fajardo, 70 F. Supp. 2d 72 (D.P.R. 1999) (holding that defamation alone does not violate an individual's liberty interest).

46. Ball v. Bd. of Trs., 584 F.2d 684, 685 (5th Cir. 1978). *See also* Burke v. Chi. Sch. Reform Bd. of Trustees, 169 F. Supp. 2d 843 (N.D. Ill. 2001).

47. Stachura v. Memphis Cmty. Sch. Dist., 763 F.2d 211 (6th Cir. 1985), *rev'd on damages issue,* 477 U.S. 299 (1986).

48. Rivera v. Cmty. Sch. Dist. Nine, 145 F. Supp. 2d 302 (S.D.N.Y. 2001).

49. *See, e.g.,* Townsend v. Vallas, 256 F.3d 661 (7th Cir. 2001) (ruling against a teacher's claim when he did not demonstrate unemployability; he continued to hold a previous part-time job and had not applied for positions in other districts).

50. *See, e.g.,* Donato v. Plainview-Old Bethpage Cent. Sch. Dist., 96 F.3d 623 (2d Cir. 1996); Vanelli v. Reynolds Sch. Dist. No. 7, 667 F.2d 773 (9th Cir. 1982); Carroll v. Robinson, 874 P.2d 1010 (Ariz. Ct. App. 1994).

held to pose no threat to a liberty interest include job-related comments such as personality differences and difficulty in working with others, hostility toward authority, incompetence, aggressive behavior, ineffective leadership, and poor performance.[51] Charges relating to job performance may have an impact on future employment but do not create a stigma of constitutional magnitude.

Liberty interests are not implicated unless damaging reasons are publicly communicated in the process of denying employment.[52] The primary purpose of a hearing is to enable individuals to clear their names. Without public knowledge of the reasons for nonreappointment, such a hearing is not required. Furthermore, a protected liberty interest generally is affected only if the *school board publicizes* the stigmatizing reasons, rather than individual, media, or another source. Accordingly, statements that are disclosed in a public meeting requested by the teacher or made by the teacher to the media or others do not require a name-clearing hearing.[53] Likewise, rumors or hearsay remarks surfacing as a result of nonrenewal do not impair liberty interests. The First Circuit noted that "in terms of likely stigmatizing effect, there is a world of difference between official charges (such as excessive drinking) made publicly and a campus rumor based upon hearsay."[54] Even when a school board publicly announces stigmatizing reasons for its action, there must be a factual dispute regarding the truth of the allegations for a hearing to be required. If a teacher does not challenge the truth of the statements, a name-clearing hearing serves no purpose.[55] A teacher, however, is not required to establish that the statements are false to be entitled to a hearing; that is the purpose of the hearing.[56]

Procedural Requirements in Discharge Proceedings

Since termination of a tenured teacher or a nontenured teacher during the contract period requires procedural due process, the central question becomes *what process is due?* Courts have noted that no fixed set of procedures apply under all circumstances.

---

51. *See, e.g.,* Lybrook v. Members of Farmington Mun. Schs. Bd., 232 F.3d 1334 (10th Cir. 2000); Hayes v. Phoenix-Talent Sch. Dist. No. 4, 893 F.2d 235 (9th Cir. 1990); Robertson v. Rogers, 679 F.2d 1090 (4th Cir. 1982); Johnson v. Indep. Sch. Dist. No. 281, 494 N.W.2d 270 (Minn. 1992).

52. *See, e.g.,* Vega v. Miller, 273 F.3d 460 (2d Cir. 2001); McCullough v. Wyandanch Union Free Sch. Dist., 187 F.3d 272 (2d Cir. 1999); Lancaster v. Indep. Sch. Dist. No. 5, 149 F.3d 1228 (10th Cir. 1998); Strasburger v. Bd. of Educ., 143 F.3d 351 (7th Cir. 1998).

53. *See, e.g.,* Schul v. Sherard, 102 F. Supp. 2d 877 (S.D. Ohio 2000).

54. Beitzell v. Jeffrey, 643 F.2d 870, 879 (1st Cir. 1981).

55. *See, e.g.,* Codd v. Velger, 429 U.S. 624 (1977); Coleman v. Reed, 147 F.3d 751 (8th Cir. 1998); *Strasburger,* 143 F.3d 351. *See also* Donato v. Plainview-Old Bethpage Cent. Sch. Dist., 985 F. Supp. 316 (E.D.N.Y. 1997) (holding on remand that an employee bears the burden of proof to show that charges are false in a name-clearing hearing).

56. *See, e.g.,* O'Neill v. City of Auburn, 23 F.3d 685 (2d Cir. 1994).

Rather, due process entails a balancing of the individual and governmental interests affected in each situation. According to the Supreme Court, a determination of the specific aspects of due process requires consideration of

> first, the private interest that will be affected by the official action; second, the risk of an erroneous deprivation of such interest through the procedures used, and the probable value, if any, of additional or substitute procedural safeguards; and finally, the government's interest, including the function involved and the fiscal and administrative burdens that the additional or substitute procedural requirement would entail.[57]

Application of these standards would require only minimum procedures in suspending a student but a more extensive, formal process in dismissing a teacher.

Minimally, the Fourteenth Amendment requires that dismissal proceedings be based on established rules or standards. Actual procedures will depend on state law, school board regulations, and collective bargaining agreements,[58] but they cannot drop below constitutional minimums. For example, a statute requiring tenured teachers to pay half the cost of a hearing that constitutionally must be provided by the school board violated federal rights.[59] In assessing the adequacy of procedural safeguards, the judiciary looks for the provision of certain basic elements to meet constitutional guarantees.[60] Courts generally have held that a teacher facing a severe loss such as termination must be afforded procedures encompassing the following elements:[61]

- Notification of charges
- Opportunity for a hearing
- Adequate time to prepare a rebuttal to the charges
- Access to evidence and names of witnesses
- Hearing before an impartial tribunal
- Representation by legal counsel
- Opportunity to present evidence and witnesses
- Opportunity to cross-examine adverse witnesses
- Decision based on evidence and findings of the hearing
- Transcript or record of the hearing
- Opportunity to appeal an adverse decision

57. Mathews v. Eldridge, 424 U.S. 319, 335 (1976).

58. *See, e.g.,* Bd. of Educ. v. Ward, 974 P.2d 824 (Utah 1999); Rich v. Montpelier Supervisory Dist., 709 A.2d 501 (Vt. 1998).

59. Rankin v. Indep. Sch. Dist. No. I-3, Noble County, Okla., 876 F.2d 838 (10th Cir. 1989). *See also* Cal. Teachers Ass'n v. State, 975 P.2d 622, 643 (Cal. 1999) (concluding that imposing half the cost of an administrative law judge "chills the exercise of the right to a hearing and vigorous advocacy on behalf of the teacher").

60. *See, e.g.,* Clark County Sch. Dist. v. Riley, 14 P.3d 22 (Nev. 2000).

61. This chapter focuses on procedural protections required in teacher terminations. It should be noted, however, that other school board decisions (e.g., transfers, demotions, or mandatory leaves) may impose similar constraints on decision making.

Beyond these constitutional considerations, courts also strictly enforce any additional procedural protections conferred by state laws and local policies.[62] Examples of such requirements might be providing detailed performance evaluations prior to termination, notifying teachers of weaknesses, and allowing an opportunity for improvement before dismissal. Although failure to comply with these stipulations may invalidate the school board's action under state law, federal due process rights *per se* are not violated if minimal constitutional procedures are provided.[63]

Except in limited circumstances, individuals are required to exhaust administrative procedures, or the grievance procedures specified in the collective bargaining agreement, prior to seeking judicial review.[64] Pursuing an administrative hearing promotes resolution of a controversy at the agency level. Furthermore, if the issue is ultimately submitted for judicial review, the court has the benefit of the agency's findings and conclusions. Exhaustion is not required, however, if administrative review would be futile or inadequate. For example, the Connecticut Supreme Court reasoned that seeking an administrative remedy would have been futile for a principal who had been constructively discharged (forced to resign by the superintendent). Since the principal had not been discharged on statutory grounds, an administrative hearing could not grant the relief sought by the principal.[65]

Various elements of due process proceedings may be contested as inadequate. Questions arise regarding issues such as the sufficiency of notice, impartiality of the board members, and placement of the burden of proof. The aspects of procedural due process that courts frequently scrutinize in assessing the fundamental fairness of school board actions are examined next.

Notice

In general, a constitutionally adequate notice is timely, informs the teacher of specific charges, and allows the teacher sufficient time to prepare a response.[66] Beyond the constitutional guarantees, state laws and regulations as well as school board policies usually impose very specific requirements relating to form, timeliness, and content of

---

62. *See, e.g.,* Spainhour v. Dover Pub. Sch. Dist., 958 S.W.2d 528 (Ark. 1998).

63. *See, e.g.,* Osteen v. Henley, 13 F.3d 221 (7th Cir. 1993); Ray v. Birmingham City Bd. of Educ., 845 F.2d 281 (11th Cir. 1988); Goodrich v. Newport News Sch. Bd., 743 F.2d 225 (4th Cir. 1984). *But see* Levitt v. Univ. of Tex. at El Paso, 759 F.2d 1224 (5th Cir. 1985) (holding that under certain circumstances, a constitutional deprivation might occur when an omission of state or local procedures results in a denial of the minimal constitutional procedures).

64. *See, e.g.,* Schuck v. Montegiore Pub. Sch. Dist. No. 1, 626 N.W.2d 698 (N.D. 2001).

65. Mendillo v. Bd. of Educ., 717 A.2d 1177 (Conn. 1998).

66. *See, e.g.,* Farley v. Bd. of Educ., 365 S.E.2d 816 (W. Va. 1988) (finding that notice of termination received by teachers one to two days prior to the hearing date set by the school board was not a "meaningful notice" to prepare for a hearing).

notice.[67] In legal challenges, the adequacy of a notice is assessed in terms of whether it meets constitutional as well as other requirements. Failure to comply substantially with mandated requisites will void school board action.

The form or substance of notice is usually stipulated in statutes. In determining appropriateness of notice, courts generally have held that substantial compliance with form requirements (as opposed to strict compliance required for notice deadlines) is sufficient. Under this standard, the decisive factor is whether the notice adequately informs the teacher of the pending action rather than the actual form of the notice. For example, if a statute requires notification by certified mail and the notice is mailed by registered mail or is personally delivered, it substantially complies with the state requirement. However, oral notification will not suffice if the law requires written notification. If the form of the notice is not specified in statute, any timely notice that informs a teacher is adequate.

Although form and timeliness are important concerns in issuing a notice, the primary consideration is the statement of reasons for an action. With termination of a teacher's contract, school boards must bring specific charges against the teacher, including not only the factual basis for the charges but also the names of accusers.[68] State laws may impose further specifications, such as North Dakota's requirement that reasons for termination in the notice must be based on issues raised in prior written evaluations.[69] If the state law identifies grounds for dismissal, charges also must be based on the statutory causes. But a teacher cannot be forced to defend against vague and indefinite charges that simply restate the statutory categories, such as incompetency or neglect of duty. Notice must include specific accusations to enable the teacher to prepare a proper defense. To illustrate, the Supreme Court of Nebraska held that a listing of statutory causes and witnesses did not inform the teacher of the factual allegations underlying the charges.[70] A Missouri appellate court found charges, such as poor organization and failure to seek remediation, to lack the specificity a teacher needed to rebut the charges.[71] Similarly, a federal district court found

---

67. *See, e.g.,* Stills v. Ala. State Tenure Comm'n, 718 So. 2d 1145 (Ala. Civ. App. 1998) (holding that when a statute specified that notice must be received by the last day of the school term, receipt of a notice three days later was inadequate); Clark County Sch. Dist. v. Riley, 14 P.3d 22 (Nev. 2000) (finding that only four days' notice with no mention of the right to a hearing violated a statute requiring 15 days' notice and the right to a hearing); Morrison v. Bd. of Educ., 47 P.3d 888 (Okla. Civ. App. 2002) (ruling that notice did not conform to statutory requirements; notice was sent by the superintendent rather than the school board and it was received on April 10 rather than *prior to* that date).

68. *See, e.g.,* Casada v. Booneville Sch. Dist. No. 65, 686 F. Supp. 730 (W.D. Ark. 1988); Simmons v. New Pub. Sch. Dist. No. Eight, 574 N.W.2d 561 (N.D. 1998). *But see* Johanson v. Bd. of Educ., 589 N.W.2d 815 (Neb. 1999) (holding that due process did not require a school district to provide a summary of the nature of the testimony of each witness).

69. Hoffner v. Bismarck Pub. Sch. Dist., 589 N.W.2d 195 (N.D. 1999). *See also* Boss v. Fillmore Sch. Dist. No. 19, 559 N.W.2d 448 (Neb. 1997) (ruling that prior to termination of a superintendent's contract, mandated statutory evaluations must be completed with an opportunity to correct noted deficiencies).

70. Benton v. Bd. of Educ., 361 N.W.2d 515 (Neb. 1985).

71. Jefferson Consol. Sch. Dist. C-123 v. Carden, 772 S.W.2d 753 (Mo. Ct. App. 1989).

that conclusory statements identifying the teacher's need to improve and ways to improve failed to provide adequate notice.[72] In some instances, state law may further require that the notice delineate the nexus between the teacher's conduct and responsibilities and duties as a teacher. Finally, only charges identified in the notice can form the basis for dismissal.[73]

Hearing

In addition to notice, some type of hearing is required *before* an employer makes the initial termination decision; posttermination hearings do not satisfy federal constitutional due process requirements. In a significant 1985 decision, *Cleveland Board of Education v. Loudermill,* the United States Supreme Court recognized the necessity for some kind of a pretermination hearing. Although the Court emphasized that a full evidentiary hearing to resolve the propriety of the discharge is not required, an initial hearing must be provided to serve as a check against wrong decisions.[74] This would entail determining if there are reasonable grounds to believe that the charges are true and that they support the dismissal. Essentially, in such a pretermination hearing, an employee is entitled to notice of the charges and evidence as well as an opportunity to respond, orally or in writing, as to why the proposed action should not be taken. If only the minimal pretermination procedures outlined by the Supreme Court are provided, a full evidentiary posttermination hearing is required.[75] Even extenuating circumstances involving severe disruption to the educational process cannot justify the omission of a preliminary determination. Under emergency conditions, however, teachers can be suspended with pay pending a termination hearing.[76]

Courts have not prescribed in detail the procedures to be followed in administrative hearings. Basically, the fundamental constitutional requirement is fair play—that is, an opportunity to be heard at a meaningful time and in a meaningful manner. Beyond this general requirement, the specific aspects of a hearing are influenced by

---

72. Wagner v. Little Rock Sch. Dist., 373 F. Supp. 876 (E.D. Ark. 1973). *See also* Stein v. Bd. of Educ., 792 F.2d 13 (2d Cir. 1986) (finding that notice specifying only date and time was inadequate).

73. *See, e.g.,* McDaniel v. Princeton City Sch. Dist. Bd. of Educ., 72 F. Supp. 2d 874 (S.D. Ohio 1999); Simmons v. New Pub. Sch. Dist. No. Eight, 574 N.W.2d 561 (N.D. 1998); Allen v. Texarkana Pub. Schs., 794 S.W.2d 138 (Ark. 1990); Farris v. Burke County Bd. of Educ., 544 S.E.2d 578 (N.C. Ct. App. 2001).

74. 470 U.S. 532 (1985). *See also* Coleman v. Reed, 147 F.3d 751 (8th Cir. 1998); Flath v. Garrison Pub. Sch. Dist. No. 51, 82 F.3d 244 (8th Cir. 1996); Fields v. Durham, 909 F.2d 94 (4th Cir. 1990).

75. *See, e.g.,* Vukadinovich v. Bd. of Sch. Trs., 978 F.2d 403 (7th Cir. 1992) (holding that a discharged teacher is not entitled to a postdeprivation hearing in addition to a full predeprivation hearing).

76. *But see* Gilbert v. Homar, 520 U.S. 924 (1997) (ruling that a temporary suspension *without* pay of an employee charged with a felony does not require a pretermination hearing when an employee occupies a position of great public trust); Mustafa v. Clark County Sch. Dist., 157 F.3d 1169 (9th Cir. 1998) (finding that a teacher who was suspended without pay for alleged sexual misconduct was not entitled to a hearing prior to suspension when he was promptly provided a hearing five days after the suspension).

the circumstances of the case, with the potential for grievous losses necessitating more extensive safeguards. According to the Missouri Supreme Court, a hearing generally should include a meaningful opportunity to be heard, to state one's position, to present witnesses, and to cross-examine witnesses; the accused also has the right to counsel and access to written reports in advance of the hearing.[77] Implicit in these rudimentary requirements are the assumptions that the hearing will be conducted by an impartial decision maker and will result in a decision based on the evidence presented. This section examines issues that may arise in adversarial hearings before the school board.

Adequate Notice of Hearing. As noted, due process rights afford an individual the opportunity to be heard at a meaningful time. This implies sufficient time between notice of the hearing and the scheduled meeting. Unless state law designates a time period, the school board can establish a reasonable date for the hearing, taking into consideration the specific facts and circumstances. In a termination action, the school board would be expected to provide ample time for the teacher to prepare a defense; however, the teacher bears the burden of requesting additional time if the length of notice is insufficient to prepare an adequate response. A notice as short as two days was upheld as satisfying due process requirements where the teacher participated in the hearing and did not object to the time or request a postponement.[78] Similarly, a one-day notice was found constitutionally sufficient when the teacher did not attend the meeting to raise objections.[79] A teacher who participates fully in the hearing process or waives the right to a hearing by failure to attend cannot later assert "lack of adequate time" to invalidate the due process proceedings.

Waiver of Hearing. Although a hearing is an essential element of due process, a teacher can waive this right by failing to request a hearing, refusing to attend it, or walking out of the hearing.[80] Voluntary resignation of a position also waives an individual's entitlement to a hearing.[81] In some states, a hearing before the school board

---

77. Valter v. Orchard Farm Sch. Dist., 541 S.W.2d 550 (Mo. 1976). *See also* McClure v. Indep. Sch. Dist. No. 16, 228 F.3d 1205 (10th Cir. 2000) (holding that a teacher was deprived of due process rights when she was not allowed to cross-examine witnesses who provided testimony by affidavit at a termination hearing); Elmore v. Plainview-Old Bethpage Cent., 708 N.Y.S.2d 713 (App. Div. 2000) (concluding that a teacher's due process rights were violated when the hearing officer forbid him to consult with his attorney during breaks in cross-examination).

78. Ahern v. Bd. of Educ., 456 F.2d 399 (8th Cir. 1972).

79. Birdwell v. Hazelwood Sch. Dist., 491 F.2d 490 (8th Cir. 1974).

80. *See, e.g.,* Conward v. Cambridge Sch. Comm., 171 F.3d 12 (1st Cir. 1999); Boner v. Eminence R-1 Sch. Dist., 55 F.3d 1339 (8th Cir. 1995); Cliff v. Bd. of Sch. Comm'rs, 42 F.3d 403 (7th Cir. 1994); Schuck v. Montefiore Pub. Sch. Dist. No. 1, 626 N.W.2d 698 (N.D. 2001); Rich v. Montpelier Supervisory Dist., 709 A.2d 501 (Vt. 1998). *See also* McKnight v. Sch. Dist. of Phila., 171 F. Supp. 2d 446 (E.D. Pa. 2001) (holding that a teacher's right to hearing was not violated when he attended but refused to participate; the school board needed only to provide an opportunity for a hearing).

81. *See, e.g.,* Lighton v. Univ. of Utah, 209 F.3d 1213 (10th Cir. 2000); Upshaw v. Alvin Indep. Sch. Dist., 31 F. Supp. 2d 553 (S.D. Tex. 1999).

may be waived by an employee's election of an alternative hearing procedure, such as a grievance mechanism or an impartial referee. For example, the Third Circuit held that an employee's choice of *either* a hearing before the school board or arbitration under the collective bargaining agreement met the constitutional requirements of due process; the school board was not required to provide the individual a hearing in addition to the arbitration proceeding.[82] Similarly, an Ohio federal district court ruled that a teacher who selected a hearing before an impartial referee was not entitled to be heard by the school board prior to its decision on the referee's report.[83]

Impartial Hearing.   A central question raised regarding hearings is the school board's impartiality as a hearing body. This issue arises because school boards often perform multiple functions in a hearing; they may investigate the allegations against a teacher, initiate the proceedings, and render the final judgment. Teachers have contended that such expansive involvement violates their right to an unbiased decision maker. Rejecting the idea that combining the adjudicative and investigative functions violates due process rights, courts generally have determined that prior knowledge of the facts does not disqualify school board members.[84] In addition, the fact that the board makes the initial decision to terminate employment does not render subsequent review impermissibly biased. Neither is a hearing prejudiced by a limited, preliminary inquiry to determine if there is a basis for terminating a teacher. Since hearings are costly and time consuming, such a preliminary investigation may save time as well as potential embarrassment.

In *Hortonville Joint School District No. 1 v. Hortonville Education Association*, the United States Supreme Court firmly established that the school board is a proper review body to conduct dismissal hearings.[85] The Court held that a school board's involvement in collective negotiations did not disqualify it as an impartial hearing board in the subsequent dismissal of striking teachers. The Court noted that "a showing that the Board was 'involved' in the events preceding this decision, in light of the important interest in leaving with the board the power given by the state legislature, is not enough to overcome the presumption of honesty and integrity in policymakers with decision-making power."[86]

Although the school board is the proper hearing body, bias on the part of the board or its members is constitutionally unacceptable. A teacher challenging the

---

82. Pederson v. S. Williamsport Area Sch. Dist., 677 F.2d 312 (3d Cir. 1982).

83. Jones v. Morris, 541 F. Supp. 11 (S.D. Ohio 1981), *aff'd,* 455 U.S. 1009 (1982).

84. *See, e.g.,* Withrow v. Larkin, 421 U.S. 35 (1975). *See also* Yukadinovich v. Bd. of Sch. Trs., 278 F.3d 693 (7th Cir. 2002) (concluding that a teacher did not establish bias in a termination hearing held in front of the school board that he had publicly criticized); Moore v. Bd. of Educ., 134 F.3d 781 (6th Cir. 1998) (finding that a superintendent's dual roles as presiding officer at the hearing and investigator did not deprive a teacher of due process).

85. 426 U.S. 482 (1976).

86. *Id.* at 496-497.

impartiality of the board has the burden of proving actual, not merely potential, bias. This requires the teacher to show more than board members' pre-decision involvement or prior knowledge of the issues.[87] A high probability of bias, however, can be shown if a board member has a personal interest in the outcome of the hearing or has suffered personal abuse or criticism from a teacher.

Several cases illustrate instances of unacceptable bias. For example, the Alabama Supreme Court invalidated a teacher termination hearing for "intolerably high bias" created by a school board member's son testifying against the teacher; the son had been the target of alleged personal abuse by the teacher.[88] The Tenth Circuit also ruled that bias was shown in the termination of a superintendent because one of the board members had campaigned to remove the superintendent from his position, and two other board members had made unfavorable statements to the effect that the superintendent "had to go."[89] The Iowa Supreme Court concluded that a school board's role of "investigation, instigation, prosecution, and verdict rendering" denied a teacher an impartial hearing, since the board used no witnesses and relied solely on its personal knowledge of the case in reaching a decision.[90] A lack of impartiality or inferences of partiality may include board members testifying as witnesses, prior announcements by board members of views and positions showing closed minds, and board members assuming adversarial or prosecutorial roles.[91]

An individual serving as prosecutor and as advisor or counsel to the board may impair due process rights. The Supreme Court of Colorado cautioned that "not only is actual fairness mandated, but the integrity of the administrative process also requires that the appearance of fairness be preserved."[92] In this case, the court found that the presence of the superintendent and principal (who initiated the charges and served as

---

87. *See, e.g.*, Sekor v. Bd. of Educ., 689 A.2d 1112 (Conn. 1997); Felder v. Charleston County Sch. Dist., 489 S.E.2d 191 (S.C. 1997). *But see* Crump v. Bd. of Educ., 378 S.E.2d 32 (N.C. Ct. App. 1989), *aff'd*, 392 S.E.2d 579 (N.C. 1990) (ruling that prehearing knowledge of the board members coupled with denial of such knowledge at the hearing substantiated impermissible bias).

88. *Ex parte* Greenberg v. Ala. State Tenure Comm'n, 395 So. 2d 1000 (Ala. 1981). *See also* Katruska v. Dep't of Educ., 727 A.2d 612 (Pa. Commw. Ct. 1999) (concluding that the testimony of a board member's wife against her principal created the appearance of bias in a hearing). *But see* Danroth v. Mandaree Pub. Sch. Dist. No. 36, 320 N.W.2d 780 (N.D. 1982) (holding that a teacher was not denied fair and proper hearing even though a board member's wife was the primary critic).

89. Staton v. Mayes, 552 F.2d 908 (10th Cir. 1977). *But see* Welch v. Barham, 635 F.2d 1322 (8th Cir. 1980) (finding that statements by two board members at trial that they could not think of any evidence that would have changed their minds about terminating the individual did not show the degree of bias necessary to disqualify a decision maker).

90. Keith v. Cmty. Sch. Dist., 262 N.W.2d 249, 260 (Iowa 1978).

91. *See, e.g.*, McClure v. Indep. Sch. Dist. No. 16, 228 F.3d 1205 (10th Cir. 2000); Cook v. Bd. of Educ., 671 F. Supp. 1110 (S.D. W.Va. 1987); Buckner v. Sch. Bd., 718 So. 2d 862 (Fla. Dist. Ct. App. 1998); Johnson v. Pulaski County Bd. of Educ., 499 S.E.2d 345 (Ga. Ct. App. 1998); Riter v. Woonsocket Sch. Dist. #55-4, 504 N.W.2d 572 (S.D. 1993).

92. deKoevend v. Bd. of Educ., 688 P.2d 219, 228 (Colo. 1984).

witnesses) during the board's closed deliberations undermined the appearance of impartiality. In addition, a school board's legal counsel serving both prosecutorial and advisory roles may create an unacceptable risk of bias or appearance of prejudice.[93] Likewise, such a situation may be created when a hearing officer and the board's counsel are from the same law firm.[94]

Evidence.   Under teacher tenure laws, the burden of proof is placed on the school board to show cause for dismissal. The standard of proof generally applied to administrative bodies is to produce a "preponderance of evidence" or "substantial evidence."[95] Administrative hearings are not held to the more stringent standards applied in criminal proceedings (i.e., clear and convincing evidence beyond a reasonable doubt). Proof by a preponderance of evidence simply indicates that the majority of the evidence supports the board's decision or, as the New York high court stated, "such relevant evidence as a reasonable mind might accept as adequate to support a conclusion."[96] If the board fails to meet this burden of proof, the judiciary will not uphold the termination decision. For example, the Nebraska Supreme Court, in overturning a school board's dismissal decision, concluded that dissatisfaction of parents and school board members was not sufficient evidence to substantiate incompetency charges against a teacher who had received above-average performance evaluations during her entire term of employment.[97]

The objective of school board hearings is to ascertain the relevant facts of the situation; the board hears evidence from both the teacher and the district officials recommending termination.[98] These hearings are not encumbered by technical, judicial rules of evidence even if charges also carry criminal liability. Termination proceedings are separate from the criminal proceedings, and, as such, dismissal might be warranted based on the evidence presented, even though such evidence would not satisfy the more stringent requirements to sustain a criminal conviction. For example, a

93. *See, e.g., Buckner,* 718 So. 2d 882. *But see* Vukadinovich v. Bd. of Sch. Trs., 978 F.2d 403 (7th Cir. 1992) (finding that a school board's attorney presiding at the hearing did not create unacceptable bias; the attorney did not participate in board deliberations); Holley v. Seminole County Sch. Dist., 755 F.2d 1492 (11th Cir. 1985) (concluding that the board's attorney was permitted to sit as hearing examiner).

94. *See, e.g.,* Hagerty v. State Tenure Comm'n, 445 N.W.2d 178 (Mich. Ct. App. 1989) (holding that no bias existed because the hearing officer and board attorney worked for the same law firm; however, the court alerted the state bar association that if a similar situation occurs in the future, a *per se* rule of reversal would be adopted because of the potential for prejudice).

95. *See, e.g.,* Lacks v. Ferguson Reorganized Sch. Dist. R-2, 147 F.3d 718 (8th Cir. 1998); Harris v. Canton Separate Pub. Sch. Bd. of Educ., 655 So. 2d 898 (Miss. 1995); *In re* Termination of Kibbe, 996 P.2d 419 (N.M. 1999); Felder v. Charleston County Sch. Dist., 489 S.E.2d 191 (S.C. 1997).

96. Altsheler v. Bd. of Educ., 476 N.Y.S.2d 281, 281 (1984). *See also* Johanson v. Bd. of Educ., 589 N.W.2d 815 (Neb. 1999).

97. Schulz v. Bd. of Educ., 315 N.W.2d 633 (Neb. 1982).

98. *See, e.g.,* Wuest v. Winner Sch. Dist. 59-2, 607 N.W.2d 912 (S.D. 2000).

teacher could be dismissed on evidence of drug use, even though criminal charges are dropped due to a defective search warrant.

Only relevant, well-documented evidence presented at the hearing can be the basis for the board's decision.[99] Unlike formal judicial proceedings, hearsay evidence may be admissible in administrative hearings.[100] Courts have held that such evidence provides the background necessary for understanding the situation. Comments and complaints of parents have been considered relevant, but hearsay statements of students generally have been given little weight.[101]

Findings of Fact. At the conclusion of the hearing, the board must make specific findings of fact. A written report of the findings on which the board based its decision is essential. Without a report of the findings of fact, appropriate administrative or judicial review would be impeded. The Minnesota Supreme Court noted that "if the trial court were to review the merits of the case without findings of fact, there would be no safeguard against judicial encroachment on the school board's function since the trial court might affirm on a charge rejected by the school board."[102] Similarly, the Oklahoma Supreme Court held that a probationary teacher's statutory entitlement to a hearing includes the right to know the rationale for the board's decision. The court admonished that "an absence of required findings is fatal to the validity of administrative decisions even if the record discloses evidence to support proper findings."[103] The findings of fact need not be issued in technical language but simply in a form that explains the reasons for the action.

If an independent panel or hearing officer conducts the hearing, the school board is bound by the panel's findings of fact but can accept or reject the panel's conclusions and recommendations.[104] Accordingly, the board can decide to terminate an individual who has been supported by the panel as long as the board bases its decision on the evidence included in the panel's factual findings.

---

99. *See, e.g.,* Goldberg v. Kelly, 397 U.S. 254, 271 (1970). *See also* Arriola v. Orleans Parish Sch. Bd., 809 So. 2d 932 (La. 2002) (finding that a teacher was afforded adequate due process in termination for drug use even though he was not able to cross-examine the laboratory technician who conducted the chemical analysis).

100. *See, e.g.,* Rogers v. Bd. of Educ., 749 A.2d 1173 (Conn. 2000); Hierllmeier v. N. Judson-San Pierre Bd., 730 N.E.2d 821 (Ind. Ct. App. 2000); Doty v. Tupelo Pub. Sch. Dist., 751 So. 2d 1212 (Miss. Ct. App. 1999).

101. *See, e.g.,* Daily v. Bd. of Educ., 588 N.W.2d 813 (Neb. 1999).

102. Morey v. Sch. Bd., 128 N.W.2d 302, 307 (Minn. 1964). *See also* Barnett v. Bd. of Educ., 654 A.2d 720 (Conn. 1995).

103. Jackson v. Indep. Sch. Dist. No. 16, 648 P.2d 26, 31 (Okla. 1982).

104. *See, e.g.,* Rogers v. Bd. of Educ., 749 A.2d 1173 (Conn. 2000); Farris v. Burke County Bd. of Educ., 544 S.E.2d 578 (N.C. Ct. App. 2001); Oleske v. Hilliard City Sch. Dist. 764 N.E.2d 1110 (Ohio Ct. App. 2001); Montgomery Indep. Sch. Dist. v. Davis, 34 S.W.3d 559 (Tex. 2000).

Dismissal for Cause

Tenure laws are designed to assure competent teachers continued employment as long as their performance is satisfactory. With the protection of tenure, a teacher can be dismissed only for cause, and only in accordance with the procedures specified by law. Tenure rights accrue under state laws and therefore must be interpreted in light of each state's provisions.

Where grounds for dismissal of a permanent teacher are identified by statute, a school board cannot base dismissal on reasons other than those specified. To cover unexpected matters, statutes often include a catch-all phrase such as "other good and just cause." Causes included in statutes vary considerably among states and range from an extensive listing of individual grounds to a simple statement that dismissal must be based on cause. The most frequently cited causes are incompetency, immorality, insubordination, and neglect of duty.

Since grounds for dismissal are determined by statute, it is difficult to provide generalizations for all teachers. The causes are broad in scope and application; in fact, individual causes often have been attacked for impermissible vagueness. It is not unusual to find dismissal cases with similar factual situations based on different grounds. In addition, a number of grounds often are introduced and supported in a single termination case. Illustrative case law is examined here in relation to the more frequently cited grounds for dismissal. Claims that dismissals impair constitutional rights are discussed in Chapter 9.

Incompetency

Courts have broadly defined *incompetency*. Although it usually refers to classroom performance, it has been extended in some instances to a teacher's private life. The term is legally defined as "lack of ability, legal qualifications, or fitness to discharge the required duty."[105] Although incompetency has been challenged as unconstitutionally vague, courts have found the term sufficiently precise to give fair warning of prohibited conduct. Incompetency cases often involve issues relating to teaching methods, grading procedures, classroom management, and professional relationships.

In general, dismissals for incompetency are based on a number of factors or a pattern of behavior rather than isolated incidents. In a Minnesota case, indicators of incompetency included poor rapport with students, inappropriate use of class time, irrational grading of students, and lack of student progress.[106] A Pennsylvania court interpreted incompetency as deficiencies in personality, composure, judgment, and attitude that have a detrimental effect on a teacher's performance.[107] Incompetency in this case was supported by evidence that the teacher was a disruptive influence in the

---

105. Henry Black, *Black's Law Dictionary*, 7th ed. (St. Paul, MN: West Publishing, 1999).

106. Whaley v. Anoka-Hennepin Indep. Sch. Dist. No. 11, 325 N.W.2d 128 (Minn. 1982). *See also* Saunders v. Anderson, 746 S.W.2d 185 (Tenn. 1987).

107. Hamburg v. N. Penn Sch. Dist., 484 A.2d 867 (Pa. Commw. Ct. 1984).

school; could not maintain control of students; and failed to maintain her composure in dealing with students, other professionals, and parents.

Dismissals for incompetency have included a wide range of charges and occasionally have involved only a single incident. To illustrate, dismissals have been upheld for incompetency where a teacher brandished a starter pistol in an attempt to gain control of a group of students[108] and an assistant principal permitted teachers to conduct a strip search of a fifth- and sixth-grade physical education class against explicit board policy.[109] A Louisiana court of appeals, however, held that a social studies teacher could not be dismissed for showing two R-rated movies; the court viewed the penalty as too harsh for a teacher with a 14-year unblemished teaching record.[110] Similarly, the South Dakota high court did not find a teacher's indiscreet answer to a fourth-grader's question about homosexual activity following a sex education video to be the type of "habitual and ongoing action" needed to support a charge of incompetency.[111]

Frequently, school boards have based charges of incompetency on teachers' lack of proper classroom management and control. Such dismissals have been contested on the grounds that the penalty of discharge was too severe for the offense. Courts have generally held that school boards have latitude in determining penalties, and their decisions will be overturned only if disproportionate to the offense. As long as evidence is presented to substantiate the board's charge, poor classroom management can result in termination.[112]

Immorality

Immorality, one of the most frequently cited causes for dismissal, is generally not defined in state laws. In defining the term, the judiciary has tended to interpret *immorality* broadly as unacceptable conduct that affects a teacher's fitness. Traditionally, the teacher has been viewed as an exemplar whose conduct is influential in shaping the lives of young students.

Sexually related conduct *per se* between a teacher and student has consistently been held to constitute immoral conduct justifying termination of employment. The Supreme Court of Colorado stated that when a teacher engages in sexually provocative or exploitative conduct with students, "a strong presumption of unfitness arises against

---

108. Myres v. Orleans Parish Sch. Bd., 423 So. 2d 1303 (La. Ct. App. 1983).

109. Rogers v. Bd. of Educ., 749 A.2d 1173 (Conn. 2000).

110. West v. Tangipahoa Parish Sch. Bd., 615 So. 2d 979 (La. Ct. App. 1993).

111. Collins v. Faith Sch. Dist. No. 46-2, 574 N.W.2d 889, 893 (S.D. 1998). *See also In re* Termination of Kibbe, 996 P.2d 419 (N.M. 1999) (ruling that a school board did not provide substantial evidence to show that a teacher's arrest for driving under the influence of alcohol was rationally related to his competence to teach).

112. *See, e.g.,* Jones v. Jefferson Parish Sch. Bd., 688 F.2d 837 (5th Cir. 1982); Linstad v. Sitka Sch. Dist., 963 P.2d 246 (Alaska 1998); Bd. of Educ. v. Kushner, 530 A.2d 541 (Pa. Commw. Ct. 1987).

the teacher."[113] Similarly, a Washington appellate court found that a male teacher's sexual relationship with a minor student justified dismissal.[114] The court declined to hold that an adverse effect on fitness to teach must be shown. Rather, the court concluded that when a teacher and a minor student are involved, the board might reasonably decide that such conduct is harmful to the school district. An Illinois appellate court, however, noted that damage to the students, faculty, or the school must be shown; the fondling of third-grade female students by a male teacher presented such damage.[115]

Teachers discharged for sexually related conduct have challenged the statutory grounds of "immorality" or "immoral conduct" as impermissibly vague. An Alabama teacher, dismissed for sexual advances toward female students, asserted that the term *immorality* did not adequately warn a teacher as to what behavior would constitute an offense. The court acknowledged the lack of clarity but rejected the teacher's contention, reasoning that his behavior fell "squarely within the hard core of the statute's proscriptions."[116] The court noted that the teacher should have been aware that his conduct was improper, and the claim of vagueness or overbreadth could not invalidate his dismissal. A Missouri federal district court conceded that the term *immoral conduct* is abstract, but, when construed in the overall statutory scheme, can be precisely defined as any conduct rendering a teacher unfit to teach.[117]

Sexual harassment involving inappropriate comments, touching, and teasing may result in termination for immorality.[118] The West Virginia high court upheld the termination of a teacher for repeated comments of a sexual nature to students; the comments had continued in spite of warnings to desist.[119] Similarly, the Supreme Court of Missouri supported a board's dismissal of a teacher for sexual harassment of the only female member of his class and for permitting male students also to harass her.[120]

---

113. Weissman v. Bd. of Educ., 547 P.2d 1267, 1273 (Colo. 1976). *See also* Hamm v. Poplar Bluff R-1 Sch. Dist., 955 S.W.2d 27 (Mo. Ct. App. 1997); *In re* Morrill, 765 A.2d 699 (N.H. 2001); Andrews v. Indep. Sch. Dist. No. 57, 12 P.3d 491 (Okla. Civ. App. 2000); Strain v. Rapid City Sch. Bd., 447 N.W.2d 332 (S.D. 1989).

114. Denton v. S. Kitsap Sch. Dist. No. 402, 516 P.2d 1080 (Wash. Ct. App. 1973). *See also* DeMichele v. Greenburgh Cent. Sch. Dist. No. 7, 167 F.3d 784 (2d Cir. 1999) (ruling that termination of a teacher for sexual misconduct with students occurring 24 years earlier did not violate his due process rights).

115. Fadler v. Ill. State Bd. of Educ., 506 N.E.2d 640 (Ill. App. Ct. 1987). *But see* Youngman v. Doerhoff, 890 S.W.2d 330 (Mo. Ct. App. 1994) (concluding that a male teacher's hugging of a 14-year-old male student was motivated by caring and concern, not by a sexual motive substantiating immoral conduct).

116. Kilpatrick v. Wright, 437 F. Supp. 397, 399 (M.D. Ala. 1977).

117. Thompson v. Southwest Sch. Dist., 483 F. Supp. 1170 (W.D. Mo. 1980).

118. *See* text accompanying note 158, Chapter 8, and notes 88–99, Chapter 10, for further discussion of sexual harassment.

119. Harry v. Marion County Bd. of Educ., 506 S.E.2d 319 (W. Va. 1998). *See also* Forte v. Mills, 672 N.Y.S.2d 497 (App. Div. 1998) (ruling that a teacher's inappropriate touching of fourth- and fifth-grade girls was sexually harassing conduct justifying termination for insubordination and conduct unbecoming to a teacher; he had received repeated warnings to desist).

120. Ross v. Robb, 662 S.W.2d 257 (Mo. 1983).

In addition to sexual improprieties with students, which clearly are grounds for dismissal, other conduct that sets a bad example for students may be considered immoral under the "role model" standard. Courts, however, generally have required school officials to show that misconduct or a particular lifestyle has an adverse impact on fitness to teach. They have recognized that allowing dismissal merely upon a showing of immoral behavior without consideration of the nexus between the conduct and fitness to teach would be an unwarranted intrusion on a teacher's right to privacy. For example, an Ohio appellate court found that school officials had not produced evidence to show that an adulterous affair with another school employee constituted immorality when it did not have a hostile impact on the school community.[121]

Teacher homosexuality has been an issue in several controversial dismissal cases. Although these cases often have raised constitutional issues related to freedom of expression and privacy, courts also have confronted the question of whether homosexuality *per se* is evidence of unfitness to teach or whether it must be shown that this lifestyle impairs teaching effectiveness.[122] Teachers, like other citizens, can be prosecuted for violating antisodomy laws;[123] diverse opinions, however, have been rendered by courts regarding the status of homosexual teachers when criminal charges are not involved. According to the Supreme Court of California, immoral or unprofessional conduct or moral turpitude must be related to unfitness to teach to justify termination.[124] Consequently, the school board must be cautious in dismissing an employee simply because it does not approve of a particular private lifestyle.

Whereas any dismissals for immorality involve sexual conduct, immorality is broader in meaning and scope. As one court noted, it covers conduct that "is hostile to the welfare of the school community."[125] Such hostile conduct has included, among other things, dishonest acts, criminal conduct, and drug-related conduct. The following cases reflect the range of misconduct resulting in charges of immorality.

Engaging in criminal conduct may constitute immorality justifying dismissal. For example, Alaska statutes define *immorality* as "an act which, under the laws of the

---

121. Bertolini v. Whitehall City Sch. Dist. Bd. of Educ., 744 N.E.2d 1245 (Ohio Ct. App. 2000). *But see* Parker-Bigback v. St. Labre Sch., 7 P.3d 361 (Mont. 2000) (upholding termination of a counselor for cohabitation with a man to whom she was not married; the court emphasized that termination did not violate the state constitution's prohibition against discrimination based on various characteristics, such as marital status, since decision was based on conduct violating Roman Catholic Church's teachings).

122. *See* text accompanying note 109, Chapter 10, for a discussion of claims of discrimination based on sexual orientation.

123. *See, e.g.,* Bowers v. Hardwick, 478 U.S. 186 (1986).

124. Morrison v. State Bd. of Educ., 461 P.2d 375 (Cal. 1969). *See also* Sch. Comm. v. Civil Serv. Comm'n, 684 N.E.2d 620 (Mass. App. Ct. 1997). *But see* Rowland v. Mad River Local Sch. Dist., 730 F.2d 444 (6th Cir. 1984) (upholding the nonrenewal of a guidance counselor who revealed her homosexuality); text with note 217, Chapter 9.

125. Jarvella v. Willoughby-Eastlake City Sch. Dist., 233 N.E.2d 143, 145 (Ohio 1967).

state, constitutes a crime involving moral turpitude."[126] The state high court held that a conviction for unlawfully diverting electricity was such a crime. Under Georgia law, conviction for submitting false tax documents was sufficient grounds to dismiss a principal for moral turpitude.[127] Other dishonest conduct found to substantiate charges of immorality includes misrepresenting absences from school as illness,[128] being involved in the sale of illegal drugs,[129] possessing cocaine,[130] and instructing a student to lie and cheat during a wrestling tournament.[131] In the absence of a statutory specification, however, the West Virginia Supreme Court held that a school board could not conclude that a conviction for a misdemeanor was *per se* immoral conduct.[132] A Pennsylvania court held that a conviction for a summary offense—threatening an individual—did not substantiate immoral conduct; the court cautioned that not all unprofessional conduct is automatically immoral conduct.[133]

Insubordination

Insubordination, another frequently cited cause for dismissal, is generally defined as the willful disregard of or refusal to obey school regulations and official orders. Teachers can be dismissed for violation of administrative regulations and policies even though classroom performance is satisfactory; school officials are not required to establish a relationship between the conduct and fitness to teach.

With the plethora of regulations enacted by school districts, wide diversity is found in types of behavior adjudicated as insubordination. Dismissals based on insubordination have been upheld in cases involving refusal to abide by specific school directives, unwillingness to cooperate with superiors, unauthorized absences, and numerous other actions. Since conduct is measured against the existence of a rule or

126. *See* Kenai Peninsula Borough Bd. of Educ. v. Brown, 691 P.2d 1034, 1036 (Alaska 1984). *See also* Toney v. Fairbanks N. Star Borough Sch. Dist., Bd. of Educ., 881 P.2d 1112 (Alaska 1994) (finding that a teacher's sexual relationship with a 15-year-old student occurring prior to his employment by the school district was a crime of moral turpitude supporting termination; the court commented that it is questionable whether such a crime could ever be too remote to be considered in determining a teacher's fitness to teach).

127. Logan v. Warren County Bd. of Educ., 549 F. Supp. 145 (S.D. Ga. 1982).

128. Riverview Sch. Dist. v. Riverview Educ. Ass'n, 639 A.2d 974 (Pa. Commw. Ct. 1994). *See also* Dohanic v. Commonwealth Dep't of Educ., 533 A.2d 812 (Pa. Commw. Ct. 1987) (holding that lying to school officials constituted immoral conduct).

129. Woo v. Putnam County Bd. of Educ., 504 S.E.2d 644 (W. Va. 1998).

130. Gedney v. Bd. of Educ., 703 A.2d 804 (Conn. App. Ct. 1997).

131. Florian v. Highland Local Sch. Dist. Bd. of Educ., 493 N.E.2d 249 (Ohio Ct. App. 1983).

132. Golden v. Bd. of Educ., 285 S.E.2d 665 (W. Va. 1981) *But see* Zelno v. Lincoln Intermediate Unit No. 12 Bd. of Dirs, 786 A.2d 1022 (Pa. Commw. 2001) (finding that a teacher could be terminated for immoral conduct based on three drunken driving convictions and two convictions for driving without a license).

133. Horton v. Jefferson County-Dubois Area Vocational Technical Sch., 630 A.2d 481 (Pa. Commw. Ct. 1993).

policy, a school board may more readily document insubordination than most other legal causes for dismissal.

Many state laws and court decisions require that acts be "willful and persistent" to be considered insubordinate. A Minnesota teacher's continuous refusal to complete program evaluation forms resulted in insubordination charges. The Minnesota Supreme Court, upholding the dismissal, defined *insubordination* as "constant or continuing intentional refusal to obey a direct or implied order, reasonable in nature, and given by and with proper authority."[134] A severe or substantial single incident may be adequate for dismissal action.[135] The Wyoming Supreme Court found that repeated refusals to obey orders were not required to justify dismissal.[136] The court concluded that termination of a teacher who refused a split assignment between two schools was proper; repeated refusals were unnecessary if other elements of insubordination were present, such as reasonableness of the order and direct refusal to obey. Similarly upheld were a New York teacher's removal of sexual harassment of female students after repeated warnings,[137] a Missouri teacher's termination after she refused to teach an assigned course,[138] and a Colorado teacher's dismissal for showing an R-rated movie without submitting a request for approval under the district's controversial materials policy.[139]

Insubordination charges often have resulted from conflicts arising from the administrator/teacher relationship. For example, a North Carolina teacher's refusal to discontinue a classroom project that the principal and curriculum specialist determined to be lacking in any educational value and her subsequent refusal to develop and implement a professional growth plan supported dismissal.[140] The dismissal of an Arkansas teacher who engaged in frequent belligerent "verbal fights" with his principal was upheld.[141] However, a Tennessee teacher, who was unable to work because of stress, fear, and intimidation resulting from incidents in the school, could not be ter-

---

134. Ray v. Minneapolis Bd. of Educ., 202 N.W.2d 375, 378 (Minn. 1972). *See also* Trimble v. W. Va. Bd. of Dirs., 549 S.E.2d 294 (W. Va. 2001) (concluding that termination for a minor incident of insubordination denied individual constitutional due process; progressive disciplinary sanctions should have been imposed to correct insubordinate conduct prior to termination proceedings).

135. *See, e.g.,* Ware v. Morgan County Sch. Dist., 748 P.2d 1295 (Colo. 1988) (finding one-time use of profanity, after being ordered not to use profanity with students, supported termination); Gaylord v. Bd. of Educ., 794 P.2d 307 (Kan. Ct. App. 1990) (upheld termination of a teacher for taking sick leave after his request for a one-day leave was denied).

136. Bd. of Trs. of Sch. Dist. No. 4 v. Colwell, 611 P.2d 427 (Wyo. 1980). *See also* Gaylord v. Bd. of Educ., Unified Sch. Dist. No. 218, 794 P.2d 307 (Kan. Ct. App. 1990).

137. Forte v. Mills, 672 N.Y.S.2d 497 (App. Div. 1998).

138. McLaughlin v. Bd. of Educ., 659 S.W.2d 249 (Mo. Ct. App. 1983).

139. Bd. of Educ. v. Wilder, 960 P.2d 695 (Colo. 1998). *But see infra* text accompanying note 156.

140. Hope v. Charlotte-Mecklenburg Bd. of Educ., 430 S.E.2d 472 (N.C. Ct. App. 1993).

141. Caldwell v. Blytheville, Ark. Sch. Dist. No. 5, 746 S.W.2d 381 (Ark. Ct. App. 1988). *See also* Yukadinovich v. Bd. of Sch. Trs., 278 F.3d 693 (7th Cir. 2002).

minated for insubordination when she failed to return to work as directed by the superintendent.[142]

Teachers cannot ignore reasonable directives and policies of administrators or
school boards. If the school board has prohibited corporal punishment or prescribed
procedures for its administration, teachers must strictly adhere to board requirements.
In upholding the termination of a Colorado teacher, the state supreme court ruled that
tapping a student on the head with a three-foot pointer supported termination when the
teacher had been warned and disciplined previously for using physical force against
school district policy.[143] Repeatedly failing to follow official directives in administering corporal punishment resulted in the termination of a Texas teacher.[144] The Eleventh Circuit found that insubordination was established when a teacher refused to take
a urinalysis drug test within two hours of the discovery of marijuana in her car in the
school parking lot, as required by school board policy.[145] The Eighth Circuit upheld
the dismissal of a teacher for violating a school board policy that prohibited students'
use of profanity in the classroom; students had used profanity in various creative writing assignments such as plays and poems.[146]

Other instances of failure to follow administrative directives justifying dismissal for insubordination include failing to follow directives designed to improve
instruction, continuing to emphasize sexual aspects of literature, and failing to acquire
board approval of supplementary materials used in the classroom.[147] The key determinant generally is whether the teacher has persisted in disobeying a *reasonable*
school policy or directive.[148]

Neglect of Duty

Neglect of duty arises when an educator fails to carry out assigned duties. This may
involve an intentional omission or may result from ineffectual performance. In a Col-

142. McGhee v. Miller, 753 S.W.2d 354 (Tenn. 1988).

143. Bd. of Educ. v. Flaming, 938 P.2d 151 (Colo. 1997). *See also* Daily v. Bd. of Educ., 588 N.W.2d 813
     (Neb. 1999) (upholding a 30-day suspension for "smacking" a student on the head in violation of a
     state law that prohibited corporal punishment).

144. Burton v. Kirby, 775 S.W.2d 834 (Tex. Ct. App. 1989). *See also* Clark v. Bd. of Dirs., 915 S.W.2d
     766 (Mo. Ct. App. 1996).

145. Hearn v. Bd. of Pub. Educ., 191 F.3d 1329 (11th Cir. 1999).

146. Lacks v. Ferguson Reorganized Sch. Dist. R-2, 147 F.3d 718 (8th Cir. 1998).

147. *See, e.g.,* Fisher v. Fairbanks N. Star Borough Sch., 704 P.2d 213 (Alaska 1985) (supplemental mate-
     rials); *In re* Proposed Termination Johnson, 451 N.W.2d 343 (Minn. Ct. App. 1990) (teaching defi-
     ciencies); *In re* Bernstein and Norwich City Sch. Dist., 726 N.Y.S.2d 474 (App. Div. 2001) (sexual
     aspects of literature); Meckley v. Kanawha County Bd. of Educ., 383 S.E.2d 839 (W. Va. 1989)
     (attendance at meetings).

148. A Tennessee appellate court noted that insubordination cannot be substantiated without an order that
     is disregarded; a principal had discouraged a teacher from entertaining students in his home but had
     not ordered him to cease the activity. Morris v. Clarksville-Montgomery County Consol. Bd. of
     Educ., 867 S.W.2d 324 (Tenn. Ct. App. 1993).

orado case, neglect of duty was found when a teacher failed to discipline students consistent with school policy.[149] A Louisiana appeals court upheld a teacher's discharge for willful neglect of duty after she locked three preschool children with disabilities in a room while attending to chores unrelated to her classroom.[150] The Supreme Court of North Carolina found that a teacher's habitual use of alcohol during the school day supported dismissal.[151]

The United States Supreme Court upheld the dismissal of an Oklahoma teacher for "willful neglect of duty" in failing to comply with the school board's continuing education requirement.[152] For a period of time, lack of compliance was dealt with through denial of salary increases. Upon enactment of a state law requiring salary increases for all teachers, the board notified teachers that noncompliance with the requirement would result in termination. Affirming the board's action, the Supreme Court found the sanction of dismissal to be rationally related to the board's objective of improving its teaching force through continuing education requirements.

The Supreme Court of Nebraska addressed what constitutes neglect of duty when a teacher allegedly had failed on several occasions to perform certain duties and at other times had not performed duties competently.[153] Evidence revealed that the teacher had not violated any administrative orders or school laws, had received good evaluations, and had been recommended for retention by the administrators. The court concluded that the facts did not support just cause for dismissal. In addition, the court cautioned that in evaluating a teacher's performance, neglect of duty is not measured "against a standard of perfection, but, instead, must be measured against the standard required of others performing the same or similar duties."[154] It was not demonstrated that the teacher's performance was below expectations for other teachers in similar positions.

In a later case, the Nebraska high court held that a superintendent's failure to file a funding form did not constitute neglect of duty to support the termination of his contract.[155] Similarly, a Louisiana appellate court held that a teacher's showing of an

---

149. Bd. of Educ. v. Flaming, 938 P.2d 151 (Colo. 1997). *See also* Knowles v. Bd. of Educ., 857 P.2d 553 (Colo. Ct. App. 1993) (holding that repeated offensive, sexually-related remarks to middle school students established neglect of duty); Childs v. Roane County Bd. of Educ., 929 S.W.2d 364 (Tenn. Ct. App. 1996) (finding that a teacher's lack of classroom control, questionable grading practices, and need for extraordinary assistance from school administrators supported neglect of duty as well as inefficiency and incompetence).

150. Cunningham v. Franklin Parish Sch. Bd., 457 So. 2d 184 (La. Ct. App. 1984). *See also* Thomas v. Cascade Union High Sch. Dist. No. 5, 780 P.2d 780 (Or. Ct. App. 1989) (finding that one incident of kicking a student substantiated neglect of duty).

151. Faulkner v. New Bern-Craven County Bd. of Educ., 316 S.E.2d 281 (N.C. 1984).

152. Harrah Indep. Sch. Dist. v. Martin, 440 U.S. 194 (1979).

153. Sanders v. Bd. of Educ., 263 N.W.2d 461 (Neb. 1978). *See also* Baker v. Bd. of Educ., 534 S.E.2d 378 (W. Va. 2000).

154. *Id.* at 465. *See also* Eshom v. Bd. of Educ., 364 N.W.2d 7 (Neb. 1985) (ruling that dismissal was supported by detailed evaluations comparing a terminated teacher with other teachers).

155. Boss v. Fillmore Sch. Dist. No. 19, 559 N.W.2d 448 (Neb. 1997).

R-rated film did not warrant dismissal for neglect of duty and incompetence.[156] The Louisiana high court concluded that a teacher bringing a loaded gun to school in his car did not substantiate willful neglect of duty to support termination.[157] The court commented that his action was certainly a mistake and possibly endangered students, but it did not involve a failure to follow orders or an identifiable school policy required for dismissal under state law.

Unprofessional Conduct

A number of states identify either *unprofessional conduct* or *conduct unbecoming a teacher* as cause for dismissal. A teacher's activities both inside and outside of school can be used to substantiate this charge when it interferes with teaching effectiveness. Dismissals for unprofessional conduct, neglect of duty, and unfitness to teach often are based on quite similar facts. Facts that establish unprofessional conduct in one state may be deemed neglect of duty in another state. Although causes for dismissal are identified in state statutes, they are defined through case law and administrative rulings in individual states. Consequently, each person must consult various sources of law in his or her state to gain a full understanding of specific statutory causes.

Most courts have defined *unprofessional conduct* as actions directly related to the fitness of educators to perform in their professional capacity. The working definition adopted by the Supreme Court of Nebraska specified unprofessional conduct as breaching the rules or ethical code of a profession or "unbecoming a member in good standing of a profession." Under this definition, the court reasoned that a teacher engaged in unprofessional conduct when he "smacked" a student on the head hard enough to make the student cry, thereby violating the state prohibition against corporal punishment.[158]

Courts have upheld dismissal for unprofessional conduct based on a number of grounds, such as permitting students to kick or hit each other for violations of classroom rules,[159] engaging in sexual harassment of female students,[160] wrapping a student in an electrical cord and verbally humiliating him in front of other students,[161]

---

156. Jones v. Rapides Parish Sch. Bd., 634 So. 2d 1197 (La. Ct. App. 1993). *See also* Kari v. Jefferson County Sch. Dist. No. 509-J, 852 P.2d 235 (Or. Ct. App. 1993) (upholding the Fair Dismissal Appeals Board's decision that a teacher's acquiescence to her husband's use of their home for the sale of marijuana did not constitute neglect of duty justifying dismissal).

157. Howard v. W. Baton Rouge Parish Sch. Bd., 793 So. 2d 153 (La. 2001). *See also* Bd. of Educ. v. Chaddock, 398 S.E.2d 120 (W. Va. 1990) (failure to remove a student with a loaded gun from the classroom did not support willful neglect of duty).

158. Daily v. Bd. of Educ., 588 N.W.2d 813, 824 (Neb. 1999). Following a hearing to consider termination of employment, the school board instead imposed a 30-day suspension on the teacher.

159. Roberts v. Santa Cruz Valley Unified Sch. Dist. No. 35, 778 P.2d 1294 (Ariz. Ct. App. 1989).

160. Conward v. Cambridge Sch. Comm., 171 F.3d 12 (1st Cir. 1999). *See also* Baltrip v. Norris, 23 S.W.3d 336 (Tenn. Ct. App. 2000).

161. Johanson v. Bd. of Educ., 589 N.W.2d 815 (Neb. 1999).

losing complete control of the classroom,[162] showing a sexually explicit film to a classroom of adolescents without previewing it,[163] and stealing pills labeled methylphenidate (generic name for Ritalin) from the school office.[164] As with dismissals based on incompetency, courts often require prior warning that the behavior may result in dismissal.

Unfitness to Teach

Unfitness to teach covers a wide array of teacher behavior. In a Montana case, the high court found nine incidents of inappropriate comments and conduct related to sex or gender to support dismissal of a teacher for unfitness even though he had an outstanding reputation.[165] An Illinois appellate court, defining *unfitness* as "conduct detrimental to the operation of the school," held that improper sexual conduct toward students constituted unfitness.[166] "Evident unfitness for service" in California law was interpreted by an appellate court to require that unfitness be attributed to a defect in temperament. As such, a number of confrontations with other teachers and administrators and sarcastic and belittling comments on student disciplinary slips supported a teacher's termination for unfitness for service.[167] The judiciary also has recognized that a determination of fitness or capacity may extend beyond actual classroom performance.[168]

Two decisions from the Supreme Court of Maine dealt with dismissals for one-time incidents that allegedly affected fitness to teach. In the first case, a teacher who was also a licensed gunsmith inadvertently brought a gun and ammunition to school in his jacket. The gun was stolen from his room but later returned. The school board initiated dismissal proceedings for "grave lack of judgment." Overturning the board action, the court held that one isolated incident does not represent such "moral impropriety, professional incompetence, or unsuitability" to constitute unfitness to teach.[169] The second case involved a teacher striking a student across the face with his hand

---

162. Walker v. Highlands County Sch. Bd., 752 So. 2d 127 (Fla. Dist. Ct. App. 2000).

163. Fowler v. Bd. of Educ., 819 F.2d 657 (6th Cir. 1987).

164. Lannom v. Bd. of Educ., No. M 1999-00137-COA-R3-CV, 2000 Tenn. Ct. App. LEXIS 133 (Tenn. Ct. App. Mar. 6, 2000).

165. Baldridge v. Bd. of Trs., 951 P.2d 1343 (Mont. 1997).

166. Lombardo v. Bd. of Educ., 241 N.E.2d 495, 498 (Ill. App. Ct. 1968). *See also* Elvin v. City of Waterville, 573 A.2d 381 (Me. 1990) (concluding that a female teacher's sexual relationship with a 15-year-old male student rendered her unfit to teach); Johnson v. Bd. of Trs., 771 P.2d 137 (Mont. 1989) (ruling that a teacher's sexual contact with two students supported dismissal for unfitness to teach and immorality).

167. Woodland Joint Unified Sch. Dist. v. Comm'n on Prof. Competence, 4 Cal. Rptr. 2d 227 (App. Ct. 1992). *See also* Palmer v. Portland Sch. Comm., 652 A.2d 86 (Me. 1995) (finding that mistreatment and humiliation of students and violation of discipline policies supported a teacher's dismissal for unfitness to teach).

168. *See, e.g., In re* Morrill, 765 A.2d 699 (N.H. 2001).

during a basketball game.[170] The blow was severe, causing the loss of one tooth, damage to another, and extensive bruises. Here, the court concluded that the single incident was sufficient to justify dismissal because of its direct impact on the teacher's effectiveness as a coach. Dismissals for one-time incidents, regardless of the grounds, are always scrutinized closely by courts.

Mental, emotional, or physical disorders can constitute unfitness or incapacity to teach. To establish incapacity, health conditions must be severe and interfere with a teacher's ability to perform in the classroom.[171] It should be noted, however, that dismissals based on physical disabilities might impair federally protected rights of employees with disabilities. As discussed in Chapter 10, the United States Supreme Court held that a teacher with tuberculosis was "handicapped" under federal antidiscrimination provisions and thus could not be summarily dismissed because of the disease.[172]

Other Good and Just Cause

Not unexpectedly, "other good and just cause" as grounds for dismissal often has been challenged as vague and overbroad. Courts have been faced with the task of determining whether the phrase's meaning is limited to the specific grounds enumerated in the statute or whether it is a separate, expanded cause. An Indiana appellate court interpreted it as permitting termination for reasons other than those specified in the tenure law, if evidence indicated that the board's decision was based on "good cause."[173] As such, dismissal of a teacher convicted of a misdemeanor was upheld even though the teacher had no prior indication that such conduct was sufficient cause. A Connecticut court found *good cause* to be any ground that is put forward in good faith that is not "arbitrary, irrational, unreasonable, or irrelevant to the board's task of building up and

---

169. Wright v. Superintending Comm., Portland, 331 A.2d 640, 647 (Me. 1975). *See also* Hall v. Bd. of Trs., 499 S.E.2d 216 (S.C. Ct. App. 1998) (concluding that failure to provide adequate supervision on a class trip and discussing the incident with other employees when directed not to discuss it by the superintendent did not constitute unfitness to teach or insubordination; the terminated teacher and the lead supervisor of the trip had agreed prior to the trip to a limited supervision role for the teacher).

170. McLaughlin v. Machias Sch. Comm., 385 A.2d 53 (Me. 1978).

171. *See, e.g.,* Smith v. Bd. of Educ., 293 N.W.2d 221 (Iowa 1980) (finding that temporary mental illness was inadequate basis for dismissal). *But see* Clarke v. Shoreline Sch. Dist. No. 412, 720 P.2d 793 (Wash. 1986) (supporting dismissal of a teacher who was sight and hearing impaired because he could not perform essential functions of teaching position).

172. Sch. Bd. of Nassau County v. Arline, 480 U.S. 273 (1987).

173. Gary Teachers Union, Local No. 4, AFT v. Sch. City of Gary, 332 N.E.2d 256, 263 (Ind. Ct. App. 1975). *See also* Hierlmeier v. N. Judson-San Pierre Bd., 730 N.E.2d 821 (Ind. Ct. App. 2000) (ruling that sexual harassment of female students and other inappropriate conduct toward students substantiated good and just cause for termination); Sheldon Cmty. Sch. Dist. Bd. of Dirs., 528 N.W.2d 593 (Iowa 1995) (finding frequent sarcastic remarks to adolescents to establish "just cause" under Iowa law). *But see* Trs. Lincoln County Sch. Dist. No. 13 v. Holden, 754 P.2d 506 (Mont. 1988) (concluding that two instances of calling students crude names did not support good cause for dismissal).

maintaining an efficient school system."[174] Terminating a teacher for altering students' responses on state mandatory proficiency tests was held to be relevant to that task.

The Second Circuit found *other due and sufficient cause* as a ground for dismissal to be "appropriate in an area such as discipline of teachers, where a myriad of uncontemplated situations may arise and it is not reasonable to require a legislature to elucidate in advance every act that requires sanction."[175] The court declined to rule on the vagueness of the term, but rather noted that courts generally assess the teacher's conduct in relation to the statutory grounds for dismissal. That is, if the specific behavior is sufficiently related to the causes specified in state law, it is assumed that the teacher should have reasonably known that the conduct was improper. In this case, where a teacher repeatedly humiliated and harassed students (and school administrators had discussed the problem with him), the court concluded that the teacher was aware of the impropriety of his conduct. The Supreme Court of Iowa supported the termination of a teacher for shoplifting under a statute permitting teachers to be terminated during the contract year for "just cause."[176] Although the teacher claimed that her compulsion to shoplift was related to a mental illness, the court found the weighing of the teacher's position as a role model, the character of the illness, and the school board's needs provided substantial evidence to terminate the teacher's employment.

Reduction-in-Force

In addition to dismissal for causes related to teacher performance and fitness, legislation generally permits the release of teachers for reasons related to declining enrollment, financial exigency, and school district consolidation. Whereas most state statutes provide for such terminations, a number of states also have adopted legislation that specifies the basis for selection of released teachers, procedures to be followed, and provisions for reinstatement. These terminations, characterized as *reductions-in-force (RIF)*, also may be governed by board policies and negotiated bargaining agreements.

Unlike other termination cases, the employee challenging a RIF decision shoulders the burden of proof. There is a presumption that the board has acted in good faith with permissible motives. Legal controversies in this area usually involve questions related to the necessity for the reductions, board compliance with mandated proce-

---

174. Hanes v. Bd. of Educ., 783 A.2d 1 (Conn. App. Ct. 2001). *See also* Oleske v. Hilliard City Sch. Dist., 764 N.E.2d 1110, 1116 (Ohio Ct. App. 2001) (concluding that a teacher's dismissal for telling dirty jokes and calling another teacher an offensive name in front of students constituted a "fairly serious matter" supporting good and just cause for dismissal).

175. diLeo v. Greenfield, 541 F.2d 949, 954 (2d Cir. 1976).

176. Bd. of Dirs. v. Davies, 489 N.W.2d 19 (Iowa 1992). *See also* Snyder v. Jefferson County Sch. Dist. R-1, 842 P.2d 624 (Colo. 1992) (holding that expiration of a teacher's certificate constituted other good and just cause for termination).

dures, and possible subterfuge for impermissible termination (such as denial of constitutional rights, subversion of tenure rights, discrimination).[177]

If statutory or contractual restrictions exist for teacher layoffs, there must be substantial compliance with the provisions. One of the provisions most frequently included is a method for selecting teachers for release. In general, reductions are based on seniority, and a tenured teacher, rather than a nontenured teacher, must be retained if both are qualified to fill the same position. Some state statutes require that both licensure and seniority be considered; a teacher lacking a license in the area would not be permitted to teach while a permanent teacher with proper credentials, but less seniority, was dismissed.[178] Along with seniority, merit-rating systems may be included in the determination of reductions. School districts in Pennsylvania use a combination of ratings and seniority; ratings are the primary determinant unless no substantial difference exists in ratings, and then seniority becomes the basis for the layoff.[179] The Nebraska Supreme Court concluded that school boards have broad discretion in deciding what factors to use in its RIF policy and how to weight those factors.[180] Guidelines or criteria established by state or local education agencies, however, must be applied in a uniform and nondiscriminatory manner.

The Fourteenth Amendment requires minimal procedural protections in dismissals for cause, but courts have not clearly defined the due process requirements for RIF. The Eighth Circuit noted that tenured teachers possess a property interest in continued employment, and thereby must be provided notice and an opportunity to be heard.[181] The District of Columbia Circuit held that due process did not require pretermination hearings when posttermination proceedings were available.[182] Specific procedural protections for employees vary according to interpretations of state law, bargaining agreements, and board policy. A Michigan court found no need for a hearing over staff reductions, because there were no charges to refute.[183] The court empha-

177. *See, e.g.,* Impey v. Bd. of Educ., 662 A.2d 960 (N.J. 1995) (holding that a school board did not need to eliminate programs or services to eliminate teaching positions; all services were provided less expensively through a contract with an external agency).

178. *See, e.g.,* DeGeorgeo v. Indep. Sch. Dist. No. 833, 563 N.W.2d 755 (Minn. Ct. App. 1997); Summers County Bd. of Educ. v. Allen, 450 S.E.2d 658 (W. Va. 1994).

179. Pa. Stat. Ann. tit. 24 § 11-1124 (Purdon, West Supp. 2002).

180. Nickel v. Saline County Sch. Dist. No. 163, 559 N.W.2d 480 (Neb. 1997). *See also* Borr v. McKenzie County Pub. Sch. Dist., 560 N.W.2d 213 (N.D. 1997).

181. Boner v. Eminence R-1 Sch. Dist., 55 F.3d 1339 (8th Cir. 1995). *See also* Chandler v. Bd. of Educ., 92 F. Supp. 2d 760 (N.D. Ill. 2000) (ruling that a teacher must be provided a notice describing the reasons for termination of employment); Westport Sch. Comm. v. Coelho, 692 N.E.2d 540 (Mass. App. Ct. 1998) (interpreting state-level arbitration to apply to performance-based dismissals not budget-induced layoffs).

182. Washington Teachers' Union v. Bd. of Educ., 109 F.3d 774 (D.C. Cir. 1997).

183. Steeby v. Sch. Dist. of Highland Park, 224 N.W.2d 97 (Mich. Ct. App. 1974). *See also* Martin v. Sch. Comm. of Natick, 480 N.E.2d 625 (Mass. 1985).

sized that the law protected the released teacher, who, subject to qualifications, was entitled to the next vacancy. In contrast, a Pennsylvania commonwealth court held that a hearing must be provided to assure the teacher (1) that termination was for reasons specified by law and (2) that the board followed the correct statutory procedures in selecting the teacher for discharge.[184]

State law or other policies may give preference to teachers who are released due to a reduction-in-force. Typically, under such requirements, a school board cannot hire a nonemployee until each qualified teacher on the preferred recall list is reemployed.[185] Although statutes often require that a teacher be appointed to the first vacancy for which licensed and qualified, courts have held that reappointment is still at the board's discretion. A Michigan appeals court recognized that a teacher could be licensed in an area, but in the opinion of the board, not necessarily qualified.[186] Additionally, a board is generally not obligated to realign or rearrange teaching assignments to create a position for a released teacher.[187]

Remedies for Violations of Protected Rights

When established that school districts or officials have violated an employee's rights protected by federal or state law, several remedies are available to the aggrieved individual. In some situations, the employee may seek a court injunction ordering the unlawful action to cease. This remedy might be sought if a school board has unconstitutionally imposed restraints on teachers' expression. Where terminations, transfers, or other adverse employment consequences have been unconstitutionally imposed, courts will order school districts to return the affected employees to their original status with back pay.

In addition to these remedies, educators are increasingly bringing suits to recover damages for actions that violate their federally protected rights. Suits are usually based on 42 U.S.C. Section 1983, which provides that any person who acts under color of state law to deprive another individual of rights secured by the Federal Con-

---

184. Fatscher v. Bd. of Sch. Dirs., 367 A.2d 1130 (Pa. Commw. Ct. 1977). *See also* Harris v. Trs. of Cascades County Sch. Dist., 786 P.2d 1164 (Mont. 1990).

185. *See, e.g.,* Harhay v. Blanchette, 160 F. Supp. 2d 306 (D. Conn. 2001); Bd. of Educ. v. Owensby, 526 S.E.2d 831 (W. Va. 1999). *See also* Davis v. Chester Upland Sch. Dist., 786 A.2d 186 (Pa. 2001) (ruling that teachers who challenged the district's failure to recall them must exhaust collective bargaining grievance procedure before filing for judicial review).

186. Chester v. Harper Woods Sch. Dist., 273 N.W.2d 916 (Mich. Ct. App. 1978). *See also* Dinan v. Bd. of Educ., 426 N.Y.S.2d 86 (App. Div. 1980).

187. *See, e.g.,* Moe v. Indep. Sch. Dist. No. 696, 623 N.W.2d 899 (Minn. Ct. App. 2001); Palmer v. Bd. of Trs., 785 P.2d 1160 (Wyo. 1990). *But see* Pennell v. Bd. of Educ., 484 N.E.2d 445 (Ill. App. Ct. 1985) (ruling that restructuring positions is not required, but bad faith realignment of positions to avoid existence of a position for a tenured teacher is prohibited).

stitution or laws is subject to personal liability. This law, which was originally enacted in 1871 to prevent discrimination against African American citizens, has been broadly interpreted as conferring liability on school personnel and school districts, not only for racial discrimination but also for actions that may result in the impairment of other federally protected rights.[188]

Suits alleging Section 1983 violations can be initiated in federal or state courts,[189] and exhaustion of state administrative remedies is not required before initiating a federal suit.[190] When a federal law authorizes an exclusive nondamages remedy, however, a Section 1983 suit is precluded.[191] This section focuses on the liability of school officials and districts for the violation of protected rights and on the types of damages available to aggrieved employees.

Liability of School Officials

Under Section 1983, public school employees acting under color of state law can be held personally liable for actions abridging students' or teachers' federal rights. The Supreme Court, however, has recognized that government officials cannot be held liable under Section 1983 for the actions of their subordinates, thus rejecting the doctrine of *respondeat superior,* even where school officials have general supervisory authority over the activities of the wrongdoers. In order to be held liable, the officials must have personally participated in, or had personal knowledge of, the unlawful acts or promulgated official policy under which the acts were taken.[192] Furthermore, the Supreme Court in 1998 ruled that public officials are absolutely immune from suit under Section 1983 for their legislative activities.[193] These actions involve discretionary, policy-making decisions, enactment of regulations, often with budgetary implications. Subsequently, courts have clarified that employment decisions related to individual employees (such as hiring, dismissal, or demotions) are administrative, not legislative, in nature.[194]

The Supreme Court has recognized that in some circumstances school officials can claim qualified immunity to shield them from personal liability when they have acted in good faith. The burden of establishing good faith immunity clearly resides with the official claiming the protection; the plaintiff does not have to prove that

---

188. Maine v. Thiboutot, 448 U.S. 1 (1980).

189. The Supreme Court has rejected the assertion that school officials are immune from a § 1983 suit initiated in a state court. Howlett v. Rose, 496 U.S. 356 (1990).

190. Patsy v. Bd. of Regents, 457 U.S. 496 (1982).

191. *See, e.g.,* Gonzaga Univ. v. Doe, 536 U.S. 273 (2002); Blessing v. Freestone, 520 U.S. 329 (1997).

192. *See* Am. Mfrs. Mut. Ins. Co. v. Sullivan, 526 U.S. 40 (1999); Rizzo v. Goode, 423 U.S. 362 (1976).

193. Bogan v. Scott-Harris, 523 U.S. 44 (1998).

194. *See, e.g.,* Canary v. Osborn, 211 F.3d 324 (6th Cir. 2000); Harhay v. Blanchette, 160 F. Supp. 306 (D. Conn. 2001).

immunity is not applicable.[195] In a 1975 student discipline case, *Wood v. Strickland,* the Supreme Court declared:

> A school board member is not immune from liability for damages under Section 1983 if he knew or reasonably should have known that the action he took within his sphere of official responsibility would violate the constitutional rights of the student affected, or if he took the action with the malicious intention to cause a deprivation of constitutional rights or other injury to the student."[196]

Subsequently, in *Harlow v. Fitzgerald* the Court eliminated the subjective test (i.e., an assessment of whether the defendants acted with malicious intentions) from the qualified-immunity standard. Under *Harlow,* "government officials performing discretionary functions generally are shielded from liability for civil damages insofar as their conduct does not violate clearly established statutory or constitutional rights of which a reasonable person would have known."[197] The Second Circuit, noting that unlawfulness must be apparent, stated:

> A right is clearly established if the contours of the right are sufficiently clear that a reasonable official would understand that what he or she is doing violates that right. The question is not what a lawyer would learn or intuit from researching case law, but what a reasonable person in the [school official's] position should know about the constitutionality of the conduct.[198]

The Ninth Circuit noted the difficulty of determining a "clearly established" violation when confronted with applying the balancing tests of *Pickering v. Board of Education*[199] for protected speech and *Mathews v. Eldridge*[200] for procedural due process in a teacher termination case. Concluding that the specific facts in this case did not show a violation of established law, the court found the school officials entitled to qualified immunity.[201] The Seventh Circuit emphasized that the individual alleging violation of a clearly established right bears the burden of demonstrating the existence of the right.[202] In determining whether a right is clearly established, the court stated that first it examines controlling Supreme Court precedent and its own circuit decisions related to the case and then reviews all relevant case law. According to the appel-

---

195. Gomez v. Toledo, 446 U.S. 635 (1980).

196. 420 U.S. 308, 322 (1975).

197. 457 U.S. 800, 818 (1982).

198. McCullough v. Wyandanch Union Free Sch. Dist., 187 F.3d 272, 278 (2d Cir. 1999).

199. 391 U.S. 563 (1968).

200. 424 U.S. 319 (1976).

201. Brewster v. Bd. of Educ., 149 F.3d 971 (9th Cir. 1998). *See also* Townsend v. Vallas, 256 F.3d 661 (7th Cir. 2001); Ulichny v. Merton Cmty. Sch. Dist., 249 F.3d 686 (7th Cir. 2001).

202. Denius v. Dunlap, 209 F.3d 944 (7th Cir. 2000). *See also* Kingsford v. Salt Lake City Sch. Dist., 247 F.3d 1123 (10th Cir. 2001); Thomas v. Roberts, 261 F.3d 1160 (11th Cir. 2001).

late court, a split among courts in assessing similar conduct points to unsettled law. Unsettled law in recent cases included the strip search of a fifth-grade class,[203] alleged retaliation against a teacher for filing a law suit,[204] and relieving a superintendent of his duties without due process while continuing to pay salary and benefits.[205]

School officials have been denied qualified immunity because of the disregard of well-established legal principles. For example, officials were not entitled to qualified immunity when they reasonably should have known that retaliating against a teacher for using her union's grievance procedure violated constitutional rights.[206] Similarly, a superintendent was not protected by qualified immunity for refusing to recommend a teacher's reemployment based on constitutionally impermissible reasons pertaining to her involvement in a divorce.[207] The Third Circuit, in remanding a case for further proceedings, noted that a superintendent who appeared to have maliciously prosecuted a teacher for theft in retaliation for the exercise of her First Amendment activities was not entitled to qualified immunity.[208] Public officials are not expected to predict the future course of constitutional law, but they are expected to adhere to principles of law that were clearly established at the time of the violation.

Liability of School Districts

In 1978, the Supreme Court departed from precedent and ruled that local governments are considered "persons" under Section 1983.[209] In essence, school districts can be assessed damages when action taken pursuant to official policy violates federally protected rights.

The governmental unit (like the individual official), however, cannot be held liable under the *respondeat superior* doctrine for the wrongful acts committed solely by its employees. Liability under Section 1983 against the agency can be imposed only when execution of official policy by an individual with final authority impairs a federally protected right.[210] The Supreme Court has held that a single egregious act of a low-level employee does not infer an official policy of inadequate training and

203. *Thomas,* 262 F.3d 1160.

204. Lytle v. Wondrash, 182 F.3d 1083 (9th Cir. 1999).

205. Harris v. Bd. of Educ., 105 F.3d 591 (11th Cir. 1997).

206. Gavrilles v. O'Connor, 611 F. Supp. 210 (D. Mass. 1985).

207. Littlejohn v. Rose, 768 F.2d 765 (6th Cir. 1985).

208. Merkle v. Upper Dublin Sch. Dist., 211 F.3d 782 (3d Cir. 2000). The court also noted that injury to reputation alone does not violate the Fourteenth Amendment; however, if the teacher is able to show damage to her reputation during the deprivation of a constitutional right, she can establish liability under § 1983 for a Fourteenth Amendment violation.

209. Monell v. Dep't of Soc. Servs., 436 U.S. 658 (1978).

210. *See, e.g.,* Collins v. City of Harker Heights, 503 U.S. 115 (1992); St. Louis v. Praprotnik, 485 U.S. 112 (1988); Pembaur v. City of Cincinnati, 475 U.S. 469 (1986); Langford v. City of Atlantic City, 235 F.3d 845 (3d Cir. 2000); Seamons v. Snow, 206 F.3d 1021 (10th Cir. 2000); Hall v. Marion Sch. Dist. No. 2, 31 F.3d 183 (4th Cir. 1994).

supervision,[211] but an agency can be liable if "deliberate indifference" in ensuring adequately trained employees is established.[212]

Although school officials can plead good faith immunity, this defense is not available to school districts. The Supreme Court has ruled that school districts and other governmental subdivisions cannot claim qualified immunity based on good faith actions of their officials. The Court acknowledged that under certain circumstances, sovereign immunity can shield municipal corporations from state tort suits, but concluded that Section 1983 abrogated governmental immunity in situations involving the impairment of federally protected rights.[213]

To avoid liability for constitutional violations, school districts have introduced claims of Eleventh Amendment immunity.[214] The Eleventh Amendment, explicitly prohibiting citizens of one state from bringing suit against another state without its consent, has been interpreted as also precluding federal lawsuits against a state by its own citizens.[215] A state can waive this immunity by specifically consenting to be sued, and Congress can abrogate state immunity through legislation enacted to enforce the Fourteenth Amendment. Such congressional intent, however, must be explicit in the federal legislation.[216]

School districts have asserted Eleventh Amendment protection based on the fact that they perform a state function. Admittedly, education is a state function, but it does not necessarily follow that school districts gain Eleventh Amendment immunity against claims of constitutional abridgments. For the Eleventh Amendment to be invoked in a suit against a school district, the state must be the "real party in interest." The Third Circuit identified the following factors in determining if a governmental agency, such as a school district, is entitled to Eleventh Amendment protection: (1)

---

211. Oklahoma City v. Tuttle, 471 U.S. 808 (1985).

212. City of Canton, Ohio v. Harris, 489 U.S. 378 (1989). For a discussion of school district liability in connection with sexual abuse of students by school employees, *see* text accompanying note 158, Chapter 8.

213. Owen v. City of Independence, Mo., 445 U.S. 622 (1980). *See* Chapter 13 for a discussion of governmental immunity under tort law.

214. Under certain circumstances, school districts may be able to use other defenses to preclude liability in a § 1983 suit. Claims that have already been decided in a state case (res judicata) or could have been litigated between the same parties in a prior state action (collateral estoppel) may be barred in a federal suit under § 1983. *See* Migra v. Warren City Sch. Dist., 465 U.S. 75 (1984); Allen v. McCurry, 449 U.S. 90 (1980).

215. *See, e.g.,* Hans v. Louisiana, 134 U.S. 1 (1890). *See also* Will v. Mich. Dep't of State Police, 491 U.S. 58 (1989) (holding that § 1983 does not permit a suit against a state; Congress did not intend the word *person* to include states).

216. Most recently, the Supreme Court held that the Family Educational Rights and Privacy Act of 1974 does not explicitly confer individually enforceable rights. Gonzaga v. Univ. Doe, 536 U.S. 273 (2002). Also, in deciding whether an individual can sue a state for money damages in federal court under the Americans with Disabilities Act of 1990, the Supreme Court ruled that Congress did not act within its constitutional authority when it abrogated Eleventh Amendment immunity. Bd. of Trs. v. Garrett, 531 U.S. 356 (2000). *See also* text with note 138, Chapter 10.

whether payment of the judgment will be from the state treasury, (2) whether a governmental or proprietary function is being performed,[217] (3) whether the agency has autonomy over its operation, (4) whether it has the power to sue and be sued, (5) whether it can enter into contracts, and (6) whether the agency's property is immune from state taxation.[218] The most significant of these factors in determining if a district is shielded by Eleventh Amendment immunity has been whether the judgment will be recovered from state funds. If funds are to be paid from the state treasury, courts have declared the state to be the real party in interest.[219]

For many states, the Eleventh Amendment question with respect to school district immunity was resolved in the *Mt. Healthy* case.[220] The Supreme Court concluded that the issue in this case hinged on whether, under Ohio law, a school district is considered an arm of the state as opposed to a municipality or other political subdivision. Considering the taxing power and autonomy of school district operations, the Supreme Court found school districts to be more like counties or cities than extensions of the state.

Remedies

Depending on employment status, judicial remedies for the violation of protected rights may include compensatory and punitive damages, reinstatement with back pay, and attorneys' fees. The specific nature of the award depends on federal and state statutory provisions and the discretion of courts. Federal and state laws often identify damages that may be recovered or place limitations on types of awards. Unless these provisions restrict specific remedies, courts have broad discretionary power to formulate equitable settlements.

Damages.   When a school official or school district is found liable for violating an individual's protected rights, an award of damages is assessed to compensate the claimant for the injury.[221] Actual injury, however, must be shown for the aggrieved

---

217. *Governmental functions* are those performed in discharging the agency's official duties; *proprietary functions* are often for profit and could be performed by private corporations.

218. Urbano v. Bd. of Managers, 415 F.2d 247, 250-251 (3d Cir. 1969).

219. Eleventh Amendment immunity covers only federal suits; it does not have any bearing on immunity in state actions.

220. Mt. Healthy City Sch. Dist. v. Doyle, 429 U.S. 274 (1977). *See also* Missouri v. Jenkins, 495 U.S. 33, 56 (1990), Stewart v. Baldwin County Bd. of Educ., 908 F.2d 1499 (11th Cir. 1990); Green v. Clarendon County Sch. Dist. Three, 923 F. Supp. 829 (D.S.C. 1996); Daddow v. Carlsbad Mun. Sch. Dist., 898 P.2d 1235 (N.M. 1995). *But see* Belanger v. Madera Unified Sch. Dist., 963 F.2d 248 (9th Cir. 1992) (holding that California school boards are indivisible agencies of the state and thus entitled to Eleventh Amendment immunity).

221. *See, e.g.,* McGee v. S. Pemiscot Sch. Dist. R-V, 712 F.2d 339 (8th Cir. 1983) (concluding that even though a teacher-coach, who was dismissed for exercising protected speech, found a higher-paying job, he was entitled to $10,000 in damages for mental anguish, loss of professional reputation, and expenses incurred in obtaining new employment).

party to recover damages; without evidence of monetary or mental injury, the plaintiff is entitled only to nominal damages (not to exceed one dollar), even though an impairment of protected rights is established.[222] Significant monetary damages, however, may be awarded for a wrongful termination if a teacher is able to demonstrate substantial losses. At the same time, individuals must make an effort to mitigate damages by seeking appropriate employment.[223]

The Supreme Court held in 1986 that compensatory damages cannot be based on a jury's perception of the value or importance of constitutional rights.[224] In this case, involving the award of compensatory damages to a teacher for his unconstitutional dismissal, the Supreme Court declared that although individuals are entitled to full compensation for the injury suffered, they are not entitled to supplementary damages based on the perceived value of the constitutional rights that have been abridged. The Court remanded the case for a determination of the amount of damages necessary to compensate the teacher for the *actual* injury suffered.

In some instances, aggrieved individuals have sought punitive as well as compensatory damages. The judiciary has ruled that school officials can be liable for punitive damages (to punish the wrongdoer) if a jury concludes that the individual's conduct is willful or in reckless and callous disregard of federally protected rights.[225] Punitive as well as compensatory damages were assessed against a principal and superintendent who, without authority, discharged a teacher in retaliation for the exercise of protected speech.[226]

In 1981, the Supreme Court ruled that Section 1983 does not authorize the award of punitive damages against a municipality.[227] Recognizing that compensation for injuries is an obligation of a municipality, the Court held that *punitive* damages were appropriate only for the *individual* wrongdoers and not for the municipality itself. The Court also noted that punitive damages constitute punishment against individuals to deter similar conduct in the future, but they are not intended to punish innocent taxpayers. This ruling does not bar claims for punitive damages for violations of

---

222. *See, e.g.,* Farrar v. Hobby, 506 U.S. 103 (1992) (concluding that an award of nominal damages is mandatory when a procedural due process violation is established but no actual injury is shown); Carey v. Piphus, 435 U.S. 247 (1978) (holding that pupils who were denied procedural due process in a disciplinary proceeding would be entitled only to nominal damages unless it was established that lack of proper procedures resulted in actual injury to the students).

223. *See, e.g.,* McClure v. Indep. Sch. Dist. No. 16, 228 F.3d 1205 (10th Cir. 2000); McDaniel v. Princeton City Sch. Dist., 114 F. Supp. 2d 658 (S.D. Ohio 2000).

224. Memphis Cmty. Sch. Dist. v. Stachura, 477 U.S. 299 (1986).

225. *See, e.g.,* Smith v. Wade, 461 U.S. 30 (1983). In 1991, the Supreme Court refused to place a limit on the amount of punitive damages that properly instructed juries can award in common-law suits, but it did note that extremely high awards might be viewed as unacceptable under the Due Process Clause of the Fourteenth Amendment. Pac. Mut. Life Ins. Co. v. Haslip, 499 U.S. 1 (1991). *See also* Standley v. Chilhowee R-IV Sch. Dist., 5 F.3d 319 (8th Cir. 1993) (holding that evidence did not support evil motive or reckless or callous indifference).

226. Fishman v. Clancy, 763 F.2d 485 (1st Cir. 1985).

227. City of Newport v. Fact Concerts, 453 U.S. 247 (1981).

federal rights in school cases, but such claims must be brought against individuals rather than against the school district itself.

The following cases illustrate the diverse circumstances that have resulted in awards of damages. An Illinois school board was required to pay a teacher $750,000 in compensatory damages for wrongfully terminating her for an out-of-wedlock pregnancy.[228] A principal's failure to respond adequately to a student's complaints of sexual abuse by a teacher resulted in an award of $350,000 against the principal.[229] The termination of a tenured New York teacher without due process merited consideration of back pay and other employment benefits but not the damages requested for emotional distress and mental anguish, because only subjective evidence of such injury was presented.[230] However, a North Carolina teacher received $78,000 in damages based on mental distress evidenced by depression and insomnia following procedural violations in his termination.[231]

Given the success teachers have had in securing damages to compensate for the violation of constitutional rights, school officials should ensure that dismissals or other disciplinary actions are based on legitimate reasons and accompanied by appropriate procedural safeguards. Courts, however, have not awarded damages unless the evidence shows that a teacher has suffered actual injury. As the Supreme Court has noted, compensatory damages are intended to provide full compensation for the loss or injury suffered but are not to be based simply on a jury's perception of the value of the constitutional rights impaired.[232]

Reinstatement.   Whether a court orders reinstatement as a remedy for school board action depends on the protected interests involved and the discretion of the court, unless specific provision for reinstatement is specified in state law. If a tenured teacher is unjustly dismissed, the property interest gives rise to an expectation of reemployment; reinstatement in such instances is usually the appropriate remedy. A nontenured teacher, wrongfully dismissed during the contract period, however, is normally entitled only to damages, not reinstatement.

---

228. Eckmann v. Bd. of Educ., 636 F. Supp. 1214 (N.D. Ill. 1986). *See also* Peterson v. Minidoka County Sch. Dist., 118 F.3d 1351 (9th Cir. 1997) (upholding a damage award of $300,000 as well as attorneys' fees for the school board's reassignment of a principal because he proposed to home school his children); Welton v. Osborn, 124 F. Supp. 2d 1114 (S.D. Ohio 2000) (awarding $177,000 in compensatory damages, $65,625 in punitive damages, and $77,747 in attorneys' fees and costs against superintendent for retaliation toward principal for exercising constitutionally protected speech).

229. Baynard v. Malone, 268 F.3d 228 (4th Cir. 2001), *cert. denied,* 122 S. Ct. 1357 (2002).

230. Cohen v. Bd. of Educ., 728 F.2d 160 (2d Cir. 1984). *But see* Alaniz v. San Isidro Indep. Sch. Dist., 742 F.2d 207 (5th Cir. 1984) (upholding a jury award of $50,000 as compensation for mental anguish and emotional distress because evidence substantiated injury).

231. Crump v. Bd. of Educ., 392 S.E.2d 579 (N.C. 1990) (awarding damages for procedural violation even though discharge was upheld). *See also* Dishnow v. Sch. Dist. of Rib Lake, 77 F.3d 194 (7th Cir. 1996) (upholding a damages award for humiliation and injury to reputation in the firing of a teacher based on the exercise of his free speech rights).

232. Memphis Cmty. Sch. Dist. v. Stachura, 477 U.S. 299 (1986).

A valid property or liberty claim entitles a teacher to procedural due process, but the teacher can still be dismissed for cause after proper procedures have been followed. If a teacher is terminated without proper procedures and can establish that the action is not justified, however, reinstatement will be ordered.[233] If proven that the actual reason for the nonrenewal of a teacher's contract is retaliation for the exercise of constitutional rights (e.g., protected speech), reinstatement would be warranted, although substantiation of such a claim is difficult.

The failure to comply with statutory requirements in nonrenewals and dismissals may result in reinstatement. When statutory dates are specified for notice of nonrenewal, failure to comply strictly with the deadline provides grounds for reinstatement of the teacher. Courts may interpret this as continued employment for an additional year[234] or reinstatement with tenure if nonrenewal occurs at the end of the probationary period. In contrast to the remedy for lack of proper notice, the remedy for failure to provide an appropriate hearing is generally a remand for a hearing, not reinstatement.

Attorneys' Fees. Attorneys' fees are not automatically granted to the teacher who prevails in a lawsuit, but are generally dependent on statutory authorization. At the federal level, the Civil Rights Attorneys' Fees Award Act gives federal courts discretion to award fees in civil rights suits.[235] In congressional debate concerning attorneys' fees, it was stated that "private citizens must be given not only the right to go to court, but also the legal resources. If the citizen does not have the resources, his day in court is denied him."[236]

To receive attorneys' fees, the teacher must be the prevailing party; that is, damages or some form of equitable relief must be granted to the teacher. The Supreme Court has held that a prevailing party is one who is successful in achieving some benefit on any significant issue in the case, but not necessarily the primary issue. At a minimum, the Court ruled that "the plaintiff must be able to point to a resolution of the dispute which changes the legal relationship between itself and the defendant."[237] If a plaintiff achieves only partial success, the fees requested may be reduced.[238]

Because Section 1983 does not require exhaustion of state administrative proceedings before initiating litigation, the Supreme Court has denied the award of attorneys' fees for school board administrative proceedings conducted prior to filing a federal suit. Unlike Title VII's explicit requirement that individuals must pursue

233. *See, e.g.,* Brewer v. Chauvin, 938 F.2d 860 (8th Cir. 1991); McGhee v. Draper, 639 F.2d 639 (10th Cir. 1981); McDaniel v. Princeton City Sch. Dist., 114 F. Supp. 2d 658 (S.D. Ohio 2000).

234. *See, e.g.,* Kiel v. Green Local Sch. Dist. Bd. of Educ., 630 N.E.2d 716 (Ohio 1994).

235. 42 U.S.C. § 1988 (2002).

236. 122 Cong. Rec. 33,313 (1976).

237. Tex. State Teachers Ass'n v. Garland Indep. Sch. Dist., 489 U.S. 782, 792 (1989). *See also* Sutton v. Cleveland Bd. of Educ., 958 F.2d 1339 (6th Cir. 1992); Farner v. Idaho Falls Schs. Dist., 17 P.3d 281 (Idaho 2000).

238. *See, e.g.,* Standley v. Chilhowee R-IV Sch. Dist., 5 F.3d 319 (8th Cir. 1993).

administrative remedies, plaintiffs can bring a Section 1983 claim directly to a federal court. In a wrongful termination case, a Tennessee teacher was awarded attorneys' fees as a prevailing litigant for the time spent on the judicial proceedings but was unsuccessful in persuading the Supreme Court that the local administrative proceedings were part of the preparation for court action.[239]

Although it has been established that the plaintiff who prevails in a civil rights suit may, at the court's discretion, be entitled to attorneys' fees, the same standard is not applied to defendants.[240] When a plaintiff teacher is awarded attorneys' fees, the assessment is against a party who has violated a federal law. Different criteria must be applied when a prevailing defendant seeks attorneys' fees. The Supreme Court has held that such fees cannot be imposed on a plaintiff unless the claim was "frivolous, unreasonable, or groundless."[241] Although awards of damages to prevailing defendants have not been common, in some situations such awards have been made to deter groundless lawsuits.

Conclusion

Through state laws and the Federal Constitution, extensive safeguards protect educators' employment security. Most states have adopted tenure laws that precisely delineate teachers' employment rights in termination and disciplinary proceedings. Additionally, in the absence of specific state guarantees, the Fourteenth Amendment ensures that teachers will be afforded procedural due process when property or liberty interests are implicated. Legal decisions interpreting both state and federal rights in dismissal actions have established broad guidelines as to when due process is required, the types of procedures that must be provided, and the legitimate causes required to substantiate dismissal action. Generalizations applicable to teacher employment termination are enumerated here.

1. A teacher is entitled to procedural due process if dismissal impairs a property or liberty interest.
2. Tenure status, defined by state law, confers upon teachers a property interest in continued employment; tenured teachers can be dismissed only for cause specified in state law.
3. Courts generally have held that probationary employment does not involve a property interest, except within the contract period.

---

239. Webb v. Bd. of Educ., 471 U.S. 234 (1985). *See also* N.C. Dep't of Transp. v. Crest St. Comm., 479 U.S. 6 (1986) (ruling that attorneys' fees could not be recovered in administrative proceedings independent of enforcement of Title VI of the Civil Rights Act of 1964).
240. *But see* Daddow v. Carlsbad Mun. Sch. Dist., 898 P.2d 1235 (N.M. 1995) (applying state law that entitles the prevailing party to an award of costs unless the court rules otherwise).
241. Christiansburg Garment Co. v. EEOC, 434 U.S. 412, 422 (1978). *See also* Bisciglia v. Kenosha Unified Sch. Dist. No. 1, 45 F.3d 223 (7th Cir. 1995).

4. A probationary teacher may establish a liberty interest, and thus entitlement to a hearing, if nonrenewal implicates a constitutional right, imposes a stigma, or forecloses opportunities for future employment.

5. When a liberty or property interest is implicated, the Fourteenth Amendment requires that a teacher be notified of charges and provided with an opportunity for a hearing that includes representation by counsel, examination and cross-examination of witnesses, and a record of the proceedings; however, formal trial procedures are not required.

6. An adequate notice of dismissal must adhere to statutory deadlines, follow designated form, allow the teacher time to prepare for a hearing, and specify charges.

7. The school board is considered an impartial hearing tribunal unless bias of its members can be clearly established.

8. The school board bears the burden of proof to introduce sufficient evidence to support a teacher's dismissal.

9. Causes for dismissal vary widely among the states, but usually include such grounds as incompetency, neglect of duty, immorality, insubordination, unprofessional conduct, and other good and just cause.

10. Incompetency is generally defined in relation to classroom performance—classroom management, teaching methods, grading, pupil/teacher relationships, and general attitude.

11. Immoral conduct, as the basis for dismissal, includes dishonest acts, improper sexual conduct, criminal acts, drug-related conduct, and other improprieties that have a negative impact on the teacher's effectiveness.

12. Dismissal for insubordination is based on a teacher's refusal to follow school regulations and policies.

13. Declining enrollment and financial exigencies constitute adequate cause for dismissing tenured teachers.

14. Wrongfully terminated employees may be entitled to reinstatement with back pay, compensatory and punitive damages, and attorneys' fees for the violation of constitutional rights.

15. An individual can recover only nominal damages for the impairment of constitutional rights unless monetary, emotional, or mental injury can be proven.

16. School officials can plead immunity to protect themselves from liability if their actions were taken in good faith; ignorance of clearly established principles of law is evidence of bad faith.

17. School districts cannot plead good faith as a defense against Section 1983 liability for compensatory damages in connection with the impairment of federally protected civil rights.

18. Punitive damages to punish the wrongdoer can be assessed against individual school officials but not against school districts.

19. Most courts have *not* considered school districts an arm of the state for purposes of Eleventh Amendment immunity from federal suits initiated by the state's citizens.

12

Labor Relations

Historically, boards of education have unilaterally controlled the management and operation of public schools. Teachers, as employees of the school board, were only minimally involved in decision making. To achieve a balance of power and a voice in school affairs, teachers turned to collective action during the 1960s and acquired significant labor rights. Labor laws and judicial rulings governing this shift in power were modeled after private-sector bargaining, resulting in labor relations in schools taking on an adversarial character.[1]

At the most fundamental level, collective bargaining juxtaposes teachers' demands for improved wages, hours, and conditions of employment against school boards' efforts to retain authority over educational policies and school operations. However, since formalized collective bargaining emerged in the early 1960s, negotiated contracts have evolved from a few pages addressing salaries to lengthy agreements that frequently are complex and impenetrable. Moreover, labor relations also are controlled by numerous other documents interpreting or amending the contract such as state labor relations board decisions, arbitration rulings, and memoranda of understanding related to the operation of the contract that often lead to limited flexibility for teachers and administrators.[2]

Diversity in labor laws and bargaining practices among the states makes it difficult to generalize about collective bargaining and teachers' labor rights. State labor laws, state employment relations board rulings, and court decisions must be consulted to determine specific rights, because there is no federal labor law covering public school employees.[3] Over two-thirds of the states have enacted bargaining laws, rang-

1. Over the past decade, pressures to reform schools have focused attention on creating collaborative negotiations processes that reduce the adversarial nature of conventional bargaining. Although some innovations have been implemented in the bargaining process, the basic legal structure explored in this chapter remains unchanged and shapes the outcome of labor relations in school districts.

2. For an analysis of this "contract behind the contract," *see* Howard Fuller, George Mitchell, and Michael Hartmann, *The Milwaukee Public Schools' Teacher Union Contract: Its History, Content, and Impact on Education* (Milwaukee, WI: Institute for Transformation of Learning, Marquette University, 1997).

3. *See infra* text accompanying note 19.

ing from very comprehensive laws controlling most aspects of negotiations to laws granting the minimal right to meet and confer. Still other states, in the absence of legislation, rely on judicial rulings to define the basic rights of public employees in the labor relations arena. This chapter examines the legal structure in which bargaining occurs and public school teachers' employment rights under state labor laws.[4]

Employees' Bargaining Rights in the Private and Public Sectors

Although there are basic differences in public and private employment, collective bargaining legislation in the private sector has significantly shaped statutory and judicial regulation of public negotiations. Similarities between the two sectors can be noted in a number of areas, such as unfair labor practices, union representation, and impasse procedures. Because private-sector legislation influences the public sector, a brief overview of its major legislative acts is warranted.

Prior to the 1930s, labor relations in the private sector were dominated by the judiciary, which strongly favored management. Extensive use of judicial injunctions against strikes and boycotts effectively countered employee efforts to obtain recognition for purposes of bargaining.[5] Consequently, courts reinforced the powers of management and substantially curtailed union development and influence. To bolster the worker's position, Congress enacted the Norris-LaGuardia Act in 1932.[6] The purpose of this federal law was to circumscribe the role of courts in labor disputes by preventing the use of the injunction, except where union activities were unlawful or jeopardized public safety and health. In essence, the legislation did not confer any new rights on employees or unions but simply restricted judicial authority that had impeded the development of unions.

Following the Norris-LaGuardia Act, Congress in 1935 passed the National Labor Relations Act (NLRA), commonly known as the Wagner Act.[7] This act created substantial rights for private-sector employees, but one of the most important outcomes was that it granted legitimacy to the collective bargaining process. In addition

---

4. As collective bargaining has matured in the public sector, state labor relations board decisions have become a substantial source of legal precedent for each state, with courts rendering fewer decisions in the labor arena. In fact, courts defer to the boards' rulings unless they are clearly contrary to law. Although specific rulings of labor boards are not included in this chapter, educators are encouraged to examine that extensive body of law if a board governs negotiations in their state.

5. For a historical discussion of the use and control of labor injunctions, *see* Benjamin Taylor and Fred Witney, *Labor Relations Law,* 4th ed. (Englewood Cliffs, NJ: Prentice-Hall, 1983).

6. 29 U.S.C. § 101 (2002). This act also rendered "yellow dog" contracts, which required employees to promise not to join a union, unenforceable by courts.

7. The Wagner Act states that "employees shall have the right to self-organization, to form, join or assist labor organizations, to bargain collectively through representatives of their own choosing, and to engage in concerted activities, for the purpose of collective bargaining or other mutual aid or protection." 29 U.S.C. § 157 (2002).

to defining employees' rights to organize and bargain collectively, the NLRA established a mechanism to safeguard these rights—the National Labor Relations Board
(NLRB). The NLRB was created specifically to monitor claims of unfair labor practices, such as interference with employees' rights to organize, discrimination against
employees in hiring or discharge because of union membership, and failure to bargain
in good faith.[8]

The NLRA was amended in 1947 by the Labor Management Relations Act
(commonly known as the Taft-Hartley Act).[9] Whereas the Wagner Act regulated
employers' activities, the Taft-Hartley Act attempted to balance the scales in collective bargaining by regulating abusive union practices, such as interfering with
employees' organizational rights, failing to provide fair representation for all employees in the bargaining unit, and refusing to bargain in good faith. Since 1947, other
amendments to the Taft-Hartley Act have further reduced union abuses. Federal legislation has restricted interference from both the employer and the union, thereby
ensuring the individual employee greater freedom of choice in collective bargaining.

Although the NLRA specifically exempts bargaining by governmental employees, a number of state public employee statutes have been modeled after this law, and
judicial decisions interpreting the NLRA have been used to define certain provisions
in public-sector laws. The recognition of the sovereign power of public employers,
however, is clearly present in public labor laws. For example, many public laws
require employers to bargain over wages, hours, and other terms and conditions of
employment as in the NLRA, but this requirement then is restricted by management
rights clauses limiting the scope of bargaining.

There are several basic differences in bargaining between the public and private
sectors. First, the removal of decision-making authority from public officials through

8. The application of private-sector labor laws to private schools, most of which are church related, has
been controversial. Only private schools with a gross annual revenue of $1 million or more come under
the jurisdiction of the NLRB; however, the majority of private schools do not reach this income level.
Furthermore, the Supreme Court has held that the NLRB does not have jurisdiction over lay faculty in
parochial schools in the absence of a clear expression of congressional intent to cover teachers in
church-related schools under the NLRA. Nat'l Labor Relations Bd. v. Catholic Bishop of Chi., 440 U.S.
490 (1979). The Second Circuit, however, concluded that Catholic schools in New York come under
the jurisdiction of the state labor relations board. Since the ruling involved bargaining activities of lay
teachers regarding only secular employment practices, no infringement of the Establishment Clause or
Free Exercise Clause of the First Amendment was found. Catholic High Sch. Ass'n v. Culvert, 753 F.2d
1161 (2d Cir. 1985). See also Hill-Murray Fed'n of Teachers v. Hill-Murray High Sch., 487 N.W.2d 857
(Minn. 1992) (ruling that church-affiliated schools are not free from the state labor law, which is a neutral regulatory law directed at secular activities); S. Jersey Catholic Sch. Teachers Org. v. St. Teresa of
the Infant Jesus Church Elementary Sch., 696 A.2d 709 (N.J. 1997) (finding that the state labor law was
a generally applicable law, neutral in its application and not intended to regulate religious conduct or
belief); N.Y. State Employment Relations Bd. v. Christ the King Reg'l High Sch., 660 N.Y.S.2d 359
(1997) (ruling that the state labor relations law in its application to lay teachers did not violate the Free
Exercise Clause or Establishment Clause).

9. 29 U.S.C. §§ 141 et seq. (2002).

bargaining has been viewed as an infringement on the government's sovereign power, which has resulted in the enactment of labor laws strongly favoring public employers. Public employees' rights have been further weakened by prohibitions of work stoppages. Whereas employees' ability to strike is considered *essential* to the effective operation of collective decision making in the private sector, this view has been rejected in the public sector because of the nature and structure of governmental services.

Bargaining rights developed slowly for public employees who historically had been deprived of the right to organize and bargain collectively. President Kennedy's Executive Order 10988 in 1962, which gave federal employees the right to form, join, and assist employee organizations, was a significant milestone for all public employees. The granting of organizational rights to federal employees provided the impetus for similar gains at the state and local levels.

Until the late 1960s, however, public employees' constitutional right to join a union had not been fully established. A large number of public employees actively participated in collective bargaining, but statutes and regulations in some states prohibited union membership. These restrictions against union membership were challenged as impairing association freedoms protected by the First Amendment. Although not addressing union membership, the Supreme Court held in 1967 that public employment could not be conditioned on the relinquishment of free association rights.[10] In a later decision, the Seventh Circuit clearly announced that "an individual's right to form and join a union is protected by the First Amendment."[11] Other courts followed this precedent by invalidating state statutory provisions that blocked union membership.[12]

The judiciary has continued to reinforce teachers' constitutional rights to participate fully in union activities. School officials have been prohibited from imposing sanctions or denying benefits to discourage protected association rights. For example, the Sixth Circuit overturned a school board's dismissal of a teacher because of union activities.[13] The Eighth Circuit held that a teacher's allegation that the superintendent placed her on probation to punish her for union activities was sufficient to establish a claim against the superintendent.[14] Similarly, the Connecticut Federal District Court

---

10. Keyishian v. Bd. of Regents, 385 U.S. 589 (1967).

11. McLaughlin v. Tilendis, 398 F.2d 287, 289 (7th Cir. 1968). *See also* St. Clair County Intermediate Sch. Dist. v. St. Clair County Educ. Ass'n, 630 N.W.2d 909 (Mich. Ct. App. 2001).

12. *See, e.g.,* Atkins v. City of Charlotte, 296 F. Supp. 1068 (W.D.N.C. 1969); Dade County Classroom Teachers' Ass'n v. Ryan, 225 So. 2d 903 (Fla. 1969).

13. Hickman v. Valley Local Sch. Dist. Bd. of Educ., 619 F.2d 606 (6th Cir. 1980). *See also* Cent. Sch. Dist. 13J v. Cent. Educ. Ass'n, 962 P.2d 763 (Or. Ct. App. 1998) (ruling that a teacher could not be discharged for exercising association rights protected under state law).

14. Springdale Educ. Ass'n v. Springdale Sch. Dist., 133 F.3d 649 (8th Cir. 1998). *See also* Ga. Ass'n of Educators v. Gwinnett County Sch. Dist., 856 F.2d 142 (11th Cir. 1988); Saye v. St. Vrain Valley Sch. Dist. RE-1J, 785 F.2d 862 (10th Cir. 1986).

found that the transfer of a teacher to another school in retaliation for using the negotiated grievance procedure was constitutionally prohibited.[15]

The United States Constitution has been interpreted as protecting public
employees' rights to organize, but the right to form and join a union does not ensure
the right to bargain collectively with a public employer; individual state statutes and
constitutions govern such bargaining rights. Whether identified as professional negotiations, collective negotiations, or collective bargaining, the process entails bilateral
decision making in which the teachers' representative and the school board attempt to
reach mutual agreement on matters affecting teacher employment. This process is
governed in 34 states by legislation granting specific bargaining rights to teachers and
their professional associations. Courts, viewing collective bargaining as within the
scope of legislative authority, have restricted their role primarily to interpreting statutory and constitutional provisions. The judiciary has been reluctant to interfere with
legislative authority to define the collective bargaining relationship between public
employers and employees unless protected rights have been compromised.

Because of the variations in labor laws, as well as the lack of such laws in some
states, substantial differences exist in bargaining rights and practices. A few states,
such as New York, have a detailed, comprehensive collective bargaining statute that
delineates specific bargaining rights. In contrast, negotiated contracts between teachers' organizations and school boards are prohibited in North Carolina. Under North
Carolina law, all contracts between public employers and employee associations are
invalid.[16] Similarly, the Virginia Supreme Court declared that a negotiated contract
between a teachers' organization and a school board is void without express enabling
legislation.[17] The board argued that its power to enter into contracts allowed it also to
bargain collectively with employee organizations, but the court concluded that such
implied power contradicted legislative intent.

In contrast to North Carolina and Virginia, other states without legislation have
permitted negotiated agreements. The Kentucky Supreme Court has ruled that a public employer may recognize an employee organization for the purpose of collective
bargaining, even though state law is silent regarding public employee bargaining
rights.[18] The decision does not impose a duty on local school boards to bargain but
merely allows a board the discretion to negotiate. This ruling is consistent with a number of other decisions permitting negotiated contracts in the absence of specific legis-

---

15. Stellmaker v. DePetrillo, 710 F. Supp. 891 (D. Conn. 1989). *See also* Morfin v. Albuquerque Pub. Sch.,
    906 F.2d 1434 (10th Cir. 1990) (recognizing a teacher's right to associate with a union and to file a
    grievance); Rockville Centre Teachers Ass'n v. N.Y. State Pub. Employment Relations Bd., 721
    N.Y.S.2d 112 (App. Div. 2001) (holding that an employee must establish a connection between an
    adverse employment decision and union activity); State Employment Relations Bd. v. Adena Local
    Sch. Dist. Bd. of Educ., 613 N.E.2d 605 (Ohio 1993) (finding that retaliation is prohibited under public
    bargaining law).

16. N.C. Gen Stat. § 95-98 (2002).

17. Commonwealth v. County Bd., 232 S.E.2d 30 (Va. 1977).

18. Bd. of Trs. v. Pub. Employees Council No. 51, 571 S.W.2d 616 (Ky. 1978). *See also* Littleton Educ.
    Ass'n v. Arapahoe County Sch. Dist., 553 P.2d 793 (Colo. 1976).

lation. The board's authority to enter into contracts for the operation and maintenance of the school system has been construed to include the ability to enter into negotiated agreements with employee organizations.

Unless mandated by statute, courts have not compelled school boards to negotiate. Whether to negotiate is thus at the school board's discretion. Once a school board extends recognition to a bargaining agent and commences bargaining, however, the board's actions in the negotiation process are governed by established judicial principles. Although the employer maintains certain prerogatives, such as recognition of the bargaining unit and determination of bargainable items, specific judicially recognized rights also are conferred on the employee organization. For example, there is a legal duty for the board to bargain in good faith. Furthermore, if the negotiation process reaches an impasse, the board may not unilaterally terminate bargaining. Also, after signing a contract, the board is bound by the provisions and cannot abrogate the agreement on the basis that no duty to bargain existed. Hence, the school board is subject to a number of legal constraints after beginning the negotiation process.

The diversity across states in protected bargaining rights for public employees has led many individuals and groups to advocate a federal bargaining law for all state and local employees. Supporting such a proposal are a number of national organizations, including the National Education Association, the American Federation of Teachers, and the American Federation of State, County, and Municipal Employees. In the mid-1970s, a federal law appeared imminent, but was abandoned by Congress with the Supreme Court's decision in *National League of Cities v. Usery* interpreting congressional authority under the Commerce Clause and within the limitations of the Tenth Amendment.[19] The Court ruled that congressional amendments to the Fair Labor Standards Act (FLSA), extending the federal minimum wage and maximum hour provisions to state and local government employees, unconstitutionally interfered with the states' rights to structure the public employer/employee relationship.

The Supreme Court, however, overturned *Usery* in 1985, concluding in *Garcia v. San Antonio Metropolitan Transit Authority* that state and municipal governments must comply with the minimum wage and overtime requirements in the FLSA.[20] The Court noted that nothing in these requirements was destructive of state sovereignty and that various checks on congressional power existed within the states. With this recognition of congressional authority, Congress again may consider uniform collective bargaining legislation. But for the immediate future, bargaining rights seem destined to be controlled by individual state legislation or, in the absence of such legislation, by the judiciary.

19. 426 U.S. 833 (1976).
20. 469 U.S. 528 (1985). Although the Supreme Court in recent years has been increasingly protective of state and local governments against various federal mandates, it has continued to recognize Congress's power to regulate these entities under the Commerce Clause. *See* Richard H. Fallon, "The 'Conservative' Paths of the Rehnquist Court's Federalism Decisions," *University of Chicago Law Review,* vol. 69 (Spring 2002): 429–494; text accompanying note 60, Chapter 1.

Teachers' Statutory Bargaining Rights

In states with laws governing teachers' bargaining rights, school boards must negotiate with teachers in accordance with the statutorily prescribed process. Generally,
public employee bargaining laws address employer and employee rights, bargaining
units, scope of bargaining, impasse resolution, grievance procedures, unfair labor
practices, and penalties for prohibited practices. Many states have established labor
relations boards to monitor bargaining under their statutes. Although the specific
functions of these boards vary widely, their general purpose is to resolve questions
arising from the implementation of state law. Functions assigned to such boards
include determination of membership in bargaining units, resolution of union recognition claims, investigation of unfair labor practices, and interpretation of the general
intent of statutory bargaining clauses.[21] Usually, judicial review cannot be pursued
until administrative review before labor boards is exhausted.[22] Thus, decisions of
labor boards are an important source of labor law, since many of the issues addressed
by boards are never appealed to courts. When the boards' decisions are challenged in
court, substantial deference is given to their findings and determinations.[23]

Most state laws define the broad criteria for determining appropriate groupings
of employees for bargaining purposes. Among the factors considered in assessing the
appropriateness of bargaining units are the similarity in skills, wages, hours, and other
working conditions of the employees; the effect of overfragmentation; the efficiency
of operations of the employer; and the employer's administrative structure. Of these
factors, similarity in skills and working conditions has been the most significant
requirement. State labor boards usually resolve disputes over the appropriateness of
bargaining units.[24]

State laws generally provide that the school board will negotiate with an exclusive representative selected by the teachers. Procedures are specified for certification
of the bargaining representative, election of the representative by employees, and recognition by the employer. Once the state labor relations board recognizes an exclusive
representative, an employer must bargain with that representative. In addition to certification, state laws also address cause and process for decertification of the exclusive
representative.

Like the NLRA, state statutes require bargaining "in good faith." *Good faith
bargaining* has been interpreted as requiring parties to meet at reasonable times and

21. *See, e.g.,* Cent. City Educ. Ass'n v. Ill. Educ. Labor Relations Bd., 599 N.E.2d 892 (Ill. 1992); Tualatin
    Valley Bargaining Council v. Tigard Sch. Dist., 840 P.2d 657 (Or. 1992).

22. *See, e.g.,* Fratus v. Marion Cmty. Schs. Bd. of Trs., 749 N.E.2d 40 (Ind. 2001).

23. *See, e.g.,* Bd. of Educ. v. State Bd. of Labor Relations, 584 A.2d 1172 (Conn. 1991); *In re* Verderber,
    795 A.2d 1157 (Vt. 2002); Dodgeland Educ. Ass'n v. Wis. Employment Relations Comm'n, 639
    N.W.2d 733 (Wis. 2002).

24. *See, e.g.,* Ohio Rev. Code § 4117.06 (A) (2002). State law not only provides that the Ohio State
    Employment Relations Board determines the appropriateness of a bargaining unit but also stipulates
    that the Board's decision is "final and conclusive and not appealable to the court."

attempt to reach mutual agreement without compulsion on either side to agree.[25] A number of states have followed the federal law in stipulating that this "does not compel either party to agree to a proposal or to require the making of a concession."[26] Good faith bargaining has been open to a range of interpretations, and judicial decisions in the public sector have relied extensively on private-sector rulings that have clarified the phrase. Failure of the school board or teachers' organization to bargain in good faith can result in the imposition of penalties.

Statutes impose certain restrictions or obligations on both the school board and the employee organization. Violation of the law by either party can result in an unfair labor practice claim. Allegations of unfair labor practices are brought before the state public employee relations board for a hearing and judgment. Specific unfair labor practices, often modeled after those in the NLRA, are included in state statutes. The most common prohibited labor practice in both public and private employment is that an employer or union will not interfere with, restrain, or coerce public employees in exercising their rights under the labor law.[27] Among other prohibited *employer* practices are interference with union operations, discrimination against employees because of union membership, refusal to bargain collectively with the exclusive representative, and failure to bargain in good faith. *Unions* are prevented from causing an employer to discriminate against employees on the basis of union membership, refusing to bargain or failing to bargain in good faith, failing to represent all employees in the bargaining unit, and engaging in unlawful activities such as strikes or boycotts identified in the bargaining law.

Upon completion of the negotiation process, the members of the bargaining unit and the school board must ratify the written agreement (usually referred to as *the master contract*). These agreements often contain similar standard contract language and clauses, beginning with recognition of the exclusive bargaining representative and union security issues (i.e., fair share fees). Management rights and association rights also are detailed. Management clauses emphasize the board's control over the establishment of educational policies, and union clauses may include the right to use school facilities or communication systems. Other provisions relate to the scope of bargaining, which is defined by the state's labor law or common law. These items include not only salary and fringe benefits but also may address grievance procedures, employee evaluations, preparation time, length of workday, class size, procedural process for employee discipline, transfers, layoff and recall procedures, assignment of duties, and procedures for filling vacancies. The range in the negotiability of these issues can be seen in the next section.

---

25. *See, e.g.,* Belfield Educ. Ass'n v. Belfield Pub. Sch. Dist. No. 13, 496 N.W.2d 12 (N.D. 1993).

26. 29 U.S.C. § 158(d) (2002).

27. *See, e.g.,* Uniontown Area Sch. Dist. v. Pa. Labor Relations Bd., 747 A.2d 1271 (Pa. Commw. Ct. 2000) (concluding that the school district committed an unfair labor practice when it did not promote a teacher to principal because of concerns about her union activities).

Scope of Negotiations

Should the teachers' organization have input into class size? Who will determine the length of the school day? How will extra-duty assignments be determined? Will reductions-in-force necessitated by declining enrollment be based on seniority or merit? These questions and others are raised in determining the scope of negotiations. *Scope* refers to the range of issues or subjects that are negotiable, and determining scope is one of the most difficult tasks in public sector bargaining. Public employers argue that issues must be narrowly defined to protect the government's policymaking role, whereas employee unions counter that bargaining subjects must be defined broadly to have meaningful negotiations.

Restrictions on scope of bargaining vary considerably among states. Consequently, to determine negotiable items in a particular state, the state's collective bargaining law, other statutes, and litigation interpreting these laws must be examined. The specification of negotiable items in labor laws may include broad guidelines or detailed enumeration of specific issues. As noted, many states have modeled their bargaining statutes after the National Labor Relations Act, which stipulates that representatives of the employer and employees must meet and confer "with respect to wages, hours, and other terms and conditions of employment."[28] A few states deal directly with the scope of bargaining by identifying each item that must be negotiated.[29] Some states specify prohibited subjects of bargaining. For example, Michigan's prohibited subjects include decisions related to the establishment of the starting date for the school year, composition of site-based decision-making bodies, interdistrict and intradistrict open enrollment opportunities, authorization of public school academies, and establishment and staffing of experimental programs.[30] Generally, statutory mandates cannot be preempted by collective bargaining agreements;[31] however, in a few states, the negotiated agreement prevails over conflicting laws, unless the laws are specifically exempted.[32]

All proposed subjects for negotiation can be classified as mandatory, permissive, or prohibited. Mandatory items must be negotiated. Failure of the school board

28. 29 U.S.C. § 158(d) (2002).

29. *See, e.g.,* Iowa Code § 20.9 (2002); Nev. Rev. Stat. § 288.150 (2002). *See also* Blount County Educ. Ass'n v. Blount County Bd. of Educ., 78 S.W.2d 307 (Tenn. Ct. App. 2002) (ruling that the state legislature did not intend to give "working conditions" a broad interpretation when it specifically listed eight mandatory bargaining topics).

30. M.C.L.A. § 423.215(3)(4) (2002). *See also* Mich. State AFL-CIO v. Mich. Employment Relations Comm'n, 538 N.W.2d 433 (Mich. Ct. App. 1995).

31. *See, e.g.,* Bd. of Educ. v. Ill. Educ. Labor Relations Bd., 649 N.E.2d 369 (Ill. 1995); Lucio v. Sch. Bd., 574 N.W.2d 737 (Minn. Ct. App. 1998); Mifflinburg Area Educ. Ass'n v. Mifflinburg Area Sch. Dist., 724 A.2d 339 (Pa. 1999); Trombley v. Bellows Falls Union High Sch. Dist. No. 27, 624 A.2d 867 (Vt. 1993).

32. *See, e.g.,* Streetsboro Educ. Ass'n v. Streetsboro City Sch. Dist., 626 N.E.2d 110 (Ohio 1994). *See also* State Dep't of Admin. v. Pub. Employees Relations Bd., 894 P.2d 777 (Kan. 1995) (holding that a collective bargaining agreement takes precedence over conflicting civil service regulations).

to meet and confer on such items is evidence of lack of good faith bargaining. Permissive items can be negotiated if both parties agree; however, there is no legal duty to consider the items. Furthermore, in most states, permissive items cannot be pursued to the point of negotiation impasse, and an employer may unilaterally change these items if no agreement is reached. Prohibited items are beyond the power of the board to negotiate; an illegal delegation of power results if the board agrees to negotiate these items. Since most statutory scope provisions are general in nature, courts or labor relations boards often have been asked to differentiate between negotiable and nonnegotiable items.[33] The following sections highlight issues related to governmental policy and specific bargaining topics.

Governmental Policy

Defining managerial rights is a key element in establishing limitations on negotiable subjects at the bargaining table. State laws specify that public employers cannot be required to negotiate governmental policy matters, and courts have held that it is impermissible for a school board to bargain away certain rights and responsibilities in the public policy area.[34] Generally, educational policy matters are defined through provisions in collective bargaining statutes, such as "management rights" and "scope of bargaining" clauses. Policy issues, such as class size and decisions related to the granting of tenure, are excluded as negotiable items in a few states; however, most states stipulate only that employers are not *required* to bargain such policy rights.

Public employee labor laws requiring the negotiation of "conditions of employment" can include far-reaching policy matters, since most school board decisions either directly or indirectly affect the teacher in the classroom. The Maryland high court noted the difficulty in distinguishing between educational policy and matters relating to teachers' employment: "Virtually every managerial decision in some way relates to 'salaries, wages, hours, and other working conditions,' and is therefore arguably negotiable. At the same time, virtually every such decision also involves educational policy considerations and is therefore arguably nonnegotiable."[35] In many states, the interpretation of what is negotiable resides with the labor relations board. Often, a balancing test is employed by these boards as well as courts, beginning with an inquiry into whether a particular matter involves wages, hours, and terms and con-

---

33. *See* Junction City Educ. Ass'n v. Bd. of Educ., 955 P.2d 1266 (Kan. 1998) (ruling that issues of negotiability should be determined initially by the state administrative agency rather than through a declaratory judgment action in a district court).

34. *See, e.g.,* Montgomery County Educ. Ass'n v. Bd. of Educ., 534 A.2d 980 (Md. 1987); Bd. of Educ. v. N.Y. State Pub. Employment Relations Bd., 555 N.Y.S.2d 659, 663 (1990); Raines v. Indep. Sch. Dist. No. 6, 796 P.2d 303 (Okla. 1990). *See also* Mich. State AFL-CIO v. Employment Relations Ass'n, 551 N.W.2d 165 (Mich. 1996) (holding that state law prohibiting bargaining over certain subjects did not implicate public employees' First Amendment speech rights).

35. *Montgomery County Educ. Ass'n,* 534 A.2d at 986.

ditions of employment. If so, then the labor board or court must determine if the matter also is one of inherent managerial policy. If not, the matter is a mandatory subject of bargaining. However, if the response is yes, the benefits of bargaining on the decision-making process must be balanced against the burden on the employer's authority.[36] Accordingly, this process entails a fact-specific analysis.

Judicial decisions interpreting negotiability illustrate the range in bargainable matters. The Supreme Court of New Jersey narrowly interpreted *conditions of employment* to mean wages, benefits, and work schedules, thereby removing governmental policy items such as teacher transfers, course offerings, and evaluations.[37] A number of courts, however, have construed the phrase in broader terms. The Nevada Supreme Court ruled that items *significantly* related to wages, hours, and working conditions are negotiable.[38] Similarly, the Pennsylvania Supreme Court concluded that an issue's *impact* on conditions of employment must be weighed to determine whether it should be considered outside the educational policy area.[39]

Although courts agree that school boards cannot be *required* to negotiate inherent managerial rights pertaining to policy matters, some states view these rights as *permissive* subjects of bargaining. That is, the board may agree to negotiate a particular "right" in the absence of statutory or judicial prohibitions.[40] If the board does negotiate a policy item, it is bound by the agreement in the same manner as if the issue were a mandatory item.[41]

36. *See, e.g.,* Cent. City Educ. Ass'n v. Ill. Educ. Labor Relations Bd., 599 N.E.2d 892 (Ill. 1992); Bay City Educ. Ass'n v. Bay City Pub. Schs., 422 N.W.2d 504 (Mich. 1988); City of Beloit v. Wis. Employment Relations Bd., 242 N.W.2d 231 (Wis. 1976). *See also* Sherrard Cmty. Unit Sch. v. Ill. Educ. Labor Relations Bd., 696 N.E.2d 833 (Ill. App. Ct. 1998) (finding that reassignment of teachers involves exercise of managerial discretion that generally is not a mandatory bargaining subject; actions of school board in directly negotiating with a teacher made it a mandatory subject).

37. Ridgefield Park Educ. Ass'n v. Ridgefield Park Bd. of Educ., 393 A.2d 278 (N.J. 1978). *See also* Carter County Bd. of Educ. v. Carter County Educ. Ass'n, 56 S.W.3d 1 (Tenn. Ct. App. 1996) (holding that the authority to appoint a principal was not subject to collective bargaining).

38. Clark County Sch. Dist. v. Local Gov't Employee-Management Relations Bd., 530 P.2d 114 (Nev. 1974).

39. Pa. Labor Relations Bd. v. State Coll. Area Sch. Dist., 337 A.2d 262 (Pa. 1975). *See also* Local 1186 v. State Bd. of Labor Relations, 620 A.2d 766 (Conn. 1993); Tualatin Valley Bargaining Council v. Tigard Sch. Dist., 840 P.2d 657 (Or. 1992).

40. *See, e.g.,* Bd. of Educ. v. Greenburgh Teachers Fed'n, 603 N.Y.S.2d 823 (1993). *But see* Colonial Sch. Bd. v. Colonial Affiliate, 449 A.2d 243 (Del. 1982) (holding that the state law does not recognize bargaining of permissive subjects); Montgomery County Educ. Ass'n v. Bd. of Educ., 534 A.2d 980 (Md. 1987) (finding no provision for permissive subjects to be bargained).

41. *See, e.g.,* DiPiazza v. Bd. of Educ., 625 N.Y.S.2d 298 (App. Div. 1995). *See also* Univ. of Haw. Prof'l Assembly v. Cayetano, 183 F.3d 1096 (9th Cir. 1999) (noting that in interpreting the requirements of a negotiated agreement, past practices are probative; the court held that the employer changing the timing of the payroll schedule raised such an issue); Bd. of Educ. v. Ward, 974 P.2d 824 (Utah 1999) (finding that although school boards have substantial discretion to interpret their policies, they do not have that discretion if the policy is part of a negotiated collective bargaining contract).

Selected Bargaining Subjects

Beyond wages, hours, and fringe benefits, states disagree as to what is negotiable. Similar enabling legislation has been interpreted quite differently among states, as illustrated by the subjects discussed next.

Class Size.   Class size has been one of the most controversial policy subjects, and one that courts and state legislatures have been reluctant to designate as negotiable. Only a few states specifically identify class size as a mandatory bargaining item,[42] and the majority of courts reviewing the issue have found it to be a nonmandatory item.[43] After the Nevada Supreme Court interpreted the state collective bargaining statute as including class size among mandatory subjects by implication,[44] the legislature responded by revising the state law to exclude class size from a detailed list of bargainable items.[45] An Illinois appellate court, however, held that class size is a mandatory issue for bargaining,[46] and several other courts have found it to be a *permissive* subject of bargaining.[47] Although the Wisconsin Supreme Court found class size to be such a permissive subject, the court held that negotiations on the impact of class size (e.g., more projects to supervise, potential for more disciplinary problems, etc.) on teachers' conditions of employment would be mandatory.[48] Similarly, a Florida appellate court concluded that class size and staffing levels are not mandatorily bargainable but noted that bargaining on the impact or effect of the implementation of these decisions would be mandatory.[49]

School Calendar.   Establishing the school calendar generally has been held to be a managerial prerogative.[50] Reflecting the judicial trend that it is a nonnegotiable man-

42. *See, e.g.,* Mass. Gen. Laws ch. 150E § 6 (2002).

43. *See* Cent. State Univ. v. Am. Ass'n of Univ. Professors, 526 U.S. 124 (1999), *on remand,* 717 N.E.2d 286 (Ohio 1999) (upholding an Ohio statute excluding faculty workload in public universities from collective bargaining).

44. Clark County Sch. Dist. v. Local Gov't Employee Mgmt. Relations Bd., 530 P.2d 114 (Nev. 1974).

45. Nev. Rev. Stat. 288 § 150.3(c)(3) (2002).

46. Decatur Bd. of Educ., Dist. No. 61 v. Ill. Educ. Labor Relations Bd., 536 N.E.2d 743 (Ill. App. Ct. 1989). *But see* 115 ILCS 5/4.5(a)(4) (2002) (specifying that bargaining about class size is prohibited in a school district whose boundaries are coterminous with a city having a population in excess of 500,000).

47. *See, e.g.,* Nat'l Educ. Ass'n-Kan. City v. Unified Sch. Dist., Wyandotte County, 608 P.2d 415 (Kan. 1980); Fargo Educ. Ass'n v. Fargo Pub. Sch. Dist., 291 N.W.2d 267 (N.D. 1980); City of Beloit v. Wis. Employment Relations Comm'n, 242 N.W.2d 231 (Wis. 1976).

48. *City of Beloit,* 242 N.W.2d 231. *See also* Tualatin Valley Bargaining Council v. Tigard Sch. Dist., 840 P.2d 657 (Or. 1992) (holding that class size was not automatically a mandatory subject under "other conditions of employment" because it related to a teacher's workload; an assessment must be made relative to its effect on working conditions).

49. Hillsborough Classroom Teachers Ass'n v. Sch. Bd., 423 So. 2d 969 (Fla. Dist. Ct. App. 1982).

50. *See, e.g.,* Pub. Employee Relations Bd. v. Wash. Teachers' Union Local 6, 556 A.2d 206 (D.C. App. 1989); Montgomery County Educ. Ass'n v. Bd. of Educ., 534 A.2d 980 (Md. 1987); Bd. of Educ. v. Woodstown-Pilesgrove Reg'l Educ. Ass'n, 410 A.2d 1131 (N.J. 1980).

agerial decision, the Maine high court stated, "The commencement and termination of the school year and the scheduling and length of intermediate vacations during the school year, at least insofar as students and teachers are congruently involved, must be held matters of 'educational policies' bearing too substantially upon too many and important non-teacher interests to be settled by collective bargaining."[51] An Indiana appellate court agreed, noting that the impact of the school calendar on students and other public interests outweighed teachers' interests.[52] Notwithstanding that the establishment of the school calendar is a managerial prerogative, the Supreme Court of New Jersey ruled that decisions affecting the days worked and compensation for those days implicate a term and condition of employment.[53] Departing from the prevailing view, the Wisconsin Supreme Court upheld a ruling of the Wisconsin Employment Relations Commission declaring the school calendar mandatorily bargainable; calendar issues were found to be more closely related to terms of employment than to policy matters.[54]

Teacher Evaluation.   Employee unions have made significant gains in securing the right to negotiate various aspects of teacher performance evaluations. Most states have not specified evaluation as a mandatory bargaining item, but a number of courts have found it to be significantly related to conditions of employment and thus negotiable. Although courts have been receptive to union proposals to negotiate the technical and procedural elements of evaluation, they have been reluctant to mandate the negotiation of evaluation criteria. In ruling that teacher evaluation was not a prohibited bargaining subject, the Supreme Court of New Hampshire noted that the contested evaluation plan provided only the procedures for evaluations, not the standards by which the teachers would be reviewed.[55] Similarly, the Supreme Court of Kansas distinguished between managerial policies and the mechanics of such policies; the mechanics of developing the evaluation procedures were found to be mandatorily

51. City of Biddeford v. Biddeford Teachers Ass'n, 304 A.2d 387, 421 (Me. 1973).

52. Eastbrook Cmty. Sch. Corp. v. Ind. Educ. Employment Relations Bd., 446 N.E.2d 1007 (Ind. Ct. App. 1983). *See also* Ind. Educ. Employment Relations Bd. v. Highland Classroom Teachers Ass'n, 546 N.E.2d 101 (Ind. Ct. App. 1989) (holding that calendar items that did not infringe on exclusive managerial powers were negotiable under a grandfather clause in the collective bargaining law); Union County Sch. Corp. v. Ind. Educ. Employment Relations Bd., 471 N.E.2d 1191 (Ind. Ct. App. 1984) (ruling that mandatory bargaining of the school calendar is not required, but under state law it is a "working condition" that must be discussed).

53. Troy v. Rutgers, 774 A.2d 476 (N.J. 2001).

54. City of Beloit v. Employment Relations Comm'n, 242 N.W.2d 231 (Wis. 1976). *But see* Racine Educ. Ass'n v. Wis. Employment Relations Comm'n, 571 N.W.2d 887 (Wis. Ct. App. 1997) (upholding the Wisconsin Employment Relations Commission's (WERC) determination that the implementation of a pilot year-round school calendar was not subject to mandatory bargaining; in balancing the employer and employee interests in this specific situation, WERC found the year-round program primarily related to educational policy).

55. *In re* Pittsfield Sch. Dist., 744 A.2d 594 (N.H. 1999). *See also* Sch. Comm. v. Boston Teachers Union, 664 N.E.2d 478 (Mass. App. Ct. 1996) (ruling that an arbitrator's authority in the nonreappointment of a teacher was limited to the agreed upon evaluation procedures).

negotiable but not the evaluation criteria, which were designated as a managerial prerogative.[56] The Supreme Court of Iowa, however, found a statutory requirement to negotiate *evaluation procedures* to encompass substantive criteria for evaluation because the term *procedures* had been interpreted broadly in previous judicial rulings.[57]

Reduction-in-Force.   With many school districts facing declining student enrollments and financial exigency, staff reductions-in-force (RIF) are threatening tenured as well as nontenured teachers. The threat has resulted in employee unions demanding input into decisions to reduce staff, criteria for reductions, and procedures for selecting teachers for release. Courts generally have held that the decision to reduce staff and the criteria used to make that decision are educational policy matters and thus not negotiable.[58] State laws also may specifically prohibit collective bargaining of reduction-in-force decisions.[59] The impact of reductions on employee rights, however, may necessitate negotiation of procedures for the reduction. The Supreme Court of South Dakota held that the decision to reduce teaching positions was a nonnegotiable managerial decision, but concluded that the mechanics of staff reductions, such as how staff would be selected and procedures for recall, were mandatorily negotiable.[60] The Supreme Court of Wisconsin found that notice and timing of layoffs had to be bar-

56. Bd. of Educ. v. NEA-Goodland, 785 P.2d 993 (Kan. 1990). *See also* Wethersfield Bd. of Educ. v. Conn. State Bd. of Labor Relations, 519 A.2d 41 (Conn. 1986).

57. Aplington Cmty. Sch. Dist. v. Iowa Pub. Employment Relations Bd., 392 N.W.2d 495 (Iowa 1986). *See also* Atlantic Educ. Ass'n v. Atlantic Cmty. Sch. Dist., 469 N.W.2d 689 (Iowa 1991) (concluding that the collective bargaining contract did not provide for arbitration of performance evaluation in the absence of negotiated performance criteria; the negotiated agreement addressed only procedural aspects, which were not contested by the teacher); Snyder v. Mendon-Union Local Sch. Dist. Bd. of Educ., 661 N.E.2d 717 (Ohio 1996) (ruling that, in the absence of a collective bargaining agreement specifying otherwise, state law governs the evaluation of a nontenured teacher).

58. *See, e.g.,* Thompson v. Unified Sch. Dist. No. 259, 819 P.2d 1236 (Kan. Ct. App. 1991); Township of Old Bridge Bd. of Educ. v. Old Bridge Educ. Ass'n, 489 A.2d 159 (N.J. 1985); N. Star Sch. Dist. v. N. Star Educ. Ass'n, 625 A.2d 159 (Pa. Commw. Ct. 1993). *But see In re* Hillsboro-Deering Sch. Dist., 737 A.2d 1098 (N.H. 1999) (ruling that the decision to release all employees in a bargaining unit to contract with a private company did not constitute a true layoff involving managerial rights and therefore it was subject to bargaining).

59. *See, e.g.,* Ill. Comp. Stat. 115 ILCS 5/4.5(a)(3) (2002). *See also* Chi. Sch. Reform Bd. of Trs. v. Educ. Labor Relations Bd., 741 N.E.2d 989 (Ill. App. Ct. 2000) (affirming the state labor board's decision upholding an arbitrator's order to reinstate a reserve teacher; the court agreed that the decision did not involve a prohibited subject since the termination of the reserve teacher was not a "layoff" involving a lack of funds or work).

60. Webster Educ. Ass'n v. Webster Sch. Dist., 631 N.W.2d 202 (S.D. 2001). *See also* Davis v. Chester Upland Sch. Dist., 786 A.2d 186 (Pa. 2001) (finding that, prior to seeking redress in court, furloughed employees contesting a school district's failure to recall them for new positions must submit the issue to an arbitrator to determine if the dispute represents a grievance under the negotiated contract).

gained, as they were primarily related to employees' interest and had "a direct impact on wages and job security."[61]

Procedures agreed upon in the collective bargaining contract must be followed. An Idaho school district argued that its contract agreement specifying notification by May 15th conflicted with a statutory requirement that districts provide notice by June 15th. The state supreme court ruled that the Idaho Code gives school trustees broad authority to negotiate "matters specified in any such negotiation agreement," which expressly enabled the district to bind itself to the earlier date.[62] Teachers, however, may possess independent statutory rights that cannot be subordinated to collective bargaining agreements. A Massachusetts appellate court held that a teacher possessed statutory "bumping" rights across the school system, not merely within her bargaining unit as specified in the collective bargaining agreement.[63] The school district argued that she could not bump a less senior teacher in another high school that involved a different bargaining unit. Ruling that state law prevailed, the appellate court noted that the legislature did not list the statute protecting seniority rights as subordinate to negotiated agreements.

Procedures negotiated by the employer and the teachers' union for staff reductions, however, must not violate the constitutional rights of any employee. The Supreme Court overturned a collective bargaining agreement that was designed to protect members of certain minority groups from layoffs.[64] The agreement ensured that the percentage of minority teachers would not fall below the percentage employed before any reduction-in-force. Without evidence of prior employment discrimination, the Court held that the plan violated the equal protection rights of nonminority teachers.

Nonrenewal and Tenure Decisions.   Decisions to retain a teacher or grant tenure clearly are managerial rights and not mandatorily bargainable.[65] If a school board negotiates procedural aspects of these decisions, however, the provisions generally are binding. For example, collective bargaining agreements may entitle nontenured

61. The court developed a balancing test for weighing employees' interests in wages, hours, and conditions of employment against the employer's right to make managerial policy decisions. If an item is "primarily related" to wages, hours, and conditions of employment, it is a mandatory subject of bargaining; if not, there is no duty to bargain. W. Bend Educ. Ass'n v. Wis. Employment Relations Comm'n, 357 N.W.2d 534, 543 (Wis. 1984). *See also* Cent. City Educ. Ass'n v. Ill. Educ. Labor Relations Bd., 599 N.E.2d 892 (Ill. 1992).

62. Hunting v. Clark County Sch. Dist. No. 161, 931 P.2d 628, 633 (Idaho 1997).

63. Ballotte v. City of Worcester, 748 N.E.2d 987 (Mass. App. Ct. 2001). *See also* Marino v. Bd. of Educ, 691 N.Y.S.2d 537 (App. Div. 1999).

64. Wygant v. Jackson Bd. of Educ., 476 U.S. 267 (1986). *See also* Milwaukee Bd. v. Wis. Employment Relations Comm'n, 472 N.W.2d 553 (Wis. Ct. App. 1991); text accompanying note 45, Chapter 10.

65. Under most state laws, reemployment of probationary teachers and tenure decisions have been found to be a prohibited subject of bargaining. *See, e.g.,* Chi. Sch. Reform Bd. v. Ill. Educ. Labor Relations Bd., 721 N.E.2d 676 (Ill. App. Ct. 1999); Honeoye Falls-Lima Cent. Sch. Dist. v. Honeoye Falls-Lima Educ. Ass'n, 402 N.E.2d 1165 (N.Y. 1980); Mindemann v. Indep. Sch. Dist. No. 6, 771 P.2d 996 (Okla. 1989). *But see* State *ex rel.* Rollins v. Bd. of Educ., 532 N.E.2d 1289 (Ohio 1988) (holding that under the collective bargaining law, a negotiated agreement prevails over another conflicting law).

teachers to procedural protections that ordinarily would not be required under state laws or the Fourteenth Amendment.[66] The Supreme Court of New Hampshire held that state law did not prevent a school board from agreeing to provide probationary teachers with a statement of reasons for nonrenewal; the board still retained its managerial prerogative not to renew the teacher's contract.[67]

School boards' failure to follow negotiated procedures has resulted in arbitrators ordering reinstatement of discharged teachers. Permissibility of such awards, however, depends on how a school board's authority is interpreted under state law. The Supreme Court of Alaska rejected an arbitrator's reinstatement of a teacher, reasoning that school boards "possess the exclusive power, not subject to *any* appeal, to decide whether to 'nonrenew' a provisional employee."[68] The court noted that a range of other remedies was available for the board's violation of the negotiated nonretention procedures. In contrast, the Supreme Court of Montana concluded that an arbitrator's reinstatement of teachers did not usurp school board authority but simply provided appropriate relief for the board's failure to abide by negotiated procedures.[69]

Under Maine law, school boards can enter into negotiated agreements containing binding grievance arbitration for employee dismissal. The state high court ruled that a school board voluntarily negotiating such an arbitration process cannot then seek to overturn an arbitrator's reinstatement decision by arguing that the decision causes the board to violate its duty to provide a safe learning environment. By agreeing to submit the dismissal to an arbitrator, the board agrees to abide by the arbitrator's interpretation of the law.[70]

66. *See, e.g.,* Kentwood Pub. Sch. v. Kent County Educ. Ass'n, 520 N.W.2d 682 (Mich. Ct. App. 1994). *But see* Bd. of Educ. v. Round Valley Teachers' Ass'n, 914 P.2d 193 (Cal. 1996) (ruling that negotiated procedures beyond statutory minimum for not rehiring probationary employees were preempted by the Education Code; when exclusive discretion is vested in the board to determine scope of procedures, the subject matter may not be subjected to mandatory or permissive bargaining).

67. *In re* Watson, 448 A.2d 417 (N.H. 1982).

68. Jones v. Wrangell Sch. Dist., 696 P.2d 677, 680 (Alaska 1985). *See also* Sch. Comm. v. Johnston Fed'n of Teachers, 652 A.2d 976 (R.I. 1995).

69. Savage Educ. Ass'n v. Trs., 692 P.2d 1237 (Mont. 1984). *See also* N. Miami Educ. Ass'n v. N. Miami Cmty. Schs., 746 N.E.2d 380 (Ind. Ct. App. 2001) (ruling that the Indiana Code allows school districts and associations to agree to binding arbitration regarding teacher nonrenewal but does not give arbitrators such authority unless specifically included in the negotiated agreement).

70. Union River Valley Teachers Ass'n v. Lamoine Sch. Comm., 748 A.2d 990 (Me. 2000). *See also* Clark County Sch. Dist. v. Riley, 14 P.3d 22 (Nev. 2000) (finding that a teacher's termination was subject to statutory law and thus judicially reviewable; collective bargaining agreement not applicable); Juniata-Mifflin Counties Area Vocational-Technical Sch. v. Corbin, 691 A.2d 924 (Pa. 1997) (upholding the arbitrator's determination that the language of the negotiated agreement evidenced intent to incorporate the statutory code, thus rendering teacher dismissal subject to grievance arbitration); Montpelier Bd. of Sch. Comm'rs v. Montpelier Educ. Ass'n, 702 A.2d 390 (Vt. 1997) (ruling that in the review of a nonrenewal decision, the arbitrator was not limited to the substantive performance of the teacher but also could include the violation of evaluation procedures within the negotiated contract in ordering reinstatement).

Union Security Provisions

To ensure their strength and viability, unions attempt to obtain various security provisions in the collective bargaining contract. The nature and extent of these provisions will depend on state laws and constitutional limitations. In this section, provisions related to union revenue and exclusive privileges are addressed.

Dues and Service Fees

When bargaining with employees, unions seek to gain provisions that require all employees either to join the association or to pay fees for its services. Since a union must represent all individuals in the bargaining unit, it is argued that such provisions are necessary to eliminate "free riders" (i.e., the individuals who receive the benefits of the union's work without paying the dues for membership). Union security provisions take several forms. The *closed shop,* requiring an employer to hire only union members, does not exist in the public sector and is unlawful in the private sector under the National Labor Relations Act and the Taft-Hartley amendments. The *union shop* agreement requires an employee to join the union within a designated time period after employment to retain a position. Although union shop agreements are prevalent in the private sector, they are not authorized by most public-sector laws and are limited or proscribed in a number of states under "right-to-work" laws.[71] The security provisions most frequently found in the public sector are *agency shop* and *fair share* agreements—terms that often are used interchangeably. An agency shop provision requires an employee to pay union dues but does not mandate membership, whereas a fair share arrangement requires a nonmember simply to pay a service fee to cover the cost of bargaining activities.

    Nonunion teachers have challenged mandatory fees as a violation of their First Amendment speech and association rights. The Supreme Court, however, has upheld the payment of fair share fees by public employees. In *Abood v. Detroit Board of Education,* the Court rejected the nonunion members' First Amendment claims, noting the importance of ensuring labor peace and eliminating "free riders."[72] Yet, the Court concluded that employees cannot be compelled to contribute to the support of ideological causes they oppose as a condition of maintaining employment as public school teachers. Accordingly, the fee for nonmember teachers who object to forced contributions to a union's political activities must reflect only the costs of bargaining and contract administration.[73]

---

71. Twenty-two states have laws that specifically declare that an individual's employment cannot be conditioned on joining a union or paying fees to a union. *See* http://nrtw.org/rtws.htm.

72. 431 U.S. 209 (1977).

73. Under Title VII of the Civil Rights Act of 1964, an employee who objects to payment of a service fee on religious grounds must be accommodated by being allowed to substitute a contribution to a charitable organization. *See, e.g.,* McDaniel v. Essex Int'l, 696 F.2d 34 (6th Cir. 1982); Tooley v. Martin-Marietta Corp., 648 F.2d 1239 (9th Cir. 1981). *See also* Wolfe v. Mont. Dep't of Labor and Indus., 843 P.2d 338 (Mont. 1992) (remanding case to determine whether the union had made a reasonable accommodation of the teacher's religious beliefs).

Although the Supreme Court's decision permits the collection of a service fee from nonunion members who raise First Amendment objections, it did not resolve a number of significant issues, such as: (1) What expenditures can unions legitimately claim as related to collective bargaining activities? (2) What procedures are adequate or necessary to protect the interests of individuals challenging the union's apportionment of costs? and (3) Can employees be discharged as a means to enforce a fair share agreement?

Under the *Abood* ruling, the nonunion employee bears the burden to object to the union's use of the agency fee,[74] and the union then must establish the proportionate service fee share related to employee representation. The Supreme Court noted the difficulty in drawing the line between collective bargaining activities and ideological activities unrelated to collective bargaining.[75] In subsequent cases, the Supreme Court and other courts have attempted to define this dividing line as well as the procedural protections necessary to respond to nonmembers' objections.

In *Ellis v. Brotherhood of Railway, Airline, and Steamship Clerks,* a private-sector case, the Supreme Court advanced a standard for determining which union expenditures can be assessed against objecting employees:

> The test must be whether the challenged expenditures are necessarily or reasonably incurred for the purpose of performing the duties of an exclusive representative of the employees in dealing with the employer on labor-management issues. Under this standard, objecting employees may be compelled to pay their fair share of not only the direct costs of negotiating and administering a collective-bargaining contract and of settling grievances and disputes, but also the expenses of activities or undertakings normally or reasonably employed to implement or effectuate the duties of the union as exclusive representative of the employees in the bargaining unit.[76]

Applying this test, the Court upheld the assessment of costs related to union conventions, social activities, and publications, but disallowed expenditures related to organizing activities and litigation unrelated to negotiations, contract administration, and fair representation.

The *Ellis* test has been employed by courts to uphold the assessment of a range of expenditures against objecting employees in the public sector such as conventions, lobbying activities, publications, and campaigns for levies to increase funds for public education.[77] In 1991, however, the Supreme Court in *Lehnert v. Ferris Faculty Associ-*

---

74. *Abood,* 431 U.S. 209. *See also* Chi. Teachers' Union Local No. 1 v. Hudson, 475 U.S. 292 (1986); Mitchell v. L.A. Unified Sch. Dist., 963 F.2d 258 (9th Cir. 1992) (ruling that only an opportunity to "opt out" was required, not affirmative consent to the deduction).

75. *Abood,* 431 U.S. at 236.

76. 466 U.S. 435, 448 (1984).

77. *See, e.g.,* Champion v. California, 738 F.2d 1082 (9th Cir. 1984); Robinson v. New Jersey, 741 F.2d 598 (3d Cir. 1984). *But see* Cumero v. Pub. Employment Relations Bd., 262 Cal. Rptr. 46 (1989) (finding that lobbying efforts were beyond the union's representational obligations under state law).

ation limited some of these charges in a Michigan public-sector case.[78] The Court upheld expenditures for conventions, selected sections of union publications, preparations for a strike,[79] and chargeable activities of state and national affiliates. But the Court ruled that unions may not assess nonmembers for lobbying and other political activities that are unrelated to contract ratification or implementation, for litigation that does not involve the local bargaining unit, and for public relations efforts to enhance the image of the teaching profession. Significant for unions, however, was the recognition that contributions to the state and national affiliates are chargeable expenditures even in the absence of a "direct and tangible impact" on the local bargaining unit.

The constitutionality of union procedures adopted to respond to nonmembers who object to the fair share fee continues to create considerable debate. Generally, after a nonmember raises an objection, unions have provided a rebate of the portion of the fee unrelated to bargaining activities. In the *Ellis* decision, however, the Supreme Court found a *pure rebate* procedure inadequate. Characterizing this approach as an "involuntary loan," the Court stated that "by exacting and using full dues, then refunding months later the portion that it was not allowed to exact in the first place, the union effectively charges the employees for activities that are outside the scope of the statutory authorization."[80] Because other alternatives such as advance reduction of dues and escrow accounts exist, the Court found even temporary use of dissenters' funds impermissible.

In *Chicago Teachers' Union, Local No. 1 v. Hudson,* the Supreme Court provided further guidance in determining the adequacy of union procedural safeguards to protect nonmember employees' constitutional rights in the apportionment and assessment of representation fees. According to the Court, constitutional requirements for the collection of an agency fee include "an adequate explanation of the basis for the fee, a reasonably prompt opportunity to challenge the amount of the fee before an impartial decision maker, and an escrow for the amounts reasonably in dispute while such challenges are pending."[81] The contested Chicago union's plan included an advance reduction of dues, but was flawed because nonmembers were required to file

---

78. 500 U.S. 507 (1991). *See also* Bromley v. Mich. Educ. Ass'n-NEA, 82 F.3d 686 (6th Cir. 1996) (ordering that defensive organizing activities designed to protect and strengthen the status of the union be treated as nonchargeable).

79. Although strikes are illegal in Michigan, preparation for a strike was viewed as an effective bargaining tool during contract negotiations. *Lehnert,* 500 U.S. 507. *But see* Belhumeur v. Labor Relations Comm'n, 735 N.E.2d 860 (Mass. 2000) (finding that expenses related to implementing a statewide strike and a demonstration highlighting lack of funding for negotiations were not chargeable to nonunion members).

80. *Ellis,* 466 U.S. at 444. *See also* Anderson v. E. Allen Educ. Ass'n, 683 N.E.2d 1355 (Ind. Ct. App. 1997) (ruling that the negotiated agreement that set the fair share fee at the full union dues amount violated teachers' First Amendment rights; because of changes in Indiana law, unions can no longer negotiate fair share agreements).

81. 475 U.S. 292, 310 (1986). *See also* Jibson v. Mich. Educ. Ass'n-NEA, 30 F.3d 723 (6th Cir. 1994) (holding that the *notice* informing nonmembers of proposed charges could not later be considered constitutionally deficient if some expenses are held to be nonchargeable).

an objection to receive any information about the calculation of the proportionate share, and they were not provided sufficient information to judge the appropriateness of the fee. The Court held that adequate disclosure required more than identification of expenditures that did not benefit objecting employees; reasons had to be provided for assessment of the fair share. In addition, the Chicago procedures did not ensure dissenting employees a prompt decision by an impartial decision maker. The Court went further than the *Ellis* prohibition on a pure rebate procedure and held that, even if an advance reduction is made, any additional amounts in dispute must be placed in escrow. This was found necessary to minimize the risk that any funds of an objector would be used for impermissible ideological activities. Subsequently, most federal appellate courts have found that escrow schemes adequately protect an individual's constitutional rights.[82]

The adequacy of unions' financial reporting practices, as required in *Hudson,* has been contested. According to the Supreme Court, financial disclosure must be adequate or sufficient, but not an exhaustive and detailed list of all expenditures. The Court specifically stated in *Hudson* that the union must provide enough detail to enable nonmembers to make an informed decision about the "propriety of the union's fee."[83] The Sixth Circuit held that this does not require unions to provide financial information audited at the "highest" available level of audit services.[84] In that case, the court upheld the union's financial disclosure—including budgets, audited financial statements, and audited supplemental schedules of the state and national associations. In 1991, the Seventh Circuit found the revised fair share notice procedures proposed by the Chicago teachers' union in response to the original *Hudson* decision to be constitutionally adequate.[85] The 32-page audited disclosure notice identified expenditures as chargeable or nonchargeable, with detailed breakdowns of expenses in each category. The level of specificity was found to be sufficient to enable nonmembers to determine if a basis existed for challenging the designated fair share fee.

---

82. *See, e.g.,* Grunwald v. San Bernardino City Unified Sch. Dist., 994 F.2d 1370 (9th Cir. 1993); Gibson v. Fla. Bar, 906 F.2d 624 (11th Cir. 1990); Crawford v. Air Line Pilots Ass'n Int'l, 870 F.2d 155 (4th Cir. 1989); Hohe v. Casey, 868 F.2d 69 (3d Cir. 1989). *But see* Tavernor v. Ill. Fed'n of Teachers, 226 F.3d 842 (7th Cir. 2000) (ruling that collecting 100 percent of the union dues from nonmembers and placing the funds in an escrow account was impermissible when the association's calculation showed that fair share generally was approximately 85 percent of full dues).

83. *Hudson,* 475 U.S. at 306. *But see* Foster v. Mahdesian, 268 F.3d 689, 694 (9th Cir. 2001) (finding that the employer has "no specific duties to employees" to ensure that each receives a *proper Hudson* notice before fees are deducted).

84. Gwirtz v. Ohio Educ. Ass'n, 887 F.2d 678 (6th Cir. 1989). *See also* Harik v. Cal. Teachers Union, 298 F.3d 863 (9th Cir. 2002) (concluding that small unions are not required to provide detailed audited statements but still must provide some independent accountant verification of expenditures); Prescott v. County of El Dorado, 204 F.3d 984, 1108 (9th Cir. 2000) (ruling that financial statements must be subjected to "some auditor verifiable methodology"); Wareham Educ. Ass'n v. Labor Relations Comm'n, 713 N.E.2d 363 (Mass. 1999) (holding that no "small union" exception existed to the *Hudson* requirement for an independent audit).

85. Hudson v. Chi. Teachers Union, Local No. 1, 922 F.2d 1306 (7th Cir. 1991).

Although the Supreme Court has upheld fair share arrangements, they may not be permitted under some state laws. The Maine high court held that forced payment of dues was "tantamount to coercion toward membership."[86] The Maine statute ensures employees the right to join a union *voluntarily,* and the court interpreted this provision as including the right to *refrain* from joining. Similarly, the Vermont Supreme Court held that fees were prohibited under the Vermont Labor Relations for Teachers Act, which specified that teachers have the right to join or not to join, assist, or participate in a labor organization.[87] Under some state labor laws, collection of fees may be forbidden. For example, Indiana amended its labor law to prohibit the payment of fair share fees or any other representation fees on all contracts negotiated after July 1, 1995.[88]

Representation fees do not violate the Federal Constitution and have been upheld in most states, but legal controversy surrounds enforcement of the provisions. Some collective bargaining agreements require employers to discharge teachers who refuse to pay the fees. In Pennsylvania, an appellate court overturned the dismissal of two teachers, stating that refusal to pay dues did not constitute "persistent and willful violation of the school laws" to justify dismissal.[89] Several courts have attempted to reconcile labor laws that authorize the negotiation of fair share fees as a condition of employment with tenure laws that permit dismissal only for specified causes. The Supreme Court of Michigan has ruled that the state labor law prevails when it conflicts with another statute.[90] Accordingly, a tenured teacher who fails to pay the agency service fee can be discharged without resort to procedural requirements of the teacher tenure law. Similarly, the California Public Employment Relations Board has held that state law authorizing a service fee permits termination of a teacher's employment.[91]

Exclusive Privileges

The designated employee bargaining representative gains security through negotiating exclusive rights or privileges, such as dues checkoff, the use of the school mail

86. Churchill v. Sch. Adm'r Dist. No. 49 Teachers Ass'n, 380 A.2d 186, 192 (Me. 1977).

87. Weissenstein v. Burlington Bd. of Sch. Comm'rs, 543 A.2d 691 (Vt. 1988). *But see* Nashua Teachers Union v. Nashua Sch. Dist., 707 A.2d 448 (N.H. 1998) (interpreting state law that permits negotiation of "other terms and conditions of employment" as authorizing agency fees to promote labor peace; court rejected argument that the fees were an unfair labor practice "encouraging" union membership).

88. Ind. Code § 20-7.5-1 (2002).

89. Langley v. Uniontown Area Sch. Dist., 367 A.2d 736 (Pa. Commw. Ct. 1977). *But see* Belhumeur v. Labor Relations Comm'n, 589 N.E.2d 352 (Mass. App. Ct. 1992) (affirming the five-day suspension of three teachers who refused to remit an agency service fee; teachers did not follow procedures for protesting the fee).

90. Bd. of Educ. v. Parks, 335 N.W.2d 641 (Mich. 1983). *See also* Whittier Reg'l Sch. Comm. v. Labor Relations Comm'n, 517 N.E.2d 840 (Mass. 1988).

91. King City Joint Union High Sch. Dist., Cal. Pub. Relations Bd., Order No. 197 (March 1982). Unions also have pursued enforcement of fair share agreements in civil actions against nonmember teachers. *See, e.g.,* Jefferson Area Teachers Ass'n v. Lockwood, 433 N.E.2d 604 (Ohio 1982); San Lorenz Educ. Ass'n v. Wilson, 654 P.2d 202 (Cal. 1982).

systems, and access to school facilities. Although exclusive arrangements strengthen the majority union and may make it difficult for minority unions to survive, they often are supported by courts as a means of promoting labor peace and ensuring efficient operation of the school system.

The exclusive privilege most often included in collective bargaining contracts is dues checkoff, a provision that authorizes employers to deduct union dues and other fees when authorized by employees. Over half of the states with public employee bargaining laws specify dues checkoff as a mandatory subject for bargaining. The Supreme Court, however, has held that employee unions have no constitutional right to payroll deductions.[92] The Fourth Circuit ruled that state legislation permitting payroll deductions for charitable organizations but not labor unions was not an infringement of the First Amendment; the law did not deny the union members the right to associate, speak, publish, recruit members, or express their views.[93] Unless prohibited by state law, most courts have upheld negotiated agreements that deny rival unions checkoff rights.

In 1983, the Supreme Court clarified one of the most controversial security rights—exclusive access to school mail facilities.[94] The case focused on an agreement between the exclusive bargaining representative and an Indiana school board denying all rival unions access to the interschool mail system and teacher mailboxes. One union challenged the agreement as a violation of the First and Fourteenth Amendments. The Supreme Court upheld the arrangement, reasoning that the First Amendment does not require "equivalent access to all parts of a school building in which some form of communicative activity occurs."[95] The Court concluded that the school mail facility was not a public forum for communication and thereby its use could be restricted to official school business. The fact that several community groups (e.g., Boy Scouts, civic organizations) used the school mail system did not create a public forum. The Court noted that, even if such access by community groups created a limited public forum, access would be extended only to similar groups—not to labor organizations. The Court's emphasis on the availability of alternative channels of communication (e.g., bulletin boards and meeting facilities), however, indicates that total exclusion of rival unions would not be permitted.

The Fifth Circuit subsequently ruled, and the Supreme Court affirmed, that denial of access to the school mail to all teacher organizations did not violate the First Amendment when other channels of communication were available.[96] However, the Court found unconstitutional a policy prohibiting individual teachers from discussing employee organizations during nonclass time or using the internal mail system or bulletin boards to mention employee organizations. Such limitations on an individual

---

92. City of Charlotte v. Local 660, Int'l Ass'n of Firefighters, 426 U.S. 283 (1976).

93. S.C. Educ. Ass'n v. Campbell, 883 F.2d 1251 (4th Cir. 1989).

94. Perry Educ. Ass'n v. Perry Local Educators' Ass'n, 460 U.S. 37 (1983). *See* text accompanying note 64, Chapter 9.

95. *Id.* at 44.

96. Tex. State Teachers Ass'n v. Garland Indep. Sch. Dist., 777 F.2d 1046 (5th Cir. 1985), *aff'd,* 470 U.S. 801 (1986).

employee's expression would be permissible only if a threat of material and substantial disruption were shown.

It appears that exclusive use of communication facilities can be constitutionally granted to the bargaining representative or that use of facilities can be denied to all employee organizations. If rival unions are excluded from specific communication channels, other avenues must be available to avoid infringement of the First Amendment. Under state laws, however, exclusive access to use of mailboxes and school facilities may be an unfair labor practice.[97]

Although a school board may provide access to mailboxes and school facilities, it cannot deliver a union's mail through its interschool mail delivery system. Under the Federal Private Express Statutes,[98] an employer is permitted to deliver only mail related to its business through the "letters of the carrier" exception to the federal law. In 1988, the Supreme Court held that this exception did not permit a union attempting to organize faculty in a university to use the university's internal mail system; the activity did not relate to the university's "current business."[99] Subsequently, the Seventh Circuit ruled that the delivery of mail of the exclusive bargaining representative did not relate to the school's current business, but rather to the union's business.[100]

In most states, school boards negotiate only with the designated bargaining representative. Under this exclusive recognition, other unions and teacher groups can be denied the right to engage in official exchanges with an employer. The Supreme Court has held that nonmembers of a bargaining unit or members who disagree with the views of the representative have no constitutional right "to force the government to listen to their views."[101] The Court concluded that a Minnesota statute requiring employers to "meet and confer" only with the designated bargaining representative did not violate other employees' speech or associational rights as public employees or as citizens, because these sessions were not a public forum. According to the Court, "The Constitution does not grant to members of the public generally a right to be heard by public bodies making decisions of policy."[102]

However, in a public forum, such as a school board meeting, a nonunion teacher has a constitutional right to address the public employer, even concerning a subject of

97. *See, e.g.,* Am. Fed'n of Teachers-Hillsborough v. Sch. Bd., 584 So. 2d 62 (Fla. Dist. Ct. App. 1991).

98. 18 U.S.C. §§ 1693 *et seq.* (2002); 39 U.S.C. §§ 601 *et seq.* (2002). These laws establish a postal monopoly and, in general, prohibit the private delivery of letters without payment to the United States Postal Service.

99. Univ. of Cal. v. Pub. Employment Relations Bd., 485 U.S. 589 (1988).

100. Fort Wayne Cmty. Schs. v. Fort Wayne Educ. Ass'n, 977 F.2d 358 (7th Cir. 1992). The case was remanded for further review to determine if some correspondence related to joint school/union committees could be characterized as the school's business.

101. Minn. State Bd. for Cmty. Colls. v. Knight, 465 U.S. 271, 283 (1984). *See also* Sherrard Cmty. Unit Sch. Dist. v. Ill. Educ. Labor Relations Bd., 696 N.E.2d 833 (Ill. App. Ct. 1998) (ruling that a school board's direct negotiation with a nonunion teacher regarding her proposed involuntary reassignment was an unfair labor practice).

102. *Knight,* 465 U.S. at 283.

negotiation. The Supreme Court concluded that a Wisconsin nonunion teacher had the right to express concerns to the school board.[103] In this case, negotiation between the board and union had reached a deadlock on the issue of an agency shop provision. A nonunion teacher, representing a minority group of teachers, addressed the board at a regular public meeting and requested postponement of a decision until further study. The Court reasoned that the teacher was not attempting to negotiate, but merely to speak on an important issue before the board—a right every citizen possesses. The Court further noted that teachers have never been "compelled to relinquish their First Amendment rights they would otherwise enjoy as citizens to comment on matters of public interest in connection with the operation of the public school in which they work."[104]

Although union security provisions such as fair share arrangements and exclusive use of specific school facilities can be negotiated, nonunion teachers' constitutional rights cannot be infringed. Teachers must be ensured an effective mechanism for challenging financial contributions that might be used to support ideological causes or political activities to which they object. If specific communication channels for nonmembers are restricted through the negotiation process, alternative options must remain open.

Grievances

Disputes concerning employee rights under the terms of a collective bargaining agreement are resolved through the negotiated grievance procedures, which generally must be exhausted before pursuing review by state labor relations boards or courts.[105] The exhaustion requirement ensures the integrity of the collective bargaining process, encouraging orderly and efficient dispute resolution at the local level. Grievance procedures usually provide for a neutral third party, generally an arbitrator, to conduct a hearing and render a decision. *Grievance* arbitration, which addresses enforcement of contract rights, differs from *interest* arbitration, which may take place in resolving an impasse in the bargaining process.[106]

Depending on state law and the negotiated contract, grievance arbitration decisions may be advisory or binding. Public employers, adhering to the doctrine of the sovereign power of government, have been reluctant to agree to procedures that might

---

103. City of Madison v. Wis. Employment Relations Comm'n, 429 U.S. 167 (1976). *See also* Ohio Ass'n of Pub. Sch. Employees v. State Employment Relations Bd., 742 N.E.2 696 (Ohio Ct. App. 2000) (ruling that the association representatives' comments at a school board meeting did not constitute negotiations under state law; the board had argued that bypassing the board's bargaining representative and negotiating directly with the board was an unfair labor practice).

104. *Id.* at 175 (quoting Pickering v. Bd. of Educ., 391 U.S. 563, 568 (1968)).

105. *See, e.g.,* Reynolds v. Sch. Dist. No. 1, 69 F.3d 1523 (10th Cir. 1995); Hokama v. Univ. of Haw., 990 P.2d 1150 (Haw. 1999); Milton Educ. Ass'n v. Milton Bd. of Sch. Trs., 759 A.2d 479 (Vt. 2000).

106. As noted in the next session, binding interest arbitration has met with resistance in the public sector as a method to resolve negotiation impasses. If it were permitted regarding monetary issues, school boards would relinquish control of the power to determine the budget.

result in a loss of public authority. Allowing grievance procedures to include final decision making by a third party significantly lessens a school board's power, effectively equating the positions of the teachers' organization and the school board. Nevertheless, as bargaining has expanded, legislative bodies have favored binding arbitration to settle labor disputes. About one-half of the states have enacted laws permitting school boards to negotiate grievance procedures with binding arbitration, and several states require binding arbitration as the final step in the grievance procedure.[107] With the widespread acceptance of grievance arbitration, it has become one of the most contested areas in collective bargaining. Suits have challenged the arbitrator's authority to render decisions in specific disputes as well as the authority to provide certain remedies.

One of the primary issues in establishing a grievance procedure is defining a *grievance*—that is, what can be grieved. In the private sector, a *grievance* is usually defined as any dispute between the employer and the employee. Teachers' grievances, on the other hand, are generally limited to controversies arising from the interpretation or application of the negotiated contract. Arbitrability of a dispute then depends on whether the school board and union agreement shows intent to settle the issue by arbitration.[108] Arbitrators generally decide arbitrability, and the decisions are presumed valid when derived from the construction of the negotiated agreement. The Supreme Court of Iowa noted that because the law favors arbitration, the court's duty is to construe the agreement broadly, recognizing arbitrability "unless it may be said with positive assurance that the arbitration clause is not susceptible of an interpretation that covers the asserted dispute. Doubts should be resolved in favor of coverage."[109]

Disputes held to be arbitrable based on specific negotiated contracts include unsatisfactory teacher performance, procedural aspects of performance evaluation, eligibility for continuing contract, reinstatement of a reserve teacher, contribution to health insurance premiums, and transfer of students to other districts on a tuition basis.[110] Although a range of issues has been found to be arbitrable, courts have ruled

---

107.   States requiring binding grievance arbitration are Alaska, Florida, Illinois, Minnesota, and Pennsylvania. *See also* Palmer v. Portland Sch. Comm., 652 A.2d 86 (Me. 1995) (holding that a discharged teacher could not compel arbitration of his dispute where he failed to exhaust his procedural remedies under the collective bargaining agreement; arbitration was the last step in the process).

108.   *See, e.g.,* Jefferson County Sch. Dist., No. R-1 v. Shorey, 826 P.2d 830 (Colo. 1992); *In re* Westmoreland Sch. Bd., 564 A.2d 419 (N.H. 1989); *In re* Bd. of Educ., 688 N.Y.S.2d 463 (1999); Davis v. Chester Upland Sch. Dist., 786 A.2d 186 (Pa. 2001).

109.   Postville Cmty. Sch. Dist. v. Billmeyer, 548 N.W.2d 558, 560 (Iowa 1996) (quoting Sergeant Bluff-Luton Educ. Ass'n v. Sergeant Bluff-Luton Cmty. Sch. Dist., 282 N.W.2d 144, 147-148 (Iowa 1979)). *See also* E. Assoc. Coal Corp. v. United Mine Workers, 531 U.S. 57 (2000) (reaffirming the strong federal policy of judicial deference to arbitration in labor disputes).

110.   *See, e.g.,* Chi. Sch. Reform Bd. of Trs. v. Ill. Educ. Labor Relations Bd., 741 N.E.2d 989 (Ill. App. Ct. 2000) (reserve teacher reinstatement); Sch. Comm. v. Boston Teachers Union, 664 N.E.2d 478 (Mass. App. Ct. 1996) (evaluation procedures); *In re* Bd. of Educ., 688 N.Y.S.2d 463 (1999) (health insurance); State *ex rel.* Williams v. Belpre City Sch. Dist. Bd. of Educ., 534 N.E.2d 96 (Ohio Ct. App. 1987) (continuing contract); Midland Borough Sch. Dist. v. Midland Educ. Ass'n, 616 A.2d 633 (Pa. 1992) (transfer of students).

that issues related to nondelegable policy matters under state law are outside the scope of arbitration. For example, impermissible issues have involved tenure decisions, employee dismissal, reappointment of nontenured teachers, evaluation of teacher qualifications, transfer of teachers, curriculum content, submission of lesson plans, teacher discipline, provision of health services to special education students, and extracurricular assignments.[111] Also, issues that are specifically excluded in the contract cannot be submitted to arbitration.

Arbitration awards or remedies also have been challenged. Courts have again adopted a narrow scope of review, with many presuming the validity of awards. The deference afforded an arbitrator's award is evident from the Supreme Court's statement that "unless the arbitral decision does not 'draw its essence from the collective bargaining agreement,' a court is bound to enforce the award and is not entitled to review the merits of the contract dispute."[112] If an arbitrator's award is rationally derived from the language and context of the agreement, courts have found that it "draws its essence" from the agreement[113] and the courts do not interfere with the award simply because they would have provided a different remedy.[114]

Negotiation Impasse

Impasse occurs in bargaining when an agreement cannot be reached and neither party will compromise. When negotiations reach such a stalemate, several options are available for resolution—mediation, fact finding, and arbitration. As discussed in the final section of this chapter, the most effective means for resolving negotiation impasse—the strike—is not legally available to the majority of public employees. Most comprehensive state statutes address impasse procedures, with provisions ranging from

111. *See, e.g.,* Chi. Sch. Reform Bd. of Trs. v. Ill. Educ. Labor Relations Bd., 721 N.E.2d 676 (Ill. App. Ct. 1999) (dismissal of teachers); Sch. Admin. Dist. No. 58 v. Mount Abram Teachers Ass'n, 704 A.2d 349 (Me. 1997) (curriculum content); Sch. Comm. v. Peabody Fed'n of Teachers, 748 N.E.2d 992 (Mass. App. Ct. 2001) (teacher transfers); Harbor Creek Sch. Dist. v. Harbor Creek Educ. Ass'n, 640 A.2d 899 (Pa. 1994) (extracurricular assignments); Raines v. Indep. Sch. Dist. No. 6, 796 P.2d 303 (Okla. 1990) (teacher discipline); Mindemann v. Indep. Sch. Dist. No. 6, 771 P.2d 996 (Okla. 1989) (teacher nonrenewal); Woonsocket Teachers' Guild v. Woonsocket Sch. Comm., 770 A.2d 834 (R.I. 2001) (health services to special education students); Pawtucket Sch. Comm. v. Pawtucket Teachers' Alliance, 652 A.2d 970 (R.I. 1995) (lesson plans).

112. W.R. Grace and Co. v. Local 759, United Rubber Workers of Am., 461 U.S. 757, 764 (1983).

113. *See, e.g.,* Scotch Plains-Fanwood Bd. of Educ. v. Scotch Plains-Fanwood Educ. Ass'n, 651 A.2d 1018 (N.J. 1995); Danville Area Sch. Dist. v. Danville Area Educ. Ass'n, 754 A.2d 1255 (Pa. 2000). *See also* Sch. Comm. v. Hanover Teachers Ass'n, 761 N.E.2d 918 (Mass. 2002) (finding that the arbitrator exceeded his authority when he did not follow the plain language of the agreement); Rochester Sch. Dist. v. Rochester Educ. Ass'n, 747 A.2d 971 (Pa. Commw. 2000) (ruling that the arbitrator's decision that the school board must work with the association in developing all policies, such as standards for student honor roll, in this case, did not draw its essence from the agreement; the board had preserved the right to develop inherent managerial policies when it signed the negotiated agreement).

114. *See, e.g.,* Union River Valley Teacher Ass'n v. Lamoine Sch. Comm., 748 A.2d 990 (Me. 2000).

allowing negotiation of impasse procedures to mandating detailed steps that must be followed. Alternatives most frequently employed to resolve impasse are identified here.

Mediation is often the first step to reopening negotiations, and may be optional or required by law. A neutral third party assists both sides in finding a basis for agreement. The mediator is selected by the negotiation teams or, upon request, appointed by a public employee relations board, and serves as a facilitator rather than a decision maker, thus enabling the school board's representative and the teachers' association jointly to reach an agreement.

Failure to reach agreement through mediation frequently results in fact finding (often called *advisory arbitration*). The process may be mandated by law or may be entered into by mutual agreement of both parties. Fact finding involves a third party investigating the causes for the dispute, collecting facts and testimony to clarify the dispute, and formulating a judgment. Because the process is advisory, proposed solutions are not binding on either party. However, since fact-finding reports are made available to the public, they provide an impetus to settle a contract that is not present in mediation.

In some states, fact finding is the final step in impasse procedures, which may leave both parties without a satisfactory solution. A few states permit a third alternative—binding interest arbitration. This process is similar to fact finding except that the arbitrator's decision related to the terms of the negotiated agreement binds both parties. States that permit binding arbitration often place restrictions on its use.[115] For example, Ohio, Oregon, and Rhode Island permit binding arbitration on matters of mutual consent;[116] Maine allows binding arbitration on all items except salaries, pensions, and insurance.[117]

It is generally agreed that mediation and fact finding, because of their advisory nature, do not provide the most effective means for resolving negotiation disputes. Since strikes are prohibited among public employees in most states, conditional binding arbitration has been considered a viable alternative in resolving deadlocks. Although a greater balance of power is achieved between the school board and the teachers' association with binding arbitration, it has not been met with enthusiasm by public-sector employers, who often view it as an illegal delegation of power. As a result, interest arbitration generally has occurred in the educational setting only on a voluntary or conditional basis.

If a collective bargaining agreement expires while the employer and the union are attempting to reach an agreement, the status quo must be maintained. Adhering to this principle means that all terms and conditions of employment remain in effect during the

---

115. To avoid strikes among certain groups of public employees, interest arbitration may be mandatory. *See, e.g.,* Ohio Rev. Code § 4117.14 (D)(l) (2002).

116. Ohio Rev. Code § 4117 (C) (2002); Or. Rev. Stat. 243 § 712 (2)(e) (2002); R.I. Gen. Laws 28 § 9.3-9 (2002).

117. Me. Rev. Stat. 26 § 979.D(4) (2002). *But see* Conn. Gen. Stat. § 10-153f (2002) (provides for submission of unresolved issues to "last best offer" arbitration).

continuing bargaining process.[118] Unless restricted by law, the majority of courts have held that this means the continuance of annual salary increments for teachers.[119] After exhausting all required impasse resolution procedures, an employer can generally implement its last and best offer, or state law may allow employees to strike.[120]

Strikes

Although it is argued there can be no true collective bargaining without the right to withhold services, which characterizes the bargaining process in the private sector, most teachers are prohibited from striking by either state statute or common law. In those states that grant public employees a limited right to strike,[121] certain conditions, specified in statute, must be met prior to the initiation of a work stoppage. Designated conditions vary but usually include (1) the exhaustion of statutory mediation and fact-finding steps, (2) expiration of the contract, (3) elapse of a certain time period prior to

118. *See, e.g.,* NLRB v. Katz, 369 U.S. 736 (1962) (establishing in the private sector that unilateral changes in terms and conditions of employment are unlawful; this principle has been applied broadly in the public sector); Denver Classroom Teachers Ass'n v. Sch. Dist. No. 1, Denver, 921 P.2d 70 (Colo. Ct. App. 1996) (ruling that the school district's failure to deduct association dues from the salaries of dues-paying nonmembers altered the conditions of employment); St. Croix Falls Sch. Dist. v. Wis. Employment Relations Comm'n, 522 N.W.2d 507 (Wis. Ct. App. 1994) (holding that the school district was required to maintain status quo regarding sick leave). *See also* Providence Teachers Union v. Providence Sch. Bd., 689 A.2d 388 (R.I. 1997) (deciding that the grievance arbitration provisions in the expired contract were not applicable to disputes arising after expiration of the agreement and unrelated to vested rights in the expired contract).

119. *See, e.g.,* Jackson County Coll. Classified and Technical Ass'n v. Jackson County Coll., 468 N.W.2d 61 (Mich. Ct. App. 1991); *In re* Cobleskill Cent. Sch. Dist., 481 N.Y.S.2d 795 (1984). *But see* Bd. of Trs. v. Assoc. COLT Staff, 659 A.2d 842 (Me. 1995) (finding that maintenance of the status quo is freezing salaries at the level existing at the expiration of the contract); *In re* Alton Sch. Dist., 666 A.2d 937 (N.H. 1995) (ruling that under state law teachers receive the annual salary increment for experience at the expiration of the negotiated contract only if the contract contains an automatic renewal clause; however, salary increases for additional training must be recognized and health benefits must be continued to maintain status quo).

120. *See, e.g.,* Mountain Valley Educ. Ass'n v. Me. Sch. Admin. Dist. No. 43, 655 A.2d 348 (Me. 1995) (holding that the school board may unilaterally implement its last best offer after impasse resolution procedures have been exhausted and negotiations are found to be at an impasse); Sisseton Educ. Ass'n v. Sisseton Sch. Dist., 516 N.W.2d 301 (S.D. 1994) (interpreting state law to require implementation of the school board's last offer at impasse); *infra* text accompanying note 121, regarding the right to strike.

121. A statutory limited right to strike exists for public employees in Alaska, Colorado, Hawaii, Illinois, Minnesota, Montana, Ohio, Oregon, Pennsylvania, Vermont, and Wisconsin. Alaska law has been interpreted as prohibiting teachers from striking even though most other public employees are permitted to strike. Anchorage Educ. Ass'n v. Anchorage Sch. Dist., 648 P.2d 993 (Alaska 1982). *See also* Martin v. Montezuma-Cortez Sch. Dist., 841 P.2d 237 (Colo. 1992) (interpreting Colorado's Industrial Relations Act to include a limited right to strike); Reichley v. N. Penn Sch. Dist., 626 A.2d 123 (Pa. 1993) (upholding the constitutionality of the statute allowing strikes by public educators; the court noted that this is a policy consideration for the legislature rather than an issue for the judicial system).

commencing the strike, (4) written notice of the union's intent to strike, and (5) evidence that the strike will not constitute a danger to public health or safety. In contrast to the few states permitting strikes, most states with public employee collective bargaining statutes have specific "no-strike" provisions.[122]

Courts consistently have upheld "no-strike" laws and generally have denied the right to strike unless affirmatively granted by the state.[123] Several early cases still represent the dominant judicial posture on public teachers' strikes. The Connecticut high court stated that permitting teachers to strike would allow them to "deny the authority of government."[124] The court in this case denied teachers the right to strike, emphasizing that a teacher is an agent of the government, possessing a portion of the state's sovereignty. The Supreme Court of Indiana issued a restraining order against striking teachers, affirming the same public welfare issue.[125] Addressing the legality of strikes, a New Jersey appellate court declared that legislative authorization for bargaining did not reflect the intent to depart from the common law rule prohibiting strikes by public employees.[126] In contrast to the prevailing common law position, the Louisiana high court declared strikes permissible for some public employees, including teachers. The court found under state law "an intent to afford public employees a system of organizational rights which parallels that afforded to employees in the private sector."[127]

A strike is more than simply a work stoppage; states define the term broadly to include a range of concerted activities such as work slowdowns, massive absences for "sick" days, and refusal to perform certain duties. For example, the Massachusetts high court found that refusing to perform customary activities, such as grading papers and preparing lesson plans after the end of the school day, constituted a strike.[128] A Missouri appellate court upheld the right of the St. Louis school superintendent to request documentation from 1,190 teachers that a "sick" day was not related to a labor dispute surrounding the negotiation of a new contract.[129] Without documentation from the teachers, the school district could deny payment for the day.

122. *See, e.g.,* Mich. State AFL-CIO v. Employment Relations Comm'n, 551 N.W.2d 165 (Mich. 1996) (upholding statutory prohibition on strikes protesting unfair labor practices; provision does not violate First Amendment free speech guarantee regardless of the employees' motivation for the strike).

123. *See, e.g.,* Passaic Township Bd. of Educ. v. Passaic Township Educ. Ass'n, 536 A.2d 1276 (N.J. Super. Ct. App. Div. 1987); Jefferson County Bd. of Educ. v. Jefferson County Educ. Ass'n, 393 S.E.2d 653 (W. Va. 1990).

124. Norwalk Teachers Ass'n v. Bd. of Educ., 83 A.2d 482, 485 (Conn. 1951).

125. Anderson Fed'n of Teachers v. Sch. City of Anderson, 251 N.E.2d 15 (Ind. 1969).

126. Passaic Township Bd. of Educ. v. Passaic Township Educ. Ass'n, 536 A.2d 1276 (N.J. Super Ct. App. Div. 1987).

127. Davis v. Henry, 555 So. 2d 457, 464-465 (La. 1990).

128. Lenox Educ. Ass'n v. Labor Relations Comm'n, 471 N.E.2d 81 (Mass. 1984). "Concerted activity" may extend beyond activities related to the negotiation of the contract. *See* Cent. Sch. Dist. 13J v. Cent. Educ. Ass'n, 962 P.2d 763 (Or. Ct. App. 1998) (ruling that "concerted activity" to enforce the rights in a union contract is protected under state law; a teacher bringing a representative of his choice to a meeting that could have disciplinary consequences was such a protected activity).

129. Franklin v. St. Louis Bd. of Educ., 904 S.W.2d 433 (Mo. Ct. App. 1995).

State laws, in addition to prohibiting work stoppages, usually identify penalties for involvement in strikes. Such penalties can include withholding compensation for strike days, prohibiting salary increases for designated periods of time (e.g., one year), and dismissal. Penalties for illegal strikes also are imposed on unions. Sanctions may include fines, decertification of the union, and loss of certain privileges such as dues checkoff.[130]

Despite statutory prohibitions on strikes, many teachers, as well as other public employees, participate in work stoppages each year. Public employers can seek a court injunction against teachers who threaten to strike or initiate such action. Most courts have granted injunctions, concluding as did the Supreme Court of Alaska that the "illegality of the strike is a sufficient harm to justify injunctive relief."[131] Failure of teachers and unions to comply with such a restraining order can result in contempt of court charges and resulting fines and/or imprisonment. For example, teachers in a Maryland school district who refused to obey an injunction were found guilty of criminal contempt.[132] In South Bend, Indiana, refusal to comply with an injunction resulted in a contempt-of-court charge and fines totaling $200,000 against two unions.[133] Establishing the level of fines involves a consideration of factors such as the magnitude of the threatened harm and the association's financial condition. A Massachusetts appellate court remanded a case where the trial judge failed to consider relevant factors in imposing a $20,000 fine for each day the union refused to return to work.[134]

Even though the injunction has been the most effective response to strikes, courts have been reluctant to impose this sanction automatically. Other factors have been considered, such as whether the board bargained in "good faith," whether the strike constituted a clear and present danger to public safety, and whether irreparable harm would result from the strike.[135] The Supreme Court of Arkansas ruled that the

130. *See, e.g.,* Buffalo Teachers Fed'n v. Helsby, 676 F.2d 28 (2d Cir. 1982); Nat'l Educ. Ass'n-S. Bend v. S. Bend Cmty. Sch. Corp., 655 N.E.2d 516 (Ind. Ct. App. 1995); E. Brunswick Bd. of Educ. v. E. Brunswick Educ. Ass'n, 563 A.2d 55 (N.J. Super. Ct. App. Div. 1989).

131. Anchorage Educ. Ass'n v. Anchorage Sch. Dist., 648 P.2d 993, 998 (Alaska 1982). *See also* Carroll v. Ringgold Educ. Ass'n, 680 A.2d 1137 (Pa. 1996) (holding that an injunction could include provisions for court-monitored bargaining between the parties). *But see* Wilson v. Pulaski Ass'n of Classroom Teachers, 954 S.W.2d 221 (Ark. 1997) (requiring proof of irreparable harm to issue a preliminary injunction). In the Arkansas case, the Eighth Circuit also declined to issue an injunction requested by the school board in order to enforce a desegregation consent decree. The court did not find that its power to enforce the consent decree gave it authority to resolve other disputes arising in the district. Knight v. Pulaski County Special Sch. Dist., 112 F.3d 953 (8th Cir. 1997).

132. Harford County Educ. Ass'n v. Bd. of Educ., 380 A.2d 1041 (Md. 1977).

133. Nat'l Educ. Ass'n-S. Bend v. S. Bend Cmty. Sch. Corp., 655 N.E.2d 516 (Ind. Ct. App. 1995). *See also* Franklin Township Bd. of Educ. v. Quakertown Educ. Ass'n, 643 A.2d 34 (N.J. Super. Ct. App. Div. 1994) (holding that the school board could be awarded attorneys' fees and damages associated with a strike and that the trial court could impose additional monetary sanctions to pressure compliance with a court order to return to work).

134. Labor Relations Comm'n v. Salem Teachers Union, 706 N.E.2d 1146 (Mass. App. Ct. 1999).

135. *See, e.g.,* Jersey Shore Area Sch. Dist. v. Jersey Shore Educ. Ass'n, 548 A.2d 1202 (Pa. 1988); Jefferson County Bd. of Educ. v. Jefferson County Educ. Ass'n, 393 S.E.2d 653 (W. Va. 1990); Joint Sch. Dist. No. 1 v. Wis. Rapids Educ. Ass'n, 234 N.W.2d 289 (Wis. 1975).

party requesting an injunction must "establish irreparable harm,"[136] regardless of whether the strike is illegal *per se*. Evidence required by school boards to demonstrate sufficient cause for an injunction has varied according to the legal jurisdiction and the interpretation of applicable state statutes.

The procedures required for dismissing striking teachers have received judicial attention. Courts have held that due process procedures must be provided, but questions arise as to the nature and type of hearing that must be afforded. The Wisconsin Supreme Court ruled that striking teachers must be provided an impartial and fair hearing, and that the board of education was not sufficiently impartial to serve as the hearing panel. Reversing this decision, the United States Supreme Court maintained that the board's involvement did not overcome "the presumption of honesty and integrity in policymakers with decision-making power."[137] The Court further held that "permitting the Board to make the decision at issue here preserves its control over school district affairs, leaves the balance of power in labor relations where the state legislature struck it, and assures that the decision whether to dismiss the teachers will be made by the body responsible for that decision under state law."[138] While noting that the Fourteenth Amendment guarantees each teacher procedural due process, the Supreme Court concluded that a hearing before the school board satisfies this requirement.

State legislatures and courts generally have refused to grant public school teachers the right to strike. Even in the few states permitting a limited right to strike, extensive restrictions have confined its use.[139] Teachers illegally participating in a strike are subject to court-imposed penalties and, in most states, to statutory penalties. Refusal of teachers to return to the classroom can result in dismissal.[140]

Conclusion

Because of the diversity in collective bargaining laws among states, legal principles with universal application are necessarily broad. Generalizations concerning collective bargaining rights that are applicable to most teachers are listed here.

1. Teachers have a constitutionally protected right to form and join a union.

---

136. Wilson v. Pulaski Ass'n of Classroom Teachers, 954 S.W.2d 221, 224 (Ark. 1997). *See also* Niles Township High Sch. Dist. v. Niles Township Fed'n of Teachers, 692 N.E.2d 700 (Ill. App. Ct. 1997).

137. Hortonville Educ. Ass'n v. Hortonville Joint Sch. Dist., 225 N.W.2d 658 (Wis. 1975), *rev'd,* 426 U.S. 482, 497 (1976). *See also* text accompanying note 85, Chapter 11.

138. *Id.,* 426 U.S. at 496.

139. *See supra* text accompanying note 121.

140. National Labor Relations Act, in the private sector, preserves the employer's right to permanently replace economic strikers; this right offsets employees' right to strike. 29 U.S.C. §§ 151 *et seq.* (2002). *See also* Van-Go Transp. Co. v. New York City Bd. of Educ., 53 F. Supp. 2d 278 (E.D.N.Y. 1999).

2. Specific bargaining rights are conferred through state statutes or judicial interpretations of state constitutions, thus creating wide divergence in teachers' bargaining rights across states.

3. School boards are not required to bargain with employee organizations unless mandated to do so by state law.

4. Collective bargaining must be conducted "in good faith," which means that the school board and teachers' organization attempt to reach agreement without compulsion on either side to agree.

5. The scope of negotiations is generally defined as including wages, hours, and other terms and conditions of employment, such as teaching load, planning time, and lunch periods.

6. Governmental policy matters are not mandatorily bargainable but are permissive subjects unless prohibited by law.

7. State legislation permitting the negotiation of a service fee (fair share) provision for nonunion members is constitutional; however, if a public employee objects to supporting specific ideological or political causes, the fee must reflect only the costs of bargaining and contract administration.

8. To collect a fair share fee from a nonunion teacher who raises First Amendment objections, the union must provide adequate information regarding the basis of the fee, procedural safeguards to ensure a prompt response to employees who may object, and an escrow account for challenged amounts.

9. Unions may constitutionally negotiate exclusive privileges such as the use of the school mail and dues checkoff; other communication options, however, must be available to rival unions.

10. Nonunion teachers have the right to express a viewpoint before the school board on an issue under negotiation between the board and union.

11. Negotiated agreements generally include a grievance procedure for resolving conflicts that arise under the terms of the contract; the procedures may provide for either advisory or binding arbitration depending on state law.

12. Impasse procedures for public-sector bargaining are generally limited to mediation and fact finding, with the public employer retaining final decision-making authority.

13. Teacher strikes, except in limited situations in a few states, are illegal and punishable by dismissal, fines, and/or imprisonment.

13

Tort Liability

Tort law offers civil rather than criminal remedies to individuals for harm caused by the unreasonable conduct of others. Generally, a *tort* is described as a civil wrong, independent of breach of contract, for which a court will provide relief in the form of damages. Tort cases primarily involve state law[1] and are grounded in the fundamental premise that individuals are liable for the consequences of their conduct that result in injury to others. Most school tort actions can be grouped into three categories: negligence, intentional torts, and defamation.[2]

Negligence

Negligence is a breach of one's legal duty to protect others from unreasonable risks of harm. The failure to act or the commission of an improper act, which results in injury or loss to another person, can constitute negligence. To establish negligence, an injury must be avoidable by the exercise of reasonable care. Additionally, each of the following four elements must be present to support a successful claim: (1) the defendant has a *duty* to protect the plaintiff, (2) the *duty is breached* by the failure to exercise an appropriate *standard of care*, (3) the negligent conduct is the *proximate or legal cause* of the injury, and (4) an actual *injury* occurs.

---

1. The only exceptions involve cases brought in the District of Columbia and actions initiated under 42 U.S.C. § 1983 (2002), which entitles individuals to sue persons acting under color of state law for damages in connection with the impairment of federally protected rights. *See* text accompanying note 188, Chapter 11.

2. A fourth category of tort cases is termed *strict liability.* This type of tort occurs when an injury results from the creation of an unusual or extreme hazard. Because such torts are uncommon in educational settings, they are not discussed in this chapter.

Duty

School officials have a common law duty to anticipate foreseeable dangers and to take necessary precautions to protect students entrusted in their care. The specific duties that school personnel owe students are to provide adequate supervision; give proper instruction; maintain equipment, facilities, and grounds; and warn students of known dangers.

Supervision.   Although state statutes require educators to provide proper supervision, school personnel are not expected to have every child under surveillance at all times during the school day or to anticipate every possible accident or incident that might occur. Moreover, there is no set level of supervision required under common law (i.e., there is no predetermined student/teacher ratio mandated by courts) for each activity or population. The level or amount of supervision required in any given situation is determined by the aggregate of circumstances, including the age, maturity, and prior experience of the students; the specific activity in progress; and the presence of external threats. Accordingly, there may be situations where no direct temporary supervision is needed (e.g., when a nondisruptive student is permitted to leave the classroom to use adjacent restroom facilities in a building with no known dangers), where close supervision is prudent (e.g., when students with histories of inappropriate behavior are assigned to the same activity-oriented classroom), and even where one-to-one supervision is required (e.g., aquatic exercise class involving students with significant physical disabilities).

In assessing if adequate supervision has been provided, courts will determine whether the events leading up to the injury foreseeably placed the student at risk and whether the injury could have been prevented by proper supervision. Two student injury cases involving rock-throwing incidents illustrate this point. In one instance, where student rock throwing had continued for almost 10 minutes before the injury occurred, the court found the supervising teacher liable for negligence.[3] But, where a teacher aide had walked past a group of students moments before one child threw a rock that was deflected and hit another child, no liability was assessed.[4] The court concluded that the teacher aide had provided adequate supervision and had no reason to anticipate the event that caused the injury.

Proper supervision is particularly important in settings that pose significant risks to students, such as vocational shops, gymnasiums, science laboratories, and school grounds where known dangers exist. In these settings, it is critical that school personnel provide both proper instruction and adequate supervision to reduce the likelihood of injury to children and staff. In a New York case, the appeals court upheld the

3. Sheehan v. Saint Peter's Catholic Sch., 188 N.W.2d 868 (Minn. 1971).

4. Fagan v. Summers, 498 P.2d 1227 (Wyo. 1972). *See also* Janukajtis v. Fallon, 726 N.Y.S.2d 451 (App. Div. 2001) (finding that even with intense supervision, officials could not have prevented a child from being injured when struck in the eye with a stick thrown by a fellow student); Dadich v. Syosset, 717 N.Y.S.2d 634 (App. Div. 2000) (identifying no negligence where a fight between two students was brief and occurred spontaneously).

apportionment of 60 percent liability to the school and 40 percent liability to the student who failed to use a catcher's mask and suffered injuries when a pitched ball tipped off the edge of the mitt and struck her in the face.[5] Safety equipment had not been made available, nor had anyone instructed her to wear a mask. A safety expert also expressed the opinion that the need to wear safety devices was greater indoors, as in this case, due to typically poor lighting.

The school district's duty to supervise also includes the duty to protect pupils and employees from foreseeable risks posed by other students or school personnel, as well as persons not associated with the district. Depending on the circumstances of a particular case, districts can meet this duty by warning potential victims, increasing the number of supervisory personnel, and/or providing increased security where assaults, batteries, or other violent acts are reasonably foreseeable. Courts do not expect schools to ensure the safety of students, but do require that officials respond promptly and professionally when confronted with potentially dangerous circumstances.[6] Minnesota school personnel failed to provide an appropriate level of supervision resulting in a student swimmer being raped in the locker room.[7] Several staff saw the rapist on campus over the course of 45 minutes to one hour. Two school employees even knew that the intruder must have accessed the girl's locker room, but neither questioned him nor had him removed.

When the alleged violator is a school employee, most courts have rejected school district liability, finding conduct such as battery and sexual assault to represent independent acts outside an individual's scope of employment.[8] The conduct of the individual violator is the proximate cause of injury and not the negligent supervision of the district. Nonetheless, districts may be found liable for negligence in hiring or in retaining employees where school officials had knowledge of prior or continuing misconduct.[9] Such knowledge was not present in an Illinois case where a school bus driver was terminated for pleading "guilty but mentally ill" to a charge of aggravated criminal sexual assault on a kindergarten boy.[10] The parents sued the district for negligent hiring and retention, among other claims. The court ruled for the district, finding that the driver's previous employment record failed to show that he represented a

---

5. Zmitrowitz v. Roman Catholic Diocese, 710 N.Y.S.2d 453 (App. Div. 2000).

6. *See, e.g.,* David XX v. Saint Catherine's Ctr. for Children, 699 N.Y.S.2d 827 (App. Div. 1999) (denying summary judgment where a 6-year-old was sexually abused by a 13-year-old during transport to school; the parents had informed officials on numerous occasions that an aide had not accompanied the driver, as was required, and that the older child had a history of aggressive sexual dysfunction). *But see* Johnson v. Carmel Cent. Sch. Dist., 716 N.Y.S.2d 403 (App. Div. 2000) (finding no notice that a student would attack another student; school personnel could not be expected to guard against all spontaneous acts of students).

7. S.W. v. Spring Lake Park Sch. Dist. No. 16, 592 N.W.2d 870 (Minn. Ct. App. 1999).

8. *See, e.g.,* Bratton v. Calkins, 870 P.2d 981 (Wash. Ct. App. 1994).

9. But failure to conduct a background check before hiring a staff member will result in liability only if such failure is shown to be the proximate cause of the injury. *See* Kendrick v. E. Delavan Baptist Church, 886 F. Supp. 1465 (E.D. Wis. 1995).

10. Giraldi v. Cmty. Consol. Sch. Dist. #62, 665 N.E.2d 332 (Ill. App. Ct. 1996).

danger to children; it supported only that he was often late to work (allegedly due to the obligations of his full-time job) and that he at times failed to navigate his route in a timely manner. Even then, a superordinate discussed his lateness with him, a supervisor rode his bus to ensure that the proper route was taken, and a "tail" was used to follow him. No improprieties of any type were discovered.

It is important to note that there may be times when students pass out of the "orbit of school authority" even though they are physically present on campus. This often occurs today, given the wide range of uses of school buildings (e.g., meetings for nonschool groups such as Scouts and Brownies). In such a case, an Indiana appeals court found that a district had no duty to supervise male students who secretly videotaped female lifeguards in their locker room in various stages of undress. The tape later was circulated at the school, and the victims claimed that the school district's negligence caused their emotional distress. The lifeguard class, although held in school facilities, was not part of the public school curriculum (i.e., it was extracurricular and sponsored by the Red Cross), and school employees neither taught nor supervised the course. Once school officials learned what had transpired, they investigated, identified, and suspended those responsible and confiscated the one remaining tape. The incident was found to be unforeseeable, and no special duty was established for the district either to provide security or to supervise the class.[11]

Supervision of students en route to and from school also has generated considerable litigation. Over the years, parents have argued that school officials are responsible for their children from the time they leave home until the time they return.[12] Although such a bright-line test would assist courts in rendering uniform decisions, in this instance it clearly would result in the placement of an unrealistic demand on school resources and an unfair burden on personnel. Unless specifically required under state statute, courts instead focus on whether the events that caused the injury were foreseeable; whether the district had an express or implied duty to provide supervision on and off school grounds both before and after school hours; and whether the child was injured due to a breach of that duty.

If a school district is not responsible for transporting a child, proper supervision still should be provided at the pick-up and drop-off area. Moreover, crossing guards should be stationed at nearby intersections for "walkers," and assistance should be provided to parents and children to help identify safe routes to and from school. If any known dangers exist that cannot be removed (e.g., criminal elements within the neighborhood, busy roads, an attractive nuisance maintained at a construction site), parents

---

11. Roe v. N. Adams Cmty. Sch. Corp., 647 N.E.2d 655 (Ind. Ct. App. 1995).

12. Some parents have unsuccessfully asserted that their respective school districts should provide supervision during private transport to school functions or even once their children arrive home. *See, e.g.,* Gylten v. Swalboski, 246 F.3d 1139 (8th Cir. 2001) (noting that there was no special duty to supervise a student who had been responsible for a traffic accident off school grounds with a nonstudent while on his way to football practice); Tarnaras v. Farmingdale Sch. Dist., 694 N.Y.S.2d 413 (App. Div. 1999) (noting that school custody ceased when the student passed out of the "orbit of school authority" and that the district was not negligent when an estranged boyfriend brutally assaulted a female youth in her home after the conclusion of the school day).

should be notified and students should be given safety instructions. Moreover, parents need to be informed as to the earliest time supervision will be provided before school (e.g., 20 minutes prior to the beginning of the school day) so that students will not arrive prior to school personnel. In such a case, no duty to supervise existed where a 12-year-old Kansas boy ran off school property before school and was hit by a car. The court reasoned that the school did not owe a duty to the student to provide supervision more than 20 minutes prior to the beginning of the school day.[13]

In cases where the district is responsible for providing transportation (e.g., school bus, disability van), officials should ensure that involved staff are properly trained and that district procedures are communicated and practiced. Such procedures should include licensure requirements, background checks, maintenance schedules, driving practices (e.g., stopping at railroad crossings), loading and unloading procedures, conduct during transport, and criteria for when an aide is to be assigned. Designated procedures were not followed in a Washington case where a bus driver was found negligent in the death of a 13-year-old who was killed by a car after she had exited the bus.[14] The driver failed to use either the stop sign or flashing lights as the student was discharged and then permitted the student to cross behind the bus instead of in front, as required by state law.

In addition, school officials also have a duty to provide supervision during field trips and school-sponsored, off-campus activities. As with other supervisory roles, school officials accompanying the students need to assess foreseeable risks associated with each activity (both planned and spontaneous) and be aware of the abilities of their students. The Supreme Court of Oregon determined that this had not occurred where a log shifted with the ocean tide and injured a student during a school outing at the beach.[15] The court concluded that the unusual wave action on the Oregon coast was a known hazard and that the teacher failed to take reasonable safety precautions.

However, when the activity is neither curricular nor school sponsored, liability is less likely, given the difficulty of identifying a continuing duty on the part of school officials to provide supervision. No continuing duty was identified in a Washington case where school officials failed to supervise students participating in a party during "senior release day."[16] A student left the party intoxicated and was killed in an accident on her way home. School personnel were not involved in planning or financing the party nor did they attend. Furthermore, knowledge that there would be a party did not create a duty to supervise.

As a general rule, school districts are not expected to protect truant and nonattending students. This is true for those who never arrive at school as well as for those who exit school grounds during the school day without permission, notwithstanding an appropriate level of surveillance of the school building and grounds as determined by the age and ability of the students. In a New York case, the court declared that "nothing short of a prison-like atmosphere with monitors at every exit could have pre-

13. Glaser v. Emporia Unified Sch. Dist. No. 253, 21 P.3d 573 (Kan. 2001).
14. Yurkovich v. Rose, 847 P.2d 925 (Wash. Ct. App. 1993).
15. Morris v. Douglas County Sch. Dist. No. 9, 403 P.2d 775 (Or. 1965).
16. Rhea v. Grandview Sch. Dist., 694 P.2d 666 (Wash. Ct. App. 1985).

vented [a student] from leaving the school grounds."[17] The court declined to require such security measures and further concluded that once a truant student is beyond the legal control of the school district, there is no duty to supervise. In fact, extreme measures to keep students at school may themselves result in liability. In Kentucky, a teacher chained a student by the ankle, and later, when he "escaped," chained him by the neck to a tree to prevent him from leaving school grounds. The student had arrived late or skipped class on numerous occasions. The appeals court determined that the lower court erred in granting a directed verdict to the teacher and that proof of emotional damages should be submitted to the jury on remand.[18]

Instruction.   Teachers have a duty to provide students with adequate and appropriate instruction prior to commencing an activity that may pose a risk of harm—the greater the risk, the greater the need for instruction.[19] Following such instruction, effort should be made to determine whether the material was heard and understood. This can be accomplished through assessments such as paper and pencil tests, oral tests, and observations, as appropriate for the activity. Proper instruction was not given in a case reviewed by the Nebraska Supreme Court where a freshman was severely burned in a welding course when his flannel shirt ignited. The school failed to make protective leather aprons available to the students, as was recommended for such activities, and the instructor had informed the students simply to wear old shirts. Perhaps most damaging to the district's case was the testimony of the instructor when he stated on four separate occasions that it was not his responsibility to ensure that students wore protective clothing. "Safety garments" as a topic was briefly mentioned in one of many handouts distributed in class, but no effort was made to determine whether students read or understood the material and on no occasion did the instructor prevent a student from participating based on the type of clothing worn.[20]

Maintenance of Buildings, Grounds, and Equipment.   Some states by law protect frequenters of public buildings from danger to life, health, safety, or welfare. These *safe place statutes* have been used successfully by individuals to obtain damages from school districts for injuries resulting from defective conditions of school buildings and grounds.[21] Moreover, school officials have a common law duty to maintain facilities and equipment in a reasonably safe condition. Districts can be held liable where they are aware of, or should be aware of, hazardous conditions and do not take the necessary steps to repair or correct the conditions. For example, school districts are

17. Palella v. Ulmer, 518 N.Y.S.2d 91, 93 (Sup. Ct. 1987).

18. Banks v. Fritsch, 39 S.W.3d 474 (Ky. Ct. App. 2001).

19. *See, e.g.,* Scott v. Rapides Parish Sch. Bd., 732 So. 2d 749 (La. Ct. App. 1999) (finding that the instructor failed to provide proper instruction to an 18-year-old student who was injured when he made a long jump at full speed and landed wrong); Traficenti v. Moore Catholic High Sch., 724 N.Y.S.2d 24 (App. Div. 2001) (upholding denial of summary judgment where a cheerleader was injured when her spotter failed to catch her; a triable issue remained as to whether adequate supervision and instruction had been provided).

20. Norman v. Ogallala Pub. Sch. Dist., 609 N.W.2d 338 (Neb. 2000).

21. *See, e.g.,* Monfils v. City of Sterling Heights, 269 N.W.2d 588 (Mich. Ct. App. 1978).

responsible for the removal or encasement of asbestos materials;[22] failure to do so can result in injury and accompanying tort suits. Because state and federal support for asbestos removal has been limited, numerous districts have sued asbestos manufacturers and suppliers to recover extraction costs.[23] Such providers typically failed either to test the materials to determine whether they were hazardous or to warn consumers of potential dangers.

The duty to provide reasonable maintenance of facilities does not place an obligation on school personnel to anticipate every possible danger or to be aware of and correct every minor defect as soon as the condition occurs. For example, a Louisiana student was unsuccessful in establishing a breach of duty in connection with an injury sustained on a defective door latch.[24] The state appeals court concluded that there was no evidence that any school employee had knowledge of, or should have had knowledge of, the broken latch. Because the risk was unforeseen, a duty to protect the student could not be imposed. Similarly, the Alabama Supreme Court did not find two teachers negligent for an injury that occurred when a student slipped on a puddle of water during a physical education class; the teachers were unaware of the puddle or the condition of the roof that led to the accumulation of water.[25]

If dangers are known, however, damages may be awarded when injuries result from unsafe building or playground conditions. A Michigan student was successful in obtaining damages for the loss of sight in one eye; the injury was sustained while playing in a pile of dirt and sand on the playground after school hours.[26] The area was not fenced, and prior to the incident parents had complained to school officials about "dirt fights" among children. The Michigan appeals court concluded that the school district breached its duty to maintain the school grounds in a safe condition.

Notwithstanding these examples, if the conduct of the injured party, rather than the unsafe condition of the grounds, is found to be the primary cause of the injury, the school district may not be liable for negligence. To illustrate, a California appeals court concluded that a district was not liable for the death of a student on school grounds after regular school hours.[27] Although the playground was accessible to the public, unsupervised, and in disrepair, the court concluded that the student's death

---

22. Asbestos School Hazard Detection and Control Act, 20 U.S.C. § 3601 *et seq.* (2002); Asbestos Hazard Emergency Response Act (AHERA) of 1986, 15 U.S.C. § 2641 *et seq.* (2002).

23. *See, e.g., In re* Asbestos Sch. Litigation, Pfizer, 46 F.3d 1284 (3d Cir. 1994); Adam Pub. Sch. Dist. v. Asbestos Corp., 7 F.3d 717 (8th Cir. 1993); Tioga Pub. Sch. Dist. #15 v. United States Gypsum Co., 984 F.2d 915 (8th Cir. 1993).

24. Lewis v. Saint Bernard Parish Sch. Bd., 350 So. 2d 1256 (La. Ct. App. 1977).

25. Best v. Houtz, 541 So. 2d 8 (Ala. 1989). *But see* Hertz v. Sch. City of E. Chi., 744 N.E.2d 484 (Ind. Ct. App. 2001) (concluding that the district had a duty to use reasonable care in removing ice and snow from its thoroughfares and was not entitled to immunity).

26. Monfils v. City of Sterling Heights, 269 N.W.2d 588 (Mich. Ct. App. 1978).

27. Bartell v. Palos Verdes Peninsula Sch. Dist., 147 Cal. Rptr. 898 (Ct. App. 1978). *See also* Oravek v. Cmty. Sch. Dist. 146, 637 N.E.2d 554 (Ill. App. Ct. 1994) (finding no evidence of willful and wanton wrongdoing on the part of the district where a 12-year-old was injured while riding her bicycle on school property after school hours).

resulted from his own conduct in attempting to perform a hazardous skateboard activity, not from defective playground conditions. A New York appeals court also held that a district was not liable for a child's eye injury incurred while playing on school grounds when school was not in session. A second student found a screwdriver and threw it at the plaintiff, causing the injury. The court noted that the screwdriver was not the property of the district and that school personnel did not know of its presence on school grounds.[28]

In addition to maintaining buildings and grounds, school personnel also are required to maintain equipment and to use it safely, whether in woodshop, science labs, or athletics.[29] In a Kentucky case, a coach was found liable for the electrocution death of a student who had been using a whirlpool. The coach had "modified" the equipment but had failed to install a ground fault interrupter, although one was required by the national electric code. His negligence was found to be the substantial factor causing the student's death.[30] Similarly, the Arizona appeals court remanded a case to determine whether a school district foreseeably and unreasonably placed elementary school children at risk when it failed to install cushioning beneath a newly constructed swing set.[31]

Duty to Warn. Courts in nearly all states today have recognized either a statutory or common law duty to warn students and/or parents of known risks they may encounter. This duty has been identified in areas such as physical education and interscholastic sport, vocational education, laboratory science, and other occasions when a student uses potentially dangerous machinery or equipment.[32] Informing, if not warning, students and parents of known dangers is necessary so that the student then may "assume" the risks associated with the activity in order to participate (see discussion of Assumption of Risk later in this chapter).

In addition to the somewhat traditional warnings connected with sports or the use of equipment, school psychologists and counselors have a duty to warn when they learn through counseling or therapy that clients intend to harm themselves or others. Those in receipt of such information are required to inform potential victims or to notify parents if the student threatens to self-injure. This requirement supersedes

---

28. Mix v. S. Seneca Cent. Sch. Dist., 602 N.Y.S.2d 467 (App. Div. 1993).

29. *See, e.g.,* Arteman v. Clinton Cmty. Unit Sch. Dist. No. 15, 740 N.E.2d 47 (Ill. App. Ct. 2000) (identifying the duty of the district to provide appropriate safety equipment to students; the injured student had been assigned "experimental" roller blades with the brake on the toe).

30. Massie v. Persson, 729 S.W.2d 448 (Ky. Ct. App. 1987).

31. Schabel v. Deer Valley Unified Sch., 920 P.2d 41 (Ariz. Ct. App. 1996). *See also* Catberro v. Naperville Sch. Dist. No. 203, 739 N.E.2d 115 (Ill. App. Ct. 2000) (reinstating a case where a student had been injured when a pole used for jump roping fell and struck his face, causing permanent injury; the pole had been purchased at a garage sale and was in disrepair).

32. Mangold v. Ind. Dep't of Natural Res., 720 N.E.2d 424 (Ind. Ct. App. 1999) (finding no negligence where a student was injured when he tried to take a shotgun shell apart using a hammer; his hunting course instructor had directed him not to handle guns or shells without parental or instructor supervision).

claims of professional ethics or discretion, therapist/client privilege, or confidentiality. In California, a university psychotherapist failed to warn a patient's former girlfriend of a death threat he made against her. Campus police interviewed the patient after they were notified of his intentions, but released him following a brief interrogation. Neither the police nor the psychotherapist took further action and the patient carried out his threat. The court held that the psychotherapist had not exercised reasonable care, particularly given his knowledge of both the seriousness of the threat and the identity of the potential victim.[33]

In Maryland, the father of a suicide victim sued two school counselors following the death of his daughter. The court held that the counselors breached their duty to inform the parent of statements his daughter allegedly made to other students regarding threatening suicide. Although the counselors claimed that they exercised professional discretion when deciding not to discuss the matter with the parent, the court reasoned that their discretion was not boundless and noted that school policy explicitly disavowed confidentiality when suicide was threatened.[34] The court observed that a simple telephone call would have satisfied this duty.

Typically, however, school officials will not be found liable when the act of suicide is unforeseeable (i.e., the threat of suicide was neither explicitly stated nor apparent), even if they knew that a particular student was under stress or seemed depressed or preoccupied. In a Wisconsin case, a student set himself afire and died. School officials had failed to inform the parents that their son had been crying at school, that he had received low grades and been removed from the basketball team, and that he failed to come to school the day of his death. The purported negligence of school personnel was found too remote to render the district liable; its actions were not the proximate cause of the student's death.[35]

Breach of Duty and Standard of Care

Once a duty has been established, the injured individual must show that the duty was breached by the failure of another to exercise an appropriate standard of care.[36] The degree of care teachers owe students is determined by the age, experience, and maturity level of the students; the environment within which the incident occurs; and the type of instructional or recreational activity. For example, primary grade students will generally require closer supervision and more detailed and repetitive instructions than high school students, and a class in woodwork will require closer supervision than a class in English literature. Variability in the level of care deemed reasonable is illus-

---

33. Tarasoff v. Regents of the Univ. of Cal., 551 P.2d 334 (Cal. 1976).

34. Eisel v. Bd. of Educ., 597 A.2d 447 (Md. Ct. App. 1991).

35. McMahon v. St. Croix Falls Sch., 596 N.W.2d 875 (Wis. Ct. App. 1999).

36. *See, e.g.,* Weber v. William Floyd Sch. Dist., 707 N.Y.S.2d 231 (App. Div. 2000) (affirming decision in favor of the defendant where a cheerleader was injured in an attempt to perform a straddle jump; she failed to show that the defendant did not exercise ordinary reasonable care).

trated in a Louisiana case where a mentally retarded student was fatally injured when he darted into a busy thoroughfare while being escorted with nine other classmates to a park three blocks from the school. The state appellate court noted that the general level of care required for all students becomes greater when children with disabilities are involved, particularly when they are taken away from the school campus. The court found the supervision to be inadequate and the selected route to be less safe than alternative routes.[37] In this and other cases, the reasonableness of any given action will be pivotal in determining whether there is liability.

Reasonable Person. In assessing whether appropriate care has been taken, courts consider whether the defendant acted as a "reasonable person" would have acted under the circumstances. The reasonable person is a hypothetical individual who has (1) the physical attributes of the defendant; (2) normal intelligence, problem-solving ability, and temperament; (3) normal perception and memory with a minimum level of information and experience common to the community; and (4) such superior skill and knowledge as the defendant has or purports to have.

Courts will not assume that a defendant possesses any predetermined physical attributes (e.g., size, strength, agility), but rather will consider each defendant's actual physical abilities and disabilities in determining whether the defendant was responsible in whole or in part for a plaintiff's injury. Accordingly, in cases where a child requires physical assistance to avoid injury (e.g., when being attacked by another student), a different expectation will exist for a physically fit teacher who is large and strong as compared to a frail teacher who is small and weak.

Although a defendant's actual physical characteristics and capabilities are used in determining whether his or her conduct was reasonable, that is not the case when considering mental capacity. Courts will assume all *adult* individuals have normal intelligence, problem-solving ability, and temperament even when the evidence indicates that they do not possess such attributes.[38] Although this may initially appear unfair, any other approach is likely to result in defense claims that are judicially unmanageable. For example, if defendants' own intellect were used, they then may argue that consideration should be given to factors such as their inability to make good or quick decisions, lack of perception or concentration, poor attention to detail, confrontational personality, or inability to deal with stress. Trying to determine each person's mental abilities and capabilities would be impractical, if not impossible, given the dearth of valid and reliable assessment instruments or techniques and the ease of those being assessed to intentionally misrepresent their abilities. The current approach (i.e., the assumption of normal intelligence) provides a more objective procedure and requires defendants (or their caregivers) to be responsible for injuries they cause others.

---

37. Foster v. Houston Gen. Ins. Co., 407 So. 2d 759, 763 (La. Ct. App. 1981).

38. W. Page Keeton, Dan B. Dobbs, Robert E. Keeton, and David G. Owen, *Prosser and Keeton on Torts,* 5th ed. (St. Paul, MN: West Publishing, 1988), p. 177.

Moreover, courts will attempt to ascertain whether a defendant "discovered that which was readily apparent"[39] in that the defendant is required to have a normal perception of the environment (e.g., be aware that the rear of the school yard is bordered by a small river) and an accurate memory of what has occurred previously within that environment (e.g., recalling that the playground floods following a heavy rain). This requirement does not assume that the defendant will know all facts, foresee all risks, or be aware of all things. Instead, it is based on the position that there exist certain facts that a reasonable adult, with normal intellect, should know.

In an effort to determine whether the defendant acted as a reasonable person, courts also will consider whether the defendant had or claimed to have had any superior knowledge or skill. Teachers, who are college graduates and state licensed, are expected to act like reasonable persons with similar education. In addition, any special training an individual has received also may affect whether a given act is found reasonable. Accordingly, a physical education instructor who is a certified lifeguard or a teacher with an advanced degree in chemistry may be held to higher standards of care than will others with lesser skills and knowledge when a student is drowning or when chemicals in a school laboratory are mixed improperly and ignite.

Invitee, Licensee, Trespasser.   In determining whether an appropriate standard of care has been provided, courts also consider whether an injured individual was an invitee, licensee, or trespasser, with invitees receiving the greatest level of care and trespassers receiving the least. In a school setting, an *invitee* is one who enters the school premises on the expressed or implied invitation of the school district or one of its agents. The district then has an affirmative duty to exercise reasonable care for the safety of invitees commensurate with the risks and circumstances involved. Furthermore, invitees must be protected against known dangers as well as those that might be discovered with reasonable care. Under most circumstances, students, teachers, and administrators are invitees of the district. Students who break into a school after hours, however, have exceeded the "period of invitation" and become trespassers.[40]

When permission to be on school premises is requested and permitted, the person becomes a licensee (e.g., requests by unsolicited visitors, salespersons, parents, newspersons). Even school children may qualify as licensees under certain circumstances (e.g., while engaged in activities of a local nonschool organization that has been permitted evening or weekend use of a school classroom; when participating in a tour of a local bakery). Such persons enter the building or grounds facing the same

39. *Id.* at 182.

40. *See, e.g.,* Howard County Bd. of Educ. v. Cheyne, 636 A.2d 22 (Md. Ct. App. 1994) (holding that 4-year-old was an invitee when she initially entered a gymnasium to attend a sports function, but that a question remained for the jury to determine whether she had exceeded the scope of her invitation at the time of the injury). *See also* Tincani v. Inland Empire Zoological Soc'y, 875 P.2d 621 (Wash. 1994) (remanding a case where a student sued a zoo after falling off a cliff during a field trip; the court questioned whether he became a licensee when he strayed beyond the area of his invitation).

conditions and threats as the occupier. Nevertheless, districts still need to warn licensees of known dangers and not injure intentionally or by willful, wanton, or reckless conduct.

Where the individual has been neither invited nor received consent, the person is guilty of trespass upon accessing school property. Although state laws often blur the distinction between licensee and trespasser, less care has to be provided for the safety of trespassers. Adult trespassers in particular have no right to a safe place and must assume the risk of what they may encounter. Generally, the owner owes no duty to trespassers other than to refrain from willfully or wantonly injuring them (e.g., by setting traps). In selected jurisdictions, however, if the owner knows that trespassers are on the premises (e.g., vagrants living in an abandoned school building), the owner must use reasonable care not to expose the trespasser to an environment that is known to be dangerous. When the trespasser is a child, as often is the case on school property, it is prudent to take additional steps to restrict access or to remove known dangers. In such narrow instances, there is little legal distinction between a trespasser and a licensee in regard to the standard of care provided.

Proximate Cause

For liability to be assessed against a school district, the negligent conduct of school personnel must be the proximate or legal cause of injury. *Proximate cause* has been defined as "that which in a natural and continuous sequence, unbroken by any efficient intervening cause, produces the injury, and without which the result would not have occurred."[41] In determining proximate cause, courts consider factors other than the defendant's conduct that contributed to producing the injury, ascertain whether the challenged conduct created a force that was in operation up to the time of the injury, and assess the lapse of time between the conduct and the occurrence of the injury. Accordingly, not every seemingly negligent act results in liability, even where an injury results, unless the act was in fact the cause of the injury. In New York, an appellate court affirmed summary judgment for the district where the sole proximate cause of the appellant's injuries was his attempt to do a back flip dismount from the playground equipment while his teacher's back was turned; the act was sudden and unforeseeable.[42] Likewise, in Montana the state supreme court affirmed a jury verdict finding no negligent supervision on the part of a special education assistant when a child let go and fell two to three feet from playground equipment, breaking her tibia. Two adult supervisors were overseeing 11 special needs students, but by the time the

---

41. Anselmo v. Tuck, 924 S.W.2d 798, 802 (Ark. 1996).

42. Ascher v. Scarsdale Sch. Dist., 700 N.Y.S.2d 210 (App. Div. 1999). *See also* Lopez v. Freeport Union Free Sch. Dist., 734 N.Y.S.2d 97 (App. Div. 2001) (concluding that the lack of supervision was not the proximate cause of a student's injury when she failed to catch hold of a jungle gym bar and fell; moreover, the playground was maintained in a reasonably safe condition and free of defects).

supervisors saw the child falling, it was too late to intervene. The alleged failure to supervise was not found to be the proximate cause of the child's injury.[43]

Injury

Legal negligence does not exist unless actual injury is incurred either directly by the individual (e.g., broken arm) or by the individual's property (e.g., broken window). Most often, an individual will know of the injury as soon as it occurs; in some instances, however, the individual may not be aware of the injury for many months or even years (e.g., development of asbestosis due to exposure to asbestos 20 years previously). In most states, there is a statute of limitations (i.e., a period of time within which suit must be filed) of one to three years on tort claims, although the actual time can be greater *if* the limitations period does not begin until the plaintiff reaches the age of majority or becomes aware of the injury. These and other exceptions to the statutory tolling period are available in several states. Such exceptions, however, can leave defendants (e.g., school districts) vulnerable to suit indefinitely or may make a defense difficult, if not impossible. Given this scenario, several states that permit expansion of their limitations period also have enacted what are called *statutes of repose*. Such statutes permit exceptions to general limitations periods, but limit what otherwise may become a perpetual right to sue, at least in regard to selected claims.

When students are injured in the school setting, school personnel have a duty to provide reasonable assistance commensurate with their training and experience. Where reasonable treatment is provided, no liability will generally be assessed even if the treatment later is proven to be inappropriate. State *Good Samaritan* laws often shield individuals from liability when they provide care in emergency situations. Acts that a reasonable person would *not* have taken, however, are not protected. In a Pennsylvania case, two teachers were held personally liable for administering medical treatment to a student by holding his infected finger under boiling water. The superior court concluded that the action was unreasonable and noted that the situation did not necessitate emergency first aid.[44]

Defenses against Negligence

Several defenses are available to school districts when employees have been charged with negligence. At times, districts have identified procedural defects (e.g., the failure to adhere to statutory requirements regarding notice of claim), or have proposed that the plaintiff's injury was caused by uncontrollable events of nature (i.e., an act of God) in an effort to thwart liability claims. More commonly, however, defenses such as

---

43. Morgan v. Great Falls Sch. Dist., 995 P.2d 422 (Mont. 2000). *See also* Williamson v. Liptzin, 539 S.E.2d 313 (N.C. Ct. App. 2000) (reasoning that the alleged negligence by the psychiatrist was not the proximate cause of plaintiff's actions—i.e., killing two people eight months after his last session).

44. Guerrieri v. Tyson, 24 A.2d 468 (Pa. Super. Ct. 1942).

immunity, contributory negligence, comparative negligence, and assumption of risk have been asserted.

Governmental Immunity. In the rare cases where governmental immunity is comprehensively applied, governmental entities (including school districts) cannot be sued for any reason. This defense is available to employees only when state law specifically confers such immunity for acts within the scope of employment, or courts interpret the law to do so. However, immunity is seldom comprehensively applied today, as nearly all states either have limited its use[45] or have qualified its application based on factors such as whether (1) the claim was related to the maintenance of the school building or property, (2) acts were governmental or proprietary, (3) decisions qualified as discretionary or ministerial, (4) school property was being used for recreational purposes, or (5) the injury was compensable under the state's workers' compensation laws (employees only).

In most jurisdictions, school districts can be held liable for injuries arising from a dangerous realty condition if authorities have knowledge of a defect and do not take corrective action (see discussion titled Maintenance of Buildings, Grounds, and Equipment) or if they maintain an attractive nuisance. An *attractive nuisance* is a facility, structure, or piece of equipment that entices the public to engage in activity that is potentially dangerous. Swimming pools and ponds on school property often are classified as attractive nuisances. Because of the potential for serious injury, school districts may claim immunity only if proper precautions are taken to prevent public access to such areas.

In some jurisdictions, a distinction has been made between governmental and proprietary functions in determining whether a school district is immune. *Governmental functions* are those that are performed in discharging the agency's official duties (e.g., hiring faculty, maintaining a building) that are generally considered immune from liability. On the other hand, *proprietary functions* are those that are only tangentially related to the curriculum, can as easily be performed by the private sector, and often require the payment of a fee (e.g., community use of school pool, catering services, plant sales); these activities have been permissible targets for tort actions. Except in the most extreme cases, however, it may prove difficult to identify activities that are proprietary, because most school endeavors in some way can be linked to the mission of the district.

---

45. For example, in Arkansas, school districts and their employees are immune from negligence suits; in Idaho, districts are immune from liability for ordinary negligence when someone who is under the supervision of district personnel is injured by another person. *See* Brown v. Fountain Hill Sch. Dist., 1 S.W.3d 27 (Ark. Ct. App. 1999) (affirming summary judgment for the school district where a high school student amputated the fingers of his right hand while operating a table saw that had its safety guard removed by the instructor; the district was immune in the negligence claim and the intentional tort claim was rejected); Coonse v. Boise Sch. Dist., 979 P.2d 1161 (Idaho 1999) (concluding that state immunity applied where a third-grade girl under the supervision of the district was assaulted by a group of older boys during recess; it was irrelevant that the boys also were under the supervision of the district).

In other states, the distinction between discretionary and ministerial functions is used to determine whether liability exists. As with governmental and propriety functions, differentiation between those that qualify as discretionary and ministerial will be obvious only when assessing extreme examples. By definition, *discretionary functions* are those that require consideration of alternatives, deliberation, judgment, and the making of a decision (e.g., the discretion used in the selection of a new teacher). In contrast, *ministerial functions* are those performed in a prescribed manner, in obedience to legal authority, and without discretion (e.g., procedures used for stopping a school bus at a railroad crossing).[46] As a rule, districts will be liable for negligence involving ministerial duties but be immune from liability for negligence associated with those that are discretionary.[47] Some states also differentiate between policy-level discretionary acts (for which immunity is granted—e.g., policy permitting the use of reasonable corporal punishment) and operational-level discretionary acts that deal with policy implementation (for which immunity is not granted—e.g., determining the number of licks to be administered and the appropriate amount of force to be used).[48]

Discretionary-function immunity was denied in an Alabama case, where a teacher was found to have acted maliciously in the administration of corporal punishment—three hard licks to an eighth-grade student for saying the word *ass*. The student had no prior record of incorrigible behavior and was severely bruised by the punishment. The teacher made no effort to first correct the student's language or to contact the principal before inflicting punishment, in contravention of district policy. The court concluded that the punishment was immoderate and malicious and qualified as battery; the district therefore was not entitled to immunity.[49]

A comparatively recent addition to immunity defenses is that for *recreational use*. Such statutes were passed to encourage property and landowners (including public-sector entities) to open their lands and waters for public recreational use. School gymnasiums, playgrounds, and athletic fields at times have been labeled as recreational facilities or areas, although state laws vary considerably.[50] Immunity for inju-

---

46. Harrison v. Hardin County Cmty. Unit Sch. Dist. No. 1, 730 N.E.2d 61 (Ill. App. Ct. 2000).

47. *See, e.g.,* Pauley v. Anchorage Sch. Dist., 31 P.3d 1284 (Alaska 2001) (granting qualified immunity to a principal who had released a student to his noncustodial mother; the good faith, discretionary decision was neither malicious nor corrupt); Trotter v. Sch. Dist. 218, 733 N.E.2d 363 (Ill. App. Ct. 2000) (concluding that the persons who were responsible for supervising a freshman swim class were entitled to discretionary function immunity in the drowning death of a student); Deaver v. Bridges, 47 S.W.3d 549 (Tex. App. 2000) (finding a Texas superintendent immune for discretionary comments he made to a newspaper about a dismissed teacher who had used racially derogatory terms).

48. Norman v. Ogallala Pub. Sch. Dist., 609 N.W.2d 338 (Neb. 2000).

49. Hinson v. Holt, 776 So. 2d 804 (Ala. Civ. App. 1998).

50. *See, e.g.,* Fear v. Indep. Sch. Dist. 911, 634 N.W.2d 204 (Minn. Ct. App. 2001) (holding that a district was not necessarily entitled to immunity when an elementary school child fell from piled snow and was injured; whether recreational immunity applied was a question to be answered at trial by applying the child trespasser standard); Auman v. Sch. Dist., 635 N.W.2d 762 (Wis. 2001) (concluding that the recreational immunity statute did not shield the district from liability for injuries to a student during mandatory recess).

ries incurred while on the property is provided unless the entrant was charged a fee for admission or was injured due to the owner's willful or wanton misconduct. In Kansas, a football player collapsed at the end of his first mandatory practice and died the following day; plaintiffs claimed that his death was caused by the failure to provide proper supervision. The court applied recreational-use immunity in regard to the ordinary negligence claim, but remanded the case for a determination of whether the defendant's conduct amounted to gross or wanton negligence.[51] If the defendant's conduct were found gross or wanton, neither recreational use nor discretionary function immunity would protect the district from liability.

Immunity also may be used as a defense when an injury is compensable under the state's *workers' compensation statute.* Workers' compensation laws are intended to reduce or eliminate negligence litigation (i.e., they do not protect employers or employees who engage in intentional torts), encourage employer interest in safety and rehabilitation, and promote the study of the causes of accidents (rather than concealment of fault), thereby reducing the occurrence of preventable accidents.[52] Under workers' compensation, liability exists regardless of negligence or fault on the part of the employer or employee, provided that the injury was accidental *and* arose out of and in the course of employment (e.g., when a kitchen employee cuts herself as she prepares finger sandwiches). Note, however, that not all injuries that occur at work are necessarily "work related." In a New Mexico case, a teacher's widow was unsuccessful in securing benefits after her adulterous husband was shot at school by another teacher's jealous husband. The court ruled that the action was taken for purely personal reasons and that the death did not arise out of, was not incident to, and did not occur in the course of the teacher's employment.[53]

A corollary issue in some states has been whether the purchase of liability insurance has impliedly waived immunity, notwithstanding explicit state statutes granting it. Courts have been divided on the matter with some maintaining immunity (in whole or in part) and others abrogating it.[54] In addition to purchasing insurance to protect district funds, a number of states have enacted legislation requiring school systems to indemnify or "save harmless" educators for potential monetary losses associated with negligent conduct that occurs during the performance of assigned duties. Coverage does not include intentional torts or acts that are willful or wanton. Although funds for such purposes can be derived from a variety of sources (e.g., sinking funds, current operations, endowments), it is common for districts to purchase insurance to help manage the financial risk associated with employee negligence. Generally, these laws

---

51. Barrett v. Unified Sch. Dist. No. 259, 32 P.3d 1156 (Kan. 2001).

52. For a related discussion, *see* Stephen B. Thomas, *Students, Colleges, and Disability Law* (Dayton, OH: Education Law Association, 2002), pp. 270–272.

53. Gutierrez v. Artesia Pub. Sch., 583 P.2d 476 (N.M. Ct. App. 1978).

54. *Compare* Brock v. Sumter County Sch. Bd., 542 S.E.2d 547 (Ga. Ct. App. 2000) (holding that the district had not waived sovereign immunity through the purchase of motor vehicle liability insurance) *with* Crowell v. Sch. Dist. No. 7, Gallatin County, 805 P.2d 522 (Mont. 1991) (holding that the purchase of insurance constituted a waiver of immunity).

require districts to assume the cost of legal representation and any resulting liability if negligence is proven.

Contributory Negligence. In states that recognize contributory negligence as a defense, plaintiffs are denied recovery if their actions are shown by the defendant to have been at least partially responsible for the injury; it makes no difference that the defendant was negligent and also at fault. Over the years, the contributory defense has been modified and weakened by courts due to a number of factors, including its harshness to injured plaintiffs, the ease of negligent defendants to avoid liability, and a change in social viewpoint (i.e., from the need to protect new industries early in the twentieth century to the desire to compensate injured persons).[55] As a result, in most jurisdictions today, a slight degree of fault will not prevent a plaintiff from prevailing; typically, the contributory negligence must be significant, although it need not be dominant.

In assessing whether contributory negligence exists, children are not necessarily held to the same standard of care as adults. Rather, their actions must be reasonable for persons of similar age, maturity, intelligence, and experience. Many courts then make individualized determinations as to whether a minor plaintiff appreciated the risks involved and acted as a reasonable person of like characteristics and abilities. Other courts have established age ranges in an effort to more objectively and uniformly determine whether children have the capacity to contribute to or cause their own injuries. Although courts vary greatly and designated ages may seem arbitrary (often based on Biblical scripture or criminal law, with little or nothing to do with child development), the most commonly used ranges are: (1) children birth to age 7 are considered incapable of negligence (although this limit sometimes is as low as age 4); (2) youth between the ages of 7 and 14 are considered incapable of negligence, but this presumption can be rebutted; and (3) students age 14 and over are generally presumed capable of negligence, although this presumption too can be rebutted. In a school setting, educational personnel have been successful in claiming contributory negligence only when they have been able to show that the injured student was sufficiently mature, intelligent, and experienced to understand the consequences of specific actions and nonetheless engaged in dangerous conduct.[56]

Comparative Negligence. Under the contributory model, only the injured party bears financial responsibility if ultimately found responsible for the act leading to an injury. With the comparative model, however, the plaintiff and/or one or more defendants bear responsibility in proportion to fault. For example, in Louisiana, a school bus driver permitted two girls to exit his bus even though he knew one had threatened

55. W. Page Keeton, Dan B. Dobbs, Robert E. Keeton, and David G. Owen, *Prosser and Keeton on Torts,* 5th ed. (St. Paul, MN: West Publishing, 1988), pp. 452–453.

56. *See, e.g.,* Aronson v. Horace Mann-Barnard Sch., 637 N.Y.S.2d 410 (App. Div. 1996) (holding that a senior who was an experienced diver and swimmer was contributorily negligent as she alone was responsible for her injuries when she executed a shallow dive).

to injure the other. He initially exited with them, held them apart, and told a teacher to summon the principal. Instead of waiting for the principal or a teacher to arrive, however, he reentered the bus to move it, because he was blocking traffic. When he pulled away, one student proceeded to stomp the other student's ankle; the injury was so severe as to require three screws to align the broken bones. The court reasoned that the driver should not have left the students unsupervised under the circumstances and assessed 15 percent liability against him.[57] Similarly, an Arizona appeals court upheld a jury verdict where a student was hit by a car when he ran into the street trying to flee another student. Liability was apportioned to the injured boy (45 percent), his parents (40 percent), and the district (15 percent) in a $6 million award. The district was aware of the conduct of the students at the bus stop, that the street was busy with fast moving traffic, and that an alternative and safer bus stop was available.[58]

Assumption of Risk.   This defense can be either express or implied. *Express assumption* occurs when the plaintiff consents in advance to take his or her chances of injury, given a known danger. For instance, signing an agreement to assume the risks associated with participation in high school football assumes, of course, that the risks have been disclosed or are apparent and are understood. *Implied assumption* occurs without an express written or oral agreement, yet is logically assumed, given the plaintiff's conduct. For example, implied assumption would exist where spectators at a baseball game elect to sit in unscreened seats; such persons assume the risk of possible injury even if they failed to sign an agreement.

Inherent risks are associated with athletics or recreation, but it cannot be assumed that all participants, regardless of age, maturity, and experience, understand those risks. As a result, school personnel must exercise reasonable care to protect students from unassumed, concealed, or unreasonably high risks. This duty can be met when participation is voluntary (i.e., there is no evidence of compulsion to participate) and the student is knowledgeable of and assumes the risks associated with the activity.[59] In Pennsylvania, the state high court remanded a student injury case for the jury to assess the student's understanding of the risks involved in preseason football conditioning and the voluntariness of his participation.[60] The student suffered permanent blindness in one eye from an injury incurred in playing "jungle football," an exercise conducted without protective equipment and involving rough body blocks and tack-

57. Bell v. Ayio, 731 So. 2d 893 (La. Ct. App. 1999) (assigning 85 percent of liability to the student responsible for the attack). *See also* Harvey v. Ouachita Parish Sch. Bd., 674 So. 2d 372 (La. Ct. App. 1996) (assigning 80 percent fault to a coach and 20 percent to a football player who failed to wear a neck roll to protect his previously injured neck; the athlete was permitted to play, notwithstanding the coach's knowledge of the athlete's prior injury and the stipulation by his parents that he wear the roll as a precautionary measure).

58. Warrington v. Tempe Elementary Sch. Dist. No. 3, 3 P.3d 988 (Ariz. Ct. App. 1999).

59. Milea v. Our Lady of Miracles Roman Catholic Church, 736 N.Y.S.2d 84 (App. Div. 2002) (holding that the student had assumed the risk of the injury when he landed on a metal cross bar attached to a portable basketball hoop; the risk did not exceed the usual dangers inherent in the sport).

60. Rutter v. Northeastern Beaver County Sch. Dist., 437 A.2d 1198 (Pa. 1981).

ling. In similar cases, but with different results, courts have found that a 19-year-old football player, who was in excellent condition, properly equipped, and well trained, had assumed the risk of injury when he continued to play and did not inform his coach of his fatigued condition;[61] that the first female high school football player in the county had assumed the risks associated with football when she was injured in her initial practice scrimmage;[62] and that an experienced 14-year-old rider assumed the risks associated with horseback riding when her horse slipped and fell for reasons unrelated to the condition of the track.[63]

Note, however, that student athletes are assuming only those risks that occur during normal participation in the sport; they are not assuming unknown risks associated with a coach's negligence. Moreover, they are not assuming that they will be exposed to intentional torts (e.g., battery) or conduct that represents a reckless disregard for the safety of others. But, penalties and poor judgment by other participants generally will not qualify as intentional torts and most often will be viewed as occurring commonly, if not routinely, in the sport (e.g., being clipped in football). In an illustrative case, the Ohio appeals court affirmed summary judgment for a school district where one soccer player collided with another, causing an injury. The student responsible for the collision was removed from the game, and her team was penalized. The court, nevertheless, reasoned that the risk of being subjected to an illegal slide tackle was a foreseeable risk of playing soccer, even if it represented a rules violation.[64] However, the court opined that had the conduct been so extreme so as to qualify as "reckless" (i.e., exceeds negligence and creates an unreasonable risk of physical harm), the penalized athlete could have been found liable.

Some educators are under the mistaken impression that parents can waive their child's right to sue for negligence by signing forms granting permission for their children to participate in particular activities. Such permission slips indicate that the student assumes normal risks associated with the activity, but parents cannot waive their child's entitlement to appropriate supervision and instruction. Accordingly, students may assume some risk of potential injury by engaging in a dangerous sport such as hockey or by participating in a field trip, but school personnel remain responsible for protecting them from foreseeable harm.

Intentional Torts

Among the more common types of intentional torts are assault, battery, false imprisonment, and intentional infliction of mental distress. Each of these torts is discussed briefly.

---

61. Benitez v. New York City Bd. of Educ., 543 N.Y.S.3d 29 (1989).

62. Hammond v. Bd. of Educ., 639 A.2d 223 (Md. Ct. Spec. App. 1994).

63. Papa v. Russo, 719 N.Y.S.2d 723 (App. Div. 2001).

64. Bentley v. Cuyahoga Falls Bd. of Educ., 709 N.E.2d 1241 (Ohio Ct. App. 1998).

Assault and Battery

Assault consists of an overt attempt to place another in fear of bodily harm; no actual physical contact need take place. Examples include threatening with words, pointing a gun, waving a knife, or shaking a fist. For there to be an assault, the plaintiff needs to be aware of the threat, and the person committing the assault needs to be perceived as having the ability to carry out the threat. In contrast, a *battery* is committed when an assault is consummated. Examples include being shot, stabbed, beaten, or struck. However, actual injury need not result for a battery claim to succeed (e.g., the person could have been punched but not injured due to a comparatively weak blow). For the plaintiff to prevail in either an assault or a battery case, the act must be intentional; there is no such thing as a negligent assault or battery.

Some school-based assault and battery cases have involved the administration of corporal punishment and other forms of discipline that require physical touching. Generally, courts have been reluctant to interfere with a teacher's authority to discipline students and have sanctioned the use of *reasonable* force to control pupil behavior. The Oregon appeals court ruled that a teacher was not guilty of assault and battery for using force to remove a student from the classroom. After the pupil defiantly refused to leave, the teacher held his arms and led him toward the door. The student extricated himself, swung at the teacher, and broke a window, thereby cutting his arm. The court concluded that the teacher used reasonable force with the student and dismissed the assault and battery charges.[65] In contrast, a Louisiana student was successful in obtaining damages.[66] The pupil sustained a broken arm when a teacher shook him, lifted him against the bleachers in the gymnasium, and then let him fall to the floor. The court reasoned that the teacher's action was unnecessary either to discipline the student or to protect himself.

Although comparatively uncommon, school personnel may initiate battery suits against students who injure them.[67] Suits are not barred simply because the person committing the tort is a minor, although the amount of the award may be capped by state statute. A Wisconsin appeals court awarded damages to a teacher when he was physically attacked outside the school building while attempting to escort a student to the office for violating a smoking ban. The court held that the student, who had five previous fighting violations, acted with malicious intent in striking the teacher numerous times and in pushing his face into the corner of a building. Both actual and punitive damages were awarded, notwithstanding the fact that the student was a minor at

---

65. Simms v. Sch. Dist. No. 1, Multnomah County, 508 P.2d 236 (Or. Ct. App. 1973). *See also* Frame v. Comeaux, 735 So. 2d 753 (La. Ct. App. 1999) (finding no battery when a substitute teacher grabbed a confrontational eighth-grade student by the arm and escorted him out of the room—the student had been talking during a test and was asked to leave).

66. Frank v. Orleans Parish Sch. Bd., 195 So. 2d 451 (La. Ct. App. 1967).

67. In addition, some negligence suits are filed by school personnel against their districts when they have been battered at work. In most cases, however, courts have found that the incidents were unforeseen and that no special duty existed on the part of the district to prevent the battery. *See, e.g.,* Genao v. Bd. of Educ., 888 F. Supp. 501 (S.D.N.Y. 1995).

the time of the battery or that the student's psychiatrist purported that a punitive award would not be a deterrent for the defendant's impulsive conduct.[68] The court also was unpersuaded by the argument that defendant's violence and anger were due to his poor self-control and that it would be inappropriate to award punitive damages given that the defendant had a learning disability. In conclusion, the court noted that if the defendant expected to continue to live freely in society, he would have to learn to control his assaultive behavior, or "appreciate" the consequences.

Self-defense often has been used to shield an individual from liability for alleged battery. An individual need not wait to be struck to engage in defensive acts, although reasonable grounds must exist to substantiate that harm was imminent. The "test" in such cases is to determine whether the defendant's conduct was that in which a reasonable person may have engaged, given the circumstances. Consideration should be given to the magnitude of the existing threat, possible alternatives to physical contact, and the time frame available to make a decision (i.e., whether the defendant acted instantaneously or had time for contemplation and deliberation).[69] Even where contact is justified, the defendant must use only force that is reasonably necessary for self-protection. Furthermore, if the alleged aggressor is disarmed, rendered helpless, or no longer capable of aggressive behavior, the defendant may not take the opportunity to engage in revenge or to punish.

In addition to self-defense, individuals accused of battery also may claim that they were acting in the defense of others. This type of tort defense is of particular importance in a school setting where educators often are called on to separate students who are fighting or to come to the aid of someone being attacked. Most jurisdictions not only permit such action on behalf of others but also consider it to be a responsibility or duty of educators, assuming good faith and the use of reasonable and necessary force.

False Imprisonment

Obviously, all restrictions on the freedom of movement or the effort to enter or exit will not qualify as false imprisonment[70] (e.g., temporarily detaining a student after school as a form of reasonable school discipline; being assigned to Saturday school to compensate for tardiness). Interestingly, to be falsely imprisoned, one need not be incarcerated; walls, locks, and iron bars are not required. Rather, imprisonment can result from being placed in a closet, room, corner, automobile, or even a circle in the middle of a football field; it can occur when confined to an entire building or when

68. Anello v. Savignac, 342 N.W.2d 440 (Wis. Ct. App. 1983).

69. The American Law Institute, *A Concise Restatement of Torts* (St. Paul, MN: West Publishing, 2000), p. 19.

70. *See, e.g.,* Harris *ex rel.* Tucker v. County of Forsyth, 921 F. Supp. 325 (M.D.N.C. 1996) (finding no false imprisonment where a student was placed for seven minutes in a holding cell in a county detention facility for continually disrupting a tour of the building; the student's behavior jeopardized the safety of the children and disrupted an otherwise orderly environment).

forced to accompany another on a walk or trip. The taking of a purse, car keys, or other property with the intent to force the person to remain also may qualify as imprisonment. Imprisonment results when physical action, verbal command, or intimidation is used to restrain and/or detain persons against their will. Tone of voice, body language, and what was reasonably understood or even implied from the defendant's conduct will be considered.

In imprisonment cases, the plaintiff need not show that physical force was used; it will suffice that the plaintiff submitted, given the apprehension of force. The plaintiff must be aware of the restraint, but need not show damages beyond the confinement itself to prevail at trial. Accordingly, any time children are unjustifiably restrained against their will, tied or taped to chairs, or bound and gagged, false imprisonment (as well as other possible violations) may be claimed.[71] Although there are times when the use of physical restraints may be necessary, educators need to document the circumstances requiring such actions and provide a narrative explaining why restraint is an appropriate and reasoned response to the behavior.

Intentional Infliction of Mental Distress

This area of tort law is comparatively new because of the historical resistance to awarding damages for a mental injury when it was not accompanied by a physical injury (e.g., pain and suffering associated with a broken leg). This reluctance purportedly was due to the difficulty of generating proof of both injury and proximate cause and then determining the appropriate amount of damages to be awarded. Nevertheless, a tort claim of intentional infliction of mental distress now is available to individuals who have experienced *severe* mental anguish. This claim, however, does not provide a remedy for every trivial indignity, insult, bad manners, annoyance, or sexist or racist comment.

Some forms of communication can result in an assault claim (e.g., a threat to strike another) or defamation suit (e.g., an unfounded claim that a teacher has been sexually involved with students); other communications might provide a basis for discrimination suits under federal laws (e.g., sexual or racial harassment). However, for the conduct to result in intentional infliction of mental distress under tort laws, it must be flagrant, extreme, or outrageous; it must go beyond all possible bounds of decency and be regarded as atrocious and utterly intolerable in civilized society.[72] No reasonable person should be expected to endure such conduct (e.g., severe and extreme acts of stalking, harassment, and assault). Moreover, in most instances, the conduct needs to be prolonged and recurring, since single acts seldom meet the necessary threshold.

---

71. *See* Gerks v. Deathe, 832 F. Supp. 1450 (W.D. Okla. 1993) (denying summary judgment for the district where a child with disabilities was locked in the school bathroom for three hours by her teacher for creating a "mess" on the floor).

72. W. Page Keeton, Dan B. Dobbs, Robert E. Keeton, and David G. Owen, *Prosser and Keeton on Torts,* 5th ed. (St. Paul, MN: West Publishing, 1988), pp. 54–66.

Given the difficulty of meeting this stringent standard, it is not surprising that few school-based claims succeed. Numerous claims have involved injured feelings or reputations, appearing trivial at best. In one such claim that bordered on disingenuous, a sixth-grade Oregon student claimed intentional infliction of mental distress when two of her teachers refused to use her nickname, Boo. "Boo" also is the street name for marijuana and was recognized as such by other students. Neither teacher had ever stated that the plaintiff used or condoned the use of drugs. In granting summary judgment for the teachers, the court concluded that no juror could reasonably find that the conduct of the teachers was an "extraordinary transgression of the bounds of socially tolerable conduct."[73] Other unsuccessful claims include a school supervisor who was callous and offensive when he ridiculed a subordinate's speech impediment;[74] a program faculty that removed a student teacher based on her unacceptable performance, unprofessional conduct, and erratic and disturbing behavior;[75] and a school administrator who sent a letter to parents and students indicating that a teacher who had made racially offensive remarks that perpetuated negative stereotypes was returning to work following a 10-day suspension.[76] None of these cases was found to have met the necessary threshold to qualify as outrageous or extreme.

In contrast, a Florida teacher was found to have supported a claim of intentional infliction of mental distress against two students. The youths had planned, edited, written, printed, copied, and distributed a newsletter that referred to the plaintiff in racially derogatory and sexually vulgar ways; threatened to rape her, her children, and their cousins; and threatened to kill her. The court distinguished the present case from those that involved mere name-calling, embarrassing photos, or harassment and concluded that the conduct here was extreme and went beyond all possible bounds of decency.[77]

Defamation

Most tort actions have involved claims for damages that were due to physical or mental injuries, but plaintiffs also have claimed injury to their reputations in the form of defamation. *Slander* is the term generally associated with spoken defamation (but also includes sign language), whereas *libel* often is used to refer to written defamation (but also includes pictures, statues, motion pictures, and conduct carrying a defamatory imputation—e.g., hanging a person in effigy).[78] In determining whether defamation has occurred, courts will consider whether (1) the targeted individual was a private or

73. Phillips v. Lincoln County Sch. Dist., 984 P.2d 947, 951 (Or. Ct. App. 1999).
74. Shipman v. Glenn, 443 S.E.2d 921 (S.C. Ct. App. 1994).
75. Banks v. Dominican Coll. 42 Cal. Rptr. 2d 110 (Ct. App. 1995).
76. Elstrom v. Indep. Sch. Dist. No. 270, 533 N.W.2d 51 (Minn. Ct. App. 1995).
77. Nims v. Harrison, 768 So. 2d 1198 (Fla. Dist. Ct. App. 2000).
78. W. Page Keeton, Dan B. Dobbs, Robert E. Keeton, and David G. Owen, *Prosser and Keeton on Torts,* 5th ed. (St. Paul, MN: West Publishing, 1988), p. 786.

public person, (2) the communication was false, (3) the expression qualified as opinion or fact, and (4) the comment was privileged.

Private and Public Persons

To prevail in a defamation case, private individuals need prove only that a false publication by the defendant was received and understood by a third party and that injury resulted. Receipt of potentially defamatory information that is not understood (e.g., receiving an unintelligible encrypted message on a computer, hearing Morse Code over a radio, or receiving a phone call in an unknown language) cannot adversely affect the plaintiff's reputation, dignity, or community standing and does not qualify as defamation. Individuals considered public figures or officials additionally must show that the publication was made with either malice or a reckless disregard for the truth. Although definitions vary considerably by state, public figures generally are those who are known or recognized by the public (e.g., professional athletes, actors), whereas public officials are those who have substantial control over governmental affairs (e.g., politicians, school board members).

Although the trend in recent years has been to broaden the class of public officials and figures, it is fortunate for teachers that the vast majority of courts have not found them to be "public," in large part because their authority typically is limited to school children.[79] Some courts, however, have found school board members, administrators, and coaches to be either public officials or figures.[80] This does not mean that all board members, administrators, or coaches even within the same jurisdiction will qualify as public persons; such a determination is made on an individual basis and is dependent on the role, responsibility, degree of notoriety, and authority of the specific individual.

Veracity of Statements

In assessing defamation claims, courts also consider whether a statement is true or false. If the statement is found to be true, or at least substantially true, judgment will generally be for the defendant, assuming that critical facts have not been omitted, taken out of context, or otherwise artificially juxtaposed to misrepresent. Educators must be particularly careful, however, when discussing students and must avoid making comments in bad faith that will result in liability. For example, if a teacher were to comment in class that a particular female student was a "slut," the comments would qualify as defamation *per se*.[81] In such cases, no proof of actual harm to reputation is required.

79. McCutcheon v. Moran, 425 N.E.2d 1130 (Ill. App. Ct. 1981). *But see* Elstrom v. Indep. Sch. Dist. No. 270, 533 N.W.2d 51 (Minn. Ct. App. 1995) (concluding that a teacher was a public official).

80. *See, e.g.,* Garcia v. Bd. of Educ., 777 F.2d 1403 (10th Cir. 1985) (school board members); Jordan v. World Publ'g Co., 872 P.2d 946 (Okla. Ct. App. 1994) (principal); Johnson v. Southwestern Newspapers Corp., 855 S.W. 2d 182 (Tex. Ct. App. 1993) (football coach).

81. *See, e.g.,* Smith v. Atkins, 622 So. 2d 795 (La. Ct. App. 1993).

In addition to proving a communication to be false, the individual must show that he or she was the subject addressed. Interestingly, the individual's identity need not be clear to all third parties (i.e., readers, viewers, or hearers of the defamation); as long as "some" third parties can identify the individual, the claim is actionable even though the individual is not mentioned by name.[82] Furthermore, the defamatory content need not be explicit; it may be implied or may be understood only by third parties with additional information.

Fact versus Opinion

Most opinions receive constitutional protection, particularly when public figures or officials are involved or the issue is one of public concern. To qualify as opinion, the communication must not lend itself to being realistically proven as true or false, and must be communicated in such a way as to be considered a personal perspective on the matter.[83] Parents may express critical opinions about a teacher (verbally or in writing) and may submit such opinions to a principal or school board.[84] Moreover, parents even have the constitutionally protected right to express negative views directly to the teacher, assuming that the expression does not amount to "fighting words"[85] or qualify as an assault.

Notwithstanding these examples, allegations that "the teacher sold drugs to a student" or that "the superintendent stole school funds" are factual statements that are capable of being substantiated and therefore may qualify as defamation unless proven true. In an Oregon case, an appeals court affirmed a damage award against parents who accused a school bus driver of sexual abuse. Even though there were no facts or evidence that supported the claim, the parents persisted in making accusations over an extended period of time by writing letters, uniting parents in protest, and attending board meetings. Their unsupported claims injured the driver's reputation, adversely affected his employability, and caused him to suffer emotional distress.[86]

82. *See, e.g.,* McCormack v. Port Washington Union Free Sch. Dist., 638 N.Y.S.2d 488 (App. Div. 1996).

83. *Compare* Milkovich v. Lorain Journal Co., 497 U.S. 1 (1990) (observing that statements made by a newspaper about a high school wrestling coach implied that the coach committed perjury in a judicial proceeding; because the statements could be proven true or false, they did not qualify as opinion) *with* Maynard v. Daily Gazette Co., 447 S.E.2d 293 (W. Va. 1994) (holding that a former athletic director was not defamed by an editorial identifying him as one of several parties responsible for the poor graduation rates of athletes; statements expressed in the newspaper were constitutionally protected opinions regarding topics of public interest).

84. *See, e.g.,* Nodar v. Galbreath, 462 So. 2d 803 (Fla. 1984) (holding that a parent's statement before the school board concerning a teacher was conditionally privileged); Ansorian v. Zimmerman, 627 N.Y.S.2d 706 (App. Div. 1995) (holding that parental claims of teacher incompetency were protected expressions of opinion and rhetorical hyperbole rather than objective fact and thus protected).

85. "Fighting words" are by their nature likely to result in an immediate breach of the peace and do not qualify as First Amendment protected speech. *See* text accompanying note 20, Chapter 4.

86. Kraemer v. Harding, 976 P.2d 1160 (Or. Ct. App. 1999).

Privilege

Whether a communication qualifies as "privileged" also may affect whether defamation is supported. Statements that are considered *absolutely privileged* cannot serve as a basis for defamation under any circumstance, even if they are false and result in injury.[87] Although less common in education than qualified privilege, an absolute privilege defense has been selectively applied in cases involving superintendents and school board members. For example, a North Dakota court held that a board member's statements at a board meeting about a superintendent were absolutely privileged.[88] Similarly, a New York court held that a superintendent's written reprimand to a coach for failure to follow regulations in the operation of the interscholastic athletic program was protected by absolute privilege.[89]

Communication between parties with qualified or conditional privilege also may be immune from liability if made in good faith, "upon a proper occasion, from a proper motive, in a proper manner, and based upon reasonable or probable cause."[90] Conditional privilege may be lost, however, if actual malice exists (i.e., where a person made a defamatory statement that he or she knew to be false, acted with a high degree of awareness of probable falsity, or entertained serious doubts as to whether the statement was true).[91] Qualified privilege was supported where a board member during a board meeting commented on the suspension of a student for marijuana possession,[92] where administrators rated school personnel,[93] and where a teacher informed school officials about the conduct of another teacher during a European trip.[94] Qualified privilege was not supported, however, where an Iowa superintendent stated during an open session board meeting that a former employee, with whom he had numerous disagreements, had created an unsafe workplace and was dangerous. Only a single incident substantiated the superintendent's position—a staff member

87. Gallegos v. Escalon, 993 S.W.2d 422 (Tex. App. 1999) (finding a superintendent absolutely immune in answering questions posed by the school board in regard to the use of a district credit card by two other district employees).

88. Rykowsky v. Dickinson Pub. Sch. Dist. # 1, 508 N.W.2d 348 (N.D. 1993). *See also* Matthews v. Holland, 912 S.W.2d 459 (Ky. Ct. App. 1995) (granting a superintendent absolute immunity for reporting reasons for a principal's nonrenewal to the state professional standards board).

89. Santavicca v. City of Yonkers, 518 N.Y.S.2d 29 (App. Div. 1987).

90. Baskett v. Crossfield, 228 S.W. 673, 675 (Ky. 1920). *See also* Phillips v. Winston-Salem/Forsyth County Bd. of Educ., 450 S.E.2d 753 (N.C. Ct. App. 1994) (holding that a board did not defame a discharged assistant superintendent since the board's communications with the superintendent were protected by qualified privilege).

91. Gallegos v. Escalon, 993 S.W.2d 422 (Tex. App. 1999).

92. Morrison v. Mobile County Bd. of Educ., 495 So. 2d 1086 (Ala. 1986).

93. *See, e.g.,* Malia v. Monchak, 543 A.2d 184 (Pa. Commw. Ct. 1988).

94. Rocci v. Ecole Secondaire MacDonald-Cartier, 755 A.2d 583 (N.J. 2000) (finding no malice, defamation, or emotional distress where a teacher sent a letter to a principal alleging that the plaintiff had acted unprofessionally on a European trip when she drank wine excessively on the flight and kept the students out late when they had early-morning responsibilities).

had received a minor bruise when she came into contact with the plaintiff as they both rushed to a file cabinet that contained "secret" records about the plaintiff. The jury found that this accidental injury did not support the superintendent's claim and held that the plaintiff had been defamed; that opinion and a $250,000 award were upheld on appeal.

Damages

Damages in tort suits can be either compensatory or punitive, and many include attorneys' fees that are typically calculated as a percent of the total award (often $33\frac{1}{3}$ to 40 percent). Compensatory damages include past and future economic loss, medical expenses, and pain and suffering. These awards are intended to make the plaintiff whole, at least to the degree that money is capable of doing so. If a plaintiff's previous injury has been aggravated, the defendant is generally liable only for the additional loss.

Although damages vary by state, it is common to cap intangibles (e.g., pain, suffering, loss of consortium, mental anguish) but not to cap actual loss. When plaintiffs prevail, it is important to note that school district assets are not subject to execution, sale, garnishment, or attachment to satisfy the judgment. Instead, judgments are paid from funds appropriated specifically for that purpose or acquired through revenue bonds. If sufficient funds are not available, it is common for states to require fiscal officers to certify the amount of unpaid judgment to the taxing authority for inclusion in the next budget. When the amounts are significant, many states permit districts to pay installments (at times up to 10 years) for payment of damages that do not represent actual loss.[95]

Furthermore, in most states, educators can be sued individually. When they are not "save harmlessed" by their school district and do not have personal insurance coverage, their personal assets (e.g., cars, boats, bank accounts) may be attached, their wages may be garnished, and a lien may be placed on their property. Where a lien is filed, the property may not be sold until the debt is satisfied. Moreover, debtors are not permitted to transfer ownership to avoid attachment (i.e., this would represent *fraudulent conveyance*). It is common for persons in law enforcement (e.g., a county sheriff) to be authorized to seize the property and hold it for sale at public auction. Because the debtor's financial worth is not a factor in calculating actual damages, the award may exceed the debtor's ability to pay. If the debtor is eventually successful in filing for bankruptcy, the plaintiff/creditor is typically paid in the same manner as other creditors.

Punitive damages are awarded to punish particularly wanton or reckless acts and are in addition to actual damages. The amount is discretionary with the jury and is based on the circumstances, behaviors, and acts. Unlike the calculation of actual

---

95. Jonathan E. Buchter, Susan C. Hastings, Timothy J. Sheeran, and Gregory W. Stype, *Ohio School Law* (Cleveland, OH: West Publishing, 2001), p. 862.

damages, the debtor's financial worth may be a factor in determining punitive amounts. When jury verdicts are seemingly out of line, the court may reduce (*remittitur*) or increase (*additur*) the amount where either passion or prejudice is a factor.

Conclusion

All individuals, including educators, are responsible for their actions and can be liable for damages if they intentionally or negligently cause injury to others. Educators have a responsibility to act reasonably, but some negligent conduct is likely to occur. Consequently, educators should be knowledgeable about their potential liability under applicable state laws and should ensure that they are either protected by their school districts or have adequate insurance coverage for any damages that might be assessed against them. To guard against liability, teachers and administrators should be cognizant of the following principles of tort law.

1. The propriety of an educator's conduct in a given situation is gauged by whether a reasonably prudent educator (with the special skills and training associated with that role) would have acted in a similar fashion under like conditions.
2. Educators owe students a duty to provide proper instruction and adequate supervision; to maintain equipment, buildings, and grounds in proper condition; and to provide warnings regarding any known dangers.
3. Educators are expected to exercise a standard of care commensurate with the duty owed—with more dangerous activities, greater care is required.
4. Foreseeability of harm is a crucial element in determining whether an educator's actions are negligent.
5. If an educator has information that a student poses a danger to self or others, parents and identifiable victims must be notified.
6. An intervening act can relieve a teacher of liability for negligence if the act caused the injury and if the teacher had no reason to anticipate that it would occur.
7. The common law doctrine of governmental immunity has been abrogated or qualified in most states (e.g., "safe place" statutes).
8. Where recognized, contributory negligence can be used to relieve school personnel of liability if it is established that the injured party's own actions were significant in producing the injury.
9. Under comparative negligence statutes, damages may be apportioned among negligent defendants, plaintiffs, and intervening actors.
10. If an individual knowingly and voluntarily assumes a risk of harm, recovery for an injury may be barred.
11. School personnel can be held liable for battery if it is determined that they used excessive force with students.
12. Unnecessary restraint and excessive detainment of students can result in false imprisonment charges.

13. In severe cases where conduct qualifies as "extreme" or "outrageous," educators or students can be found liable for the intentional infliction of mental distress.

14. Public officials can recover damages for defamation from the media for statements pertaining to public issues only if malice or an intentional disregard for the truth is shown.

15. Educators generally are protected from defamation charges by "qualified privilege" when their statements about students are made to appropriate persons and are motivated by proper intentions.

14

Summary of Legal Generalizations

In the preceding chapters, principles of law have been presented as they relate to specific aspects of teachers' and students' rights and responsibilities. Constitutional and statutory provisions, in conjunction with judicial decisions, have been analyzed in an effort to depict the current status of the law. Many diverse topics have been explored, some with clearly established legal precedents and others where the law is still evolving.

The most difficult situations confronting school personnel are those without specific legislative or judicial guidance. In such circumstances, educators must make judgments based on their professional training and general knowledge of the law as it applies to education. The following broad generalizations, synthesized from the preceding chapters, are presented to assist educators in making such determinations.

Generalizations

The Legal Control of Public Education Resides with the State as One of Its Sovereign Powers. In attempting to comply with the law, school personnel must keep in mind the scope of the state's authority to regulate educational activities. Courts consistently have held that state legislatures possess plenary power in establishing and operating public schools; this power is restricted only by federal and state constitutions and civil rights laws. Of course, where the federal judiciary has interpreted the United States Constitution as prohibiting a given practice in public education, such as racial discrimination, the state or its agents cannot enact laws or policies that conflict with the constitutional mandate unless justified by a compelling governmental interest. In contrast, if the Federal Constitution and civil rights laws have been interpreted as permitting a certain activity, states retain discretion in either restricting or expand-

497

ing the practice. Under such circumstances, standards vary across states, and legislation becomes more important in specifying the scope of protected rights.

For example, the Supreme Court has rejected the assertion that probationary teachers have an inherent federal right to due process prior to contract nonrenewal, but state legislatures have the authority to create such a right under state law. Similarly, the Supreme Court has found no Fourth Amendment violation in blanket or random drug testing of public school students who participate in extracurricular activities; however, state law may place restrictions on school authorities in conducting such searches. Also, the Supreme Court has found no Establishment Clause violation in the participation of sectarian schools in state-supported voucher programs to fund education, but these programs might run afoul of state constitutional provisions prohibiting the use of public funds for religious purposes.

Unless constitutional rights are at stake, courts defer to the will of legislative bodies in determining educational matters. State legislatures have the authority to create and redesign school districts, to collect and distribute educational funds, and to determine teacher qualifications, curricular offerings, and minimum student performance standards. With such pervasive control vested in the states, a thorough understanding of the operation of a specific educational system can be acquired only by examining an individual state's statutes, administrative regulations, and judicial decisions interpreting such provisions.

Certain prerequisites to public school employment are defined through statutes and state board of education regulations. For example, all states stipulate that a teacher must possess a valid teaching license based on satisfying specified requirements. State laws also delineate the permanency of the employment relationship, dismissal procedures for tenured and nontenured teachers, and the extent to which teachers can engage in collective bargaining.

State laws similarly govern conditions of school attendance. Every state has enacted a compulsory attendance statute to ensure an educated citizenry. These laws are applicable to all children, with only a few legally recognized exceptions. In addition to mandating school attendance, states also have the authority to prescribe courses of study and instructional materials. Courts will not invalidate such decisions unless constitutional rights are abridged. Comparable reasoning also is applied by courts in upholding the state's power to establish graduation requirements, including the use of proficiency tests as a prerequisite to receipt of a diploma. Courts have recognized that the establishment of academic standards is within the state's scope of authority.

It is a widely held perception that local school boards control public education in this nation, but local boards hold only those discretionary powers conferred by state law. Depending on the state, a local board's discretionary authority may be quite broad, narrowly defined by statutory guidelines, or somewhere in between. School board regulations enacted pursuant to statutory authority are legally binding on employees and students. For example, school boards can place conditions on employment (e.g., continuing education requirements, residency requirements) beyond state minimums, unless prohibited by law.

In some states, policy-making authority in certain domains (e.g., curriculum, personnel) has been delegated to school-based councils, and the relationship between local boards and school-based councils is still being defined. Courts will not overturn decisions made by school boards or site-based councils unless clearly arbitrary, discriminatory, or beyond their scope of authority.

School board and/or council discretion, however, may be limited by negotiated contracts with teachers' associations. Negotiated agreements may affect terms and conditions of employment in areas such as teacher evaluation, work calendar, teaching loads, extra-duty assignments, and grievance procedures. It is imperative for educators to become familiar with all these sources of legal rights and responsibilities.

All School Policies and Practices That Impinge on Protected Personal Freedoms Must Be Substantiated as Necessary to Advance the School's Educational Mission.   The state and its agents have broad authority to regulate public schools, but policies that impair federal constitutional rights must be justified by an overriding public interest. Although courts do not enact laws as legislative bodies do, they significantly influence educational policies and practices by interpreting constitutional and statutory provisions. Both school attendance and public employment traditionally were considered privileges bestowed at the will of the state, but the Supreme Court has recognized that teachers and students do not shed their constitutional rights at the schoolhouse door. The state controls education, but this power must be exercised in conformance with the Federal Constitution.

It is important to keep in mind that the Bill of Rights places restrictions on governmental, not private, action that interferes with personal freedoms. To illustrate, the Establishment Clause prohibits public school employees from directing or condoning devotional activities in public education. However, student-initiated religious groups in secondary schools that do not represent the public school must be treated like other student groups in terms of school access during noninstructional time. Furthermore, community religious groups, even those involved in religious instruction targeting elementary school children, must be treated like other community groups in terms of access during nonschool hours.

In balancing public and individual interests, courts weigh the importance of the protected personal right against the governmental need to restrict its exercise. For example, courts have reasoned that there is no overriding public interest to justify compelling students to salute the American flag if such an observance conflicts with religious or philosophical beliefs. In contrast, mandatory vaccination against communicable diseases has been upheld as a prerequisite to school attendance, even if opposition to immunization is based on religious grounds. Courts have reasoned that the overriding public interest in safeguarding the health of all students justifies such a requirement.

Restrictions can be placed on students' activities if necessary to advance legitimate school objectives. For example, the judiciary has recognized that students' constitutional rights must be assessed in light of the special circumstances of the school. Consequently, school authorities can restrict attire inconsistent with the school's objectives and can impose dress codes, even uniforms, if shown to advance those objectives rather than directed at stifling expression. School authorities, although considered state officials, can conduct warrantless searches of students based on reasonable suspicion that contraband posing a threat to the school environment is concealed. Similarly, vulgar expression that might be protected by the First Amendment for adults can be curtailed among public school students to further the school's legitimate interest in maintaining standards of decency. Student expression that gives the appearance of representing the school also can be censored to ensure its consistency with educational objectives. And even personal student expression of ideological views that merely happens to take place at school can be restricted if linked to a disruption of the educational process.

Similarly, constraints can be placed on school employees if justified by valid school objectives. Prerequisites to employment, such as examinations and residency requirements, can be imposed if necessary to advance legitimate governmental interests. Furthermore, restrictions on teachers' rights to govern their appearance and make lifestyle choices outside the classroom can be justified when it impinges on their effectiveness in the classroom. Although teachers enjoy a First Amendment right to express views on matters of public concern, expression relating to private employment grievances can be the basis for disciplinary action. Even teachers' expression on public issues can be curtailed if it impedes the management of the school, work relationships, or teaching effectiveness.

Every regulation that impairs individual rights must be based on valid educational considerations and be necessary to carry out the school's mission. Such regulations also should be clearly stated and well publicized so that all individuals understand the basis for the rules and the penalties for infractions.

School Policies and Practices Must Not Disadvantage Selected Individuals or Groups.   The inherent personal right to remain free from governmental discrimination has been emphasized throughout this book. Strict judicial scrutiny has been applied in evaluating state action that creates a suspect classification, such as race. In school desegregation cases, courts have charged school officials with an affirmative duty to take whatever steps are necessary to overcome the lingering effects of past discrimination. Similarly, intentional racial discrimination associated with student grouping practices, testing methods, or suspension procedures, as well as with employee hiring or promotion practices, has been disallowed.

However, neutral policies, uniformly applied, are not necessarily unconstitutional even though they may have a disparate impact on minorities. For example, prerequisites to employment, such as tests that disqualify a disproportionate number of minority applicants, have been upheld as long as their use is justified by legitimate employment objectives and not accompanied by discriminatory intent. Also, the placement of a disproportionate number of minority students in lower instructional tracks is permissible if such assignments are based on legitimate educational criteria that are applied in the best interests of students. Likewise, school segregation that results from natural causes rather than intentional state action does not implicate constitutional rights.

In addition to racial classifications, other bases for distinguishing among employees and students have been invalidated if they disadvantage individuals. Federal civil rights laws, in conjunction with state statutes, have reinforced constitutional protections afforded to various segments of society that traditionally have suffered discrimination. Indeed, the judiciary has recognized that legislative bodies are empowered to go beyond constitutional minimums in protecting citizens from discriminatory practices. Accordingly, laws have been enacted that place specific responsibilities on employers to ensure that employees are not disadvantaged on the basis of gender, age, religion, national origin, or disabilities. If an inference of discrimination is established, employers must produce legitimate nondiscriminatory reasons to justify their actions. School officials can be held liable for damages if substantiated that benefits have been withheld from certain individuals because of their inherent characteristics.

Federal and state mandates also stipulate that students cannot be denied school attendance or be otherwise disadvantaged based on characteristics such as gender, disabilities, national origin, marriage, or pregnancy. Eligibility for school activities, such as participation on interscholastic athletic teams, cannot be denied to a certain class of students. In addition, disciplinary procedures that disproportionately disadvantage identified groups of students are vulnerable to legal challenge. Educators should ensure that all school policies are applied in a nondiscriminatory manner.

Courts will scrutinize grouping practices to ensure that they do not impede students' rights to equal educational opportunities. Nondiscrimination, however, does not require identical treatment. Students can be classified according to their unique needs, but any differential treatment must be justified in terms of providing more appropriate services. Indeed, judicial rulings and federal and state laws have placed an obligation on school districts to provide appropriate programs and services to meet the needs of children with disabilities and to eliminate the language barriers of those with English-language deficiencies.

Due Process Is a Basic Tenet of the United States System of Justice—The Foundation of Fundamental Fairness. The notion of due process, embodied in the Fifth and Fourteenth Amendments, has been an underlying theme throughout the discussion of teachers' and students' rights. The judiciary has recognized that due process guarantees protect individuals against arbitrary governmental action impairing life, liberty, or property interests and ensure that procedural safeguards accompany any governmental interference with these interests.

In the absence of greater statutory specificity, courts have held that the United States Constitution requires, at a minimum, notice of the charges and a hearing before an impartial decision maker when personnel actions impair public educators' property or liberty rights. A property claim to due process can be established by tenure status, contractual agreement, or school board action that creates a valid expectation of reemployment. A liberty claim to due process can be asserted if the employer's action implicates constitutionally protected rights (e.g., freedom of speech), damages the teacher's reputation, or forecloses the opportunity to obtain other employment. Many state legislatures have specified procedures beyond constitutional minimums that must be followed before a tenured teacher is dismissed. The provision of due process does not imply that a teacher will not be dismissed or that sanctions will not be imposed. But it does mean that the teacher must be given the opportunity to refute the charges and that the decision must be made fairly and supported by evidence.

Students, as well as teachers, have due process rights. Students have a state-created property right to attend school that cannot be denied without procedural requisites. If this right to attend school is withdrawn for disciplinary reasons, due process is required. The nature of the proceedings depends on the deprivation involved, with more serious impairments necessitating more formal proceedings. If punishments are arbitrary or excessive, students' substantive due process rights may be implicated. Children with disabilities have due process rights in placement decisions as well as in disciplinary matters. Since school authorities are never faulted for providing too much due process, at least minimum procedural safeguards are advisable when making any nonroutine change in a student's status.

Inherent in the notion of due process is the assumption that all individuals have a right to a hearing if state action impinges on personal freedoms. Such a hearing need not be elaborate in every situation; an informal conversation can suffice under some circumstances, such as brief student suspensions from school. The crucial element is for all affected parties to have an opportunity to air their views and present evidence that might alter the decision. Often, an informal hearing can serve to clarify issues and facilitate agreement, thus eliminating the need for more formal proceedings.

Educators Are Expected to Follow the Law, to Act Reasonably, and to Anticipate Potentially Adverse Consequences of Their Actions. Public school personnel are presumed to be knowledgeable of federal and state constitutional and statutory provisions as well as school board policies affecting their roles. The Supreme Court has emphasized that ignorance of the law is no defense for violating clearly established legal principles. For example, ignorance of the Supreme Court's interpretation of Title IX restrictions under the Education Amendments of 1972 would not shield a school district from liability for school authorities' failure to respond to student complaints of sexual harassment.

Educators hold themselves out as having certain knowledge and skills by the nature of their special training and certification. Accordingly, they are expected to exercise sound professional judgment in the performance of their duties. Reasonable actions in one situation may be viewed as unreasonable under other conditions. To illustrate, in administering pupil punishments, teachers are expected to consider the student's age, mental condition, and past behavior as well as the specific circumstances surrounding the rule infraction. Failure to exercise reasonable judgment can result in dismissal or possibly financial liability for impairing students' rights.

Teachers also are expected to make reasonable decisions pertaining to the academic program. Materials and methodology should be appropriate for the students' age and educational objectives. If students are grouped for instructional purposes, teachers are expected to base such decisions on legitimate educational considerations.

In addition, educators are held accountable for reasonable actions in supervising students, providing appropriate instructions, maintaining equipment in proper repair, and warning students of any known dangers. Teachers must exercise a standard of care commensurate with their duty to protect students from unreasonable risks of harm. Personal liability can be assessed for negligence if a school employee should have foreseen that an event could result in injury to a student.

Educators also are expected to exercise sound judgment in personal activities that affect their professional roles. Teachers do not relinquish their privacy rights as a condition of public employment, but private choices that impair teaching effectiveness or disrupt the school can be the basis for adverse personnel action. As role models for students, teachers and other school personnel are held to a higher level of discretion in their private lives than expected of the general public.

Conclusion

One objective of this book has been to alleviate educators' fears that the scales of justice have been tipped against them. It is hoped that this objective has been achieved. In most instances, courts and legislatures have not imposed on school personnel any requirements that fair-minded educators would not impose on themselves. Reasonable policies and practices based on legitimate educational objectives consistently have been upheld by courts. If anything, legislative and judicial mandates have clarified and supported the authority as well as the duty of school personnel to make and enforce regulations that are necessary to maintain an effective and efficient educational environment. The federal judiciary in the late 1960s and early 1970s expanded constitutional protection of individual liberties against governmental interference. Since the 1980s, however, federal courts have exhibited more restraint and reinforced the authority of state and local education agencies to make decisions necessary to advance the school's educational mission, even if such decisions impinge on protected personal freedoms. Courts do continue to invalidate school practices and policies if they are arbitrary, unrelated to educational objectives, or impair protected individual rights without an overriding justification.

Because reform is usually easier to implement when designed from within than when externally imposed, educators should become more assertive in identifying and altering those practices that have the potential to generate legal intervention. Internet censorship, peer sexual harassment, as well as bullying and other intimidating behavior are a few issues now requiring educators' attention. Furthermore, school personnel should stay abreast of legal developments, since new laws are enacted each year and courts are continually reinterpreting constitutional and statutory provisions.

In addition to understanding basic legal rights and responsibilities, educators are expected to transmit this knowledge to students. Pupils also need to understand their constitutional and statutory rights, the balancing of interests that takes place in legislative and judicial forums, and the rationale for legal enactments, including school regulations. Only with increased awareness of fundamental legal principles can all individuals involved in the educational process develop a greater respect for the law and for the responsibilities that accompany legal rights.

Glossary

absolute privilege protection from liability for communication made in the performance of public service or the administration of justice.

appeal a petition to a higher court to alter the decision of a lower court.

appellate court a tribunal having jurisdiction to review decisions on appeal from inferior courts.

arbitration (binding) a process whereby an impartial third party, chosen by both parties in a dispute, makes a final determination regarding a contested issue.

assault the placing of another in fear of bodily harm.

battery the unlawful touching of another with intent to harm.

certiorari a writ of review whereby an action is removed from an inferior court to an appellate court for additional proceedings.

civil action a judicial proceeding to redress an infringement of individual civil rights, in contrast to a criminal action brought by the state to redress public wrongs.

civil right a personal right that accompanies citizenship and is protected by the Constitution (e.g., freedom of speech, freedom from discrimination).

class action suit a judicial proceeding brought on behalf of a number of persons similarly situated.

common law a body of rules and principles derived from usage or from judicial decisions enforcing such usage.

compensatory damages monetary award to compensate an individual for injury sustained (e.g., financial losses, emotional pain, inconvenience) and restore the injured party to the position held prior to the injury.

concurring opinion a statement by a judge or judges, separate from the majority opinion, that endorses the result of the majority decision but offers its own reasons for reaching that decision.

consent decree an agreement, sanctioned by a court, that is binding on the consenting parties.

consideration something of value given or promised for the purpose of forming a contract.

contract an agreement between two or more competent parties that creates, alters, or dissolves a legal relationship.

criminal action a judicial proceeding brought by the state against a person charged with a public offense.

damages an award made to an individual because of a legal wrong.

declaratory relief a judicial declaration of the rights of the plaintiff without an assessment of damages against the defendant.

de facto segregation separation of the races that exists but does not result from action of the state or its agents.

defamation false and intentional communication that injures a person's character or reputation; slander is spoken and libel is written communication.

defendant the party against whom a court action is brought.

de jure segregation separation of the races by law or by action of the state or its agents.

de minimis something that is insignificant, not worthy of judicial review.

de novo a new review.

dictum a statement made by a judge in delivering an opinion that does not relate directly to the issue being decided and does not embody the sentiment of the court.

directed verdict   the verdict provided when a plaintiff fails to support a prima facie case for jury consideration or the defendant fails to produce a necessary defense.

discretionary power   authority that involves the exercise of judgment.

dissenting opinion   a statement by a judge or judges who disagree with the decision of the majority of the justices in a case.

en banc   the full bench; refers to a session where the court's full membership participates in the decision rather than the usual quorum of the court.

fact finding   a process whereby a third party investigates an impasse in the negotiation process to determine the facts, identify the issues, and make a recommendation for settlement.

friend-of-the-court briefs   briefs provided by nonparties to inform or perhaps persuade the court (also termed *amicus curiae* briefs).

governmental function   activity performed in discharging official duties of a federal, state, or municipal agency.

governmental immunity   the common law doctrine that governmental agencies cannot be held liable for the negligent acts of their officers, agents, or employees.

impasse   a deadlock in the negotiation process in which parties are unable to resolve an issue without assistance of a third party.

injunction   a writ issued by a court prohibiting a defendant from acting in a prescribed manner.

in loco parentis   in place of parent; charged with rights and duties of a parent.

liquidated damages   contractual amounts representing a reasonable estimation of the damages owed to one of the parties for a breach of the agreement by the other.

mediation   the process by which a neutral third party serving as an intermediary attempts to persuade disagreeing parties to settle their dispute.

ministerial duty   an act that does not involve discretion and must be carried out in a manner specified by legal authority.

negligence   the failure to exercise the degree of care that a reasonably prudent person would exercise under similar conditions; conduct that falls below the standard established by law for the protection of others against unreasonable risk of harm.

per curiam   a court's brief disposition of a case that is not accompanied by a written opinion.

plaintiff   the party initiating a judicial action.

plenary power   full, complete, absolute power.

precedent   a judicial decision serving as authority for subsequent cases involving similar questions of law.

preponderance of evidence   a standard that requires more evidence to support than refute a claim; it also is termed the *51 percent rule*.

prima facie   on its face presumed to be true unless disproven by contrary evidence.

probable cause   reasonable grounds, supported by sufficient evidence, to warrant a cautious person to believe that the individual is guilty of the offense charged.

procedural due process   the fundamental right to notice of charges and an opportunity to rebut the charges before a fair tribunal if life, liberty, or property rights are at stake.

proprietary function   an activity (often for profit) performed by a state or municipal agency that could as easily be performed by a private corporation.

punitive damages   a monetary punishment where the defendant is found to have acted with either malice or reckless indifference.

qualified immunity   an affirmative defense that shields public officials performing discretionary functions from civil damages if their conduct does not violate clearly established statutory or constitutional rights.

qualified privilege   protection from liability for communication made in good faith, for proper reasons, and to appropriate parties.

reasonable suspicion   specific and articulable facts, which, taken together with rational inferences from the facts, justify a warrantless search.

remand   to send a case back to the original court for additional proceedings.

respondeat superior   a legal doctrine whereby the master is responsible for acts of the servant; a governmental unit is liable for acts of its employees.

save harmless clause   An agreement whereby one party agrees to indemnify and hold harmless another party for suits that may be brought against that party.

stare decisis   to abide by decided cases; to adhere to precedent.

statute   an act by the legislative branch of government expressing its will and constituting the law within the jurisdiction.

substantive due process   requirements embodied in the Fifth and Fourteenth Amendments that legislation must be fair and reasonable in content as well as application; protection against arbitrary, capricious, or unreasonable governmental action.

summary judgment   disposition of a controversy without a trial when there is no genuine dispute over factual issues.

tenure   a statutory right that confers permanent employment on teachers, protecting them from dismissal except for adequate cause.

tort   a civil wrong, independent of contract, for which a remedy in damages is sought.

ultra vires   beyond the scope of authority to act on the subject.

vacate   to set aside; to render a judgment void.

verdict   a decision of a jury on questions submitted for trial.

Selected Supreme Court Cases

Abood v. Detroit Bd. of Educ., 452–453

Adarand Constructors v. Pena, 357

Adler v. Bd of Educ., 327, 392

Agostini v. Felton, 59–60

Aguilar v. Felton, 59

Albemarle Paper Co. v. Moody, 354

Allen v. McCurry, 397

Ambach v. Norwick, 273

American Mfrs. Mut. Ins. Co. v. Sullivan, 426

Ansonia Bd. of Educ. v. Philbrook, 375

Arizona Governing Comm. for Tax Deferred Annuity & Deferred Comp. Plans v. Norris, 370

Ashcroft v. ACLU, 88

Ashcroft v. Free Speech Coalition, 88

Attorney Gen. of N.Y. v. Soto-Lopez, 279

Baker v. Owen, 241

Bartnicki v. Vopper, 336

Baynard v. Alexandria City Sch. Bd., 181

Beilan v. Board of Pub. Educ., 328

Bethel Sch. Dist. No. 403 v. Fraser, 108–110, 130

Bishop v. Wood, 399–400

Board of Curators v. Horowitz, 89, 244

Board of Educ. v. Allen, 58

Board of Educ. v. Dowell, 159–160

Board of Educ. v. Earls, 136, 262

Board of Educ. v. Grumet, 61

Board of Educ. v. Mergens, 43, 126

Board of Educ. v. Pico, 85–86

Board of Educ. v. Rowley, 194

Board of Regents v. Roth, 396–397, 398

Board of Regents v. Southworth, 117

Board of Trs.v. Fox, 113

Board of Trs. v Garrett, 23, 429

Bob Jones Univ. v. United States, 58

Bogan v. Scott-Harris, 426

Bolger v. Youngs Drug Prods. Corp., 113

Bowen v. Massachusetts, 208

Bowers v. Hardwick, 342, 415

Boy Scouts of Am. v. Dale, 128, 372

Branti v. Finkel, 328

Brentwood Acad. v. Tennessee Secondary Sch. Athletic Ass'n, 14, 134

Broadrick v. Oklahoma, 331

Brown v. Board of Educ. (I), 22, 147, 149, 187

Brown v. Board of Educ. (II), 149

Burlington Industries v. Ellerth, 369

Burlington Sch. Comm. v. Massachusetts Dep't of Educ., 202

California Fed. Savings & Loan Ass'n v. Guerra, 366

Camara v. Municipal Court of City and County of S.F., 12, 248

Cantwell v. Connecticut, 13, 25

Capitol Square Review & Advisory Bd. v. Pinette, 39, 108

Carey v. Piphus, 267–268

Cedar Rapids Cmty. Sch. Dist. v. Garret F., 207

Chandler v. Miller, 278, 338

Chicago Teachers' Union, Local No. 1 v. Hudson, 454–455

Christiansburg Garment Co. v. EEOC, 434

City of Boerne v. Flores, 28

City of Canton, Ohio v. Harris, 429

City of Charlotte v. Local 660, Int'l Ass'n of Fire-fighters, 457

City of L.A. Dep't of Water & Power v. Manhart, 369

City of Madison, Joint Sch. Dist. No. 8 v. Wisconsin Employment Relations Comm'n, 317, 459

City of Newport v. Fact Concerts, 431

City of Richmond v. J.A. Croson Co., 357

Clark v. Jeter, 145, 347

Cleveland Bd. of Educ. v. LaFleur, 366

Cleveland Bd. of Educ. v. Loudermill, 406

Cole v. Richardson, 273, 327

Collins v. City of Harker Heights, 428

Committee for Pub. Educ. & Religious Liberty v. Nyquist, 61, 63

Committee for Pub. Educ. & Religious Liberty v. Regan, 58–59
Connick v. Myers, 307–310, 320
Cooper v. Aaron, 10, 149
Cornelius v. NAACP Legal Def. & Educ. Fund, 114
County of Allegheny v. ACLU, 27, 39
Crawford v. Board of Educ., 154
Crowell v. Benson, 18
Cumming v. Richmond County Bd. of Educ., 147

Davis v. Monroe County Bd. of Educ., 182
DeShaney v. Winnebago County Dep't of Soc. Servs., 301

Edwards v. Aguillard, 55–56, 81
Ellis v. Brotherhood of Ry., Airline, and S.S. Clerks, 453–454
Elrod v. Burns, 328
Employment Div. v. Smith, 28
Engel v. Vitale, 29
Epperson v. Arkansas, 55, 81
Evans v. Romer, 370
Everson v. Board of Educ., 26, 58

Faragher v. City of Boca Raton, 369
Farrar v. Hobby, 431
Firefighters Local Union No. 1784 v. Stotts, 358
Florence County Sch. Dist. Four v. Carter, 203
Franklin v. Gwinnett County Pub. Schs., 180, 301
Franks v. Bowman Transp. Co., 358
Freeman v. Pitts, 160
Furnco Constr. Corp. v. Waters, 349

Garcia v. San Antonio Metro. Transit Auth., 11, 441
Gebser v. Lago Vista Indep. Sch. Dist., 181, 301–302
Geduldig v. Aiello, 365
General Elec. Co. v. Gilbert, 365
Gilbert v. Homar, 406
Ginsberg v. New York, 110
Gitlow v. New York, 13, 25
Givhan v. Western Line Consol. Sch. Dist., 307
Gomez v. Toledo, 427
Gong Lum v. Rice, 148
Goss v. Board. of Educ., 149
Goss v. Lopez, 235–237, 268
Gonzaga Univ.v. Doe, 16, 98, 426, 429
Good News Club v. Milford Cent. Sch., 45–46
Graham v. Richardson, 144, 347
Green v. County Sch. Bd., 150, 160

Gregory v. Ashcroft, 377
Griffin v. County Sch. Bd. , 149
Griggs v. Duke Power Co., 354
Griswold v. Connecticut, 97, 126
Grove City Coll. v. Bell, 16

Harlow v. Fitzgerald, 427
Harrah Indep. Sch. Dist. v. Martin, 277, 419
Harris v. Forklift Sys., 368
Hazelwood Sch. Dist. v. Kuhlmeier, 87, 115–116, 118, 320
Hazelwood Sch. Dist. v. United States, 358
Hazen Paper Co. v. Biggins, 377, 381, 382
Healy v. James, 125, 326
Helvering v. Davis, 10
Honig v. Doe, 212
Hooper v. Bernalillo County Assessor, 246, 279
Hortonville Joint Sch. Dist. No. 1 v. Hortonville Educ. Ass'n, 408, 466
Howlett v. Rose, 267, 426
Hunt v. McNair, 59
Hunter v. Erickson, 144, 347

Indiana *ex rel.* Anderson v. Brand, 286, 394
Ingraham v. Wright, 240–241, 266
International Union, United Auto., Aerospace, & Agric. Implement Workers of Am. v. Johnson Controls, 365
Irving Indep. Sch. Dist. v. Tatro, 207

Johnson v. New York State Educ. Dep't, 78–79
Kadrmas v. Dickinson Pub. Schs., 78
Katz v. United States, 250
Kelly v. Johnson, 333–334
Keyes v. School Dist. No. 1, Denver, 151
Keyishian v. Board of Regents, 108, 273, 327, 439
Korematsu v. United States, 144, 347
Kimel v. Florida Bd. of Regents, 23, 377

Lamb's Chapel v. Center Moriches Union Free Sch. Dist., 27, 44
Lau v. Nichols, 164
Lee v. Weisman, 27, 31–32
Lehnert v. Ferris Faculty Ass'n, 453–454
Lemon v. Kurtzman, 26–27, 61
Levitt v. Committee for Pub. Educ. & Religious Liberty, 59
Lynch v. Donnelly, 38

Maine v. Thiboutot, 426
Mapp v. Ohio, 248
Marbury v. Madison, 21

Marsh v. Chambers, 30
Martin v. Wilks, 357
Mathews v. Eldridge, 403, 427
McCarthy v. Philadelphia Civil Serv. Comm'n, 278
McCollum v. Board of Educ., 48
McDonnell Douglas Corp. v. Green, 349, 378
McLaurin v. Oklahoma State Regents for Higher Educ., 148
Memphis Cmty Sch. Dist. v. Stachura, 324–325, 401, 431–432
Meritor Savings Bank v. Vinson, 368
Meyer v. Nebraska, 81
Migra v. Warren City Sch. Dist., 429
Miller v. California, 110
Milliken v. Bradley (I), 154–155
Milliken v. Bradley (II), 155, 158
Minnesota State Bd. for Cmty. Colls. v. Knight, 458
Miranda v. Arizona, 236, 265
Mississippi Univ. for Women v. Hogan, 145, 178, 347
Missouri v. Jenkins, 155, 158
Missouri *ex rel.* Gaines v. Canada, 148
Mitchell v. Helms, 60–61
Monell v. Department of Soc. Servs., 428
Mt. Healthy City Sch. Dist. v. Doyle, 306–307, 313–314, 383, 397, 430
Mueller v. Allen, 58, 62–63
Murphy v. United Parcel Serv., 189, 385

Nashville Gas Co. v. Satty, 366
National Educ. Ass'n v. South Carolina, 273, 354
National Gay Task Force v. Board of Educ., 315–316, 342
National League of Cities v. Usery, 11, 441
National Treasury Employees Union v. Von Raab, 261, 338
NCAA v. Smith, 173
New Jersey v. T.L.O., 248–250, 253, 264, 337
Nixon v. Shrink Mo. Gov't PAC, 326
NLRB v. Catholic Bishop of Chi., 438
NLRB v. Katz, 463
North Carolina Dep't of Transp. v. Crest St. Comm., 434
North Carolina State Bd. of Educ. v. Swann, 153
Northeastern Fla. Chapter of the Associated Gen. Contractors of Am. v. City of Jacksonville, 357
Norwood v. Harrison, 58

O'Connor v. Ortega, 337

Ohlson v. Phillips, 273
Oklahoma City v. Tuttle, 428–429
Oncale v. Sundowner Offshore Servs., 180, 367
Oubre v. Entergy Operations, 379
Owasso Indep. Sch. Dist. v. Falvo, 98–99
Owen v. City of Independence, Mo., 429

Pacific Mut. Life Ins. Co. v. Haslip, 431
Pasadena City Bd. of Educ. v. Spangler, 152
Patsy v. Board of Regents, 426
Perry v. Sindermann, 397–398
Perry Educ. Ass'n v. Perry Local Educators' Ass'n, 114, 316, 457
Personnel Adm'r of Mass. v. Feeney, 350
PGA Tour v. Martin, 211
Pickering v. Board of Educ., 306, 309, 314, 427
Pierce v. Society of Sisters, 57, 68
Plessy v. Ferguson, 147
Plyler v. Doe, 74–75, 145

R.A.V. v. St. Paul, 122
Rankin v. McPherson, 308
Reeves v. Sanderson Plumbing Prods., 380
Regents of Univ. of Mich. v. Ewing, 243
Rendell-Baker v. Kohn, 14, 393
Reno v. ACLU, 88
Roemer v. Board of Pub. Works, 59
Rogers v. Paul, 149
Rosenberger v. Rector & Visitors, 47–48
Rutan v. Republican Party of Ill., 328
San Antonio Indep. Sch. Dist. v. Rodriguez, 9, 19, 145
Santa Fe Indep. Sch. Dist. v. Doe, 34–36
Schenck v. United States, 108
School Bd. v. Arline, 189, 278, 387, 422
School Dist. v. Ball, 59
School Dist v. Schempp, 29, 53
Shapiro v. Thompson, 144
Shelton v. Tucker, 328
Sipuel v. Board of Regents, 148
Skinner v. Oklahoma, 144
Skinner v. Railway Labor Executives' Ass'n, 261, 338
Sloan v. Lemon, 61
Sony Corp. v. Universal City Studios, 297
St. Mary's Honor Ctr. v. Hicks, 350, 355
Stone v. Graham, 37
Sutton v. United Airlines, 189, 385
Swann v. Charlotte-Mecklenburg Bd. of Educ., 150, 156
Sweatt v. Painter, 148

Terry v. Ohio, 249–251
Texas v. Johnson, 108
Texas Dep't of Cmty. Affairs v. Burdine, 360
Texas State Teachers Ass'n v. Garland Indep. Sch. Dist, 316, 433, 457
Tilton v. Richardson, 59
Tinker v. Des Moines Indep. Sch. Dist., 2, 117–119, 125, 268
Torcaso v. Watkins, 373
Toyota Motor Mfg. v. Williams, 385
Trans World Airlines v. Hardison, 374
Trans World Airlines v. Thurston, 381
Troxel v. Granville, 68

United Air Lines v. McMann, 381
United States v. Chadwick, 251
United States v. Darby, 2
United States v. Montgomery County Bd. of Educ., 156–157
United States v. Place, 259
United States v. Virginia, 178
United States Civil Serv. Comm'n v. National Ass'n of Letter Carriers, 331
University of Cal. v. Public Employment Relations Bd., 458
University of Penn. v. EEOC, 294

Vail v. Board of Educ. of Paris Union Sch. Dist. No. 95, 398
Vernonia Sch. Dist. 47J v. Acton, 136, 261–262

Village of Arlington Heights v. Metropolitan Hous. Dev. Corp., 151, 347

Wallace v. Jaffree 30
Walters v. Metropolitan Educ. Enters., 348
Walz v. Tax Comm'n, 26
Washington v. Davis, 347, 352
Waters v. Churchill, 308, 310
Webb v. Board of Educ., 434
West Virginia State Bd. of Educ. v. Barnette, 50, 107–108
White v. Dougherty County Bd. of Educ., 333
Widmar v, Vincent, 43
Wieman v. Updegraff, 327
Will v. Michigan Dep't of State Police, 429
Wisconsin v. Yoder, 28, 50, 71
Withrow v. Larkin, 408
Witters v. Washington Dep't of Servs. for the Blind, 58
Wolman v. Walter, 61
Wood v. Strickland, 24, 226, 267, 427
W.R. Grace & Co. v. Local 759, United Rubber Workers of Am., 461
Wygant v. Jackson Bd. of Educ., 157, 280, 358, 450

Zelman v. Simmons-Harris, 63–64
Zobel v. Williams, 279
Zobrest v. Catalina Foothills Sch. Dist., 59–60
Zorach v. Clauson, 48
Zucht v. King, 72

Index

Academic freedom (*see also* Censorship)
  community objections to classroom
    materials, 325–326
  expressing views in the classroom,
    321–322
  in general, 318
  selection of course content, 318–321
  teaching strategies, 322–326
Academic sanctions
  absences, 244–245
  misconduct, 245–248
Accidents (*see* Tort liability)
Accreditation of schools, 3–4
Actual notice, 181, 405
Advertising in public schools, 113–114
Affirmative action (*see* Discrimination in
  employment)
Age classifications (*see also* Discrimination
  in employment)
  admission to programs, 170–171
  condition of participation in extracurricular
    programs, 171
  entitlement to special education services,
    171
Age discrimination (*see* Discrimination in
  employment)
Age Discrimination Act, 170
Age Discrimination in Employment Act,
  348–349, 377–382
Age of majority, 197
Agency shop/fair share agreements
  bargaining expenses, 453–454
  constitutionality of, 452–453
  definition of, 452
  enforcement, 456
  procedures for rebate, 453–455
Aid for families with dependent children, 208

AIDS
  employees, 384, 388
  instruction about, 84
  students, 73–74
Americans with Disabilities Act, 16, 348
Appearance, grooming, and dress codes
  students, 128–134
  teachers, 333–334, 373–374
Arbitration, 461–462
Arm of the state, 377, 383, 430
Asbestos abatement
  Asbestos Hazard Emergency Response
    Act, 474
  Asbestos School Hazard Detection and
    Control Act, 474
  liability for asbestos-related injuries,
    473–474
Assault and battery
  administration of corporal punishment,
    240, 243
  defined, 487
  in general, 487–488, 492
Association
  expressive, 372
  loyalty oaths, 273, 327
  political activity, 329–333
  political affiliation, 327–329
  student clubs, 125–128
  subversive activities, 327–328
  union membership, 439–440
Assumption of risk, 485–486
Assurance of compliance, 188
Athletics (*see* Extracurricular activities)
Attendance (*see* Compulsory Attendance)
Attorneys' fees, 268, 433–434
At-will employee, 379
Available labor market, 157

Bargaining (*see* Collective bargaining)
Bible
  distribution of, 46–47
  objective study of, 40–41
  reading of, 29
Bilingual/bicultural education
  application of Title VI Civil Rights Act of
    1964, 154, 164, 165
  Bilingual Education Act, 15
  Equal Educational Opportunities Act, 145,
    153, 163, 165
Bill of Rights, in general, 11–14
Black English, 163
Boards of education (*see also* School-based
    councils)
  local
    appointment of teachers, 276–277
    elections, 5–6
    meetings, 6–7
    membership, 6
    powers, in general, 5–8
  state
    authority, in general, 4–5
    membership, 4
Bona fide occupational qualification, 348,
    361, 372–373, 378, 380
Boston Latin School, 162, 179
Boy Scouts of America, 372
Brown mandate, 149
Business necessity standard, 348, 350, 354,
    359, 366, 387

Censorship (*see also* Academic freedom)
  course content, 54–57, 84
  electronic media, 87–88
  instructional materials, 82–88
  removal of library books and materials,
    83–87
  student expression, 109–117
Charter schools, creation of, 2–3, 161
Child abuse, molestation
  definition, 299–300
  duty to report, 300–301
  school employees, allegations of abuse,
    301–303, 356
  state laws, 300
Child Online Protection Act, 87–88
Children's Internet Protection Act, 88

Choice plans, 63–65
Church/State relations
  Bible reading, 29
  Bible study courses, 40–41
  child-benefit doctrine, 58
  coercion test, 27
  creation science, 55–56
  curriculum challenges, 54–57
  distribution of religious literature, 46–48
  endorsement test, 27
  Equal Access Act, 43–44, 126–127
  Establishment Clause, in general, 26–27
  evolution, teaching of, 55–56
  financial aid to private schools, 57–65
  Free Exercise Clause, in general, 27–28,
    375
  graduation ceremonies, 31–36
  Halloween observances, challenges to, 38
  instruction about religion, 40–42
  New Age theology, 54
  Pledge of Allegiance, 50–51
  prayer, 29–36
  proselytization in the classroom, 39–42
  reading series, challenges to, 56–57
  regulation of private schools, 57–58
  release time for religious instruction,
    48–49
  religion, defined, 53–54
  religious displays, 37–39
  religious exemptions from public school
    activities, 50–53
  Religious Freedom Restoration Act of
    1993, 28
  religious holiday observances, 37–38
  religious materials in course assignments,
    41–42
  school access, community groups, 44–46
  secular humanism, 54
  sex education classes, 54–55
  silent meditation, 30–31
  student absences for religious reasons,
    49–50
  student-initiated devotional meetings,
    43–44
  student-initiated religious expression,
    32–36, 42–44, 46–48
  tax relief measures for private school costs,
    62–63

Ten Commandments, posting of, 37–38
textbooks and instructional materials, aid
  for, 58, 60–62
Title I and other services, provision of,
  59–60
transportation services, aid for, 58, 62
tripartite (*Lemon*) test, defined, 26
vouchers, 63–65
Circumstantial evidence, 349
Citizenship, requirement for licensure, 273
Civil Rights Act of 1964
  Title IV, 153
  Title VI, 145, 163, 164,165
  Title VII
    gender, 359–363, 365–369
    in general, 346–352
    race, 352, 354, 357–358
    religion, 372–375
    sexual harassment, 181
    statutory standards, treatment and
      impact, 349, 350
Civil Rights Act of 1871, Section 1983, 16
Civil Rights Act of 1866, Section 1981
  in general, 16, 352
  liability of school districts, 428–430
  liability of school officials, 16, 426–428
Class action, 358
Class size, scope of negotiations, 447
Collective bargaining
  agency shop/fair share agreement,
    452–456
  arbitration awards, 461
  bargaining laws, in general, 442
  dues check-off, 457
  exclusive privileges, 456–459
  exclusive representative, 442
  Executive Order 10988, 439
  First Amendment protection, 439
  good-faith bargaining, 442–443
  grievances, 459–461
  impasse procedures
    arbitration, 461–462
    fact-finding, 462
    mediation, 462
  injunctions, 465–466
  interest arbitration, 459, 460
  labor relations boards, 442
  managerial rights, 445–446

master contracts, in general, 443
National Labor Relations Act, 437–438
National Labor Relations Board, 438
Norris LaGuardia Act, 437
private schools, status of bargaining, 438
private sector, overview of bargaining,
  437–439
scope of negotiations
  class size, 447
  in general, 444
  governmental policy, 445–446
  nonrenewal decisions, 450–451
  reduction-in-force, 449–450
  school calendar, 447–448
  teacher evaluation procedures, 448–449
  tenure, 450–451
state legislation, 440–441
strikes, 463–466
Taft-Hartley Act, 438
unfair labor practices, 443
union shop, 452
use of school mail facilities, 457–458, 459
Commerce Clause, 11, 441
Community groups, use of public schools,
  44–46
Community service requirements, 82
Comparative negligence (*see* Tort liability)
Competency testing (*see* Proficiency testing)
Compulsory attendance
  age requirement, 170
  alternatives to public schooling, 68–71
  exceptions, 71–72
  health requirements, 72–74
  home instruction, 69–71
  requirements, in general, 67–68
Condom distribution, 74
Consent decree, 351
Conservative citizen groups, 83
Constructive notice, 181
Contracts, personnel, 282–283
Contributory negligence (*see* Tort liability)
Copyrighted material
  computer software, 297–299
  Copyright Act, 295–296
  fair use, defined, 295
  fair use, guidelines, 295–296
  videotaping, 297
Corporal punishment

assault and battery, 240, 243
federal constitutional issues, 240–242
guidelines, 243
reasonableness, 241–242
remedies for inappropriate use, 243
school board policies, 241–243
state laws, 242–243
teacher dismissal, for inappropriate use,
    242–243, 418
Courts (*see* Judicial system)
Creation science, teaching of, 55–56
Curriculum (*see also* Instruction)
censorship, 54–57, 82–89
evolution, challenges to, 55–56
No Child Left Behind Act, 80
pupil protection laws, 103–104
religious conflicts, 41–42, 54–57
requirements for public schools, 80–82
sex education, challenges to, 54–55

Defamation (*see* Tort Liability)
Defense of Marriage Act, 370
Deliberate indifference, 182, 371
Department of Education, 17, 382
Department of Health, Education, and
    Welfare, 151
Department of Justice, 191, 383
Department of Labor, 349
Desegregation
affirmative action, 150, 157
all deliberate speed, 149, 152
de facto segregation, 151, 154, 155
de jure segregation, 146, 148, 151, 152,
    154, 155, 156, 158, 159, 166
discriminatory intent, 151, 155
ending judicial supervision, 160–161
fiscal responsibilities, 157–159
Green criteria, 150, 160
higher education, 148
options (permissible and impermissible)
    altering attendance zones, rezoning, 149
    busing, 151, 152, 153, 154, 159
    consolidating schools/districts, 151, 152
    freedom of choice/open enrollment, 150,
        154, 161
    interdistrict remedies, 154–156
    magnet schools, 154, 157, 158, 159, 161
    neighborhood schools, 159

no majority of any minority, 152
one-grade-per-year, 149
pairing schools, 151
racial quotas, 151, 156, 157
voluntary transfer, 149, 153, 154, 155,
    158, 161
separate but equal, 147, 148, 149, 177
staff desegregation, 150, 156, 157
standards
    diverse student body, 161
    extent practicable, 156
    maximum potential, 155–156
    narrowly tailored, 156, 157, 161, 162
unitary status, 149, 150, 156, 160, 161
vestiges of past discrimination, 160, 162
white flight, 154
zone jumping, 154
Direct evidence, 220, 349, 359, 373, 378
Directed verdict, 349
Disabilities (*see* Discrimination in employ-
    ment; Students with disabilities)
Discipline
academic sanctions
    absences, 244–245
    misconduct, 245–248
conduct codes, in general, 225–230
conduct off school grounds, 228
corporal punishment, 240–243
expulsions
    children with disabilities, 214–216
    due process requirements, 230–233
    grounds, 230
    guidelines, in general, 229–230
    Gun-Free Schools Act of 1994, 234
    weapons, possession of, 234
    zero-tolerance policies, 234–235
liability, 266–268
remedies for violations of protected rights,
    266–268
suspensions
    children with disabilities, 213–214
    due process requirements, 235–238
    Goss requirements, 236–237
    in-school suspension, 238
transfers, 238–239
Discovery, defined, 218
Discrimination against students (*see*
    Desegregation; Gender-based

classifications; Students with
  disabilities)
Discrimination in employment
  age
    adverse actions, 379–380
    Age Discrimination in Employment Act,
      377–382
    compensation and benefits, 378–379
    constructive discharge, 379–380
    early retirement incentive programs, 381
    Employee Retirement Income Security
      Act, 381
    harassment, 380
    hiring and promotion, 378
    reduction-in-force, 379–380
    retaliation, 377, 380–381
    retirement, 381–382, 377
  disabilities
    Americans with Disabilities Act,
      382–384, 388, 389
    average person in the general
      population, 385
    communicable diseases, 387
    constructive discharge, 389
    essential functions of the job, 386, 387,
      388
    major life activity, 385, 389
    mitigating or corrective measures, 385
    otherwise qualified, 382, 386–390
    qualifying as disabled, 384–387
    reasonable accommodation, 382, 383,
      387, 388, 389
    Rehabilitation Act of 1973, Section 504,
      382, 289
    substantially limits, 385, 386, 389
    termination and nonrenewal, 389
    undue hardship, 382, 387, 388
  gender
    comparable worth, 363
    compensation, 361–363
    Equal Pay Act, 351, 361–363
    hiring and promotion, 359–361
    pregnancy-related policies, 365–366
    retirement benefits, 369–370
    sexual harassment, 367–369
    Title VII Civil Rights Act, 367–369
  in general
    affirmative action, 346, 357

bona fide occupational qualification
  (BFOQ), 348, 361, 372–373, 378, 380
burden of proof, 347, 349, 350
business necessity standard, 348, 350,
  354, 359, 366, 387
constitutional standards, 347, 352, 359,
  370, 372, 377, 382
diversity, 358, 361
four-fifths rule (80 percent rule),
  354
job related, 350
jury trials, 351
McDonnell Douglas test, 349, 378
make-whole remedy, 351–352
mixed motive cases, 352
payroll method, 348
qualified relevant labor market, 358
qualifying as an employer, 348–349
remedies/relief, 351–352
retaliation, 349–351, 375
reverse discrimination
role model theory, 358, 361, 364
statutory standards
use of quotas, 358
  race or national origin
    adverse decisions, 355–356
    hiring and promotion, 352, 355
    test requirements, 352–355
  religious
    accommodations, 372–376
    hiring and promotion, 372–373
    leave, 374–375
  sexual orientation
    access to benefits, 283, 370
    adverse employment decisions, 371–372
    harassment, 371
Dismissal (*see* Teacher dismissal)
Disparate impact, 347, 349, 350, 353–355,
  363, 377
Disparate treatment, 349, 352, 359, 377, 381,
  389
Down-size, 157, 158, 346, 357, 379
Dress (*see* Appearance, grooming and dress
  codes)
Dropout/dropout rate, 165
Drug testing
  employees, 338–340
  students, 261–263

Due process (*see also* Discipline; Teacher
      dismissal)
   defined, 393
   hearing, 406–411
   in general, 231–232, 392–394
   notice, 236, 404–406
   students
      expulsion, 230–235
      suspension, 235–240
   teachers
      contract nonrenewal, 284, 394–396
      dismissal, 394
      liberty interests, 396–397, 400–402
      procedures, in general, 402–404
      property interests, 397, 398–400

Educational malpractice, 93–96
Elementary and Secondary Education Act of
      1965, 14–15, 59–61, 168
Eleventh Amendment immunity, 362, 377,
      383, 429–430
Employee Retirement Income Security Act,
      381
Employment (*see also* Teacher dismissal)
   assignment, 272–282, 375–376
   contracts
      basic elements, 282–283
      supplemental, 287–289
      tenure, 284–287
      term, 284
   demotion, 280–281, 355
   evaluation, 289–291
   health and physical requirements,
      277–278, 387
   leaves of absence, 289, 374–375
   licensure, 272–273
   loyalty oaths, 273
   noninstructional duties, 281–282
   records, 292–294
   requirements for employment, 277–279,
      353
   residency requirements, 278–279
Equal Access Act, 43–44, 126–127
Equal Educational Opportunities Act, 145,
      153, 163, 165, 177
Equal Employment Opportunity
      Commission, 347, 348, 350, 353–354,
      357, 377, 383

Equal Pay Act, 351, 361–363
Equal protection guarantees
   fundamental interest/right, 144
   standards
      intent, 144, 347
      intermediate scrutiny, 144, 145, 347
      rational basis test, 144, 347
      strict scrutiny review, 144, 347
      suspect classification, 144
Essential functions of the job, 375
Evaluation of teachers
   negotiated agreements, 448–449
   procedures, 290–291
   standardized tests used in hiring and
      promotion, 353–355
Evolution, teaching of, 55–56
Expression (*see* Freedom of expression)
Expulsion (*see* Discipline)
Extracurricular activities
   academic conditions, 138–139
   age and length of eligibility restrictions,
      137–138
   attendance and training regulations,
      135–136
   criteria for selection, 136–139
   defined, 134
   denial of participation, 134–138
   drug testing, 136, 261–263
   fees, 139–140
   gender discrimination, 147–152
   health requirements, 136
   home-schooled students, 71
   residency requirements, 136–137
   sports, 171–176
   students with disabilities, participation of,
      136, 209–212
   Title IX Education Amendments of 1972,
      application of, 172–177

Facial discrimination, 143, 146, 347
Facially neutral discrimination, 145, 166, 347
Facilities, public school
   access, generally, 146
   access for community religious groups,
      44–46
   access for student-led groups, 43–44,
      126–127
Fair Employment and Housing Act, 371

Fair Labor Standards Act, 441
False imprisonment, 488–489
Family Educational Rights and Privacy Act,
    97–102
Family Medical Leave Act, 349
Federal Constitution
    in general, 9–10
    major provisions affecting education,
        10–14
Federal courts
    courts of appeal, 20–21
    district courts, 20
    structure, 20–21
    United States Supreme Court, 18–19,
        21–22
Federal legislation
    civil rights laws, in general, 15–17
    funding laws, in general, 14–15
Fees
    courses, 79–80
    extracurricular activities, 139–140
    supplies, 79–80
    textbooks, 78–79
    transportation, 78
Field trips, liability for negligence, 472, 486
Fifth Amendment, 12–13, 352
Fighting words, 492
Flexible schedule, employment, 373–374
Fourteenth Amendment, figure, 144
Fourth Amendment
    in general, 12
    search and seizure, 248–251
Fraudulent conveyance, 494
Freedom of association (*see* Association)
Freedom of expression (*see also* Academic
        freedom; Equal Access Act; Student-
        initiated clubs; Student publications)
    students
        anti-harrassment policies, challenges to,
            122–123
        commercial speech, 113–114
        defamation, 109
        demonstrations, 121–122
        electronic expression, 123–124, 228
        forums, types of, 114–115
        in general, 107–109
        hate speech, fighting words, 111–112
        Hazelwood principle, 115–117

inflammatory expression, 111–112
        lewd and vulgar expression, 109–111
        obscene expression, 109
        prior restraints, 119–120
        private expression, 117–125
        school-sponsored expression, 114–117
        student-initiated clubs, 43–44, 125–128
        time, place, and manner restrictions,
            124–125
        Tinker principle, 117–118
        unprotected conduct and expression,
            109–112
        viewpoint discrimination, 36, 44–48,
            122–123
    teachers
        application of constitutional principles,
            309–315
        balancing of interests, 313–315
        channel rules, 316–317
        Pickering principle, 306–307
        political expression, 312, 329–331
        prior restraints, 315–316
        private expression to superiors, 307
        private grievances, 309–310
        protected expression on issues of public
            concern, 306–307, 310–312
        time, place, and manner restrictions, 318
Freedom of press (*see* Student publications)
Freedom of religion (*see* Church/State
        relations)
Fundamental right, 144

Gender-based classifications (*see also*
        Discrimination in employment)
    admission criteria, 179–180
    athletics (*see also* Extracurricular
        activities)
        contact sports, 172–173
        gender-segregated teams, 172–173
        modified sports for women, 176
        noncontact sports, 174
Gender-segregated programs and schools,
    177–179
General Welfare Clause, 10–11
Gifted and talented students programs, 145,
    166, 168, 169, 171
Good Samaritan laws, 480
Goss requirements, 235–237

Governmental immunity, 429–430, 481
Graduate Record Examination, 355
Green criteria, 150, 160
Grievance procedures
  arbitrator awards, 461
  definition of, 459
Gun-Free Schools Act of 1994, 234

Hairstyle
  students, 128–130
  teachers, 333–334
Hatch Act (employment), 331
Hatch Amendment (student privacy),
    103–104
Hate speech, fighting words, 111–112
Hazelwood principle, 115–117
Head of household, 361
Hearings, in employee dismissal
  adequate notice, 407
  evidence, 410–411
  findings of fact, 411
  in general, 406–407
  impartial hearing, 408–410
  waiver of hearing, 407–408
Hearsay evidence, 219, 411
Home education, 69–71
Homosexuality
  employee, expression about, 315–316
  harassment, 371
  teacher dismissal, basis for, 371, 415
Honor societies, selection for, 100
Houston, Charles, 148

Illegal aliens, students, 74–75
Illegitimacy, 145
Immorality (*see* Teacher dismissal)
Immunity
  Eleventh Amendment immunity, 429–430
  governmental immunity for tort actions,
    481–484
Immunization, as prerequisite to school
    attendance, 72–73
Inclusion, 200
Incompetency (*see* Teacher dismissal)
Individuals with Disabilities Education Act,
    192–193
Injury (*see* Tort liability)
Instruction (*see also* Curriculum)

academic achievement, 82, 89–93
  curricular requirements, 81–82
  prescribed textbooks, 82
  proper instruction, tort action, 373
Instructional negligence, 93–96
Insubordination (*see* Teacher dismissal)
Intentional infliction of mental distress,
    489–490
Irrebuttable presumption, 366

Jacob K. Javits Gifted and Talented Students
    Education Act, 168
Judicial system
  federal courts, 20–22
  general role, 17–19
  powers of review, 20–21
  state courts, 20
  trends, in general, 22–23

Labor relations (*see* Collective bargaining)
Labor unions (*see also* Collective bargaining)
  exclusive privileges, 456–459
  right to join, 439
  security provisions, 452–456
Language barriers, 163, 164
Least restrictive environment, 200–201
Legislative power, in general, 2–3
Lewd and vulgar student expression,
    109–111
Liability (*see also* Immunity; Tort liability)
  school districts
    damages, 430–432, 494, 495
    Eleventh Amendment immunity,
      429–430
    Section 1983, Civil Rights Act of 1871,
      425–429
  school officials
    damages, 430–432
    Section 1983, Civil Rights Act of 1871,
      426–428
Libel, 490
Liberty rights
  employees, 396–397, 400–402
  in general, 393
  students, 238, 239
Licensure (*see also* Testing of employees)
  requirements, 272–274
  revocation, 275–276

types of, 274
Limited-English proficient students, 164, 165, 166
Linguistic minorities, 163
Liquidated damages, 377, 380–382
Local boards of education (*see* Boards of education, local)
Lottery, admission to school, 161, 169
Loyalty oaths, 273, 327

Malpractice, 93–96
Major life activity, defined, 189
Marriage, discrimination based on, 365
Marshall, Thurgood, 148
Maximize a child's potential, 169, 194, 208
McDonnell Douglas test, 349, 378
Mediation
    employment, 461, 462
    students with disabilities, 218–219
Medicaid, 208
Mental impairment, defined, 189
Minimum competency testing (*see* Proficiency testing)
Minority role models, 157
Mitigating or corrective measures, 189, 385

Narrowly tailored (employment), 347, 352, 357–358, 361
National Association for the Advancement of Colored People, 148
National Honor Society, 183
National Labor Relations Act, 437–438
National Labor Relations Board, 438
National Teachers Examination, 272–273, 354–355
Native language, 163–167, 197
Neglect of duty (*see* Teacher dismissal)
Negligence (*see* Tort liability)
Negotiations (*see* Collective bargaining)
Newspapers (*see* Student publications)
Ninth Amendment, in general, 13
No Child Left Behind Act, 15, 80, 89, 168
Nonpublic schools (*see* Private schools)
Nonrenewal of teachers, 394–396
Norris LaGuardia Act, 437

Obligation of Contracts Clause, 11
Obscene expression, 109

Office for Civil Rights, 17, 191, 382
Office of English Language Acquisition, 163
Office of Special Education Programs, 192, 218
Otherwise qualified, under Section 504, 365, 190, 382, 386–390

Parens patriae, 57–58
Parental rights laws, 103–104
Pedophile, 371, 384
Personnel files, 292–294
Physical impairment, defined, 189
Political activity, employees
    affiliations, 327–329
    campaigning, 329–331
    Hatch Act, 331
    holding public office, 331–333
    patronage dismissals, 328–329
Prayer (*see* Church/State relations)
Precedent, defined, 18
Pregnancy
    employees, 365–366
    Pregnancy Discrimination Act, 365
    maternity leave, 365–366
    students, 183–184
Preponderance of evidence, 220, 361, 362
Principle wage earner, 361, 367
Privacy rights (*see also* Search and seizure)
    students
        Family Educational Rights and Privacy Act, 97–102
        Hatch Amendment, 103
        Protection of Pupil Rights Amendment, 104
        records, 97–103
    teachers
        breastfeeding of child, 336
        drug testing, 338–340
        evaluation, 336
        health-related issues, 336
        personnel files, 292–294
        sexual orientation, 342–343
        sexual relationships, 341–342
        unwed, pregnant status, 341
Private schools
    comparable services, 59–60
    state aid to, 58–65
    tax relief measures, 62–63

voucher plans, 63–65
Procedural due process (*see* Due process)
Proficiency testing
    home-schooled students, 69–70
    students, in general, 89–93, 166–167
    students with disabilities, 92–93
Property rights
    employees, 394, 397, 398–400
    in general, 393
    students, 230, 235–236, 238, 239
Proselytization of students, 39–42
Proximate cause, 479–480, 489
Publications (*see* Student publications)
Pupil protection laws, 103–104

Quantity or quality of production, 362

Race discrimination (*see* Desegregation;
    Discrimination in employment)
Reasonable force, 487
Record of impairment, 189
Records
    Family Educational Rights and Privacy
        Act, 97–102, 293
    personnel, 292–294
    students, 97–103
Reduction-in-force
    dismissal of teachers, 157, 158, 358, 364,
        379, 423–425
    negotiated agreements, 449–450
Regarded as having an impairment, 189
Rehabilitation Act of 1973, Section 504 (*see*
    Discrimination in employment;
Students with disabilities)
Religion (*see* Church/State relations)
Religious discrimination in employment (*see*
    Discrimination in employment)
Religious exemptions, 50–53
Religious Freedom Restoration Act of 1993,
    28
Religious influences in public schools, 29–48
Remedies for violating protected rights (*see*
    also Liability)
    in general, 425–426
    students, 266–268
    teachers
        attorneys' fees, 433–434
        civil rights legislation, 425–429

damages, 430–432
    reinstatement, 432–433
Residency requirements
    athletics, 136–137
    school attendance
        in general, 74–77
        illegal aliens, 74–75
        nonresident students, 75–76
        open enrollment, 76
        special education, 196–197
Respondeat superior, 181
Retirement, 369–370
Revocation of license, 275
Rightful place, employment discrimination,
    357–358

Safe place statutes, 473
Salary schedule, 283, 378–379
Save-harmless laws, 494
School-based clinics, 74
School-based councils
    authority, 8–9
    composition of, 8
School boards (*see* Boards of education)
School calendar
    negotiations topic, 447–448
    religious absences, 374
School districts
    accreditation of, 3–4
    creation of, 2
Search and seizure
    employees
        drug testing, 338–340
        reasonableness standard, 337–338
    students
        consent, 257
        drug-detecting canines, 258–261
        drug testing, 261–263
        Fourth Amendment, 248–249
        guidelines, 266
        individualized suspicion, in general, 250
        informants, 250
        locker searches, 251–253
        metal detectors, 257–258
        personal possessions, 253–255
        personal searches, 255–257
        police involvement, 263–266
        reasonableness standard, 249–253

strip searches, 256–257
T.L.O. tests, 249
Secret societies, 126
Segregation (*see* Desegregation)
Self-defense, 488
Seniority, in employment, 357–358, 362, 363, 373–375, 379
Sensitivity training, 371
Sex-based classification (*see* Gender-based classifications)
Sex education, 54–55
Sexual harassment (*see also* Discrimination in employment)
employees, 367–369
students, 180–183, 301–303, 386
Sexual molestation or abuse of students, liability for, 301–303, 492
Sexual orientation discrimination, 342–343
Sheltered English immersion, 165
Sign language/Sign-language interpreter, 163, 199, 375–376, 387
Slander, 490
Social Security Act, 208
Societal discrimination, 358
Special education (*see* Students with disabilities)
Speech (*see* Freedom of expression)
Sports (*see* Extracurricular activities)
State board of education (*see* Boards of education, state)
State department of education, 5
State judicial system, 20
State legislative power, 2–3
Strikes (*see also* Collective bargaining)
definition of, 464
dismissal of striking teachers, 466
injunctions, 465–466
limited right to strike, 463–464
"no strike" laws, 464
penalties, 465
Student achievement
educational malpractice, 93–96
proficiency testing, 89–93
Student appearance
attire, 130–134
hairstyle, 128–130
Student discipline (*see* Discipline)

Student-initiated clubs
Equal Access Act, 43–44
open membership, 126–128
secret societies, 126
Student publications (*see also* Freedom of expression)
off-campus distribution, 122
prior review, 119–120
school sponsorship, 115–117
unofficial student publications, 118–121
Student records (*see* Records)
Students with disabilities
accessible facilities, 190
age of majority, 197
AIDS as a disability, 207
Americans with Disabilities Act of 1990, 191–192
assessment and evaluation
in general, 197–199, 215
second and independent evaluations, 198
assistive technology devices, services, 193
behavioral management/intervention, 213–214
child find, 196
contagious disease as a disability, 189, 384
defined, 192
discipline, 192, 212–216
extended school year, 208–209
free appropriate education, 193–195
identification of
in general, 196–197
qualifying ages, 193
qualifying as disabled, 193
residency, 196–197
zero reject, 196
Individuals with Disabilities Education Act, 192–193
placement
bright-line test, 207
change of placement, 202, 205, 214
continuum of alternative placements, 200, 201, 217
extended school year, 208, 209
financial issues, 193, 207–208
full inclusion, 200
individualized education program, 193, 195–199, 209, 210

individualized education program team, 199, 201, 214, 218
interim alternative educational setting, 214
least restrictive environment, 193, 199, 200, 201, 215, 217
maximum extent appropriate, 200
neighborhood school, 194
private placement, 193, 200
related services, 193, 205–209
residential placement, 200, 201
respite care, 203
reverse mainstream, 200
sports, 209–212
supplemental aids and services, 193
then current placement, 215–216
transitional services, 193
unilateral placement by parents, 202–205, 218
procedural safeguards
administrative hearings, 198
confidentiality pledge, 218
copy of, 216
disclosure, 219
exhaustion of administrative remedies, 191, 213, 218, 220
informed consent, 205, 197, 218
judicial review, 217, 220
manifestation determination, 214–215
mediation, 217–219
notice, 204, 205
record of hearings, 219
remedies and fees, 191, 202, 203, 221–222
state review, 217, 220
statute of limitations, 221
stay-put provision, 212, 216–218
surrogate parent, 199
tier system, 217, 219
Rehabilitation Act of 1973, Section 504, 188–191
services available in private schools, 204
supplementary aids and services, 193
time-out, 213–214
Subdivision of the state, 377, 383
Substantial evidence, 214
Substantially limits a major life activity, 189
Substantive due process, defined, 13–14
Suicide, liability for, 476

Summary judgment, defined, 350
Supplemental security income, 208
Suspension of students (*see* Discipline)
Statutes of respose, 480

Taft-Hartley Act, 438
Teacher dismissal (*see also* Remedies for violating protected rights)
causes
immorality, 371, 413–416
incompetency, 412–413
insubordination, 416–418
neglect of duty, 418–420
other just cause, 422–423
reduction-in-force, 423–425
statutory provisions, in general, 412
unfitness to teach, 421–422
unprofessional conduct, 420–421
defined, 412
due process
defined, 393
dismissal, 394
liberty interests, 396–397, 400–402
nonrenewal, 284, 394–396
property interests, 397, 398–400
remedies for wrongful dismissal, 425–434
Teacher evaluation (*see* Evaluation of teachers)
Teachers' bargaining rights (*see* Collective bargaining)
Tenth Amendment, in general, 1–2
Tenure
award of, 284–285
board authority, 285
collective negotiations issue, 450–451
denial of, 364, 394
dismissal for cause, 284, 412–425
types of contracts, 282–284
Test of English as a Foreign Language, 153
Testing (*see* Proficiency testing)
Testing of employees, 272–273, 353–355
Test-taking phobia, as disability, 386
Textbooks
challenges to, 54, 56–67
fees, 78–79
loan to religious schools, 58, 60–62
prescribed, 82
Threats by students, 111–112, 124
Tinker principle, 117–118, 125

Title IV Civil Rights Act of 1964 (*see* Civil Rights Act of 1964)
Title VI Civil Rights Act of 1964 (*see* Civil Rights Act of 1964)
Title VII Civil Rights Act of 1964 (*see* Civil Rights Act of 1964)
Title IX Education Amendments of 1972, 172–183
Tort liability (*see also* Educational malpractice)
  accidents, 469
  attractive nuisance, 481
  damages, 494–495
  defamation
    fact versus opinion, 492
    libel, 490
    malice, 493
    privileged and unprivileged communication, 493–494
    public versus private persons, 491
    reckless disregard for the truth, 491
    slander, 490
    veracity of statements, 491–492
  defined, 468
  discretionary functions, 482
  duty to warn, 475
  governmental functions, 481
  insurance, 494
  intentional torts
    assault, 243, 367, 487, 492
    battery, 243, 367, 487
    false imprisonment, 488–489
    intentional infliction of mental distress, 367, 371 489–490, 493,
  ministerial functions, 482
  negligence
    assumption of risk, 485–486
    breach of duty, 476–479
    comparative, 484–485
    contributory, 484
    defenses, 480–486
    duties, 469–476
    elements identified, 468–486
    foreseeability, 469, 470, 471, 472, 474, 475, 476, 479, 486
    injury, 480
    instructional (*see* Educational malpractice)

invitee, licensee, trespasser, 478–479, 482
    proximate cause, 479–480, 489
    reasonable person, 477–478
    safe place statutes, 473
    save harmless statutes, 494
    standard of care, 476–477
  proprietary functions, 481
  recreational use, 482
  strict liability, 367, 468
Tracking schemes, 166–167
Transfer (*see also* Desegregation/options)
  students
    disciplinary, 238–239
    extracurricular requirements, 136–137
    open enrollment, 76
  teachers, 280, 355–356, 375–376, 379, 380, 387, 388
Truancy
  academic sanctions, 243–248
  compulsory attendance, 67–68
  resulting in injury, 472
Tuition
  private school placement for students with disabilities, 202–204
  public school courses, 78–80
Tuition tax credits and deductions, 62–63

Undue burden/hardship, 208, 373–375
Uniforms for students, 133–134
Unions (*see* Collective bargaining)
United States Constitution (*see* Federal Constitution)
United States Supreme Court
  jurisdiction, 21–22
  role, 20–21
Urinalysis (*see* Drug testing)

Vaccination 72–73
Virginia Military Institute, 178
Vouchers, 63–65

Wagner Act, 437–438
Weapons, possession of, 234–235
Workers' compensation, 483–484

Zero reject, 196
Zero-tolerance discipline policies, 215, 234–235